Pop Perspectives

Pop Perspectives

READINGS TO CRITIQUE CONTEMPORARY CULTURE

Laura Gray-Rosendale
Northern Arizona University

McGraw Hill

Boston   Burr Ridge, IL   Dubuque, IA   Madison, WI   New York
San Francisco   St. Louis   Bangkok   Bogotá   Caracas   Kuala Lumpur
Lisbon   London   Madrid   Mexico City   Milan   Montreal   New Delhi
Santiago   Seoul   Singapore   Sydney   Taipei   Toronto

Higher Education

Published by McGraw-Hill, an imprint of The McGraw-Hill Companies, Inc., 1221 Avenue of the Americas, New York, NY, 10020. Copyright © 2008. All rights reserved. No part of this publication may be reproduced or distributed in any form or by any means, or stored in a database or retrieval system, without the prior written consent of The McGraw-Hill Companies, Inc., including, but not limited to, in any network or other electronic storage or transmission, or broadcast for distance learning.

This book is printed on acid-free paper.

1 2 3 4 5 6 7 8 9 0 DOC/DOC 0 9 8 7

ISBN: 978-0-07-293365-9
MHID: 0-07-293365-8

Editor-in-chief: *Emily Barrosse*
Publisher: *Lisa Moore*
Sponsoring editor: *Christopher Bennem*
Editorial coordinator: *Jesse Hassenger*
Marketing manager: *Tamara Wederbrand*
Development editor: *Julie McBurney*
Production editor: *Jean R. Starr/Mel Valentin*
Design manager: *Marianna Kinigakis/Kim Menning*
Text designer: *Ellen Pettengell*
Cover designer: *John Resh*
Art editor: *Ayelet Arbel*
Photo research: *PhotoSearch, New York*
Photo research coordinator: *Alexandra Ambrose*
Media producer: *Alexander Rohrs*
Production supervisor: *Randy Hurst*
Composition: *9.5/12 Century Book by Newgen-Austin/G&S*
Printing: *R. R. Donnelley/Crawfordsville*

Cover: © Peter Gridley/Taxi/Getty Images

Credits: The credits section for this book begins on page 665 and is considered an extension of the copyright page.

Library of Congress Cataloging-in-Publication Data

Gray-Rosendale, Laura.
  Pop perspectives : readings to critique contenporary culture / Laura Gray-Rosendale. —
[1st ed.]
    p. cm.
  ISBN-13: 978-0-07-293365-9 (alk. paper)
  ISBN-10: 0-07-293365-8 (alk. paper)
  1. College readers. 2. Readers—Popular culture. 3. English language—Rhetoric—
Problems, exercises etc. 4. Critical thinking—Problems, exercises, etc. I. Title.
PE1417.G66 2007
808'.0427—dc22
                                                                    2007009625

The Internet addresses listed in the text were accurate at the time of publication. The inclusion of a Web site does not indicate an endorsement by the authors or McGraw-Hill, and McGraw-Hill does not guarantee the accuracy of the information presented at these sites.

www.mhhe.com

To my husband Steve and my brother Dave—this one is for you. To life, language, and no more biffing.

Contents

PART I Analytical Concepts and Writing Strategies 1

PART II Reading Ourselves, Reading Others 109

Reading Visuals and Other Media

About the Author

Laura Gray-Rosendale is Associate Professor of English at Northern Arizona University where she directs a writing program in conjunction with the Multicultural Student Center. She has published scholarly books and articles about basic writing, contemporary rhetoric, feminism, autobiographical writing, visual and cultural studies, and politics. Gray-Rosendale makes her home in Flagstaff with her husband Steve and their dog Max.

Preface

Reading and Writing about Popular Culture

Pop Perspectives: Readings to Critique Contemporary Culture *provides students with crucial knowledge about culture and criticism, rhetoric, as well as argumentation; shows students how to utilize and practice these analytic strategies; and engages students in applying their new skills to a broad range of multimedia texts.*

Constant changes in visual literacy, technological developments, as well as the ever evolving shape of our political and economic landscape increasingly pose real challenges for introductory composition teachers and our students. Teachers know that our students—many of whom are thoughtful, socially conscious, and technology savvy Generation Xers and Millennials—need critical skills in rhetoric, argument, as well as active reading and writing to succeed in college as much as in their professional lives. We want to prepare our students to navigate and analyze this new world, a terrain dominated by shifting communication demands and complex multimedia texts. However, teachers also understand that truly effective skills-building can be accomplished only if we captivate our students' imaginations—allow our writing courses to be places where students can take hold of their interests, a space where they might formulate their own thoughts, goals, and dreams. Our students constantly show us that they want to directly engage the world around them in ways that they find meaningful, to make contemporary cultural issues, events, and phenomena a central part of their studies.

A CLASSICAL CONTEMPORARY TEXTBOOK

Years ago when I first began teaching composition classes with these goals in mind, my students and I researched advertising, consumer culture, style, film, music, sports, spaces, technology, and television. Of course, I did what most busy composition teachers do: I made a hopeful and exhaustive search for a comprehensive textbook.

If a textbook was going to really meet my own and my students' demands, I knew it had to accomplish three important things:

1. Provide students a strong intellectual basis in critical thinking, reading, and response; rhetoric; and argumentation
2. Explain to students in interesting, easy-to-understand ways how and why precisely to use such analytic techniques

3. Offer a wide variety of lively readings covering timely, entertaining, and contemporary topics—from diverse perspectives—about popular culture

In short, it had to be a *classical contemporary* composition textbook—one that taught classical, traditional, and essential skills through a contemporary, popular culture approach. While there were some strong textbooks available, I quickly discovered that no text fully combined these three crucial features.

The realization that no such text existed left me in a bit of a quandary. Like many teachers, I wished that the rhetoric and argumentation books included readings that more fully ignited my students' interests. At the same time, I also wanted the popular culture readers to supply a more integrated, thorough analytic and pedagogical component so that I would not be required to spend hours filling in the missing pieces by creating various worksheets. I needed material that carefully taught my students how to analyze both written and visual texts through models and encouraged them to develop their skills through exercises. Finally, I sought a reader that incorporated essays that were not only compelling and wide ranging, but also truly distinct—both in terms of the artifacts they examined and the cultural and ethnic groups' voices they incorporated.

My search for a textbook that fulfilled these needs never ended. Years later—after having taught thousands of introductory writing students across New York and Arizona at various kinds of colleges and universities, students from diverse backgrounds and with different comfort levels around reading and writing—I still had yet to find a textbook that really satisfied my own or my students' needs. As a result, when I was hired to direct a summer writing program, I did what many writing teachers do: I cobbled together my own text—a combination of revised worksheets, lectures, exercises, and readings—and I updated it several times a year. This text eventually became the foundation of a thriving writing curriculum, one in which scores of students and their teachers have now participated. Drawing from my own knowledge and experiences designing and teaching the course as well as their superb suggestions, the textbook and the program continue to change and, I hope, become more and more effective. *Pop Perspectives: Readings to Critique Contemporary Culture* is the classical contemporary textbook that is at the heart of our writing program. *Pop Perspectives* attempts to offer what is often missing from today's popular culture readers for composition classes. It provides both teachers and students with critical classical tools, tools that are more essential now than they have ever been. Just as importantly, *Pop Perspectives* teaches students how to use these tools across various media, creating the habits of mind necessary to tackle today's important cultural issues—whether our students come across them in writing, sciences, technology, or business classrooms; the workplace; or the many other complex worlds they will encounter in the future.

TAKING ACTION

Teachers of writing often struggle over one central question: How do we maintain the intellectual integrity of our composition courses while still endeavoring to reach our students where they live? As a teacher and scholar of composition I am ever more convinced that our students learn new concepts best when they can apply them to what they already know. Our students are often extremely well informed about the intricacies of popular culture. They know Disney, *Survivor*, The Body Shop, Britney Spears, Dell Computers, and Starbucks. Through *Pop Perspectives: Readings to Critique Contemporary Culture* students are able to enhance their reading and writing skills by utilizing them to comprehend pop culture texts that they already find fascinating. Along the way, they gain greater insight into the place of pop culture in the world at large, and into their own important place in that world.

Teaching critical reading and writing through the study of popular culture is among our best intellectual approaches available. Cultural Studies is assuming an ever larger presence in academic environments, and for good reason. It represents a respected scholarly field of study with a long history—in which thoughtful monographs and books are being published at an alarming rate—that draws in research from a variety of disciplines. The most successful work of this type combines the engaging aspects of popular culture with the rich intellectual tradition of rhetoric and argumentation. I have emulated that approach in writing this textbook: Both inviting and challenging, *Pop Perspectives* aims to weave classical skills together with contemporary issues in order to meet the needs of today's teachers and students alike. As you make this text a part of your writing curriculum, I very much look forward to hearing about your own and your students' experiences as well as integrating your suggestions for additions and improvements.

Pop Perspectives has two sections. Part I, "Analytical Concepts and Writing Strategies," offers students an initiation into the world of crucial analytic concepts and writing strategies. It contains three chapters. The first chapter teaches students about culture and skills in critical thinking, reading, and response. The second chapter explains how to use rhetoric to analyze others' work and teach students crucial prewriting techniques that create bridges between reading others' texts and writing about them. The third chapter provides students with tools to understand arguments and gives them the skills to write polished argumentative and research papers of their own. These three chapters prepare students well for the demands of writing courses as well as for the kinds of writing they may encounter in their other classes and their lives outside college. In addition, these chapters are student-centered in meaningful ways. All of the chapters begin with "*Pop* Profiles," introductions to a few of my former writing students—now established in their respective careers—who describe how they use these skills in their jobs and everyday lives. Likewise, all of the chapters present compelling student examples as models and guides.

Chapter 1, "Introduction: Culture and Criticism," furnishes students with critical thinking, reading, and response tools. This chapter familiarizes students with various definitions of culture, and explains *Pop Perspectives's* goals and its structure. Then students learn how to adopt a critical perspective: to engage in critical thinking, reading, and response. Students trace how one former student uses various critical strategies—previewing, annotating, paraphrasing, summarizing, analyzing, and evaluating—to respond to a newspaper editorial about U.S. efforts in Iraq. Moreover, students receive useful checklists for critical thinking, reading, and response that they can utilize to analyze any text. Finally, students apply their new knowledge to a written text, an editorial about the merits of eating broccoli, as well as a number of visual texts, specifically websites about various endangered species and the efforts of the World Trade Organization.

Chapter 2, "Rhetoric and Reading to Write," provides more complex critical approaches. It walks students through two types of rhetorical analysis assignments they will encounter—rhetorical analysis of a written text (a speech by President George W. Bush) and rhetorical analysis of a visual text (the Calvin Klein Obsession advertising campaign). In both of these cases, the book supplies easy-to-follow, step-by-step instructions and checklists for how to read and analyze texts that have both written and visual components, presenting useful student models. Students examine the transition from critical reading of texts to critical writing about texts—specifically, they learn the importance of prewriting strategies such as taking notes, freewriting, mapping, clustering, scratch outlining, and formal outlining. Finally, students encounter two different types of exercises throughout this chapter that will call upon them to test their new knowledge. The first one encourages students to apply what they have learned and apply it to a written text about violence in the schools. The second invites students to harness all of the skills they have uncovered thus far to examine a wide range of pop culture texts including advertisements, rituals and spaces, commercials, television shows, and films. Students move from more informal types of writing to more formal prose and, finally, create their own spoof advertisements.

Chapter 3, "Argument, Research, and Writing," helps students discover how to analyze, evaluate, and write even more skillfully by studying the elements of argument. They learn both how to read others' arguments and write their own. Students gain knowledge about logical reasoning by exploring models by Stephen Toulmin and Aristotle, view arguments according to their main parts (i.e., the research question, claim, support, and warrants), and investigate the potential logical fallacies that would undermine their own arguments as well as help them to dismantle others' arguments. Then they turn their attention toward applying this new knowledge to conducting research and writing essays, investigating the later stages of the writing process—drafting, reflecting, and revising.

The chapter walks students through an example of one student's entire writing process as he constructs a research essay about *The Jerry Springer Show*. Students observe how he considers a central research question, examines primary sources, narrows his focus, creates a working thesis and outline, constructs a full rough draft, reflects on that draft by commenting on how to improve his own work, consults secondary sources, composes a revision, and prepares to revise the essay once more with the help of his instructor. This chapter also presents a user-friendly final revision checklist. And, as with the first two chapters, Chapter 3 offers exercises throughout so that students can apply their new knowledge of argumentation to a range of popular culture texts. They encounter two kinds of exercises. In the first they are asked to apply their knowledge of logical reasoning and fallacies to both written and visual texts, including an article from *The Onion*, advertisements, ad spoofs, and websites. In the second they create drafts of their own arguments about cultural texts such as malls, music, and sports; reflect on them; and revise them.

By the end of Part I, students have gained significant knowledge about culture and criticism, rhetoric, as well as argumentation; discovered how to utilize these analytic strategies; and learned how to apply these techniques to various multimedia texts. In addition, since the final exercises in Chapter 3 invite students to write cultural criticism arguments of their own—much like those they are about to read in the second part of the book that are written by professional writers and thinkers—they have effectively entered an exciting community of other writers and thinkers. At this point they are more than ready to take the invigorating next steps: applying their skills to the readings about popular culture in Part II.

Part II of *Pop Perspectives* supplies an intriguing set of readings about pop culture, an arena where students can hone their analytic skills and explore many examples of argumentative writing in action. It includes seven chapters of readings. Each chapter contains a spectrum of essays, providing intelligent, interesting, and diverse perspectives on a broad range of concerns in popular culture. There are essays that offer very positive readings of popular cultural texts, pieces that provide negative assessments, and selections that scrutinize both the potential positive and negative elements. The quality and variety of these essays allow teachers the chance to cluster readings easily and to capture their students' varied interests.

Part II includes two sections, "Reading Ourselves, Reading Others" and "Reading Visuals and Other Media." The first takes up issues related to students, their lives, and their senses of themselves in the world—identities and work; spaces, rituals, and styles; and sports. The second addresses concerns related to the popular media and how it impacts us—print advertising and commercials; television; movies, and music; as well as cyberculture and gaming. Visuals are included throughout each section.

The first section in Part II, "Reading Ourselves, Reading Others," contains three chapters. Chapter 4, "Understanding Lives and Jobs," includes two sets of readings. The first incorporates perspectives from a wide range of cultural backgrounds—Native American, "white," Hispanic, African American, mixed-race or inter-ethnic, and Asian American. In creative nonfiction essays, these writers discuss how identity and cultural diversity intersect with critical issues such as community, environment, economic status, ethnicity, and generational affiliations. The second includes pieces about work life in contemporary culture—texts about the effects of Wal-Mart on small-town living; the emergence of a new working class; the ways in which websites such as "Facebook" and "MySpace" are impacting employment; and "Dilbert" cartoonist Scott Adams' reflections on the corporate world.

Chapter 5, "Imagining Spaces, Rituals, and Styles," has two sections. The first integrates topical essays on Generations X and Y as well as malls as critical cultural spaces; comedian George Carlin's thoughts on the problems of finding places to put our "stuff"; supermarkets as well as the proliferation of screens in other spaces we encounter everyday; proms as rituals that support certain cultural narratives and attitudes about masculinity, femininity, and youth culture; the various cultural functions of ghetto cityscapes; as well as how public and private spaces are created in Disney World. The second centers upon issues of style, including essays about job security, masculinity, dress, and social status; the role of Martha Stewart and style in American culture; the growth of the "metrosexual" consumer; how street styles have reflected as well as impacted African American masculinity; and the history of clothing as well as how fashion can be read just like other cultural text. Chapter 5 includes several visual analysis exercises throughout.

Chapter 6, "Playing Sports," encompasses intriguing essays about rethinking sports in terms of social issues as well as critical innovations and celebrities. The first part looks at sports and issues of homophobia; how fixed notions of masculinity, race, and ethnicity are constructed and deconstructed through sports; as well as how various perspectives on femininity are reproduced through the rules that govern and the media surrounding sports. The essays focus particularly on softball, baseball, and figure skating. The second part of the chapter offers pieces that address the growing popularity of sports video games; racism, class status, and the NBA; the increasingly vocal debate around the present and past use of sports team mascots; the celebrity phenomenon of Tiger Woods; the marketing machine around today's sports, including sports programming on the radio; and the cultural imperialism and the colonizing impulses found in the United States' participation in Olympic sports. The essays cover, among other things, football, basketball, golf, and soccer.

The second section of Part II, "Reading Visuals and Other Media," contains four chapters. Chapter 7, "Analyzing Print Ads and Commercials," has three parts. The first part incorporates intriguing essays about advertising. These include a piece by Kalle Lasn, the creator of AdBusters: a politically oriented culture jamming group that creates ad spoofs; the beneficial, positive values of advertising certain products and services—particularly those related to health care and drugs; the ways in which sexual appeals work in fashion advertising as well as specific analytic tools for how to read both print advertising and commercials; the pragmatic aspects of how ad campaigns and product placement are approached by advertising companies; and the complicated notion of "branding" as well as the effects of global links between corporations. The second examines images of diversity in print ads and commercials, centering on the history of Pepsi's ad campaigns and racism and addiction issues; historical representations of people of color in ads, particularly specific ad campaigns featuring African Americans, Latinos/as, Asians, and Native Americans; as well as the pros and cons of how advertisers are now targeting gay consumers. The third takes up the history of how ad campaigns represent gender issues, tracing changes from the 1950s to the present; the ways in which advertising and violent white masculinity converge; and how young boys have been ushered into complex understandings of what it means to be a male (as well as African American) through the cult of Joe Camel. The essays in this chapter might be read in conjunction with the "Ad Analysis" assignments and full-color advertisements included at the end of Chapter 7 so that students can test their critical reading skills.

Chapter 8, "Watching Television," includes a compelling section on the latest television trend—talk shows and reality television shows such as *Oprah, Survivor, The Bachelor, The Swan,* and others. This first section highlights how such shows address concerns of race, class, gender, ethnicity, and age. The second section features essays about other popular television images—from *The Unit* to *The Simpsons*—with pieces that show both the positive as well as negative aspects of television in American culture. The final section of the chapter examines how television news programs function in our culture, often mimicking and reinforcing other entertainment genres; how homeshopping networks are designed to promote user-friendly comsumerism, a technique now being employed quite successfully by the Internet as well; and how infomercials are increasingly using reality media forms such as the television talk show format to obscure their main purpose—to sell.

Chapter 9, "Seeing Movies and Listening to Music," has two parts. The first part centers on film and offers essays about changing constructions of masculinity in films such as *As Good As It Gets*, *Good Will Hunting*, and *Magnolia*; how issues of race and ethnicity operate in *Rush Hour*; the ways in which the lesbian gaze functions in contemporary films such as *Being John Malkovich*; the history of the gangster and gangsta film genres; the explosion of the "high school" or "teen" movie genre; and the ways in which the movie *Nurse Betty* takes up issues of race, gender, class, and ethnicity. The second part provides pieces on a wide variety of musical genres. The essays center the political potentials of punk music; the importance of hip-hop music and culture; the complex issues surrounding the creation and media promotion of so-called Latin music; Britney Spears's life and music as well as the ways in which it depends upon racist notions of femininity and the Old South; the changing landscape of country music and its ethnic and cultural history; rap music's attempts at political empowerment and the effects of rap's growing commercialism as well as technological innovations; and a distressed father's discussion with his daughters concerning how race, class, gender, and age are represented in today's music videos.

The book closes with Chapter 10, "Surfing in Cyberculture and Gaming," a chapter about contemporary technology. The first section encourages the reader to examine and rethink the intersections of gender, race, ethnicity, and class within cyberspace and gaming. The essays tackle the problems and possibilities of gender-specific Internet interest groups; the anonymity of the web interactions and the impacts this has on issues of masculinity and femininity; the problems in access to the Internet that some African American communities have experienced; the positive and negative potentials of Internet interactivity and gaming that target young girls; the growth of virtual combat and representations of warfare in gaming; and issues of sovereignty, fraud, and identity for Native American–owned web organizations. The second section traces recent innovations in technology. The pieces examine constructions of "reality" and gaming; the impact of IM (instant messaging or texting) on how we communicate and what this reveals about changes in our culture; gaming's creative possibilities for storytelling and the ways in which our advertising-based culture effectively undermines these potentials; as well as how one writer is coping with an increasingly contagious online "illness," eBay addiction.

POP PERSPECTIVES AND YOUR CLASS

Pop Perspectives embraces essays and visuals—some drawn from popular sources and some from academic sources—that address topics of real interest in popular culture. As much as possible, I have tried to select readings that are timely, thought-provoking, and engaging. In addition, I have aimed to present a wide range of texts by authors speaking from diverse communities. All of the essays are among the most current available, and some of the essays have been written and updated expressly for this volume. They serve as outstanding models for student writing about popular culture, and all of the selections—textual and visual—supply material on which students can test their analytic skills.

The readings are designed to provoke a range of student responses, from energizing discussions and short written responses to more formal, developed research projects. Each chapter begins with a reader-friendly and informative introduction that encourages student involvement. The introduction to each chapter also provides overviews of the selections, allowing both instructors and students to get a sense of the texts at a glance. Within each chapter, subsections are arranged according to common themes or issues, making clustering and assigning related essays easier.

The readings in each chapter are accompanied by three sorts of material: biographical sketches about the authors and their works, a set of detailed questions that move from simple reaction to considered analysis titled "Exercising Your Skills," and a capstone assignment called "Taking Action" that requires students' to synthesize, analyze, and evaluate concerns relevant to the reading as a group.

"Exercising Your Skills" assignments includes several components. *Before Reading* questions prepare students to consider their own experiences in preparation for the upcoming reading. They are designed to encourage students to start thinking about the issues that the readings will raise and can serve as excellent ways to prompt informal responses and class discussions. *After Reading* questions require students to offer detailed analyses of the essay's rhetorical appeals, purpose, audience, claims, warrants, support, and logical fallacies. Then they ask students to synthesize and analyze that information to make short persuasive arguments of their own. The *After Reading* questions are separated into those related to "Critical Perspective," "Rhetoric and Argument," and "Analysis." Students discover how to apply all of the classical analysis and writing skills that they have learned to unravel a reading, one step at a time.

Taking Action questions conclude each reading. Like *Pop Perspectives* itself, these questions encourage students' active engagement, inviting them to take responsibility for their own learning and knowledge-building; to form support systems, communities, and teams with their peers around the readings' topics; as well as to integrate their interpretations into broader, more meaningful patterns that will help them to make sense of the media-centered world as well as their place in it. *Taking Action* questions enable students to consider their analyses in terms that are useful for completing larger writing projects as well as contemplating the relationships between their analyses and wider social and cultural issues. These questions also foster an active and social learning environment, preparing students for the team-writing and team-presentation situations they increasingly encounter in today's academic environments and workplaces.

All of these questions—*Before Reading*, *After Reading*, and *Taking Action*—can be used to advance class discussion, short writing assignments, and formal writing. Just as the introductory chapters that model skills-building move from simple tasks to more complex ones, the reading questions for each text move from students' experiences and basic reading knowledge of the text to students' own detailed analyses and argumentative writings.

Pop Perspectives's flexible pedagogical scaffolding within both the introductory chapters and the readings portion enables it to adapt to a wide variety of teacher and student needs. The book is meant to be dynamic—to move, stretch, and grow to accommodate the interests individual teachers and students bring to it. It provides great opportunities for teachers to play more interactive roles in the classroom and for students to develop outstanding team-building skills. My great hope is that by making the book widely available, teachers and students will enjoy and be able to effectively use these materials, materials that my colleagues and I have found invigorating and powerful.

ACKNOWLEDGMENTS

Many people's hard work made this book possible. Thank you first and foremost to Steve for all your love and support through it all. I am grateful to each and every one of them. Thank you to the very talented Lisa Moore for supporting the book from start to finish. Christopher Bennem, Victoria Fullard, Julie McBurney, and Alexis Walker's editorial suggestions were invaluable throughout. Thanks also to McGraw-Hill's Alexandra Ambrose, Deborah Anderson, Jesse Hassenger, Sharon O'Donnell, Jean Starr, and Mel Valentín for bringing it all together.

Many, many thanks to my former students at Syracuse University, Cortland State College, and Northern Arizona University for sharing their work with us: Tanya Alvarez-White, Christine Dugas, Sergio Gregorio, Matt Hutchinson, Kimberly Kaplan, John Rider, and Bryan Villescas. Much appreciation to the S.T.A.R. students at Northern Arizona University, especially my own 2005 and 2006 groups: Charlotte Aden, Dania Lisette Allen, Keshia K. Beyale, Jarrett Blackwater, Alicia Brown, Caitlin Castillo, Chris Cole, Sherry Gilmore, Ashley Laverne Hardin, Olivia Jara, Zinnabah Xiochitl Jim, Brianna King, Karen Kinsel, Ryan M. Moore, Cosme Morales, Krystal Pope, Jhered R. Roberson, Maria Magdalena Rosales-Martinez, Monica Scobee, Amy C. Shea, Rose Sutton, Amy Tidwell, and Kathryn A. White. Thank you to all of the excellent teachers who have contributed so much to the curriculum over the years: Charlene Adams, Mohammed Albakry, Mary Anderson, Samantha Andrus-Henry, Sanaa Bengholam, Kendra Birnley, Kyle Boggs, Cori Brewster, Judith Bullock, Desiree Butterfield, Stephanie Capaldo, Levia DelQuadro, James Higuera, Noah Hilgert, Danny Iberri-Shea, Jacob Lesandrini, Katherine MacKinnon, Ellen Manos, Dan McMillan, Don Olson, Ann Shaheen, Chris Vassett, Matt Volz, and Josh Zimmerman.

Thanks also to the following people and groups for their support: John Ackerman, Linda Adler-Kassner, Linda Martin Alcoff, the American Popular Culture Associations, Mike Amundson and Nellie, Dawn Armfield, Damian Baca, Kathleen Baca, Marlia Banning, the Basic Writing Conference at the Conference on College Composition and Communication, Jeff Berglund, Loyola Bird, Dorothy Briggs, Monica Brown, Lisa Cahill, Lelani Carreno, Kesia Ceniceros, the Composition and Cultural Rhetoric Program at Syracuse University, Geoff Chase, LaNaia Colbert, James Comas, John Crowley, the CTEL staff at Northern Arizona University, Scott Denton, Aaron Dunckel, Jennifer and John Fieldhouse, Grenetta Thomassey Fink, Ann Fitzsimmons, David Franke, Sherry Greene Gelinas, Sharon Gorman, the Grays (David, Sandy, and Robert), Keith Gilyard, Henry Giroux, Greg Glau, David Grant, Tara Green, Nance Hahn, Lauren Hallal, Gil Haroian-Guerin, Dayle Hardy-Short, Susanmarie Harrington, Kris-ten Harris, Traci Harvey, Thomas Henry, Wendy Hesford, Margaret Himley, Deborah Holdstein, Lori Hull, Seth Khan-Egan, Cynthia Kosso, the Kerlens (Faith, Katlyn, Rachel, Deb, and Mike), Anne Harvey Kilburn, Joyce Kincannon, Hilda Ladner, Ken Lindblom, Cindy Linden, Deborah Lindquist, Carol Lipson, my Literary, Technology, and Professional Writing colleagues at Northern Arizona University, Tina Luffman, Andrea Lunsford, Scott Lyons, Steven Mailloux, Elaine Maimon, Max Squax, the McGraw-Hill Teaching Basic Writing List members, Peter McLaren, Dean Mellow, Amy Modahl, Derek Owens, Shane Pablo, Louise Wetherbee Phelps, Tom Peele, Jody Pelusi, Clarissa and Mauricio Perez, the Pozens (Olivia, Audrey, Dan, Heather, Jeremy, Heather, and Janet), Nalisha Rangel, Emily Robertson, Carol Rodriquez, Duane Roen, the Rosendales (Katia, Matt, Natalya, Alex, Tim, Lisa, Dave, Abbie, Nella, and Richard), Robert Rufo, Debi Saldo, Eileen Schell, Anne Scott, the Shaeffers (Hank, Gilly, and Pauline), Leta Sharp, Erin Shelley, Austin Shepard, Dawn Skorczewski, Catherine Smith, Trudy Smoke, Craig Stern, Sandy Raymond, Steve Thorley, Karen Uehling, Karen Underhill, the entire Verde Valley Medical Center Sedona Oncology Staff (especially Karen Aldridge, Jane Bakash, Karen Freriks, Brenda Horton, Barbara Lacey, Robyn Muscanya, and Cheryl Raab), Victor Villanueva, Stacey White, Anne Winn, Ed White, Mark Wood, Allen Woodman, Jane Armstrong Woodman, the Writing Program at Cortland State College, the Writing Program at Syracuse University, James Zebroski, Cori Zoli, and Jean Zukowski-Faust.

Much gratitude to all the excellent writers who have contributed their original essays as well as republished works to this book. In addition, a very special thank you goes out to Vic Bulluck and the NAACP's Hollywood Office for generously allowing me to include their work here.

Lastly, many, many thanks to the reviewers of the book for their tremendously thoughtful comments and suggestions along the way:

Suzanne Ashe, *Cerritos College*
Patrick S. Brennan, *University of Florida*
Jennifer Brezina, *College of The Canyons*
T. Fredrick Burack, *University of Iowa*
Paul Carbonaro, *Sinclair Community College*
Eric Cash, *Abraham Baldwin College*
J. Brian Chambley, *Ohio State University*
Bill Church, *Missouri Western State College*
Kevin Davis, *East Central College*
Samir Dayal, *Bentley College*
Joshua Dickinson, *Jefferson Community College*
Loren Glass, *University of Iowa*
M. Todd Harper, *Kennesaw State University*
Ellen Hudgins Hendrix, *Georgia Southern University*
Karen J. Jacobsen, *Valdosta State University*
Lori Jacobson, *SUNY Buffalo*
Dennis G. Jerz, *Seton Hall University*
Tiel Lundy, *University of Denver*
Ben McCorkle, *Ohio State University*

Kay Mizell, *Collin County Community College*
Bev Neiderman, *Kent State University*
Alyssa O'Brien, *Stanford University*
Seiwoong Oh, *Rider University*
Jonas Prida, *Tulane University*
Deborah Rard, *California State University, Hayward*
Alex Reid, *SUNY Cortland*
John E. Ribar, *Southeastern University*
Vivian Rice, *Syracuse University*
Tristan Destry Saldana, *Los Angeles City College*
Myra Seaman, *College of Charleston*
Phillip Serrato, *Fullerton College*
Grant T. Smith, *Viterbo University*
Julius Sokenu, *Quinebaug Valley Community College*
John Vanderslice, *University of Central Arkansas*
James Ray Watkins, *Eastern Illinois University*
Larry Weirather, *Clark College*
Ed Wiltse, *Nazareth College*
William Wolff, *University of Texas*
Xiaoye You, *Purdue University*

PART ONE

Analytical Concepts
and Writing Strategies

CHAPTER ONE

Introduction: Culture and Criticism

POP PROFILE: CULTURE AND CRITICISM

Meet Kimberly Kaplan

I studied chemistry as an undergraduate, focusing specifically on preforensics. I also completed an internship at the Maricopa Office of the Medical Examiner in Arizona. I am currently attending graduate school at Washington State University where I am working toward a doctoral degree in analytical chemistry. Eventually I may become a professor in this field or work for the government and industry designing and constructing instruments.

The instrument behind me is an ion mobility spectrometer time of flight (IMS-TOF) used for detecting small molecules in biological samples such as blood or bacteria. This instrument can also detect explosives, drugs, chemical warfare, etc. My great hope is to be able to miniaturize instruments that are already available full size and make them into handheld devices. This would allow analysis on site instead of having to transport samples back to the lab.

Today I still find the critical reading, writing, and thinking skills I learned in my writing class to be very valuable in my work. Paraphrasing, summarizing, and analysis are strategies I cannot live without. Every day I have to be able to dissect science journals to discover what the author is saying and to think about how I want to respond. Likewise whenever I write up articles of my own, I rely heavily on these skills. I simply could not meet my life and career goals without them.

We consciously "read" all the time—books at our desks, gossip magazines about celebrities while standing in the supermarket checkout line, sports sections from local newspapers on the bus, and the nutrition information on our cereal boxes at breakfast. However, even when we are not aware of it, we are also constantly reading other things—interpreting and decoding them—such as paintings, graffiti, and murals; piercings, tattoos, and clothing styles; popular music videos, daytime soap operas, advertisements, baseball games, websites, and films; the expression on our best friend's face as we share exciting news; or the way our professor greets us on the first day of class. Just as we read and evaluate written texts for our classes and in our everyday lives, we read and evaluate many other "texts" of our culture as well—the swoosh of the Nike logo, eBay, *The O.C.*, iPods, *Nacho Libre*, the Superbowl, headlines about Brad Pitt and Angelina Jolie, a Sprite bottle, PlayStation 3, *Everybody Hates Chris*, and even Donald Trump in an expensive suit loudly exclaiming, "You're fired!"

The primary aim of *Pop Perspectives* is to present you with the tools necessary for reading and responding to *all* texts carefully, as well as to allow you to test your abilities by examining a wide range of texts. It will make you a better reader and at the same time teach you how to become a more effective and persuasive writer. The book accomplishes this by teaching you some fundamental strategies—ones that have a distinguished history that can be traced back to the ancient Greeks and form the basis of much that gets done in the university world—for analyzing texts, conducting research, and writing your own essays. However, *Pop Perspectives* is unique because it teaches you these well-established strategies by applying them not to older texts about which you may know relatively little but rather to contemporary ones, texts about which you may already know a great deal and find meaningful: those images, issues, and events of our everyday world.

What you learn here will also help you to respond more effectively to any text that you encounter during your college career—be it in history, information studies, sociology, engineering, business, microbiology, art appreciation, or chemistry. It will make you a more thoughtful employee and, most importantly, a more thoughtful human being. It will encourage you to carefully consider your own responses to the social and political issues you may encounter and to discern the impact of all of the choices you make—the things you buy, the living spaces you inhabit, and the television shows you watch.

CONSIDERING CULTURE

However, before we discover anything about those crucial reading and writing tactics or begin the task of applying them to texts, we need to define some important key terms that may help us along the way.

We often call this everyday world around us **culture.** Yet what exactly do we mean when we say *culture?*

"Culture" originates from the verb *colere* which means to inhabit, cultivate, as well as protect. You will not be surprised to learn that the word "culture" has often been associated with **high culture,** which refers to privileged or elite social forms and their values (i.e., opera, ballet, classical music, museums). In fact, in 1869 the poet and literary critic Matthew Arnold wrote in support of this view of culture, declaring in the preface to his book *Culture and Anarchy* that to have culture is to "know the best that has been said and thought in the world."[1]

However, today the word "culture" has another, more commonly held meaning, that associated with **popular culture.** "Popular" originates from *popularis* which means "belonging to the people." Popular culture comprises the common images, traditions, customs, and knowledge shared by large groups of people. In 1958 the literary and media scholar Raymond Williams argued that this was another, equally valid view of culture. In his essay "Culture Is Ordinary" Williams contended that culture is "a whole way of life" or the very "common meanings and directions" that make up our everyday conversations.[2] Williams believed that culture also includes our jokes, idioms, the way we dress, our rituals, how we behave, and the many kinds of media—instant messaging, television shows, emails, news, movies, sports, advertising—that we create and use.

Williams suggested, along with many other thinkers, that an awareness of how popular culture both reflects and shapes our world is crucial to leading thoughtful, fulfilling lives. This awareness is often referred to as **cultural and media literacy.** Such knowledge helps us to perform basic functions—it indicates when it's appropriate to laugh at people's foibles and when not; when to wear dress shoes to a job interview and when to wear Vans; as well as when to greet someone with an informal "Yo, dawg" and when to use the more formal "Pleased to meet you." This kind of knowledge also helps us to better make crucial decisions that affect our welfare and the lives of those we care about. If you are not aware that hackers are sending emails spoofing large companies, you may reveal all of your personal information to people who could ruin your credit record and steal your identity. If you and your family have not heard through media sources that certain drugs have been pulled by the FDA, your health may be compromised. If you are not familiar with print advertisements for cell phone services and their use of small print, you and your friends may get charged more than you can afford.

[1]Matthew Arnold. "Preface." *Culture and Anarchy.* 3rd edition. New York: Macmillan and Co., 1882 (originally published 1869), 4.

[2]Raymond Williams. "Culture Is Ordinary." *Studies in Culture: An Introductory Reader.* Eds. Ann Gray and Jim McGuigan. London: Arnold, 1997 6.

Without this cultural and media literacy, not only would we all experience great difficulties being active, productive members of this common culture. We might also be subject to its whims—the desires of hackers, drug companies, and the cell phone services. Worse yet, we might cease to have the power to impact, affect, or change this common culture: to better protect our personal information and catch hackers, to make drug companies accountable, or to keep cell phone companies from charging unreasonable rates.

American popular culture itself can be broken down into smaller parts or vital **subcultures,** more specific groups marked by region, economic status, gender identification, ethnic or racial background, customs or habits, and other factors (e.g., southerners, nouveau riche, Native American tribes, skater punks, bloggers).

Right now you might be wondering, even though popular culture is very interesting, what place does it have in your writing course? What connection does this have to reading and writing? The detailed analysis of popular culture (how it is produced, disseminated, and consumed) is actually a very specific kind of writing, **cultural criticism**. This writing helps us to become more aware of the impact our surroundings have on us and to better understand our world. It also sometimes aims to help us understand and/or resist culture's negative impacts: Cultural criticism investigates beliefs and assumptions we hold in common, contradictions and conflicts that exist between social groups, and images as well as messages that influence and reflect who we want to be. Those who engage in cultural criticism—writers in universities, comedians in stand-up sketches, editorial writers for newspapers, writers for animated series, newscasters on comedy news programs—closely examine and offer thoughtful perspectives on the images and written language of popular texts. They hope to discover (among other things) the *myths* (e.g., the myth of male superiority) that dominate our culture; the *values* and *ideologies* (e.g., patriotism) that inform it; the *desires* and *anxieties* (e.g., the desire to be sexually attractive and the anxiety or fear of not being so) that cause us to consume (e.g., buy things); and the *representations* of various groups (e.g., men, women, racial and ethnic groups, different regional communities, various generations, different abilities, and people of different economic classes).

UNDERSTANDING *POP PERSPECTIVES*

This book is, in part, a work of cultural criticism. It aims to help you examine all texts more carefully and thoroughly, and to respond to them in ways that are effective and persuasive to your audience. It strives to teach you tools that will allow you to better make sense of the world around you and your important place in it. It makes connections between using these techniques for reading, analyzing, and writing about popular culture—with careful attention to words and images—and using these very same techniques for reading, analyzing, and writing all sorts of texts for all sorts of audiences.

Pop Perspectives has two sections.

Part I introduces you to crucial analytic concepts and writing strategies. It contains three chapters. This introduction chapter teaches you skills in critical thinking, reading, and writing. The second chapter explains how to read and analyze others' work as well as introduces you to prewriting strategies. The third chapter provides you with tools to understand arguments, conduct research, and write arguments of your own. Taken together, these three chapters will prepare you well for the demands of your writing course as well as for the kinds of writing you may encounter in other classes and in your lives outside college.

Chapter 1, "Introduction: Culture and Criticism," provides you with introductory techniques in critical thinking, reading, and responding. As you have just seen, this chapter reveals various definitions of culture and explains the textbook's goals and structure. Then you will learn how to adopt a critical perspective—to engage in critical thinking, reading, and responding. You will investigate how one student uses various critical strategies—previewing, annotating, paraphrasing, summarizing, analyzing, and evaluating—to respond to a newspaper editorial about U.S. efforts in Iraq. Likewise, you will encounter useful checklists for critical thinking, reading, and responding that you can use to analyze any text. Finally, you will harness your new knowledge, putting all you have learned into practice. You will encounter exercises that ask you to use your critical perspective techniques to analyze both written and visual texts.

Chapter 2, "Rhetoric and Reading to Write," gives you access to some more complex critical approaches. It walks you through two types of rhetorical analysis assignments you will encounter: rhetorical analysis of a written text and rhetorical analysis of a visual text. You will learn step-by-step instructions for how to read and analyze texts that have both written and visual components. You will also examine one student's transition from critical reading of texts to critical writing about texts—or *how to read in order to write*. Specifically, you will learn the importance of taking notes, freewriting, mapping, clustering, scratch outlining, and formal outlining. Finally, you will encounter several different types of exercises throughout this chapter that will call upon you to test your new knowledge. The first type encourages you to take what you have learned and apply it to a written text. The second type invites you to examine a wide range of pop culture texts as well as to move from more informal types of writing to more polished prose.

Chapter 3, "Argument, Research, and Writing," introduces you to the principles of argument and guides you through the entire writing process, reviewing how to use prewriting strategies as well as teaching you about drafting and revision. In the sections on argument, you will investigate strategies for recognizing and employing claims, evidence, and warrants as well as for detecting logical fallacies. In the sections on writing, you will study an example of one student's entire writing process as he constructs a research essay about *The Jerry Springer Show*. You will read an in-depth account of this writer's process as he considers a central research question, examines primary sources, narrows his focus, creates a working thesis and outline, constructs a full rough draft, reflects on that draft (commenting on how to improve his own work), consults secondary sources, and composes a revision. As with the first two chapters, this chapter offers several sorts of exercises throughout so that you can test your new knowledge. The first asks you to apply your knowledge of logical fallacies to both written and visual texts. The second welcomes you to create arguments of your own about cultural texts, reflect on them, and revise them.

After the first three chapters you will have discovered crucial knowledge about culture and criticism, rhetoric, as well as argumentation; learned how to employ these analytic strategies; and discovered how to use these strategies to understand various multimedia texts. In combination, Chapters 1 through 3 give you the strong analytic and writing skills necessary to move to the next important step in *Pop Perspectives*—applying your new knowledge to reading argumentative texts about popular culture and writing arguments about them.

Part II is the anthology or readings portion of this book. It provides a set of readings about pop culture, or an arena where you can hone your analytic skills and examine many examples of argumentative writing in action. It includes seven chapters of readings accompanied by three kinds of questions that involve exercising your skills—*Before Reading* questions, which ask you to briefly reflect on general issues the text raises in terms of your own life and experiences; *After Reading* questions, which invite you to answer specific questions about the essay that are related to issues of critical perspective, rhetoric and argument, as well as analysis; and *Taking Action* questions, which encourage you to take what you have learned to the next level and to incorporate what you have read into your own broader view of American culture.

Part II incorporates two distinct sections, "Reading Ourselves, Reading Others" and "Reading Visuals and Other Media." The first takes up issues related to your lives and your sense of yourselves in the world—identity and cultural diversity, work, spaces, rituals, styles, and sports. The second addresses concerns related to the popular media and how it impacts us—advertising, television, movies, music, cyberculture, and gaming. Although you will encounter two kinds of texts throughout the readings portion of the book, they address these same issues in different ways. The first, **popular cultural criticism,** often speaks to a general audience and can be found in popular venues such as magazines, newspapers, and popular books. These essays tend to be written in response to topical issues in the media and offer readings written for mass consumption. Generally they reflect social and political perspectives held by wide groups of people—conservative or liberal, traditional or new, receptive to accepted policy or opposed to it. **Academic cultural criticism** is written more specifically for students, teachers, and scholars. These essays can be found in academic journals and books. They tend to be more complicated than popular cultural criticism, contain more quotations from experts, and often use a more "objective" tone. Like pop cultural criticism, they also reflect social and political perspectives. These may be theoretical or interpretive perspectives based in such ideologies as feminism, Marxism, and/or critical race theory.

When we read any text, be it texts for our classes or jobs; our spaces, rituals, and styles; our sports; our print advertising and commercials; our television; our movies and music; or our cyberculture and gaming critically—that is, carefully, consciously, and deliberately—we engage in an active dialogue with it. When we adopt a **critical perspective**, we use critical thinking, reading, and responding skills to understand, analyze, and evaluate others' texts and perspectives. We do not simply take the "facts" of any text at face value. Instead, we act as detectives, questioning a text's use of definitions, explanations, assumptions, and structure. We break down the text and ask how and whether its pieces fit together adequately. We study the ways in which the creator of the text supports her or his main ideas and the kinds of assumptions he or she makes. Then, we decide what we think about the text and respond to it. We do not merely absorb knowledge or accept ready-made approaches to the problem: We think through and finally create our own tentative answers to problems. Finally, adopting a critical perspective about a text means that we are no longer just reading that text; instead, in some real sense we have contributed to an understanding of that text and, in so doing, made that text our own.

A CRITICAL PERSPECTIVE: STRATEGIES FOR THINKING, READING, AND RESPONDING

Critical thinking, reading, and responding are a lot like sleuthing. These skills are important for your overall success, both in your personal and academic lives. They will help you to read your favorite newspapers, websites, 'zines, books, and magazines more carefully, but they will also enable you to better understand academic texts, job ads, memos, reports, interview situations, and exchanges with coworkers. As you will see, adopting a critical perspective requires that you understand various aspects of a text: its **author** (the person or persons who created it), **audience** (the people it was created for and the people who are likely to examine it—and these may be different groups), **context** (the specific text and/or place where the piece first appeared and when or in what historical context), **purpose** (why it was created and what its goals are), **title** (what the text is named), **structure** (how it is arranged), and its **main point** (the central issue it sets out to prove).

John is an engineering student who has a minor in business. He hopes one day to design equipment for an energy company and eventually to create his own firm. John believes that critical thinking, reading, and writing skills are crucial for his major—and for his future work life. John also believes that these skills are important in his everyday life: "Knowing how to read, write, and think critically is essential for all of the work I do for my engineering and business classes. It's also really important for all of the classes I take outside my major. Everything I read requires that I adopt a critical perspective on it—so that I can understand what the experimenter or writer intended and hypothesized as well as what I think about what that person has said and the results. Engineering is really all about being able to see a problem from many perspectives so that you can think all the possibilities through. I think adopting a critical perspective is important in terms of what I do outside of school, too—whether I choose to take one route up a rock face or another, make a specific move or another while playing a video game, pick one line down a hairy hill while mountain biking or another, visit one company Web site or another." When John is not in class, he can be found playing video games, watching movies, listening to hip-hop, or enjoying downhill mountain biking or rock climbing.

In an attempt to exercise our sleuthing skills for looking at texts, we will examine the informal work of one student, John. We will watch as he uses reading and responding strategies—previewing, annotating, paraphrasing, summarizing, analyzing, and evaluating—to get beneath the surface of the text.

This text is a "Letter to the Editor," written by Bernard Bellush that appeared in *The New York Times* on October 30, 2003. This text might be understood as an example of pop cultural criticism, criticism of U.S. military policy and practices, the president's actions, and popular media images.

Letter to *The New York Times* (Oct. 30, 2003)

To the Editor:

Looking at the Oct. 29 front-page picture of two huge American soldiers towering over an Iraqi child and examining his pockets did two things for me. On the one hand, it made me wince to see what some of our soldiers are being forced to do in Iraq. On the other hand, it recalled for me a sharply contrasting picture of earlier G.I.'s, including me, handing out pieces of chocolate bars to newly liberated, joyous French children some 60 years ago.

It happened during the days and weeks after our D-Day landing on Omaha Beach in France. As members of the 616th Ordnance Ammunition Company, we not only fulfilled our original military goal of setting up the first American ammunition depot in France, but we also later became what we always should be, ambassadors of good will and conveyors of the best of the American dream.

I weep as I look at today's picture.

BERNARD BELLUSH
Valhalla, N.Y., Oct. 29, 2003

Taking Out the Magnifying Glass—Previewing

Before really delving into the text, try to get an overview of it, taking one step at a time. In some sense you are preparing to read the text more carefully. To preview effectively, skim the text and try to answer the questions that involve taking up a critical perspective in the following checklist:

CHECKLIST FOR PREVIEWING

☐ *Author*: Study headnotes and any introductory text, figuring out what you can about the author. What is the author's background? Does it make him or her especially qualified to write the piece? Does it suggest any bias or other predisposition with regard to the topic?

☐ *Context*: Consider the context in which the text first appeared. If it was published, in what kind of publication did it appear—for example, a popular magazine, like *Time*; a mainstream newspaper, like *USA Today*; a scholarly journal, like *Tikkun?* In what historical moment was it published, and how does this shape how we read it? What does the context suggest about the piece's intended audience and its purpose?

☐ *Audience*: Think about whom the writer hoped to reach. What do you know about those people? What assumptions do they share? Are they likely to be persuaded? Why or why not?

☐ *Purpose*: Why did the writer write this piece? What was the writer setting out to show or prove to the reader?

☐ *Title*: Consider the title. What, if anything, does it reveal about the topic and the author's attitude toward it? What is its tone? What kind of language does it use?

☐ *Structure*: Note the structure and other formal conventions of the piece. Are there any headings in the piece? If so, how is the topic divided? In what order are the subtopics presented? Is there any significance to this order? Does it look like a researched piece (i.e., does it have footnotes or a list of outside sources consulted)? Does it resemble any recognizable form of writing (e.g., a letter, a legal document, a lab report, an email, etc.)?

☐ *Main Point*: Read the text for its main point. Then, try to determine your overall impression of what the writer is trying to convey.

Previewing the Oct. 30, 2003, Letter to The New York Times

Author: There are no headnotes or introductions to the piece. We can see below his signature that he lives in Valhalla, New York. I researched a bit about Bellush and learned that he is a well-known writer on labor issues and a former history professor.

However, he seems to be writing this more as a concerned citizen and not just as an author or teacher.

Context: Bellush is writing to *The New York Times* in response to a photo that appeared on the front page of that day's edition of the paper. It is important to think about the larger historical context, too. The United States' military has been stationed in Iraq since March 2003 and is attempting to rebuild the country's political framework.

Audience: It is addressed "to the editor" of the *Times*—but letters like these are typically written for other readers, right? Many of the people who read this newspaper, I would guess, are college educated and concerned about contemporary political and social issues.

Purpose: Bellush wants to comment on the picture and tell the readers of the *Times* what it makes him think and feel.

Title: There is no title. Editorials don't usually have titles.

Structure: It looks like a typical letter—starts with "To the Editor" and ends with a signature.

Main Point: The last sentence tells us that he "weeps" at the picture. I'm not sure why yet . . . . Maybe this is because he believes that the responses of the locals to U.S. presence in Iraq and WWII are very different.

Delving In—Reading and Annotating

After previewing, it's time to do your first careful reading of the text. It is almost always a good idea to read the piece once from start to finish, even if you come across ideas or language that trips you up at first. Never read without a pen or pencil in hand, however, and don't skip over unfamiliar ideas or phrases. Instead, do the following:

CHECKLIST FOR READING AND ANNOTATING

☐ *Mark Up the Text*: Mark up the text, circling ideas that are confusing and words you don't know so that you can look them up later.

☐ *Underline or Highlight*: Underline what seem to be the main points of the text. Pay particular attention to the author's introduction and conclusion, where main ideas are often explicitly stated.

☐ *Record Your Response*: Record any ideas with which you agree or disagree. Jot notes in the margin to capture your preliminary reactions.

☐ *Talk Back to the Text*: Talk back—or write back—to passages that interest you, confuse you, or irritate you. Ask questions in the margin and write responses.

☐ *Examine Support*: Note the kinds of support the author provides for his or her main ideas. For example, does the author quote experts? Does he or she cite statistics?

Reading and Annotating the Letter

Letter to *The New York Times* (Oct. 30, 2003)

To the Editor:

Looking at the Oct. 29 front-page picture of two huge American soldiers towering over an Iraqi child and examining his pockets did two things for me. On the one hand, it made me wince to see what some of our soldiers are being forced to do in Iraq. On the other hand, it recalled for me a sharply contrasting picture of earlier G.I.'s, including me, handing out pieces of chocolate bars to newly liberated, joyous French children some 60 years ago.

It happened during the days and weeks after our D-Day landing on Omaha Beach in France. As members of the 616th Ordnance Ammunition Company, we not only fulfilled our original military goal of setting up the first American ammunition depot in France, but we also later became what we always should be, ambassadors of good will and conveyors of the best of the American dream.

I weep as I look at today's picture.

BERNARD BELLUSH
Valhalla, N.Y., Oct. 29, 2003

So, Bellush is probably a reader of the paper, and he cares about what he reads.

Readers of the *NYT* tend to be well educated and up-scale. He wants to reach those people.

This language is very powerful (i.e., "huge" and "towering"). It makes the soldiers seem scary. In using this language, Bellush echoes the kid's point of view.

Bellush uses the word "winces."—He really hates what he sees. But Bellush says it's not the soldiers' fault: They are "forced" to do it.

He uses the phrase "Sharply constrasting." Bellush means that "earlier" G.I.s weren't "towering" or "huge"—they gave chocolate to "joyous" children. What is Bellush's evidence? He was one of them!

Does he mean that there's a picture of the earlier G.I.s somewhere? Or, is he referring to a picture in his mind? This happened 60 years ago now. Are variables—such as children being used as combatants—different in this situation than in WWII?

Bellush is a little more specific here about where and when he had his "contrasting" experience as a G.I. He also includes more about what they accomplished (i.e., a military depot and "good will").

Bellush uses strong language here (i.e., he "weeps"). What makes Bellush so sad? He doesn't state so explicitly, but he seems to be claiming that things in Iraq are the opposite of how they were in France in his day. Maybe he is suggesting that there is a lack of friendliness and/or that the military's goals in Iraq have not yet been accomplished.

Restating the Case—Paraphrasing

Once you have a good understanding of the text, often the next step is to put it into your own words. Paraphrases are not meant to be brief. Rather, they offer a translation of complex ideas into more understandable language. Writing paraphrases helps you to gain a better handle on a text. When you paraphrase a complex text, you are re-wording that text sentence-by-sentence so that you can better comprehend the meaning conveyed. While this step is time-consuming, it teaches discipline of the mind and helps you to develop your critical analysis.

CHECKLIST FOR PARAPHRASING

☐   *Reread*: Reread the text to be paraphrased and look up any unfamiliar words in a dictionary.

☐   *Translate*: Translate the passage or put it into your own words. Be sure to put quotations marks around any phrases that you are citing from the text.

Paraphrasing the Letter

The Oct. 29 picture in *The New York Times* featured two American soldiers standing over an Iraqi kid. They appear to be going through his pockets. I had two reactions to this image. First, I was disturbed to see what U.S. soldiers have to do in Iraq. Second, I noticed how different this image is from images during WWII of U.S. soldiers giving chocolate to French kids (after D-Day landing on Omaha Beach in France)—during WWII. I was one of those guys.

We did a good job. We created the first American ammunition depot in France. We also brought caring and kindness to the people there. We embodied the American dream.

This picture makes me sad.

Cutting to the Chase—Summarizing

After you have previewed and annotated a text (and perhaps paraphrased it, especially if the ideas are complicated), your next step should be to summarize its main ideas. A summary presents a short restatement of the text's central point, and it may explain how the main ideas in the text support the central point. The chief aim of a summary, however, is to supply the overarching concepts conveyed by a text, and not to take up any minor details it mentions. All good summaries are brief and to the point, complete, and do not pass judgment on the issues the author addresses. Writing a summary will help you to grasp what you have read and allow you to use the information to support, refute, or reexamine the text in light of your own thoughts.

CHECKLIST FOR SUMMARIZING

☐   *Examine Your Annotations*: Look at your notes. This will help you to consider the most important parts of the text and its structure.

☐   *Pinpoint Main Ideas*: Write a short paragraph that presents the author's main point, mostly in your own words. Be sure to reread sections of the original text as necessary, placing the original text in quotation marks.

Summarizing the Letter

Bellush's letter examines a photo that appeared in *The New York Times*. It depicts two U.S. soldiers frisking an Iraqi child. He asserts that this experience is nothing like his experience as a soldier in France after World War II. Bellush implies that America is not achieving its goals in Iraq.

Weighing the Evidence—Analyzing and Evaluating

After you summarize and paraphrase a text, you are ready to **analyze** it. When you analyze a text, you ask more detailed questions about how the writer supports her or his ideas as well as whether the text is persuasive or not and why.

CHECKLIST FOR ANALYZING

☐ *Kinds of Support*: What kinds of support does the author use for his or her ideas?
- Is the evidence reliable? For example, if she or he quotes experts, are these experts credible? Why or why not? If he or she cites statistics, do they seem trustworthy? How can you tell? What was the sample from which the data were taken?
- Is there enough evidence? Citing a single expert who supports the author's claims or only one image might not be enough, for example.

☐ *Logical Reasoning*: How does the author connect ideas and support? Are there any obvious flaws in the author's reasoning?

☐ *Assumptions*: What assumptions does the author make about the issues raised in the text? Is the writer biased in any ways? Or, are the assumptions reasonable?

☐ *Tone*: What is the author's tone or attitude? Does the writer exercise humor, sarcasm, or irony? Does the writer attempt to elicit the audience's emotions or utilize objectivity to draw in the audience? How does the writer's attitude affect the presentation of his or her ideas?

Analyzing the Letter

Bellush contrasts the U.S. presence in Iraq today with its presence in France after World War II. He seems to want to focus on the roles of soldiers in the military and what they are "being forced to do." His main forms of evidence for these differences include his own memories and experiences as a soldier. Bellush also gives historical references. In particular, Bellush mentions D-day and landing on Omaha Beach in France. In order to compare the situations of Iraq in 2003 and France then he offers the evidence of soldiers' different interactions with children (the situation in the featured picture versus a "sharply contrasting picture of earlier G.I.s" that we do not see). Bellush is banking on the fact that this is enough information on which to base a comparison. His tone is effective in large part because it seems pretty personal and heartfelt (soldiers are "huge," "towering," and he "weeps"). One could argue that Bellush makes some compelling points and supports them with strong evidence. He wants us to understand that the situation in Iraq is worth getting upset about, and I think he accomplishes this. Still, one could also argue that all of these factors make Bellush's editorial open to the charge that he does not provide enough evidence and that he is not being objective enough.

Cracking the Case—Evaluating the Text

Now that you have previewed, annotated, summarized, and analyzed the text, you can assess how well the text works. Ask yourself the following questions:

CHECKLIST FOR EVALUATING

☐ *Convincing or Not*: Is the author's central point clear? Is it convincingly argued? Why or why not? Have my own views—or might other people's views—changed as a result of this text?

☐ *Your Views:* What are your thoughts on the topic? How can you support them? How do they relate to the ideas expressed in the author's text and his or her method of presenting them?

Evaluating the Letter

I can make a few tentative evaluative assertions about Bellush's editorial. First, Bellush's use of language is extremely effective, and it has the possibility of having a very strong impact on his audience. However, the drawback of his approach is that such language choices may make his assertions seem too dramatic or inflammatory to readers who are already likely to disagree with him. Second, Bellush uses two kinds of support for his perspectives—his own experiences, memories, and relevant historical references as well as the specific example of the child and soldiers in the featured photograph versus the "sharply contrasting picture of earlier G.I.s" that the reader cannot see. Bellush's personal experiences and memories are very persuasive forms of evidence. The featured visual only bolsters his support. However, the drawback of Bellush's approach is that he does not bring in other forms of evidence to support his views and thus opens himself to the charge of being biased. I would argue that Bellush's text is very persuasive—especially to those who find his language choices and use of evidence convincing. However, those who are predisposed not to agree with him would be more likely to be swayed by his claims if he acknowledged the potential differences between the Iraq and WWII situations, if he tempered his language, and if he included other sorts of evidence. This having been said, I believe doing so might go directly against Bellush's purposes—to really evoke emotions and cause the reader to think about the issues he raises. I also think that if he made all of these changes his editorial would have probably been too long for the space the newspaper could give him. For these reasons, I believe his argument accomplishes what it sets out to accomplish and does so very persuasively.

CULTURE AND CRITICISM: **EXERCISING YOUR SKILLS**

Now that we have watched John apply his skills in critical thinking, reading, and responding—previewing, annotating, paraphrasing, summarizing, analyzing, and evaluating—you are ready to use these same skills.

Analyze an Editorial

Put your new skills into practice as you examine an editorial from the *Chicago Tribune* about children eating their vegetables. First, preview, anno-tate, paraphrase, and summarize the piece. When you have finished, offer your own short analysis and evaluation of the text as well as the issues it addresses.

Chicago Tribune

Back Off on the Broccoli*

June 16, 2006

You can lead a kid to broccoli but you can't make him eat it. If that's your parenting style, then scrape those untouched veggies into the garbage disposal and try again tomorrow. And dump the guilt down the drain, too: Your kids are less likely to be overweight than kids who grow up in a clean-your-plate household, according to a new study.

Just in time for the 25th anniversary DVD edition of "Mommie Dearest," a study in the June issue of the journal *Pediatrics* finds that strict disciplinarian mothers are even more likely to raise chubby kids than those derelict moms who let their youngsters graze on Pringles and M&Ms. Moms who set clear rules and enforce them with flexibility and respect are least likely to have overweight youngsters.

The study of 872 families divided mothers into four groups—authoritarian, permissive, neglectful and flexible—and checked the kids' body mass indexes two years later. Roughly 10 percent of 1st graders with permissive or neglectful mothers were overweight, compared with 17 percent of those with strict disciplinarian mothers and less than 4 percent of those with flexible moms.

This makes perfect sense to anyone who was forced as a child to sit for hours at the dinner table, staring sullenly at a pile of cold lima beans long after everyone else had finished their dessert. Far from encouraging healthy eating habits, that sort of discipline fostered a lifelong hostility to lentils and a rebellious tendency in adulthood to eat Ben & Jerry's straight out of the carton, often instead of dinner.

But today's kids aren't waiting 'til they grow up to get fat. About a third of children ages 2–19 are overweight—three times as many as in the mid-1960s, with the biggest increases coming since 1990. Doctors also are seeing an alarming number of children with typically adult health problems such as diabetes and hypertension.

It's no wonder some mothers, especially the ones who are predisposed to micromanage their kids' lives, react by declaring the house a fat- and sugar-free zone. But good intentions can backfire. Too much anxiety in the home can cause kids to overeat for comfort or escape—if it doesn't trigger eating disorders like bulimia and anorexia.

Kids who are allowed judicious access to the cookie jar, though, sometimes forget it's there. And the ones who aren't force-fed asparagus are more inclined to try it, perhaps not the first time it appears on their plates, but eventually. Given choices—and limits—kids can learn to self-regulate. The lesson for moms is that in parenting, as in dieting, moderation is the key.

The study drew no conclusions about fathers because precious few of them participated. Our unscientific observation is that when it comes to nutrition, Dad is often either the good cop or the bad example . . . or both. Someone ought to do a study about that.

*The full text can be found at http://www.chicagotribune.com/news/opinion/chi-0606160311jun16,01119641.story?coll =chi-newsopinion-hed.

Analyze Websites

Using these same skills—previewing, annotating, paraphrasing, summarizing, analyzing, and evaluating—examine the two sets of websites that follow. Look at each website's layout; organizational structure; navigational flags and indexes; search tools; use of icons or buttons; use of columns, tables, charts, and graphs; use of fonts; headers and footers; headings and subheadings; bulleted and numbered lists; text wrapping; decorative elements; pop-up windows; and digital illustrations and graphics. (See "Rhetoric in Visual and Multimedia Texts" for additional tips for analyzing websites.)

The first set of websites is for two environmentally oriented programs to save endangered species. The second set is designed to represent the World Trade Organization (http://www.wto.org and http:www.gatt.org).

Begin by previewing the two websites in each set and annotating them. In particular, make note of the various similarities and differences between them. Then answer the following questions for each set of websites: What assertions might you be able to support about the similarities and differences between the two websites? What is the relationship between these two websites? In what ways are they each effective for their purposes?

Websites: Set 1

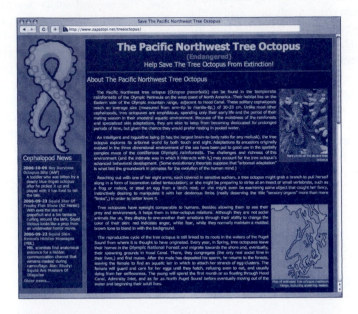

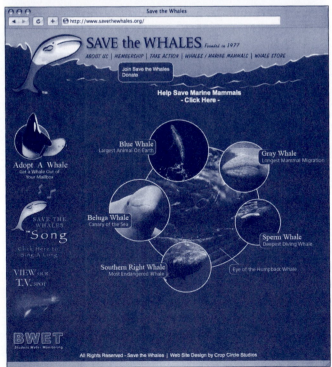

Websites: Set 2

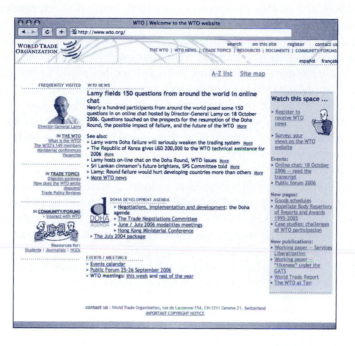

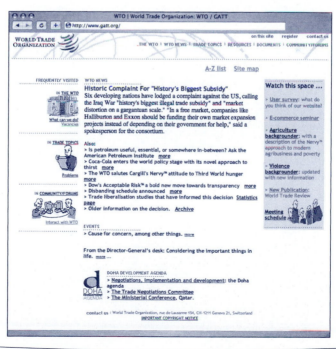

CHAPTER SUMMARY

In Chapter 1 of *Pop Perspectives* you have learned about studying culture, and you have gained important access to tools for adopting a critical perspective—critical thinking, reading, and responding—that will be helpful to you in all of your college classes as well as in your work and other experiences outside the classroom.

You have also watched how John applied his skills in critical thinking, reading, and responding through previewing, annotating, paraphrasing, summarizing, analyzing, and evaluating. In order to reinforce your new skills, you have also completed the exercises to apply what you have learned. You are now ready to discover more about critical analyses of written as well as visual and multimedia texts and to apply what you learn to your writing.

In Chapter 2, "Rhetoric and Reading to Write," you will learn how to offer even more careful, detailed analyses of written as well as visual and multimedia texts. In addition, you will learn about how your critical thinking and reading skills can make you a stronger writer—how you can *read to write*. In particular, you will examine the early stages of the writing process. These include freewriting, mapping, clustering, scratch outlining, and formal outlining. Chapter 2 offers exercises to test and apply what you have learned. All of this will help you get ready to fully analyze others' texts as well as to carefully create strong, persuasive texts of your own.

CHAPTER TWO

Rhetoric and Reading to Write

POP PROFILE: RHETORIC AND READING TO WRITE

Meet Matthew Hutchinson

As an undergraduate I studied English as well as film production, motion graphics design, and digital animation. I received a master's degree in communication and I was awarded the Woodruff Fellowship in Media Innovation and Responsibility by the Georgia State University. I coproduced Flashbang!, an international motion graphic animation festival based in Atlanta and taught undergraduate courses in film aesthetics/analysis and film production. I am currently an associate producer and writer for Turner Broadcasting in Atlanta. I also continue to write, direct, and produce independent films and music videos. Some of my music videos have been featured on the Black Entertainment Television program.

The ability to analyze and decode the rhetoric of contemporary visual culture has been one of the greatest gifts of my life. In college and graduate school, I focused much of my academic attention on breaking down and critically examining the messages of mass media and television. Now that I work in television, I've found that these analytic skills are instrumental in producing compelling writing and imagery. Having a larger sense of rhetorical perspective and self-analysis about my own work as a producer is most certainly a professional, and I believe emotional, advantage. As a writer and filmmaker, my creative process is absolutely dependent on rhetorical analysis.

In Chapter 1 we learned about the varied definitions of culture—be it those in which the opera, high tea, a palatial estate, the symphony, and Shakespeare are central or those that consider The Donnas, Cheerios, Abercrombie and Fitch, Nickelback, and *The Fast and the Furious* just as significant. In addition, we discovered how to adopt a critical perspective through using some introductory techniques in critical thinking, reading, and responding. We investigated how to utilize previewing, annotating, paraphrasing, summarizing, analyzing, and evaluating. And we applied our new knowledge to several texts.

However, we have yet to unearth all of the key questions to ask while analyzing a text. In fact, so far we have just scratched the surface. A critical thinker, reader, and writer needs more equipment in her or his toolbox in order both to interpret and assess others' work effectively as well as to write her or his own texts persuasively. One of the most essential critical thinking, reading, and writing tools is a knowledge of **rhetoric**—the skills of effective writing and speaking that help us to inform and persuade others, and sometimes even to encourage them to take action. We use rhetoric when we attempt to explain to a friend various politicians' views on specific issues, to convince her that one candidate ought to be supported over another, and maybe even to coax her to take a bus, subway, or car to the polls to cast her vote.

Chapter 2 will teach you some more complex critical approaches for both reading and writing. You will examine two types of ways to analyze rhetoric: rhetorical analysis of a written text (a speech by President George W. Bush) and rhetorical analysis of a visual text (the Calvin Klein Obsession advertising campaign). You will learn how to read and analyze texts that have both written and visual components. Then, you will observe one student's transition from critical reading of texts to critical writing about texts—specifically, you will see the importance of prewriting strategies such as taking notes, freewriting, mapping, clustering, scratch outlining, and formal outlining. Finally, you will encounter two different types of exercises throughout this chapter. The first one asks you to take what you have learned and apply it to a written text. The second invites you to harness all of the skills you have learned thus far, in both Chapters 1 and 2, to investigate a wide range of pop culture texts, moving from informal types of writing to more formal prose.

RHETORIC

Even though you may not have recognized it at the time, the issues we examined in Chapter 1—previewing, annotating, paraphrasing, summarizing, analyzing, and evaluating—were also actually partly concerned with rhetoric. They were helping us to explore how a text is constructed so as to inform, persuade, and perhaps encourage others to take action.

What is rhetoric? Rhetoric gets its earliest meanings from the Greek words *rhema*, or "word," and *rhetor*, originally referring to a teacher. Today a **rhetor** indicates a person who employs any means to inform and persuade (the classical Greek scholar Aristotle's definition) as well as encourages others to take action through symbols or language. Scholars generally consider rhetoric to be the study and use of language (written and spoken), images, and concepts to inform, persuade, and possibly move an audience. We can witness rhetoric operating virtually everywhere, in the popular media, in our everyday habits and rituals, and in the written texts (appearing within any discipline) that make up our culture.

When we rhetorically analyze a text, we take our understanding of texts one step further, looking at how they use language and visuals in even more detail. We once again consider issues related to the author, context, audience, purpose, and structure. However, this time we delve into them in more detail, also looking at two other rhetorical concerns, **constraints** and **intertextuality.** Constraints are the limitations with which the author has to contend in producing images and writing texts. For example, editorial writers have only a small amount of space within which to make their points; they have to adhere to the rules of editorial writing, a form of writing that is often more opinion based than evidence based; and they have to respond in a timely fashion so that other readers understand the context that prompted this response. Intertextuality describes the other sources or cultural references upon which the text draws. Often such references point to other texts, concepts, or events. For instance, popular websites sometimes reference other resources, related texts, as well as relevant events and news. Sometimes they also include advertisements for other products and services.

THE APPEALS

When rhetoric is at work, very real issues are at stake. Studying rhetoric and responding to it require us to ask questions about why we choose to be certain kinds of people and not other kinds; why we claim membership in certain cultural, historical, political, or institutional groups and not others; why we believe particular ideas to be true and others to be false; why we align ourselves with certain kinds of causes and against others; and why we understand specific things as "normal" and other things as "abnormal."

Once we have carefully considered the issues of author, context, audience, purpose, structure, constraints, and intertextuality in a text, our final step is to distinguish how the text is constructed to appeal to this particular audience in this particular context. The classical Greek scholar Aristotle contended that there are three major appeals to the audience at work in most texts and that multiple appeals can occur within one text—even within a single quotation in a text—simultaneously: **ethos, pathos,** and **logos.**

Ethos

The Greek word *ethos* is related to our English word "ethics." It refers to the trust-worthiness of a rhetor—the writer, speaker, or image creator—based upon how others perceive her or his character. Aristotle believed that intelligence, character, and good will were the attributes that produce credibility. For our purposes, ethos most often describes an appeal a rhetor makes to the audience based on her or his authority or credibility. For instance, the audience is more likely to listen to the rhetor if she or he is considered to be a reliable source of information, has a positive preexisting reputation, has good will, or is an acknowledged expert. Ethos can also refer to the presumed character of the audience, as it is constructed by the rhetor. For instance, a rhetor can make assumptions about her or his audience's ethos—such as the audience's own integrity, honesty, trustworthiness or, conversely, the audience's own combativeness, deceitfulness, and disloyalty.

How Is Ethos Created? Ethos can be established through having knowledge about the issues, demonstrating fairness, having the best interests of the listeners in mind, and building a relationship with the audience. In addition, there are other methods. Here are several specific means of establishing ethos:

- *Position*: In some cases, the rhetor's prior behavior, position or role in the community, and knowledge or expertise guarantee credibility.
- *Self-Presentation*: Some methods of self-presentation make rhetors more or less believable—tone, word choice, appearance (when relevant), and other factors contribute to self-presentation.
- *Identification*: If the rhetor identifies with the values of the community, her or his rhetoric might be more effective.
- *Perspective*: An effective rhetor needs to assume the right position vis-à-vis his or her audience at the right moment—Greek rhetoricians termed this *kairos* (timeliness). For instance, when a rhetor uses the word "I," it can create a friendly, personal relationship with the reader/viewer in one context; in another context, the use of "I" can seem biased, or overly reliant on personal experience. Similarly a person's use of "we" can either construct a shared set of relations between the rhetor and the audience—a very powerful connection—or create a false intimacy.
- *Language Choices*: A rhetor's choice of style and specific language choices can lend (or detract from) credibility as well, depending on the level of authority, reliability, experience, and knowledge these choices imply.
- *Cultural Status*: In certain contexts, a rhetor's background—gender, sexual preference, race and ethnicity, age, class status, abilities, or membership in another culturally determined group—can affect how particular audiences view her or his ethos.

Letters to the editor provide some superb examples of ethos in action. A writer will often attempt to establish her ethos by articulating her own background and position to seem credible. Likewise, sometimes a writer will establish ethos by constructing a "we" to which she belongs. She may use vivid or contrasting language to help establish her ethos. Finally, a writer may use her cultural status to impact her ethos. The fact that she has had relevant experience or has related expertise may add to the persuasiveness of her assertions.

Pathos

The word "pathos" emerges from the greek *pathe*, which means emotions, and is related to the English words "pathetic," "sympathy," and "empathy." Pathos depicts an appeal to the reader's or viewer's emotions. It refers to the ability to evoke feelings in readers and viewers through a combination of concrete language and vivid examples. Aristotle mentions emotions such as anger, calmness, enmity, hate, fear, confidence, shame, shamelessness, kindliness, unkindliness, pity, indignation, envy, and emulation.

How Is Pathos Created? While pathos can certainly be used to manipulate, it remains one of the most effective ways to move people to action. Pathos is an appeal that we experience in many places—in newspaper editorials, advertisements, paintings, murals, sculptures, films, television shows, and political speeches. Context, values, and social status also influence the kinds of emotions that can be elicited and how they are elicited. A rhetor often tries to evoke emotion from her or his audience so as to be more persuasive, as well as to get the reader to do what he or she wants him or her to do. Appeals to pathos are achieved through the following:

- *Concrete Language/Detailed Descriptions*: Carefully chosen language (e.g., word choice, imagery, metaphors, and analogies) as well as visuals can stir the audience's emotions.
- *Strategic Examples and Illustrations*: Oftentimes a person focuses on stories, examples, and illustrations to give a text power. Appeals to pathos may appear as part of support for a claim or, since they can draw in the reader, in the introductions and conclusions to arguments.

Advertisements offer some excellent examples of pathos in action. They often use concrete language and detailed descriptions to appeal strategically to their audience's emotions. Sometimes they utilize captions, superimpositions (words placed on top of images), logos, footnotes, fine print, watermarks, motifs, allusions, inset quotes, or headlines. Likewise, the visuals in ads can appeal to an audience's emotions through the images themselves as well as how they are arranged on the page.

Logos

The term *logos* emerges from the Greek word meaning "word." It consists of an appeal to the audience's logic or reason and proposes a logical position, which it supports with evidence. Logos also frequently refers to the parts of an essay that depend upon rational appeals.

How Is Logos Created? A writer attempts to appeal to the reader's logic with evidence such as statistics and diagrams, standard argumentative structures, well-reasoned examples, and expert testimony that is field or discipline dependent. Logos relates to the formal logic of rhetoric.

Appeals to logos are most often made through formal argumentation, a subject that will be discussed at length in the next chapter. However, when beginning to look for appeals to logos in a text, examine the following:

- *Credibility*: Well-selected experts and scholarship from credible sources can make an assertion more persuasive.
- *Evidence*: The rhetor's claims should be supported with solid, reliable evidence that backs up her or his assertions.
- *Logic*: One part of the argument should necessarily lead to the next. There should not be any flaws in the logic of the argument.
- *Counterarguments*: The argument should consider and anticipate counter-arguments that might be made against such a position.

Essays in academic journals—about sociology, engineering, film, health sciences, chemistry, ecology, journalism, forestry, or any other professional field or discipline—furnish some of the best examples of logos in action. These texts will often use logos through establishing author credibility. There may be information about the writer that indicates her or his credentials to write about the subject. Logos may also be created through use of evidence—referencing previous studies and citing the words of experts. The text may use examples, statistics, charts, and other forms of support. Appeals to logos can also often be found in the actual structure of these texts. Most points will lead logically from one to the next, from general to more and more specific—such that evidence and information for each element are included. Finally, a writer may use logos by referencing opposing positions, acknowledging their existence and possibly challenging them.

CHECKLIST FOR RHETORIC IN WRITTEN TEXTS

Remember, when you analyze the rhetoric of a written text (or even a text that is primarily written but also has some visual components—like a website), you will want to examine all of the issues addressed in previewing, annotating, paraphrasing, summarizing, and analyzing. Additionally, though, ask yourself these questions:

CHECKLIST FOR RHETORIC IN WRITTEN TEXTS

☐ *Constraints*: What are the limitations with which the rhetor has to contend in producing this text? In what ways might the context or purpose shape (or compel) the kinds of texts that the rhetor produces?

☐ *Intertextuality*: What other sources or cultural references does this text draw upon? How do you know? What names, ideas, and concepts are discussed by this text? How does referring to such sources lend credibility to the text or perhaps detract from it?

☐ *Ethos*: How does the rhetor represented in the text reflect credibility, good will, and strong moral character? Is the rhetor successful in doing so? How does the rhetor use position, self-presentation, identification, perspective, language choices, and cultural status to achieve this? Does the rhetor construct an "ethos" for her or his audience as well?

☐ *Pathos*: What language choices, examples, and illustrations are employed to stir the audience's emotions? What emotions do they elicit and how?

☐ *Logos*: Does the rhetor use credible experts, evidence, and logic as well as references and refutations of counterarguments?

READING TO WRITE: PREWRITING

As you can see, adopting a critical perspective and engaging in rhetorical analysis are not only modes of reading, but also forms of active and critical *writing*. As we gain crucial distance from texts, in a sense we are already beginning to formulate our responses to those texts in writing—whether in our highlighted portions of the text, our sticky notes on the pages, the filled margins of the texts, the notes in our notebooks, or even in the ideas taking shape in our own minds. When we act as critical writers, we are always talking back to texts, asking tough questions of them and their authors, starting to write down—even if in only the most informal ways—our own evaluations.

In the next chapter we will move to the more detailed forms of writing: drafting, reflecting, and revising. In addition, we will discover more fully that when we begin to write in earnest, we also find that we need to apply to our own work the same critical thinking tools we are learning here. We will ask ourselves whether the parts of our essays fit together as well as they might, whether our main idea is in fact clear and well supported, whether the logic of our prose holds, whether we have adequately defined the terms we use, whether we have reliable sources to back up our thoughts, whether our own assumptions are valid, whether our word choices are persuasive, whether our language is concise enough not to obscure our purpose and our point, as well as whether our structure and arrangement best support our thoughts.

Before we can move to these later stages in the writing process, however, we will first need to examine how a critical perspective and knowledge of rhetoric can help us to begin to write critically. In order to do this, we need to learn some crucial **prewriting** strategies or ways to write down our general ideas on a topic. Prewriting can include techniques such as **freewriting, mapping, clustering, scratch outlining, and formal outlining.** When we freewrite, we write down all that occurs to us on a certain topic; when we map, we create an image of the main points in the text and their relationships; when we cluster ideas, we take what seem like distinct or unrelated pieces and find their commonalties, grouping them together to formulate our own assertions about the text; when we make a scratch outline, we jot down our main points and the key ideas that will support them; and when we make a formal outline, we flesh out these key ideas and consider which quotations from the text we will select to back up our ideas.

RHETORIC IN ACTION: ANALYZING A WRITTEN TEXT

Now we will examine President George W. Bush's address on Veteran's Day, November 11, 2003.

> *Tanya is an information science and technologies major. She plans to pursue a career in library science and data systems management. Tanya believes that skills in rhetorical analysis are very important for all of her career interests: "People who work in information technology need to be extremely strong writers—we have to be able to write concise reports and memos, manage digital graphics and design, create data bases, offer multi-media reports, and design web pages. All of this involves really understanding rhetoric—how context, audience, purpose, structure, and the appeals can make a text persuasive. Without this knowledge, I might be able to design a multi-media report that contains the correct information. But would it win over my clients? Without attention to those rhetorical elements, probably not." In her spare time, Tanya enjoys designing graphics and websites for friends and family, working as a volunteer writing tutor for "at risk" children in her community, and dancing with a modern jazz dance group.*

Watch how one student, Tanya, employs critical reading and responding skills, as well as her knowledge of rhetoric. First she briefly skims and previews the text. Then Tanya reads and annotates it. Next Tanya paraphrases and summarizes the essay. In an effort to analyze and evaluate the text, she begins the writing process by prewriting.

As you read Bush's text alongside Tanya's detailed commentary, notice how her annotations take into consideration author, context, audience, purpose, structure, constraints, intertextuality, ethos, pathos, and logos.

Reading and Annotating

President Bush Discusses Iraq in Veteran's Day Address[1]

THE PRESIDENT: Ed, thank you very much. It's an honor to be here. I appreciate your invitation. I want to thank you for your decades of leadership in the conservative movement. Presidents come and go, except here at the Heritage Foundation. (Laughter.) I appreciate being with your good bride, Linda; the trustees of the Heritage; the longtime Heritage supporters; and the Ronald Reagan Fellow at Heritage, a man who is a fine leader and a fine Attorney General, Ed Meese. (Applause.)

It's appropriate that we gather in the building named for Ronald Reagan. The Heritage Foundation emerged as an important voice in Washington during the Reagan years. The American people gave Ronald Reagan his mandate for leadership. Yet, it was the Heritage Foundation, with a book by that title, from which he drew ideas and inspiration. Ever since, in the councils of Washington, Heritage has been an advocate for free enterprise, traditional values and the advance of liberty around the world. My administration has benefited from your good work, and so has our country. Thank you for what you do. (Applause.)

We meet on Veterans Day, and I know there are many veterans in this room. On behalf of the nation, I thank you for your service to our country. (Applause.) The title of veteran is a term of great respect in America. All who served, whether for a few years or for many, have put the nation's needs above their own. All stood ready, if the order came to risk everything for their country's cause.

Author: Most likely Bush is not the author of this speech, but he delivered it. Bush is the president, and a member of the Republican party. He is also financially conservative, supportive of the Christian right, anti-abortion, etc.—white, upper middle class, male, from a political family, and a Yale grad.

Context: Bush delivers this speech in the nation's capitol, at the Heritage Foundation (also a conservative group). They value principles such as free enterprise, individual freedom, and strong national defense. The speech is given on Veteran's Day, 2003; U.S. troops are still in Iraq even though the war has been declared over. Bush has come under criticism for keeping the military in Iraq.

Bush shows good will—he uses humor (laughter), politeness ("thank you," "appreciate"), compliments (i.e., "an honor," "good bride," "fine leader," "fine Attorney General," "important," "Thank you.")—to draw in his audience.

Tone: I think Bush sounds polished, polite, and formal.

Audience: Bush is trying to persuade various audiences—the people in the room, veterans, the Republican Party, the American people, and international political leaders. Bush establishes a positive relationship with his immediate audience—use of "longtime" and "fine."

Ethos: Bush uses his position as president; self-presentation as a reliable person; identification with his audience, Reagan, and the Heritage Foundation; and language choices to build his credibility.

Purpose: Bush has a number of purposes that are working simultaneously. I think Bush wants to praise the efforts of his own party and veterans, persuade various audiences that U.S. efforts in Iraq are going well, refute those who oppose him, and warn terrorists that the U.S. will not back down.

[1]The full speech can be found at http://www.whitehouse.gov/news/releases/2003/11/200311111-10 .html. See http://www.whitehouse.gov/president/ for access to President Bush's other speeches and policy statements.

Our wars have taken from us some of our finest citizens, and every hour of the lifetimes they hoped to live. And the courage of our military has given us every hour we live in freedom. (Applause.)

Pathos: Bush chooses concrete language to say that veterans are deserving of "great respect," will "risk everything," and are our "finest citizens" who have "courage." He directly connects military service to "freedom" here. It seems like he is making an emotional appeal to his various audiences—to their senses of themselves as good, patriotic Americans. This is a really smart move, but it also may reveal a bias.

Intertextuality: Bush refers to WWII, a war in American history that people generally thought was just. Notice how Bush uses really vivid images here to draw in veterans.

Constraints: I'm not sure about this. However, maybe Bush is limited by two different interests—he needs to discuss Iraq but also to talk about Veteran's Day—so he links the two. I'm not sure if this link really holds, though. Should it?

Intertextuality: This reminds me of other famous speeches by presidents and senators over the years that have set up an "us" and a "them." I am not sure which specific examples I could point to yet, though. This tactic just sounds really familiar to me.

Okay. Now it's really clear. There is a definite "us" and "them" thing being created—those soldiers who work for American ideals and those enemies who are "ruthless."

Intertextuality: This sort of echoes Thomas Paine's famous quotes in 1776 as he attempted to convince Americans to stay the course when they were considering reconciling with Great Britain after many difficult battles: "what we obtain too cheap, we esteem too lightly, 'tis dearness only that gives everything its value."

Intertextuality: Bush refers to Arlington Cemetery, which makes people think of bravery and heroism. He wants to connect U.S. troops' efforts in Iraq with these same qualities—and possibly to prepare the American people for more deaths.

In every generation, members of the Armed Forces have been loyal to one another, and faithful to the ideals of America. After the second world war, returning veterans often said they had just been doing their jobs, or didn't talk about their service at all. Yet they knew the stakes of the fight they had been in, and the magnitude of what they had achieved. Long after putting away his uniform, one American expressed his pride in having served in World War II. He said, "I feel like I played my part in turning this from a century of darkness into a century of light." This is true of all who served and sacrificed in the struggles of the 20th century. They maintained the greatest fighting force in the world. They kept our country free, and we're grateful to them all. (Applause.)

We come to this Veterans Day in a time of war. And today's military is acting in the finest traditions of the veterans who came before them. They've given all that we've asked of them. They are showing bravery in the face of ruthless enemies, and compassion to people in great need. Our men and women in uniform are warriors and they are liberators, strong and kind and decent. By their courage, they keep us safe; by their honor, they make us proud. (Applause.)

When we lose such Americans in battle we lose our best. And the time—this time of brave achievement is also a time of sacrifice. Not far from this place, at Army and Navy medical centers, young service members are recovering from injuries of war. Not far from here, at Arlington National Cemetery, as in home towns across America, we have laid to rest young men and women who died in distant lands. For their families, this is a terrible sorrow, and we pray for their comfort. For the nation, there is a feeling of loss, and we remember and we honor every name. (Applause.)

Our people in uniform know the cost and risk of war. They also know what is at stake in this war. Army Command Sergeant Major Loakimo Falaniko recently lost his son, Private Jonathan Falaniko, in an attack near Baghdad. Father and son both served in Iraq, in the same unit, the 1st Armored Division's Engineer Brigade. At his son's memorial service, Command Sergeant Major Falaniko said this: "What our country brings to Iraq is a chance for freedom and democracy. We're making a difference every day. My son died for a good cause. He answered the nation's call."

Our mission in Iraq and Afghanistan is clear to our service members—and clear to our enemies. Our men and women are fighting to secure the freedom of more than 50 million people who recently lived under two of the cruelest dictatorships on Earth. Our men and women are fighting to help democracy and peace and justice rise in a troubled and violent region. Our men and women are fighting terrorist enemies thousands of miles away in the heart and center of their power, so that we do not face those enemies in the heart of America. (Applause.) Our men and women are fighting for the security of America and for the advance of freedom, and that is a cause worth fighting for. (Applause.)

> *Logos and Pathos:* Bush supports his point that the efforts of soldiers in Iraq are heroic using testimonial evidence (logos). But, here's the odd thing. This choice also seems to allow him to appeal to the audience's emotions (pathos). I guess he is doing both at the same time!
>
> Bush suggests that we all know what we are doing in Iraq—that the reasons for the war are "clear." I think he's trying to allay his audience's fears here.
>
> *Pathos:* I notice that Bush utilizes contrasting imagery a lot. American ideals are about "peace" and "justice" and "causes," but Iraq is a "troubled" and "violent" region under one of the "cruelest dictatorships."
>
> *Pathos:* Bush tends to repeat phrases like "the failure of democracy" to drive home the idea that if democracy is important, U.S. efforts in Iraq are important. This seems really effective rhetorically. And, in a speech this repetition is probably helpful. But is he overstating the case? I'm not sure.

The work we are in is not easy; yet it is essential. The failure of democracy in Afghanistan and Iraq will condemn every advocate of freedom in those two countries to prison or death, and would extinguish the democratic hopes of millions in the Middle East. The failure of democracy in those two countries would provide new basis for the terrorist network and embolden terrorists and their allies around the world. The failure of democracy in those two countries would convince terrorists that America backs down under attack, and more attacks on America would surely follow.

The terrorists cite the examples of Beirut and Somalia as evidence that America can be made to run. Five years ago one of the terrorists said that an attack could make America retreat in less than 24 hours. The terrorists are mistaken. (Applause.) The United States will complete our work in Iraq and in Afghanistan. Democracy in those two countries will succeed. And that success will be a great milestone in the history of liberty.

A democratic revolution that has reached across the globe will finally take root in the Middle East. The stagnation and isolation and anger of that region will give way to progress and opportunity. (Applause.) America and the world will be safer from catastrophic violence because terror is not the tool of the free. (Applause.)

The United States has made an unbreakable commitment to the success of freedom in Afghanistan and Iraq. We have a strategy to see that commitment through. In Afghanistan, we're helping to build a free and stable democracy, as we continue to track down and destroy Taliban and al Qaeda forces. Following years of cruel oppression, the Afghan people are living with hope and they're making steady progress.

In Iraq, the terrorists have chosen to make a stand and to test our resolve. Their violence is concentrated in a relatively small area of that country. Yet, the terrorists are dangerous. For the sake of Iraq's future, for the sake of America's security, these killers must be defeated. (Applause.)

After the swift advance of our coalition to Baghdad and the removal of Saddam Hussein from power, some remnants of the regime fled from the battlefield. Over time, Baath Party and Fedayeen fighters and other Saddam loyalists have organized to attack our forces, to terrorize international aid workers and to murder innocent Iraqis. These bitter holdouts would rather see Iraqis dead than see them free.

Logos: Now Bush anticipates counterarguments and refutes them ("The terrorists are mistaken").

Bush blends appeals to logos and pathos here, reinforcing the idea that the U.S. will not back down—almost as if "we" are being bullied and won't stand for it. I have to think more about whether I think this a fair approach. Again, appealing to pathos, Bush puts two opposites together: "democratic revolution" and "catastrophic violence." In addition, Bush asks his audience to believe that they are part of this "we" he mentions. Moreover, here's that opposite language again—"stable democracy" versus "cruel oppression."

Pathos: I think Bush uses a lot of vivid language to evoke audience emotions (i.e., "test our resolve," cruel oppression, "terrorists," and "killers").

Logos: Bush is trying to provide evidence that the situation in the Middle East is a dire one in need of U.S. intervention. This is an appeal to logos. He also tries to establish the common goals of the two terrorist groups and the idea that they might be linked—both acting as enemies of the U.S. But, does he prove this connection or just assume it? I have to think more about that.

Foreign jihadists have arrived across Iraq's borders in small groups with the goal of installing a Taliban-like regime. Also present in the country are some terrorists from Ansar Islam and from al Qaeda, who are always eager to join in the killing and who seek revenge after their defeat in Afghanistan. Saddam loyalists and foreign terrorists may have different long-term goals, but they share a near-term strategy—to terrorize Iraqis and to intimidate America and our allies.

Recent reporting suggests that despite their differences, these killers are working together to spread chaos and terror and fear. Since the fall of Saddam Hussein, 93 percent of terror attacks have occurred in Baghdad and five of Iraq's 18 provinces. The violence is focused in 200 square miles known as the Baathist Triangle, the home area to Saddam Hussein and most of his associates. Here, the enemy is waging the battle, and it is here that the enemy will be defeated. (Applause.)

In the last few months, the adversary has changed its composition and method, and our coalition is adapting accordingly. We're employing the latest battlefield technology to locate mortar positions and roadside bombs. Our forces are moving against specific targets based on intelligence gathered from Iraqis. We're conducting hundreds of daily patrols. Last month alone we made 1,500 raids against terrorists. The recent operations have resulted in the capture or death of more than a thousand killers, the seizure of 4,500 mortar rounds; 1,600 rocket-propelled grenades have been seized, thousands of other weapons and military equipment. Our coalition is on the offensive in Iraq, and we will stay on the offensive. (Applause.)

The long-term security of Iraq will be assured by the Iraqis, themselves: 118,000 Iraqis are now serving as police officers and border guards, civil defense personnel and in the facilities protection service. Iraq's security forces join in operations with our troops and they patrol towns and cities independently. Some 700 troops

Logos: Notice the language choice here to define "the enemy." What was two groups a moment ago has now become one. Also look at how "killers" and "the enemy" have become interchangeable, creating pathos in the audience. This is really effective rhetorically. But I also wonder if it isn't a little sneaky.

Here Bush also uses facts and statistics to support his idea that the U.S. troops' efforts in Iraq are successful. Now Bush gets really specific in his appeal to logos—providing evidence for what the U.S. is doing in Iraq that is valuable (i.e., "latest battlefield technology," "moving against specific targets," "conducting hundreds of daily patrols," "capture or death of . . . killers," and "seizure of 4,500 mortar rounds"). The idea of the death of killers is interesting. How is the death of killers not accomplished by a killer? Hmm . . . .

Bush also uses logos to show and establish the Iraqis' own role. Why is this important to the rest of his text and its purposes? I have to think about this more.

Okay. Here I think Bush is anticipating a counterargument: He knows that Americans (and people across the world) many want the U.S. troops to pull out of Iraq and that they want Iraq to govern itself. So, he's trying to deal with that potential assertion head-on. But, does he do this effectively?

are now serving in the new Iraqi army. Thousands more are being trained, and we expect to see 35,000 Iraqi troops in the field by the end of next year. Increasingly, the Iraqi people are assuming the responsibilities and the risks of protecting their own country. And their willingness to accept these duties is one of the surest signs that the Iraqis want freedom, and that the Iraqis are headed toward self-government. (Applause.)

Under our strategy, increasing authority is being transferred to the Iraqi people. The Iraqi Governing Council has appointed ministers who are responsible for the day-to-day operations of the Iraqi government. The Council has also begun the process that will lead to a new constitution. No friend or enemy should doubt Iraq liberty will find a lasting home.

Logos and Pathos: Bush counters the charges that the U.S. is spending too much time in Iraq and that the Iraqis do not want the U.S. there. Notice the appeal to pathos again: "we're offering aid and self-rule and hope for the future; the terrorists offer nothing but oppression and death." This also sets up a further contrast between the U.S. (better) and the "terrorists" (much worse).

Notice how Bush grants the point here—that "democracy will not spring up in a matter of months." Bush is using a lot of logos and pathos here. By allying himself with all that is good and just, he is also trying to reestablish his own ethos as someone we can trust.

Iraqis are a proud people and they want their national independence. And they can see the difference between those who are attacking their country and those who are helping to build it. Our coalition is training new police; the terrorists are trying to kill them. We're protecting pipelines and power plants for the good of the Iraqi people; the terrorists are trying to blow them up. We're turning authority over to Iraqi leaders; the terrorists are trying to assassinate them. We're offering aid and self-rule and hope for the future; the terrorists offer nothing but oppression and death. The vast majority of Iraqis know exactly what is going on in their country today. Having seen the worst of tyranny, the Iraqi people will reject the return of tyranny. (Applause.)

After decades of dictator's sustained assault on Iraq's society and dignity and spirit, a Jeffersonian democracy will not spring up in a matter of months. We know that our Baathist and terrorist enemies are ruthless and cunning. We also know that the lives of Iraqis have improved greatly in seven short months. Yet, we know the remaining tasks are difficult.

We also know a few things about our own country. America gained its own independence and helped free much of the world by taking on difficult tasks. We're a confident people, and we have a reason to be confident. Our Armed Forces are skilled and powerful and humane. They're the best in the world. (Applause.) I will keep them that way. (Applause.)

We've got good friends and allies serving with us in Iraq. There are 32 countries standing beside our troops. Our commanders have the capabilities they have requested, and they're meeting a changing enemy with flexible tactics. The Congress has provided the resources we need to support our military and to improve the daily lives of newly-liberated people. Other nations and organizations have stepped up to provide more than $18 billion to the emerging democracies of Afghanistan and Iraq. The peoples of those two countries are sacrificing for their own liberty. And the United States once again is fighting in the cause of our nation, the great cause of liberty. And we know that the cause of liberty will prevail. (Applause.)

Much is asked of us, and we have answered this kind of challenge before. In the summer of 1948, the Soviet Union imposed a sudden and total blockade on the city of Berlin in order to force the allies out. More than 2 million people would soon be without food or fuel or medicine. The entire world watched and wondered if free peoples would back down—wondered whether free people would abandon their commitments. It was at the outset of the Cold War, and the will and the resolve of America were being measured.

> **Logos:** Here Bush provides a real case as an example, the outset of the Cold Wars. This seems like a wise choice. But does the example support his claim? Does the analogy/comparison really work?
>
> **Intertextuality:** Bush creates a connection between the situation with Iraq, the Soviet Union's actions in 1948, and Reagan's efforts during the Cold War. He is linking the Iraqi effort to the fight against communism. I don't know what I think about this link. Is the situation really the same? I am not sure. I think I need to learn more about both situations before I can say for sure.

In an urgent meeting, all the alternatives were discussed, including retreat. When the moment of decision came, President Harry Truman said this: "We stay in Berlin, period. We stay in Berlin, come what may." By the determination of President Truman, America and our allies launched the Berlin Airlift, and overcame more than 10 months of siege. That resolve and the daring of our military saved a city, and held back the communist threat in Europe.

Nearly four decades later, Ronald Reagan came to West Berlin with the same kind of resolve, and vision beyond the Cold War. When he called on the Soviets to tear down that wall, he was asserting a confident new doctrine. He believed that communism can not only be contained, but transcended; that no human barrier could hold back the spread of human liberty. The triumph

Structure: Bush's text depends upon both building points and soliciting responses throughout. He begins by establishing ethos and complimenting his immediate audience. Then he outlines the importance of veterans. Bush links the situations of all veterans during all wars—and, specifically brings up WWII. Bush provides evidence that U.S. troops need to be in Iraq. He also establishes the fact that we have allies in what we are doing. He refutes potential counterarguments. He makes a historical reference that links the fights against terrorism and against communism. He ends by reconnecting with his larger audience—all American people—and suggesting that we are fighting for "freedom" in our efforts in Iraq. This parallelism between the beginning and the end is important in making his argument seem persuasive and also in making his audience feel involved. It also gives the audience a sense of closure.

Here Bush makes reference to religion and God—probably trying to connect with Christians in particular, but probably all who believe in God.

of that vision eventually turned enemies into friends, healed a divided continent, and brought security and peace to Europe and America.

Two years into the war on terror, the will and resolve of America are being tested, in Afghanistan and in Iraq. Again, the world is watching. Again we will be steadfast; we will finish the mission we have begun, period. (Applause.)

We are not only containing the terrorist threat, we are turning it back. We believe that freedom is the right of every person. We believe that freedom is the hope of every culture. We believe that freedom is the future of every nation in the Middle East. And we know as Americans that the advance of freedom is the surest path to peace.

May God bless you all. (Applause.)[1]

Paraphrasing

I think Bush is trying to convince various audiences—the people in the room (including veterans), the American people, and an international audience—that (1) veterans are people worthy of honor and respect in American culture, and (2) that the war in Iraq is a just war (that it will bring liberty and democracy to the Iraqi people). He knows that some people listening might disagree with his policy to keep U.S. troops in Iraq. I think Bush tries to refute their positions and to convince them that in order for democracy to win, the U.S. troops and our allies need to be in Iraq.

Summarizing

The main point of Bush's speech is that we ought to stay in Iraq because we are freeing the Iraqis from a "cruel dictatorship," and we should value veterans from wars past, present, and future—the ones here at home in the U.S. as well as the ones fighting in Iraq. The U.S. has been victorious in wars before and will be so in Iraq.

Now we will watch how Tanya begins to put her ideas together in preparation to write a paper about the text. She starts the writing process by prewriting—freewriting, mapping, clustering, scratch outlining, and formal outlining.

Freewriting

When you freewrite you do not worry about how your words sound or what your text looks like. You write continuously for a period and express many of your ideas about a topic.

> Bush understands his audience well—the people in the room, the international people, and the American people. Okay. I got that. I think that he is telling them what he knows they want to hear in order to persuade them to accept his argument. Sometimes I think his purpose makes sense and sometimes I think the links are weird. Like does the war in Iraq really have that much to do with veterans who have served in other wars? Is he just using this as an opportunity to cover himself? I don't know. His use of context makes sense. Bush knows how he has to respond given who he's talking to and when. The thing that gets me about the text is that he really mixes a lot of logos and pathos together and he doesn't really always provide support for his ideas. Yet he seem to reference potential arguments one might make against him and then refute them with short, unsupported statements. One could contend that Bush is not really refuting those counterarguments but just reasserting his own ideas one more time. Then there's the problem of the structure of his text being a little confusing. I think this may be because he is juggling so many purposes and audiences at one time. Bush jumps around between defending himself and making new points. I guess the thing that concerns me most about the rhetoric of this essay is how all of this opposite imagery gets used—like Americans as embodying "peace," "values," and "democratic revolution" versus Iraqis as "troubled," "violent," and under "cruel oppression." Is any group of people or country all good or all evil? I am not sure that I trust that kind of language—even though it could be a very persuasive rhetorical technique. Maybe it's just me, but I think that maybe things are more complicated than that.

Mapping

Mapping a text helps you to better think through relationships between ideas. When you map a text, you take its central ideas or themes and jot down how other ideas in the essay are related to it. This can help you chart the structure of a writer's text. You can also use this technique to assess the connections between ideas in your own essay.

Notice how Tanya maps the relationships between the main ideas in Bush's speech and the connections between these ideas, as well as subordinate concepts and examples.

> Bush's speech makes links between U.S. presence in Iraq, veterans, and liberty or the fight for democracy. Sometimes these connections work logically and sometimes they don't. His evidence comes from examples and analogies, some which are persuasive and seem to work, others which could be refuted (even when he has anticipated and acknowledged them) and therefore may be less rhetorically effective. Bush's language choices are sometimes persuasive and yet sometimes he blurs categories and ideas. I think that this undermines his assertions.

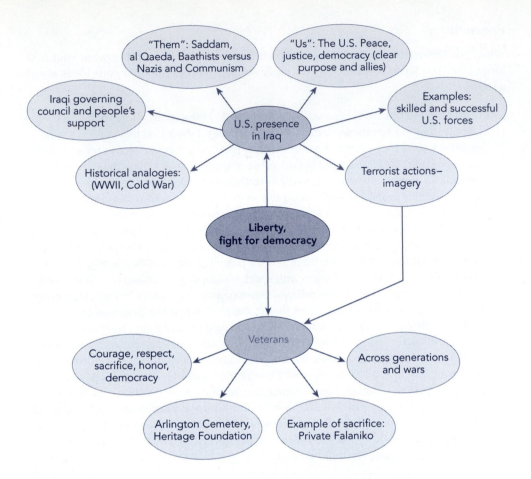

Clustering

Clustering helps you to begin to make connections between your close reading, free-writing, and mapping of the text (its use of rhetoric as well as its main points and themes) and the kinds of specific points you want to make about the text (your own assertions, interpretations, and evaluations). When you cluster ideas, as you can see from Tanya's example above, you take what may otherwise seem like distinct or unrelated pieces and find their commonalties, grouping them together in ways that will help you formulate your own assertions—and finally your own written essay—about the text.

My Key Idea: Some of the speech is quite rhetorically effective. Some of it is not as rhetorically effective.

What Works Well

Pathos: In his intro Bush uses concrete language to describe the Republican Party, veterans, and military service and to appeal to people's desire to be liked and respected and to be good, democratic Americans; he creates an "us" and "them" throughout (effective rhetorical move but leaves him open to the charge of painting the situation too simplistically); he uses contrasting imagery; and he connects audience patriotism to U.S. efforts in Iraq.

Context: Bush deals with the fact that it is Veteran's Day appropriately. He references where he is giving this speech, for what reasons, and deals with the immediate historical context—the fact that troops are still in Iraq despite the fact that the war has officially been declared over.

Audience: Bush makes references to many potential audiences, giving his speech wide appeal. This could also mean that he is not able to satisfy any one audience fully. He tries to persuade the people in the room, veterans, the Republican Party, the American people, international political leaders, and maybe even "terrorists" who may hear pieces of his speech.

Purpose: Bush juggles several different purposes and attempts to appeal to a wide variety of groups (to applaud the efforts of veterans, to justify U.S. efforts in Iraq, to gain support of U.S. efforts in Iraq); and he praises the efforts of party, veterans, Iraqi people; and challenges efforts of terrorists. This gives his text wide appeal, but it also may mean that Bush will not be able to fully satisfy any one purpose.

Ethos: Bush establishes credibility using politeness and good will in his introduction with various groups. Throughout the text Bush indicates that he is a reliable person who has knowledge about history, the current situation in Iraq, and terrorism in general. Bush also creates an identification with his audience and reestablishes and reinforces his credibility at the end by connecting his ethos to issues of his freedom and Christian values.

What Could Work Better

Logos: Bush often supports his points but with singular cases and examples that are designed to appeal mainly to the audience's emotions. For instance, consider the testimonial evidence of Sergeant Falaniko. Bush often anticipates and refutes counterarguments but does not provide the evidence necessary to back up his refutations. For example, he asserts that "the terrorists cite examples and yet that the terrorists are mistaken."

Structure: While there is a clear structure for Bush's speech, the fact that it has multiple purposes and audiences makes it seem like it is jumping around a bit.

Constraints: Bush has two very different interests, but the constraints of his situation force him to link them—the situation in Iraq and Veteran's Day. These may or may not be analogous situations, but Bush does not explore the differences as well as the similarities. Instead, he assumes that they are much the same, and this could open him to criticism.

Intertextuality: Bush uses lots of intertextuality, but does not always reference his sources. Bush also makes analogies between other wars and the situation in Iraq that may or may not hold. Likewise, he makes links between Arlington Cemetery, bravery, and continued deaths in Iraq that may not hold. Bush also creates a connection between the situation in Iraq and the Soviet Union's actions in 1948 during the Cold War, linking the Iraqi effort to the war against communism—again, an analogy and intertextual reference that may not hold.

Scratch Outlining

Once you have a general idea of the main points in your paper, scratch outlining helps you begin to create an informal, tentative structure for your paper. Watch how Tanya considers how to arrange her ideas.

Main Point One: Bush's speech is rhetorically effective in some important ways.

> *How?*

Use of pathos and ethos (introduction, conclusion, vivid language)

> The speech utilizes specific language choices to honor veterans, to establish the validity of U.S. actions in Iraq, and to argue for continued actions in Iraq. Bush establishes a strong ethos because he can speak to multiple audiences (e.g., Republican Party, veterans, American people, international community, Iraq).

Use of purpose and audience

The speech has multiple purposes—to value veterans and to make a case for U.S. troops remaining in Iraq. It also has multiple audiences—veterans, Republicans, international politicians, American people, Iraqis, and terrorists.

Appropriate for context

His speech addresses where and when it is given. It makes reference to his actual contemporary context and relevant historical contexts.

Main Point Two: Bush's speech is not rhetorically effective in some important ways.

How?

Use of structure

The speech's introduction and conclusion are solid. But Bush jumps around a bit, confusing his multiple purposes and sometimes blurring them. (It could be positive to have multiple purposes but not so good to overlap them.)

How he deals with constraints

Bush is in a tight spot. This may force him to reference counterarguments and refute them with a sentence or an example. But is this enough for these comparisions?

Use of intertextuality

The speech uses lots of analogies between historical events, cases, and actions. But does Bush provide adequate and logical references for these comparisons?

Use of logos

Bush's reasoning is sometimes less clear than it could be. Likewise, Bush's appeals to the audience's emotions may override his points.

Formal Outlining

Once you have completed a scratch outline, you are ready to consider a more formal outline for your paper. Notice how Tanya's formal outline does not include quotations, but suggests where she needs to include them in her text. This reminds Tanya to back up her views when she actually writes her paper.

I. *Introduction:* Here I explain what my paper sets out to prove: While Bush's speech is rhetorically effective in many ways, his speech's structure, constraints, intertextual references, and appeals to logos undermine his assertions.

II. *Main Point One:* Bush's speech to veterans on November 11, 2003, is a complicated composition, one that is rhetorically effective in a number of critical ways. First, Bush strategically uses pathos and ethos to draw in his audience. Second, he directs his speech to multiple purposes and at multiple audiences rather adeptly. Third, Bush's speech usefully acknowledges the context within which he is speaking.

   A. *Bush's effective use of ethos and pathos.* In the introduction Bush attempts to establish a rapport with his audience (appealing to their desire to be liked and respected) and to establish himself as credible by acknowledging their own as well as his efforts. I will use quotes from Bush's essay to back up my ideas.

B. *Bush's effective use of purpose and audience.* For instance, Bush's purpose is clear, even if it is two pronged: to value veterans and to make a case for U.S. troops remaining in Iraq. He also is sure to address different audiences in different ways. Bush talks about how other countries view the United States in order to speak to both his national and international audiences, for example. I will use quotes from Bush's essay to back up my ideas.

C. *Bush's effective understanding of context.* For instance, Bush acknowledges that he is speaking on Veteran's Day, that he is speaking in the Heritage Foundation, and that the country is still at war with Iraq. I will use quotes from Bush's essay to back up my ideas.

III. *Main Point Two:* Despite these strengths, Bush's speech could be more persuasive. It is not structured as persuasively as it might be, Bush does not always handle the constraints of his situation as well as he could, his intertexual references are not always helpful to his case, and Bush's appeals to logos are sometimes too dependent upon appeals to pathos, ones that are not always believable.

A. *Bush's sometimes confusing use of structure.* Bush's speech jumps around a lot. Even though he has a clear introduction and conclusion, from there things break down a bit. In places Bush provides examples that rely on pathos and set a tone but don't really back up his ideas that veterans should be valued and that the U.S. troops' presence in Iraq is a good thing. I will use quotes from Bush's essay to back up my ideas.

B. *Bush's handling of constraints.* Bush knows that his approval rating is dropping and so he tries to make a number of counterarguments against those who disagree with him. However, since Bush does not really refute these charges, his own assertions are not as convincing. I will use quotes from Bush's essay to back up my ideas.

C. *Bush's intextextual references and analogies.* Bush makes a comparison between the situation in Iraq with WWII and the Cold War that may not necessarily hold. I will use quotes from Bush's essay to back up my ideas.

D. *Bush's use of logos and his dependency on pathos.* Even though Bush gives examples of how effective U.S. troops are in Iraq, all of this is mixed in with his images of America as democratic and just and Iraqi terrorists as evil. I would contend that the situation is not that simple. I will use quotes from Bush's essay to back up my ideas.

IV. *Conclusion:* My conclusion will reveal what my paper has proven: The rhetorically effective elements of Bush's speech are overshadowed by a number of problems. If Bush hopes to protect himself from these potential criticisms and disputes, he might usefully (1) clarify his structure, (2) make sure that appeals to pathos do not override other appeals, (3) more fully acknowledge and refute the arguments against him, (4) consider his references and analogies, (5) make sure appeals to logos are fully substantiated, (6) use language that is less likely to seem overly simplistic, and (7) acknowledge both differences and similarities between his various audiences' needs as well as the multiple purposes of his speech.

RHETORIC IN WRITTEN TEXTS: **EXERCISING YOUR SKILLS**

Now that we have seen Tanya apply critical reading and responding (e.g., previewing, annotating, paraphrasing, summarizing, analyzing, and evaluating), rhetoric (e.g., author, context, audience, purpose, constraints, intertextuality, and the three appeals—ethos, pathos, and logos), and prewriting (e.g., freewriting, mapping, clustering, scratch outlining, and formal outlining) to another text, you are ready to apply these same skills. Be sure to look back through the earlier sections of the chapter and review each of these steps before you begin this section.

Put your new skills into practice as you read David Greenberg's "Students Have Always Been Violent," an essay prompted by contemporary incidents of school violence such as Columbine. It appeared in the May 6, 1999, issue of the magazine *Slate*. Much like the students featured in the book, you will want to dedicate some thoughtful care and attention to analyzing this essay.

Preview the essay first. Then read through it carefully, making detailed notes and annotations in the margins about how each of the rhetorical tactics are operating. When you have finished reading, answer the questions at the end.

Students Have Always Been Violent:
They're Just Better Armed Today

Judging by the histrionic Columbine massacre coverage, you'd think that children are by nature innocent, free of violent or sexual thoughts until corrupted by our culture. That schools have traditionally been safe. That the recent spate of killings is unprecedented.

History says otherwise. In every era, American schoolchildren—especially teen-agers—have been unruly and destructive. As late as the 17th century, those "children" we now call teen-agers were considered adults. And preteens swore, drank, had sex, even dueled with guns. If school violence wasn't a problem back then, it's only because few children went to school.

In colonial America, most young children were taught at home. Those who attended school were just as prone to be disorderly as today's youths. Teachers kept problem children in line with corporal punishments that seem positively barbaric today: They tied children to whipping posts and beat them or branded students for their crimes—a "T" for thievery, a "B" for blasphemy. Occasionally children were put to death.

Branding fell from favor in the 18th century, but students were still flogged or tied to chairs (for more on corporal punishment, click http://slate.msn.com /toolbar.aspx?action=print&id=27715" \l "27717#27717"). In the early 19th century, school reformer Horace Mann reported that he saw 328 floggings in one school during the course of a week. As the principles of humanitarianism spread and the era of mass schooling arrived, Mann and others replaced or supplemented the elite academies with taxpayer-supported "common schools," which admitted young students from all walks of life. (Later, attendance became compulsory.) In the Gilded Age, as immigrants and migrants flooded the cities, public elementary schools proliferated. Finally, the Progressives championed the view of adolescence as a stage of childhood, and high schools (the first of which opened in the 1820s) multiplied as well.

It appears that more students meant more violence. In 1837, Mann noted that almost 400 schools across Massachusetts had to be shut down because of disciplinary problems. In most institutions, keeping order took precedence over teaching. One observer in 1851 likened the typical American school to "the despotic government of a military camp." In the colleges, where the teen-age students were bigger and less docile, violence was even worse. Princeton University, to take just one example, witnessed six major riots between 1800 and 1830, including the burning of the library in 1802 and a rash of campus explosions in 1823 that caused half of one class to be expelled.

School violence persisted into the 20th century, taking different forms according to the climate of the day. In politically charged times, students became violent in the name of political causes. In 1917, for example, when New York City introduced a "platoon" system to deal with an influx of pupils, students rebelled—literally. Between 1,000 and 3,000 schoolchildren picketed and stoned P.S. 171 on Madison Avenue and attacked nonstriking classmates. Similar riots erupted across the city, resulting in furious battles between student mobs and the police. Likewise, the civil rights movement and anti-Vietnam War protests brought different forms of "political" violence to places ranging from Little Rock Central High in Arkansas to Kent State University in Ohio.

More politically sedate times didn't translate into student acquiescence, however. In the post-World War II years, urban strife and suburban anomie gave rise to school violence of the sorts broadly rendered by

Hollywood in the 1955 films *Rebel Without a Cause* and *Blackboard Jungle*. The nation waxed hysterical over "juvenile delinquency," as the vogue phrase had it—alienated adolescents unaccountably sullen in the bountiful Eisenhower years. Though history had recorded public concern over bands of violent teen-agers ever since the beginning of the republic, the fear of "gangs" (a term coined in the 1930s) caught the nation's fancy. *Time* magazine headlined a story, "Teen-agers on the Rampage," which detailed a weeklong outbreak of violence in high schools from Maine to California. Congress held hearings on the delinquency epidemic, calling comic-book artists to testify about whether their drawings inspired children to violence.

Youth rebelliousness surged in the 1960s. While crime grew overall, juvenile crime grew faster. Sociologists, social workers, and policy wonks turned their attention en masse to offenses ranging from vandalism to gang-related crime, from drug use to student-upon-student assaults. Schools implemented safety plans, bringing in adult hall monitors and setting up bodies for hearing student grievances. Urban schools hired professional security agents—and later adopted the surveillance cameras, metal detectors, locker searches, and other measures more commonly seen in prisons. But a major study conducted in 1978 confirmed what experience had been teaching. Teen-agers were more likely to be victims of crime at school than anywhere else.

If student violence has now been a major concern for decades now, what seems to distinguish '90s violence is the suburban- or rural-school massacre. West Paducah, Ky.; Jonesboro, Ark.; Pearl, Miss.; Moses Lake, Wash.; Springfield, Ore.; and now Littleton, Colo.—in each case, young students, armed with guns, committed multiple murders in or near the school itself. To be sure, similar atrocities have occurred in the past. In 1927, a 55-year-old school-board official detonated three bombs in the Bath, Mich., schoolhouse, killing 45 people. And to be sure, the string of recent killings in fact reveals nothing, statistically speaking, about our society. Yet they remind us that the number of children killed by guns skyrocketed in the '80s and while tailing off in the '90s remains far higher than in decades past. According to one recent study, the growing trend of violent altercations ending in death is attributable "almost entirely" to the proliferation of guns among children.

History makes it clear that children and teen-agers are no strangers to violent impulses. There have always been, and always will be, maladjusted or deranged students who unleash those impulses. That they do so is inevitable. How they do so may be within our control.

Author and Text

Do a bit of research on the web about David Greenberg and *Slate* magazine. What do you now know about the author and the journal? How is what you have learned reflected in the specific kinds of language choices Greenberg makes?

Audience

Who are the potential audiences for this text? How do you know?

Context

Describe the context(s) in which Greenberg writes this text and the potential audience(s) to whom he directs it. What quotations can you find from the text that support your views?

Purpose

What is the main purpose of Greenberg's text? How can you tell? What assumptions does he seem to be making? Be sure to offer examples from the text to back up your thoughts.

Structure

Characterize the structure of this essay. Do you think that this is a rhetorically effective structure given Greenberg's context and purpose? Why or why not? Provide textual evidence for your perspective.

Constraints

Describe the potential constraints placed upon Greenberg as he was writing this text. Where and how might these be reflected in the language of the text itself?

Intertextuality

Write down all of the examples of intertextuality that are operating in this text. Why and how does Greenberg use them? Do you find them persuasive? Why or why not?

The Appeals

Examine Greenberg's text according to the three rhetorical appeals. Where and how does he establish ethos, pathos, and logos in this essay? Does Greenberg utilize these appeals persuasively? How yes? How no? Offer specific quotations to back up your points.

Creating Your Own Rhetoric

After you have completed your rhetorical analysis, consider whether you agree with Greenberg's assertions. What is your position on such matters? After evaluating his essay, determine whether you believe that Greenberg's piece is persuasive (i.e., rhetorically effective) or not and why. Using the prewriting techniques—freewriting, mapping, clustering, scratch writing, and formal outlining—write a short essay in which you make an assertion about the rhetorical effectiveness or lack of effectiveness of certain elements of Greenberg's text. Support your views with quotes from his text.

RHETORIC IN VISUAL AND MULTIMEDIA TEXTS

After examining Tanya's use of rhetorical analysis as well as completing a rhetorical analysis of your own, you now have a good sense of how rhetorical considerations can help you to read written texts and begin to write about them. However, the printed or spoken word is not the whole of rhetoric: visual and multimedia rhetoric can be equally, and sometimes even more, significant. Just like written texts, these popular cultural texts—advertisements, commercials, television shows, film, websites, as well as cultural rituals and spaces—need to be previewed, read, and annotated. Visual texts also require that we examine author and text, audience, context, purpose, structure, constraints, intertextuality, and appeals. As with written texts, understanding how rhetoric works in visual and multimedia texts can help you to make sense of them and start to analyze and evaluate them. Likewise, these same skills are essential to creating successful media forms themselves—be they websites, print advertising, multimedia presentations, video productions, film editing, or commercial work.

Analyzing visual texts is much like analyzing written texts. However, since all visual texts—print ads, commercials, television shows, films, websites, as well as cultural rituals and spaces—often contain genre-specific rhetorical components, we need additional analytic strategies to interpret them. Below are some tips for beginning to observe the rhetoric at work in some of the most common visual and multimedia texts:

✔ *Print Ads:* When we analyze a print ad, we look at its composition or layout— what we would call structure or arrangement in a written text. We observe the content of the image(s); how the visual attributes are arranged; patterns, dominant colors, harmony, balance, proportion, movement, contrast, unity, overlapping shapes and lines, symmetry and asymmetry, repeated forms, as well as variations in form; from what perspective each image is presented and how it was generated; and how the image is "framed." In addition, we examine how the visuals relate to the written text; what the type/font looks like; what paper stock is used; how the print is laid out on the page; whether there are captions, superimpositions (words placed on top of images), logos, footnotes, fine print, watermarks, motifs, allusions, inset quotes, headlines, embedded images, and white space; and how the medium contributes to the rhetorical impact of the text. We also ask ourselves what kinds of cultural narratives (stories about ourselves, our culture, our beliefs, our habits, our anxieties, and our values)—which function much like intertextuality does in a written text—are at work in the print ad. We look at the worldviews and feelings they evoke, and the codes or symbols they employ to draw the audience into these cultural narratives. Finally, we examine how women, children, ethnic and racial minorities, lower-class people, individuals who are differently abled, and other groups are represented as well as what this reveals about American culture.

✔ *Commercials*: When we interpret commercials, we consider all of the same rhetorical issues we would in a print ad (composition or layout, use of written text, and cultural narratives). However, in addition, we need to examine sound—which works much like word choice or rhythm does in a written text. We think about whether there are jingles, music, dialogue, soundtracks, voiceovers, or subliminal sounds that operate as critical components of the texts. In addition, we need to observe the camera work—which operates like a certain ethos or point of view does in a written text, directing the audience's attention to certain elements over others. We look at whether the camera fades in and out, cuts quickly between other images, slices across images, tracks a single image, zooms in and out, goes in and out of focus, as well as superimposes one image on another. We examine lighting and editing, actors and actresses (dress, mannerisms, gender, cultural background, class status, age, nationality).

✔ *Television Shows*: When we analyze television shows, we examine all of the same rhetorical issues we would in a commercial (composition or layout, use of written text, cultural narratives, sound, and camera work). In addition, we need to consider how the genre of the television show impacts its rhetorical features. News programs require different rhetorical elements than situation comedies. In a news program we would need to look at how the stories are framed and in what order they occur, what role the newscasters play, and how commercials interact with the news text. Situation comedies require that we examine dialogue and character development closely, the use of laugh tracks, the sorts of humor the shows promote, and the kinds of commercials that air alongside the show. Dramatic series require different analytic strategies than game shows. In dramatic series we would examine narrative, the rise and fall of plot and character development, as well as commercial placement. In game shows we would look at the role of the host, the studio audience, the audience at home, the set, the narrative structure, and use of commercials. We could also incorporate relevant aspects of analyzing film into our analysis of television. See that information below.

✔ *Films*: When we interpret films, we examine all of the same visual rhetorical issues we would in a television show (composition or layout, use of written text, cultural narratives, sound, camera work, and genre distinctions). In addition, we look at different camera shots—long shot (used often in epic films where locale plays an important role), full shot (just barely includes the human body in full), medium shot (contains a figure from the waist up), close-up shot (shows little of the locale and concentrates on one object), and deep-focus or wide-angle shot (involves close, medium, and long shots simultaneously). We also observe camera angles—the bird's-eye view (directly overhead as if from an omniscient perspective), the high angle (provides a general overview from a height just above the actors' heads), the eye-level shot (camera directly faces the action), the low angle shot (shot from below to increase verticality and make performers seem larger), and the oblique angle (provides a lateral view in which the horizon is skewed). We also view use of light and dark to create moods (high lighting, low lighting, back lighting, overexposure, special lenses, filters); color symbolism (cool colors to suggest tranquility and serenity, bold colors to suggest stimulation or violence);

density of visual images (how much visual information is packed into a scene); character placement (what part of the screen's frame the characters occupy); typical movement (pans, tilts, crane shots, dolly shots, zoom shots, handheld shots, and aerial shots) and movement distortion (animation, fast motion, slow motion, reverse motion, and freeze frames); sound (to provide support for the film's narrative or to provide contrast); set (style, location, period, class, and size); and costumes (age, fabric, color, body posture, and attitude). We also analyze narrative structure—realistic (the narrator is barely visible, rejects glib endings, avoids melodrama); classical (there is a shaping hand in the storyline but no overt narrator, the narrative rises to a climax and then there is a resolution); or formalistic (there is an overtly manipulative narrator, the plot's structure is heightened, and time is often rearranged). Finally, we interpret the political perspective of the film (democratic or hierarchy-based, cultural versus natural, outsiders versus insiders, international versus nationalistic).

✔ *Websites*: When we analyze websites, we examine all of the same visual rhetorical issues we would in a film (composition or layout, use of written text, sound, cultural narratives, generic distinction, and use of visual aspects such as shots). In addition, we need to consider whether the website's organizational structure is linear, hierarchical, interlinked, or some combination. We look for links (to home page and other pages), navigational flags and indexes, search tools, and whether the users need to click more than three times to get to what they are looking for. We think about the appearance and sounds of icons or buttons; the use of columns, tables, charts and graphs; as well as the alignment of similar elements, chunking or clustering used to visually separate like elements, fonts, page numbers, specific line lengths, headers and footers, headings and subheadings, bulleted and numbered lists, captions and bylines, marginal glosses and pull quotes, sidebars, spacing, indentation, justification, text wrapping, and decorative elements. We also look at what kind of different paths the site makes available to the viewer; what kinds of pop-up windows, digital illustrations and graphics, as well as plug-ins are used; and whether specific imaging techniques are used such as wipes (quick replacement of one image with another), dissolves (slow replacement of one image with another), fade-outs (image gradually fades to black), fade-ins (image appears from an empty screen), flip-frames (image flips into a new sequence), cuts (a sequence is stopped to show a new image), or defocus shots (one scene ends and moves out of focus as the other comes into focus, connecting the scenes).

✔ *Cultural Rituals and Spaces*: When we examine cultural rituals and spaces we are analyzing events in which many people engage and places that many people frequent, ones that say something important about our culture and how we perceive it. Cultural rituals often include happenings such as sporting events, concerts, parties, pageants, festivals, as well as daily habits and behaviors. Cultural spaces reference locations such as malls, museums, restaurants, apartments and houses, gardens, and neighborhoods. Analyzing cultural rituals and spaces often requires us to make use of every rhetorical strategy we have examined thus far—from those used to analyze print ads to websites—because they are both visual and interactive. In addition, they also sometimes contain a component that others do not: The interaction with a space or ritual is often live, immediate, involves others, and happens on a repetitive basis that we often take for granted. When we analyze a ritual, then, we utilize all of the tools already discussed. But we also need to examine who participates; what rules govern the ritual; what roles people play (participants, audiences; official figures) and why; what exactly occurs in such a ritual, in what order and why; when and where it occurs; and what this reveals about American values, anxieties, fears, and desires. When we analyze a space, we need to consider how it is organized and why, its look and feel, where it appears and when, how people interact with each other in that space, as well as what this reveals about American culture.

CHECKLIST FOR RHETORIC IN VISUAL AND MULTIMEDIA TEXTS

As discussed, analyzing a written text rhetorically requires that you look at author and text, context, audience, and purpose. In order to examine the rhetoric of various visual and multimedia texts fully, however, you must take up several rhetorical issues not always present in written texts. In addition to consulting the genre-specific rhetorical components for print ads, commercials, television shows, films, websites, and cultural rituals and spaces, ask yourself these questions:

CHECKLIST FOR RHETORIC IN VISUAL AND MULTIMEDIA TEXTS

☐ *Composition or Layout*: What is the composition of this text?

☐ *Written Text*: What role does the written word play in this text?

☐ *Sound*: How does sound function in this text?

☐ *Cultural Narratives, Codes, and Conventions*: Which cultural narratives, codes, and conventions are operating in this text? What do they reveal about American culture's fears, desires, values, and anxieties? How are various groups represented?

☐ *Camera Positioning, Movement, and Editing*: How do camera positioning, movement, and editing impact this text?

☐ *Genre Distinctions*: How does the genre of the text affect the text's shape and tone?

☐ *Use of Specific Visual Elements*: How do the specific visual elements of the text contribute to its message and effectiveness?

☐ *Interactivity*: Is human interaction encouraged by the text? If so, how does the rhetoric of the text accomplish this?

RHETORIC IN ACTION: ANALYZING A VISUAL TEXT

Composition/Camera:
Wet hair slicked back to reveal face– post-shower scene? She's just turning around.

Composition:
Dark, murky background. Something's there but it's unclear what.

Composition/Camera:
Very little white space; text superimposed on image; camera positioning–spying.

Composition:
Pale skin against dark hair and background contrast.

Cultural Codes/Conventions:
Black-and-white photography; grainy yet high art; no color; history of taboo images of the female body versus history of art and the female nude.

Composition/Camera:
Looks right at viewer; disarming, brings viewer into image.

Composition/Cultural Codes/ Conventions:
Lips dark and slightly parted– about to speak to the viewer? Caught unexpectedly and scared? Is she inviting the viewer or warning the viewer away?

Composition:
Name of perfume in capitals; white against black for contrast. "O" is bigger than the rest. Thin font. Name of perfume takes up the whole length of page. Reading left to right, catches the viewer's attention.

Composition/Perspective:
Frame within a frame (light, then dark) draws the viewer's eye in more.

Context/Composition:
Name of company also in white, smaller font. Note that ad appeared in a *Vogue* magazine.

Composition:
"Parfum"–a very small font to tell viewer what product actually is. Why use the French word? Seems more elite, global, and chic?

Cultural Codes/Conventions:
Bare shoulder, arm, back, and part of chest– towel around her draped hastily? Shading on back highlights her thin torso.

Christine is a dual major in communication, specializing in journalism and advertising, as well as English. Her main interest centers on multiethnic literature as well as representations of women of color. She hopes one day to be a newscaster. Christine is both captivated by the rhetoric of advertisements and bothered by it. "I think all people should learn how rhetoric operates in visual texts. If you are in advertising, you have to know how rhetoric works in order to make an effective ad. And people in advertising need to look at the ethics of their rhetorical approaches. If you are a consumer, you want to understand rhetoric so that you won't be at the whims of advertisers' desires instead of your own. That's really, really important. I am especially concerned about how the media represents women, and it's one of the things I want to work on when I pursue my goal of becoming a newscaster." When Christine is not busy studying to complete her two majors, she enjoys painting, writing in her journal, blogging, and running cross-country.

Thus far we have focused primarily on how to create a rhetorical analysis of a written text.[2] Christine, a student who is familiar with rhetoric in multimedia texts, has applied the same tools for critical reading and responding to the primarily visual text above. She has previewed, read, and annotated an advertisement for Calvin Klein's Obsession perfume.

We will watch now as Christine skillfully begins to analyze and evaluate this ad rhetorically (note that paraphrase and summary have less relevance for visual texts).

Analyzing and Evaluating

Author: This was created by an advertising firm hired by Calvin Klein. I need to find out who specifically?

Context: The Obsession ad appeared in women's fashion magazines such as *Vogue* and *Glamour* primarily. These magazines often contain lots of ads for fashion and beauty products. Next to an Obsession ad one might find articles targeting women that have to do with intimate relationships, fitness, and fashion. This ad was first used by Calvin Klein in the mid-1990s as part of a larger set of black-and-white ads. The ad also contributed to the celebrity of model Kate Moss (and later to a lively discussion about "heroin chic" and female body image). I need to learn more about this. I will search on the web and look in journals about advertising. Kate Moss has been featured in some more recent CK ads as well.

Audience: The intended audience for the advertisement is complicated, I think. The ad appeared mainly in women's fashion magazines, but was presumably designed to appeal both to men and women—men were supposed to find her sexually attractive, and women would want to be like her. Male viewers are encouraged to be both paternalistic and protective toward her, and to see her as a possible sexual conquest. In contrast, women are asked to identify with her, as well to adopt the male gaze of desire toward her—to want to be like her, to look like her, and to possess her. The viewer is called upon to look narcissistically at this image (to want to be her) as well as voyeuristically (to want to watch her—to catch her unawares).

I think audience is pretty complicated here. Some male viewers may feel disconnected from this image—particularly if they don't find Moss desirable or if they identify with Moss's role in the picture. Similarly, some female viewers—asked to identify with the male gaze around which the ad is structured (to desire Moss as an object) or to identify with her subjection to male desire—may feel uncomfortable with this image. In many cases, though, it's a fair bet that men would remember the ad thanks to its connection with sexual desire—and purchase this product for a girlfriend or wife. Women, associating the desirable female image with the product, would purchase it for themselves. The advertiser asks male and female viewers alike to objectify—or, to make a "thing" of—the female body depicted in the ad. This may be an effective way to sell a product, but I don't agree that is an ethical approach to representing women.

Purpose: The main purpose of the ad, of course, is to persuade the viewer to purchase the perfume. However, the visuals in the ad appear not to address qualities of perfume, but sexuality.

[2]See http://pobox.upenn.edu/~davidtoc/calvin.html.

Constraints: I think that the advertisers were constrained by the fact that they could only hint at nudity in this ad rather than show it. While Moss appeared nude in Calvin Klein ads in Europe (notice that cultural norms shift depending upon local!), in the United States public opinion required that she emerge semi-clothed, seemingly wrapped in a towel. The advertisers were also constrained by the public outcry against a related ad campaign launched by Calvin Klein, this one featuring children and adolescents, also in various stages of undress and staring provocatively at the viewer. Many people thought that such images were akin to child pornography.

Intertextuality: This ad evokes other images or ideas in the audience. I think it suggests all of Kate Moss's other ad campaigns, her role as a supermodel and icon. I think some could argue that it also evokes the pornographic because it is grainy and black-and-white. And, it also suggests the artistic because it is black-and-white. This is a powerful combination.

Rhetorical Appeals

Ethos: If we're in the right target audience, this ad appeals to our ethos, our sense of ourselves—particularly to our sense of ourselves as sexual beings. That's often a strong emotional appeal. No wonder we see it in so many ads. The black and white photography's association with the artistic and the upper class culture allows the viewer to feel like she or he is a part of that elite world. It also allows the viewer to feel a bit daring, risky, and adventurous since there is something taboo about looking at the image. The ad also constructs a specific ethos for Moss—the viewer is supposed to think of her as sexual, sensual, and maybe even vulnerable (see her body posture and facial expression).

Pathos: This ad also appeals to many of our emotions (pathos)—our desire for intimacy, sex, comfort, control, adventure, and our desire to transgress taboos (voyeurism). The expression on Moss's face might be one of surprise, even fear. She is turning to face the camera as if caught unawares. Here's what I think. For me, Moss's pose calls to mind that of a caged animal. This indication of the figure's vulnerability might, it could be argued, contribute to the erotic tone.

Logos: While the advertisement certainly employs both ethos and pathos, there seems to be little or no appeal to logos. So here is my question: Why, rationally, should the ad persuade us to buy the perfume? The advertisers are banking on the fact that the appeals to ethos and pathos will be strong enough to achieve their purpose. And, they are probably right!

Visual Components

Structure/Composition: The ad is very spare. There is a simple dark backdrop and the word "Obsession" running horizontally across Moss's body. The viewer is led to ask the question, Is she obsessed with us or are we obsessed with her? The words "Calvin Klein" appear, not incidentally, right below her partially exposed chest with the French word "parfum" in an even smaller font directly underneath. The use of French references the value that elite American culture has historically bestowed upon European culture—by extension implying that if one purchases this perfume, one may also be purchasing an elite and supposedly more fulfilling lifestyle. Is this true? Probably not. However, this hooks us. The placement of Moss's head, slightly tilted above the word "Obsession," requires that the viewer's eye move from her eyes to the name of the product and then to the company name, reinforcing an association for the viewer between her sexuality, her role as an object of desire, and the company itself.

Sound: There is no sound.

Camera Positioning: The fact that the photograph is in black-and-white contributes to the tone of the ad. Black-and-white photography, particularly of "the nude," is thought by many to be artistic, tasteful, and aesthetically pleasing—more so than color photography, which is often considered more "commercial." However, the use of black-and-white, one might argue, also makes the photo seem somewhat seedy like a grainy underground pornographic picture or video. The subtle rhetorical combination of these two very different contexts enables the viewer to simultaneously experience both the comfort of participating in "high-culture" elitism and the thrill of engaging in something illicit. This technique is used over and over again in perfume ads. She is also looking right at the viewer, inviting the viewer in or expressing shock at the viewer's presence.

Cultural Narratives, Codes, and Conventions: This ad relies upon the idea that a partially clad female body is thought to be erotic and even artistic. Many fashion ads feature women in sexually explicit positions. Many ads targeting men do the same. This ad also relies upon the notion that direct eye contact in ads often signals fear or desire. Looking at the viewer draws us in. Finally, the ad relies upon a cultural narrative that ads do not have to convince us to buy products through logical reasoning but instead can persuade us by tapping our fears, anxieties, beliefs, desires, and values. And, they do often this very effectively!

Prewriting: I will use freewriting, mapping, clustering, scratch outlining, and formal outlining to clarify my ideas. However, I do have a few thoughts about my paper right now. After this rhetorical analysis, I could reasonably assert that the ad sells the product by making the female body seem like an object that can be possessed (along with a bottle of perfume). And/or I could also say this: The ad becomes more persuasive by alluding to several powerful cultural myths that we see in American culture a lot—women are either inexperienced or provocative; nudity is either artistic or pornographic; making the right purchase can lead to membership among the cultural elite as well as underworld street culture. Either way, I think I have a lot of evidence from my rhetorical analyses to support either or both approaches.

RHETORIC IN VISUAL TEXTS: **EXERCISING YOUR SKILLS**

Now that we have watched Christine apply her rhetorical skills to help her understand a visual text, you are ready to use the same skills. Put your new skills to use as you examine how rhetoric works in a variety of texts including spoof advertisements, cultural rituals and spaces, commercials, television shows, and films. Then you will use your knowledge to create a spoof advertising campaign of your own. Consult the two checklists—"Checklist for Rhetoric in Written Texts"

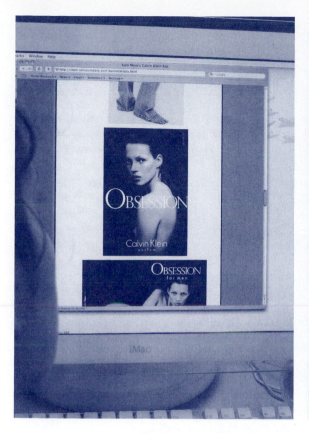

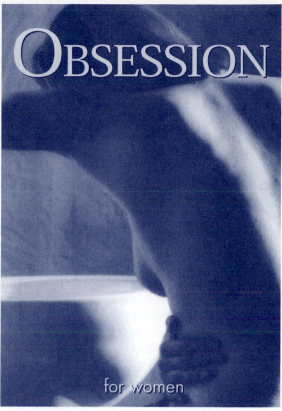

and "Checklist for Rhetoric in Visual and Multimedia Texts"—for help, and be sure to pay attention to the relevant genre conventions of the text you are examining.

Critical Reading and Responding: Ad and Ad Spoof

Take a look at the AdBusters spoof next to the original Obsession ad that Christine analyzed. Think about how the producers of this image aim to confront many of the central rhetorical and cultural ploys used in the original ad campaign. Employing your critical reading and responding skills—previewing, annotating, paraphrasing, summarizing, analyzing, and evaluating—determine what changes the creators of this ad made to the original ad's composition, including the visual

image and the placement of the written text, in order to alter its meaning. Look at the content of the images; how the visual attributes are arranged; patterns, dominant colors, harmony, balance, proportion, movement, contrast, unity, overlapping shapes and lines, symmetry and asymmetry, repeated forms, as well as variations in form: Create detailed analysis of both texts.

Rhetorical Analysis: Cultural Rituals and Spaces

Examine the rhetoric of a cultural ritual or space of your choosing. How do rhetorical issues operate in this cultural text? Consider how issues of authorship or expertise, context, audience, purpose, structure, constraints, and intertextuality work. Be sure to think about the visual and interactive elements. Utilize all of the relevant tools discussed in the "Checklist for Rhetoric in Visual and Multimedia Texts" and think about the genre conventions of the text you are examining. For a cultural ritual, examine who participates; what rules govern the ritual; what roles people play (participants, audiences, official figures) and why; what exactly occurs—in what order as well as when and where it occurs; and what this reveals about American values, anxieties, fears, and desires. For a cultural space, look at how it is organized and why as well as consider its look and feel, where it appears and when, how people interact with each other and with that space, and what this reveals about American culture. Then ask yourself the following questions: What worldviews, identifications, or cultural status are afforded to those performing the ritual or those living and/or working in the spaces? How, for example, might this ritual or space support or undermine cultural conventions about masculinity and femininity, age, the environment, race, ethnicity, disability, and class?

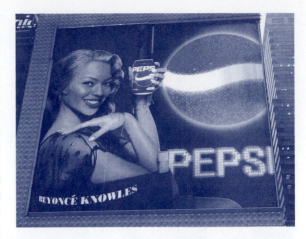

want the audience to associate with the product? How, for example, might this commercial support or undermine cultural conventions about masculinity and femininity, age, the environment, race, ethnicity, disability, and class? Does there seem to be a disconnection between the product and the means of targeting the audience?

Rhetoric and Multimedia Visual Texts: Television Commercials

Consider how you might read a television commercial according to its rhetorical appeals. Watch any commercial that airs during primetime television—for example, this Pepsi campaign featuring Beyonce Knowles.[3] Investigate what is being sold. What sorts of appeals to ethos, pathos, and logos does this advertisement make? How does it get the viewer's attention? Now look at rhetorical issues such as composition, sound, camera positioning, as well as cultural narratives, codes, and conventions. Use all of the relevant tools discussed in the "Checklist for Rhetoric in Visual and Multimedia Texts" and look at the genre conventions of the text you are examining. What ideas about the world and other people does the advertiser

Critical Reading into Informal Writing: Television Shows

Apply your rhetorical skills to reading a television show.[4] Watch a long-running television program such as *The Simpsons* or any another. Pick one or two significant scenes for analysis. What can you tell about each of these characters and the roles they adopt? In what ways might these characters and the plots of the show challenge conventional readings of culture—using humor, sarcasm, and irony—and to what degree do they support them? Look at as many rhetorical issues in the show as you can, including author and producer, context, purpose, structure, constraints, intertextuality, ethos, pathos, and logos, composition, sound, camera positioning, as well as cultural narratives, codes, and conventions.

[4]See the official website for *The Simpsons* at http://www.thesimpsons.com/.

Look at all of the relevant tools discussed in the "Checklist for Rhetoric in Visual and Multimedia Texts" and consider the genre conventions of the text you are examining. Then, use your freewriting, mapping, clustering, scratch outlining, and formal outlining skills to compose a short, informal paper. Offer an assertion about whether these rhetorical choices are effective or not, and offer quotations from the text to provide evidence for your perspectives.

Critical Reading into Formal Writing: Films

Think about how you might read a film rhetorically. Watch any film that interests you. You might choose one particularly gripping scene for analysis, or you could look at multiple scenes, tracing the similarities and differences between them. Look at rhetorical issues in the film such as author and producer, context, audience, purpose, structure, constraints, intertextuality, ethos, pathos, and logos, composition, sound, camera positioning, as well as cultural narratives, codes, and conventions. In addition, examine different camera shots, camera angles, use of light and dark, color symbolism, density of visual, use of move-

ment, set, and costumes. Analyze the shape of the narrative and interpret the political perspective of the film. What stories or narratives are promoted by this film, and what arguments is the film making? In what ways do they question as well as sustain conventional readings of our culture? Is the film a parody of other films or cultural references? Does it rely on stereotyping? Then, use your freewriting, mapping, clustering, scratch outlining, and formal outlining skills to create a formal paper that offers a careful analysis and evaluation of the film. Be sure to provide quotations from the text to support your assertions. In addition, select at least two reputable outside sources from the Internet (ones that also appear in magazines or journals) from which you can offer quotations so as to back up your views.

Create Your Own Rhetoric

Now that you have analyzed and written about the rhetorical tactics employed in a variety of visual texts, here is your chance to put rhetoric into practice. Find an ad campaign that has been quite successful and popular. Collect as many ads from this campaign as you can. Make note of their specific rhetorical choices. Now create your own spoof ad for the product—you can use computer graphics and digital programs, photographs, illustrations, visuals from magazines, your own artwork—to foreground some of the potential problems as well as positive possibilities you see at work in the ads' rhetoric, the company, and the product. The four AdBusters spoofs shown on page 60 refer to very recognizable ad campaigns.[5] Review those ad spoofs for ideas. In addition, visit the AdBusters website for specific prewriting suggestions that will help make your spoof ad as effective as possible. Consider placement of the ad, communication objective, target audience, format, concept, visual, headline, copy, and mistakes to avoid.[6]

[5]See http://adbusters.org/creativeresistance/spoofads/printad/.

Less cars, more world. **Drivers wanted.®**

Fresher! Cleaner!

NEW IMPROVED LIFE!

Better Than Ever!

#1 America's #1 Selling Drug!

Prozac

MOOD BRIGHTENER

Wash Your Blues Away!

OBSESSION

Calvin Klein

for men

Grease

CHAPTER SUMMARY

In this chapter of *Pop Perspectives* you have gained important access to tools for rhetorical analysis. You have discovered how being a critical reader and responder can make you a better interpreter and evaluator of texts. In addition, you have discovered the ways in which being a more thoughtful reader will make you a better writer. Watching Tanya's example, you have learned how to analyze the rhetoric of a written text using the "Checklist for Rhetoric in Written Texts" and how to begin prewriting, the early stages of the writing process—including freewriting, mapping, clustering, scratch outlining, and formal outlining. Likewise, you have studied how to offer careful rhetorical analyses of visual and multimedia texts by observing Christine's example and studying the "Checklist for Rhetoric in Visual and Multimedia Texts" for analyzing print ads, commercials, television shows, films, websites, as well as cultural rituals and spaces. In order to reinforce your new skills, you have also used the exercises to apply what you have learned. You are now ready to discover more about the writing process—how other writers conduct research and construct polished, persuasive texts—as well as how you apply their techniques to your own writing.

In Chapter 3, "Argument, Research, and Writing," you will investigate how to analyze, evaluate, and write arguments in more detail. You will identify how to view arguments according to their main parts (i.e., the research question, claim, support, and warrants), and view potential flaws in logic that can undermine arguments. Likewise, you will find out about the later stages of the writing process—drafting, reflecting, and revising. As with the first two chapters, Chapter 3 provides exercises throughout so that you can apply your new knowledge of argumentation to a range of popular culture texts. Learning about argument and research will help you to create more polished texts, making you the most persuasive, effective thinker and writer that you can be.

CHAPTER THREE

Argument, Research, and Writing

POP PERSPECTIVES PROFILES: ARGUMENT, RESEARCH, AND WRITING

Meet Sergio Gregorio

My undergraduate degree was in broadcast journalism. I received a law degree from Howard University in Washington, DC. Today I am an attorney with Willkie Farr & Gallagher in Washington, DC, a New York–based international law firm with a sizable litigation practice. I practice law and I cohost a television show about local politics called Clout, which airs on DC cable.

Contrary to popular belief, most lawyers do not spend their days in court. Rather, we spend our days in the library and at our desks researching and writing. Excellent argumentation skills are essential to everything I do. I use words and images—or, rhetoric—to persuade my audience, usually a panel of judges. But, most importantly, I use logic and careful arguments to make my case. Much of the time this involves comparing and contrasting the salient points of an older case with the important facts in the case I am arguing.

In my television work, I also rely heavily on my argumentation skills. I meet weekly with producers of Clout to talk about everything from guests, wardrobe, and lighting to interview questions and potential interview responses. Since politicians can spend a lot of time rumbling through talking points, I use my skills to encourage them to answer **my** *questions. In doing so, I am able to "connect" to them and make them comfortable enough to open up during the interviews.*

In Chapter 1 we discovered the importance of reading culture—be it an essay in our textbook, the World Series, podcasts, Domino's pizza, the *MTV Music Awards,* or our best friend's wardrobe choices—from a critical perspective, one that entails critical thinking, reading, and writing. Then, in Chapter 2 we learned a good deal about rhetoric—the skills of effective writing and speaking that help us to inform and persuade others, and sometimes even to encourage them to take action. We realized that rhetoric is really at work everywhere—in films such as *Scary Movie,* the comedic sketches of Dave Chappelle, instant text messaging between friends, the lyrics to Nine Inch Nails' songs, the television show *America's Next Top Model,* and web-based advertisements for Barnes and Noble. We also examined various prewriting strategies that will set us up well for writing formal papers.

Chapter 3 builds upon what you have learned in the first two chapters. Here you will discover how to analyze, evaluate, and write even more skillfully by studying **argument,** or the specific branch of rhetoric that deals with the appeal to logos. You will study both how to read others' arguments and write your own. You will find out about logical reasoning by exploring models by Aristotle and Stephen Toulmin, learn how to view arguments according to their main parts (e.g., the research question, claim, support, and warrants), and investigate the potential flaws in logic that would undermine your own arguments as well as help you to dismantle others' arguments. Next you will turn your attention toward applying this new knowledge to conducting research and writing essays, learning about the later stages of the writing process— drafting, reflecting, and revising. The chapter walks you through an example of one student's entire writing process as he constructs a research essay about *The Jerry Springer Show.* You will see how he considers a central research question, thinks about primary sources, narrows his focus, creates a working thesis and outline, constructs a full rough draft, reflects on that draft (commenting on how to improve his own work), consults secondary sources, and composes a revision. As with the first two chapters, Chapter 3 offers exercises throughout so that you can apply your new knowledge of argumentation to a range of popular culture texts.

LOGICAL REASONING

Logical reasoning is a mode of critical thinking, reading, and writing that operates in most texts that seek to persuade—whether written, visual, or some combination. It is at the heart of what encourages readers to view an arguer's assertions as valid.

Western modes of logical reasoning usually work in one of two ways: by induction or by deduction.

What Is Induction?

Induction begins with specific observations and ends with a generalized conclusion. Inductive reasoning often does not definitively prove something, but instead arrives at a conclusion based on the available evidence. Induction is an important mode of logical reasoning for scientific experimentation and law enforcement. After a crime has been committed on the television show *CSI*, for example, detectives begin with the evidence at the scene—they take copious photographs, dust for fingerprints, use cotton swabs to take samples—in order to devise theories about who committed the crime and why.

What Is Deduction?

Deduction starts with a generalization and proceeds to a conclusion based on this generalization. A deductive argument rests on a fundamental truth, value, or right, rather than on specific pieces of evidence.

For example, the campus-based, student activist organization No Sweat argues against the use of sweatshops by multinational corporations owned by U.S. interests. The main assumption that underpins their arguments is that sweatshops create unsafe working conditions and low wages for workers. The fundamental truth that the deductive argument depends upon is that this treatment of human beings is unjust. As with all good premises, this premise is reasonable and likely to be accepted. Of course, the severity of the problem and the methods by which we can solve the problem might be debated.

Definition, Language, and Audience

In any argument it is important to define all vague or ambiguous terminology, clarify complex issues or concepts, and employ language clearly and concisely. If we do not do this, our argument will suffer logically and we may lose credibility with the reader. In addition, in order for a text to be persuasive, we must have a good sense of who our audience is, what their ideas, attitudes, needs, values, and desires may be, and how to relate to them most effectively. As writers of argument, we are often responding to the views of others—both those who oppose and support our views. If our audience is likely to concur with our perspectives, perhaps less support is necessary. If our audience is unlikely to agree with our perspectives, we may need additional support and to anticipate counterarguments more effectively. Along with those issues about audience addressed earlier, we may want to examine the following:

- What is the audience's relationship to the subject matter?
- How much knowledge does the audience have about the subject?
- What views does the audience likely hold about this subject?

- What investments (e.g., emotional, aesthetic, psychological, personal, moral, intellectual, status based) does the audience have in the subject?

Aristotle's Model for Logical Reasoning

The Syllogism. The Greek philosopher **Aristotle** outlined the syllogism or syllogistic logic, one critical model for logical reasoning upon which much contemporary argumentation depends. A **syllogism** is a logical formulation that suggests that if a major premise is true and a minor premise is true, then the combination of the two must be true (i.e., if A and B, then C). Consider this set of sentences, for example:

Singer Courtney Love is a woman. All women are mortal.
Courtney Love is mortal.

A. *Major Premise:* All women are mortal.
B. *Minor Premise:* Singer Courtney Love is a woman.
C. *Conclusion:* Courtney Love is mortal.

Based on syllogistic logic, we determine that if all women are mortal and Courtney Love is a woman, then Love must be mortal. Though hardcore Hole fans may disagree, if they agree with A and B, they must consent to C because the truth of the conclusion is contained in the premises.

The Enthymeme. Aristotle noted that people who create arguments often do not spell out their argumentative premises. This might happen because the creator of the argument is rushed, or because he or she wants to hide one of the (possibly dubious) premises to make an argument more persuasive.

This incomplete truncated syllogism, or **enthymeme,** indicates that if A is true, C must be true and demands that the audience fill in the "B" term on its own. Many of our contemporary arguments, particularly those that emerge in popular culture, are based on enthymemes. Consider this set of sentences, for example, and the complex issues they raise about ethics, murder, and the death penalty:

Scott Peterson has been tried and found guilty of killing his wife, Laci,
and their unborn child. Therefore, he should receive the death penalty.

A. *Major Premise:* Scott Peterson has been tried and found guilty of killing his wife, Laci, and their unborn child.
B. *Minor Premise:* [Not stated]
C. *Conclusion:* Therefore, he should receive the death penalty.

The missing premise is as follows: Those who have committed murder should receive the death penalty. If we do not believe that this suppressed premise is viable (i.e., if we do not think that committing murder necessitates the death penalty or we think that the evidence against Peterson was questionable), we may not agree that this argument is valid. Perhaps we believe that there were mitigating circumstances that led to the murder of his wife, Laci, or that Peterson may have larger psychological problems that can be addressed through incarceration and counseling. Exposing the ways in which the unstated premise might be considered flawed, then, might be one significant way to challenge the argument itself.

Stephen Toulmin's Practical Model

Since Aristotle's time, many scholars of argument have expanded his models for reasoning. One of the most significant critical responses to Aristotle's work in this area was offered by philosopher Stephen Toulmin in the 1950s. **Toulmin** questioned models of argument based on Aristotelian formal logic, contending that the syllogism with its three-part structure was too rigid a model, instead calling for a more practical understanding of reasoning. He was concerned that the syllogistic logic articulated by Aristotle sometimes failed to account for the variability, relativity, and mutability of arguments in our everyday lives. In place of the Aristotelian model, then, Toulmin created an audience-based, field-based, courtroom model. Toulmin asserted that while we do we argue about facts and judgments of taste, we also importantly argue about opinions. As a result, Toulmin also felt that the audience for any argument had a much greater role in how a given argument was received than Aristotle had originally suggested. Toulmin argued that as we create arguments, we have to effectively anticipate counterarguments and question our own assumptions. He also stressed that opposing arguments must be given real thought and consideration.

In Toulmin's scheme, a given **claim** must be based on specific **data.** Take the following claim: Mariah Carey is a Latin musical artist. We base this claim on data—in this instance, that one of Carey's parents is Venezuelan. To establish the connection between the claim and the data, we may cite a **warrant.** Thus, Mariah Carey is a Latin musical artist (claim) by virtue of having a parent from Venezuela (data), because people with Spanish ancestry are usually termed "Latin" (warrant). Often a warrant may need support or **backing.** In this example we could cite analogous instances of other musicians with Spanish heritage and how they have been categorized as "Latin" despite having ancestors that come from a wide range of Spanish-speaking countries—such as Jennifer Lopez, Mark Anthony, Christina Aguilera, Ricky Martin, Enrique Iglesias, or Shakira. Oftentimes, a claim also has a **qualifier** such as *surely*, *likely*, or *perhaps*. In our example, for instance, we might say that Mariah Carey could perhaps (qualifier) be categorized as a Latin musical artist (claim) because people with Spanish ancestry are usually termed "Latin" (warrant).

THE MAIN PARTS OF AN ARGUMENT

While Aristotle, Toulmin, and other contemporary rhetoric scholars have offered crucial ideas about argumentation, a combination of their theories may best help us to get at the most important features of contemporary arguments. Today's often complicated arguments—ones that increasingly take up issues of personal, social, political, and ethical significance—require that we have various tools for analysis. Therefore, when we examine arguments, we will look at the **research question, claim, support,** and **warrants.**

> **The Research Question:** The query or obstacle that a creator of argument wants to answer or solve.
>
> **The Claim:** The proposition the arguer sets out to prove.
>
> **The Support:** Information used to back up a claim.
>
> **The Warrants:** Inferences or assumptions that the arguer takes for granted and that underlie his or her argumentative claims.

The Research Question

The research question is a query or obstacle that a creator of argument wants to answer or solve. The specific ways in which the arguer understands and phrases the question will result in certain kinds of responses or claims instead of others. As a result, understanding the kind of question that gives rise to the claim is critical. One example of a research question is the following: "Does the video game, 'Grand Theft Auto,' have an impact on children's understandings of morality and violence?" Remember, asking an objective question is critical to obtaining unbiased evidence. As part of researching this question one could read journal articles in psychology and sociology to determine what experts have said. One might also perform case studies about specific children, tracing their reactions to the video game.

Claims

The argumentative claim is a proposition the arguer sets out to prove. Often the main claims of an essay are thesis statements. Subclaims are subthesis statements that help to support the main claim. There are various kinds of claims. Creators of arguments employ different sorts of claims depending upon what kinds of outcomes they desire.

Kinds of Claims

Factual Claims: Factual claims assert that a condition has existed, exists, or will exist. The support that they draw on largely involves factual information such as statistics, examples, or other forms of testimony that are verifiable. Examples of factual claims include the following: "*Friends* was among the most watched television shows in viewing history" and "Four out of five dentists recommend Trident sugarless gum for their patients who chew gum." Examples of television watching polls and demographic studies might support this claim about *Friends*. Examples of surveys, interviews, and statistics about dentists' views would help support this claim about Trident gum.

Judgment Claims: Judgment claims express approval or disapproval and may establish that an action, belief, or condition is right or wrong, good or bad, beautiful or ugly, worthwhile or undesirable. Judgment claims tend to take up concerns of aesthetics and morality, so the arguer usually needs to establish carefully the standards for discussion and to define her or his terms. Examples of judgment claims include comments such as "Celine Dion is a much better singer than Avril Lavigne" and "*Kill Bill Vol.1* and *2* have made cinematic history." Examples of Dion's vocal training background, comments from other singers recognized as the best in their chosen genre and discussion of her vocal range might help to support the claim that she is a better singer than Lavigne. Analyses of the roles of women in the films, the graphic but stylized images of violence, and the innovative use of camera angles, and choreographed fight sequences might help support this claim about the *Kill Bill* movies.

Proposal Claims: Proposal claims assert that a certain course of action should be adopted. Examples of proposal claims include the following: "In order to decrease death rates in car accidents, we must increase seat belt laws nationally" and "Independent films need to be marketed more effectively in order to secure larger viewing audiences." Examples of particular states that have adopted seat belt laws and evidence that reveals how their death rates due to car accidents have gone down would help support this claim about the need to increase such laws. Examples of independent films with large and skillful marketing campaigns could be compared to those that were not promoted as much in order to support this claim about how independent films might gain larger audiences.

Evaluating Claims

Evaluating claims requires that we look at them carefully and determine whether they are valid and clear, specific, and relevant.

CHECKLIST FOR EVALUATING CLAIMS

☐ *Evaluate Viability*: Is this a reasonable, logical claim? Examine the likelihood that this claim is workable, whether it might be acceptable to people, and whether they will find it to be truthful.

☐ *Evaluate Potential Opposition*: Does the claim establish common ground with the opposition? Does it take the opposition's views into account?

☐ *Evaluate Scope*: Is this claim specific enough to be proven, but general enough that people will find it significant?

☐ *Evaluate Contribution*: Does the claim contribute to an ongoing discussion? Does it address concerns relevant to the people who will read it? Does it provide evidence for a gap in the research?

Support

The support is the information utilized to back up a claim. Its aim is to convince the audience that the arguer's claim is credible and true. Typically, support consists of a combination of evidence and the rhetorical appeals we studied earlier. Evidence often involves facts, statistics, personal observations, and testimony from expert sources (examples of logos). Other rhetorical appeals include ethos and pathos.

Kinds of Support

Evidence: Evidence can require facts from various sources such as magazines, newspapers, books, and articles. According to Toulmin, the kind of evidence most effective to support a claim depends on the field and on the audience. For example, if you wanted to convince a group of nursing students that rapid-weight-loss diets can be hazardous to their health you might find some excellent support in medical journals. In addition, evidence can sometimes involve statistics. For instance, if you wanted to show politicians that child labor was a growing problem in Asian countries exporting materials to the United States, you could locate statistics that indicated how many child workers in Asia could be found making products for U.S. companies in 1990 as opposed to those today. Likewise, evidence can entail using personal observations (along with interviews, surveys, and questionnaires). For example, if you wanted to argue that your community needed a better bike trail system, you could take note of how many vehicle–bike accidents had occurred, study pollution levels, and show the limitations of the current path system. Finally, evidence can also include expert sources. For instance, if you wanted to prove that global warming was contributing to the extinction of certain plants, you could go to the library, find essays recently written by scientists who study global warming, and quote their views.

Rhetorical Appeals: Support can come in the form of rhetorical appeals. Pathos is often used. For example, if you wanted to prove that people should adopt a vegetarian diet, you could support this claim with the notion that it causes animal suffering, citing examples of commercial farms keeping animals in small cages and feeding them poorly. This would evoke feelings of sadness, pity, anger, and fear at the potential abuse of animals. Ethos is also sometimes employed as a form of support. For instance, if you wanted to show that health care should be universalized, you would want to appear credible. This might entail arguing from a strong base of knowledge about the various issues, quoting experts in the field, and pointing to examples, personal experiences, statistics, and other data. As a result of your knowledge, you would appear more trustworthy and your argument would appear more viable.

Evaluating support is not always easy. Here are some guidelines to follow:

CHECKLIST FOR EVALUATING SUPPORT

☐ *Evaluate Facts*: Is the evidence current, sufficient, relevant, and accurate? Are the examples representative?

☐ *Evaluate Statistics*: Do the statistics come from trustworthy sources? Are the terms clearly defined? Has any significant information been omitted?

☐ *Evaluate Personal Observations*: Are the experiences (interviews, surveys, and questionnaires) cited unbiased, viable, and representative?

☐ *Evaluate Testimony*: Is the source of the opinion worth listening to? Why or why not? Is the source biased? What is the basis of the source's opinion?

☐ *Evaluate Rhetorical Appeals*: Do the rhetorical appeals support the argument or undermine it?

Warrants

Warrants, also sometimes called **inferences** and **assumptions,** are thoughts, often unexpressed, that operate in every argument and that guarantee the sound relationship between the claim and the evidence. The reader is likely to believe the claim only if she or he finds the warrant believable.

These are the main warrants that typically exist in arguments. Frequently more than one is used:

Kinds of Warrants

Warrant of Authority: These are assumptions that are based on the credibility of outside research, third parties, or sources. The audience is led to believe that a claim is supported because of the strength of the testimony of experts. For example, if we are told that Martin Scorsese could argue that Stanley Kubrick was one of the best American film directors, we might be inclined to believe in Kubrick's excellence. This would be due in large part to the strength of Scorsese's own credentials as a director, and our belief that one director is a good judge of another. The warrant in this case would be Scorsese's authority. If we had serious evidence that undermined Scorsese's credibility in this regard, this warrant might be found to be false and this argument could be open to refutation.

Warrant of Verifiable Fact: These are assumptions dependent upon the reliability of verifiable, factual evidence. For example, consider the claim that more children between the age of five and eight watch *Spongebob Squarepants* than those between the age of nine and twelve. Imagine that this claim is supported by a demographic study that reveals higher numbers of younger viewers. This evidence is verifiable. If it can be shown to be true, the claim will be adequately supported by the evidence. The warrant in this instance would be that this demographic study is a viable indicator of who watches *Spongebob Squarepants*. If, for instance, this study is shown to be poorly done (i.e., poor sampling, poorly derived statistics), the warrant could be shown to be false and the argument might be challenged.

Warrant of Rhetorical Appeal: These are assumptions that are based on the values of the audience and the arguer. The audience is asked to agree that a claim is supported because of persuasive rhetorical appeals to ethos, pathos, and/or logos. For instance, imagine an ad for a pet insurance company that features a picture of a forlorn puppy. The implicit claim in the ad is that we should buy the insurance. For us to believe that this claim is valid, we have to be influenced by this strong rhetorical appeal to pathos. The warrant in this case would be that caring for, protecting, and loving our pets means being economically prepared to take care of their potential illnesses. If we dispute that insurance itself is necessary for taking care of our pets altogether or feel manipulated by this strong appeal to pathos, then we might challenge the ad's warrant of rhetorical appeal and the implied claim of the ad.

Evaluating Warrants

Much like evaluating evidence, analyzing warrants can be difficult. We need to ask questions like the following:

CHECKLIST FOR EVALUATING WARRANTS

☐ *Evaluate Understandability*: Is the warrant understandable? Is it clearly articulated in the text or is it implicit?

☐ *Evaluate Validity*: Is this warrant true and valid? Is the opposition likely to offer a counterexample? Are there better warrants that one might use?

☐ *Evaluate Relevance*: Is the warrant relevant, given the claim and the evidence offered?

☐ *Evaluate Context and Community*: Does the warrant make sense given the context in which it appears and the community it is addressing?

Understanding research questions, claims, supports, and warrants will help us to better analyze and evaluate others' arguments as well as make more persuasive arguments of our own.

DISMANTLING AN ARGUMENT

We should always begin analyzing an argument by looking at whether the premises hold, the research question is pertinent, the claim is valid, the support is strong, and the warrants are verifiable. In some cases, the claim may be strong but the evidence weak. In other cases, the claim may be weak and the evidence strong. In still other cases, the warrants may be questionable.

Logical Fallacies

After you have addressed these other concerns, ask whether the argument contains any **logical fallacies**—flaws in logic that often involve faulty facts and misrepresentations. Knowing where and how logical fallacies operate in an argument can help you to successfully dispute that argument. Here are some of the main ones:

- *Ad Hominem Argument: Ad hominem* is Latin for "against the man." An **ad hominem** argument attacks the personal character or the reputation of one's opponents, usually ignoring the meaning and content of the opponents' arguments. For example, one might argue that we should not purchase Marilyn Manson's music because his lyrics are troubling. In order to support this claim, one may direct attention toward personal information about him—his dress and make-up, his politics, and his religious beliefs. While this information may be true, the argument itself is not valid. A more logically sound way of making such an argument would involve not criticizing the man and his life but rather revealing why his lyrics themselves are disturbing.

- *Ad Populum Argument: Ad populum* is Latin for "argument to the crowd." In the **ad populum** argument one attempts to make an audience trust that her or his argument is valid, not through logical proof, but through appealing to broad beliefs shared with the audience. Such approaches often dominate political debates in which candidates connect their campaign platforms to the voters' desires and concerns. For instance, imagine that a politician claims "I deserve to be voted president of the United States." Directly after saying this, he states the following: "We need to take back the power of the presidency for the people. We must give the power of the government back to the younger generation." While few people would disagree that people should have a say in the presidency, particularly the younger generation, in this statement no real evidence is offered for why the candidate should in fact become president. Actual policy statements used as evidence would provide better support for this politician's candidacy.

- *Straw Man*: The **straw man** type of argument attacks an opponent, setting up her or him as a "straw man" or an easy target, by misrepresenting his or her position (often by exaggerating it). Consider the following set of statements: "Military service should be legally mandatory. People don't want to enter the military because they find it an inconvenience. However, they should realize that there are more important things than convenience." To say that people might not want to join the military because of "inconvenience" exaggerates and misrepresents the situations of actual people who both choose to enter the military and those who do not. It also overlooks why people in both groups might have trouble with such a legal mandate. In order to best support an argument for compulsory military service, one needs to offer evidence for the importance of such service—to one's community, country, the world. Likewise, perhaps one would also do well to draw a valid analogy between other successful legal mandates and this proposed one.

- *Non Sequitur*: In Latin this means "it does not follow." While this is clearly a part of most logical fallacies, it usually refers to a conclusion that does not follow from the premises of the argument. Even more specifically, it can refer to a sentence in which there is a subordinate clause that has little to do with the main clause. Consider the following statement that offers an example of the first type: "*Survivor* demands that people be able to survive in the natural elements. No one who comes from a big city could ever win the million dollars." While it may be true that wilderness experiences might be helpful to winning the show, it does not necessarily follow that urban dwellers do not have such experiences or that they do not have other skills useful to succeeding on the show. In order to make such an argument work, one would have to fill in the missing logical pieces and avoid an exaggerated term like "no one."

- *Hasty or Faulty Generalization*: This is a logical fallacy in which the arguer draws conclusions without sufficient evidence or based on too few examples. An example of a **hasty or faulty generalization** is as follows: Imagine that you listen to one song by Linkin Park for the first time and then, based upon hearing that one song, proclaim to your friends that you are a devoted fan of the band's music. Having not listened to the rest of the group's songs, your friends might rightly say that you are making a hasty or faulty generalization. Perhaps there are some songs by the group that you will not like. In order to avoid making a hasty or faulty generalization, you would do well to familiarize yourself with a good deal of the band's music—providing you with more evidence and therefore more expertise with which to judge.

- *False Dilemma*: In a **false dilemma** the person constructing an argument sets up an either–or situation, causing the reader or viewer to choose between two possibilities by implying that no other viable options exist (e.g., "You're either for us or against us"). Consider the following comment made by a car salesperson: "Look, you need to decide. Either you choose that you can afford this new car, or you will have to walk everywhere for the rest of your life." Note that other options are not being considered here—such as purchasing a used car, using public transportation, or buying a different vehicle such as a bike or motorcycle. In order to avoid this logical fallacy, be sure that the dilemma being set up takes all possibilities into consideration.

- *False Analogy*: In a **false analogy** the arguer suggests that two situations or things are analogous when they might not be. Writers of newspaper editorials often use analogies between one thing and another in order to make their points. For instance, various writers have compared the situation in Iraq with WWII or Vietnam, often depending on their political perspectives. However, for many reasons—differences in historical context, terrain, public sentiment, policy, and purpose—these analogies may not hold. In order to make sure an analogy is viable, the writer should explain why the points of comparison are valid.

- *Begging the Question* and *Jumping to Conclusions*: These fallacies depend upon circular reasoning—restatement of a claim rather than proof of it. In **begging the question,** the creator of the argument expects people to accept as given a premise that's actually controversial. For example, imagine the following statements: "Gay marriage should be legal because not making it so violates the U.S. Constitution." Notice that the arguer is failing to acknowledge that gay marriage's violation of the Constitution is a controversial matter that has inspired much debate and discussion. While this is a valuable claim, one could make a more persuasive argument by acknowledging and explaining this controversy in detail or basing the argument for legality on some other, less controversial, premise. In **jumping to conclusions,** one may assert a claim and reach a conclusion without providing ample evidence. One well-known example is as follows: "God exists because the Bible says so. The Bible is a reliable source because it is the word of God." While God may exist and the Bible may well be a very reliable source of information, one might argue that the argument is jumping to conclusions because no factual evidence is offered for either assertion. In order to avoid this logical fallacy one would need to provide evidence. Doing so might be difficult because matters of faith, while important, are almost impossible to prove with empirical evidence.

- *Faulty Use of Authority*: Although logical arguments often depend upon expert witness as evidence, sometimes the experts cited do not have the necessary expertise to support the claim proffered. **Faulty use of authority** can also occur when a worthy authority cited is inaccurately quoted, misinterpreted, or quoted out of context. For instance, consider the following: "Dr. Phil, a well-known counselor and television personality, recommends that you purchase a Trek bicycle." Note that while Dr. Phil may be an expert on relationships, he is not an expert on cycling; therefore, his authority on the subject has little relevance. In order to make the argument that a Trek bike is worth purchasing, it would be better to cite a cycling expert, such as Lance Armstrong, who used the actual product to win the Tour de France.

- *Slippery slope*: The creator of a **slippery slope** argument predicts one step will lead to a series of other undesirable steps, without providing adequate causal evidence for this. Consider the following example: "If we let children spend too much time on the Internet, they will become less intelligent, more prone to suicide and depression, and more likely to commit violent crimes." Notice that each of these conditions is worse than the first and none are substantiated. In order to make such an argument, one would have to provide verifiable evidence for each assertion. Since this would be quite difficult to accomplish, one might do just as well to avoid overstating the case.

- *Appeal to Tradition*: In **appeal to tradition** the arguer maintains that something should exist because it is a tradition, no matter how unexamined it might be. This is a logical fallacy not because traditions do not have their place in arguments, but because the negative aspects of traditions are not taken into consideration. Take the following statement as an example: "Women have never been in the PGA. Sure, it's a form of exclusion. However, that's how it's always been, and that's how it needs to stay." While the first and second statements might be verifiable and accurate, tradition does not necessarily dictate that these conditions should continue to exist. In order for such an argument to hold, one might do better to consider the reasons why women have not been part of the PGA in the past and whether any of these reasons are themselves justifiable in this current historical context.

- *Appeal to Change*: In **appeal to change** the arguer maintains that change must occur, despite significant costs and substantial evidence to the contrary. This is a form of logical fallacy, not because new policies are not often valuable but because supporting them at all costs may entail overlooking potential negative repercussions. For instance, one might claim the following: "Since technology now allows classes to be taught on the web, all teachers should teach as many of their classes on the Internet as possible." While this might be exciting new technology, perhaps some courses would suffer as a result of not being taught in classrooms. Consider language classes, for instance, in which students' pronunciation and teacher feedback are key to learning. Just because the technology is available, we need not necessarily use it.

LOGICAL REASONING AND FALLACIES: **EXERCISING YOUR SKILLS**

Logical Reasoning: Ad and Ad Spoof

Consider this milk ad featuring Elle McPherson. You may also want to consult http://www.whymilk.com/ for other milk ads. Then, look at the ad in light of the AdBusters spoof ad. What kind of logical reasoning do these ads depend upon—inductive or deductive? How can you tell? Consider each of these ads as syllogisms. What are their major premises, minor premises, and conclusions?

Analyze and Dismantle Arguments: Ad and Spoof

Consider what specific argumentative claims, support, and warrants are operating in the real ad versus the spoof ad. Are there any logical fallacies at work? If yes, what are they? Do you think that they detract from the arguments that the ads make?

Create Your Own Argument About Ads

Reflect on the argumentative claim you might make about how this milk ad—and others you examine on the website—and how they operate rhetorically and argumentatively. What support from the ads could you use to back up your views? What additional evidence might you need to locate? Use the prewriting strategies you have learned to create a rough draft.

Create Your Own Argument About Websites

Go to the National Park website shown at http://www.nps.gov/ and explore the various links (consult the "Checklist for Rhetoric in Visual and Multimedia Texts" in Chapter 2 for help with your analysis). After you have done this, examine the 1997 version of the site and read the tongue-in-cheek essay about the subject from *The Onion*. Using humor and sarcasm, this essay takes issue with changes that were made to the National Park Service's website in 1997 that have since been changed back to how they originally looked. As you read, look at the images you see on today's website and compare them to the 1997 images.[1] Outline the writer's argumentative claim, support, and warrants—determining what kinds are at work. Consider the rhetorical tactics being used by the essay's writers. In addition, make note of

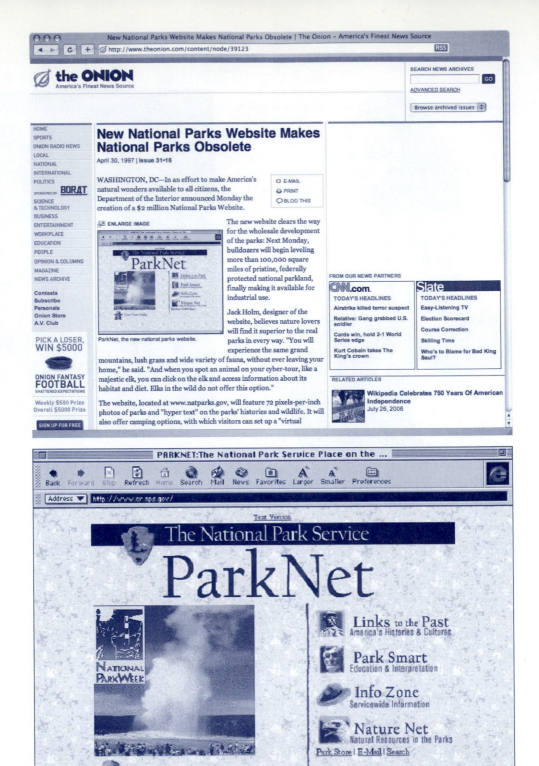

the ONION
America's Finest News Source

New National Parks Website Makes National Parks Obsolete

April 30, 1997 | Issue 31•16

WASHINGTON, DC—In an effort to make America's natural wonders available to all citizens, the Department of the Interior announced Monday the creation of a $2 million National Parks Website.

☒ E-MAIL
🖶 PRINT
🔲 BLOG THIS

🖾 ENLARGE IMAGE

ParkNet, the new national parks website.

The new website clears the way for the wholesale development of the parks: Next Monday, bulldozers will begin leveling more than 100,000 square miles of pristine, federally protected national parkland, finally making it available for industrial use.

Jack Holm, designer of the website, believes nature lovers will find it superior to the real parks in every way. "You will experience the same grand mountains, lush grass and wide variety of fauna, without ever leaving your home," he said. "And when you spot an animal on your cyber-tour, like a majestic elk, you can click on the elk and access information about its habitat and diet. Elks in the wild do not offer this option."

The website, located at www.natparks.gov, will feature 72 pixels-per-inch photos of parks and "hyper text" on the parks' histories and wildlife. It will also offer camping options, with which visitors can set up a "virtual any logical fallacies operating in the article. Next, make your own argument about the two websites and the article. What do you think about the article? Do you prefer the rhetoric of today's website or the 1997 version? Examine the use of images and text—and support with evidence as well as the article. Use the prewriting strategies you have learned to create a rough draft.

New National Parks Website Makes National Parks Obsolete

WASHINGTON, DC—In an effort to make America's natural wonders available to all citizens, the Department of the Interior announced Monday the creation of a $2 million National Parks Website.

The new Website clears the way for the wholesale development of the parks: Next Monday, bulldozers will begin leveling more than 100,000 square miles of pristine, federally protected national parkland, finally making it available for industrial use.

Jack Holm, designer of the Website, believes nature lovers will find it superior to the real parks in every way. "You will experience the same grand mountains, lush grass and wide variety of fauna, without ever leaving your home," he said. "And when you spot an animal on your cyber-tour, like a majestic elk, you can click on the elk and access information about its habitat and diet. Elks in the wild do not offer this option."

The Website, located at www.natparks.gov, will feature 72 pixels-per-inch photos of parks and "hyper text" on the parks' histories and wildlife. It will also offer camping options, with which visitors can set up a "virtual campsite" inside a national park and watch a quick-time movie of the setting sun while RealAudio playback of crickets and coyotes runs at 44.1 kilohertz.

"We digitally enhanced actual recordings of coyotes from Arizona's Saguaro National Park," Holm said. "It should sound better than the real thing."

According to National Parks Destruction Chief Lew Hoffson, countless grizzlies, moose and bison will be incinerated when the 750,000-acre Yellowstone National Park is slash-burned to make room for what he says will be the nation's largest factory outlet mall.

"Yellowstone, like the other national parks, has proven to be a huge financial burden to taxpayers, costing more than $200 million a year to maintain," Hoffson said. "The new Yellowstone Factory Shoppes, on the other hand, are privately funded and should be immensely profitable right from the word go. It just makes sense."

The economic advantage of massive, unregulated development of the parks was only one reason for the Website move. Safety was also a factor.

"Every year, between 30 to 40 national parks visitors are killed in accidents, ranging from animal attacks to falls off cliffs," Holm said. "The Website will be far safer, with the greatest danger posed to visitors being possible neck and back strain from prolonged sitting at the computer station." To avoid such discomfort when visiting the new cyber-parks, Holm strongly advised taking a "stretch break" every 15 to 20 minutes.

Yet another advantage of web-based camping will be the chance for visitors to enjoy interacting with talking, anthropomorphic wildlife, such as PC Puffin, a friendly, wise-cracking aquatic cartoon bird who gives visitors tours of Alaska's Denali National Park. "Non-cyber-parks do not feature puffin-led tours, for in real life animals do not talk," Holm said.

U.S. Parks Department officials said the department is also planning an endangered-species Website, enabling people to observe and study rare species on their computers.

Once the Website is up and running, the actual endangered animals will either be allowed to die out naturally in captivity or be killed off wholesale by poachers.

U.S. Sen. Spencer Abraham (R-MI), who sponsored the legislation, said that he and

his family are planning a trip to the National Parks Website this July. "We've never been to Yellowstone," he said, "and I understand we'll be able to download a sound effect of hot, splashing water digitally recorded right at Old Faithful. We're very excited."

RESEARCH AND WRITING ON POPULAR CULTURE: PREWRITING, DRAFTING, AND REFLECTING

Bryan is a microbiology student working toward a degree in dentistry. Bryan has found argumentative skills to be very important to his success in college and his major: "Knowing how to make an argument has been essential to me when I have applied for scholarships. Simply put, I would not be able to go to college without them. When I write letters of intent, they are mini-arguments. I have to think carefully about my claim, support, and warrants. I have to know what rhetorical tactics I will use and why. Then I have to consider the writing process—think about what I am going to write, make a rough draft, do final adjustments, and then come up with a final product. My main aim is to make my point as clearly as possible." Bryan adds, "You don't have to be an English major to want to improve your skills and to enjoy writing. Knowing how to use critical perspective, rhetorical analysis, and argumentation to communicate persuasively is fundamental to being successful in life." Even though he knew that the topic was controversial, Bryan chose to make an argument about The Jerry Springer Show *because he was disturbed by the show, concerned by how popular it is, and fascinated with how Jerry functioned as a mediator while also belittling his audience. Bryan spends his free time working as a mentor to other students, playing guitar and drums, snowboarding, and skateboarding.*

Researching and writing your own cultural criticism requires that you consider a specific research question, examine primary sources, create a working thesis and outline, consult secondary sources, and draft as well as revise the paper (not necessarily in this order). We will watch how one student, Bryan, accomplishes this while writing about *The Jerry Springer Show.*

Earlier in the book we examined rhetoric, critical reading, and responding techniques, as well as prewriting strategies such as freewriting, mapping, and outlining. Here we will turn our attention more fully to the later stages of the writing process—**drafting, reflecting,** and **revising.** In the drafting stage, we use our prewriting as the foundation upon which to build an essay. In the reflecting stage we put time and distance between ourselves and our working drafts (and we may consult secondary source material), allowing us the ability to reconsider our thoughts as well as to come up with new ideas. In the revising stage we make our ideas as clear as they can be, restructure the text to maintain our logic, and perhaps modify our thesis.

Bryan provides a good, beginning model for how you might compose your own essay. His techniques will prove useful to you for any research paper you may write during your college career. In addition, these same skills have value for creating other media forms—be they websites, print advertising, multimedia presentations, video productions, commercials, or even television shows themselves.

Prewriting

When you begin prewriting for a paper of this kind, you may follow the steps Bryan uses below: Create a research question; read, reread, and take detailed notes on your primary text; and construct a working thesis and outline. In this case Bryan watches, rewatches, as well as takes detailed notes about a television show episode.

Preliminary Research Question:

What might a close analysis of *The Jerry Springer Show* reveal about the participants, Jerry, our culture, and the show's viewers?

Notes on the Primary Text ("Cheaters on the Run"—Specific Episode of Jerry Springer)

- *Introduction to Show:* Jerry appears in a business suit. Camera swings around from audience to Jerry. Lights behind him. Lights in audience. Billowing fog. The audience shouts "Jerry!" The announcer says, "the eighth wonder of the world" as he introduces Springer.

- *Show Topic: "Cheaters on the Run":* This is a very typical topic for the show—exposing problems in relationships, especially people deceiving each other, getting violent with each other, shouting at each other. Jerry roams the crowd and shakes hands. Jerry introduces guests and various "love triangles." Relationships: Tom and April (John); Bob and Sarah (Allan); Wesley and Tara (Mike); Cory and Apryl (Jason). Dress of people tight and minimal. This accentuates differences between body types. Clothes also seem inexpensive. Speech is often stilted. Is this an attempt to represent a stereotype of the "lower class"?

- *Examples of Interactions:* There are many examples of violent exchanges. Bob, Sarah, and Allan have a violent exchange and so do Cory, Apryl, and Jason. The show's "bodyguard" Steve interrupts in both cases. Audience's reaction is strange, goading—"Kick his butt!", "Steve, Steve, Steve!", and "Jerry, Jerry, Jerry!"

- *Show within the Show:* The show often has some sort of exposé in which viewers are encouraged to act as voyeurs. Jerry's crew, with Tom, follows April and John to river. Tom sees couple in river and burns clothes. John puts on half-burnt underwear. Tom and April fight. Tom chases John down the street naked. Over-the-top violence and anger, plus taboo nakedness. People treat each other really poorly, quick to fight. Does the presence of the crew exacerbate this?

- *Examples of Interactions:* Deception on the show often seems to lead to violence. Wesley reveals to Tara that he has been seeing Mike. Mike and Tara fight each other about what they can offer to Wesley in a relationship.

- *Jerry's Role:* Jerry seems supportive yet patronizing to his guests. When the guests are explaining their current situation, Jerry gives them his undivided attention. Yet when we are watching Tom and John chasing each other through the streets, Jerry makes several sarcastic comments. "What the hell was that? It's a good thing you were in good shape!" Crowd laughs. Jerry also taunts Wesley, Tara, and Mike. Mike declares that Tara is not attractive enough to warrant Wesley's interest. Jerry, in an "innocent" attempt to get a laugh says, "He [Wesley] left you for a toothless bitch [Tara]? How inconsiderate of him!"

- *Audience in Studio:* The audience behaves in a cruel way, and is encouraged to do so. They shape or are maybe meant to mirror our responses as viewers at home. One audience member says to John, "Yeah, I got a question for the fatso in the blue shirt. Are you the poster-boy for the Pillsbury doughboy?" Audience laughter. Another woman from the audience makes a lewd comment to April, saying, "Yeah, I have a question for the fat whore fighting with the two tubs of lard! Who's fatter, you or you boyfriend?"

- *Jerry's "Final Thought":* Jerry's final words seem like an attempt to bring order to the chaos. However, I think that something else is happening here. This segment allows him to patronize the guests once more and make an apparent appeal to logos—but what evidence has he provided for his claims? Jerry sounds sincere when tells us—the audience at home—that we should be good to one another, not resort to such physical violence, not be dishonest in our relationships, and not get involved in sexual relationships when we are committed to other people. But has he done anything to create harmony or has he just fostered more discord?

Working Thesis and Outline

I. *Introduction:* Describe the show, draw in reader, and set scene for show (1–2 paragraphs).

II. *Main Claim/Thesis Statement: The Jerry Springer Show* is troubling because it encourages angry debate and physical violence. It also patronizes and mocks people based upon their physical, gender, and class differences. The show's success relies upon the viewers' desires to feel successful, controlled, and "normal" in comparison to the guests and even the audience depicted on the show itself. The participants sometimes become scapegoats against which the viewers can define themselves. The show reveals American cultural myths, fears, anxieties, desires, and values about violence and scapegoating, physical appearance and gender identity, as well as class relations.

III. *Background/Setting the Stage—The Guests:* Explain all of participants' relationships and how Jerry introduces them. Provide quotes from the show to back this up.

IV. *Evidence/Violence and Scapegoating:* Offer examples of how Jerry, the audience, and Steve instigate violence and mock guests. Give quotations from the show to support this.

V. *Evidence/Reinforcing Cultural Stereotypes—Physical Appearance and Gender:* Provide examples of how women and homosexual men are represented in troubling ways on the show. Give quotations from the show to back this up.

VI. *Evidence/Reinforcing Cultural Stereotypes—Class Relations:* Offer examples of how lower-class people are represented on the show. Provide quotations from the show to back this up.

VII. *The Role of the Studio Audience and How Jerry's 'Final Thought' Segment Secures the Stereotypes:* Give instances of how the audience supports limited views of appropriate physical types, class, and gender relations and how Jerry reinforces this. Furnish examples for support.

VIII. *My Final Thoughts on* The Jerry Springer Show: Reinforce thesis by restating it. Use slightly different language. Connect thesis and argument as clearly as possible to broader cultural issues. Explain why argument is significant to how we view television as well as how television views us (exactly how this show and others like it perpetuate those particular American cultural myths, fears, anxieties, desires, and values discussed earlier). Indicate why this is troubling and how it could impact participants' and viewers' habits, thoughts, and life choices that in fact may be at cross purposes with their true intentions—to have enriching, rewarding, and fulfilling lives. Will come back to conclusion and rethink it after collecting evidence for the argument itself. Looking at evidence may change my conclusion.

When you move from prewriting to drafting, consider your audience and the main claim about which you want to persuade that audience. Think about issues such as thesis statements, introductions, supporting paragraphs, evidence, and conclusions. Drawing from his outline, Bryan creates a very rough draft of his own argument and analysis of *The Jerry Springer Show.* Next, Bryan reads his text aloud to himself. As he does so, Bryan "talks back" to his own draft after he composes it, making comments in the margins that indicate what he tried to accomplish with the draft and areas where it could be improved.

Drafting

Bryan's Rough Draft

The Jerry Springer Show and American Culture

One night you decide to relax and watch some television. Remote in hand, you stumble upon one show. At first it appears as if the cameraman is being attacked by a person in a wild frenzy. Then, suddenly, the camera stops and focuses on a lone figure standing, dressed in a business suit. Next the camera dodges up and over the backstage crew as if they were obstacles in a race with no obvious goal. It then pans across a huge audience of people who are standing there clapping wildly and grinning. What are they chanting? "JERRY! JERRY! JERRY!" However, before you have a chance to think about what is happening or even to consider turning the channel, a deep, commanding voice announces, "Ladies and gentlemen, the eighth wonder of the world . . . Jerry Springer!"

You have trouble pulling yourself away from the show—even though what you are seeing truly disturbs you. What keeps you watching while no one is watching you is that you cannot shake a set of questions: What am I watching? Who is this Jerry character? Why are all these people calling his name? What also keeps you watching is the fact that, while there are tons of reality shows on television, you have never seen anything quite like this. While it is extremely strange and uncomfortable to observe, there is something captivating about the show at the same time. You stay tuned for the reason millions of people watch *The Jerry Springer Show* every day. You wish you did not have to admit this. However, you too want to see what will happen next.

Though *The Jerry Springer Show* keeps us watching, is this necessarily a good thing? I am not so sure. I think that the show

Title: I'm pretty sure that this title reflects my initial focus. Once my main claim becomes more detailed, I will make my title more specific as well.

Introduction: Here I am trying to engage my reader by using "you" and descriptive language. Maybe I should include more description. I am a little worried, though, that my thesis may not be as clear as I want it to be. I think I need to get to it more quickly.

I am wondering if "I" and "you" are too informal here. I will need to doublecheck with my Instructor to make sure that this approach is okay.

Main claim: This is where I should make my main claim. It still seems too vague to me. I also don't think that I am really analyzing the show for its logical fallacies yet. When I revise my paper it will be important for me to do that.

encourages anger and physical violence and it mocks people. The show's success relies upon the viewers' desire to see "dirt." Why does seeing "dirt" make us feel good, though? More importantly, however, what does our need for such dirt say about American culture?

The Guests

In order to get at these questions, it is important to take a look at one particular episode. Although there are many episodes one might select, "Cheaters on the Run," airing on June 20, 2001, offers a good representative example.

Tom knows that his girlfriend of a year and a half, April, is cheating on him with his best friend, John. Bob and his wife Sarah have been married for four years. She is cheating on him with their roommate Allan. Wesley plans to introduce his girlfriend Tara to his gay lover Mike. Cory and Apryl (not to be confused with the first April) have been dating for the past two years. Apryl wants to confess that she has been cheating on Cory with Jason.

What do all of these guests have in common? Each couple is involved in some act of infidelity and is about to confess it on national TV. Within the format of the show each couple is made to seem ridiculous in some way. The audience seems to enjoy hooting and jeering at them. The very structure of the show makes the participants seem somehow cartoonish—forcing the audience to see them as walking stereotypes rather than real human beings. It's a form of tasteless programming and it reveals some strange things about our culture and maybe even us as viewers.

Subtitles: I use subtitles to help me organize my essay. I will need to get clearer about my divisions and subtitles for the final draft. I think my subtitles should reflect my argumentative subclaims much more.

Logical Fallacies/Ad Hominem: When I read through my essay and think about logical fallacies, I realize that *The Jerry Springer Show* is full of flawed logic. For instance, aren't all of these nasty jibes examples of *ad hominem* arguments? All of this irrelevant personal information is brought in to undermine the character and reputation of the participants. Jerry does this to the guests and the guests do this to each other. I need to add something about this in my essay.

About Jerry: Jerry's ethos as the "ring leader" is key. His suit, demeanor, what he says, and his credentials set this up. The participants' ethos is often represented as somewhat untrustworthy—again, through dress, behavior, word choice, use of violence and obscenity, etc. The studio audience's attitude is also important. The things they shout, the way they dress, how they talk to the participants versus how they talk to Jerry—all of this is crucial. Then there's the reaction of the audience at home to consider. How does the show appeal to the viewers at home? Are the viewers at home somehow made to feel that they are better than the people who appear on the show? If yes, how and why?

Problems With My Assignment: What am I trying to argue in this section? I guess I want to look at the following: Why were these guests chosen and not others? Why/how do we respond to them? I need to make sure that everything I write in these sections helps to back up my main claim. In addition, I need to be careful in representing these guests that I am not doing what the show does itself—representing people in troubling ways.

I am restating my claim here. However, it still feels fuzzy to me. I am not sure that just restating it here is going to be enough. I need to find a way to make a clearer claim about the show and its cultural impacts. I think that I also need to offer my main claim in one place in my essay rather than scattering it throughout my introduction.

I also need to go back through my text to revise and make sure I don't use sentence fragments or run-on sentences. I also need to doublecheck grammar, style, and spelling as I revise.

Quotes: All of this would definitely be made stronger if I could provide more evidence, more quotes from the show.

I am also worried that my own language might be offensive here. I really don't want to perpetuate the same kind of language choices that I am criticizing. I need to find better ways to talk about my subtitles and subclaims. It's hard to get outside "Jerry's language"! I guess that's why the show has such a huge audience.

Logical Fallacies: I think I am onto something here! As I am rereading my paper I am realizing that this little film within the film misrepresents and exaggerates these people's lives and experiences for the purposes of mockery and supporting Jerry's and the audience's views of these people. Who are the actual people and what are their actual experiences? We will never know! Instead we just get a particular slice of their lives here—and it is designed to be one-sided and unflattering. One could assert that in doing so Jerry is using a *straw man* argument.

Violence

All of the guests shout, swear, and attack each other. For example, the scenario involving Bob and his wife Sarah, who is cheating with their roommate Allan. The first thing the couple does is get into a swearing match. To make matters worse, Allan is introduced onto the stage along with the fighting couple. Instantly, the two men lunge for each other. Before they can even think of hitting each other, they are stopped by a 185-pound barricade named Steve (the show's "bouncer"). As the battle continues on the stage, the rowdy crowd perpetuates in the humiliation of the show's participants, screaming chants such as "Kick his ass!" "Steve, Steve, Steve!" and "Jerry, Jerry, Jerry!"

Why does the audience cheer them on? The show seems to encourage violence, along with the idea that cheating is something that happens a lot in American culture. At the same time, the show suggests that the participants are subhuman, and that they are there to perform for the audience, like circus animals.

Obese People

The treatment of our first couple, Tom and April, makes fun of people struggling with weight issues. April wants to confess that she has been cheating with Tom's best friend John. In a segment filmed earlier, Tom brings Jerry's camera crew with him to spy on them. As Tom is walking with the camera crew down the river, they come across a pile of clothes and a picnic basket. As the camera turns toward the river we see the two people in the river: April and John. Tom lights their clothes on fire. John runs out of the water naked and starts stomping on the clothes. Tom shouts at April, and John pulls a piece of burnt underwear from the fire and puts it on, then runs out of the viewer's sight; then Tom chases after John. The two men are filmed by Jerry's camera crew as they breathe heavily and attempt to run through the streets in their underwear, trying to kill each other. The audience roars, ignoring the message the show is sending—the notion that there is one standard of beauty to which the guests do not adhere.

Class

"White trash" or "rednecks" are common terms on the show. Just as the participants on the show are ridiculed for not measuring up to some arbitrary standard of physical attractiveness, they are also ridiculed for their lower-class status. Jerry Springer mocks his guests repeatedly, reinforcing the notion over and over again that they are from the lowest class, and that Jerry is from the highest.

Jerry's "Final Thought"

Appearing alone on the stage at the end of show, Jerry offers his opinion concerning what battling couples should do instead of resorting to verbal and physical violence. As we listen, we are encouraged once more to look down upon the lives and actions of the show's participants, who are represented as violent, not typically attractive, and lower class. In effect this sends a signal to the audience that lower-class people and those who do not adhere to arbitrary standards of beauty are somehow inferior or immoral.

> Throughout the show it seems like Jerry is making arguments to the crowd. He appeals to broad beliefs shared by the audience—but he does not offer much logical proof. One could argue that this is an *ad populum* argument. He just panders to the audience's desires and concerns—both at home and in the studio audience.
>
> I think that the whole conclusion of the show, Jerry's "Final Thought," is a logical disconnect from what has come before in the show too. One might argue that this is an example of a *non sequitur*. Does Jerry's conclusion that we should not resort to this verbal and physical violence follow from what has happened in the show before? Didn't he just egg on the participants and the audience? One could also contend that he makes a *hasty generalization* because Jerry provides too few examples to support this conclusion—skewed examples that suit his own purposes. What about the rest of these people's lives? What about the real difficulties they experience? Finally, it could be argued that all of the logic in this show is based on a *slippery slope* view—that if one behaves or dresses in a certain way, a troubled life is sure to follow. Is this always accurate? Is it a fair representation of these people and their lives? I don't know if I want to add all of this into my next draft, but these are interesting things to notice!

> ### "Final Thoughts" on *The Jerry Springer Show*
>
> The show encourages angry debate, physical violence, and the mockery of people based on their physical characteristics and class status. The guests are represented in stereotypical ways. They are at the mercy of an audience—and a host—both of whom feel superior to them. I think the show reveals a lot that is ugly about American culture. We'd probably all be better off if it were taken off the air.

Reflecting

Now that you have written a rough draft of your paper, you need time and space to reflect on your essay. This means putting some distance between you and your writing—ideally for a day or so. This will give you a more objective stance on your essay so that you may reconsider issues such as your essay's main claim, structure, audience, or evidence. Many writers use this time to work on other projects, to go for a run, or to clean their rooms.

Bryan's Reflection Process

Once I wrote this rough draft I made some notes on it. Then I set my paper aside for a few days. In between I went to my other classes and did some recreational things like playing guitar and picking up a game of basketball with friends. I also read a couple of academic essays and chapters in books about talk shows. This gave me the time to think about my paper—how to clarify my main claim, how to get rid of the holes in my own logic and better support my views, and how to polish my own writing and tone. As a result, I had a lot of new ideas when I returned to my paper.

ARGUMENT IN ACTION: REVISING

Revising

After you have put some distance between yourself and your writing (and perhaps reviewed secondary sources), you are ready to revise your draft. When you revise, you restructure and rephrase your ideas for clarity and logical flow, refine your main points, and bring in additional evidence. You can make revision easier by working from a typed or printed text, reading your draft aloud (as Bryan did), and having your peers read your work. Watch as Bryan maps out his ideas for revision and then drafts a new version of his paper. As you read Bryan's revision you will see two sets of comments, Bryan's comments on his text and his instructor's responses to his comments.

Ideas for Revision:

- *Introduction:* Make my own position and claim much clearer. I also need to try to make my claim in one place in my text—and very directly. What do I want to claim about what the show says about American cultural myths, fears, anxieties, desires, and values? What do I want to say specifically about the show's representations of violence, obesity, and class? Is there more that I want to say about the show and its flawed logic? I also need to strike a balance between detailed description that captivates the reader and a very clear argumentative claim.

- *Audience:* Use my introduction and argument to better consider my own audience. While my audience for this text is my teacher, my audience also includes a college-level, general group with an interest in television. However, I cannot expect that they know anything about the show or see the value of my argument.

- *Opposition:* Better anticipate and refute my opposition from the beginning. Who are they? They seem to include two potential groups: (1) Pro the show: people who may think the show is positive because people like it—it isn't "highbrow," and (2) Against the show: people might not see any value in analyzing a television show at all because it is merely "entertainment." I need to anticipate and refute their positions. There is also a third potential group—people who may agree with my analysis but may not agree with me that the show is necessarily emblematic of our culture. I need to think about this possible opposition, too, and suggest why the show itself is indicative of larger trends in American culture.

- *Precision/Defining Terms:* I know what I want to say but I'm having some trouble saying it. Maybe that's because the argument I want to make is a little complicated. I think some of what I read in my secondary sources about "spectacle" and "scapegoating" might help me clarify my claims. I also think that these other thinkers' discussions of "dominant value systems" could support my argument very well.

- *Expert Testimony/Evidence:* Bring in secondary sources to support my claims. Though I think my argument makes sense, expert testimony and examples will help me to better back up my views. The additional reading I have done and notes I have taken will help me here. Watching the show again several more times closely and writing down relevant quotations will also be very important.

- *Examples/Evidence:* Give more examples from the show. The more actual quoting from the show, expert testimony, and/or examples of behavior I offer, the more convincing my argument will be.

- *Expand:* Right now I have three main parts—violence, obesity, and class. This analysis seems a bit uneven to me. In addition, I think I can bring in some of my ideas on how gender operates on the show. How are female guests treated differently than male guests? How are homosexual guests treated differently than heterosexual?

- *Conclusion:* Work on my conclusion. Right now it feels really weak. I usually have trouble writing strong conclusions until I have completed many drafts of my paper. I want to end the paper with a bang, while still admitting to my reader that this is only a partial analysis.

- *Final Comment:* Even if I am able to make all of these revisions to my draft, I know that there will be lots of other things I could do to make the paper stronger. Continuing to draft, reflect, and revise over and over again is what will make my paper more persuasive.

Bryan's Latest Draft

How *The Jerry Springer Show* Reinforces Negative Cultural Stereotypes

At night you find yourself relaxing while watching some television. Remote in hand, you stumble upon one show. At first the jittery camera angles make you wonder if the camera-man is being attacked by a person in a wild frenzy. Then, suddenly, the camera stops and focuses on a lone figure standing erect, dressed in a casual business suit. He builds an ethos in that moment—appearing reflective, thought-ful, and worthy of our respect. His head is bowed slightly, as if in prayer. The studio lights contribute to this image's spiritual overtones, illuminating his head from above. When the camera finally reveals his face, his expression appears to be one of utter confidence. Now it seems as if the brief moment of contemplation was only an attempt to prepare himself for what is to come—the battle that lays before him.

Bryan: This title is a lot more specific than in my rough draft. However, I still think it could better reflect what I am trying to prove.

Instructor: Great points, Bryan. I think this title does characterize the general claim you make much better—but it does not yet tell the reader what you are proving exactly. It also does not draw in your reader as much as it could. Keep thinking about other options as you revise your paper.

Instructor: Bryan, as you rewrite your essay, look at the di-rections for analyzing television's generic conventions found in our book. For instance, be sure that you have adequately addressed issues such as composition or layout, use of writ-ten text, cultural narratives, sound, and camera work (see the ideas about how to analyze camera work in films, too, since they are relevant to your analysis of television). In ad-dition, consider how the genre of the television show im-pacts its rhetorical features. What are the specific rhetorical features of the talk show? Are there rises and falls in plot and character development? Is there a method to commercial placement? How do the show's segment lead-in graphics and graphics between commercials, the host, the studio audi-ence, the audience at home, the set, the narrative structure, and the use of commercials shape how we view the show?

Bryan: I have tried to add more description here. I could do even more to focus on the role of Springer. I also added a bit more narrative to draw in the reader. I've noticed that a lot of cultural critics use this rhetorical technique—and that it can be quite effective. I could probably do more of this and expand my introduction quite a bit more.

Instructor: Bryan, I think you have done a nice job revis-ing and adding to your initial description of the show. This draws in your reader quite well. In addition, as you note, this is a very successful rhetorical technique that cultural critics use. In your next revision, however, I urge you to arrive at your claim more quickly and to make it more suc-cinctly. In this way, your reader will have a better sense of what you plan to prove in your text from the beginning.

Bryan: Is it okay if I use "you" here? I tried other techniques but they did not have the same immediacy.

Instructor: Writers in the genre of cultural criticism often use this technique. Of course, not all genres allow this—so you need to ask that question of every writing genre you encounter. In this case, though, I think this is an effective strategy. The key is that if you establish this relationship with your audience early on, you need to maintain it throughout your text.

Instructor: Try to avoid the use of excess words here. How about "the camera steadies itself"?

Bryan: Here is where I move from a description of the show to preparing the reader for my own argumentative claim. Is it working?

Instructor: Yes, this is much better, Bryan. However, I still think the transition could be smoother. If you make a point of getting to your argumentative claim more quickly, some of the transition problems you are having here will become easier to negotiate. This is something you will need to work on in your next draft.

Bryan: I know I need to work on the transition between paragraphs here. It's still a little rough.

Instructor: You have some excellent sources here, Bryan. I agree with your comment. Now you do want to better transition between ideas and better contextualize your quotes. This is a problem all writers encounter when we begin to introduce secondary sources. It is a good rule of thumb to follow these general steps:

1. Introduce subclaim
2. Contextualize quotation
3. Offer quotation and necessary citation
4. Provide close analysis of quotation for your reader
5. Connect your analysis back to the subclaim

Instructor: Your main claim is much clearer! However, in your next version, Bryan, I would like to see you assert it more quickly and directly. You might want to consider providing your readers with a mini-outline of the whole paper. In addition, be careful that your outside sources do not take over your own voice. Remember, it's your argument your reader wants to hear, not your outside sources'.

The camera then jets away dramatically into the studio halls, floats through a billowing fog, and then dodges up and over the backstage crew. You, the viewer, feel what you are meant to feel. The camera angles, lighting, and sound are strategically designed to appeal to the emotions of the audience watching in the studio and at home—arousing excitement, interest, and anticipation. You and the studio audience cannot wait to see what will happen next. Finally, the unsteady camera rights itself, finding its home on the main stage of the show. Through the eyes of the camera that pan the studio crowd, a chant begins and grows ceremoniously: "JERRY! JERRY! JERRY!" Suddenly the "JERRY" chant shifts to maniacal screams, whistles, and clapping. A deep voice announces, "Ladies and gentlemen, the eighth wonder of the world . . . Jerry Springer!"

Undoubtedly all of these images are quite engrossing. Yet after watching for several minutes, questions invariably occur to the viewer: What exactly am I witnessing? Who is this Jerry character? Why are all these people calling his name? The television show is very strange and yet oddly appealing at the same time. What keeps you watching is the fact that, while there are many reality shows on television, you have never seen anything quite like this. Even though the show is extremely uncomfortable to watch, there is something captivating about the show at the same time. You stay tuned for the reason millions of people watch *The Jerry Springer Show* every day. While you may be loathe to admit it, you too cannot wait to see what will happen next.

Like all television shows, as defined by the Museum of Television Archives, *The Jerry Springer Show* serves as a forum "in which society tests out and comes to terms with the topics, issues, and themes that define its basic values, what it means to be a 'citizen,' a participating member of society" (5). However, the success of *The Jerry Springer Show* is particularly unique because it depends upon several disturbing elements: employing logical fallacies, encouraging physical violence, and reproducing gender and class inequities. Moreover, the show's success relies upon the studio audience's and home viewers' desires to feel successful, controlled, and "normal" by comparison. Each guest is what critic Elizabeth Birmingham in "Fearing the Freak: How Talk TV Articulates Women and Class" refers to as a "scapegoat Other," or one who is sacrificed to the viewers' egos (134) to make them feel better in comparison.

Setting the Stage: The Guests

Although there are many episodes one might select in order to support the aforementioned claims about *The Jerry Springer Show,* "Cheaters on the Run," airing on June 20, 2001, offers a good representative example. As usual the show commences with Jerry roaming through the crowd, greeting all of his guests with a firm handshake and a "welcome"—sort of like a host greeting his guests at a party, or maybe a manager shaking hands with his employees at a company picnic. "Today we are going to talk about individuals who cheat on their loved ones," booms Jerry. Then Jerry introduces

Instructor: See "Each guest is what critic Elizabeth Birmingham in 'Fearing the Freak: How Talk TV Articulates Women and Class' refers to as a "scapegoat Other." How can you state this more clearly? Consider "As critic Elizabeth Birmingham argues in 'Fearing the Freak: How Talk TV Articulates Women and Class,' the show depends upon having a 'scapegoat Other'. . . ."

Instructor: As you reread your paper, look at your conclusion once more. Can you bring some of these good points into your introduction and restructure your paper accordingly? In addition, you will want to work on the way you integrate Birmingham's ideas about the "scapegoat Other into your introduction and throughout your paper." Be sure to address her article more directly. Also, look at my earlier suggestions for how to effectively use outside sources so that you can transition between your ideas more smoothly here.

Bryan: I have tried to make these subtitles reflect what I am doing in each section more precisely. Should I leave them in the final draft? Should they get even more specific in the next version?

Instructor: Yes, these are getting more and more specific and reflective of your argumentative subclaims. As your argument becomes more and more specific, of course, your subclaims and therefore your subtitles may get even clearer. Very nice work!

Instructor: Good points! There are also lots of graphics at the beginning of this show and in between commercial segments that warrant commentary. Can you build this information into your analysis as well? These examples seem to further support your claims (i.e., use of lightning bolts, fire, neon signs).

Instructor: I see that you have now added more quotations from your primary source to make your argument more persuasive. Very good, Bryan. I encourage you to do even more of this as you continue to revise your paper. Likewise, you should add additional quotations from secondary sources to support your subclaims.

Bryan: I don't like some of my transition between paragraphs at all yet. I will need to transition more smoothly between my sources and my own commentary.

Instructor: Excellent reflections, Bryan. One other thing you will want to consider: Why is the fact that this depends upon a straw man argument an important point for you to make here? How does it support your subclaim in this section? Can you make that connection clearer for your reader? If not, you may want to take it out of your paper. Anything that does not support your main argument, of course, detracts from its overall effectiveness.

Instructor: I wonder if you could give more detailed descriptions of each person before you get to their "plot lines." My concern is that the reader may be introduced to the characters a bit too quickly. In order to keep your reader with you, you may sometimes need to "pause" a bit more in your writing. Without the necessary lead-in and contextualizing information, this part of your essay may feel rushed to the reader and you may lose her or him at a pivotal point in your argument.

Instructor: This final sentence should touch back upon the earlier ideas in the paragraph. As of yet, the connections are not as clear as they might be.

the show's guests and their dramatic predicaments, one by one.

The very structure of *The Jerry Springer Show* itself displays and encourages logical fallacies. Short introductions of each person and his or her predicament take her/his situation out of context, depending upon a straw man argument. Tom knows that his girlfriend of a year and a half, April, is cheating on him with his best friend, John. He is on the show to confront her. Bob and his wife Sarah have been married for four years. She is cheating on him with their roommate Allan. On the show Sarah plans to divulge her indiscretion to Bob and ask for forgiveness. Wesley plans to introduce his girlfriend Tara to his lover Mike. Cory and Apryl (not to be confused with the first April) have been dating for the past two years. Apryl wants to confess that she has been cheating on Cory with Jason, and hopes to remain in her relationship with Jason. What do all of these guests have in common? Not only is each couple involved in some act of infidelity that will—according to the dictates of the show—require a public confession, but each of the guests is also far enough from the comfortable "norms" of American behavior and appearance that they can be mocked and patronized. As television critic David Plotz contends, *The Jerry Springer Show* is designed strategically, purposely seeking out "guests who are too confused and too angry to address their problems rationally and too inarticulate to address them verbally" (92). As the show exposes the differences between the participants on the show and the studio and home audiences, the audience members' egos will be flattered at the expense of the guests.

Violence and Scapegoating

All the guests have problems—and, presumably, they're on the show to resolve them. As Kathleen S. Lowney asserts in *Baring Our Souls: TV Talk Shows and the Religion of Recovery, The Jerry Springer Show* suggests that public confession is the way to settle complex problems. However, the show appears to do little more for the guests than persuade them to use violence and profanity toward one another.

Examples of violence and scapegoating are ubiquitous on *The Jerry Springer Show*. For instance, on this particular episode, the scenario involving Bob and his wife Sarah, who is cheating with their roommate Allan, leads to a rather violent exchange. Sarah begins by telling Jerry and the audience about how she has been sleeping with their roommate. Then, presumably in hopes of a reconciliation, Bob is introduced and walks onto the stage. The couple immediately gets into a swearing match, battling each other with a set of ad hominem arguments designed to direct attention away from the meaning of their opponents' claims and toward things like dress, sexual history and the like. When Bob finally is introduced to the stage, he and Allan instantly lunge for each other. They are stopped by a 185-pound barricade named Steve (the show's "enforcer"). As the battle continues, albeit somewhat more subdued, the rowdy crowd more directly participates in the humiliation of the show's participants, screaming chants such as "Kick his butt!" "Steve, Steve, Steve!" and "Jerry, Jerry, Jerry!"

Other guests, such as Cory and his girlfriend Apryl, show the same tendency toward violence as well as scapegoating—and receive the same response from the audience—as Bob, Allan,

Instructor: Bryan, as with the last section, here you have two ideas for your subclaim that should be incorporated and stated together in the first paragraph. For instance, you might rewrite this as follows: "While the show presumably functions to solve guests' problems, in actuality it exploits the guests by supporting violence and scapegoating."

Bryan: I think I need to offer more in my paper about Steve's role as "the enforcer," as Jerry's counterpart on the show. Since Jerry cannot "get his hands dirty" and still appear as better than the guests, Steve has a pivotal role.

Instructor: Absolutely! There are multiple layers here that you should lay out clearly for your reader: (1) the characters, (2) the studio audience, (3) Steve, (4) the audience at home, and (5) Jerry. You also will want to explain the connections and relationships between them. What are the power hierarchies among these people? How do you know? What effect does this have on the viewer of the show itself? The studio audience often displays a more extreme reaction to the characters than the audience at home. Since Steve is the enforcer (the muscle), Jerry is able to stay seemingly above the fray. Discuss all of this in more detail as you revise your draft.

Instructor: I think that you need to define this term "human spectacle" a bit more. I know that you mean to suggest that these people are there to be looked at by the audience, not to look at us, and that they are set up as objects for the audience to judge. In your next revision, look up Birmingham's reference to cultural critic Guy Dehord's work on spectacle. See Debord, Guy. *Society of the Spectacle.* Detroit: Black and Red, 1983.

Bryan: Do I need more quotes from the show to support my views? I think that this could help me to make my argument stronger here.

Instructor: Yes, Bryan. This will make your argument that much more persuasive. Before you write your next draft of the paper, be sure to watch the episode several more times and make certain you have all of the quotations from the show that you will need to back up each of your points. In addition, though, offer careful transitions between your quotations from secondary sources. Here you move a bit too quickly between them.

Instructor: Consider this sentence: "In effect, the show encourages audience members to 'rubber neck' and have this be socially acceptable." Can you state this more clearly? For example, "The show makes audience 'rubber necking' socially acceptable" might better capture your meaning.

Sarah. When Cory appears on the stage after Apryl confesses to cheating on him with Jason, she callously informs him about how worthless he is, and how she hopes to maintain her relationship with her lover instead. When Jason emerges on the stage, he smashes into Cory like two cars in a head-on collision. Once again, Steve, the ever-present bouncer for this raucous party gone out of control, breaks them apart. Again the crowd chants, encouraging the violence on the stage and ridiculing the show's participants. Yet again, though, no movements toward any productive resolutions of conflicts have in fact occurred.

Certainly *The Jerry Springer Show*'s structure as well as its use of violence and scapegoating indicate that the participants are subhuman, and not like those of us in either the studio or at home audience. However, such tactics are not altogether new. As rhetoric scholar Jon Bruschke argues, *The Jerry Springer Show*'s rhetorical strategies have a long history, mimicking the Roman royalty's interest in gladiators: "Just like the Roman emperors watching gladiators fight and die for no greater reward that the amusement of the royalty, the entire event is staged for the benefit of the observers and to the detriment of the combatants" (8). The guests are merely there to perform for the audience, to be nothing but what Birmingham terms a "human spectacle," an event created for our pleasure (135). In this way, the members in the studio audience—and also perhaps at home—seem to have the best of both worlds: they get to distinguish themselves from the subhuman, violent behaviors of the studio guests, while still enjoying the "charge" of witnessing the violent behavior their own jeers elicit. In effect, the show allows audience members to "rubber neck" and have this be socially acceptable. As television critic Janice Kaplan writes of similar shows, in fact "watching these shows is the moral equivalent of staring at a train wreck" (14).

Reinforcing Cultural Stereotypes: Physical Appearance and Gender

In addition to being encouraged in self-destructive, violent behavior, guests are also exploited in other ways. The structure of the show forces them to inhabit and exhibit stereotypes about physical types, gender, and class—and then turns around and ridicules them for this. The participants, like walking cartoons, are encouraged to engage in behaviors that are portrayed as ludicrous, if not outright grotesque.

The treatment of our first couple, Tom and April, offers a good example. Tom, April, and John are all struggling with their weight and do not conform to the arbitrary, normative standards of physical attractiveness or the typical cultural definitions of what should constitute proper masculine and feminine behaviors. In an exposé filmed prior to the show but airing during the show itself, a suspicious Tom brings Jerry's camera crew with him to spy on them as they "picnic" down by a river. Laura Grindstaff's book about the production of television talk shows, *The Money Shot: Trash, Class, and the Making of TV Shows,* indicates that this phenomenon of the film clip within the television show is becoming an ever more frequent part of talk show formats as audiences' desires to know previously hidden, intimate details become greater and greater. Grindstaff suggests that this phenomenon is due to audiences' increasingly higher threshold for confessional media forms.

As Tom is creeping carefully along with the camera crew in tow down to the river and he lights upon a pile of clothes and a picnic basket. The camera pans toward the river and we see two people in the water: April and John. Furious at witnessing this infidelity, Tom sets their clothes on fire. Then Tom chases after John. A stunned John runs out of the water naked and starts stomping on the clothes, while Tom confronts April and they

Bryan: As I reread this it sounds kind of awkward to me. I need to rephrase this—it's the show itself that encourages the behavior.

Instructor: Great catch, Bryan! How about "Guests are not only forced to be self-destructive and violent. They are also exploited in more insidious ways"?

Instructor: After reading your "Notes for Revision," I know that you are very much aware that you need to anticipate your opposition's views and refute them carefully. You will need to do even more of this in your revision. One counterargument you will want to anticipate is that this show is entirely "staged." Even if it is, though, the fact that it is staged is telling in just the same ways that you argue here. However, it would be good to better anticipate this particular counterclaim.

Instructor: Here you aim to provide evidence for your subclaim. More quotations from the show would help make this more persuasive, I think.

scream every profanity one could imagine at each other (though, of course, they are bleeped out). John then salvages a scrap of burnt underwear from the fire. Putting it on, he runs out of the viewer's sight, shouting hysterically, Tom chasing him. The scene becomes yet more absurd when the two men are next filmed by Jerry's camera crew, breathing heavily and running through the streets, now both in their underwear and trying to kill each other. The audience roars, readily imbibing the troubling message the show is sending—the notion that there is indeed one real standard of beauty—and one view of proper masculine and feminine behaviors—to which the guests do not adhere.

As with many other instances in the show, its humor and structure depend upon logical fallacies. In particular, Jerry uses an ad populum logical fallacy when he offers commentary on the video clip, appealing to the broad beliefs of his audience rather than providing logical proof for his assertions. He utters sarcastic remarks as the two figures pursue each other: "What the hell was that?" Jerry quips. Then he follows up with a statement meant entirely to poke fun at the men's weight—to reinforce the fact that they are somehow "abnormal": "It's a good thing you were in good shape!" After Jerry says this, the crowd erupts into hysterical laughter, collaborating with Jerry in ridiculing the participants for not adhering to normative standards of weight and physical beauty.

However, not only is the notion that there are appropriate physical types and aberrant ones as well as proper masculine and feminine behaviors and improper ones reinforced by the show; more specific stereotypes about gender are also bolstered through the way in which guests are depicted. Women on the show are typically represented only according to their roles as objects and sexual beings, alternately as being either frigid or nymphomaniacs. For example, the "love" triangle among John, Tom, and April is characterized as initiated and then spurred on by April's

Instructor: As you revise, consider whether the logical fallacies are evidence for the stereotyping or whether the issue of logical fallacies themselves should have its own subclaim. Right now you seem to be moving between these two different perspectives about how the problem of logical fallacies should function in your argument.

Instructor: Nice work! I imagine that there are many other examples of how the show uses ad populum logical fallacies. Could you mention a few others to back up your points?

Bryan: This is yet another example of a straw man argument. I could expand on this.

Instructor: Excellent point! Be sure to bring this into your revision.

insatiable appetite for sexual liaisons. Another troubling gender stereotype on the show involves the depiction of homosexual and lesbian guests. Gays and lesbians are represented in stereotypical ways that undermine their life choices and reinforce homophobia. One instance of this occurs on the show when Wesley, his girlfriend Tara, and his gay lover Mike are introduced to the audience. First, Wesley confesses to Tara that he has been having an affair with Mike for five months. When Mike is finally introduced to the audience, the importance of Wesley and Mike's relationship is never broached. Instead, Mike becomes the scapegoat figure, represented problematically as sexually promiscuous and uncaring. Tara easily gains the audience's support against Wesley and Mike. As a result, homosexuality itself becomes a straw man as the audience is led to assume without thought or discussion that homosexuality is "abnormal." Then, as if Tara feels that she must reinforce typical heterosexual codes, she reveals her breasts. While this act may serve to reinforce the false notion that homosexuality is abnormal, however, it does not cement her desirability as a heterosexual woman. Instead, the crowd goes wild, showing nothing but revulsion that a 55-year-old woman would expose herself—and revealing the show's attitude about women's identities: They amount to little more than a set of body parts that, once again, need to conform to normative, limited understandings of beauty in order to be acceptable.

> **Bryan:** I definitely need more quotations here.

> **Instructor:** I think so too, Bryan. In addition, sometimes these descriptions get a bit too "plot-driven" and you are in danger of not attending enough to the actual language the participants use. In addition, this takes you away from true *analysis* of the show and tends to make you focus a bit too much on *summary*. Likewise, in this section, try to make your longer, more embedded sentences clearer. A good rule of thumb is to intersperse more complicated constructions with simple sentences that follow the "subject-verb-object" format.

> **Instructor:** You may want to flesh out this example and give more quotations to back up your views throughout this section. You make some great points about how gender operates on the show. However, right now you stop short of a full, thorough analysis. As you note, it's an important part of the show. Birmingham's work is particularly good on this. I urge you to reread her article.

Reinforcing Cultural Stereotypes: Class Relations

Just as the participants on the show are ridiculed for not measuring up to some arbitrary standard of physical attractiveness and limited conceptions of gender, they are also ridiculed for their lower-class status. Most of the guests that appear on the show are

Bryan: I need to figure this out—how does this connection get made? It seems obvious, but how do I explain it? I think that this might be an example of *false dilemma* to some degree along with *ad hominem* and *straw man*. People are either "attractive" or worthy of ridicule. This perspective is really troubling to me.

Instructor: Yes, I think you are right that this example is some combination of these logical fallacies. However, you might characterize this as a cultural prejudice or bias as well. How are the normative standards of beauty constantly perpetuated and reinforced? How does this keep traditional cultural power relations in place and also reinforce them?

Instructor: Bryan, here you hint at the fact that you would argue that the show is often dependent upon the *false dilemma* fallacy. Sometimes there may be real dilemmas that are more complicated—such as how money impacts these people's lives, or troubling oppression caused by ethnic or racial or gender differences. You may want to consider this more at this point in your argument. The show sets up people as either "normal" or "abnormal." However, people's real lives are far more complicated. Are there other options that justify people's behaviors—such as the fact that they find themselves in difficult situations and this may cause them to behave in certain ways? Be sure to cover all of this in your next revision.

depicted as coming from lower-class backgrounds. The studio audience frequently uses terms such as "white trash" and "redneck" to describe them. The participants are mocked for not being able to afford better things—for their poor choice in clothes, or poor dental care, and hygiene.

It's not only the audience that makes fun of the guests' lower-class attributes. As with physical attractiveness and gender issues, Jerry does as well. In this way, Jerry continually emphasizes his own distance from the guests, as a middle-class, presentable, and well-educated man. Jerry provides the perfect example of the talk show host Birmingham describes in her essay, one who "provide[s] a contrast to the guests, both physically in terms of dress and appearance, and socially, in terms of education and decorum" (138). For example, when Mike declares that "Wesley left me for a fat-ass, toothless bitch!" Jerry, in an "innocent" remark, retorts, "He [Wesley] left you for a toothless bitch [Tara]? How inconsiderate of him!" The audience roars—in part, at least, because of the contrast between the uneducated language Mike uses ("fat-ass, toothless bitch") and the "classy" language Jerry uses ("inconsiderate").

As with representations of violence, gender, and physical attractiveness, the guests are presented as "different" from the studio audience and the audience at home in terms of class. They are depicted as more excessive in every way and therefore worthy of contempt. In effect, this sends a signal to the audience that lower-class people are somehow inferior or immoral. In laughing at them with Jerry, the audience in the studio and at home reinforces and cements this disturbing stereotype.

The Studio Audience and Jerry's "Final Thought" Secure the Stereotypes

Toward the end of the show, the studio audience gets a chance to ask questions and state their opinions of the guests and their dilemmas. Much like public flogging ceremonies or town stonings of the past, on *The Jerry Springer Show* the guests are continuously jeered at by the crowd, whose anger, rage, and ridiculing tone grows ever greater. Most of the questions they ask, of course, are not really questions at all. Instead, they are designed to mock the guests and to bolster the audience's sense (both in the studio and at home) of their own self-worth.

For example, one audience member offers the following "question" to John: "Yeah, I got a question for the fatso in the blue shirt. Are you the poster-boy for the Pillsbury doughboy?" Jerry laughs along with the studio audience in response to this question, exercising his authority in a disturbing way. The insult results in peals of laughter from the audience. Another woman from the audience makes a lewd comment to April, saying, "Yeah, I have a question for the fat whore fighting with the two tubs of lard! Who is fatter, you or your boyfriend?" While these comments are calculated to get laughs, they inevitably reduce the guests to mere stereotypes, reinforcing normative notions about physical types, gender, and class status. The audience continuously plays the role of the chorus in a traditional Greek drama, passing judgment on the various players, and telling the audience at home what they should think and feel.

Instructor: Here is part of your subclaim for this section: "Toward the end of the show . . ." The second part of your subclaim comes later. Try to put it together and make sure that it appears in one place.

Bryan: I need a much better transition here between paragraphs.

Instructor: Good point, Bryan. I think you will want to consider why this is significant. In addition, this is a good place in your text to "pause" and remind your reader of your main points. A transition sentence to begin the next paragraph such as the following might help: "There are many disturbing examples of such public flogging that occur on the show."

Bryan: I think this analogy of the "chorus" and the "studio audience" is worth looking at more. However, I need to include more about how the chorus works—maybe even give an example from Greek drama to make this clearer. In addition, I think I could make the purposes of this more obvious.

Instructor: Yes, this is a superb point. Take a brief look at some of the traditional Greek dramas. In many such cases, the chorus is meant to do the following: (1) provide and reflect emotional reactions to the main narrative, (2) engage in dialogue with the play's main characters, (3) help compress the action of the play so more plot developments can occur more quickly, and (4) help fill in missing pieces due to off-stage action that cannot be quickly or easily represented. Sophocles' *Oedipus Rex* and *Antigone* offer some good examples. Don't spend too much time finding ways to build those texts into your argument. However, do look at them to familiarize yourself with just how this traditional form of response works.

Instructor: The second part of your subclaim is "It's clear that the 'Final Thought' segment . . ." Build this second part of your subclaim into the first part that I mentioned earlier in my comments. Likewise, here you might need to write more about how the show limits the behaviors of those of us watching at home as well. We feel that we cannot be too overweight, too lower class, too sexually "different." What effects does this have on those of us watching from home, do you think?

Those looking for some peaceful resolution to all of these problems might reasonably turn to Jerry's "Final Thought" for solace. Appearing at the end of each show, Jerry offers his opinion concerning what the battling couples should do. In his expensive blazer, dress pants, and shoes, a bespectacled Jerry tells us in a fatherly tone that we should be good to one another, not resort to such physical violence, not be dishonest in our relationships, and not get involved in sexual relationships when we are committed to other people. As we listen, we are encouraged once more to look down upon the lives and actions of the show's participants, to feel a kinship with Jerry over and against these people whom the show has ridiculed for being physically unattractive, not fulfilling gender expectations, or behaving immorally. It's clear that the "Final Thought" segment has only one real message for all of us: Whatever you do, don't be like these people who fail to measure up to the societal standards of physical attractiveness, gender, and class.

Instructor: Here might be another good place for you to reiterate your counterpoint to the potential opposition I mentioned before. Try to combat the argument that "all of this is fake so why should we care?"

Final Thoughts on *The Jerry Springer Show*

Many in the mainstream media, particularly those with conservative political agendas, have argued that *The Jerry Springer Show* is tasteless and unethical, and I would agree with this assessment. Some of these critics, however, focus their criticism on the behavior of the guests: Ellen Goodman, for example, calls daytime television "a waste site of abnormality and amorality" (A5), but focuses her critique on the lives of the people on display onstage rather than on how the show reinforces troubling societal views about violence and scapegoating, physical stereotypes, gender, and class. While I certainly don't applaud the guests' choices as they are often portrayed, I believe that there is a deeper, more disturbing problem at work in *The Jerry Springer Show.* The show reinforces

Instructor: This is part of your subclaim for this section. The other green portion is also part of your subclaim. Try to bring these together and state this more clearly early on in this section.

oppressive stereotypes in American culture, and encourages our taste for angry debate and physical violence, and for the exploitation of people based upon physical traits, gender, and class.

Many progressive television critics share my perspective. Yet, they have also often asserted that the show is an important model of progressive politics, a view with which I do not concur. For instance, Joshua Gamson argues in *Freaks Talk Back: Tabloid Talk Shows and Sexual Nonconformity* that the mere fact of exposing such "differences" on television programs may itself be a good thing—increasing visibility and presenting a critical forum for otherwise underrepresented groups. Unfortunately, I am not quite so optimistic that greater visibility alone can heal long-standing social inequities. While the show poses as a "self-help" show that entertains, as I have argued, the show is in fact a powerfully repressive force. In making us feel good about what we're not and keeping our energies focused on despising those who are "different," the show does little more than help maintain a very disturbing status quo or lowest common denominator, a world where social inequalities based upon physical traits, gender, and class are not only tolerated but enthusiastically reinforced over and over again.

Instructor: What does this indicate about how American cultural myths operate on the show? You need to expand on this here.

Bryan: I think this is what I want to say, but it probably needs to be reworked. Likewise, after rereading my conclusion I wonder if I should bring some of my concluding ideas into my introduction. Should I bring these ideas to the front and reorganize my paper?

Instructor: I completely agree with your reflection here, Bryan. One way to get to your argument more quickly would be to begin the paper with an analysis of the two main responses to the show—the ones you outline here. Then you might briefly outline your position and what you hope to prove. If you have your main claim and mini-outline established early in the paper, then you can give a rich description of the show and not lose your reader. Revising the paper along these lines may involve getting rid of many of the places in your text early on where you address the reader directly.

Instructor: As you rewrite your paper, you will need to rethink your subclaims and streamline them. This will help you to revise each subsection and let your argumentative points more clearly drive the paper's structure.

Now you just need to make the structure clearer. As I read your paper, here is one possible structure that emerges. Consider this possibility, and then we can discuss it further:

Main Claim: The success of *The Jerry Springer Show* is unique because it depends upon several disturbing elements: employing logical fallacies, encouraging physical violence, as well as reproducing gender and class inequities.

Subclaim 1: The setup and structure of the show display and encourage some troubling logical fallacies.

Subclaim 2: While the show presumably functions to solve guests' problems, in actuality the show exploits the guests, supporting violence and scapegoating.

Subclaim 3: The show reinforces the notion that there are appropriate and inappropriate physical types as well as masculine and feminine behaviors.

Subclaim 4: The show ridicules guests for their lower-class status.

Subclaim 5: The "Final Thought" encourages the audience to laugh at the guests while reinforcing arbitrary societal standards of physical attractiveness, gender, and class.

Subclaim 6: While it poses as a "self-help" show that entertains, the show is in fact a powerfully repressive force. By making us feel good about what we're not and keeping our energies focused on despising those who are "different," the show does little more than help maintain a world in which social inequalities based upon physical traits, gender, and class are not only tolerated but enthusiastically reinforced over and over again.

Bryan: I am using Modern Language Association citation here. I think I may still want to find additional sources.

Works Cited

Birmingham, Elizabeth. "Fearing the Freak: How Talk TV Articulates Women and Class." *Journal of Popular Film and Television* 28.3 (2000): 133–39.

Bruschke, Jon. "A Critical Analysis of *The Jerry Springer Show*." http://commfaculty.fullerton.edu/jbrushke/a_critical_analysis _of_the_jerry.htm. Dec. 2004. 1–19.

"Cheaters on the Run." *The Jerry Springer Show*. Host and prod. Jerry Springer. Universal Domestic Television, Chicago. 20 June 2001.

Gamson, Joshua. *Freaks Talk Back: Tabloid Talk Shows and Sexual Nonconformity*. Chicago: Chicago UP, 1999.

Goodman, Ellen. "Trash TV." *Des Moines Register* 18 Mar. 1995: 5A.

Grindstaff, Laura. *The Money Shot: Trash, Class, and the Making of TV Shows*. Chicago: Chicago UP, 2002.

Kaplan, Janice. "Are Talk Shows Out of Control?" *TV Guide* 1–7 Apr. 1995: 13–16.

Lowney, Kathleen S. *Baring Our Souls: TV Talk Shows and the Religion of Recovery.* Berlin and New York: Aldine de Gruyter, 1999.

Plotz, David. "Jerry Springer: Once the Talk Show Host Was Mayor of Cincinnati. Now He's Mayor of Sodom." http://slate.msn.com/id/1857. Dec. 2004. 1–16.

"Talk Shows." The Museum of Television Archives. Dec. 2004. http://www.museum.tv/archives/etv/T/htmlT/talkshows/talkshows.htm.

Instructor's Final Comments: I applaud your thorough revisions. Great job, Bryan! Your final product will be much more persuasive as a result.

As you revise, consider the following:

1. Introduction: I very much like your introduction. It is rich, detailed, and draws in your reader. The trouble is that it keeps you from getting to your argumentative claim and mini-outline for the paper as quickly as you might. In my commentary I have mentioned some alternative formats and ideas for you to consider as you revise the introduction. Let's talk more about this as you continue revising your paper.

2. Thesis/Main Claim: Make your argumentative claim earlier in your text. While the detailed description of the show is excellent, do not let it obscure your own argument. If your reader has to wait too long before you get to your argumentative claim, she or he may lose interest. This change may mean shortening the description and adding it into your text after your argument is mapped out. It also may mean moving some of the ideas you offer in your conclusion and making them more central to your analysis as well as how you organize your argument. Once you have clarified your introduction and main claim, you may decide that not all of your subclaims are relevant or that new ones must be incorporated. As you consider this, we can discuss how you might excise certain portions and add in others.

3. Use of Primary Sources: Be sure that you provide enough quotations from the participants on the show. Right now you are relying more on "plot lines" to convey your points. The danger here is that you will spend more time *summarizing* than *analyzing*. Watch the episode several more times and be sure you have accurate quotations by the participants to add into each section.

4. Use of Secondary Sources: Work on providing more support for your subclaims—particularly quotations and descriptions to back them up. When you do offer quotations, be sure to follow the suggestions for introducing outside sources that I mention in my marginal commentary. In addition, I urge you to consult some of the secondary sources I mention in my marginal commentary. I think that having familiarity with these sources may help you during the revision process. As you revise, make sure that you continue to avoid any hint of plagiarism and give credit to all of your outside sources.

5. Subclaims: Reread each of your body paragraphs and identify the subpoints you make. They should occur early in each section, ideally in the first or second paragraphs. How can you make them clearer? How can you better establish the relationship between them and your main argumentative claim? One approach you could take is to create a map of your own argument as it is. What is your main claim? How does each subsection and subclaim connect back to the main claim? If it does not, you will need to revise the subclaim or consider discarding it.

6. Body Paragraphs: You are now ready to consider more micro-level concerns in your next revision: Does each paragraph connect logically to the next? Are you offering good transitions between ideas within paragraphs? Are you varying your paragraph and sentence length to keep your audience with you?

7. Transitions between Paragraphs: In many places throughout your essay you transition quite well from idea to idea. However, there are places that you and I have both noted require some more work. Make sure that you echo your subclaim in a given paragraph before moving right to providing evidence in the form of "For example" or "For instance." Remind your reader what you are setting out to prove in this section.

8. Conclusion: What you state in your conclusion of this revision of your essay is likely going to reframe your entire argument in your next revision. This will leave you room in the conclusion to write more about what relevance your analysis of the show has for how we understand American culture as well as how we understand the genre of cultural criticism. Your thesis is a very interesting one because it is not an entirely negative or positive evaluation of the show. Now you will want to address the following issues: How does your approach differ from that of other cultural critics? Why do you think that this view is important to consider? You always want to leave your reader with the sense that you have proven what you set out to prove—and that she or he will leave your text with something to ponder. How can you incorporate this into your conclusion?

9. Style Issues: Once you do all of the above, you will be very close to having a final, polished version. At that point make sure that you have accomplished the following: varied your word choice, created a welcoming tone for your reader, mixed simple and complex sentences, and proofread several times to catch your grammar and spelling errors.

Summary: This is an excellent draft, Bryan. Once you make these revisions your paper will be a very strong final product! I look forward to seeing your next version.

Like Bryan, you will likely have substantive ideas for revision—ones you discover, ones your peers point out, as well as ones your instructor recommends—and produce many drafts of your paper before you are finished. As your essay is reaching completion, consult this final revision checklist to make sure that it as persuasive and well written as it can be. If you find your paper lacking in any area on the checklist, go back to your paper and rework that section.

FINAL REVISION CHECKLIST INTRODUCTION

☐ Does your paper begin in a way that grabs the reader's attention and introduces the paper's purpose?

☐ Does the introduction provide a general overview of the issue at hand and connect to the thesis?

☐ Does the introduction close with a narrowly defined thesis in the form of a statement that links directly to the body paragraphs?

SUPPORTING PARAGRAPHS AND CONCLUSION

☐ Do each of your supporting paragraphs have a main idea, subthesis, or subclaim that relates back to the thesis in your introduction?

☐ Does each paragraph lead logically to the next point?

☐ Do the body paragraphs have logical connections and smooth transitions between them?

☐ Do you vary paragraph length to avoid losing your audience?

☐ Do you provide adequate and appropriate evidence—details, examples, facts, statistics, expert authority, or personal observations—to support your points?

☐ Do you use convincing quotes from secondary sources to back up your views, and do you credit these outside sources to avoid the charge of plagiarism?

☐ Does your conclusion go beyond merely restating the thesis, instead giving your audience something important to ponder?

STYLE AND MECHANICS

☐ Have you varied your word choice and tried to avoid clichés?

☐ Have you created a tone in the paper that is appropriate to your particular topic and audience?

☐ Have you employed a mixture of simple and complex sentences to maintain your audience's interest?

☐ Have you reread, proofread, and edited your paper carefully so that you have caught any grammar or spelling errors?

ARGUMENT, RESEARCH, AND WRITING: **EXERCISING YOUR SKILLS**

Create Your Own Argument About Malls

Public spaces can be analyzed much like advertisements or television shows. Begin by conducting primary research. Spend several hours at your favorite mall. First, take notes as people walk by—examine the use of space, patterns in people's behavior, what they are wearing, saying to each other, carrying, and the like. Then focus most of your analysis on one store in particular. Examine how the store is set up, how its windows are designed to entice consumers, where specific merchandise is sold in the store, how the salespeople behave, and where the products are made. Then, using your primary research as well as secondary sources about mall culture, make an argument about how this store sells products to consumers. What identities does it offer consumers? How does the way in which the store is arranged reinforce this? Be sure to point to specific evidence from your close analysis of the store. Use the prewriting, drafting, and reflecting strategies you have learned to create a rough draft.

Create Your Own Argument About Music

Music videos, lyrics, and CD inserts can also be analyzed in order to create cultural criticism arguments. As with the earlier mall example, begin by conducting primary research. Spend several hours watching and reviewing a music video of your choosing. First, take notes as you watch—examine the dress, mannerisms, and visuals depicted in the video. What narratives about gender, race, class, ethnicity, and age are put forward in this video? Then, using your primary research as well as secondary sources about cultural criticism and music, make an argument about what an analysis of this artist, video, and lyrics reveals about American cultural myths, fears, anxieties, desires, and values. What worldviews, images, and fantasies do these visual and written texts provide for viewers? Use the prewriting, drafting, and reflecting strategies you have learned to create a rough draft.

Create Your Own Argument About Sports

Sporting events and other public rituals can also be analyzed. As with the previously mentioned mall and music examples, begin by conducting primary research. Spend several hours watching a particular sporting event. First, take notes as you observe—examine the way that the rules function, the use of uniforms, off-field behavior among teammates and coaches and referees, audience behavior, and the like. Then, using your primary research as well as secondary sources about cultural criticism and sports, make an argument about what the rituals of this sporting event reveal about American cultural myths, fears, anxieties, desires, and values. What worldviews, images, and fantasies do this team and sport offer to viewers? What identities do they provide viewers? Use the prewriting, drafting, and reflecting strategies you have learned to create a rough draft.

Create Your Own Extended Cultural Criticism Argument

Thus far you have offered brief cultural criticisms of websites, ads, malls, music, and sports. It is time to take the next step. Now you will compose an extended argument—complete with argumentative claim, support, and warrants—about a cultural phenomenon entirely of your own choosing. You will use a close rhetorical analysis of the cultural artifact as a primary source and as evidence for your argument. Be sure to avoid making logical fallacies. Select a cultural text from this range of choices: advertising, consumer culture, style, film, music, sports, spaces, technology, and television. Next, use the prewriting, drafting, and reflecting strategies you have learned to create a rough draft. Consult secondary sources and incorporate them into your paper. Then, revise this draft according to peer feedback and/or your instructor's comments. Consider the final revision checklist as you complete your final draft. The product should be a polished, extended paper.

CHAPTER SUMMARY

In Chapter 3 you have built upon what you studied in Chapters 1 and 2—how to develop critical thinking, reading, and responding skills as well as how to apply your knowledge of rhetoric to analyzing all kinds of texts. In this chapter you have learned some key principles for logical reasoning—or the appeal to logos. You have also investigated how insufficient claims, evidence, warrants, as well as logical fallacies can undermine an argument. Additionally, you have observed how Bryan drafts, reflects upon, and then revises his own paper. Then you applied your skills to analyze other arguments as well as research and write your own arguments about various kinds of texts. These principles—a critical perspective, rhetorical analysis, and argumentation—will be very useful to you in any situation in school or on the job where you will be called upon to interpret, challenge, or write persuasive arguments of your own.

These approaches have value for analyzing as well as creating other media forms, be they websites, print advertising, multimedia presentations, video productions, film editing, or commercial work. Using these strategies also further develops your cultural and media literacy—your awareness of how popular culture both reflects and shapes our world. Above all, what you have learned thus far in the book has prepared you to be a fuller contributor to our culture itself, to be a more thoughtful citizen and consumer.

You have now successfully completed Part I of *Pop Perspectives*. You are more than ready to take the exciting next step. Now you will apply these skills to readings about popular culture in Part II of *Pop Perspectives*, hone your analytic abilities, investigate many examples of argumentative and cultural criticism writing in action, and build even more persuasive, compelling arguments of your own.

PART TWO

Reading Ourselves, Reading Others

CHAPTER FOUR

Understanding Lives and Jobs

INTRODUCTION

Considering Identities and Work

Imagine that a publisher—interested in the stories you have to tell—has invited you to write an autobiography of your life. What unique anecdotes might you share about yourself, your habits and behaviors, as well as your everyday experiences? How might you characterize your race and ethnicity, class, gender, language, politics, age, region, and religion?

These many identifications are critical in shaping who we are—how we perceive American culture, ourselves, and our place in that culture—as well as how others view us. We may identify as African American, Latina/o, Asian American, European American, Native American, or as some combination; as upper class, middle class, lower class, or somewhere in between; masculine, feminine, or metrosexual; as one who uses Spanish and African American vernacular or a mixture of Yiddish and Polish; as heterosexual, homosexual, or bisexual; as Republican, Democrat, Independent, Libertarian, Green Party, or Socialist; as Generation X, Generation Y (Millennials), or a baby boomer; as from the middle of the United States, the eastern shores, the West Coast; as Muslim, Christian, or Jewish; or other possibilities.

While race and ethnicity, class, gender, sexual preference, language, politics, disability, age, job, region, and religion shape our identities, since we spend a good deal of our lives preparing to enter the workforce, looking for jobs, and working, our identities are also oftentimes influenced by the jobs we hold. We hope to make a living wage; have a safe and attractive place to live; develop a "career"; create a simpler, more humane life; climb the ladder; give back to others; get raises; as well as experience peaceful downtime and exciting vacations. At various points in our lives we may be factory workers, lawyers, fast-food restaurant servers, teachers, retail workers, engineers, stay-at-home parents, or doctors. With each job come different responsibilities, different social contexts, different perceptions of free time and leisure, and different understandings about wages and bosses. Although I am a writer and professor now, more than twenty years ago I worked in a very different environment. I had to ride my bicycle fifteen miles each way every morning to McDonald's where I donned a polyester uniform and uttered phrases such as "May I take your order, please?" and "Would you like fries with that?"

Identities and work are important aspects of our American culture. We read identities—what a person's race and ethnicity, class, gender, sexual preference, language, politics, disability, age, region, and religion are—every day as we try to make sense of ourselves and others in the world. We consider work, as well as the kinds of wages, working conditions, leisure time, and social status that come with working, as we make many decisions every day. To some degree, the various differences between our identities and our work lives shape our current realities and our future possibilities.

Overview of Selections: Identities

In this chapter of *Pop Perspectives: Readings to Critique Contemporary Culture* you will read about how people's lives and experiences impact who they are and how they are viewed. These pieces are written by some people with whom you may deeply identify—whose voices and experiences are remarkably similar to your own—and other people from cultural backgrounds and experiences with which you may have few commonalties and are less familiar.

The first section is titled "Identities." Here you will consider how race and ethnicity, class, gender, sexual preference, language, politics, disability, age, job, region, and religion play a crucial part in how we view ourselves and how others view us.

The chapter starts with a compelling chapter by Debra CallingThunder, a Native American editor, columnist, and member of the Northern Arapaho tribe, who has spent most of her life on the Wind River Indian Reservation in Wyoming. Calling-Thunder's poetic language traces her cultural and familial history through the stories that have been passed down to her from her elders. She describes how—due to issues of race and ethnicity, class, language, politics, region, and religion—her family continues to be impacted by events from the Sand Creek Massacre in Colorado in 1894. CallingThunder also asks us to examine various contemporary acts of oppression against Native Americans by the American government.

Next is an essay by Torri Minton, who was an award-winning journalist, college instructor, and staff writer for the *San Francisco Chronicle*. [Minton passed away in 2004.] In her thoughtful piece, Minton examines the recent turn to investigate "whiteness" within both social and educational circles. Recounting the experiences of Edward Ball, a former New York reporter, who comes from a white, Southern family (as he traces his family roots for his book *Slaves in the Family*), Minton exposes the complicated nature of defining whiteness. Minton also takes us through the history of whiteness studies. She considers many people's fears that this relatively new area of research and personal discovery will do little more than support white supremacist positions. Minton also relays many people's hopes that studying whiteness will allow people to better understand how white privilege works in our culture and in our personal lives as well as to combat its negative effects.

Nell Bernstein, the editor of *YO!* magazine (a magazine on teen life), offers a considerable contrast to the aforementioned essays by considering how some white suburban teenagers are dressing and behaving like inner-city teenagers of color. Bernstein calls this "claiming," assuming an identity as your own that may be different from the cultural identity into which you were born. She investigates what motivates teenagers to "go gangsta" or "choose cholita" by interviewing and telling the life stories of a number of these teenagers and their families. Bernstein also discloses how people of color are reacting to this phenomenon. She contemplates whether this is a positive development (the result of moving to an increasingly multiracial American population) or a negative development (a symptom of the fact that white teenagers do not have a ready cultural identity of their own).

An intriguing essay by Chicano professor of history and writer Tomás Sandoval then appears. His text looks at issues of race and ethnicity, class, language, politics, age, job, and region. Sandoval leads us through his own very personal and sometimes painful experiences of becoming a "Chicano," or a Mexican American concerned about political issues, particularly equal rights, for his people. Sandoval divulges the ways in which he has felt ostracized because of his Mexican American heritage. He also reveals how being considered "different" or "other" finally led him to make a career of working with Chicano students and studying Chicano history. Sandoval calls upon us to value the wide range of experiences that all students of color bring to college settings—and to let their experiences shape communities of higher learning.

Next Kiflin Turner, a news writer for *The Observer*, a newspaper serving the University of Notre Dame and St. Mary's College, furnishes a powerful discussion about the lives of African American college students and the ways in which they continue to suffer every day from racial stereotyping. After pointing to African American students' own words and experiences, Turner then calls upon colleges and universities to create more programs that foster community and promote the investigation of cultural identity among African American students. He also maintains that students need more African American role models on campuses who will support their personal and intellectual lives—pointing a finger at his own university for not going far enough. While Turner's references center mainly on the Notre Dame University campus, his argument has relevance for all students and all college environments.

Melissa Algranati then presents a revealing text about her complex identity. Her piece tackles concerns about race and ethnicity, class, gender, language, politics, age, region, and religion. While Algranati is now a mother and professional working for Girl Scouts of America, here she writes about her early adult years, recounting her personal experiences as the product of two immigrant families—and her identity as a "Puerto Rican, Egyptian Jewish woman." Algranati discusses the difficulties she has experienced because of her mixed-race heritage and describes the ways in which her identity is too often not accounted for or rendered invisible by mainstream American culture. Since Algranati does not "look" Puerto Rican, she has often overheard racist and anti-religious comments by people who assume she's a member of their ethnic group. Algranati describes how her "inter-ethnic" identity has led her to check "other," a category too often invisible in American culture, when confronted with identification categories on forms.

The final essay featured in this section is an important work written by an undergraduate student writer and political activist at the University of Pennsylvania,

Olivia Chung. Her chapter illuminates concerns related to race and ethnicity, class, gender, language, politics, age, and region. Chung describes how much her identity as a Korean American has involved trying to "look the part" of an American. Chung chooses an innovative method for making her argument: moving between a careful analysis and a rich, interior monologue. In particular, Chung explores the various pressures she experiences from both American and Asian cultures, pressures that are exemplified in the suggestion that her eyelids be more "Americanized" through plastic surgery.

Overview of Selections: Work

The second section of Chapter 4, "Work," describes the many ways in which jobs shape us. Here you will encounter essays about how jobs function in various people's lives as well as how such jobs are represented in the media.

This portion commences with a significant essay by writer Sarah Anderson who has written a number of books about economic policy. Anderson characterizes the growing Wal-Mart empire and its negative impacts on her family, her neighbors, and small-town, rural life in Litchfield, Minnesota. While Anderson sees the value of the money that large companies can bring into poorer communities, she contends that large corporations shouldn't take over Mom 'n' Pop shops in rural communities, forcing individuals to rely on them exclusively for their livelihoods. Instead, Anderson calls for a return to small businesses and neighborhood markets.

Then Rebecca Piirto Heath, a contributing editor to *American Demographics* and a freelance writer, provides an influential examination about how definitions of the working class in American culture have changed and developed over time. She is interested in why, within a "supposedly classless society, nearly half of Americans consistently identify themselves as working class." In order to answer this question, Heath investigates representations of working-class life in the media as well as surveys about shifts in class status over time, revealing that who the working class was in the past is not who the working class is today. While the working class is more diverse than ever, Heath maintains that the upper class is still less diverse than it should be. Likewise, with increased globalization and less job security, the working class is becoming a broader and broader social category—one that includes everyone from factory workers to Borders bookstore clerks. Uncovering the growing trend of temporary or contingent workers as well as the unsteady nature of jobs in the corporate sector, Heath also charts the role that unions have played in aiding workers of all kinds.

Next, Eddie R. Cole Jr., a writer for the *Black College Wire*, presents an absorbing essay about the effects that popular websites like "Facebook" and "MySpace" are having not only on students' social lives but also on their chances for employment. He interviews a wide range of people—including students, employers, and the owners of such sites—to learn about the ways in which this technology can be accessed. Cole gives us examples of how personal sites are being used for employers to learn more about potential applicants: not only what they do with their free time but also their race, class, gender, and sexual orientation. Cole suggests that although such sites can be enjoyable, this new technology may give employers increased access to students' behaviors, habits, and lives. Cole contends that this can be positive if used strategically but devastating if it is not.

The section closes with an engrossing essay by business executive turned cartoonist, Scott Adams, about his popular cartoon "Dilbert." Interspersing humorous images of the cartoon with his own critical analyses of work life, Adams outlines how workers are treated, how bosses behave, and how all working people receive poor compensation for their work. Adams exposes us to the "Dilbert Principle" of management in today's work world. He offers a list of criteria by which people can judge their abilities as bosses and workers. In the end, Adams recommends that humor is one crucial avenue through which we can all challenge and combat the difficulties of the American economy as well as our work environments.

As you read this chapter, think about your own identity and the multiple functions work has in your life. In what ways might your own background—your race and ethnicity, class, gender, sexual preference, politics, disability, age, job, region, and religion—shape your experiences, attitudes, and behaviors? How do issues such as wage fairness, corporate globalization, working conditions, leisure time, and possibilities for advancement impact your past and present work life as well as your future career plans?

IDENTITIES

DEBRA CALLINGTHUNDER

"Voices of the Invisible"

Debra CallingThunder is a member of the Northern Arapaho tribe. She lives on the Wind River Indian Reservation in Wyoming. CallingThunder has edited The Wind River News *and has been a columnist for the* Salt Lake Tribune.

EXERCISING YOUR SKILLS

Before Reading

CallingThunder's essay makes the experiences of people who have often felt invisible visible. Have you ever felt invisible—as though no one noticed you? Did this situation involve issues of race and ethnicity, class, gender, sexual preference, language, politics, disability, age, region, and/or religion? Think about the specific situation and the issues that contributed to your feelings. How did you respond to being on the outside, to being "different"? Was your response taken seriously? Why or why not? Similarly, have you ever suspected that your thoughts, ideas, or cultural values were not adequately represented in your class textbooks, popular television, or movies? If yes, what were these ideas, and why do you think that they may have been excluded?

There are voices behind the wall—our voices, disembodied, spoken as if by beings unseen.

From the silence arise words conjured from invisible mouths, and laughter without smiles, and songs without celebration, and wailing without tears.

The air is crowded with words—wondrous and beautiful words that rise invisible and unheard and then are swallowed by time. The air is crowded with words—words that bind us to eternity, that carry the stories and dreams which are gifts from generations unseen, the songs of victory and mourning which compel us to seek tomorrow.

We are the invisible ones, the People of the Sky, the people of dreams whose voices cannot be bound by pain. We are the people of prayers, who stand small before the Creator, who entreat him, so that the strand of time that holds us to eternity might not be cut and our words slip into silence.

I give this song to Our People, to all the generations, and empty my soul before them.

Words are gifts, our grandparents say, and they give us many words so that we will remain a nation, a circle of people.

My grandmother, Cleone Thunder, is nearly ninety now, an age she says is not so old. Days disappear, falling furiously into time, but love remains, and words and songs and stories.

She tells us the stories of our beginning when the Creator above rejoiced and we and many others came to exist, and the circle of our lodges grew large. Only a short time ago, she says, Our People roamed the Earth, following the great buffalo herds that stormed across the plains, across an expanse of time and dreams.

The buffalo sang to us, and their song was their life. The buffalo sang to us so that we would grow strong. And the Old People would gather together many words to make prayers to the Creator. They would gather words as they walked a sacred path across the Earth, leaving nothing behind but prayers and offerings.

Now the buffalo days are gone, and we are here, living on a reservation in houses, no longer in a circle of tipis, but still as a tribe. Many of us have fallen into material poverty, but we are rich in relatives and songs and beauty.

The transmission of these words is how we keep the oral tradition alive, the gift of the Old People who loved us from long ago even though we did not yet exist upon the Earth. The words of the grandparents have bound us together, those of us who are like a victory song, like an eagle feather, like the thunder when it laughs.

When my grandmother was young, she lived in the old way—in a tipi near the Wind River, the river we love—with her great-great-grandmother, Hoh-dah-wan, who gathered wood although she was old.

Hoh-dah-wan, the grandmother of Chief Black Coal, lived during a time when the people wandered the Earth, starving because the buffalo were nearly gone. She gave my grandmother the stories of the Sand Creek Massacre of 1864, when the U.S. Cavalry attacked a Cheyenne and Arapaho camp under a white flag of truce and an American flag. . . .

She saw the people fleeing in the snow, running to the riverbanks, hoping the Earth would shelter them from the nightmare.

After it was done, the soldiers looted the camp, stealing sacred objects and human bodies—including those of my grandmother's two uncles. The elders say that the loss of sacred objects continues to hurt the tribe.

The U.S. Army used the beheaded bodies for medical research. It later gave some of the remains to the Smithsonian Institution in Washington, D.C.—our national museum—for display as curios.

In October 1992, a Smithsonian anthropologist came to talk to the spiritual elders of our tribe about the repatriation of Arapaho human remains and funerary and sacred objects. My grandmother and I were there.

The Smithsonian has made the return of the massacre victims' remains a priority, he told us that day nearly 128 years after the massacre. He said that the government began taking the remains of tribal people to continue medical studies begun on the bodies of Civil War soldiers.

No, my grandmother told him, it was because white people considered us savage and uncivilized. But they were wrong.

My grandmother is among the first Arapahos to know only the confines of a reservation and not to learn the sacred ways of the women's Quill Society.

Her mother, Grass Woman, the daughter of Black Coal, was one of the last of the seven medicine women who carried the Quill Society's medicine bundles. Until her time, the women had passed on knowledge of the society to successive generations.

The seven medicine women supervised the making of quill ornaments used to decorate tipis, moccasins, buffalo robes, and cradles with designs representing prayers for health and long life. The women made gifts of the quillwork so that blessings would follow the people as they traveled the four hills of life.

The ceremonies of the society have disappeared with other aspects of Arapaho life, and our grandparents say they long for the old ways. There is a loneliness for Arapaho words, they say—the quiet, flowing words of the storytellers that spilled into the thin, winter light and into the hearts of the people, the words that bound generations and were stronger than death.

In 1878, the Northern Band of Our People settled on a reservation in Wyoming that they share with an enemy tribe, the Shoshone. The federal government set about turning them into farmers and Christians by allotting families land and outlawing the tribe's ceremonies. Smallpox threatened the tribe, which numbered only several hundred.

Black Coal, one of our last traditional chiefs, gave part of his land allotment to the Catholic Church for a school. That way, he said, the children would no longer be sent to faraway boarding schools, banished from the words of Our People.

His son, Summer Black Coal, had been one of the first Arapahos to be taken to a boarding school, where the children were punished for speaking their tribal languages. The sons of the Arapaho chiefs and subchiefs were taken so that the people would no longer fight and the future leaders would not learn Our People's way.

After the school at St. Stephen's Mission was built, the elders, the chiefs, and the warriors would go into the classrooms and tell the children to get a white man's education. The buffalo days are gone, they told them, and you are the ones who will make a new life for the people.

In 1958, the federal government and the state of Wyoming put a radioactive-waste dump near the school. It wasn't cleaned up until thirty years later.

The children were not sacred to them.

In 1890, Smithsonian ethnologist James Mooney described Our People as "devotees and prophets, continuously seeing signs and wonders."

The government had sent him to study our tribe, because it expected us to become extinct and our words to fall into silence. It was during this time that many of the sacred societies, including the Quill Society, began to die out, and soon their ceremonies slipped away and their prayers were heard no more upon the Earth. It was also during this time that Our People began to follow the way of the Ghost Dance,[1] crying out to the Creator, for the return of the buffalo and a way of life.

Have pity on us, Father, they prayed. Have pity on us, for we have nothing left.

We buried my cousin last month. He was seventeen.

Before we buried him, the priest said words, incantations. He told us that all of us were to blame for his death because we failed to speak, we failed to listen. He said that we loved alcohol too much and our young ones too little.

His words cut into the silence and into our hearts.

Then, we heard the songs given to us by the Old People, the healing words that rose above the circle of the drum. They sang so that we would be strong and the people endure. We have done it many times before—given our young ones back to the Earth who catches our tears and to the Creator above.

We have done it many times before, we, the Sky People who are tied together by time and blood, who have shared laughter and tears, life and death.

In July 1992, my family visited the Plains Indian Museum in Cody, Wyoming, where traditional cradleboards were on display, including an Arapaho cradleboard made around 1890 from sackcloth and dyed porcupine quills.

A little girl asked her mother what the quill ornaments were.

Toys, her mother said.

She did not know that they were the captive prayers the grandmothers had prepared for the young ones.

She did not know that like the sacred prayers of the grandmothers and the songs of the buffalo, too many of our children have fallen silent.

---

[1] *Ghost Dance:* The name given to two religious dances, particularly in the 1870s and 1890s. Ghost Dance participants focused on the hope that, by performing a circular dance and other ceremonies, the Indian way of life and Indian lands would be restored.

After Reading

Critical Perspective

1. Think carefully about your reaction to this text. What effects did reading Calling-Thunder's words have on you? Why do you believe her words made you react this way?

Rhetoric and Argument

2. What sorts of rhetorical tactics—context, intertextuality, constraints, ethos, pathos, and logos—does CallingThunder employ to persuade her audience? Be sure to supply detailed examples from the text.
3. What is CallingThunder's main claim in her text? Would you be able to discern the author's identity by her writing style or by the warrants or assumptions she makes? If yes, how so?
4. What kinds of evidence does CallingThunder employ to back up her assertions? Do you find this support persuasive? Why or why not? Also, determine whether you can locate any logical fallacies in her text. Offer quotes from the text that substantiate your position.
5. How would you describe the organization of CallingThunder's text? Where does the largest shift in tone and focus occur? What is the effect of CallingThunder's choice?
6. Several times in her text CallingThunder refers to white representations of Native Americans and how they have impacted her and her family. List as many of these as you can find in her text. What implicit critique do they furnish about American myths and values as well as about American history? Provide evidence from the text to support your analysis. What do you think about the validity of her argument and her use of support?

Analysis

7. In a short argumentative response, address the following questions: In what ways does CallingThunder's writing reconceive or challenge traditional argumentative formats and structures? Why do you think that she notices this strategy? Is it effective or not? Be sure to provide details and quotes from the text as well as library and Internet resources to support your views.

Taking Action

CallingThunder's essay examines how representations of Native peoples impact our everyday lives, how we treat each other, how we perceive that others view us, and how we view ourselves.

Get into a small group. Discuss some very specific representations of Native Americans that you have experienced in the mainstream media—in advertising, television, and film. What do you like about these images? What concerns you about them? What challenges do you think CallingThunder's text poses for such images?

Write an informal essay as a group in which you offer an argumentative claim about one significant representation—positive, negative, or something in between—of Native Americans in the American media. Provide close rhetorical analyses and quotes from this representation as evidence for your ideas. Include library and Internet sources to support your assertions. Consider sharing your work with other groups both inside and outside the campus community.

TORRI MINTON

"Search for What It Means to Be White: More and More Look to Ethnic Identity"

Torri Minton was a staff writer for the San Francisco Chronicle. *This piece is one of a series of articles in "About Race," a yearlong public journalism project examining various aspects of race relations in the Bay Area. Minton passed away in 2004.*

EXERCISING YOUR SKILLS

Before Reading

Minton's text raises issues about what it means to be "white." Have you ever considered how "whiteness" is defined in American culture? If you have, what made you consider this? If not, why do you think you have never examined this issue before? How is whiteness represented in the American media? Give examples of images of white characters on television shows, in music videos, and in films. How do we know that they are white? What does whiteness mean exactly? Historically, how has whiteness been valued? When and where has it been a "burden" or, conversely, an "asset"?

Edward Ball grew up hearing stories about his eccentric ancestors and the 25 rice plantations they owned in South Carolina.

What he did not hear stories about were the Ball family's other property—nearly 4,000 human beings.

Ball set out to uncover his missing history, mirroring a quest that many white Americans have just begun.

"I was trying to understand my identity as a white person," said Ball, a former New York reporter who writes of his search in a new book, *Slaves in the Family*.

"I believe the legacy of slavery shapes the identities of white people as powerfully as it shapes the identities of black people," he said.

Until recently, white Americans have not had to think much about what it means to be white.

Successive waves of immigrants came to the United States from Ireland, Italy and other European countries, often sharply divided by language, culture and religion. But over time, the differences among white ethnic Americans blurred.

Now, as the population becomes increasingly made up of ethnic minorities, white people like Ball are beginning to feel their whiteness and to seek their own cultural identity.

The search includes a hard look at how white people are affected by racism and where they fit in a multiethnic society. The quest for a white identity has generated an academic discipline and more than a dozen books on whiteness in the last year alone.

"Some people say, 'Oh my God, this is white supremacy,'" said Jeff Hitchcock, founder of the Center for the Study of White American Culture in New Jersey.

"It is not," Hitchcock said. "It is a conscious attempt to look at the racial structure in our society. Is it being used to support white privilege?"

In 1996, the center held the first National Conference on Whiteness.

In the past two years, a string of similar events ensued, including, "The Making and Unmaking of Whiteness," sponsored by the University of California at Berkeley, and "Outing Whiteness," sponsored by the Claremont Colleges in Southern California.

Because it is so hard to draw generalizations, defining whiteness is tricky. White culture is the invisible American norm—the standard of the majority against which all others are measured, scholars say.

As a result, whiteness studies classes and seminars tend to ponder more questions than answers about what it means to be white in the United States. They have broad titles like "Whiteness in the U.S. Imagination" and "Establishing the Fact of Whiteness," and "'Wonder Breading' in America: On the Hidden Injuries of Whiteness."

"I find a lot of my white students are vexed by that question," said Matt Wray, a doctoral student at the University of California at Berkeley, who studies white identity. "As whites, we don't think of race as something that belongs to us. But we have special privileges that come to us by virtue of having white skin."

Psychologist Judith Katz takes the definition of whiteness a step further, listing characteristics she says are generally associated with white people, including rugged individualism, emotional control, a penchant for strict time schedules, belief in Christianity and a culture that romanticizes war.

Whiteness studies has its critics on the left and right. Some warn that developing a white identity could lead to racial divisiveness. Others say it could resurrect notions of biological race differences.

Chip Berlet, whose liberal organization in Somerville, Mass., studies political conservatism, fears that the white identity movement could further entrench white supremacists.

"I don't think they understand how strong the resurgence of white nationalism is," said Berlet, senior analyst at Political Research Associates and author of *Eyes Right,* an anthology on right-wing ideology. "Be clear that white identity throughout history has been based on supremacy and the oppression of black people—and also be aware that there are many people willing to hijack the discussion and move it toward the idea that democracy only works in separate nations."

Other critics insist the very idea of whiteness should be abolished altogether in the name of ending white racial dominance.

Advocates of the study of whiteness disagree. Many argue that an understanding of what it means to be white in the United States is a necessary step to honest dialogue about race—and to fighting racism.

"You have to be an ostrich not to see that white people are culturally and economically dominant in this society," Ball said. "You have to be willfully ignorant not to see that this is a direct result of the legacy of slavery."

For white people, Ball said, "this creates a neurotic oscillation between a sense of entitlement and a sense of unearned privilege."

It is difficult to develop a positive sense of whiteness "when there is not a lot to be proud of," said Pamela Perry, a doctoral student in sociology at UC Berkeley.

Perry observed teenagers develop their white identities during a year at two East Bay high schools—one multiracial and urban and the other mostly white suburban. She declined to name the schools.

The white students at the multiracial school developed a much stronger group identity, Perry found, underscoring the assumption that people who find themselves in a minority are more apt to seek a group identity.

White students at the multiracial school preferred punk and rock 'n' roll over rap, explaining candidly that "It speaks more to my experience as a white person."

Such sports as skateboarding were also considered "white."

Even when white students adopted the typical costume of baggy pants like everyone else, Perry found, they modified the style to their group identity.

For example, the pants might be cut off at the hem in imitation of skateboarders.

The white teenagers who did listen to rap music were those who identified with the black students, Perry found.

At the suburban school, where white students were in the majority, they appeared to have less of a need to develop a group identity, Perry said.

White students were more likely to listen to rap music, but they associated it with being hip, tough and urban, not specifically black.

The search for a white identity has been explored in pop culture as well as academic discourse. It may even help explain the popular fascination with the "white trash" personality celebrated on television shows such as "Roseanne" and the "Jerry Springer Show," sociologists say.

"I don't think you can point to many periods in history where white trash has been held up as a defiant countercultural hero," said Wray, co-editor of a book called *White Trash.*

On the Internet, "White Trash Online" features Cheetos, race cars and Elvis.

Steve McGrew's White Trash Web page calls Wal-Mart "white trash heaven," beer "white trash blood," and Elvis the "king of white trash."

Beyond the stereotypes and Spam, much of whiteness studies is about recognizing the privilege that many whites unconsciously take for granted.

It is a delicate subject.

Lauren Kucera grew up in white suburban Burlingame, but she felt pretty knowledgeable about race. Her mother was active in the civil rights movement, and every summer, Kucera went off to a multicultural center.

"I figured, 'Aren't I exposed? Aren't I cured?'" said Kucera, now a cross-cultural communications educator.

Four years ago, she started attending workshops about race and racism. Among the white participants, she said, she found "a great deal of taboo and insecurity."

"One of the ultimate fears is to be called a racist," said Kucera. "But how can you help but be racist in a society that is racist?"

Edward Ball also grew up in a segregated neighborhood, seeing black people as the distant and mysterious "other."

"All white folks have a certain amount of fear that we internalize from childhood—fear of other racial groups," he said.

Ball conceded that he was afraid the African American slave descendants—some of whom were his own blood relatives—would hate him.

"One of the reasons I embarked on this effort was to release that fear," he said. "I succeeded."

Across the country, students, in particular, are beginning to ask what it means to be white.

"They want to know who they are and who they can be, without the national chauvinism, the racial arrogance and supremacy," said Benjamin Bowser, sociology professor at California State University at Hayward and co-editor of the book *Impacts of Racism on White Americans*.

"This is a marvelous, marvelous exploration," Bowser said. "We need to respond."

One Man's Search for a Plantation Past

Edward Ball waded through 10,000 pages of family papers spanning 400 years in his search to find the stories of the thousands of slaves his ancestors owned.

He exchanged tears, hard words and horrific memories with some of the nearly 100,000 African Americans in the United States today who are descendants of Ball family slaves.

"My life had been shaped by the legacy of those plantations," Ball said. "I took benefit from them."

It was not a financial, but cultural benefit, he said, like "being first in line for jobs, housing and education. Most white people, I think, sense something about that."

Ball sought to make amends, although many of the descendants of his family's slaves viewed his apologies as irrelevant. One man credited him with being "man enough" to try.

Some of the families were not aware of their ancestry. Others were angry. Many accepted him into their homes.

"The first impression they had of me was one of shock," Ball said.

"First, that I existed, and second, that I was there."

Many said they never thought they could put a face on a slave master—until they met Ball.

"This was an intensely perverse gift," Ball said. "Because it enabled them, and also me, to make contact with those families long dead who had suffered incomprehensibly, and bring them to life, pay them respect, confer dignity on their lives."

After they got to know each other, Ball said many of the families became intensely interested in finding out what had happened to their relatives. From 1698 to 1863, the Balls of South Carolina were one of the largest slave-holding families in the South.

The Ball family myth enshrined the slave-owning clan as benevolent masters. But Ball found records of sexual violence, hangings and mutilation.

"I'm talking about sitting down with black people at a kitchen table to talk about what our ancestors did to and with each other," Ball said.

"I'm not suggesting that everyone is able to do it, but I found that talking about the tragic events that families share . . . it gives relief."

After Reading

Critical Perspective

1. Why do you think Minton is particularly concerned with whiteness as a concept? What is her main claim about whiteness? What rationale does Minton provide for her concern? Do you find this viable? Why or why not? Be sure to provide examples from her text to back up your views.

Rhetoric and Argument

2. What kinds of rhetorical appeals does Minton make in her text? Give textual examples of her audience and purpose as well as her use of ethos, pathos, and logos. Do you find these appeals persuasive? Why or why not? Which appeal appears to be the strongest?
3. Minton indicates that some argue that studying constructions of whiteness can help challenge racism while others think it can further racist propaganda. What do you believe about this? What do you believe Minton thinks? Furnish examples from her text to support your claims.
4. Minton cites examples of how white students adopt different group identities when they find themselves in different contexts—particularly when they are in the majority versus when they are in the minority. Why do you think that Minton utilizes these examples? Provide quotes from her essay to back up your ideas.

Analysis

5. Much like many articles that appear in newspapers and magazines, Minton's essay relies upon many others' quotes to make its case. Now consider Minton's argument—her implicit or explicit claims, support, and warrants. Write a short text about whether you agree with them or not. Explain your position in detail. Do you think that Minton's text exhibits any biases or logical fallacies? Give quotes from the text as well as library and Internet sources to support your thoughts.

Taking Action

Minton's essay raises many complex and controversial issues about how whiteness as well as how other racial and ethnicity categories function in American culture.

Form a small group. Apply or challenge the ideas Minton's argument raises through taking part in an exercise. Interview a group of people from your writing class or from your circle of friends. Ask them to tell you as much as they can about their cultural and ethnic heritages. Remember, you may have different views within your small group about these issues; be sure to record these as well.

Ask the people you interview to answer the following questions: In the global world (global commerce, global communication) in which we all now live, how do we determine who exactly is "white" and who is "not white"? How should the terms be defined? Do you self-identify as white? If so, what does such an identification mean? Or, do people self-identify in other ways? What are the personal, cultural, and political ramifications of these identifications? Do you feel as if you have a responsibility to understand your family's historical relationship to racist practices? If so, should this be pursued as Edward Ball chose to pursue it? What stands to be gained and what stands to be lost?

If "white" seems like an inadequate identity category to some people you interview, inquire as to whether other identification categories might be more appropriate or not. Are these other categories determined in similar or different ways? Are they likely to pose as many potential problems as whiteness? Why or why not?

Get back into the larger class group. Based upon your small group's research, determine what kinds of argumentative claims you could make about college students and the issue of whiteness. How might you support them? What library and Internet sources might you consult?

Nell Bernstein

"Goin' Gangsta, Choosin' Cholita"

Nell Bernstein is editor of YO!, *a San Francisco–based journal for teens published by the Pacific News Service. She has also published work in* Glamour, Woman's Day, Salon, *and* Mother Jones.

EXERCISING YOUR SKILLS

Before Reading

Bernstein's text examines the issue of claiming an identity with which a person was not born. Have you—or anyone else you have known—ever wanted very badly to be part of a specific group to which you did not belong? What were you willing to say and do to become part of that group? What things were you willing to change about yourself? What things did you resist changing? Why? Reflect a bit upon your choices and how you look back upon them now. Would you alter anything about the choices made? Why or why not?

Her lipstick is dark, the lip liner even darker, nearly black. In baggy pants, a blue plaid Pendleton, her bangs pulled back tight off her forehead, 15-year-old April is a perfect cholita, a Mexican gangsta girl.

But April Miller is Anglo. "And I don't like it!" she complains. "I'd rather be Mexican."

April's father wanders into the family room of their home in San Leandro, California, a suburb near Oakland. "Hey, cholita," he teases. "Go get a suntan. We'll put you in a barrio and see how much you like it."

A large, sandy-haired man with "April" tattooed on one arm and "Kelly"—the name of his older daughter—on the other, Miller spent 21 years working in a San Leandro glass factory that shut down and moved to Mexico a couple of years ago. He recently got a job in another factory, but he expects NAFTA to swallow that one, too.

"Sooner or later we'll all get nailed," he says. "Just another stab in the back of the American middle class."

Later, April gets her revenge: "Hey, Mr. White Man's Last Stand," she teases. "Wait till you see how well I manage my welfare check. You'll be asking me for money."

A once almost exclusively white, now increasingly Latin and black working-class suburb, San Leandro borders on predominantly black East Oakland. For decades, the boundary was strictly policed and practically impermeable. In 1970 April Miller's hometown was 97 percent white. By 1990 San Leandro was 65 percent white, 6 percent black, 15 percent Hispanic, and 13 percent Asian or Pacific Islander. With minorities moving into suburbs in growing numbers and cities becoming ever more diverse, the boundary between city and suburb is dissolving, and suburban teenagers are changing with the times.

In April's bedroom, her past and present selves lie in layers, the pink walls of girlhood almost obscured, Guns N' Roses and Pearl Jam posters overlaid by rappers Paris and Ice Cube. "I don't have a big enough attitude to be a black girl," says April, explaining her current choice of ethnic identification.

What matters is that she thinks the choice is hers. For April and her friends, identity is not a matter of where you come from, what you were born into, what color your skin is. It's what you wear, the music you listen to, the words you use—everything to which you pledge allegiance, no matter how fleetingly.

The hybridization of American teens has become talk show fodder, with "wiggers"—white kids who dress and talk "black"—appearing on TV in full gangsta regalia. In Indiana a group of white high school girls raised a national stir when they triggered an imitation race war at their virtually all-white high school last fall simply by dressing "black."

In many parts of the country, it's television and radio, not neighbors, that introduce teens to the allure of ethnic difference. But in California the influences are more immediate. The California public schools are the most diverse in the country: 42 percent white, 36 percent Hispanic, 9 percent black, 8 percent Asian.

Sometimes young people fight over their differences. Students at virtually any school in the Bay Area can recount the details of at least one "race riot" in which a conflict between individuals escalated into a battle between their clans. More often, though, teens would rather join than fight. Adolescence, after all, is the period when you're most inclined to mimic the power closest at hand, from stealing your older sister's clothes to copying the ruling clique at school.

White skaters and Mexican would-be gangbangers listen to gangsta rap and call each other "nigga" as a term of endearment; white girls sometimes affect Spanish accents; blond cheerleaders claim Cherokee ancestors.

"Claiming" is the central concept here. A Vietnamese teen in Hayward, another Oakland suburb, "claims" Oakland—and by implication blackness—because he lived there as a child. A law-abiding white kid "claims" a Mexican gang he says he hangs with. A brown-skinned girl with a Mexican father and a white mother "claims" her Mexican side, while her fair-skinned sister "claims" white. The word comes up over and over, as if identity were territory, the self a kind of turf.

At a restaurant in a minimall in Hayward, Nicole Huffstutler, 13, sits with her friends and describes herself as "Indian, German, French, Welsh, and, um . . . American"; "If somebody says anything like 'Yeah, you're just a peckerwood,' I'll walk up and I'll say 'white pride!' 'Cause I'm proud of my race, and I wouldn't wanna be any other race."

"Claiming" white has become a matter of principle for Heather, too, who says she's "sick of the majority looking at us like we're less than them." (Hayward schools were 51 percent white in 1990, down from 77 percent in 1980, and whites are now the minority in many schools.)

Asked if she knows that nonwhites have not traditionally been referred to as "the majority" in America, Heather gets exasperated: "I hear that all the time, every day. They say, 'Well, you guys controlled us for many years, and it's time for us to control you.' Every day."

When Jennifer Vargas—a small, brown-skinned girl in purple jeans who quietly eats her salad while Heather talks—softly announces that she's "mostly Mexican," she gets in trouble with her friends.

"No, you're not!" scolds Heather.

"I'm mostly Indian and Mexican," Jennifer continues flatly. "I'm very little . . . I'm mostly . . ."

"Your mom's white!" Nicole reminds her sharply. "She has blond hair."

"That's what I mean," Nicole adds. "People think that white is a bad thing. They think that white is a bad race. So she's trying to claim more Mexican than white."

"I have very little white in me," Jennifer repeats. "I have mostly my dad's side, 'cause I look like him and stuff. And most of my friends think that me and my brother and sister aren't related, 'cause they look more like my mom."

"But you guys are all the same race, you just look different," Nicole insists. She stops eating and frowns. "OK, you're half and half each what your parents have. So you're equal as your brother and sister, you just look different. And you should be proud of what you are—every little piece and bit of what you are. If you were Afghan or whatever, you should be proud of it."

Will Mosley, Heather's 17-year-old brother, says he and his friends listen to rap groups like Compton's Most Wanted, NWA, and Above the Law because they "sing about life"—that is, what happens in Oakland, Los Angeles, anyplace but where Will is sitting today, an empty Round Table Pizza in a minimall.

"No matter what race you are," Will says, "if you live like we do, then that's the kind of music you like."

And how do they live?

"We don't live bad or anything," Will admits. "We live in a pretty good neighborhood, there's no violence or crime. I was just . . . we're just city people, I guess."

Will and his friend Adolfo Garcia, 16, say they've outgrown trying to be something they're not. "When I was 11 or 12," Will says, "I thought I was becoming a big gangsta and stuff. Because I liked that music, and thought it was the coolest, I wanted to become that. I wore big clothes, like you wear in jail. But then I kind of woke up. I looked at myself and thought, 'Who am I trying to be?'"

They may have outgrown blatant mimicry, but Will and his friends remain convinced that they can live in a suburban tract house with a well-kept lawn on a tree-lined street in "not a bad neighborhood" and still call themselves "city" people on the basis of musical tastes. "City" for these young people means crime, graffiti, drugs. The kids are law-abiding, but these activities connote what Will admiringly calls "action." With pride in his voice, Will predicts that "in a couple of years, Hayward will be like Oakland. It's starting to get more known, because of crime and things. I think it'll be bigger, more things happening, more crime, more graffiti, stealing cars."

"That's good," chimes in 15-year-old Matt Jenkins, whose new beeper—an item that once connoted gangsta chic but now means little more than an active social life—goes off periodically. "More fun."

The three young men imagine with disdain life in a gangsta-free zone. "Too bland, too boring," Adolfo says. "You have to have something going on. You can't just have every-day life."

"Mowing your lawn," Matt sneers.

"Like Beaver Cleaver's house," Adolfo adds. "It's too clean out here."

Not only white kids believe that identity is a matter of choice or taste, or that the power of "claiming" can transcend ethnicity. The Manor Park Locos—a group of mostly Mexican-Americans who hang out in San Leandro's Manor Park—say they descend from the Manor Lords, tough white guys who ruled the neighborhood a generation ago.

They "are like our . . . uncles and dads, the older generation," says Jesse Martinez, 14. "We're what they were when they were around, except we're Mexican."

"There's three generations," says Oso, Jesse's younger brother. "There's Manor Lords, Manor Park Locos, and Manor Park Pee Wees." The Pee Wees consist mainly of the Locos' younger brothers, eager kids who circle the older boys on bikes and brag about "punking people."

Unlike Will Mosley, the Locos find little glamour in city life. They survey the changing suburban landscape and see not "action" or "more fun" but frightening decline. Though most of them are not yet 18, the Locos are already nostalgic, longing for a Beaver Cleaver past that white kids who mimic them would scoff at.

Walking through nearly empty Manor Park, with its eucalyptus stands, its softball diamond and tennis courts, Jesse's friend Alex, the only Asian in the group, waves his arms in a gesture of futility. "A few years ago, every bench was filled," he says. "Now no one comes here. I guess it's because of everything that's going on. My parents paid a lot for this house, and I want it to be nice for them. I just hope this doesn't turn into Oakland."

Glancing across the park at April Miller's street, Jesse says he knows what the white cholitas are about. "It's not a racial thing," he explains. "It's just all the most popular people out here are Mexican. We're just the gangstas that everyone knows. I guess those girls wanna be known."

Not every young Californian embraces the new racial hybridism. Andrea Jones, 20, an African American who grew up in the Bay Area suburbs of Union City and Hayward, is unimpressed by what she sees mainly as shallow mimicry. "It's full of posers out here," she says. "When *Boyz N the Hood* came out on video, it was sold out for weeks. The boys all wanna be black, the girls all wanna be Mexican. It's the glamour."

Driving down the quiet, shaded streets of her old neighborhood in Union City, Andrea spots two white preteen boys in Raiders jackets and hugely baggy pants strutting erratically down the empty sidewalk. "Look at them," she says. "Dislocated."

She knows why. "In a lot of these schools out here, it's hard being white," she says. "I don't think these kids were prepared for the backlash that is going on, all the pride now in people of color's ethnicity, and our boldness with it. They have nothing like that, no identity, nothing they can say they're proud of.

"So they latch onto their great-grandmother who's a Cherokee, or they take on the most stereotypical aspects of being black or Mexican. It's beautiful to appreciate different aspects of other people's culture—that's like the dream of what the 21st century should be. But to garnish yourself with pop culture stereotypes just to blend—that's really sad."

Roland Krevocheza, 18, graduated last year from Arroyo High School in San Leandro. He is Mexican on his mother's side, Eastern European on his father's. In the new hierarchies, it may be mixed kids like Roland who have the hardest time finding their place, even as their numbers grow. (One in five marriages in California is between people of different races.) They can always be called "wannabes," no matter what they claim.

"I'll state all my nationalities," Roland says. But he takes a greater interest in his father's side, his Ukrainian, Romanian, and Czech ancestors. "It's more unique," he explains. "Mexican culture is all around me. We eat Mexican food all the time, I hear stories from my grandmother. I see the low-riders and stuff. I'm already part of it. I'm not trying to be; I am."

His darker-skinned brother "says he's not proud to be white," Roland adds. "He calls me 'Mr. Nazi.'" In the room the two share, the American flags and the reproduction of the Bill of Rights are Roland's; the Public Enemy poster belongs to his brother.

Roland has good reason to mistrust gangsta attitudes. In his junior year in high school, he was one of several Arroyo students who were beaten up outside the school at lunchtime by a group of Samoans who came in cars from Oakland. Roland wound up with a split lip, a concussion, and a broken tailbone. Later he was told that the assault was "gang-related"— that the Samoans were beating up anyone wearing red.

"Rappers, I don't like them," Roland says. "I think they're a bad influence on kids. It makes kids think they're all tough and bad."

Those who, like Roland, dismiss the gangsta and cholo styles as affectations can point to the fact that several companies market overpriced knockoffs of "ghetto wear" targeted at teens.

But there's also something going on out here that transcends adolescent faddishness and pop culture exoticism. When white kids call their parents "racist" for nagging them about their baggy pants; when they learn Spanish to talk to their boyfriends; when Mexican-American boys feel themselves descended in spirit from white "uncles"; when children of mixed marriages insist that they are whatever race they say they are, all of them are more than just confused.

They're inching toward what Andrea Jones calls "the dream of what the 21st century should be." In the ever more diverse communities of Northern California, they're also facing the complicated reality of what their 21st century will be.

Meanwhile, in the living room of the Miller family's San Leandro home, the argument continues unabated. "You don't know what you are," April's father has told her more than once. But she just keeps on telling him he doesn't know what time it is.

After Reading

Critical Perspective

1. Why do you think that Bernstein felt it was important to write this essay? Do you agree with the concerns she raises? Be sure to provide evidence from the text to back up your views.

Rhetoric and Argument

2. This essay offers several different scenarios from real people's lives in order to make its points. Do you think that this was an effective rhetorical strategy? Why or why not? Make note of the specific things that each person asserts, specifically which points stick with you after reading the essay. What about these examples is particularly memorable?

3. This piece raises questions about whether people have the right to claim a racial or ethnic identity to which they were not born as well as whether people have the right to claim one of their racial or ethnic identities over others. What do you think about these ideas? What potential real societal benefits might there be if people "embraced the new racial hybridism"? What potential negative repercussions might there be if people did so? Explain your position by pointing to the text for evidence as well as referencing your own experiences.

4. Observe the rather different statements made by Jesse Martinez and Andrea Jones in this essay. When describing the growing phenomenon of the white cholita, Jesse states, "'It's not a racial thing. . . . It's just all the most popular people out here are Mexican. We're just the gangstas that everyone knows. I guess those girls wanna be known.'" However, Andrea says, "'It's full of posers out here'" and articulates that they have "'no identity, nothing they can say they're proud of.'" Whose position do you agree with more? Why? Draw from textual examples and your own experiences to support your views.

Analysis

5. In a short essay, consider ads, commercials, television shows, and movies that depict the white cholita and gangsta identities. How are they represented in these media images? Why do you think that this is the case? Do you think that these are fair and balanced depictions? Why or why not? Offer quotes from library and Internet sources to back up your views.

Taking Action

April Miller and her father assume very different views on her adoption of a Mexican identity. Form into two class groups—one group assuming April's position, the other her father's. Each group should find detailed evidence to support its claims as well as be prepared to refute the claims made by the other group. Be sure to be sensitive to differences in perspective within the class, and to be willing to argue a case with which you may not agree.

When you have completed this debate, form the large class group again. Discuss your reactions to the exercise as well as the specific claims and evidence offered by each group. Then talk as a class about how you think race and ethnicity in American culture ought to be defined and why. As part of this discussion, recall April Miller's comment that she would "rather be Mexican" as well as Andrea Jones's assertion that white students are "posers" who "have no identity" and adopt someone else's identity as a result. How do their views shape or fail to shape your definition of race and ethnicity?

TomÁs Sandoval

"On the Merits of Racial Identity"

Tomás Sandoval is a professor in the History Department at California State University–Monterey Bay. Much of his research centers on the Latino/a community formation in San Francisco from 1945 to 1970. Sandoval's scholarship involves an investigation into oral histories and the examination and contestation of certain stereotypes.

EXERCISING YOUR SKILLS

Before Reading

Sandoval reveals how his own experiences in college and graduate school have shaped who he is today. Spend a few minutes freewriting. Consider how your own identity characteristics (race and ethnicity, class, gender, sexual preference, language, politics, disability, age, region, and/or religion) shape who you are, how others view you, and how you perceive other people. Make a list of specific attributes and variables that contribute to your own unique identity. How might you have been a different person, made different choices, or held different perspectives if you did not have this background and these identity traits?

As a teaching assistant at UC Berkeley, I have had the rare opportunity to work with students who are at a crucial intellectual point in their lives. In their first or second year of college education, at a time when their identity is beginning to take concrete and passionate shape, they encounter me in the discussion section of some history class dealing with the intersection of race, culture, class, and politics. What they learn, I hope, is to think critically of the world around them and to strive for an intellectual position that questions the simplistic notions that dominate this world. Especially with issues concerning race, I tell them, it is all too easy for us to fall into the essentialist constructs of past generations of minority activists and further impede their well-intentioned goal: progress for all people of color.

What I learn, however, is something even more profound. They remind me that you can't overlook the obvious in your quest for intellectual growth, even if it turns out to be a little limited or even wrong. Sometimes, just sometimes, we acquire a strength that can be used for a greater good if we learn to understand race in ways that go beyond or even contradict the skills we develop as scholars. Ultimately, there still is a difference between the "real" world and the intellectual one. What makes sense in one doesn't always make sense in the other. No matter what intellectual constructs come from academia, however persuasive and sensible they may seem when applied to observations about the world outside the university, people living in that world continue to hold fast to their own belief systems.

In a race-conscious world, this is still true today. More and more intellectuals agree in their criticisms of essentialist identity politics. The notion that people of a certain ethnicity must conform to certain political ideals, maintain some specific cultural standard, and be "true to their race" is too simplistic when considered with a complex understanding of how "race" itself is a social construct. But the experiences of many of my students and myself suggest that sometimes it is good to be too simplistic. Often, these experiences suggest a need for holding onto some of the simplistic notions of the past for the purpose that they serve. I can make this easier to understand with the example of my own story.

I am a Chicano. The second of three children born to two second-generation Americans, I grew up in a typical Los Angeles suburb of tract housing and strip malls. Perhaps not so typically, people of my ethnicity all but dominated the landscape. Whether in our schools, supermarkets, malls, or playgrounds we always seemed to be surrounded by people of Mexican descent. Of course, people of other ethnicities shared the same spaces with us. Yet, undoubtedly, in the greater La Puente area of the 1980's I was part of a Mexican majority.

Then, in 1990, I began my undergraduate career at a small, liberal arts college in a place called Claremont, California. While it was only about fifteen miles farther east from LA than the town in which I grew up, Claremont seemed like an entirely different planet. Tree-lined streets, classic well-maintained homes, and a small shopping square in the town center which closed every evening after sunset characterized this "little bit of New England out West." While Claremont was completely different from where I grew up, it only took me about five minutes to acculturate myself to a city whose careful development over two generations produced a neighborhood where Beaver Cleaver himself could have lived. I mean, you could walk barefoot on the streets without fear of stepping in, or on, anything that might seriously ruin your day or worse. Yet, the population of that town, or more specifically, my microcosm within it, was quite another thing to get used to. For you see, at Claremont McKenna College I was part of a small Mexican minority in a primarily wealthy, Anglo student population.

In actuality, that's when I became a "Chicano." That is to say, that's when my ethnicity began to take a more developed, precise, and political meaning for me personally. The name Chicano became the name that I, like the politicized generation of Mexican Americans before me, chose to reflect that change. Before that, I (like all of the people around me) was a "Mexican." At times we were "Mexican Americans," some of us were even "Hispanics," but the terms rarely served to describe more than our historical nationality and, at times, level of acculturation. Of course, even those qualities have a very real political aspect to them. The difference was that those names for our identity, at that time in my life, didn't have to be political. When people used one of them to describe themselves, they didn't necessarily mean to say something about their racial politics.

No matter what we called ourselves, we related to our ancestries in different ways and at different levels. My Mexicanness differed from that of my second generation friends as it did from others who were racially mixed or immigrants. We were not being cultural relativists. We lived in a world of cultural standards. In the eyes of many of the Mexican adolescents around me some of us were more Mexican than others. Sometimes being too Mexican or too American caused some social anxiety. Still, we all shared some ambiguous connection to each other, perhaps best expressed through our cultural practice, our speech habits, and the foods we all ate.

The bond between us became more clear when we joked around with our Filipino and Anglo friends. Because we lived in a mixing ground of cultures, race became the topic of running jokes among my group of friends. Any cultural stereotype was free game as we took the opportunity to break up into ethnic teams and make fun of each other. Of course, the Mexicans rarely lost. We were the majority. In some ways, our status produced a culture to which other students had to acculturate themselves. On some level then, acceptance was gained by assuming some level of a Mexican American culture. (And all of this still existed within a greater society which acculturated all of us to a confused "Americanness" too!) Yet, whatever we called ourselves, whatever that meant to us individually, my Mexican friends and myself always had our common and free-floating status as Mexicans all but secured.

In Claremont, however, there were very few of "us." I suddenly found that my views in the classroom, particularly on issues concerning race, produced a different effect than they had previously. I, like my twenty or so other college mates, represented the "Mexican view." White students, many of whom had surprisingly never had much contact with Mexicans of any sort, listened to our views on these matters not as merely another opinion but as the "Mexican opinion." In some respects this new aspect of classroom learning inspired confidence in my own beliefs. Who I was and what I thought were more than the mere product of what I had learned in books or through my parents. They were products of my culture and other life experiences. By observing how others considered my views, I was able to grow in my understanding of what made me different from the students around me and what did not.

Even more striking were the few opportunities where "our" views were actually desired. Whereas before in my education teachers never avoided race in their lessons, probably because it was all around them, I now found that professors rarely included it in their discussions except as some sidenote or special case. How can one teach about the welfare system and not include some discussion of the way race seems to interplay with the realities of class? How can you discuss civil rights and not include Mexican Americans and their struggles of the sixties and seventies? Simply put, my professors didn't teach many of these things because it was not part of their experience. Because of that, few of my non-Mexican professors and classmates exhibited a strong inclination to learn these things on their own.

It was at Claremont that I first began to truly appreciate the way that societies can mask their acknowledgment of the racial "other" and, at the same time, portray a knowledge that is as singularly complete as any. I came to accept that most people approach the learning of what they don't know through the gaze of what they do. For people who never had to experience strong emotions because of their race or ethnicity, ignoring those aspects in other aspects of their life was a natural consequence. That didn't mean that their learning was flawed compared to mine, just different. So, what rang "true" to the majority of students in a class seemed increasingly flawed through my eyes because my past made me see things in a different light.

The journey these frustrations led me on is one I continue today. Feeling that my experiences and views were absent in many of my classes, I not only tried to assert them more vociferously in discussions, I also began to feel some sort of obligation to make sure that they were as right as they could be. Unexpectedly, I began to feel some sort of weight upon me when I realized that when I shared my views in class, I spoke for those whom I had never met yet were tied to me by blood and history. What once was only a loose association with other Mexicans whom I didn't know, now became a firmer and more political bond in an environment which took my views and the views of my other Mexican classmates as indicative of all "our people."

The way that my views indicated the views of all Mexicans to my classmates naturally contributed to my cultural nationalism. This occurred not only because they were willing to invest in me the authority to speak for my community but because I, as one of the few who even tried, became perfectly willing to do so. By trying to understand how my views and experiences were different from others I was naturally learning more about who I was and where I came from. I was also increasingly becoming aware of how all of that fit into society as a whole as well as in the smaller world of university life. My ethnicity produced a clash with the world I encountered in Claremont. That world reduced it to a reflection of my "race." I quickly realized that politically, and personally, it was more advantageous to go with the flow rather than to fight it.

In short, I began to study Chicano history. If professors wouldn't include the information in their classes, I made a point to speak up with the information I had learned on my own. Every opportunity I had to write a term paper, I tried to focus it on some aspect of the Chicano experience. In discussions where race and culture naturally fit in, and at my school they rarely did, I made an effort to at least try to make others consider discussing them. A major preoccupation of my classroom demeanor became to insert Chicanos every place that I could both to satisfy my own standards for the "truth" and to complicate everyone else's.

As I moved onward in my studies, both my educational environment and my own self-education produced a person who was more critical and balanced than many of my fellow students. I began to feel advantaged not only because of the body of knowledge I accumulated on the Chicano experience but because I lived in a society that made me learn it in order to feel normal and content. I felt that the world that ignored my race was hardly race-blind. Instead, it was a white, upper-class social environment. In that respect I felt that I had the upper hand. By ignoring race altogether, the majority was failing to fully grasp the way that they themselves were racial beings.

These intellectual changes also made me closer to many of the other minority students at Claremont. We all shared feelings, both of marginalization and of the burden of being representative of our larger communities, at least in the eyes of many of our classmates. We all also shared an experience of cultural withdrawal as we found ourselves missing what we had previously been used to on a daily basis. As these sentiments met with the frustrations of higher education, the meanings of our minority identity became more public and the way in which those meanings were conveyed became even more significant to our peace of mind and feelings of solidarity. In the process, ethnicity became political, as well as culturally essentialized.

It's difficult to explain but that's how I became a Chicano. The title that I now ascribed to my ethnicity suggested much more than culture to me and, I hoped, to those who knew of it. It meant that I was conscious of the history of my community. It expressed a strong pride in who I was and a commitment to making sure that those aspects of myself would not be ignored or devalued. Furthermore, it meant that I shared the views of those political activists who first began to use the title widely during the Chicano Civil Rights Movement of the late sixties and early seventies. By calling myself Chicano, I was telling the world not only who I was culturally but what that meant to me politically and professionally.

The meaning of this identity has continued to evolve for me during my studies at UC Berkeley in the department of history. As before, the classroom has helped to transform me. Except this time it has not been as the student but as the instructor. What I have learned is a product of the conflict between what I have increasingly come to accept on an intellectual level and what I have come to hold increasingly dear on an emotional one.

In graduate school we are taught to be critical thinkers who can challenge the simplistic notions of the past. In areas of culture and cultural history, this has produced a revolution in thinking. The more I learned in this new environment, the more intellectually sophisticated I felt. My own experiences already suggested some of these new currents. Since I had become more conscious of the political aspects of my race, I had also become more conscious of the ways that my varied environments helped to build them. I knew that there wasn't anything essential about being Mexican. The more that I learned about Chicano history the better positioned I was to see the variety of experience and culture within my own community. In fact, my life in a "white" college had done more to narrow down the meaning of my Mexicanness than anything else, as it helped me to understand the way that whites, who are typically assumed to belong to a non-race, are also racial.

Once these loose beliefs took concrete shape in classes, I wanted others to appreciate the complexity of these common assumptions we make about race in our society. When I stood before my students, I sought to lead them down the same path that I now walked. By complicating what it meant to be "Chicano," by trying to make them understand that we shouldn't have to conform to society's ideas about who we are or the ones imposed upon us by our own communities, and by emphasizing that our goal should be to form a multiracial, inclusive movement rather than a narrow, nationalistic one, I hope that I have been at least partially successful. But recently, I have realized that it is important not to lead them down this path too rapidly.

It is me that has changed. It finally hit me this past semester that my students are going through what I did at Claremont. Instead of providing them with an environment where they were free to develop and express some form of nationalism so that they could draw their own conclusions, I was trying to make them bypass where I had been so that we could all begin from the same place. I wanted to spare them what I went through, but I couldn't. Every person of color in this society will have to confront many of these emotions at sometime in his/her life. Society sees and acts through race. Eventually, we all have to make sense of our ethnicity and its place in our lives.

For many, making sense of it means becoming somewhat culturally nationalistic. Now I don't think that all of the assumptions underlying cultural nationalism as a political stance are true. I'm not sure that in the long-run cultural nationalism will be the best tack to take for achieving a better society. But it is necessary on two levels: as part of the process of becoming culturally (and politically) aware and as a means of survival. On some level, because the world works from simplistic beliefs about race and culture it is vital that we make sense of our place in that world from within those beliefs before we deconstruct them into oblivion.

In the so-called "real world" members of my family call themselves everything from Mexican to Hispanics. Happily, more and more of them use the term Chicano or Chicana and in so doing accept many of the political beliefs that I have. But no matter what my cousins or aunts or uncles call themselves, they, like all Mexicans in the United States, will come to some realization of how their race affects their experiences in this nation. The conclusions they draw and the strategies they choose for survival may not be all the same, but they will not be void of political significance.

And they should not be. To separate the two is to place oneself at a disadvantage. In my classes, I now encourage strategic simplicity along with a critical appraisal of race. I do it for my students, so that they can gain confidence in knowing who they are and where they came from. It is important for those of us who are Chicano and Chicana and are in graduate programs to acknowledge our race to show our students that they are not alone and that they too can do what we have done. I do it for class dialogue, so that none of our discussions will ever be limited to the intellectual at the expense of the experiential. But I don't do it just for my Chicano and Chicana students. Everyone I teach can better learn about themselves when all of our pasts are told and appreciated.

And, when all is said and done, I do it for myself. I've learned that I can't separate my politics from my race or from my profession. The personal is truly political. But so is my profession as a scholar and teacher. The most important thing that I've learned, though, is that the political development of my students is as worthwhile to them as their critical understanding of race. To fully understand race we must understand it in all of its manifestations and, on some level, we must learn to accept why people situate themselves where they do. It is their right to make that decision. And it is my responsibility as an educator to come to terms with it.

After Reading

Critical Perspective

1. What exactly does Sandoval want to change about how students of color are taught in university settings? How does he propose to do this? Do you agree with Sandoval's perspectives? What do you like about them? What would you change about them?

Rhetoric and Argument

2. Sandoval writes about his own cultural heritage and ethnic background a great deal in this essay. Do you think that this builds a credible ethos for him as a writer? Are there ways in which it detracts from his ethos? Do you think that this was a persuasive way to make an argument? Why or why not? Be sure to offer examples from the text to support your views.

3. What is Sandoval's main claim in his essay and where does he make it? How does this assertion tie into Sandoval's sense of the responsibility teachers have for their students' lives and learning? Give textual evidence to support your thoughts.

4. What sorts of evidence does Sandoval use to support his ideas? Do you find this evidence persuasive? Why or why not? Offer examples from the essay to provide support for your views. How do his evidence and his rhetorical appeals work together strategically?

5. Are there ways in which Sandoval's argument may be biased, have faulty warrants or assumptions, or employ any logical fallacies? Where might you point to in his text to support your ideas? Similarly, if you think that his argument is not biased and does not have any logical fallacies, provide evidence to support your perspectives.

Analysis

6. Think about media images in film, television, and advertising that represent Chicana/o people. In a short argumentative text, address the following questions: What positive images, particularly of Chicanos, have you seen in the media and how have they affected you? If you have witnessed negative images, how have these impacted you? What would you change about them specifically?

Taking Action

Sandoval is very interested in creating a university curriculum that is diverse and supports cultural differences.

In a short freewrite, point to specific educational experiences of your own—ones in history as well as other sorts of classes—that have supported the importance of diversity and cultural differences. Remember, your experiences may be markedly different from those Sandoval discusses, depending on the geographical region as well as the neighborhood within which you grew up. What did you learn as a result of your experiences and why? If you have had few or no experiences like this, write about why this may have occurred, how this makes you feel, and if there is anything you might have liked to see done instead. Give examples from your own experiences to back up your views.

Now meet in a small group and share all of your ideas. Outline a set of university classes that you have not encountered (in your major or in your electives) but might be additionally useful in accomplishing this goal. What kinds of books might you read, trips might you take, and assignments might be used? Include library and Internet sources to support your suggestions. Write up your group's notes and present them to the rest of the class. Consider sharing your work with other groups both inside and outside the campus community.

KIFLIN TURNER

"Identity Beyond Stereotypes: African-American Students Search to Find a Niche Beyond the Confines of Racial Myths"

Kiflin Turner is a staff writer for The Observer, *a newspaper dedicated to independent journalism at the University of Notre Dame and St. Mary's College.*

EXERCISING YOUR SKILLS

Before Reading

Kiflin's essay exposes some of the problems that result from stereotyping. In a five-minute freewrite exercise, consider the ways in which you or those you care about have been stereotyped by others based upon religion, race and ethnicity, age, class, or any other identity category. Once you have completed this task, take another five minutes to try to determine why you were stereotyped in this way as well as whether or how you challenged these stereotypes. How did these experiences affect you? In what ways have these stereotypes been used to belittle and hurt people historically?

Patrick Parks was a little surprised when one of his dormmates thought he played football.

That's because he's short.

But Parks, a senior African-American student at Notre Dame, frequently gets mistaken for an athlete because of his skin color. Parks' dark skin is frequently a signal to other students that he's an athlete—but he's not.

"[My dormmate] just assumed that because I was black, I played football," Parks said, adding that his size should have been a consideration, but was overshadowed by his skin color.

Racial profiling of minority students is a disturbing everyday occurrence where minority students are categorized as being athletes or intellectually inferior.

"Sometimes there's a lot of talk that only people who are black are characterized as automatically student athletes and that's not necessarily true," said Susan Creary, a sophomore African-American student.

Racial profiling of African-American students as athletes is a major misconception that is an obstacle for minority students' acceptance in the Notre Dame community.

"There's definitely room for improvement, there's always that stereotype of all African-Americans on campus being athletes, and unfortunately a lot of times it holds true because a lot of them are athletes," said Thomas Gilbert, a biracial walk-on member of the track and field team.

Mistaken Identity

Gilbert's experience is familiar to other minority students. Sophomore Justin Ruiz is no stranger to racial discrimination in his dorm and in the classroom.

Ruiz recalled one incident where a resident in his dorm repeatedly hesitated to speak with him, regardless of Ruiz's efforts to initiate friendly conversation.

"I'll say hi to him and he won't say anything back—and I don't know if he's intimidated or I don't know if he's [not] used to people of color," said Ruiz.

The same situation also occurs elsewhere on campus, Ruiz said.

"For the most part, people say hello back, but sometimes they just kind of shrug their shoulders and keep on walking," Ruiz said.

In the classroom setting, many African-American students are singled out because of their race, and expected to be "the voice" for the community. This often puts many students in an uncomfortable learning environment where their individual experiences are often misunderstood as the majority opinion.

This can cause many minority students to feel self-conscious in the classroom and prevent them from actively participating in classroom discussions. Some students even feel singled out because of their race, and labeled as intellectually inferior. While some of the stereotyping comes from professors, in actuality, most of it comes from his fellow classmates.

"I do feel uncomfortable in certain classes where I'm the only minority and everybody looks at me. When I speak everyone listens—It's like 'Oh the minority is speaking, everybody listen,'" said Ruiz.

One of the obstacles to combating these incidents is they frequently go unreported and unnoticed by the majority of students at Notre Dame.

"There are daily occurrences that happen many of which we don't hear about in the dorm [and] in the classroom that still makes it very clear to me that we have a lot of work to do," said Iris Outlaw Director of Multicultural Student Programs and Services (MSPS). "Students who are historical minorities continue to struggle with being in predominately majority communities," said Outlaw.

While Outlaw said most minorities are strong enough to survive and to break through the barriers of daily prejudices, some students are not. Negative experiences that penetrate the African-American community are not only harmful to currently enrolled minority students, but may deter potential prospects from attending the University. If current minority students are not happy with their experience, they are likely to communicate those negative experiences to prospective students.

"The tenor is changing," said Chandra Johnson, co-chair of the University recruitment and retention committee. "But the reason that it is so difficult at this point in time is
because sometimes [African-Americans] expect the University to do our recruiting—how
students come is by word of mouth from those who have gone here.

"Those of us who are African Americans who are alumni here are not recruiting. There
are some who are and who work very hard at it, but there is a lot more that needs to be
done. And until the experience is enhanced, then it's difficult to even invite people to want
to follow after us," said Johnson.

Struggling to Stay

The University may find it difficult to recruit when many African-American students are
leaving the University after enrolling freshman year.

The number of African-American students who leave after sophomore year is alarming
to some University officials who say that financial strain and academics may be key proponents in low student return rates rather than social maladjustment problems. In a given
year, up to 16 percent of African-American students leave the University before the start
of the junior year, while up to 4 percent of majority students leave the University.

"Sometimes students come to Notre Dame and their financial aid packages change and
some of them get overwhelmed with a cost that they just can't pay," said Outlaw.

Another reason that may contribute to students not returning is the breadth of academic progress.

"For some students of color their first year is really their roughest year and it's not a
reflection of their intelligence," Outlaw said. "When they come here they may not have a
strong enough background for some of the courses that all first year [students] have to take."

While Outlaw cited financial and academic difficulties as the major reasons that lead up
to a student's discontinuation of their education at Notre Dame, Outlaw said the feeling of
isolation is another factor.

"Sometimes students in historical minorities are caught between which group to be a
part of," Outlaw said. "What happens is when they don't form a community around themselves, the isolation factor is so deep and so inculcated that it affects everything—G.P.A.,
one's ability to concentrate, one's ability to be sociable, one's ability to just exist," said
Outlaw.

Making the Experience Worthwhile

While some experiences demonstrate [that] racial discrimination is apparent on campus,
other African-American students feel the climate at Notre Dame is accepting. Sophomore
Nikki McCord, a member of the University committee for retention and recruitment, said
her experiences were generally positive.

"I like the climate here on campus, and the main reason is because I have been able to
get involved in different types of activities," said McCord.

By initiating contact with all students, regardless of race, McCord said that the Notre Dame experience is dependent on the actions a student takes to build her/his own personal experiences.

"One thing that separates Notre Dame from any other school is the people that we accept—and we accept very educated, broad-minded people," McCord said. "Because of that, I think that helps people to be accepting of different cultures and different ethnicities."

Finding visible African-American role models on campus can be problematic for students seeking to identify with others in their racial group. A recent trend of minority leadership on Notre Dame's campus is beginning to provide more role models for African-American students.

African-American students in the community have other prominent figures who they can relate to like leprechaun Michael Brown (Notre Dame's official mascot), Steven Smith, president of the glee club, and Tambre Paster, a drum major in the Notre Dame marching band. Johnson thinks that more African-American students will consider applying to Notre Dame because of this leadership trend.

"We've had some wonderful icons at the University and prospects are going to go up," said Johnson.

The overall percentage of African-Americans remains at a low 3.2 percent, and minority students struggle to find others who share similar interests and experiences.

"I wish [there] were more African-American people here, but I don't know if it's just not a lot of African-Americans applying here to get in, or if the University is not accepting them because their credentials aren't good enough," said Charles Thomas, an African-American player on the men's basketball team. "I think [there] could be more here, but I don't know what they could do to increase it."

Recent efforts have been made to create a more open environment for African-Americans on campus. These efforts will hopefully take steps to improve minority visibility and to make the campus climate more accepting.

In the last three years the University has made an institutional mandate to establish programs to facilitate the development of African-American cultural identity and increase the number of role models and icons. The development of various programs shows that the University is taking measures to expand the minority community at Notre Dame.

"Within the last three years the University has grown in leaps and bounds to make it an institutional mandate in perceptions," said Johnson.

Another change is the institution of a mandatory diversity education program. The program, offered by the office of student affairs to freshmen, is a peer coordinated program that promotes discussion on the cultural diverse aspects of the University.

Programs such as these generate an open dialogue between not only minority students, but also all students on campus. The first two years of this program have been successful, Outlaw said.

"[F]or two years now we've had a mandatory diversity workshop that all first year students have to attend this is another step forward in trying to provide a welcoming environment for not only under-represented groups, and students of color, but [also] for those students who possibly may be gay or lesbian," said Outlaw.

For students like Parks, the experience of racial tension on campus is an opportunity to bring about discussion and change. As a result of an anthropology grant, Parks is studying minority educational inequality in predominantly white post-secondary institutions like Notre Dame.

"When I got to the heart of things, it was basically about my experience at Notre Dame," said Parks. "I can say I have had an equal amount of both positive and negative [experiences], but the intensity of the negatives that I have experienced propelled me to help others."

After Reading

Critical Perspective

1. Consider the experiences shared by Patrick Parks, Thomas Gilbert, and Justin Ruiz. What do these men's stories help Turner to claim about identity issues on college campuses? Give textual evidence to back up your assertions.

Rhetoric and Argument

2. What kinds of rhetorical appeals does Turner make in his text? Provide textual examples of his audience, purpose, ethos, pathos, and logos. Do you find these appeals persuasive? Why or why not? Which of the three appeals seems the strongest?
3. Turner mentions that many African American students leave Notre Dame after their sophomore year. What evidence does he provide for why this is the case? Are there other reasons for why students may be leaving that Turner does not mention? Provide quotes to support your views.
4. What solutions does Turner provide to the problems of stereotyping that his essay investigates? Do you find these solutions persuasive? In what ways are they possible? What problems might they pose? Give examples from his text to back up your ideas.

Analysis

5. Think about Turner's essay—his claims, support, and warrants. Write a short argumentative text about whether you agree with them or not. Explain your position in detail. Do you believe that his text exhibits any bias or logical fallacies? Offer quotes from the text as well as library and Internet sources to support your thoughts.

Taking Action

Turner's essay raises concerns about identity and stereotyping that have relevance for all students. Write a short draft of an article for your school newspaper in which you advance your own argument about how to change various forms of stereotyping on the college campus related to race and ethnicity, class, gender, sexual preference, language, politics, disability, age, region, and/or religion. Include detailed interviews from various members of the college campus—students, teachers, and administrators—to support your views.

Then make copies of each class member's draft, create a book out of them, and share them with the rest of the class. After you have all read through the book, have a discussion about which essays surprised you, disturbed you, or taught you the most. Consider revising the essays with your peers' and teachers' feedback and then creating a more polished version of the book by the end of the course.

MELISSA ALGRANATI

"Being an Other"

Melissa Algranati is a graduate of the State University of New York at Binghamton and has a master's degree from Columbia University. Her work has been published in Thomas Dublin's Becoming American, Becoming Ethnic: College Students Explore Their Roots.

EXERCISING YOUR SKILLS

Before Reading

Algranati's essay describes her experiences not fitting easily into any particular identity category. She has a long yet accurate way to describe her identity—a "Puerto Rican, Egyptian Jew." Why do you think that it might be important to characterize one's identity using this detailed language? What experiences have you had (or, actions have you taken) that undermined, stretched, or challenged the identity categories to which you belong: your understanding of your own race and ethnicity, class, gender, sexual preference, language, politics, abilities, age, region, and/or religion? How did the people around you respond? Why do you think they acted in this way? How did this make you feel?

Throughout my whole life, people have mistaken me for other ethnic backgrounds rather than for what I really am. I learned at a young age that there are not too many Puerto Rican, Egyptian Jews out there. For most of my life I have been living in two worlds, and at the same time I have been living in neither. When I was young I did not realize that I was unique, because my family brought me up with a healthy balance of Puerto Rican and Sephardic customs. It was not until I took the standardized PSAT exam that I was confronted with the question: "Who am I?" I remember the feeling of confusion as I struggled to find the right answer. I was faced with a bad multiple-choice question in which there was only supposed to be one right answer, but more than one answer seemed to be correct. I did not understand how a country built on the concept of diversity could forget about its most diverse group, inter-ethnic children. I felt lost in a world of classification. The only way for me to take pride in who I am was to proclaim myself as an other, yet that leaves out so much. As a product of a marriage only a country like America could create, I would now try to help people understand what it is like to be a member of the most underrepresented group in the country, the "others."

My father, Jacques Algranati, was born in Alexandria, Egypt. As a Sephardic Jew, my father was a minority in a predominantly Arab world. Although in the minority, socially my father was a member of the upper middle class and lived a very comfortable life. As a result of strong French influence in the Middle Eastern Jewish world, my father attended a French private school. Since Arabic was the language of the lower class, the Algranati family spoke French as their first language. My whole family is polyglot, speaking languages from the traditional Sephardic tongue of Ladino to Turkish and Greek. My grandfather spoke seven languages. Basically, my father grew up in a close-knit Sephardic community surrounded by family and friends.

However, in 1960 my father's world came to a halt when he was faced with persecution on an institutional level. As a result of the Egyptian-Israeli conflict, in 1956 an edict was issued forcing all foreign-born citizens and Jews out of Egypt. Although my father was a native-born citizen of the country, because of a very strong anti-Jewish sentiment, his citizenship meant nothing. So in 1960 when my family got their exit visas, as Jews had done since the time of the Inquisition, they packed up and left the country as one large family group.

Unable to take many possessions or much money with them, my father's family, like many Egyptian Jews, immigrated to France. They proceeded to France because they had family who were able to sponsor them. Also, once in France my family hoped to be able to receive a visa to America much sooner, since French immigration quotas to the United States were much higher than those in Egypt. Once in France my family relied on the generosity of a Jewish organization, the United Jewish Appeal. For nine months my father lived in a hotel sponsored by the United Jewish Appeal and attended French school until the family was granted a visa to the United States.

Since my father's oldest brother came to the United States first with his wife, they were able to sponsor the rest of the family's passage over. The Algranati family eventually settled in Forest Hills, Queens. Like most immigrants, my family settled in a neighborhood filled with immigrants of the same background. Once in the United States, my father rejoined many of his old friends from Egypt, since most Egyptian Jewish refugees followed a similar immigration path. At the age of fourteen my father and his group of friends were once again forced to adjust to life in a new country, but this time they had to learn a new language in order to survive. Like many of his friends, my father was forced to leave the comforts and luxuries of his world for the hardships of a new world. But as he eloquently puts it, once his family and friends were forced to leave, there was really nothing to stay for.

Like my father, my mother is also an immigrant; however my parents come from very different parts of the world. Born in Maniti, Puerto Rico, my mom spent the first five years of her life in a small town outside of San Juan. Since my grandfather had attended private school in the United States when he was younger, he was relatively proficient in English.

Like many immigrants, my grandfather came to the United States first, in order to help establish the family. After securing a job and an apartment, he sent for my grandmother, and three weeks later my mother and her fourteen-year-old sister came.

Puerto Ricans are different from many other people who come to this country, in the sense that legally they are not considered immigrants. Because Puerto Rico is a commonwealth of the United States, Puerto Ricans are granted automatic U.S. citizenship. So unlike most, from the day my mother and her family stepped on U.S. soil they were considered citizens. The only problem was that the difference in language and social status led "real" Americans not to consider them citizens.

As a result of this unique status, my mother faced many hardships in this new country. From the day my mother entered first grade her process of Americanization had begun. Her identity was transformed. She went from being Maria Louisa Pinto to becoming Mary L. Pinto. Not only was my mother given a new name when she began school, but a new language was forced upon her as well. Confronted by an Irish teacher, Mrs. Walsh, who was determined to Americanize her, my mother began her uphill battle with the English language. Even until this day my mother recalls her traumatic experience when she learned how to pronounce the word "run":

"Repeat after me, run."
"Rrrrrrrrrun."
"No, Mary, run."
"Rrrrrrrrrun."

No matter how hard my mother tried she could not stop rolling her "r's." After several similar exchanges Mrs. Walsh, with a look of anger on her face, grabbed my mother's cheeks in her hand and squeezed as she repeated in a stern voice, "RUN!" Suffice it to say my mother learned how to speak English without a Spanish accent. It was because of these experiences that my mother made sure the only language spoken in the house or to me and my sister was English. My parents never wanted their children to experience the pain my mother went through just to learn how to say the word "run."

My mother was confronted with discrimination not only from American society but also from her community. While in the United States, my mother lived in a predominantly Spanish community. On first coming to this country her family lived in a tenement in the Bronx. At the age of twelve my mother was once more uprooted and moved to the projects on the Lower East Side. As one of the first families in a predominantly Jewish building, it was a step up for her family.

It was not her environment that posed the biggest conflict for her; it was her appearance. My mother is what people call a "white Hispanic." With her blond hair and blue eyes my mother was taken for everything but a Puerto Rican. Once my mother perfected her English, no one suspected her ethnicity unless she told them. Since she was raised to be above the ghetto, never picking up typical "Hispanic mannerisms," she was able to exist in American society with very little difficulty. Because of a very strong and protective mother and the positive influence and assistance received from the Henry Street Settlement, my mother was able to escape the ghetto. As a result of organizations like Henry Street, my mother was given opportunities such as fresh air camps and jobs in good areas of the city, where she was able to rise above the drugs, alcohol, and violence that consumed so many of her peers.

As a result of her appearance and her upbringing, my mother left her people and the ghetto to enter American society. It was here as an attractive "white" female that my mother and father's two very different worlds merged. My parents, both working on Wall Street at the time, were introduced by a mutual friend. Since both had developed a rather liberal view, the differences in their backgrounds did not seem to be a major factor. After a year of dating my parents decided to get engaged.

Although they were from two different worlds, their engagement seemed to bring them together. Growing up in the midst of the Jewish community of the Lower East Side, my mother was constantly influenced by the beauty of Judaism. Therefore, since my mother never had much connection with Catholicism and had never been baptized, she decided to convert to Judaism and raise her children as Jews. The beauty of the conversion was that no one in my father's family forced her to convert; they accepted her whether she converted or not. As for my mother's family, they too had no real objections to the wedding or conversion. To them the only thing that mattered was that my father was a nice guy who made my mom happy. The most amusing part of the union of these two different families came when they tried to communicate. My father's family is descended from Spanish Jewry where many of them spoke an old Castilian-style Spanish, while my mother's family spoke a very modern Caribbean-style Spanish. To watch them try to communicate in any language other than English was like watching a session of the United Nations.

It was this new world, that of Puerto Rican Jewry, my parents created for me and my sister, Danielle. Resembling both my parents, having my mother's coloring with my father's features, I have often been mistaken for various ethnicities. Possessing light hair and blue eyes, I am generally perceived as the "all-American" girl. Occasionally I have been mistaken for Italian since my last name, Algranati, although Sephardic, has a very Italian flair to it. I have basically lived a chameleon-like existence for most of my life.

As a result of my "otherness," I have gained "acceptance" in many different crowds. From this acceptance I have learned the harsh reality behind my "otherness." I will never forget the time I learned about how the parents of one of my Asian friends perceived me. From very early on, I gained acceptance with the parents of one of my Korean friends. Not only did they respect me as a person and a student, but her father even went so far as to consider me like "one of his daughters." I will always remember how I felt when I heard they made one of their daughters cancel a party because she had invited Hispanics. Even when my friend pointed out that I, the one they loved, was Hispanic they refused to accept it. Even today to them, I will always be Jewish and not Puerto Rican because to them it is unacceptable to "love" a Puerto Rican.

Regardless of community, Jewish or Puerto Rican, I am always confronted by bigots. Often I am forced to sit in silence while friends utter in ignorance stereotypical responses like: "It was probably some spic who stole it," or "You're just like a Jew, always cheap."

For the past three years I have worked on the Lower East Side of Manhattan at the Henry Street Settlement. Basically my mother wanted me to support the organization that helped her get out of the ghetto. Unlike when my mother was there, the population is mostly black and Hispanic. So one day during work I had one of my fellow workers say to me "that is such a collegian white thing to say." I responded by saying that his assumption was only partially correct and asked him if he considered Puerto Rican to be white. Of course he doubted I was any part Hispanic until he met my cousin who "looks" Puerto Rican. At times like these I really feel for my mother, because I know how it feels not to be recognized by society for who you are.

Throughout my life I do not think I have really felt completely a part of any group. I have gone through phases of hanging out with different crowds trying in a sense to find myself. Basically, I have kept my life diverse by attending both Catholic-sponsored camps and Hebrew school at the same time. Similar to my parents, my main goal is to live within American society. I choose my battles carefully. By being diverse I have learned that in a society that is obsessed with classification the only way I will find my place is within myself. Unfortunately, society has not come to terms with a fast-growing population, the "others." Therefore when asked the infamous question: "Who are you?" I respond with a smile, "a Puerto Rican Egyptian Jew." Contrary to what society may think, I am somebody.

After Reading

Critical Perspective

1. What specific sorts of difficulties—particularly stereotypes about their respective cultures—did Algranati's parents have to overcome and work against in order to be accepted by mainstream American culture? To what degree were they successful, do you think? Do you think that this is a worthy goal? Why or why not?

Rhetoric and Argument

2. Discuss Algranati's use of various rhetorical tactics: audience, purpose, ethos, pathos, logos, intertextuality, context, and constraints. Do you think her rhetorical strategies are persuasive? Give quotes to back up your position.
3. Characterize how Algranati begins her essay. Do you believe that this is an effective approach given her topic? Why or why not?
4. What main claim does Algranati make in this text? Where exactly does this claim appear? In what ways does this text adhere to standard modes of argumentative organization and what ways does it deviate?
5. Describe the kinds of evidence that Algranati utilizes to substantiate her main assertion. What sort of evidence is it? Do you find this kind of evidence persuasive given her claim? Point to the text to back up your perspectives.
6. What kinds of warrants or assumptions does Algranati make in her text? Do you find them plausible? Why or why not?

Analysis

7. In a short argumentative response, address the different sorts of difficulties Algranati has encountered because of her inter-ethnic or mixed-race heritage. What does she claim about this heritage as a result? What do you think about this assertion? Be sure to support your analyses with quotes from the text as well as library and Internet sources.

Taking Action

Reread Algranati's essay, looking carefully at when she is confronted by a fellow coworker who tells her "that is such a collegian white thing to say." At this moment Algranati's body is falsely being read as "white." This person is making many assumptions about Algranati's beliefs, her ethnic heritage, her values, and her ideals.

Meet in a small group. Address the following questions: Think back upon your own experiences. When has your body (your dress, habits, attitudes, or the like) been read inaccurately by others? In what context or contexts did this occur? Explain the circumstances, your reactions, as well as the others' response. Why do you think that this happened? What did these experiences reveal about you and the others who misperceived you? What do your experiences indicate about American culture and appearances?

Describe and define the "collegian white" attitude as you have experienced it in your own life. What values, beliefs, anxieties, mannerisms, and behaviors distinguish it from other attitudes one might have? What kinds of dress, styles, and tastes are associated with it? In what ways do you adhere to it, and in what ways do you deviate from it? Be sure to provide evidence from library and Internet sources as well as your own experiences. Share your findings with the rest of the class.

Olivia Chung

"Finding My Eye-dentity"

Olivia Chung is an undergraduate student at the University of Pennsylvania where she does activist work, writes, and listens to hip-hop music. She is from a second-generation Korean American family and is originally from Silver Spring, Maryland.

EXERCISING YOUR SKILLS

Before Reading

Chung writes about her identity as an Asian American student who grew up in Spring Silver, Maryland. In this essay she describes how people in her family and cultural background sometimes act as if it's necessary to change their physical appearance in order to better fit into mainstream American culture.

How do you define what it means to be an "American"? Can you think of ways in which people you know (you, your friends, your family) act, dress, behave, and so on, in order to better fit into the images of "Americanness"? What are some other ways in which people alter their appearances to more fully conform to America's gender, race, class, ethnic or other stereotypes and standards?

Olivia, you wanna get sang ka pul?

I'm driving my mother to work, when she randomly brings up the eyelid question. The question that almost every Korean monoeyelidded girl has had to face in her life. The question that could change the future of my naturally noncreased eyelids, making them crease with the cut of a cosmetic surgeon's knife.

You know your aunt? She used to have beany eyes just like you! She used to put on white and black eyeliner every morning to make them look BIG. Then she went to Korea and got the surgery done. Now look! She looks so much better! Don't you want it done? I would do it. . . .

I think this is about the 346,983,476th time she has brought this topic up. Using the exact same words. You would look so much more prettier with bigger eyes! she says. *You know, because they look kind of squinty and on top of that you have an underbite, so you look really mean. . . .* She explains while narrowing her eyes and jutting out her jaw in emphasis of her point.

A couple of years ago, I would have taken her suggestion seriously. I remember reading a section of *Seventeen* magazine, where the once-did-funky-makeup-for-100-anorexic-white-girls-on-runways beauty expert revealed the secret to applying eye makeup. As a desperate preteen girl seeking beauty advice, I remember it perfectly. Put dark shadow right over the eyelashes, light powder all over, medium shadow over the edge of the crease of your eyelid. That's where I always tripped up. Crease? Umm . . . excuse me? These so-called beauty experts never gave me enough expertise to figure out how to put makeup on my face without looking like a character in a kabuki play. I tried to follow the beauty experts' advice. But I decided it wasn't working when people asked me if I had gotten a black eye.

My friends suggested training my eyelids to fold with tape. *My mother did that and now she has a real crease, one of my friends told me.* I, however, never learned the magic behind that, and always felt too embarrassed to ask. Another friend once excitedly showed me how she had bought a bottle of make-your-own-eye-crease glue from Korea. I let her try it on me too. I could barely open my eyes, thanks to the fierce stinging sensation resulting from the glue that got on my eyeball. And when I finally did take a quick glimpse of myself in the mirror, I saw a stranger with uneven eyelids.

The first time I remember being insulted was when I was little. . . .

In kindergarten, I believe. Oh, it was classic. A little blond kid pulled the edges of his eyes out, yelling, *Ching chong chinaman!* I, being new to this game, could only make a weak comeback. *I'm not Chinese . . . I'm KOREAN.* I remember feeling confused and hurt, realizing that I looked different and not understanding why being different was bad.

Couldn't we all just get along? I had learned that God loves people as they are, as different as they are. I learned that He looks at the heart, and that it really doesn't matter how a person looks. I think my belief in this, combined with my fear of a sharp object cutting the skin above my eye, kept me away from the *sang ka pul* surgery. Yet, I continued to receive comments on my "chinky" eyes, and I always emerged from these situations feeling confused and angry . . . without ever really knowing why. Why couldn't I be accepted with my so-called chinky eyes? Why in the world were they even called "chinky" eyes? If they meant to insult Chinese, all the Chinese people I knew had huge eyes. With the crease.

As I grew older, the childish "ching chong"s came with less frequency. Still, the magazines continue to give me unhelpful directions on how to apply makeup. Still, I witness my own friends getting the surgery done in an effort to be "more beautiful." Still, my mother continuously confronts me with the dreaded eyelid question. *You wanna get* sang ka pul? I always answer her with an *are-you-crazy?* but simple *no*. All the things I wish I could have told her come flowing on this page with my pen. . . .

Umma, my mother, don't you see that my noncreased eyes are beautiful? Asian eyes are beautiful. Your eyes are beautiful. My eyes are beautiful. Asian is beautiful. After all these years of wanting to open up my eyes with tape and glue and surgery, I have opened up my eyes to a different definition of beauty. A broader definition of beauty, one that embraces differences and includes every girl, who can hold her head up, *sang ka pul*-less and chinky-eyed, because being *Asian is beautiful*.

After Reading

Critical Perspective

1. Describe Chung's use of tone in this piece. Where does she convey this tone, and is it effective in making her point? What emotions does this essay evoke in you? Which specific images and word choices does Chung employ in order to make you feel these feelings?

Rhetoric and Argument

2. Chung utilizes italics throughout her essay to convey different voices that she is using. What are the rhetorical effects of making this choice? Do you find this effective? Why or why not? Also examine Chung's use of audience, purpose, ethos, pathos, logos, intertextuality, context, and constraints.
3. Chung employs a somewhat unconventional structure in order to make her argument. Do you find this structure persuasive? What is her main claim and how does she support it? Be sure to quote from the text to support your position.
4. Examine contemporary media images of Asian Americans in advertisements in television, and film. Which images effectively open our eyes "to a different definition of beauty," as Chung has done? Which images reproduce notions about beauty that do not support and celebrate ethnic and racial differences?

Analysis

5. Write a short argumentative essay in which you answer the following questions: Do you think that all women are subject to particular standards of beauty in Amer-

ican culture? If yes, what are they? What struggles do women from various backgrounds face in trying to live up to these standards? Be sure to provide evidence from the essay as well as library and Internet sources to support your claims.

Taking Action

Form a small group. Look through a series of women's magazines for advertisements for beauty products. Select a wide range that depict women from various backgrounds. What rhetorical features do these ads utilize? What images of beauty do these ads convey to women? What other images of beauty are missing?

Then discuss similarities and differences in the ads that you have selected. Come up with answers to the following questions: How do these ads use context, purpose, composition, constraints, intertexuality, cultural codes, as well as rhetorical appeals (ethos, pathos, logos)? What claims about women, sexuality, race and ethnicity, class status, as well as beauty do these ads seem to advance? What do you think about this? Include library and Internet sources to support your views.

After you have answered these questions, work together in your small group to construct your own ad for a woman's beauty care product that provides a different definition of beauty in order to sell its product. Share with the rest of the class why you made the rhetorical choices in your ad that you made, what new definitions of beauty you are trying to convey in your ad, and how you think beauty should be represented differently in future ad campaigns.

WORK

SARAH ANDERSON

"Wal-Mart's War on Main Street"

Sarah Anderson is a writer for The Progressive. *She has also been a fellow of the Institute for Policy Studies and the director of the Global Economy Project at the Institute for Policy Studies in Washington, DC. She is also the coauthor (with John Cavanagh and Thea Lee) of* Field Guide to the Global Economy.

EXERCISING YOUR SKILLS

Before Reading

Anderson reveals her own experiences with her family's business, Wal-Mart, and small town life. Make a list of large companies, not locally owned businesses, that can be found around the country. How is the arrival of large chain stores in small towns is impacting these communities' economic livelihoods negatively? Have you witnessed any of this firsthand? If yes, where and how? On the other hand, in what ways has the presence of these stores impacted communities positively? Make a list of both the potential negative and positive effects specific big businesses and corporations can have on communities, the people who live there, and people's habits and behaviors. As you consider these issues, also list some of the concerns as well as potentially positive possibilities such businesses might offer for other countries—where many of the goods are now made.

The basement of Boyd's for Boys and Girls in downtown Litchfield, Minnesota, looks like a history museum of the worst in children's fashions. All the real duds from the past forty years have accumulated down there: wool pedal-pushers, polyester bell-bottoms, wide clip-on neckties. There's a big box of 1960s faux fur hats, the kind with the fur pompon ties that dangle under a girl's chin. My father, Boyd Anderson, drags all the old stuff up the stairs and onto the sidewalk once a year on Krazy Daze. At the end of the day, he lugs most of it back down. Folks around here don't go in much for the retro look.

At least for now, the museum is only in the basement. Upstairs, Dad continues to run one of the few remaining independent children's clothing stores on Main Street, USA. But this is the age of Wal-Mart, not Main Street. For every Wal-Mart opening, there is more than one store like Boyd's that closes its doors.

Litchfield, a town of 6,200 people sixty miles west of Minneapolis, started losing Main Street businesses at the onset of the farm crisis and the shopping-mall boom of the early 1980s. As a high-school student during this time, I remember dinner-table conversation drifting time and again toward rumors of store closings. In those days, Mom frequently cut the conversation off short. "Let's talk about something less depressing, okay?" Now my family can no longer avoid the issue of Main Street Litchfield's precarious future. Dad, at sixty-eight, stands at a crossroads. Should he retain his faith in Main Street and pass Boyd's down to his children? Or should he listen to the pessimists and close up the forty-one-year-old family business before it becomes obsolete?

For several years, Dad has been reluctant to choose either path. The transition to retirement is difficult for most people who have worked hard all their lives. For him, it could signify not only the end of a working career, but also the end of small-town life as he knows it. When pressed, Dad admits that business on Main Street has been going downhill for the past fifteen years. "I just can't visualize what the future for downtown Litchfield will be," he says. "I've laid awake nights worrying about it because I really don't want my kids to be stuck with a business that will fail."

I am not the aspiring heir to Boyd's. I left Litchfield at eighteen for the big city and would have a rough time readjusting to small-town life. My sister Laurie, a nurse, and my sister-in-law Colleen, who runs a farm with my brother Scott, are the ones eager to enter the ring and fight the retail Goliaths. Both women are well suited to the challenge. Between them, they have seven children who will give them excellent tips on kids' fashions. They are deeply rooted in the community and idealistic enough to believe that Main Street can survive.

My sisters are not alone. Across the country, thousands of rural people are battling to save their local downtowns. Many of these fights have taken the form of anti-Wal-Mart campaigns. In Vermont, citizens' groups allowed Wal-Mart to enter the state only after the company agreed to a long list of demands regarding the size and operation of the stores.

Three Massachusetts towns and another in Maine have defeated bids by Wal-Mart to build in their communities. In Arkansas, three independent drugstore owners won a suit charging that Wal-Mart had used "predatory pricing," or selling below cost, to drive out competitors. Canadian citizens are asking Wal-Mart to sign a "Pledge of Corporate Responsibility" before opening in their towns. In at least a dozen other U.S. communities, groups have fought to keep Wal-Mart out or to restrict the firm's activities.

By attacking Wal-Mart, these campaigns have helped raise awareness of the value of locally owned independent stores on Main Street. Their concerns generally fall in five areas:

- Sprawl Mart—Wal-Mart nearly always builds along a highway outside town to take advantage of cheap, often unzoned land. This usually attracts additional commercial development, forcing the community to extend services (telephone and power lines, water and sewage services, and so forth) to that area, despite sufficient existing infrastructure downtown.
- Wal-Mart channels resources out of a community—studies have shown that a dollar spent on a local business has four or five times the economic spin-off of a dollar spent at a Wal-Mart, since a large share of Wal-Mart's profit returns to its Arkansas headquarters or is pumped into national advertising campaigns.
- Wal-Mart destroys jobs in locally owned stores—a Wal-Mart-funded community impact study debunked the retailer's claim that it would create a lot of jobs in Greenfield, Massachusetts. Although Wal-Mart planned to hire 274 people at its Greenfield store, the community could expect to gain only eight net jobs, because of projected losses at other businesses that would have to compete with Wal-Mart.
- Citizen Wal-Mart?—in at least one town—Hearne, Texas—Wal-Mart destroyed its Main Street competitors and then deserted the town in search of higher returns elsewhere. Unable to attract new businesses to the devastated Main Street, local residents have no choice but to drive long distances to buy basic goods.
- One-stop shopping culture—in Greenfield, where citizens voted to keep Wal-Mart out, anti-Wal-Mart campaign manager Al Norman said he saw a resurgence of appreciation for Main Street. "People realized there's one thing you can't buy at Wal-Mart, and that's small-town quality of life," Norman explains. "This community decided it was not ready to die for a cheap pair of underwear."

So far Litchfield hasn't been forced to make that decision. Nevertheless, the town is already losing at least some business to four nearby Wal-Marts, each less than forty miles from town. To find out how formidable this enemy is, Mom and I went on a spying mission to the closest Wal-Mart, twenty miles away in Hutchinson.

Just inside the door, we were met by a so-called Wal-Mart "greeter" (actually the greeters just say hello as they take your bags to prevent you from shoplifting). We realized we knew her. Before becoming a greeter, she had been a cashier at a downtown Litchfield supermarket until it closed early this year. I tried to be casual when I asked if she greets many people from Litchfield. "Oh, a-a-a-ll the time!" she replied. Sure enough, Mom immediately spotted one in the checkout line.

Not wanting to look too suspicious, we moved on toward the children's department, where we discreetly examined price tags and labels. Not all, but many items were cheaper than at Boyd's. It was the brainwashing campaign that we found most intimidating, though. Throughout the store were huge red, white, and blue banners declaring BRING IT HOME TO AMERICA. Confusingly, the labels on the children's clothing indicated that they had been imported from sixteen countries, including Haiti, where an embargo on exports was supposed to be in place.

Of course, Wal-Mart is not Main Street's only foe. Over coffee at the Main Street Cafe, some of Litchfield's long-time merchants gave me a litany of additional complaints. Like my dad, many of these men remember when three-block-long Main Street was a bustling social and commercial hub, with two movie theaters, six restaurants, a department store, and a grand old hotel.

Present-day Litchfield is not a ghost town, but there are four empty storefronts, and several former commercial buildings now house offices for government service agencies. In recent years, the downtown has lost its last two drugstores and two supermarkets. As a result, elderly people who live downtown and are unable to drive can no longer do their own shopping.

My dad and the other merchants place as much blame for this decline on cut-throat suppliers as on Wal-Mart. The big brand names, especially, have no time anymore for small clients. Don Brock, who ran a furniture store for thirty-three years before retiring in 1991, remembers getting an honorary plaque from a manufacturer whose products he carried for many years. "Six months later I got a letter saying they were no longer going to fill my orders."

At the moment, Litchfield's most pressing threat is a transportation department plan to reroute the state highway that now runs down Main Street to the outskirts of town. Local merchants fear the bypass would kill the considerable business they now get from travelers. Bypasses are also magnets for Wal-Mart and other discounters attracted to the large, cheap, and often unzoned sites along the bypass.

When I asked the merchants how they felt about the bypass, the table grew quiet. Greg Heath, a florist and antique dealer, sighed and said, "The bypass will come—it might be ten years from now, but it will come. By then, we'll either be out of business or the bypass will drive us out."

The struggles of Main Street merchants have naturally created a growth industry in consultants ready to provide tips on marketing and customer relations. Community-development experts caution, though, that individual merchants acting on their own cannot keep Main Street strong. "Given the enormous forces of change, the only way these businesses can survive is with active public and government support," says Dawn Nakano, of the National Center for Economic Alternatives in Washington, D.C.

Some of the most effective efforts at revitalization, Nakano says, are community development corporations—private, nonprofit corporations governed by a community-based board and usually funded in part by foundation and government money. In Pittsburgh, for example, the city government and about thirty nonprofit groups formed a community development corporation to save an impoverished neighborhood where all but three businesses were boarded up. Today, thanks to such financing and technical assistance, the area has a lively shopping district.

Although most community development corporations have been created to serve low-income urban neighborhoods, Nakano feels that they could be equally effective in saving Main Streets. "There's no reason why church, civic, and other groups in a small town couldn't form a community development corporation to fill boarded-up stores with new businesses. Besides revitalizing Main Street, this could go a long way toward cultivating a 'buy local' culture among residents."

The National Main Street Center, a Washington, D.C.–based nonprofit, provides some of the most comprehensive Main Street revitalization services. The Center has helped more than 850 towns build cooperative links among merchants, government, and citizens. However, the Center's efforts focus on improving marketing techniques and the physical appearance of stores, which can only do so much to counter the powerful forces of change.

No matter how well designed, any Main Street revitalization project will fail without local public support. Unfortunately, it is difficult for many rural people to consider the long-term, overall effects of their purchases, given the high levels of rural unemployment, job insecurity, and poverty. If you're worried about paying your rent, you're not going to pay more for a toaster at your local hardware store, no matter how much you like your hometown.

Another problem is political. Like those in decaying urban neighborhoods, many rural people have seen the signs of decline around them and concluded that they lack the clout necessary to harness the forces of change for their own benefit. If you've seen your neighbors lose their farms through foreclosure, your school close down, and local manufacturing move to Mexico, how empowered will you feel?

Litchfield Mayor Ron Ebnet has done his best to bolster community confidence and loyalty to Main Street. "Every year at the Christmas lighting ceremony, I tell people to buy their gifts in town. I know everyone is sick of hearing it, but I don't care." Ebnet has whipped up opposition to the proposed bypass, with strong support from the city council, chamber of commerce, the newspaper editor, and the state senator. He also orchestrated a downtown beautification project and helped the town win a state redevelopment grant to upgrade downtown businesses and residences.

Ebnet has failed to win over everyone, though. Retired merchant Don Larson told me about a local resident who drove forty miles to get something seventeen cents cheaper than he could buy it at the Litchfield lumberyard. "I pointed out that he had spent more on gas than he'd saved, but he told me that 'it was a matter of principle.' I thought, what about the principle of supporting your community? People just don't think about that, though."

Mayor Ebnet agrees, "Many people still have a 1950s mentality," he says. "They can't see the tremendous changes that are affecting these small businesses. People tell me they want the bypass because there's too much traffic downtown and they have a hard time crossing the street. And I ask them, but what will you be crossing to? If we get the bypass, there will be nothing left!"

Last summer, with the threat of the bypass hanging over his head, Dad became increasingly stubborn about making a decision about the store. His antique Underwood typewriter was never more productive, as it banged out angry letters to the state transportation department.

My sisters decided to try a new tactic. While my parents were on vacation, they assaulted the store with paintbrushes and wallpaper, transforming what had been a rather rustic restroom and doing an unprecedented amount of redecorating and rearranging.

The strategy worked. "At first, Dad was a bit shocked," Laurie said. "He commented that in his opinion, the old toilet-paper dispenser had been perfectly fine. But overall he was pleased with the changes, and two days later he called for a meeting with us and our spouses."

"Your dad started out by making a little speech," Colleen said. "The first thing he said was, 'Well, things aren't how they used to be.' Then he pulled out some papers he'd prepared and told us exactly how much sales and profits have been over the years and what we could expect to make. He told us what he thinks are the negative and the positive aspects of the job and then said if we were still interested, we could begin talking about a staffing date for us to take over."

Dad later told me, "The only way I could feel comfortable about Laurie and Colleen running the store is if it was at no financial risk to them. So I'm setting up an account for them to draw from—enough for a one-year trial. But if they can't make a good profit, then that's it—I'll try to sell the business to someone else. I still worry that they don't know what they're getting themselves into. Especially if the bypass goes through, things are going to be rough."

My sisters are optimistic. They plan to form a buying cooperative with Main Street children's clothing stores in other towns and have already drafted a customer survey to help them better understand local needs. "I think we're going to see a big increase in appreciation of the small-town atmosphere," Colleen says. "There are more and more people moving to Litchfield from the Twin Cities to take advantage of the small-town way of life. I think they might even be more inclined to support the local businesses than people who've lived here their whole lives and now take the town for granted."

Small towns cannot return to the past, when families did all their shopping and socializing in their hometown. Rural life is changing and there's no use denying it. The most important question is, who will define the future? Will it be Wal-Mart, whose narrow corporate interests have little to do with building healthy communities? Will it be the department of transportation, whose purpose is to move cars faster? Will it be the banks and suppliers primarily interested in doing business with the big guys? Or will it be the people who live in small towns, whose hard work and support are essential to any effort to revitalize Main Street?

In my hometown, there are at least two new reasons for optimism. First, shortly before my deadline for this article, the Minnesota transportation department announced that it was dropping the Litchfield highway bypass project because of local opposition. (My dad's Underwood will finally get a rest.) The second reason is that a new teal green awning will soon be hanging over the front door of Boyd's—a symbol of one family's belief that Main Street, while weary, is not yet a relic of the past.

After Reading

Critical Perspective

1. How does reading about Anderson's experiences make you react? Have you noticed similar patterns in your own communities?

Rhetoric and Argument

2. In what ways does Anderson establish an ethos for herself as a writer in this text? Where does she accomplish this? Also examine Anderson's use of audience, purpose, ethos, pathos, logos, intertextuality, context, and constraints. Do you think this makes her argument more effective? Offer evidence from the text to support your assertions.

3. Anderson commences her argument somewhat unconventionally. Describe the tactic she uses here and how it appeals to the audience's ethos and pathos. Be sure to give quotes from the text to support your views.

4. What kind of evidence does Anderson present for her claims? Do you find this evidence persuasive? Why or why not? Are there any faulty assumptions or logical fallacies in her text? Point to particular parts of the essay to support your thoughts.

5. Anderson engages in some "research" for this piece. Describe this research in detail. What does Anderson learn from it? Do you think this research aids or hinders her argument?

Analysis

6. In a short essay, reflect upon the following: What kinds of answers does Anderson provide to the problems or questions that she outlines? How do Anderson's questions prompt the reader to offer certain kinds of responses? Do you agree with her thoughts or disagree? What other concerns would you raise? Be sure to consult library and Internet sources.

Taking Action

Form a small group. Spend several hours at a large department store like Wal-Mart, Target, Sears, Mervyns, or JCPenney. Make note of how the store is designed, laid out, how the cashiers operate, and the various kinds of advertising used within the store. You may also want to speak with the people who work there.

Now write an informal essay in which you make an argumentative claim about this store—its floor plan, how the various departments are organized, how the store functions, what the workers do throughout the store and at what times of day, and what this reveals about the cultural functions as well as changes in American businesses and communities. Include library and Internet sources to support your assertions.

Answer the following questions: What specifically does the store do to attract and keep consumers? Is it effective? Why or why not? What potential negative as well as positive possibilities does the store embody? What do you notice about the class status of the people who work and shop there? Why might this be significant? How do the prices of the items compare to other area retailers? What effects might this have on neighboring communities and neighborhood retailers? What do you think about this?

Discuss your research with the class. Consider sharing your work with other groups both inside and outside the campus community.

REBECCA PIIRTO HEATH
"The New Working Class"

Rebecca Piirto Heath is a contributing editor of American Demographics *and a regular contributor to* Marketing Tools. *She is author of* Beyond Mind Games: The Marketing Power of Psychographics. *Heath lives and works as a freelance writer in Rocklin, California.*

EXERCISING YOUR SKILLS

Before Reading

Heath investigates how class status and jobs operate in contemporary American culture. How do you define the term "working class"? Reflect upon whether you can point to images of working class life in advertising, television, film, radio, or the like. What do these images share in common? In what ways are they different? How do such images reflect or fail to capture how class identity operates in people's day-to-day working lives?

As recently as two years ago, leading newspapers were announcing the death of the working class. That obituary now seems premature. Although the structure of the working class is shifting, its spirit is thriving. What's changing is the working-class stereotype of a hard-hatted, blue-collared, middle-aged, white man. As the industrial age becomes more of a dim memory, the image of the group of people who drive the economy is changing, too. Indicators suggest that the working core of Americans is becoming younger, more ethnically diverse, more female, somewhat more educated, and more alienated from its employers.

Trying to pinpoint the precise nature of this shift, however, is a prickly proposition. The difficulty comes from our uniquely American view of class. The common belief on these shores is that America, unlike Europe, is a classless society. We admit to racial, ethnic, gender, and cultural divisions. But to class? Most Americans think of class the same way they think of the British monarchy—something foreign.

Economic indicators show a steady polarization between incomes of the top-earning households and the lowest-income households. Only the richest Americans have seen any real income growth in the last decade. Incomes of the top 5 percent of Americans grew 37 percent between 1984 and 1994, compared with a meager 1 percent increase on the bottom.

Despite this evidence, many Americans find it most comfortable to believe that class divisions, if they exist at all, are minor obstacles. Even supposedly jaded baby-boomer parents still teach their children they can be anything they want to be. Despite growing rumbles of doubt, most of us still believe the old adage that an individual with enough gumption can pull himself up by his bootstraps, especially with a little hard work and a good education.

"No one wants to be working class in America," says Peter Rachleff, professor of history at Macalester College in St. Paul, Minnesota. For those who take issue with that statement, Rachleff asks another question: "When was the last time you saw a U.S. film about the working class?" British films, on the other hand, are full of working-class heroes. "We are bombarded by so much popular culture that tells us continually that this is a middle-class society," says Rachleff.

Michael Moore, author of *Downsize This* and a popular director and producer, has made a name for himself by poking fun at America's "classlessness." *Roger & Me* was a surprise hit documentary about Moore's attempts to track down General Motors CEO Roger Smith to ask him why the company's auto plant in Flint, Michigan, was closing and laying off thousands of loyal longtime workers. Moore says that getting a distributor for his films has always been an uphill battle. "There's something about working-class satire and irony that seems to be missing from our national language," he says.

This lack is ironic in itself, considering the relative novelty of a large middle class in this country. "The middle class didn't even exist until this century," says Moore. So what's behind all this American denial of its working-class roots? "It all started to change after World War II, when working-class people were able to own a home, buy a car or two, take extended summer vacations, and send their kids to college. Once they got some of the trappings of wealth, they got the illusion that they were like the man who lived in the house on the hill," says Moore.

Class in a Classless Society

One reason why many surveys don't reveal the state of the working class is that they don't ask about it. Many definitions of the middle class are based on income. By one definition, the middle class includes households with incomes of $15,000 to $75,000. Such socioeconomic categories rarely include an explicit working-class group.

One survey that does is the General Social Survey (GSS), conducted by the National Opinion Research Center. Since 1972, it has asked Americans to classify themselves as lower, working, middle, or upper class. In 1994, 46 percent of American adults said they were working class, virtually equal to the 47 percent who claimed middle-class status. These proportions have varied little over the past several years.

In an effort to get at the characteristics underlying class affiliation, Mary Jackman, a professor of sociology at the University of California-Davis, and her husband, political scientist Robert Jackman, published *Class Awareness in the United States* in 1986. It was based on a landmark survey conducted by the University of Michigan's Survey Research Center in 1975. The study has been called "the most important study of class identification since Richard Center's 1949 *Psychology of Social Classes.*" The Jackmans intentionally crafted the question to include five class divisions—poor, working, middle, upper-middle and upper. "This way middle was truly in the middle, which is more how people think of it," says Jackman. With this grouping, 8 percent identified with the poor, 37 percent with the working class, 43 percent with the middle class, 8 percent with upper-middle, and 1 percent with the upper class.

The Jackmans went on to analyze why people classified themselves the way they did. They asked them to rate the relative importance of attributes such as income, education, and occupation, as well as lifestyle and attitudes. Topping the list for most people was occupation, followed by education and people's beliefs and feelings. Up to 49 percent rated the kind of family a person came from as not important at all. "It seems that, for most people, social class is a combination of fairly hard-core economic attributes that you can identify pretty quickly and other cultural and expressive attributes that you can't identify quite so quickly—their lifestyles, values and attitudes," says Jackman.

Income turned out to be less valuable a predictor than occupation or education. "Education ends up being so important because it's a piece of social capital that reflects Americans' longterm focus," Jackman says. Occupations also played a role, although a less clear one. "The occupations that caused the most confusion about working- or middle-class status were the upper-level blue-collar jobs or skilled tradesmen," says Jackman. Lower-level clerical jobs also created confusion. But there was no debate over assembly-line workers and seven other solidly blue-collar occupations.

The occupational line is blurring even more today. With more companies downsizing, outsourcing, and turning to temporary workers, some highly qualified workers have been marginalized and are underemployed or working for lower pay and fewer benefits. At the same time, formerly semi-skilled blue-collar jobs demand higher-level skills. Even auto mechanics, a solidly working-class occupation in the 1970s, now require sophisticated knowledge of electronics. "For most functions, you just can't use a mechanic anymore. You really need technicians who can solve problems at a much higher level than in the past," says Myron Nadolski, dean of automotive and technical training at American River College in Sacramento, California.

Today's Working Class

The work force isn't the same as it was 40 years ago. Neither is the working class. Since the Jackmans' study hasn't been updated and the General Social Survey doesn't ask respondents why they label themselves the way they do, differences between working- and middle-class Americans must be inferred by their answers to other questions.

The average age of working- and lower-class Americans is declining, while the age of the middle and upper classes is increasing in line with national trends. On the other hand, the working class has become more average in its gender mix. The proportion of working-class Americans who are female increased from 48 percent in 1974 to 54 percent in 1994. The other classes have been predominantly female all along.

One of the most significant changes in the working class that is also in line with national trends is its increasing racial diversity. Back in the mid-1970s, Jackman found a clear delineation between the races in class attitudes. "You really have to deal separately with blacks and whites because the distribution is so different," Jackman says. This is because, historically, blacks were left out of the economy altogether and have only recently begun to rise into the working and middle classes.

Racial diversity among the lower, working, and, to a lesser extent, middle class is increasing, while the upper class is becoming less racially diverse. Between 1974 and 1994, the proportion of whites who claimed working-class status decreased 9 percent, while the proportion of blacks grew 3 percent and those of other races rose 5 percent. The shift was even more pronounced for the lower class, and somewhat less so for the middle class. Meanwhile, the proportion of whites claiming upper-class status increased, while the proportion of blacks decreased.

The GSS supports the notion that income level plays an unclear role in class identification. In 1994, 74 percent of the working class and 63 percent of the middle class reported household incomes between $15,000 and $74,999. But 10 percent of the upper class also reported making less than $15,000, and 4 percent of the lower class reported making over $50,000 a year.

Educational level is a more reliable indicator that rises steadily with social class, although educational level for all groups has increased. The upper and middle classes still have the preponderance of bachelor's and graduate degrees, but higher degrees are becoming more common among the working class. The proportion of bachelor's degrees held by working-class adults more than doubled between 1974 and 1994, from 4 percent to 10 percent. The proportion of two-year degrees held by working-class respondents increased by 5 percentage points, to 6.5 percent. Two percent of the working class had graduate degrees in 1994.

Similarly, the occupations that make up the working class are less clear-cut. Between 1988 and 1996, the proportion of managers and professionals in the working class increased by 4 percent, to reach 17 percent in 1996. The proportion of technical, sales and administrative workers also rose slightly. Conversely, the proportions of service employees, farm workers, and craft and skilled workers have declined. (It is not possible to compare occupations before 1988 because the classification scheme changed.) In addition, the number of part-time workers has increased across the board, but part-timers remain most prevalent in the lower and working classes.

What does all this mean? Changes in the working class reflect changes in the work environment itself, says David Knoke, professor of sociology at the University of Minnesota, who is currently conducting a panel study of 1,000 work environments around the country to measure shifts in outsourcing, part-time and temporary employment, and cutbacks. "The number of people involved in non-full-time work has quadrupled in the past decade," says Knoke. Up to 30 percent of all U.S. workers are now "contingent" workers—temporaries, part timers, sub-contractors or independent consultants, according to Knoke.

Knoke and colleagues theorize that increased global competition has forced the elimination of companies' internal job markets. "It used to be that if you got a job with IBM out of college, you were set for life," Knoke says. "A series of job ladders was built into the organization that allowed people to count on a slow but steadily rising standard of living."

The likely effect of these shifts on workers is already being seen. "People involved in part-time work have a looser stake in the organization. There's more of a sense of having to fend for themselves," Knoke says. "People see themselves as more working class and having less of a stake in the middle class." Jackman agrees. "I believe there has been a hardening of awareness of class boundaries in the last 10 or 15 years because the situation for American workers has gotten grim, and it's happened so quietly."

The [recent] UPS strike crystallized these issues for American workers, which is one reason why the 180,000 striking teamsters had such overwhelming support from the public. "Workers across the country could identify with the striking UPS workers because they're all feeling the same pinch," says Deborah Dion, AFL-CIO spokesperson.

Union Resurgence?

Not surprisingly, interest in organized labor is one of the attributes most common among the working class. "You can be working class without being a union member, but it's difficult to think of a union member who is not aware of working-class issues," says Rachleff of Macalester College. This relationship is borne out in GSS data. Union membership is one of the clearest delineators between the working and other classes. Although union membership among U.S. workers has fallen across the board, for the last 25 years it has remained highest among those who claim working-class status.

Unions understand the changing structure of the new working class and are targeting somewhat younger, more ethnic, better-educated workers, and different occupations than they did 25 years ago. Coincidentally, just around the time UPS capitulated to strikers' demands for more full-time jobs and a better pension arrangement, the AFL-CIO launched a five-city pilot ad campaign to help boost sagging union membership. More than one-third of all American workers belonged to unions in 1950. By 1997, less than 15 percent of workers (only 10 percent of nongovernment workers) were union members.

A recent AFL-CIO poll found that 44 percent of the general public employed in a nonsupervisory job said they would vote to form a union at their workplace. Another 20 percent were less certain but still positive, saying it was better to join together at a work site to solve problems. "That 20 percent is made up of the same people we're trying to reach with our campaign—minority groups, young people, and women," says Dion.

The ads are four personal stories from real union members. Mike, a construction worker, represents the traditional white, male, blue-collar core of the membership, but with a twist—he's young. A young black nurse named Arthereane talks about her love of helping children and her conviction that hospitals run best when they're run by doctors and nurses, not the profit motive. Erin, a working mother, balances family and her job as a chef with the help of her union. Michael, a worker at a Harley-Davidson plant, sings the union's praises for keeping the company from closing the plant, and making jobs more secure and the company more profitable. The tag line is: "You have a voice, make it heard; today's unions."

"These issues are the key because they are issues that workers everywhere are concerned about. Everything's going up except workers' fair share—the stock market's going up and executive salaries are skyrocketing," Dion says. She believes this is a pivotal time for unions to get this message out to people who may not realize the historic power of unions to raise wages and secure better benefits for workers.

Filmmaker Michael Moore also sees this as a pivotal period. "I think we're going to see a resurgence in interest in unions," he says. "In the last five years, it's dawned on a lot of people that unions have been asleep at the wheel. They really don't have that much in common with the man on the hill."

Moore features some of the newest members of the United Food and Commercial Worker Union in his film, *The Big One*. The 45 booksellers who start at $6 an hour at the Borders Books store in Des Moines, Iowa, voted in the union in December 1996. They are mostly young, with bachelor's or even graduate degrees. Many came to Borders from other professions—teaching, the arts, or independent bookstores driven out of business by the big chains. They say it's not about money so much as it is about respect.

"The way they pay us and treat us is a paradox," says employee organizer Christian Gholson. "On one hand, they say the employees are the reason for Borders' success, then they say this is a transitional job and you aren't worth more than $6.50 an hour." So far only four of Borders' 200-plus stores have organized, but Gholson sees it as a worthwhile struggle. "In my perfect world, I'd like to make $8.00 an hour. That's not so much when you see the volume of business that goes through this store," he says.

The trend toward unionization is growing among health-care professionals as well as among upscale service businesses that depend on younger workers. Stores in the Starbucks Corporation and Einstein/Noah Bagel Corporation chains have also voted for union representation [recently]. As for Gholson, their issues are better wages, full-time hours, health benefits—and respect.

Social scientists see historic similarities between today's labor issues and those of the 1930s. "After the Depression, everybody's job became a lot more insecure," says labor historian Rachleff. "There were a lot of efforts by white-collar workers to unionize. The intervention of anti-communism stopped that and threw the labor movement back onto a much narrower social foundation." Knoke says that the contract between employers and workers has once more ended. "For a lot of people, it's turned into something like it was before World War II," he says. "There is great uncertainty. People are being forced out of jobs that are disappearing."

If globalization is creating a working class with a wider social base, what does a person like Gholson, who considers himself a writer and a poet, have in common with an auto-plant assembly-line worker? It seems like a clash of cultures. "It's very funny watching these enthusiastic young kids trying to get the old fogies of the union to take action and get involved," says Mike Moore.

The Jackman's study found that beliefs and feelings were an important determinant of class in the 1970s. For today's working class, the commonality just might be age-old issues such as job security, autonomy on the job, occupational prestige, and the belief that hard work should be rewarded. The working class has always been the group most likely to rate job security as the most important reason for taking a job, according to GSS data. "There are differences between us and the old union people," admits Gholson. "But there's a middle ground where we all agree."

The mere fact that working-class identification has stayed so stable over the last 20 years, despite myriad macro economic and social changes, is significant in itself. "If we find people continuing to identify themselves as workers, there must really be something going on socially," says Rachleff, "because there's so much stacked against their doing that."

After Reading

Critical Perspective

1. Heath's essay suggests that while Americans oftentimes do not focus on class issues and employment—instead considering America a classless society—class impacts us more than we think. Do you believe that Heath is correct about this? Be sure to furnish evidence from her text and from your own experiences to support your views.

Rhetoric and Argument

2. What rhetorical tactics—use of audience, purpose, ethos, pathos, logos, intertextuality, context, and constraints—are at work in Heath's essay? Do you think that she employs them effectively? Why or why not?
3. What is Heath's main assertion about class relations and employment in her text? Where in her essay does she offer this claim? Do you find her claim persuasive? Why or why not? Offer textual evidence for your perspectives.
4. Look at the kinds of examples that Heath utilizes to support her claim. Do you feel that each one gives adequate support for her argument? Why or why not? Provide quotes to back up your views.
5. Are there examples from the contemporary media—other than the ones to which Heath refers—that you can point to that support her claim? Conversely, are there examples from the contemporary media that you can point to that refute Heath's claim? Be as specific as possible.

6. Heath closes with some examples of how union organizing is becoming important for today's contingent workers. What roles do you think unions can have in the lives of today's workers and why? Offer examples from your own life as well as the text to support your thoughts.

Analysis

7. Which Heath mentions a few examples of contemporary media in her analysis. New television shows and films have been released since she originally wrote this essay. In a short essay, make an argument about whether Heath's thoughts about depictions of working-class people in the media are still valid. Or, do you think that the representations of class in today's media have changed slightly? What evidence from primary texts as well as library and Internet sources might you point to in order to support your views?

Taking Action

Get into a small group. In a jointly written informal response, make an argumentative claim about how class issues are depicted in one specific, contemporary film and what you believe this reveals about how contemporary class relations in American culture operate. Be sure to give a brief overview of the film's plot, provide close analyses of scenes as well as quotes from the text to support your views, and include library and Internet sources. Share your responses with each other in the larger class group.

Eddie R. Cole Jr.

"Guess Who Else Is Reading Those 'Facebook' Entries?"

Eddie R. Cole Jr. is editor-in-chief at the Tennessee State University student newspaper, The Meter. *He has worked as an intern at* The Macon (GA) Telegraph, Mobile (AL) Press-Register, *and the* Nashville Pride *weekly newspaper. Cole's online publications have appeared in blackcollegewire.org, nytimes-institute.com, blackamericaweb .com, and tsumeter.com.*

EXERCISING YOUR SKILLS

Before Reading

Cole examines the effects that "Facebook" and "MySpace" are having on students' employment opportunities. Consider the various methods through which employers can learn about their potential employees. How much does an employer have a right to know about you and why? Do you think that an applicant should share her or his "Facebook" or "MySpace" pages with an employer? Why or why not?

Tondia Payne is one of more than 4,830 Tennessee State University students registered with facebook.com, which calls itself an Internet directory that "connects college students worldwide through social networks."

And those Tennessee State students are among 12 million college students worldwide registered to the site. Unbeknownst to most of them, employers are using Facebook entries as a view into job applicants' characters, a trend that increasingly worries college administrators.

Dennis Gendron, vice president for technology and administrative services at Tennessee State, said the issue has become a concern at the national meetings of his colleagues.

"A lot of times, students are short on their context," Gendron said, referring to students' placing personal information in their profiles. "Nobody is trying to discourage Facebook, but it's just like anything else. You give a kid a car and they drive at 80 miles per hour, but you try to tell them to drive at 60 miles per hour instead. Everything has limitations."

"Employers can get access through students and faculty to use Facebook to view kids' profiles," he said. "Monster.com," an online career management site, "is who you portray you are, but Facebook is who you really are."

Yet Chris Hughes, co-founder of Facebook, said the chance of an employer getting access to Facebook is slim.

"Several factors would have to line up to make it possible," Hughes said in an e-mail. "First, the employer would have to be a graduate of the particular school that the interviewee is attending. Second, that particular school would be able to distribute .edu e-mail addresses to its alumni. Finally, the individual undergrad would have had to configure her privacy settings to specifically make her profile available to alumni.

"The likelihood that all three of those factors line up makes the chances of this happening low. If students don't want a potential alumnus looking at their profiles, they can just change their privacy settings so that they're not available to alumni. Simple as that."

But that does not ease administrators' fears, which go beyond job applicants. For example, after October's football game against rival Ohio State, hundreds of Penn State fans rushed the field after a 17–10 victory.

That led to a melee and resulted in two arrests, according to a Jan. 26 report in the *Chronicle of Higher Education*.

Less than a week later, Tyrone Parham, the Penn State assistant director of police, was tipped off about students posting pictures of themselves rushing the field and a Facebook discussion group titled, "I Rushed the Field after the OSU Game (And Lived!)," according to the *Chronicle*.

Days later, nearly 50 students were referred to the Penn State Office of Judicial Affairs.

Payne, the Tennessee State student who has been a registered Facebook member since December, said those who use Facebook are making judgments based on students' fun time.

"I don't feel that people should use [the book] to find character, because when people put crazy pictures up, they are just doing it for fun so their friends can see what they are up to," said the junior social work major from Memphis. "Just because an employer sees those pictures doesn't mean they are judging character."

Is it fair not to hire a job applicant based on his or her social life?

"Once an employer gets into the system, you don't get to ask that question," Gendron said.

Employers Can Learn Race, Religion, Gender

As a result of Title VII of the 1964 Civil Rights Act, employers are prohibited from discriminating based on race, color, religion, sex or national origin.

Facebook can provide viewers all of that information.

Faheem Goree, a Tennessee State senior from Atlanta majoring in mass communications, isn't taking any chances.

"I won't put anything extra personal on my page because of the job I have; people might want to look me up and I wouldn't want them to see pictures of me in an unprofessional state," said Goree, who also works at Nashville's WUBT-FM.

Rodriquous Rhodes, a junior sports science major from Memphis, said he can understand an employer's reasoning.

"I wouldn't blame a company for using the Facebook to find character," said Rhodes, who identified himself as a limited user of the site. "You are putting this stuff on the Internet and you know that others will see it. Although it is your personal life, employers have to think about [whether] the lifestyles you are living will affect your work habit[s]."

Corporate Thinking

Nickie Singleton, a product specialist in the medical sales department for Siemens Medical Solutions, said she could understand why a company would use Facebook as a reference.

"It's hard to get an idea of who a person is," Singleton said. "You can get a paper picture of a person, but that's why we get to have face-to-face interviews."

She also said employers look for something unique and Facebook might be a way to distinguish between two equally qualified job applicants.

"It gives them a picture of a person outside of a resume," Singleton said. "Facebook is more candid and honest, because people lie on their resume all the time."

Inman E. Otey, director of the Tennessee State University Career Center, said students should continue to embrace new technology, but must be careful.

"Students must utilize all of these marvelous ways of informing others," Otey said. "But they must know that there are abusive people out there and be aware of where they put this personal information. There are so many people with evil intentions.

"Just be careful with what you do, [and] how you say it and you don't have to worry about it coming back to haunt you."

Employers and others should use Facebook in its context, she said.

"You do things in college that you wouldn't do when out of school," Otey said.

Ramifications Go Beyond Not Getting the Job

Even in school, however, Facebook entries can lead to trouble.

At Duquesne University, a student was asked to write a paper after a group he started on Facebook was judged to be homophobic, according to the *Chronicle of Higher Education* report. At Northern Kentucky University, students were charged with having a keg in a dorm room after university officials saw a picture of the keg online.

Virginia Commonwealth University will be training students about Internet safety starting in October, Vice Provost Henry G. Rhone told the *Chronicle*.

"Online privacy is becoming a huge issue on a lot of campuses and I think we're just beginning to have our eyes opened to it," Rhone said.

For Tennessee State student Carl Erskine Davis Jr., the thought of strangers viewing his personal information on Facebook was enough for him to stop using it.

"I was on the Facebook, but I removed my profile because I just couldn't get [over] knowing people that I don't even know could look up my profile and find things out about me," said Davis, a junior mass communications major from Memphis. "It was just too random."

After Reading

Critical Perspective

1. Cole's piece—a piece written for students and teachers on college campuses—takes a journalistic approach. What do you believe Cole thinks about "Facebook" and how students should conduct themselves on it? How can you tell? How would you characterize his main claim? Do you agree with him? Why or why not?

Rhetoric and Argument

2. What rhetorical strategies—audience, purpose, ethos, pathos, logos, intertextuality, context, and constraints—does Cole use to draw in his audience? Do you find these tactics effective? Why or why not? Be sure to offer quotes from the text to back up your thoughts.

3. Look at the kinds of evidence Cole utilizes throughout his piece. Do you think that such evidence is persuasive? Are there any potential logical fallacies at work in his text? Provide textual evidence to back up your views.

4. What solutions, if any, does Cole offer to the problems his essay reveals? If he does offer explicit or implicit suggestions for change, where in his text does he make them? Do you have additional ideas that could add to his argument? Be as specific as you can.

Analysis

5. Have you ever heard about or witnessed discrimination—or other problems—that potential employees or students on college campuses have suffered due to their "Facebook" or "MySpace" pages? Write a short essay in which you try to recount and research such examples. Answer the following questions: What general situations emerged? What role did these sites play? If discrimination or potential harm occurred, why was this the case? What do you think needs to be done to protect students from these problems? Draw from your own experiences as well as library and Internet sources.

Taking Action

Meet in a small group. Your goal as a team is to investigate how sites like "Facebook" and "MySpace" operate in today's college and university environments—particularly your own. Interview one member from each of the following campus groups: students, staffs, teachers, and administrators. Ask them about their thoughts about these sites, how they are used, and how they ought to be used. If they are willing to go on record, audiotape or videotape their thoughts and their own stories.

After you have completed this interview process, arrange the stories in a user-friendly format by editing your material and providing a voice-over that carries a narrative thread and argumentative claim. Share your products with your other class members. Explain to the rest of the class what you hoped to show about the ways such sites operate on your campus. Then have a discussion about the positives and negatives—advancing potential solutions to these problems.

Scott Adams

"The Dilbert Principle"

Scott Adams is the creator of "Dilbert." His comic strips are based on personal experience. Adams held a series of technology and finance jobs at corporations such as Crocker National Bank and Pacific Bell. For many years he worked a day job while doing the "Dilbert" comic strip mornings, evenings, and weekends.

EXERCISING YOUR SKILLS

Before Reading

Adams writes and draws "Dilbert," a comic strip that humorously explores the plight of the white-collar worker (see http://www.unitedmedia.com/comics/dilbert/). Familiarize yourself with the comic strip. What images and words do you find humorous and why? Examine and describe in detail the wide range of social commentaries Scott Adams offers about the American workplace through his comic strips.

I use a lot of "bad boss" themes in my syndicated cartoon strip "Dilbert." I'll never run out of material. I get at least two hundred e-mail messages a day, mostly from people who are complaining about their own clueless managers. Here are some of my favorite stories, all allegedly true:

- A vice president insists that the company's new battery-powered product be equipped with a light that comes on to tell you when the power is off.
- An employee suggests setting priorities so the company will know how to apply its limited resources. The manager's response: "Why can't we concentrate our resources across the board?"
- A manager wants to find and fix software bugs more quickly. He offers an incentive plan: $20 for each bug the Quality Assurance people find and $20 for each bug the programmers fix. (These are the same programmers who create the bugs.) Result: An underground economy in "bugs" springs up instantly. The plan is rethought after one employee nets $1,700 the first week.

Stories like these prompted me to do the first annual Dilbert Survey to find out what management practices were most annoying to employees. The choices included the usual suspects: Quality, Empowerment, Reengineering, and the like. But the number-one vote-getter in this highly unscientific survey was "Idiots Promoted to Management."

This seemed like a subtle change from the old concept by which capable workers were promoted until they reached their level of incompetence—best described as the "Peter Principle." Now, apparently, the incompetent workers are promoted directly to management without ever passing through the temporary competence stage.

When I entered the workforce in 1979, the Peter Principle described management pretty well. Now I think we'd all like to return to those Golden Years when you had a boss who was once good at something.

I get all nostalgic when I think about it. Back then, we all had hopes of being promoted beyond our levels of competence. Every worker had a shot at someday personally navigating the company into the tar pits while reaping large bonuses and stock options. It was a time when inflation meant everybody got an annual raise; a time when we freely admitted that the customers didn't matter. It was a time of joy.

We didn't appreciate it then, but the much underrated Peter Principle always provided us with a boss who understood what we did for a living. Granted, he made consistently bad decisions—after all he had no management skills. But at least they were the informed decisions of a seasoned veteran from the trenches.

Example

Boss: "When I had your job I could drive a three-inch rod through a metal casing with one motion. If you're late again I'll do the same thing to your head."

Nitpickers found lots of problems with the Peter Principle, but on the whole it worked. Lately, however, the Peter Principle has given way to the "Dilbert Principle." The basic concept of the Dilbert Principle is that the most ineffective workers are systematically moved to the place where they can do the least damage: management.

This has not proved to be the winning strategy that you might think.

Maybe we should learn something from nature. In the wild, the weakest moose is hunted down and killed by dingo dogs, thus ensuring survival of the fittest. This is a harsh system—especially for the dingo dogs who have to fly all the way from Australia. But

nature's process is a good one; everybody agrees, except perhaps for the dingo dogs and the moose in question . . . and the flight attendants. But the point is that we'd all be better off if the least competent managers were being eaten by dingo dogs instead of writing Mission Statements.

It seems as if we've turned nature's rules upside down. We systematically identify and promote the people who have the least skills. The usual business rationalization for promoting idiots (the Dilbert Principle in a nutshell) is something along the lines of "Well, he can't write code, he can't design a network, and he doesn't have any sales skill. But he has very good hair. . . ."

If nature started organizing itself like a modern business, you'd see, for example, a band of mountain gorillas led by an "alpha" squirrel. And it wouldn't be the most skilled squirrel; it would be the squirrel nobody wanted to hang around with.

I can see the other squirrels gathered around an old stump saying stuff like "If I hear him say, 'I like nuts' one more time, I'm going to kill him." The gorillas, overhearing this conversation, lumber down from the mist and promote the unpopular squirrel. The remaining squirrels are assigned to Quality Teams as punishment.

You may be wondering if you fit the description of a Dilbert Principle manager. Here's a little test:

1. Do you believe that anything you don't understand must be easy to do?
2. Do you feel the need to explain in great detail why "profit" is the difference between income and expense?
3. Do you think employees should schedule funerals only during holidays?
4. Are the following words a form of communication or gibberish:

   The Business Services Leadership Team will enhance the organization in order to continue on the journey toward a Market Facing Organization (MFO) model. To that end, we are consolidating the Object Management for Business Services into a cross strata team.

5. When people stare at you in disbelief do you repeat what you just said, only louder and more slowly?

Now give yourself one point for each question you answered with the letter "B." If your score is greater than zero, congratulations—there are stock options in your future.

(The language in question four is from an actual company memo.)

After Reading

Critical Perspective

1. Why do you think that people find "Dilbert" humorous? What about the comic strip makes us laugh? What does this suggest to you about how work functions in Americans' lives?

Rhetoric and Argument

2. What rhetorical strategies—purpose, ethos, pathos, logos, intertextuality, context, and constraints—does Adams utilize to draw in his audience? How do you know?
3. What does Adams claim about today's workplace and the role of management? Do you agree with his assertion? Why or why not? Try to provide examples from your own experiences to back up your views.
4. Look at the kinds of support that Adams employs to substantiate his claim. Do you feel that such evidence is persuasive? In what ways might it fail to convince some readers? Provide evidence from the text to back up your views.
5. Who is the real audience for Adams's text—workers, bosses, or both? How do you know? Do you feel that you are part of that audience? Why or why not?
6. Do you think that Adams's text is meant to be an argument, an editorial, or a bit of both? What makes you think this? If it is an argument, are there any potential logical fallacies at work in his text?

Analysis

7. Do you know a boss who fits the description of the "Dilbert Principle"? Write a short essay in which you try to recount experiences in your own life (or experiences from those you know) that might be the basis of an interesting "Dilbert" car-

toon. Answer the following questions: How did the Dilbert Principle boss behave? How did you or those you know respond? In what ways do these experiences support or refute Adams's notion that the least skilled get promoted to managerial positions? Draw from your own experiences as well as library and Internet sources.

Taking Action

Meet in a small group. Take a look at the work of other popular cartoonists in newsprint strips, television, and film. What kinds of social commentaries do they make about work life as well as race, ethnicity, class, disability, gender, or other identity traits? Which kinds of social commentaries are central and which appear to be missing? Why is this significant? How do they use rhetorical ploys to accomplish this?

Discuss similarities and differences in the cartoons that you have selected. As a group, come up with answers to the following questions: How do these cartoons use context, purpose, composition, constraints, intertextuality, cultural codes, as well as rhetorical appeals (ethos, pathos, logos) to make comments about American culture? What do you think about this? Include library and Internet sources to support your conclusions.

After you have answered these questions, work as a small group to construct your own comic strip (using print and multimedia resources) that aims to provide a particular social commentary through humor. Then share your comic strip with the whole class and explain why you made these rhetorical choices, what social commentary you are trying to convey in your comic strip, and how you have tried to use humor in order to accomplish this.

CHAPTER FIVE

Imagining Spaces, Rituals, and Styles

INTRODUCTION

Considering Spaces, Rituals, and Styles

Do you frequent large department stores? Do you travel there only to shop for something specific, or are there other reasons why you go visit them? What specific activities play a part of your morning ritual before going to school or work? Why do you choose these particular activities rather than others? How would you describe your individual style—are you hip-hop, grunge, alternative, punk, preppy, athletic, hippy granola? Or, do you define your style in opposition to any of these groups?

Our sense of ourselves and the world around us is often created by our interactions with various spaces, rituals, and styles. Stores in malls are certain kinds of spaces, arranged in colorful, attractive ways to encourage our eyes to wander and our credit cards to fly out of our wallets and pocket books. Hot Topic, American Eagle, PacSun, and Victoria's Secret can be seen alongside JC Penney, Sears, Macys, and Bloomingdales. When my friends and I wander the stores in outlet malls and look for bargains, music blaring at us, each store with a different ambience, we often become overwhelmed by just how much stuff there is in the world: all those things you know you want and all those things you never knew you wanted.

College life depends on many kinds of rituals. On many campuses, for instance, every fall brings Homecoming weekend. A queen and king are crowned. Parades with bands and floats move through the streets. There is an important football game with a rival team. Alumnae, family members, and friends flood the campus. People create signs, dress in school colors, scream chants, and have tailgate parties. For some this ritual is an initiation into college life. For others this is a familiar cultural event that recurs every year, part of the rhythm of the academic schedule.

Hip-hop culture has given us certain styles. Artists such as Jay Z, Notorious B.I.G., Sean "P. Diddy" Combs, and Missy Elliot are now often embodied in brands such as TommyGirl, Roxy, Cool, Fox, ONeill, Billabong, and Nike. The link between the importance of style and hip-hop music could not be more evident than when Raekwon of the Wu-Tang Clan integrates the appropriate clothing choices into songs for the album "Criminology": "Phonograph hip-hop put me on top / 'Lo wears, and Tommy Hil fly with a knot."

Spaces, rituals, and styles are critical parts of our American culture. The differences between kinds of spaces, rituals, and styles are important, and they indicate things about the people who participate in them. We read spaces—whether they are rural or urban, expansive or confining. We read rituals—whether they require controlled applause (a theater performance), the holding of Bic lighters (a James Taylor concert), or outright screaming (a Stain'd show); whether they are crucial rights of passage (getting a driver's license) or relatively unimportant incidents (eating dinner). We read styles—the way people wear their hair (buzz cuts, mohawks, shaved clean, long and straight, streaked or permed); the kinds of clothes they don (men's Claiborne dress shirts, Hollister tops, Ann Taylor dresses, Levi's jean jackets); the kind of computer they use (iMac, Dell, IBM, or a lesser known brand); their facial expressions and mannerisms (smiles, carriage of head, use of arm movements while talking); their jewelry (hemp bracelets, diamond earrings, class rings); their tattoos and piercings (images of anchors, flowers, or family members; nose rings, earrings, belly button piercings); the sorts of cars they drive (a 1985 Trans Am, a BMW, a Volkswagen beetle); and their other personal belongings—in order to make sense of others and our relationships to them.

Overview of Selections: Spaces and Rituals

In this chapter of *Pop Perspectives*: *Readings to Critique Contemporary Culture* you will be introduced to different spaces and rituals as well as styles—from malls to shopping for groceries to specific clothing, attitudes, and behaviors.

The first section is entitled "Spaces and Rituals." Here you will scrutinize the various myths, ideologies, and practices associated with different elements of consumer culture in America: malls, spaces for "stuff," supermarkets and screens, prom events, neighborhood spaces, and the construction of Disney World. You will consider the ways in which who we are and how we view ourselves are becoming ever more connected to such constructed environments.

An intriguing essay on the shifting nature of mall space and culture by writer James Morrow begins the chapter. Morrow investigates the death of the conventional mall and the emergence of the new mall as what is being termed a "lifestyle center." He examines how the needs of various generations—Y, X, and baby boomers—are impacting the shifting perspective on malls and therefore how malls are built. He quotes Paco Underhill, founder and managing director of the commercial research firm Envirosell and author of the book *The Call of the Mall* as suggesting that mall developers can no longer see themselves as "landlords" but rather must understand their roles as "creators of spaces." Morrow reveals that perhaps the greatest challenge today is fostering a mall environment that caters to the needs of Generation X—a generation whose needs are very different from those of past generations. This requires mall creators to "demall" their malls: to create new consumer spaces that foster community and innovative streetscapes that afford shoppers independence.

Next a hilarious stand-up skit or essay is provided for us by the well-known comedian and social critic George Carlin. In this text Carlin discusses how much stuff Americans accumulate, the problems around finding spaces for all of that stuff, and the ways in which rabid consumption forces us to accumulate and then get rid of perfectly usable things just to have the latest, most popular versions. He describes how every time we visit someone we have to find a new place for our stuff. Carlin suggests that finding space for our things can become a constant preoccupation. In the end Carlin asks us to consider our own tendency to gather goods more carefully and to think about our reasons for doing this.

Then there is an entertaining yet disturbing piece by an independent filmmaker and instructor who teaches a Trash Cinema and Youth Culture course at the USC School of Cinema-Television, Dan Leopard. Leopard leads us through an account of his typical daily experiences in a supermarket. Leopard exposes the extent to which we are surrounded by different screens all the time. While this may appear on the surface to be an innovative technological advancement, Leopard asserts that these screens operate strategically—to ward us away from shoplifting, to dispense money, and to entertain us. Despite the fact that not all of them appear to be about surveillance, he contends that they are in fact policing our actions, or needs, and our behaviors.

Next is an Ad Analysis exercise. The featured ad is geared toward the ritual of teenagers getting ready for the prom. It frames an important essay by Amy L. Best, a professor of sociology, that advances an analytical view of how proms function in American culture—the media representations in music, magazines, film, and television that prepare us for them as well as the cultural narratives we tell ourselves about proms as well as masculinity and femininity. Best interviews teenagers about their prom experiences and the complexities of being initiated into the adult world. Best reveals that proms are too often about adults' ideas about adolescence rather than kids' views about themselves and their own experiences.

The next essay is offered by the famous photographer of and writer about American culture, Camilo José Vergara. Vergara is perhaps best known for capturing haunting images of the World Trade Center's Twin Towers following September 11, 2001. Vergara's compelling text takes us into various spaces he has visited: "green ghettos," "institutional ghettos," and "new immigrant ghettos." These are relatively new spaces in our American cultural landscape, the result of suburban sprawl and city growth. The presence of these spaces also reveals social and cultural inequities among various populations. Vergara's text describes how communities are built and fail to be built around these spaces, as well as the living conditions of people who inhabit these spaces.

The final piece centers on Disney World, and provides an important look at how it operates. Susan Willis, a professor of English who specializes in minority literature and cultural studies at Duke University, draws upon her own experiences at the park and additional research. Willis argues that the success of a space like Disney World ironically depends upon its erasure of spontaneity and play. She shows us that "conformity," "purposeful consumption," and homogeneity among and between families are what dominate instead. The landscape of Disney World is "commodified" or makes everything into something for profit—including our memories. Willis closes with the idea that the "magic of Disney World" is not really magic at all but rather a highly structured event. While it may appear seamless and perfect, it really depends upon what is not visible in order to function.

Overview of Selections: Styles

The second section of Chapter 5, "Styles," focuses entirely on style issues, including dress, mannerisms, behaviors, and attitudes.

The section starts with an instructive essay by John Molloy, a very popular writer of self-help books on dress and an image consultant to corporate executives. Molloy proffers that the "socio-economic value of a man's clothing is important in determining his credibility within certain groups." Molloy runs experiments to reveal to us how people view the class status of men wearing different colored raincoats. The results are similar every time. Tan coats signify high class status and black coats signify lower class status. Molloy's study exposes the ways that men must dress in order to be perceived in positive ways by others, and offers some conclusions based upon his study that he suggests all males need to follow if they are to be successful.

Next is an Ad Analysis exercise about Martha Stewart. This exercise can be completed in conjunction with the essay that follows by writer Margaret Talbot about Martha Stewart. Employing humorous anecdotes and descriptions, Talbot investigates Stewart's domestic empire for us—her books, magazines, and columns; her merchandising at Kmart, paint at Sherwin Williams, and furniture at Bernhardt; and her "The Catalog for Living" as well as various websites devoted to merchandise and flower sales. Talbot contends that Stewart has created a style for working women in America that is nearly impossible to achieve. With it comes a valuing of white, upper-class mores and the traditional roles for women of nurturers and caregivers. Talbot's claims may be examined in light of Stewart's indictment on charges of obstructing justice and lying to the government about ImClone stock sales; as well as her new media ventures (including her prime-time reality show *The Apprentice: Martha Stewart*, her daytime show *Martha*, and her radio ventures).

Then Warren St. John examines a relatively new and intriguing style and marketing trend that dominates much of today's art and design, fashion, home décor, cooking, and architecture: metrosexuality. With the popularity of television shows such as *Queer Eye for the Straight Guy*, the role of the well-coiffed, well-dressed metrosexual—the heterosexual male who is very concerned with hair, clothes, and physique—has hit the mainstream. To St. John this reveals shifts in how masculinity may be functioning for many men as well as women. The metrosexual is now a hip consumer group that is being targeted directly by advertisers. St. John traces this phenomenon for us and makes some intriguing claims about the effects that this new style is having on consumers of American culture.

Richard Majors and Janet Mancini Billson, professors who research African American studies issues, offer their crucial essay next. They write about how style—dress, possessions, attitudes, and behaviors—operates within some black communities. Explaining how hustling and making a life on the streets operate, they contend that these are significant stylistic and social tactics that fight racism and oppression. Clothes, jewelry, pants, shoes, and cars make important statements about a person's identity and power in the world. Styles, according to these writers, are not just about putting forward images but are also a necessary part of changing social inequities.

In the last selection Alison Lurie presents a detailed analysis about the symbolic and linguistic function of clothing. Providing a thoughtful history concerning the kinds of meanings attributed to various styles and forms of dress, Lurie argues that we are always constantly reading other people's identities, attitudes, values, thoughts, desires, and fears when we look at how they are dressed. Clothing itself is not just a casual choice. Instead, how we dress is a language of its own; it speaks to who we want to be, who we want others to think we are, and how we want the world to view us. Lurie argues that this has always been the case—our style choices are signs that signify many things about us—things we want to signify and things about which we may be unaware.

As you peruse this chapter, reflect upon how spaces, rituals, and styles impact you every day. What kinds of spaces do you travel through, how are they set up, why are they arranged in this way, and what are the effects of such spaces? Are these spaces large and open or small and confining? Do these spaces have comfortable seats, and how are they placed in the spaces? What kinds of rituals do you participate in every day, such as sitting in class, going for a run, eating lunch at the cafeteria, hanging out with your friends, or studying at the library? What kinds of styles do you choose? Why do you elect to wear certain clothes and not others? What do the products you use and outfits you wear convey about your identity—your race and ethnicity, class, gender, sexual orientation, language, politics, disability, age, region, and religion as well as the groups to which you belong?

SPACES AND RITUALS

JAMES MORROW
"X-It Plans"

James Morrow is a freelance journalist based in Sydney, Australia. He writes for various journals and edits The Weekly James.

EXERCISING YOUR SKILLS

Before Reading

Morrow's essay examines the relationships between Generation X and mall culture. Think about your own experiences at malls. Why do you go to them? How would you describe your experiences and their effects on you? What stores do you choose to shop at and why? What kinds of ethos do these stores construct for their shoppers? What sorts of appeals to pathos do these stores make in order to draw in consumers? How are these stores designed in order to facilitate this? In what ways might our senses of identification, community, self-worth, and cultural status be connected to our mall experiences?

The week of August 31, 2003, was a typically slow news week wrapping up the dog days of summer, but it may go down as a watershed moment for the retailers, designers, developers and architects who work in the fast-changing world of shopping malls. In Sunnyvale, Calif., the beginning of that week saw the final curtains drawn on the Sunnyvale Town Center, a traditional box-style shopping center that opened in 1979, which had been slowly drowning in the middle of a vast sea of empty parking spaces before going under following anchor tenant J.C. Penney's decision to weigh anchor.

The headline in a local newspaper: "Sunnyvale mall a goner."

A few days later and 2,500 miles east, in Richmond, Va., the local press was very different. In that city's suburb of Henrico County, locals and officials gathered to cut the ribbon on the new Short Pump Town Center, one of a new breed of shopping venues known broadly in the business as "lifestyle centers." Late architect Victor Gruen, who popped the notion of America's mall out of his own brain and, in so doing, helped bring to life Baby Boomers' picture of the American Dream, must be turning in his grave. Departing radically from the traditional mall concept, the Short Pump Town Center was the latest entry in a broader retail trend being led by members of Generation X.

While Baby Boomers still have higher incomes than their younger Gen X counterparts, they are spending fewer and fewer dollars on retail purchases as their disposable cash gets eaten up by everything from college tuitions to "bracket creep"—and their spending will continue to decrease as they head into retirement.

The feted Generation Y, while bigger in terms of numbers, only contributes about 5 percent of consumer spending and thus doesn't have the economic oomph to cause planners and developers to, literally, re-landscape urban and suburban America.

That task has fallen to Generation X. Now between ages 27 and 39, this demographic represents the vanguard of the powerful married-with-kids market (controlling 18 percent of the GDP), who are seeing their careers take off toward peak income, and are in a position to make retailers and designers wake up to what has been brewing for some time: the death of the traditional shopping mall.

The Mall Is Dead—Long Live the Mall!

But are developers getting the message? Yes and no. On one hand, about 60 lifestyle centers have been built around the country, and 20 more are slated to open over the next two years (in comparison to only five regional malls that are thought to be on the drawing board. A 2001 study by PriceWaterhouseCoopers estimates that 400 of these retail behemoths could be obsolete by the end of next year). Further economic motivation: the average lifestyle center turns over about $500 per square foot in sales per year, compared with just $211 for a typical old-style shopping mall.

At the same time, "Mall developers are not doing enough to capture Generation X," says Wendy Liebmann, president of New York City–based WSL Strategic Retail, a global marketing and retail consulting firm. "I think that one of the huge issues malls are facing is that the people behind them do not understand the way the younger generation of shoppers shop. They're still trying to attract their parents and grandparents."

For the first time in decades, shopping centers—where Americans dispose of 49 percent of the nearly $2.5 trillion they spend on non-automotive retail items every year, and whose new construction starts eclipsed $3.15 billion in 2003—are poised for the biggest revolution since the first fully enclosed mall opened outside Minnesota in 1956, amid the Baby Boom.

Now it's Boomers' kids who are having their say, and what these shoppers want is "another reason to walk in the doors." Just filling some immediate consumer need may have been enough up to now, but not tomorrow. Xers, the smartest shoppers on the face of the earth, want to do more than just buy stuff—whether it be to have a proper sit-down meal (not in a food court), see a movie or get some work done on their laptop while having a cup of coffee. Indeed, the biggest issue facing builders today is "the migration of the development community from being landlords to creating spaces," says Paco Underhill, founder and managing director of commercial research firm Envirosell and author of *The Call of the Mall* (Simon & Schuster, 2004).

Providing this place-like experience is becoming increasingly imperative for retailers and developers. The International Council of Shopping Centers recently issued a report entitled "Tapping the 25- to 34-year-old Consumer," which, while skewed toward the junior end of Gen X, underlined the need to capture this market. This is not just because Generation X has money to spend (and they do), but because their attitudes represent a fundamental shift in shopping culture, one which will be seen for decades to come. As the report's authors put it, "As teens of today move into the next age cohort, the 25- to 34-year-old population will accelerate rapidly over the next 10 years. Mall tenants, in particular, could potentially exploit the fact that 25- to 34-year-olds spend the highest at mall stores per trip among the age groups. This implies that retailers targeting this segment today are poised to reap benefits tomorrow."

Easier said than done. "Traditional mall anchors like department stores are not getting the younger shoppers," says Liebmann, and alienate "people in their teens, 20s and 30s." Because of these giants' inability to draw customers into malls, says David Kass, president of the Cincinnati-based Continental Retail Development, "specialty retailers have been looking for venues that are more economical for them, and where they don't have to subsi-dize anchor tenants with higher rents."

Thus, says Kass, whose company has built several such shopping environments around the country, lifestyle centers have become a popular option with retailers as well as shoppers.

Besides lifestyle centers, which tend to feature clusters of specialty chain retailers such as Pottery Barn and Crate & Barrel along with movie theatres and restaurants, mall designers are turning to other new concepts, says Mark Costandi, himself a 35-year-old Gen Xer who is also a project architect and designer at retail branding and interior design giant FRCH in Cincinnati. But one general rule tends to apply to just about all new devel-opments that successfully capture this Generation X market: according to Costandi, "they turn the mall inside-out."

"Whether it is the 'main street' concept, lifestyle centers, 'de-malling,' mixed, or multi-use properties, the story is the same," he says. "Certainly we're seeing more and more glorified strip centers with nicer tenants for those developers that aren't that daring, but others are going further." Those that own malls are "de-malling," which is a jargony way to describe tearing everything down except for anchor stores at either end and then rebuild-ing from the middle out.

Alternatively, some choose to keep the existing structure and scab exterior pads onto the old anonymous box of the mall, giving the retail outlets and restaurants inside an exte-rior presence, such as at the Kenwood Mall in Ohio.

Mixing It Up, or, the Suburban Jungle

For a developer to capitalize on the Gen X market and create a new sort of mall (or what Liebmann describes as a "multi-format shopping center experience"), more is needed than to put new signage and doors on an old anonymous box. Location, functionality, variety and experience must all combine to create the environment Generation X wants. Even if the stores seem ubiquitous, the successful retailers who target Gen X in these environ-ments are ones who sell products that seem less mass-marketed and more retro, while also being affordable.

"People in Generation X like the trend of being able to walk down a main street under one 'non-roof', which gives them a cozy traditional feel that is also very big at the moment," says Liebmann. But that's only part of the battle. "There is an issue of things being more urban in feel rather than an extension of the 'burbs, a cultural mindset relevant to this audience that doesn't want to be stuck way out there."

One company that has been working to do this is Federal Realty Investment Trust (FRIT). During the 1980s and 1990s, they put together a string of properties across the U.S. in closed-in suburbs of the sort favored by the young professionals and start-up fami-lies of Gen X who don't want to live in the outer rings of their parents. Although they say they do not market specifically to the Gen X cohort, "we do cater to many of the character-istics of Gen Xers," says Vikki Quinn, FRIT's director of marketing. "Since they are more likely to be health-conscious, some of our properties have gyms. We also try to offer things that Gen Xers like. Since a lot of them are young and looking for social outlets, we have outdoor concerts."

Quinn cites two of her company's properties: Bethesda Row just outside of Washington, D.C., and Santana Row, in San Jose, Calif., as prime examples of shopping centers that fit this model. (Being in the Silicon Valley area, Santana Row also offers something that is showing up in more shopping centers around the country: wireless Internet hot spots.)

The key to the thinking behind places like these, says Quinn, is that they don't just appeal to shoppers: "These are for people on a date, people with families looking to do something outside, a whole range of people," she says. "Some of our retailers are staying open later, because people like to wander into the bookstore or art gallery after dinner to hang out. Retailers are definitely recognizing this and capitalizing on it."

As part of this trend, which might be called the urbanization of the mall, canny developers are adding residential and office space to their shopping centers—meaning that, ideally, customers could both earn and spend just about all of their money in one place (FRIT's Bethesda and San Jose properties both have housing components.)

You Never Know Your Luck in a Big City

"Generation X has a real need to establish community, and we tend to be more urban" notes Costandi, and says the best of these venues combine these values to create transparent streetscapes that let shoppers (and residents) go where and do what they want, and form their own relationships and habits organically, without being directed by planners. "My biggest push as a designer is to capture these residential aspects, and it's great when you can incorporate residential and even office life into these centers so that they don't just sit there in the middle of a sea of parking," he says, echoing Gruen, who originally envisioned his malls surrounded by housing as well.

But this is only the beginning. Experts say that the next wave of shopping mall urbanization will be more dramatic, mirroring development seen for a decade in other countries. While Americans may have invented the concept of the traditional, shopping mall, it is overseas that architects, designers and developers are working to create the mall of the future. The U.S. market "is still very old paradigm," says Liebmann, born and raised in Australia, where she says some very innovative non-anchored shopping centers are being built, especially in traditional downtown areas where developers have feared to tread over the past several decades.

"Retail has to follow housing trends," adds Underhill. "While the mall and the lifestyle center followed the population to a suburban setting, today, as the problems of crime and pollution have largely been solved in a lot of cities, we are witnessing the re-population of downtowns." The key question for developers looking to capture Gen X shoppers becomes: How do I better service the young, the rich and the childless who are living downtown?

The answer, says Underhill, is in the latest developments like the recently opened Time-Warner Center in Manhattan, where customers are going to arrive both by escalators from street level below and by elevator from their condos above.

Time pressures are also part of this urbanization trend, and Underhill says that malls will have to change their marketing strategies to take advantage of Gen X's preoccupation with getting things done efficiently and conveniently—a need that will only get more acute over the next decade. Already the ICSC has found that shoppers at lifestyle centers tend to be more pop-in, pop-out shoppers than those visiting traditional malls, spending 57 minutes versus 78 minutes on average per trip, according to one survey they conducted of 1,500 shoppers at five such centers around the country. Although their shopping time was shorter, it was also more valuable to retailers, with lifestyle center customers spending $79.80 per visit, or $84 an hour, versus $57.70 per visit, or just about $60 an hour, at malls.

To take advantage of this desire of shoppers to save time, "there will be a better union between a store, its catalog and the Web," predicts Underhill. "The implications are going to be major in terms of how retailers market themselves." Among the future scenarios he sees are the end of traditional coupons, in-store circulars and newspaper ads for sales, to be replaced by "personalized direct mail over the Internet, where what the shopper gets is based on his own relationship to the store."

Furthermore, he says, more and more stores will be an extension of their catalog, whereby they won't necessarily have all their inventory in stock but will be able to provide delivery within a short time. And retailers will be more organized around providing one-stop lifestyle solutions, "whether it be a studio apartment store where everything is miniature and bundled, or a grocery store that offers complete meal-in-a-box kits."

Whether willingly or simply because they have no other choice, developers and retailers are waking up to the challenges of serving Gen X, the first cohort to be both alienated enough and affluent enough to make a real difference in how the country shops. As Costandi, who designs and shops in the next generation of shopping centers, says, "a successful mall needs to give us a bit of life, the excitement our generation is looking for—we're not mall walkers!"

After Reading

Critical Perspective

1. According to Morrow, how have traditional mall spaces operated? Based upon your own experiences, characterize how specific display windows, food courts, elevators, escalators, and arcades are set up to perpetuate and augment the buying and selling of goods. In what ways do these spaces foreground that malls are spaces for consumerism? In what ways do they attempt to alter this perception?

Rhetoric and Argument

2. What critical rhetorical choices does Morrow make in his text? Describe his use of audience, purpose, ethos, pathos, logos, intertextuality, context, and constraints. What rhetorical appeals does Morrow offer and where? Are these convincing? Why or why not?

3. Consider the question or main concern that propels Morrow to write this text. How do you know what it is? Provide textual evidence to back up your claim.

4. According to Morrow, what have historically been the basic attributes of mall culture? What are the new attributes of mall culture that are now emerging and why? Be sure to point to the essay for support.

5. What assumptions or warrants are at work in Morrow's argument? Do you find these viable? Why or why not? How does Morrow employ support from experts to back up his claim? Do you find this strategy effective? How so or how not?

6. Do you think that Morrow's essay is well structured and persuasive? Why or why not? What evidence can you furnish to substantiate your views?

Analysis

7. Write a short argumentative essay in response to Morrow's text: Do you agree with his assertion that mall spaces are undergoing radical changes right now—and they will need to change even more drastically in order to capture the Generation X and Y markets? Provide examples from your own experiences as well as from library and Internet sources to support your thoughts.

Taking Action

Get into a small group. Go to a mall for one hour. If there are no malls nearby, select a large department store. Position yourselves in good viewing locations. Then make note of the various cultural considerations that you see at work. How do people dress? How do they interact with each other? Where do they shop? Do these issues seem to differ at all depending on people's identities—issues such as race and ethnicity, class, gender, and the like? How do visual rhetorical concerns operate within a mall or large department store space?

As a result of your findings, deliberate on what assertions you might make about the myths and power structures supported by the spatial arrangement and organization of the space or spaces you are examining. What might you contend about the specific kinds of stores or departments there? What values and ideologies are supported by mall or department store life? What representations and behaviors do you witness and why? What critical signs and codes are at work? You may also want to consult additional library and Internet sources for information. Write up your findings and share them with the rest of the class.

George Carlin
"A Place for Your Stuff"

George Carlin is a stand-up comedian and social critic who grew up in Bronx, New York. Carlin published a best-selling book from which this essay was taken, titled Brain Droppings. *He is also the author of* Napalm and Silly Putty. *In addition, throughout his career, Carlin has taken on a number of comedic roles in films such as* Outrageous Fortune, Bill & Ted's Bogus Journey, The Prince of Tides, *and* Dogma.

EXERCISING YOUR SKILLS

Before Reading

In his text Carlin makes note of Americans' problems finding spaces to put all of their stuff. Comedians are often some of American society's best and most persuasive cultural critics. Watch some stand-up shows on *Comedy Central* or a series of videos featuring Jon Stewart, Chris Rock, George Carlin, George Lopez, Ellen DeGeneres, Dave Chappelle, or any other comedian whose performances you enjoy. You may choose to watch a performance of this skit. What aspects of American culture do these comedians ridicule, satirize, or speak about ironically? Examine how stand-up comedians use rhetorical choices (e.g., purpose, context, constraints, tone, intertextuality, audience, and arrangement). How might they utilize these rhetorical tactics, along with ethos, pathos, and logos, differently than other kinds of cultural critics? What could be particularly valuable about these kinds of rhetorical choices?

Actually this is just a place for my stuff, ya know? That's all, a little place for my stuff. That's all I want, that's all you need in life, is a little place for your stuff, ya know? I can see it on your table, everybody's got a little place for their stuff. This is my stuff, that's your stuff, that'll be his stuff over there. That's all you need in life, a little place for your stuff. That's all your house is: a place to keep your stuff. If you didn't have so much stuff, you wouldn't need a house. You could just walk around all the time.

A house is just a pile of stuff with a cover on it. You can see that when you're taking off in an airplane. You look down, you see everybody's got a little pile of stuff. All the little piles of stuff. And when you leave your house, you gotta lock it up. Wouldn't want somebody to come by and take some of your stuff. They always take the good stuff. They never bother with that crap you're saving. All they want is the shiny stuff. That's what your house is, a place to keep your stuff while you go out and get . . . more stuff!

Sometimes you gotta move, gotta get a bigger house. Why? No room for your stuff anymore. Did you ever notice when you go to somebody else's house, you never quite feel a hundred percent at home? You know why? No room for your stuff. Somebody else's stuff is all over the place! And if you stay overnight, unexpectedly, they give you a little bedroom to sleep in. Bedroom they haven't used in about eleven years. Someone died in it, eleven years ago. And they haven't moved any of his stuff! Right next to the bed there's usually a dresser or a bureau of some kind, and there's NO ROOM for your stuff on it. Somebody else's shit is on the dresser.

Have you noticed that their stuff is shit and your shit is stuff? God! And you say, "Get that shit offa there and let me put my stuff down!"

Sometimes you leave your house to go on vacation. And you gotta take some of your stuff with you. Gotta take about two big suitcases full of stuff, when you go on vacation. You gotta take a smaller version of your house. It's the second version of your stuff. And you're gonna fly all the way to Honolulu. Gonna go across the continent, across half an ocean to Honolulu. You get down to the hotel room in Honolulu and you open up your suitcase and you put away all your stuff. "Here's a place here, put a little bit of stuff there, put some stuff here, put some stuff—you put your stuff there, I'll put some stuff—here's another place for stuff, look at this, I'll put some stuff here . . ." And even though you're far away from home, you start to get used to it, you start to feel okay, because after all, you do have some of your stuff with you. That's when your friend calls up from Maui, and says, "Hey, why don'tchya come over to Maui for the weekend and spend a couple of nights over here."

Oh, no! Now what do I pack? Right, you've gotta pack an even SMALLER version of your stuff. The third version of your house. Just enough stuff to take to Maui for a coupla days. You get over to Maui—I mean you're really getting extended now, when you think about it. You got stuff ALL the way back on the mainland, you got stuff on another island, you got stuff on this island. I mean, supply lines are getting longer and harder to maintain. You get over to your friend's house on Maui and he gives you a little place to sleep, a little bed right next to his windowsill or something. You put some of your stuff up there. You got your Visine, you got your nail clippers, and you put everything up. It takes about an hour and a half, but after a while you finally feel okay, say, "All right, I got my nail clippers, I must be okay." That's when your friend says, "Aaaaay, I think tonight we'll go over the other side of the island, visit a pal of mine and maybe stay over."

Aww, no. NOW what do you pack? Right—you gotta pack an even SMALLER version of your stuff. The fourth version of your house. Only the stuff you know you're gonna need. Money, keys, comb, wallet, lighter, hanky, pen, smokes, rubber and change. Well, only the stuff you HOPE you're gonna need.

After Reading

Critical Perspective

1. How does Carlin start his text? How does this impact you as a reader? Do you think his uses of sarcasm and exaggeration help or hinder his argument? Why or why not?

Rhetoric and Argument

2. What other kinds of rhetorical choices—his use of audience, purpose, ethos, pathos, logos, intertextuality, context, and constraints—does Carlin make from the very beginning of his text? Do you find these choices to be persuasive? Why or why not? Be sure to point to the places in the text that best support your views.
3. Discuss how this text deviates from a traditional academic argument. What is Carlin's main argumentative claim? Where does he make it in his text? What kind of claim is it?
4. How does Carlin support his claim? Do you find this evidence convincing? Why or why not? What assumptions or warrants does Carlin make in his text? Are they reasonable ones to make? Why or why not?
5. Look around your room or apartment. Make a list of your "stuff," in order of priority. What stuff do you find to be most important to you, and why? How does the relevance of your stuff alter from occasion to occasion? For instance, what stuff has to come with you when you go home to visit your family over a holiday? How is this stuff different from the stuff you might take with you when you go on a trip

with friends? Write a short argument about what your stuff means to you, what it says about you, and what it reveals about the beliefs, desires, myths, anxieties, and values of American culture.

Analysis

6. Take a few moments to analyze and evaluate Carlin's text. Are there any logical fallacies, gaps, or unsubstantiated warrants and support are at work in Carlin's text? In what ways might these argumentative flaws undermine the success of his argument? How could they augment it? What gives you this sense? Write a short argument in which you provide quotes from the text to support your work as well as offer additional library and Internet sources.

Taking Action

Form a small group. Your task is to create a comedy sketch of your own that reveals something important about how a specific space, ritual, or style functions in American culture. Brainstorm ideas, come up with a workable concept, and then outline and write up your skit. Once you have revised it as carefully and thoroughly as possible, perform your comedy sketch for the whole class. After your performance, discuss the cultural criticism you tried to make and what rhetorical and argumentative tactics you employed. You might also choose to videotape all of the class comedy sketches and share them with other groups in the campus community.

Dan Leopard
"Micro-Ethnographies of the Screen: The Supermarket"

Dan Leopard has a doctorate from the University of Southern California in Los Angeles and an MFA from the School of the Art Institute of Chicago. He has worked as an independent filmmaker and has taught teens to produce television in the San Francisco Bay Area. Leopard currently teaches on Trash Cinema and Youth Culture at the USC School of Cinema-Television and is completing a book on transformations of educational practice and school culture in response to screen technologies and entertainment media.

EXERCISING YOUR SKILLS

Before Reading

Leopard's essay examines how screens function in one public space where we often shop, supermarkets. He also provides quick in-motion snapshots of these screens. In preparation for reading his text, go to another commercial space that requires consumers to use or be seen by multiple screens (stores, companies, sports arenas, concerts, or other spaces). As you observe how the screens work, think about what functions these screens have—or what their purposes are. In what ways do these screens operate similarly? In what ways do they operate differently? In what ways do these screens add to or detract from your experience of being in these spaces? How do the various screens make you behave, and what specific attitudes and feelings do they foster in you as a person and consumer? Take detailed notes about your experiences with these spaces and how they utilize screens.

As I enter my neighborhood supermarket, I pass beneath a television monitor mounted about five feet above my head. I glance up at the screen and see myself enter the store, the sliding glass door to my back and a rather bored looking young security guard, arms crossed leaning against the lotto machine, to my side. A small camera attached to the base of the monitor provides a continuous stream of images throughout the day. I suppose this screen must serve to warn any potential thieves that they are being watched. As a subject of the camera and its screen, I am now either a dissuaded thief or, perhaps most likely, an oblivious innocent as I notice that most shoppers entering through this door fail to look up at the surveillance screen. Whatever intention the store managers had in displaying this screen at this location, it goes for the most part unseen. I only notice this surveillance screen because I have come to this store with the express intent of seeing the screens that I normally ignore or overlook.

I grab a shopping cart and begin my trip through the aisles. At the rear of the store, past the bottles of organic juice, baggies of instant salad, and cartons of lactose free milk, stands a bank machine idling next to a full service teller window for a large bank chain. Whereas the shopper in relation to the screen display at the store entrance is given over to the identity of proto-thief or would-be bandit, the screen of the bank machine performs a routine function—dispensing cash, accepting deposits, informing on account balances, and the like. While the bank screen differs from the surveillance screen in that there is no starring role for the subject on the screen itself, the user does become the focus of the screen during the transaction. The screen directly addresses the user by delivering an instruction or by asking a series of questions. Insert card. Instant cash? Do you want to print a statement of your last ten transactions? Graphics appear on the screen, short animations that serve to entertain—if you can call it that—and to provide the user with a logo-like branding of the bank's identity. Figure 1 provides a sample screen shot of the image as it flits past the viewer/user. To this screen, I am one of the bank's valued customers.

Concluding my business at the bank machine, I load my shopping cart with food and arrive at the checkout line. The final screen that presents itself is a flat screen monitor mounted on a pole above the cash register about eye level with me as I transfer my food selections to a conveyor belt leading to the cashier. This screen rather loudly advertises items

Figure 1: Bank Machine Screen.

for sale in the store, local businesses, and upcoming programs on the Food Network while providing recipes for shoppers who have remembered to bring their notepads to the line. This "check-out" screen signals the eventual demise of the ubiquitous, decades old magazine rack located at the end of most cashier aisles (Figure 2). While in the past one has been offered the opportunity to glance through, and hopefully purchase, *Time, Newsweek,* or the *Weekly World News,* now one may gawk at a video screen conveniently placed for consumption. I recently became excited by the teaser for the season premier of *Emeril Live* and learned how to cook a nutmeg flavored, orange glazed ham (although I failed to bring my pocket notepad, so I have forgotten several of the steps in the process).

Figure 2: Checkout Line Screen.

While each of these supermarket screens participates in the ritual of grocery shopping, each serves a different function and ascribes a different subjectivity to the shopper. The screen mounted overhead at the entrance door serves to warn away shoplifters. Its image is silent, blurry, and continuous. The bank machine screen interacts with the shopper signaling activity through a series of beeps and music. Its image is both fragmented and functional. Finally, the checkout screen serves to distract shoppers as they wait in line to pay for their chosen food stuff. It is bright, sharp, loud, and rapidly edited. If the other two screens dissolve into the designed environment of the supermarket—each item for sale and each surface for display beckons to me while feigning a ubiquitous naturalness—then this final screen proclaims its need to seduce and distract me. In so doing, like an insecure performer on stage, it displays its newness to the supermarket scene. The design of product packaging and display advertising draws on a lineage leading back to the beginnings of consumer capitalism, while this checkout screen stands uneasily as a bastard hybrid of the magazine rack, the candy display, and the television commercial.

As media theorist Vincent Mosco [2004] suggests: "the real power of new technologies does not appear during their mythic period, when they are hailed for their ability to bring world peace, renew communications, or end scarcity, history, geography, or politics; rather, their social impact is greatest when technologies become banal." Public screens, even as they address us, attempt to blend in, to deflect our attention. During my previous trips to this supermarket, I had ignored the surveillance screen, cursed the bank screen for non-responsive buttons, and shielded my eyes from the checkout screen. Yet, nevertheless, each of these screens had called to me and I had on previous trips responded with the subjectivity that they—or to be less anthropomorphic, their designers—intended for me to display. What this micro-ethnographic glance—a frame of mind rather than a research method—reveals to the subject of these screens (in this case myself) is that these screens make us do things—refrain from shoplifting, withdraw cash, bake a ham.

Bibliography

Vincent Mosco. *The Digital Sublime: Myth, Power, and Cyberspace.* Cambridge, MA: MIT Press, 2004, p. 19.

After Reading

Critical Perspective

1. Read the first paragraph of Leopard's text. Now address the following questions: What kind of mood or tone is Leopard attempting to create for the reader? Why do you think a writer would make this choice? How does this approach make you feel?

Rhetoric and Argument

2. What specific language choices does Leopard make that impact you as a reader? Examine his use of audience, purpose, ethos, pathos, logos, intertextuality, context, and constraints. Do you find these choices to be persuasive? Why or why not? Be sure to point to the places in the text that best support your views.

3. Leopard's essay provides a creative approach to offering an academic argument. What is Leopard's main argumentative claim? Where does he make it in his text? What kind of claim is it? Do you think that this is a viable claim? Why or why not?

4. What kinds of evidence does Leopard utilize to support his claim? Do you find his use of support persuasive? Why or why not? Are there any logical fallacies at work in Leopard's essay? If yes, explain how and where they operate.

5. During the course of one week, make note of every form of interactive media you encounter, where you encounter it, and how it functions in your life. Using Leopard's essay as a model, write a creative piece about your experiences, then present a claim of cultural criticism that explains why these experiences are significant—what they say about changes in American culture, how spaces are being constructed differently, and the ways in which this is impacting us as a society.

Analysis

6. Examine Leopard's essay closely. Do you agree with his argumentative claim? Why or why not? Write a short argument in which you make an analytic claim about Leopard's essay, offering quotes from the text, and library and Internet sources to support your work.

Taking Action

Get into a small group. Your job is to create a short documentary about the ways in which screens and other fast-moving media images are shaping people's daily lives. Rather than going into this project with specific findings in mind, let what you learn along the way guide your inquiry.

Select businesses you will frequent to get observations and footage. Consider the people you will interview. Then, begin asking people from various age groups, class backgrounds, as well as different gender, race, or ethnicity categories to tell you about their experiences.

Once you have obtained your footage, examine it all and determine the sorts of themes and patterns you notice. What tentative assertions might you make about how media interaction in different spaces shapes people's experiences? Do people's backgrounds lead them to have different responses and thoughts about their media interaction? You may also want to consult additional library and Internet sources for information. When you are ready, share your documentary with the rest of the class and have a discussion about what you have all discovered.

Ad Analysis

Take a look at the ad on page 194 that appeared in *Seventeen* magazine in a March issue—right before high school prom season. Analyze this ad argumentatively as well as rhetorically. What is the main claim of the ad? How does the ad support that main claim? What assumptions or warrants does the ad hold to be true? Then look at the language and visuals in more detail. What specific language choices tell you that this ad is aimed at a young female audience? What appeals to pathos, particularly the audience's fears, desires, anxieties, values and beliefs, is this ad making? How does this ad work to construct particular notions about femininity and masculinity? Give specific evidence from the ad to support your views.

After you have read Best's essay, return to this ad. What claims might Best make about the specific narratives that this ad depends upon? What evidence might you find within this ad to support her claims?

AMY L. BEST

"Coming of Age at the Prom: Adolescence and Popular Culture"

Amy L. Best is a professor of sociology at San José State University. She has authored Prom Night: Youth, Schools, and Popular Culture *from which this essay comes. She has also written "Ugly Duckling to Swan" in* Constructions of Deviance *with D. Heckert.*

EXERCISING YOUR SKILLS

Before Reading

Best's piece is taken from a book in which she investigates proms as cultural rituals. How do you think that proms are represented in television, film, and advertisements? What specific examples can you point to in order to support your thoughts? Now think back to your own prom experiences. How did your experiences match the expectations proffered by the media?

As you consider how the prom operated at your particular school, discuss how the prom was described and treated differently by specific cliques within your school. In what ways did people's views of the prom expose their values, beliefs, and ideologies?

If you did not attend your prom, why did you specifically choose not to, and what were the results of your choice? If you did attend your prom, what did you wear, what kinds of music did you listen to, and what sort of car did you or your friends drive? What do these events and memories suggest to you about high school proms as ritualistic *events?* How might they reinforce myths and assumptions about youth culture as well as cultural narratives about masculinity and femininity?

Proms are a big deal. A much anticipated event for juniors and seniors, proms tend to take on a larger-than-life importance for many students, parents, and communities. It is not uncommon for preprom planning to begin early in the year. Teachers and students assemble after school to decide on the most important prom decisions: the theme, the location, the decorations, the menu, the remembrance gifts, the price of tickets, and the music (band or DJ?). By the time spring arrives, proms are the focal point of school life. The flurry of talk about who's taking whom, who's wearing what, and plans for after the prom often fills the halls between classes and spills over into the cafeterias. Most public schools and many private and parochial schools today organize a junior and senior prom each year. By the time students graduate from high school many have attended several proms; one young woman in this study had gone to ten proms by the time she graduated!

The appeal of the prom is understandable. For many high school kids the prom represents a momentary break in the monotony of daily school life; a departure from what are often considered mundane school routines. For others, the prom provides an occasion to shed one's school identity and become someone else, even if for only one night. Yet there is more here: the overwhelming messages from popular culture, parents, and teachers make it clear that the prom is an important cultural rite of passage. These messages shape how students come to think of the prom and its significance to their lives. Students often feel that they *must* go to the prom, that if they don't go somehow they have missed a once-in-a-lifetime chance. The message conveyed in films, television shows, prom magazines, and advertisements is that the prom is the most momentous night of the year. Don't squander this once-in-a-lifetime chance to make memories by not attending this significant social rite! Make the prom a night to remember!

Constructing the prom as an important cultural rite works to ensure that students will go to the prom. Subtle social controls are at work here in shaping how kids come to think of the prom and, subsequently, of themselves. Examining how proms are constructed through popular cultural texts, such as magazines, films, and television shows, the first portion of this essay identifies the discourses that have helped to define how proms are understood. The second portion explores the ways kids use the prom narratives presented in popular culture to talk about their proms. Particular consideration is given to how these narratives work to give meaning to youth identities.

A Night to Remember: Reading Proms in Contemporary Cultural Life

Proms are a part of our everyday cultural imagery, possibly more so now than ever before. A range of media have provided a bevy of images of the prom, testifying to its importance not only in the lives of high school students but to American cultural life as well. The 1980s witnessed an explosion of teen films organized around high school life and, most notably, the prom. Films like *Carrie, Pretty In Pink, Fast Times at Ridgemont High, Valley Girl. Back to the Future, Grease, Just One of the Guys, Teen Wolf,* and *Footloose* provided our culture with a collective imagination of the prom. Just as in the 1980s, movie theaters in the late 1990s were inundated with box office hits that either develop entirely around the prom (*10 Things I Hate About You, Trippin', Never Been Kissed, American Pie,* and *She's All That*—all released in 1999), or include prom scenes as a major part of their plot development (*Jawbreaker, Something About Mary, Dance till Dawn, The Rage: Carrie 2, Romy and Michele's High School Reunion, Grosse Point Blank,* and *Mean Girls*). Many television shows, such as *Beverly Hills 90210, Roseanne, That Seventies Show, The Simpsons, Boy Meets World, Saved by the Bell, Friends, Sabrina the Teenage Witch, The Golden Girls,* and *Buffy the Vampire Slayer* have also incorporated the prom into their story lines.

These films and television shows identify the key players of the prom. The prom queen tends to receive an inordinate amount of airtime. She is both adored and reviled, envied and scorned. She is pretty and popular, fashionably dressed, usually rich, and almost always white. She is consumed with her appearance and the appearance of others. She spends most of her time with her exclusive entourage of girlfriends, ruthlessly stepping on the little people. Then, there are the minor players, the teachers and parents. Teachers serve as reminders that proms are institutionally linked to schools. They are the chaperones, there to ensure that students don't dance too close together, to keep a watchful eye out for any tomfoolery, to make sure the punch hasn't been spiked.

Images of the prom and its attendants are everywhere in today's popular media. In the course of my research, I was struck repeatedly not only by the pervasiveness of prom images (the prom has been used to market *Tide* laundry detergent), but by how proms are framed around particular discourses of contemporary adolescent life. How proms are portrayed in popular media has everything to do with the current notions of the "adolescent."

It is not surprising that different narratives of adolescent life are employed to give the prom meaning; the prom is, after all, an event *for* adolescents. And just as there is not a single version of what an adolescent is, there is neither a single version of what a prom is. Images of the prom rely upon opposing and contestable readings of youth's worlds and realities, emerging as competing narratives. The narrative of nascent romance, for example, is central to how proms are understood culturally. But equally salient is the narrative of sex on prom night. Is the prom about romance or sex, good clean fun or wild abandon? [1] Based upon the media images of proms, it is difficult to know—though certainly the allure of heterosexual romance, in general, is often linked to the prom. What is always clear, however, as pointed out earlier, is that the prom is a rite of passage; for better or worse, the prom is not to be missed.

Images of proms, as varied as they are, provide a basis through which "adolescence" is culturally defined, interpreted, and made meaningful as a socially organized experience. Through these cultural representations, both the young and old are educated about the social role of adolescence, and what "adolescence" means via its relation to adulthood. In effect, we become readers of a generation of youth through these images. [2] What is significant about these images, however, is that they actually tell us little about how youth see and define themselves. Their importance as cultural artifacts lies in the fact that they speak volumes about how youth continue to be defined by the adult world. Cultural ideology is at work here, providing us as consumers of culture with an all-too-often limited number of meanings of youth's lives and realities. [3]

Coming of Age: Constructing the Teen

While representations of proms are laced with symbols of youth cultures, most also harbor adult agendas and anxieties about how youth should or should not organize themselves. Within a context in which youths themselves are increasingly seen as social liabilities, most films and TV shows reflect adult concerns for the development of youth into upstanding, morally correct adults. Teen violence, teen pregnancy, and youth crime are regularly broadcast on the nightly news. In the wake of these increased (and inflated) representations of demonized and morally impoverished youth, the prom is often nostalgically and reverently celebrated as a tiny capsule of youthful innocence and hope. In a recent article in *Harper's* magazine titled "Home After Dark: A Funeral for Three Girls in Kentucky," a feature about three girls who were shot by a fourteen-year-old student as they left the regular morning prayer session at their high school, it is worth noting that one of the girls, Kayce, was buried in her prom dress. The girl's mother explained to the mourners at the service that, "She's thankful Kayce went to her first prom last year. At the time it seemed almost overblown, the flowers, the pictures, the dress and preparation, but the memory of those preparations are her only indication of what it might have been like to plan a wedding for Kayce, with Kayce."[4] In this way, we can see that the prom is memorialized as an event that offers the promise to reclaim honor and youthful innocence (and possibly youth redemption).

In other cases, the prom is depicted as an important though somewhat trivial part of the process of coming of age. The following passage, taken from Jean Shepard's short story "Wanda Hickey's Night of Golden Memories," tells the tale of Shepard's high school prom. Shepard threads together the series of awkward, often painful and humiliating adolescent moments he endured not only to gain entrance to the prom but to ensure its success, noting, in retrospect, "I leafed through the pages [of the high school yearbook] . . . suddenly there it was—a sharply etched photographic record of a true puberty rite among a primitive tribe in Northern Indiana. The caption read: 'The Junior Prom was heartily enjoyed by one and all. The annual event was held this year at the Cherrywood Country Club. Mickey Eisley and his Magic Music Makers provided the romantic rhythms. All agreed it was an unforgettable evening, the memory of which we will cherish in the years to come.' True enough. In the gathering gloom of my Manhattan apartment, it all came back."[5] Drawing upon a similar discourse, *People* magazine, in one article featuring photos of Hollywood celebrities at their proms, enabled its readers to look on and "remember when," saying, "Ah, Spring! It's the time of year when a high schooler's thoughts turn from SATs and fake IDs to that other adolescent rite of passage: the prom. Years and even decades later, mere mention of the event, for those who have partaken, can conjure memories of baby-blue tuxes, big hair and really, really bad cover bands faster than you can hum the opening notes of 'Stairway to Heaven.'"[6]

The idea that the prom is a significant social event specific to being an adolescent permeates these cultural images. Whether the kids are fighting for their "right" to experience this rite of passage, as in the popular 1984 movie *Footloose,* or mark their coming of age by the loss of their virginity on prom night, as in the 1999 film *American Pie,* these images of kids at the prom rely upon and recuperate the idea that coming of age is a natural, incremental, and essential progression.[7] In Susan Shadburne's recent documentary *Street Kids and Tuxes,* about the lives of street kids in Oregon and their journey to a prom held for homeless youth, the promotional brochure reads as follows: "Here, for one brief night, they strut, eat, dance, laugh and forget their lives in the only traditional rite of passage they will probably ever know."[8]

In the popular 1999 teen film *She's All That,* about a young woman's struggle to "find" herself, her journey to selfhood culminates at the prom. Laney Boggs (Rachel Leigh Cook), is a slightly offbeat girl, disinterested in the daily banter of "popularity," disaffected from school, and alienated from her peers. By Hollywood standards, she is not your "typical" teen. Rather than shopping endlessly and fixating on romance like other (Hollywood) girls, Laney spends much of her time alone in the basement of her father's house, where she painstakingly pores over her politically inspired artwork, awaiting the arrival of adulthood. The meager social life she maintains exists outside of school.

When not painting, Laney spends her time watching over her younger brother, Simon, and her well-intentioned but inept widower father. Mired in the responsibilities of adult life, Laney hardly has time for such trivial matters as being a teen. In the opening scene of the film, we find Laney outside Simon's bedroom door, beckoning him to get out of bed; they are already late for school, she warns. In her hand she is holding a glass of orange juice for him. She pounds on his door, pleading with him, but he is slow to stir. Just as we are convinced that she is the maternal figure to Simon, and our remorse for her lost adolescence begins to wax, she hocks up a "loogey," threatening her brother that she will deposit the phlegm in his orange juice if he doesn't get out of bed. Alas, she is just a teen after all.

From this opening scene and throughout the movie, it is clear that Laney is responsible for the care of her family. Without the direction of a mother, it is she who must maintain family life and manage even its most mundane features. The tension between normative ideas of "adulthood" (real responsibility) and "adolescence" (carefree fun) underlies this film as a coming of age tale.

Laney's life, however, takes a sudden turn when Zack Syler (Freddie Prinze, Jr.), the most popular boy in school (who recently had been "dumped" by his horribly wicked longtime girlfriend and anticipated prom queen) accepts a bet wagered by his best friend that he can turn even the most pitiful wallflower into the prom queen. Laney, unequivocally recognized as the weirdest girl in school, is chosen for the bet. With a mere six weeks left before the prom, Zack gets to work: he enlists his younger sister to make her over into a teen beauty queen, and takes Laney to parties attended exclusively by the popular clique.

Determined to win the bet, Zack relentlessly pursues her. Inevitably (and predictably), both Zack and Laney begin to realize their emerging affections for one another. But eventually Laney learns the truth, that her newfound popularity has been a ruse and the mysterious but welcomed attentions of Zack Syler are the result of a cruelly inspired bet between two boys. Defeated, she returns to her artist's perch in the basement, and denounces "teen" life. She is determined not to attend her prom, even though she has been nominated for prom queen. On the night of the prom, we find Laney down in the basement, dressed in the disheveled, paint-splattered uniform of a "serious" artist, completing her self-portrait, when she is interrupted by her father. "Don't you have a prom or something to go to?" he asks.

"No, I'm not going," she replies. Disquieted by his daughter's decision not to attend her prom, and what it might mean for him as a "suitable" father, he pauses for a moment before he begins his "Father Knows Best" speech: "Sometimes I think you take on so much, so you don't have to deal with the business of being a kid. I can't imagine being seventeen is easy, especially with your mother not around. I'm just afraid if you keep putting off your life like this, you're gonna wake up eighty-five years old, sitting on a porch somewhere [he pauses evidently unsure what he should say next] . . . looking for your teeth."

"Thanks Dad," she replies, "That was graphic." Yet, she is sufficiently persuaded by her father's not-so-compelling treatise on coming of age that she trades in her artist's smock for a black-sequined, floor-length gown, attends her prom and is all the wiser for doing so, even though she is not elected prom queen and the promise of romance at the prom never materializes.[9] Stories such as these, depicting proms as modern-day Cinderella tales of transformation from disheveled, drab girlhood to sexy and glamorous femininity are common. *Pretty in Pink, Carrie,* and *Never Been Kissed* are all versions of this tale. Such tales work to secure femininity in our culture as well as the importance of heterosexual romance. While Laney is not elected prom queen and seems as if she couldn't care less, she still submits to the trappings of an idealized feminine image. She trades in her nonconformist style for a fashion makeover straight out of the pages of *Seventeen* magazine.

The prom is also constructed here as a quintessentially important part of the business of being a kid. Implicit is the idea that one cannot legitimately speak about the experience of high school—or of growing up, for that matter—if one is unable to reference the prom. In other words, having missed the prom, one might as well have missed all of what's important about high school. The prom is the capstone of teen life.

While relying upon a particular understanding of adolescence as a distinct stage in the life course, these images also naturalize what it means to be an adolescent. Equally significant, the construction of adolescence only becomes meaningful in relation to the construction of adulthood. In this way adolescence, more than being defined by what it is, is defined by what it is *not*.

It is also worth noting that these prom images, because they are based fundamentally on an all-American teen rite, revolve around white, middle-class teens. While narratives on proms vary, the characters in these films rarely do. Representations of youth in prom films are totalizing images; they work to erase class and racial differences among youth. They resecure the idea that the typical teen is white, suburban, and middle-class. By providing a narrow vision of youth, these images of kids at the prom reproduce prevailing cultural notions that adolescence is ahistorical and universal.

Prom as Horror Story: Teen Angst and Disaster

Proms occupy a precarious place. They are celebrated, packaged in particular ways that serve to designate them as important life events, but they are also easily satirized. The prom is an event adults may remember, but it is attended by teenagers only. Because of this, the prom is frequently depicted as an event that we adults may have taken seriously as teens, but only because we were "silly" teens, preoccupied with such ignoble and frivolous issues as "popularity" and "self-image." In popular films, as well as everyday talk, the prom is mockingly constructed as a moment besieged by teen angst and tumult—so profound disaster and disappointment are inevitable. One news radio talk show I listened to asked callers to call in with their most "horrifying prom episodes."[10] The idea that proms are riddled with disappointment, to be rendered inconsequential once we reach adulthood, was easy to recognize as part of our culture's coming-of-age lore.

The popular comedy *Something About Mary* is a film about an ill-fated prom whose narrative depends upon the notion that the teen years are a period of abject humiliation and social awkwardness. The story develops around Ted Stroemann (Ben Stiller), a caricature of male adolescence—nerdy, pimply, and with a mouth full of braces—who is beguiled by the pretty, popular, and smart Mary (Cameron Diaz). Like other high school geeks, he admires her from afar. On a whim, he musters up enough courage to ask Mary to the prom. Much to his astonishment, she actually says yes. On the awaited day, Ted arrives at her house outfitted in a brown tuxedo with a brown-trimmed frilly tuxedo shirt to pick her up. Mary descends the stairs, dressed in a sky-blue floor-length frock. She is an image of loveliness, embodying all that is innocent and pure: her long blond hair cascades over her shoulders, her blue eyes sparkle.[11] Just when Ted thinks on this night of nights that nothing could go wrong, it does. Before they leave for the prom, he visits the bathroom; as he is zipping up his pants, he catches his penis in the zipper. Not only painful, it is painfully humiliating. In an effort to salvage what appeared to be a magical evening, he struggles to gain composure; he is determined to resolve this dire situation, but in the end only makes matters worse. Before long, Mary is alerted to Ted's most compromising predicament, as are her mother and father! The scene concludes with him strapped to a stretcher, surrounded by a small crowd, before being carried off in an ambulance to the hospital, his one chance of love lost. We find Ted ten years later, pining away in a bar with a bunch of dimwitted pals and wondering, What if? What if they had made it to the prom, had had that special dance—would Mary have realized that he was her prince?

In many of these representational forms, proms are constructed through a filter of adult memory; in fact, the narrator is often an adult. While understood as an important event for youth, the prom also occupies a privileged place in the individual and collective memories of American adults.[12] Proms tend to be events that adults remember, which may help to explain why the themes of adolescent disappointment, fragility, and embarrassment are recurring themes in these texts. Proms, then, are a part of how adults remember and re-write their pasts (even so for those who didn't go to their proms). Adults get to define their current self in relation to their past self; who adults were then shapes who they are now.

In the prom film *Never Been Kissed* this theme presents itself again. The story revolves around Josey Geller (Drew Barrymore), who eight years after her high school prom works as a copy editor for her hometown newspaper. Just as in high school, she is plain, shy, and meek—in short, nothing special. She is given the opportunity to return to high school, this time as an undercover, investigative reporter; she eagerly accepts her assignment. Once there she is reminded of the torture and ridicule she had endured at the hands of her merciless peers (even as a twenty-five-year-old she still can't pass as "cool"). Through a series of flashbacks, we gain a sense of Josey's former high school self. In the first flashback, we see Josey in school—painfully awkward and drearily dull. In the background we hear a cacophony of voices chanting "Josey Grossey" (her nickname in high school). That she was repeatedly taunted and tormented by her classmates is a theme established early in the film. In the second flashback, Josey learns she has been asked to the prom by the most popular boy in school, on whom she has a secret crush. Not realizing she is being set up for disappointment and humiliation, she readies herself for her prom. She twirls before the mirror as she admires the image she sees before her—a lucky girl who is about to be whisked off to her prom by a popular boy. The phone rings; it is her date calling her outside. Filled with the promise of a wondrous night of fairy-tale romance, she rushes out to her front stoop and awaits his arrival. Yet instead of being presented with a corsage, as she had hoped, she is assaulted with raw eggs by her date. Devastated by this unexpected turn of events, she drops to the ground in tears as her date drives off with another girl to the prom.

Harboring this memory, years later she admits she has never fully recovered. "All I wanted was to be accepted and they tortured me . . . I lived a lifetime of regret after my first time at high school," she explains. Unlike her real high school days, her second chance at high school eventually brings her popularity, the man of her dreams (her English teacher), a date for the prom, and the much coveted honor—the throne. While she was prevented from attending her first prom, at her second she is crowned prom queen. Unlike the wallflower she was, she finds herself this time the unexpected recipient of male attention.

On prom night, we find her once again on her front stoop awaiting the arrival of her date. As he nears in the limo, she shudders as the painful memory of her past prom is momentarily relived. Unlike last time, she is presented with that long-awaited corsage, finally getting to attend the prom escorted by a dream date! What is significant is that as she reconstructs her past, she is also able to reconstruct her present. As an adult returning to high school, Josey Geller is given the opportunity to rewrite and renarrate her high school history, and significantly her prom. Only after she returns to high school, eight years after she has graduated, has she finally blossomed. She is hardly able to recognize her former self.

Not to Be Missed

Despite the inevitable disappointment that accompanies the prom, it is generally assumed that proms are events not to be missed. In the popular John Hughes movie *Pretty in Pink,* the older and wiser Iona (Annie Potts) tries to cajole the young Andie (played by then teen star Molly Ringwald) into attending her prom:

Andie: Did you say you went to your prom?

Iona: Yeah, sure.

Andie: Was it the worst?

Iona: Yeah, but it's supposed to be. You have to go. Right?

Andie: Well, you don't have to. It's not a requirement.

Iona: I had this girlfriend who didn't go to hers and every once in a while she gets this really terrible feeling something is missing. She checks her purse, she checks her keys, she counts her kids. She goes crazy and then she realizes nothing is missing. She decided it was side effects from skipping her prom.

Even if a terrible time is had, the prom is still supposed to be remembered. While this framing is resolutely patterned by an adult ideology, reflecting how adults define and remember their own proms and themselves as adolescents, kids I interviewed also used this discourse to make sense of the prom:

I wanted to show face so I can say twenty years from now, oh like, when we have our twenty-year reunion, you know like, "I went to my prom." I wanted to go and get dressed up and just showcase anyway, you know. (African-American female student)

In my school, going to the prom was a big deal. Everybody couldn't wait to show off their new clothes, limo, and their date. The prom was considered to be the event of the year. Some go for the once-in-a-life-time experience, while others go so they can tell their grandchildren they went. My reason for going to the prom was for obvious reasons. All my friends were going. Other reasons included that feeling of regret. I felt if I didn't attend my prom, that I one way or another would regret it in the future. (Asian-American female student)

Themes of regret, of the prom being an important social rite, of it being a night to make memories pervaded kids' accounts as they discussed their prom experiences:

It was May 27 and I still couldn't believe the long-awaited day was finally here. When we arrived we took more pictures. We walked into the dining area where we were given the most grotesque food ever imaginable. Somehow the food wasn't even important. Too many things were going on at the time. Friends were socializing, camera flashes were being shot and excitement saturated the air. We all danced the night away. The entire night seemed to breeze by like it was only one hour, if that long. I couldn't believe the night was gone. I knew in my heart that although it was gone, the memories of my friends, boyfriends, and fellow classmates would stay with me forever. (Asian-American female student)

The lingering feeling of regret in having missed the prom is so powerful that many of those who do not attend their proms operate with a similar understanding of what proms are and the significance they have for American culture and the overall life course. The regret that one African-American woman expressed about not going to the prom again testifies to the cultural notion that the prom is an important milestone in the process of becoming adults:

> When I first began high school I was under the impression that my senior year would be one of the best years of my life. I held onto this hope until approximately my junior year, where everything went downhill. I hated school more than ever. I really couldn't wait until my senior year and not for any other reason except the fact that it was to be my final year of school ever. I had no plans of going on to college at this point. Prom preparations began the first day of classes for most of the senior girls. But not for me. I was not interested in anything that had to do with school whatsoever. I was not banning the prom for reason of rejection from a potential prom date. I basically knew I could get a date and that made it worse. As the prom time neared I began to feel slight regret about my decision not to attend, but it was too late to turn back now. All the good dresses would have been taken, and all the good dates would have been taken. So prom night came and went for me just like any other night. I was alone because everyone I knew was attending our senior prom. I look back on my decision and I must admit I regret it. I regret that I missed out on many high school activities simply because of my negative feelings toward everything. I definitely know if I could turn back time I would have attended my prom.

The sense of fatalism expressed here points to how social controls work in this space. The fear of having missed the prom is harnessed as a mechanism to gain students' consent to this event and the material and ideological conditions it secures. As in cultural representations, the prom is interpreted here as a critically important part of the coming-of-age process.

A Time to Remember

In popular representations and in kids' talk, the prom is often thought to be especially meaningful because it represents one of the last times kids can appreciate their connection with students who share similar histories of place and space. "It's the last time you get to be with your friends, have fun," one student offered. "I really enjoyed the night. It was a night to remember, a night to remember." This theme pervaded students' narratives:

> My prom for me was very special. It was the last night I'd spend with my friends from home. It was a lot of fun because we were on a boat and the DJ started playing many old school songs, the Electric Slide, Doing The Butt among others. It was so much fun doing all our old dances and just reminiscing on the old days. It made us wonder how different things were going to be once we were all apart when we went to school. (African-American female student)

Proms are supposed to capture heartfelt emotions about leaving and loss, the disbanding of a unified class of students who are moving on. It is not surprising, then, that songs with titles like "We've Got Tonight," "Hold On to the Night," "Make it Last Forever," "Sweet Days," and "Only Time Will Tell" will be used as prom night themes year after year.[13] The song chosen for the last dance of the night often incorporates themes of change, continuity, remembrance, and commemoration. Consider these lyrics from Billy Joel's "A Time To Remember," which was a favorite when I attended high school in the 1980s, and continues to be a popular choice as a prom theme today:

> This is the time to remember, cause it will not last forever
> These are the days to hold onto, cause we won't although we'll want to
> These are the days, but times are gonna change
> You've given me the best of you and now I want the rest of you.
> Some day we will both look back and laugh
> We've lived through a lifetime and the aftermath.

Another song by Billy Joel, "Just the Way You Are," is also another of the popular prom songs:

> I would never leave you in times of troubles
> We never could have come this far.
> I took the good times, I'll take the bad times
> I'll take you just the way you are.

The prom is celebrated as a moment of togetherness, as a place of belonging to a group of students who share a collective history of the past.[14] (Of course, what is often overlooked is the fact that proms, like everyday life in school, are beset with divisions and distinctions.) The imminent departure from high school and entrance into an adult world is crystallized in the prom. The prom signifies a bridge between the past—life in high school—and an unknown future.[15] Two students responded:

> *Being a very tight-knit class we went through a lot together. The class of '95 always got along well. Our senior prom would be one of the last times our class would be together in its entirety. We were determined to make the most out of this night so we could look back and have very fond memories of everything and everyone. My senior prom was unforgettable. We made the most of one of our last times together and the memories we made will bond the members of my class for life. (White female student)*

> *It was like, "Ah, remember this and how funny was this?" It was basically the fact that like . . . the senior prom weekend was really like the end of the year. Everybody gets back and after a weekend like that, who wants to think about school, you know? It's usually like school is ending in like a month. And for us that weekend just like ended it. You know, because like before prom weekend it was like, "At least we have prom weekend coming up," you know? And then like, after that the only thing you have coming up is like graduation. So there's nothing, like, to look forward to, you know, because school's pretty much done with. (African-American male student)*

Many students talked about the prom as a moment in which to come together. A student from Woodrow High School, drawing a parallel between the prom and a dance ritual celebrating solidarity in a tribal society, told me the prom highlighted the harmonious coming together of diverse groups in their celebration of difference.

As is the case in popular cultural texts, kids' talk works to reconstruct adolescence as a universally shared experience; even across their differences these kids belong to a "common culture." What is assumed here is that all young people come to this space in similar ways, but of course they don't. Relations formed around race, class, gender, and sexuality shape the types of investments kids make in this space and how they ultimately define it. These kids' narratives privilege age over other social relations and in doing so elide attention to these differences.

Proms as Popular Cultural Sites: Representation and Everyday Life

What is the consequence of the repeated invocation of the theme of the prom as a rite of coming of age? Sociologists have long argued that ritual serves to stabilize the current organization of cultural and social life because it forcefully "unites a particular image of the universe with a strong emotional attachment to it."[16] While structuring kids' investments in the prom, these images also shape *how* kids read the prom. As I have shown the construction of the prom as an important cultural event relies upon prevailing definitions of adolescence as a distinct stage in the life course. Not only do these images *depend* upon our culture's willingness to accept adolescence as a "natural" given, but these images *confirm* and *reify* this reality. In other words, these images resecure the notion that to be a teenager is to be something entirely different from being an adult. Proms have been made meaningful in the wider culture through this lens, a lens that belongs fundamentally to adults, not to kids. However, kids do use these narratives to narrate their proms, as is clearly demonstrated here.

How, then, should the relationship between everyday life and these representational systems be understood and theorized? Since most of these prom representations are narrated by adults, the prom is interpreted through a discourse that defines adolescence by its relation to adult life and in so doing belies consideration of the series of ongoing relations that make the prom a complex and multilayered space of meaning. These images, while providing us with a clear sense of the cultural currency proms have, tell us little about the way kids invest in or define the prom. What an examination of these images does offer is a framework through which to understand what youth respond to as they fashion their identities at the prom. As kids make sense of who they are, they are profoundly aware that history and reality already has been defined for them. The challenge youth face as they solidify and articulate their identities (as working-class youth, white youth, middle-class youth, gendered youth, youth of color) is the struggle against these discursive and material forces that limit the possibility for meaningful self-representation. For this reason, understanding how youths' lives are shaped by adult agendas and ideologies, and how youth negotiate and struggle against them in local settings, is critically important at this historical moment. Popular culture may be made through these representational systems, but popular culture is also made through everyday local life.[17]

Notes

1. Equally significant is the possibility for multiple readings. I am not arguing here that these texts only can be read in one way. There is always the possibility for oppositional readings (Daspit and Weaver, 1999).
2. For more extensive analyses on teen films see Bernstein, 1997; Lewis, 1992.
3. Steinberg and Kincheloe, 1997.
4. Phillips, 1998:75.
5. Shepard, 1971:299–301.
6. "Dance Fever," 1996:42.
7. Kett, 1977; Lesko, 1996; Steinberg and Kincheloe, 1997.
8. That a prom is held for homeless kids further supports the argument I make here. Implicit is that this is an event that all youth, regardless of the conditions under which they live, should experience.
9. The analysis I offer here focuses on the ways in which this film sustains a narrow construction of the teen; however, the film can be read in a number of different ways. It also provides a rich, gendered narrative on what constitutes youth romance. In other ways, the film offers an alternate reading of femininity. It is clear that Laney in some ways is developing a feminist consciousness as she struggles to make sense of her newfound popularity. At the prom she is not elected prom queen. Surprisingly, she isn't crushed by her defeat. My purpose in making this point is to highlight the varied ways in which this film can be interpreted.
10. Significantly, two popular teen horror films, *Carrie* and *Prom Night,* center on the prom.
11. Of course, this image is racialized. Mary's presentation as "a dream date" is convincing in part because she is the embodiment of white purity (for more on this notion, see hooks, 1995).
12. In the course of researching this project, I heard scores of stories by adults about their proms. Adults were eager to share with me their tales (of disaster—most were horror stories), often unsolicited. The number of times I heard "Have I got a prom story for you" are too numerous to count. And there is more: a friend of mine was invited to a bachelorette party for a bride to be, for which all guests were requested to wear their 1980s prom dresses. I also learned of a self-help group that hosts a prom for its members. What underlies this adult event is the idea that participants can revisit their prom and rewrite its story in any way they wish.
13. www.proms.net.
14. Vinitzky-Seroussi, 1998.
15. For many of these kids, leaving high school is accompanied by greater "adult" responsibilities and the possibility for greater freedom and autonomy (at least in some measure). Many youth feel conflicted about finishing high school. Though schools exercise

enormous control over their lives, for some kids schools also serve as sanctuaries. This seems to be especially pronounced for white middle-class kids, whose adolescent experience is structured largely around securing their protection from an external world (Gaines, 1994).

16. Stoeltje, 1996:15.

17. For more information on popular culture, *what* it is and *where* it is, see Daspit and Weaver, 1999; Fiske, 1989a, 1989b; Roman and Christian-Smith, 1988.

References

Bernstein, Jonathan. 1997. *Pretty in Pink: The Golden Age of Teenage Movies*. New York: St. Martin's/Griffin.

"Dance Fever." 1996. *People,* May 27, 42–52.

Daspit, Toby and John A. Weaver, eds. 1999. *Popular Culture and Critical Pedagogy: Reading, Constructing, Connecting*. New York: Garland.

Fiske, John. 1989a. *Understanding Popular Culture*. Boston: Unwin Hyman.

———. 1989b. *Reading The Popular*. Boston: Unwin Hyman.

Gaines, Donna. 1994. "Border Crossing in the U.S.A." *Microphone Fiends: Youth Music and Youth Culture,* ed. Andrew Ross and Tricia Rose. New York: Routledge.

Hooks, Bell. 1995. *Reel to Real: Race, Sex and Class at the Movies*. New York: Routledge.

Kett, Joseph F. 1977. *Rites of Passage: Adolescence in America, 1790 to the Present*. New York: Basic Books.

Lesko, Nancy. 1996. "Denaturalizing Adolescence: The Politics of Contemporary Representation." *Youth and Society* 28:2 (139–61).

Lewis, Jon. 1992. *The Road to Romance and Ruin: Teen Films and Youth Culture*. New York: Routledge.

McCoy, Liz. 1995. "Activating the Photographic Text." *Knowledge, Experience and Ruling Relations: Studies in the Social Organization of Knowledge,* ed. Marie Campbell and Ann Manicom. Toronto: University of Toronto Press.

Phillips, Jayne Anne. 1998. "Home After Dark: A Funeral for Three Girls In Kentucky." *Harper's,* November, 73–83.

Roman, Leslie G. and Linda Christian-Smith, eds. 1988. *Becoming Feminine: The Politics of Popular Culture*. London: The Falmer Press.

Shepard, Jean. 1971. *Wanda Mickey's Night of Golden Memories and Other Disasters*. New York: Doubleday.

Steinberg, Shirley and Joe L. Kincheloe, eds. 1997. *Kinder-Culture: The Corporate Construction of Childhood*. Boulder, CO: Westview Press.

Stoeltje, Beverly. 1996. "The Snake Charmer Queen: Ritual Competition and Signification in American Festival." *Beauty Queens On The Global Stage: Gender, Contests and Power,* ed. Colleen Ballerino Cohen, Richard Wilk, and Beverly Stoeltje. New York: Routledge.

Vinitzky-Seroussi, Vered. 1998. *After Pomp and Circumstance: High School Reunion as an Autobiographical Occasion*. Chicago: University of Chicago Press.

After Reading

Critical Perspective

1. What did you like about Best's text? What did you not like about Best's text? Do you think that there is any other information she should have included in order to make her text more persuasive? If yes, provide examples.

Rhetoric and Argument

2. What rhetorical tactics such as use of audience, purpose, ethos, pathos, logos, intertextuality, context, and constraints do you see in this essay? Provide textual evidence for this. Do you think these tactics help bolster her argument? Why or why not?

3. Best argues that the ways in which prom rituals are represented in popular television and movies is through adults' eyes. She contends that these representations reinforce stereotypes about America's youths. Examining her argument closely and also thinking about your own experiences, do you find her claim convincing? Why or why not?

4. What kinds of evidence does Best utilize to back up her claim? Can you think of other relevant examples from which she might draw, including those based on your own experiences or the experiences of your friends? Are there examples that you can think of that might undermine her argument?

5. Are there any logical flaws in Best's argument that you can detect? Are there any specific assumptions that she makes with which you disagree? Be sure to point to evidence from her text to support your assertions.

Analysis

6. Best asserts that in most media images the prom queen, prom king, and the prom situation are depicted as homogeneous—most people are white, middle class, and conform to Western standards of "beauty." In a short essay, explain your thoughts: Do you agree with this assessment? Why or why not? What problems might her assertion pose? Provide examples from your own experiences as well as library and Internet sources.

Taking Action

Meet in a small group. Think about other rituals and important rites of passage in teenagers' lives beside the prom (i.e., first significant time away from your family, first best friend, first love interest, first driver's license and road trip, first acceptance to college). How do advertisers, and television show and film creators, use these rites of passage to encourage young consumers to purchase their products (e.g., clothing and food, video games, flowers and candy cars, computers and books)?

What narratives do these media forms tell us about who teenagers and twenty-somethings are, what they believe, and what is important to them? In what ways do these images represent you? In what ways do these images fail to capture what these events meant to you? Be sure to record all of the different thoughts and reactions of group members. Consult library and Internet sources if useful. Consider sharing your work with other groups outside your class, both inside and outside the campus community.

Camilo José Vergara
"The Ghetto Cityscape"

Camilo José Vergara is a photographer and writer. He has written essays for The New York Times, The Nation, Architectural Record, *and* The Atlantic Monthly. *This essay appeared in his book* The New American Ghetto. *He has also published* Unexpected Chicanoland, Twin Towers Remembered, *and* Silent Cities: The Evolution of the American Cemetary.

EXERCISING YOUR SKILLS

Before Reading

In this essay Vergara writes about ghettos as important cultural spaces. As a photographer, he has spent a lot of time in various spaces, observing people. Visit an area that you would categorize as having either urban or rural poverty. Spend a number of hours there taking detailed notes on what you see and experience. What kinds of houses, stores, green areas, and the like are available for people? What messages might the ways in which space is laid out send about issues of poverty? What do you think about such messages?

If you were among the nearly eleven thousand people who lived in two-story row houses in North Camden in the 1960s, you could walk to work at Esterbrook Pen, at Knox Gelatin, at RCA, or at J. R. Evans Leather. You could shop on Broadway, a busy three-mile-long commercial thoroughfare, nicknamed the "Street of Lights" because of its five first-run movie theaters with their bright neon signs.

After J. R. Evans Leather was abandoned and almost completely demolished, its smokestack stood alone in a vast field by the Delaware River, a symbol of the demise of industry in Camden. Hundreds of row houses—once counted among the best ordinary urban dwellings in America—have been scooped up by bulldozers, their debris carted to a dump in Delaware. Walking along North Camden's narrow streets, one passes entire blocks without a single structure, the empty land crisscrossed by footpaths. The scattered dwellings that remain are faced with iron bars, so that they resemble cages.

With nearly half of its overwhelmingly Latino population on some form of public assistance, this once thriving working-class neighborhood is now the poorest urban community in New Jersey. In 1986, former mayor Alfred Pierce called Camden a reservation for the destitute. The north section of the city has become the drug center for South Jersey, and it hosts a large state prison.

North Camden is not unique. Since the riots of the 1960s, American cities have experienced profound transformations, best revealed in the spatial restructuring of their ghettos and in the emergence of new urban forms. During the past decade, however, the "underclass" and homelessness have dominated the study of urban poverty. Meanwhile, the power of the physical surroundings to shape lives, to mirror people's existence, and to symbolize social relations has been ignored. When scholars from across the political spectrum discuss the factors that account for the persistence of poverty, they fail to consider its living environments. And when prescribing solutions, they overlook the very elements that define the new ghettos: the ruins and the semi-ruins; the medical, warehousing, and behavior-modification institutions; the various NIMBYs, fortresses, and walls; and, not least, the bitterness and anger resulting from living in these places.

Dismissing the value of information received through sight, taste, and smell, or through the emotional overtones in an informant's voice, or from the sensation of moving through the spaces studied, has led to the creation of constructs without character, individuality, or a sense of place. And although the limitations of statistical data—particularly when dealing with very poor populations—are widely acknowledged, our great dependency on numbers is fiercely defended. Other approaches are dismissed as impressionistic, anecdotal, as poetry, or "windshield surveys."

Yet today's ghettos are diverse, rich in public and private responses to the environment, in expressions of cultural identity, and in reminders of history. These communities are uncharted territory; to be understood, their forms need to be identified, described, inventoried, and mapped.

An examination of scores of ghettos across the nation reveals three types: "green ghettos," characterized by depopulation, vacant land over grown by nature, and ruins; "institutional ghettos," publicly financed places of confinement designed mainly for the native-born; and "new immigrant ghettos," deriving their character from an influx of immigrants, mainly Latino and West Indian. Some of these communities have continued to lose population; others have emerged where a quarter-century ago there were white ethnic blue-collar neighborhoods; and sections of older ghettos have remained stable, working neighborhoods or have been rebuilt.

The Green Ghetto: Return to Wilderness?

Green ghettos, where little has been done to counter the effect of disinvestment, abandonment, depopulation, and dependency, are the leftovers of a society. Best exemplified by North Camden, Detroit's East Side, Chicago's Lawndale, and East St. Louis in Illinois, they are expanding outward to include poor suburbs of large cities such as Robbins, Illinois, and are even found in small cities such as Benton Harbor, Michigan.

Residents, remembering the businesses that moved to suburban malls, the closed factories, the fires, complain of living in a threatening place bereft of jobs and stores and neglected by City Hall. In many sections of these ghettos, pheasants and rabbits have regained the space once occupied by humans, yet these are not wilderness retreats in the heat of the city. "Nothing but weeds are growing there" is a frequent complaint about vacant lots, expressing no mere distaste for the vegetation, but moral outrage at the neglect that produces these anomalies. Plants grow wildly on and around the vestiges of the former International Harvester Component Plant in West Pullman, Chicago. Derelict industrial buildings here and in other ghettos have long ago been stripped of anything of value. Large parcels of land lie unkempt or paved over, subtracted from the life of the city. Contradicting a long-held vision of our country as a place of endless progress, ruins, once unforeseen, are now ignored.

Institutional Ghettos: The New Poorhouses

In New York City, Newark, and Chicago, large and expensive habitats—institutional ghettos—have been created for the weakest and most vulnerable members of our society. Institution by institution, facility by facility, these environments have been assembled in the most drug-infested and destitute parts of cities. They are the complex poorhouses of the twenty-first century, places to store a growing marginal population officially certified as "not employable." Residents are selected from the entire population of the municipality for their lack of money or home, for their addictions, for their diseases and other afflictions. Nonresidents come to these institutions to pick up medications, surplus food, used clothes; to get counseling or training; or to do a stint in prison. Other visitors buy drugs and sex.

As Greg Turner, the manager of a day shelter on the Near West Side of Chicago, puts it: "They say, 'Let's get them off the streets and put them together in groups.' It is like the zoo: we are going to put the birds over here; we are going to put the reptiles over there; we are going to put the buffalo over here; we are going to put the seals by the pool. It is doing nothing to work with the root of the problem, just like they do nothing to work with the children, to teach them things so they don't grow up and become more homeless people or substance abusers."

Although the need for individual components—for instance, a homeless shelter or a waste incinerator—may be subject to public debate, the overall consequences of creating such "campuses" of institutions are dismissed. The most important barrier to their growth is the cost to the taxpayers of building and maintaining them.

Such sections of the city are not neighborhoods. The streets surrounding Lincoln Park in south Newark, for example, an area that includes landmark houses, grand public buildings, and a once-elegant hotel, were chosen by two drug treatment programs because six of its large mansions would provide inexpensive housing for a residential treatment program. On the northwest corner of the park, a shelter for battered women just opened in another mansion, and a block north in a former garage is a men's shelter and soup kitchen. The largest structures overlooking the park, the hotel and a former federal office building, house the elderly, who fear going out by themselves. No children play in the park; no parents come home from work. This is a no-man's-land devoted to the contradictory goals of selling drugs and getting high, on the one hand, and becoming clean and employed on the other.

Sterling Street, Newark, 1980.

New Immigrant Ghettos: Dynamic and Fluid

In other parts of New York and Chicago a community of recent immigrants is growing up, but this type of ghetto is most visible in South Central Los Angeles and Compton, where the built environment is more intimate than in older ghettos, the physical structures are more adaptable and it is easier for newcomers to imprint their identity. Here paint goes a long way to transform the appearance of the street.

The new immigrant ghettos are characterized by tiny offices providing services such as driving instruction, insurance, and immigration assistance; by stores that sell imported beer, produce, and canned goods; and by restaurants offering home cooking. Notable are the businesses that reflect the busy exchange between the local population and their native country: money transfers, travel agencies, even funeral homes that arrange to have bodies shipped home.

To get by, most residents are forced to resort to exploitative jobs paying minimum wage or less and usually lacking health benefits. For housing they crowd together in small, badly maintained apartments, cinder-block garages, or in trailers.

Not being eligible for public or city-owned housing may in the long run prove to be a blessing for the newcomers. Although forced to pay high rents, immigrants tend to concentrate in neighborhoods that are part of the urban economy, thus avoiding the extreme social disorganization, isolation, and violence that characterize other types of ghettos. Because of the huge influx of young people with expectations that life will be better for

Sterling Street replaced by a parking lot, 1994.

their children and grandchildren, these ghettos are more dynamic and fluid, resembling the foreign-born communities of a century ago.

After Reading

Critical Perspective

1. Describe how Vergara begins his text. What kinds of language choices does he make? In what ways might these be significant to Vergara's larger argument?

Rhetoric and Argument

2. Examine Vergara's rhetorical strategies—his use of audience, purpose, ethos, pathos, logos, intertextuality, context, and constraints. Characterize why you think that they are effective or ineffective. Be sure to provide quotes from the text to back up your views.
3. Consider Vergara's use of subtitles in his text. Why do you think he employs them? What textual evidence can you point to in order to support your thoughts? Do you think that this choice is persuasive?
4. What do you think Vergara is arguing about ghettos? What makes you think this? Where in his text do you find evidence to support your thoughts? Do you agree with him? Why or why not?

Analysis

5. Write a short argumentative essay in which you address the following questions: Why does Vergara think that writers and scholars have previously overlooked these various kinds of cityscapes? What have been the effects of this neglect? Do you think that Vergara is accurate? Why or why not? In order to support your views, be sure to provide evidence from his text as well as from additional library and Internet sources.

Taking Action

Form a small group to discuss a series of questions. Be sure to record your answers. Think about the neighborhood in which you grew up. Does it fall into any of the categories outlined by Vergara? If yes, how so? If no, how is your neighborhood different? What are the various pros and cons of living in this kind of neighborhood? What kinds of communities, relationships, and experiences does it foster? What kind of relationships between people does it make more difficult? Consult relevant library and Internet sources as needed. Then get into the larger class group to share your findings.

SUSAN WILLIS

"Disney World: Public Use/Private State"

Susan Willis is a professor of English at Duke University. She is the author of Specifying: Black Women, Writing the American Experience, *and a book on mass culture,* A Primer for Daily Life. *Willis is also coauthor of* Inside the Mouse: Work and Play at Walt Disney World.

EXERCISING YOUR SKILLS

Before Reading

Willis provides a very detailed reading of how Disney World's space functions. Examine one of the Disney communities or explore another planned community in your area. Make note of the specific features of this community (what services are there) as well as the specific features that appear to be absent. What do you like about this community? What don't you like? Why?

At Disney World, the erasure of spontaneity is so great that spontaneity itself has been programmed. On the "Jungle Cruise" khaki-clad tour guides teasingly engage the visitors with their banter, whose apparent spontaneity has been carefully scripted and painstakingly rehearsed. Nothing is left to the imagination or the unforeseen. Even the paths and walkways represent the programmed assimilation of the spontaneous. According to published reports, there were no established walkways laid down for the opening-day crowds at Disneyland.[1] Rather, the Disney Imagineers waited to see where people would walk, then paved over their spontaneous footpaths to make prescribed routes.

The erasure of spontaneity has largely to do with the totality of the built and themed environment. Visitors are inducted into the park's program, their every need predefined and presented to them as a packaged routine and set of choices. "I'm not used to having everything done for me." This is how my companion at Disney World reacted when she checked into a Disney resort hotel and found that she, her suitcase, and her credit card had been turned into the scripted components of a highly orchestrated program. My companion later remarked that while she found it odd not to have to take care of everything herself (as she normally does in order to accomplish her daily tasks), she found it "liberating" to just fall into the proper pattern, knowing that nothing could arise that hadn't already been factored into the system. I have heard my companion's remarks reiterated by many visitors to the park with whom I've talked. Most describe feeling "freed up" ("I didn't have to worry about my kids," "I didn't have to think about anything") by the experience of relinquishing control over the complex problem-solving thoughts and operations that otherwise define their lives. Many visitors suspend daily perceptions and judgments altogether, and treat the wonderland environment as more real than real. I saw this happen one morning when walking to breakfast at my Disney resort hotel. Two small children were stooped over a small snake that had crawled out onto the sun-warmed path. "Don't worry, it's rubber," remarked their mother. Clearly only Audio-Animatronic simulacra of the real world can inhabit Disney World. A real snake is an impossibility.

In fact, the entire natural world is subsumed by the primacy of the artificial. The next morning I stepped outside at the end of an early morning shower. The humid atmosphere held the combination of sun and rain "Oh! Did they turn the sprinklers on?" This is the way my next-door neighbor greeted the day as she emerged from her hotel room. The Disney environment puts visitors inside the world that Philip K. Dick depicted in *Do Androids Dream of Electric Sheep?*—where all animal life has been exterminated, but replaced by the production of simulacra, so real in appearance that people have difficulty recalling that real animals no longer exist. The marvelous effect of science fiction is produced out of a dislocation between two worlds, which the reader apprehends as an estrangement, but the characters inside the novel cannot grasp because they have only the one world: the world of simulacra. The effect of the marvelous cannot be achieved unless the artificial environment is perceived through the retained memory of everyday reality. Total absorption into the Disney environment cancels the possibility for the marvelous and leaves the visitor with the banality of a park-wide sprinkler system. No muggers, no rain, no ants, and no snakes.

Amusement is the commodified negation of play. What is play but the spontaneous coming together of activity and imagination, rendered more pleasurable by the addition of friends? At Disney World, the world's most highly developed private property "state" devoted to amusement, play is all but eliminated by the absolute domination of program over spontaneity. Every ride runs according to a computerized schedule. There is no possibility

[1] Scott Bukatman, "There's Always Tomorrowland: Disney and the Hypercinematic Experience." *October 57* (Summer 1991). pp. 55–78.

of an awful thrill, like being stuck at the top of a ferris wheel. Order prevails particularly in the queues for the rides that zigzag dutifully on a prescribed path created out of stanchions and ropes; and the visitor's assimilation into the queue does not catapult him or her into another universe, as it would if Jorge Luis Borges fabricated the program. The Disney labyrinth is a banal extension of the ride's point of embarkation, which extends into the ride as a hyper-themed continuation of the queue. The "Backstage Movie Tour" has done away with the distinction between the ride and its queue by condemning the visitor to a two-and-a-half-hour-long pedagogical queue that preaches the process of movie production. Guests are mercilessly herded through sound stages and conveyed across endless back lots where one sees the ranch-style houses used in TV commercials and a few wrecked cars from movie chase scenes. Happily, there are a few discreet exit doors, bail-out points for parents with bored children. Even Main Street dictates programmed amusement because it is not a street but a conduit, albeit laden with commodity distractions, that conveys the visitor to the Magic Kingdom's other zones where more queues, rides, and commodities distinguish themselves on the basis of their themes. All historical and cultural references are merely ingredients for decor. Every expectation is met programmatically and in conformity with theme. Mickey as Sorcerer's Apprentice does not appear in the Wild West or the exotic worlds of Jungle and Adventure, the niches for Davy Crockett and Indiana Jones. Just imagine the chaos, a park-wide short circuit, that the mixing of themed ingredients might produce. Amusement areas are identified by a "look," by characters in costume, by the goods on sale: What place—i.e., product—is Snow White promoting if she's arm in arm with an astronaut? The Utopian intermingling of thematic opportunities such as occurred at the finale of the movie *Who Framed Roger Rabbit?,* with Warner and Disney "toons" breaking their copyrighted species separation to cavort with each other and the human actors, will not happen at Disney World.

However, now that the costumed embodiment of Roger Rabbit has taken up residence at Disney World, he, too, can expect to have a properly assigned niche in the spectacular Disney parade of characters. These have been augmented with a host of other Disney/Lucas/Spielberg creations, including Michael Jackson of "Captain EO" and C3PO and R2D2 of *Star Wars,* as well as Disney buyouts such as Jim Henson's Muppets and the Saturday morning cartoon heroes, the Teenage Mutant Ninja Turtles. The Disney Corporation's acquisition of the stock-in-trade of popular culture icons facilitates a belief commonly held by young children that every popular childhood figure "lives" at Disney World. In the Utopian imagination of children, Disney World may well be a never-ending version of the finale to *Roger Rabbit* where every product of the imagination lives in community. In reality, the products (of adult imaginations) live to sell, to be consumed, to multiply.

What's most interesting about Disney World is what's not there. Intimacy is not in the program even though the architecture includes several secluded nooks, gazebos, and patios. During my five-day stay, I saw only one kiss—and this a husbandly peck on the cheek. Eruptions of imaginative play are just as rare. During the same five-day visit, I observed only one such incident even though there were probably fifty thousand children in the park. What's curious about what's not at Disney is that there is no way of knowing what's not there until an aberrant event occurs and provokes the remembrance of the social forms and behaviors that have been left out. This was the case with the episode of spontaneous play. Until I saw real play, I didn't realize that it was missing. The incident stood out against a humdrum background of uniform amusement: hundreds of kids being pushed from attraction to attraction in their strollers, hundreds more waiting dutifully in the queues or marching about in family groups—all of them abstaining from the loud, jostling, teasing, and rivalrous behaviors that would otherwise characterize many of their activities. Out of this homogeneous "amused" mass, two kids snagged a huge sombrero each from an open-air stall at the foot of the Mexico Pavilion's Aztec temple stairway and began their impromptu version of the Mexican hat dance up and down the steps. Their play was clearly counterproductive as it took up most of the stairway, making it difficult for visitors to enter the pavilion. Play negated the function of the stairs as conduit into the attraction. The kids abandoned themselves to their fun, while all around them, the great mass of visitors purposefully kept their activities in line with Disney World's prescribed functions. Everyone but the dancers seemed to have accepted the park's unwritten motto: "If you pay, you shouldn't play." To get your money's worth, you have to do everything and do it in the prescribed manner. Free play is gratuitous and therefore a waste of the family's leisure time expenditure.

Conformity with the park's program upholds the Disney value system. Purposeful consumption—while it costs the consumer a great deal—affirms the value of the consumer. "Don't forget, we drove twenty hours to get here." This is how one father admonished his young son who was squirming about on the floor of EPCOT's Independence Hall, waiting for the amusement to begin. The child's wanton and impatient waste of time was seen as a waste of the family's investment in its amusement. If a family is to realize the value of its leisure time consumptions, then every member must function as a proper consumer.

The success of Disney World as an amusement park has largely to do with the way its use of programming meshes with the economics of consumption as a value system. In a world wholly predicated on consumption, the dominant order need not proscribe those activities that run counter to consumption, such as free play and squirming, because the consuming public largely polices itself against gratuitous acts which would interfere with the production of consumption as a value. Conformity with the practice of consumption is so widespread and deep at Disney World that occasional manifestations of boredom or spontaneity do not influence the compulsively correct behavior of others. Independence Hall did not give way to a seething mass of squirming youngsters even though all had to sit through a twenty-minute wait. Nor did other children on the margins of the hat dance fling themselves into the fun. Such infectious behavior would have indicated communally defined social relations or the desire for such social relations. Outside of Disney World in places of public use, infectious behavior is common. One child squirming about on the library floor breeds others; siblings chasing each other around in a supermarket draw others; one child mischievously poking at a public fountain attracts others; kids freeloading rides on a department store escalator can draw a crowd. These playful, impertinent acts indicate an imperfect mesh between programmed environment and the value system of consumption. Consumers may occasionally reclaim the social, particularly the child consumer who has not yet been fully and properly socialized to accept individuation as the bottom line in the consumer system of value. As an economic factor, the individual exists to maximize consumption—and therefore profits—across the broad mass of consumers. This is the economic maxim most cherished by the fastfood industry, where every burger and order of fries is individually packaged and consumed to preclude consumer pooling and sharing.

At Disney World the basic social unit is the family. This was made particularly clear to me because as a single visitor conducting research, I presented a problem at the point of embarkation for each of the rides. "How many in your group?" "One." The lone occupant of a conveyance invariably constructed to hold the various numerical breakdowns of the nuclear family (two, three, or four) is an anomaly. Perhaps the most family-affirming aspect of Disney World is the way the queues serve as a place where family members negotiate who will ride with whom. Will Mom and Dad separate themselves so as to accompany their two kids on a two-person ride? Will an older sibling assume the responsibility for a younger brother or sister? Every ride asks the family to evaluate each of its member's needs for security and independence. This is probably the only situation in a family's visit to Disney World where the social relations of family materialize as practice. Otherwise and throughout a family's stay, the family as nexus for social relations is subsumed by the primary definition of family as the basic unit of consumption. In consumer society at large, each of us is an atomized consumer. Families are composed of autonomous, individuated consumers, each satisfying his or her age- and gender-differentiated taste in the music, video, food, and pleasure marketplace. In contrast, Disney World puts the family back together. Even teens are integrated in their families and are seldom seen roaming the park in teen groups as they might in shopping malls.

Families at Disney World present themselves as families, like the one I saw one morning on my way to breakfast at a Disney resort hotel: father, mother, and three children, small to large, each wearing identical blue Mickey Mouse T-shirts and shorts. As I walked past them, I overheard the middle child say, "We looked better yesterday—in white." Immediately, I envisioned the family in yesterday's matching outfits, and wondered if they had bought identical ensembles for every day of their stay.

All expressions of mass culture include contradictory Utopian impulses, which may be buried or depicted in distorted form, but nevertheless generate much of the satisfaction of mass cultural commodities (whether the consumer recognizes them as Utopian or not). While the ideology of the family has long functioned to promote conservative—even reactionary—political and social agendas, the structure of the family as a social unit signifies communality rather than individuality and can give impetus to Utopian longings for communally defined relations in society at large. However, when the family buys into the look of a family, and appraises itself on the basis of its look ("We looked better yesterday"), it becomes a walking, talking commodity, a packaged unit of consumption stamped with the Mickey logo of approval. The theoretical question that this family poses for me is not whether its representation of itself as family includes Utopian possibilities (because it does), but whether such impulses can be expressed and communicated in ways not accessible to commodification.

In its identical dress, the family represents itself as capitalism's version of a democratized unit of consumption. Differences and inequalities among family members are reduced to distinctions in age and size. We have all had occasion to experience the doppelganger effect in the presence of identical twins who choose (or whose families enforce) identical dress. Whether chosen or imposed, identical twins who practice the art of same dress have the possibility of confounding or subverting social order. In contrast, the heterogeneous family whose members choose to dress identically affirms conformity with social order. The family has cloned itself as a multiple, but identical consumer, thus enabling the maximization of consumption. It is a microcosmic representation of free market democracy where the range of choices is restricted to the series of objects already on the shelf. In this system there is no radical choice. Even the minority of visitors who choose to wear their Rolling Stones and Grateful Dead T-shirts give the impression of having felt constrained not to wear a Disney logo.

Actually, Disney has invented a category of negative consumer choices for those individuals who wish to express nonconformity. This I discovered as I prepared to depart for my Disney research trip, when my daughter Cassie (fifteen years old and "cool" to the max) warned me, "Don't buy me any of that Disney paraphernalia." As it turned out, she was happy to get a pair of boxer shorts emblazoned with the leering images of Disney's villains: two evil queens, the Big Bad Wolf, and Captain Hook. Every area of Disney World includes a Disney Villains Shop, a chain store for bad-guy merchandise. Visitors who harbor anti-Disney sentiments can express their cultural politics by consuming the negative Disney line. There is no possibility of an anticonsumption at Disney World. All visitors are, by definition, consumers, their status conferred with the price of admission.

At Disney World even memories are commodities. How the visitor will remember his or her experience of the park has been programmed and indicated by the thousands of "Kodak Picture Spot" signposts. These position the photographer so as to capture the best views of each and every attraction, so that even the most inept family members can bring home perfect postcard like photos. To return home from a trip to Disney World with a collection of haphazardly photographed environments or idiosyncratic family shots is tantamount to collecting bad memories. A family album comprised of picture-perfect photo-site images, on the other hand, constitutes the grand narrative of the family's trip to Disney World, the one that can be offered as testimony to money well spent. Meanwhile, all those embarrassing photos, the ones not programmed by the "Picture Spots," that depict babies with ice cream all over their faces or toddlers who burst into tears rather than smiles at the sight of those big-headed costumed characters that crop up all over the park—these are the images that are best left forgotten.

The other commodified form of memory is the souvenir. As long as there has been tourism there have also been souvenirs: objects marketed to concretize the visitor's experience of another place. From a certain point of view, religious pilgrimage includes aspects of tourism, particularly when the culmination of pilgrimage is the acquisition of a transportable relic. Indeed, secular mass culture often imitates the forms and practices of popular religious culture. For many Americans today who make pilgrimages to Graceland and bring home a mass-produced piece of Presley memorabilia, culture and religion collide and mesh.

Of course, the desire to translate meaningful moments into concrete objects need not take commodified form. In Toni Morrison's *Song of Solomon,* Pilate, a larger-than-life earth mother if there ever was one, spent her early vagabondage gathering a stone from every place she visited. Similarly, I know of mountain climbers who mark their ascents by bringing a rock back from each peak they climb. Like Pilate's stones, these tend to be nondescript and embody personal remembrances available only to the collector. In contrast, the commodity souvenir enunciates a single meaning to everyone: "I was there. I bought something." Unlike the souvenirs I remember having seen as a child, seashells painted with seascapes and the name of some picturesque resort town, most souvenirs today are printed with logos (like the Hard Rock Cafe T-shirt), or renderings of copyrighted material (all the Disney merchandise). The purchase of such a souvenir allows the consumer the illusion of participating in the enterprise as a whole, attaining a piece of the action. This is the consumerist version of small-time buying on the stock exchange. We all trade in logos—buy them, wear them, eat them, and make them the containers of our dreams and memories. Similarly, we may all buy into capital with the purchase of public stock. These consumerist activities give the illusion of democratic participation while denying access to real corporate control which remains intact and autonomous, notwithstanding the mass diffusion of its logos and stock on the public market. Indeed the manipulation of public stock initiated during the Reagan administration, which has facilitated one leveraged buyout after another, gives the lie to whatever wistful remnants of democratic ownership one might once have attached to the notion of "public" stocks.

Disney World is logoland. The merchandise, the costumes, the scenery—all is either stamped with the Disney logo or covered by copyright legislation. In fact, it is impossible to photograph at Disney World without running the risk of infringing a Disney copyright. A family photo in front of Sleeping Beauty's Castle is apt to include dozens of infringements: the castle itself. Uncle Harry's "Goofy" T-shirt, the kids' Donald and Mickey hats, maybe a costumed Chip 'n Dale in the background. The only thing that saves the average family from a lawsuit is that most don't use their vacation photos as a means for making profit. I suspect the staff of "America's Funniest Home Videos" systematically eliminates all family videos shot at Disney World; otherwise prize winners might find themselves having to negotiate the legal difference between prize and profit, and in a larger sense, public use versus private property. As an interesting note, Michael Sorkin, in a recent essay on Disneyland, chose a photo of "[t]he sky above Disney World [as a] substitute for an image of the place itself." Calling Disney World "the first copyrighted urban environment," Sorkin goes on to stress the "litigiousness" of the Disney Corporation.[2] It may be that *Design*

[2]Michael Sorkin. "See You in Disneyland," *Design Quarterly* (Winter 1992), pp. 5–13.

Quarterly, where Sorkin published his essay, pays its contributors, thus disqualifying them from "fair use" interpretations of copyright policy.

Logos have become so much a part of our cultural baggage that we hardly notice them. Actually they are the cultural capital of corporations. Pierre Bourdieu invented the notion of cultural capital with reference to individuals. In a nutshell, cultural capital represents the sum total of a person's ability to buy into and trade in the culture. This is circumscribed by the economics of class and, in turn, functions as a means for designating an individual's social standing. Hence people with higher levels of education who distinguish themselves with upscale or trendy consumptions have more cultural capital and can command greater privilege and authority than those who, as Bourdieu put it, are stuck defining themselves by the consumption of necessity. There are no cultural objects or practices that do not constitute capital, no reserves of culture that escape value. Everything that constitutes one's cultural life is a commodity and can be reckoned in terms of capital logic.

In the United States today there is little difference between persons and corporations. Indeed, corporations enjoy many of the legal rights extended to individuals. The market system and its private property state are "peopled" by corporations, which trade in, accumulate, and hoard up logos. These are the cultural signifiers produced by corporations, the impoverished imagery of a wholly rationalized entity. Logos are commodities in the abstract, but they are not so abstracted as to have transcended value. Corporations with lots of logos, particularly upscale, high-tech logos, command more cultural capital than corporations with fewer, more humble logos.

In late twentieth-century America, the cultural capital of corporations has replaced many of the human forms of cultural capital. As we buy, wear, and eat logos, we become the henchmen and admen of the corporations, defining ourselves with respect to the social standing of the various corporations. Some would say that this is a new form of tribalism, that in sporting corporate logos we ritualize and humanize them, we redefine the cultural capital of the corporations in human social terms. I would say that a state where culture is indistinguishable from logos and where the practice of culture risks infringement of private property is a state that values the corporate over the human.

While at Disney World, I managed to stow away on the behind-the-scenes tour reserved for groups of corporate conventioneers. I had heard about this tour from a friend who is also researching Disney and whose account of underground passageways, conduits for armies of workers and all the necessary materials and services that enable the park to function, had elevated the tour to mythic proportions in my imagination.

But very little of the behind-the-scenes tour was surprising. There was no magic, just a highly rational system built on the compartmentalization of all productive functions and its ensuing division of labor, both aimed at the creation of maximum efficiency. However, instances do arise when the rational infrastructure comes into contradiction with the onstage (park-wide) theatricalized image that the visitor expects to consume. Such is the case with the system that sucks trash collected at street level through unseen pneumatic tubes that transect the backstage area, finally depositing the trash in Disney's own giant compactor site. To the consumer's eyes, trash is never a problem at Disney World. After all, everyone dutifully uses the containers marked "trash," and what little manages to fall to the ground (generally popcorn) is immediately swept up by the French Foreign Legion trash brigade. For the consumer, there is no trash beyond its onstage collection. But there will soon be a problem as environmental groups press Disney to recycle. As my companion on the backstage tour put it, "Why is there no recycling at Disney World—after all, many of the middle-class visitors to the park are already sorting and recycling trash in their homes?" To this the Disney guide pointed out that there is recycling backstage: bins for workers to toss their Coke cans and other bins for office workers to deposit papers. But recycling onstage would break the magic of themed authenticity. After all, the "real" Cinderella's Castle was not equipped with recycling bins, nor did the denizens of Main Street, U.S.A., circa 1910, foresee the problem of trash. To maintain the image, Disney problem solvers are discussing hiring a minimum-wage work-force to rake, sort, and recycle the trash on back lots that the environmentally aware visitor will never see.

While I have been describing the backstage area as banal, the tour through it was not uneventful. Indeed there was one incident that underscored for me the dramatic collision between people's expectations of public use and the highly controlled nature of Disney's private domain. As I mentioned, the backstage tour took us to the behind-the-scenes staging area for the minute-by-minute servicing of the park and hoopla of its mass spectacles such as firework displays, light shows, and parades. We happened to be in the backstage area just as the parade down Main Street was coming to an end. Elaborate floats and costumed characters descended a ramp behind Cinderella's Castle and began to disassemble before our eyes. The floats were alive with big-headed characters, clambering off the super structures and out of their heavy, perspiration-drenched costumes. Several "beheaded" characters revealed stocky young men gulping down Gatorade. They walked toward our tour group, bloated Donald and bandy-legged Chip from the neck down, carrying their huge costume heads, while their real heads emerged pea-sized and aberrantly human.

We had been warned *not* to take pictures during the backstage tour, but one of our group, apparently carried away by the spectacle, could not resist. She managed to shoot a couple of photos of the disassembled characters before being approached by one of the tour guides. As if caught in a spy movie, the would-be photographer pried open her camera and ripped out the whole roll of film. The entire tour group stood in stunned amazement; not, I think, at the immediate presence of surveillance, but at the woman's dramatic response. In a situation where control is so omnipresent and conformity with control is taken for granted, any sudden gesture or dramatic response is a surprise.

At the close of the tour, my companion and I lingered behind the rest of the group to talk with our tour guides. As a professional photographer, my companion wanted to know if there is a "normal" procedure for disarming behind-the-scenes photographic spies. The guide explained that the prescribed practice is to impound the cameras, process the film, remove the illicit photos, and return the camera, remaining photos, and complimentary film to the perpetrator. When questioned further, the guide went on to elaborate the Disney rationale for control over the image: the "magic" would be broken if photos of disassembled characters circulated in the public sphere; children might suffer irreparable psychic trauma at the sight of a "beheaded" Mickey; Disney exercises control over the image to safeguard childhood fantasies.

What Disney employees refer to as the "magic" of Disney World has actually to do with the ability to produce fetishized consumptions. The unbroken seamlessness of Disney World, its totality as a consumable artifact, cannot tolerate the revelation of the real work that produces the commodity. There would be no magic if the public should see the entire cast of magicians in various stages of disassembly and fatigue. That selected individuals are permitted to witness the backstage labor facilitates the word-of-mouth affirmation of the tremendous organizational feat that produces Disney World. The interdiction against photography eliminates the possibility of discontinuity at the level of image. There are no images to compete with the copyright-perfect onstage images displayed for public consumption. It's not accidental that our tour guide underscored the fact that Disney costumes are tightly controlled. The character costumes are made at only one production site and this site supplies the costumes used at Tokyo's Disneyland and EuroDisney. There can be no culturally influenced variations on the Disney models. Control over the image ensures the replication of Disney worldwide. The prohibition against photographing disassembled characters is motivated by the same phobia of industrial espionage that runs rampant throughout the high-tech information industry. The woman in our tour group who ripped open her camera and destroyed her film may not have been wrong in acting out a spy melodrama. Her photos of the disassembled costumes might have revealed the manner of their production—rendering them accessible to non-Disney replication. At Disney World, the magic that resides in the integrity of childhood fantasy is inextricably linked to the fetishism of the commodity and the absolute control over private property as it is registered in the copyrighted image.

As I see it, the individual's right to imagine and to give expression to unique ways of seeing is at stake in struggles against private property. Mickey Mouse, notwithstanding his corporate copyright, exists in our common culture. He is the site for the enactment of childhood wishes and fantasies, for early conceptualizations and renderings of the body, a being who can be imagined as both self and other. If culture is held as private property, then there can be only one correct version of Mickey Mouse, whose logo-like image is the cancellation of creativity. But the multiplicity of quirky versions of Mickey Mouse that children draw can stand as a graphic question to us as adults: Who, indeed, owns Mickey Mouse?

What most distinguishes Disney World from any other amusement park is the way its spatial organization, defined by autonomous "worlds" and wholly themed environments, combines with the homogeneity of its visitors (predominantly white, middle-class families) to produce a sense of community. While Disney World includes an underlying Utopian impulse, this is articulated with nostalgia for a small-town, small-business America (Main Street, U.S.A.), and the fantasy of a controllable corporatist world (EPCOT). The illusion of community is enhanced by the longing for community that many visitors bring to the park, which they may feel is unavailable to them in their own careers, daily lives, and neighborhoods, thanks in large part to the systematic erosion of the public sector.

In the last decade the inroads of private, for-profit enterprise in areas previously defined by public control, and the hostile aggression of tax backlash coupled with "me first" attitudes have largely defeated the possibility of community in our homes and cities.

Whenever I visit Disney World, I invariably overhear other visitors making comparisons between Disney World and their home towns. They stare out over EPCOT's lake and wonder why developers back home don't produce similar aesthetic spectacles. They talk about botched, abandoned, and misconceived development projects that have wrecked their local landscapes. Others see Disney World as an oasis of social tranquility and security in comparison to their patrolled, but nonetheless deteriorating, maybe even perilous neighborhoods. A[n] essay in *Time* captured some of these sentiments: "Do you see anybody [at Disney World] lying on the street or begging for money? Do you see anyone jumping on your car and wanting to clean your windshield—and when you say no, getting abusive?"[3]

Comments such as these do more than the class anxiety of the middle strata. They poignantly express the inability of this group to make distinctions between what necessarily constitutes the public and the private sectors. Do visitors forget that they pay a daily use fee (upwards of $150 for a four-day stay) just to be a citizen of Disney World (not to mention the $100 per night hotel bill)? Maybe so—and maybe it's precisely *forgetting* that visitors pay for.

If there is any distinction to be made between Disney World and our local shopping malls, it would have to do with Disney's successful exclusion of all factors that might put the lie to its uniform social fabric. The occasional Hispanic mother who arrives with extended family and illegal bologna sandwiches is an anomaly. So too is the first-generation Cubana who buys a year-round pass to Disney's nightspot, Pleasure Island, in hopes of meeting a rich and marriageable British tourist. These women testify to the presence of Orlando, Disney World's marginalized "Sister City," whose overflowing cheap labor force and overcrowded and under-funded public institutions are the unseen real world upon which Disney's world depends.

After Reading

Critical Perspective

1. Characterize the sorts of word choices that Willis makes in her text. What does this tell you about how she views her audience? Give textual evidence to back up your views.

Rhetoric and Argument

2. Reflect on Willis's rhetorical choices—her use of audience, purpose, ethos, pathos, logos, intertextuality, context, and constraints. Explain why you think that they are persuasive or not. Be sure to give support quotes from the text to back up your thoughts.

[3]"Fantasy's Reality," *Time,* 27 May 1991, p. 54.

3. Consider Willis's discussion of souvenirs and logos in her text. Why do you think she dedicates a good deal of time to these topics? Do you think that these choices help her argument? Why or why not?

4. What do you think that Willis is asserting about how Disney World works—or the kind of space it really is? What makes you assert this? Where in her text do you find support to substantiate your viewpoints? Do you agree with her? Why or why not?

Analysis

5. Write a short argumentative essay in which you address the following questions: What criticisms does Willis make about Disney World? Do you think that her claims are valid? Why or why not? In order to back up your views, be sure to provide evidence from her text as well as from additional library and Internet sources.

Taking Action

As a class, create a detailed list of the attributes you would want to have in an ideal neighborhood or community. To what degree do the ever growing Del Webb communities—and other self-contained neighborhoods—attain this ideal? To what degree do they fall short? Share your answers and responses with the rest of the class as you try to determine whether this ideal is possible or desirable. Consult relevant library and Internet sources.

STYLES

JOHN MOLLOY

"Dress for Success"

John Molloy is The New York Times *best-selling author of various self-help books, including* Dress for Success *and* The New Woman's Dress for Success Book. *Molloy lives in Florida and now works as an image consultant and corporate speaker.*

EXERCISING YOUR SKILLS

Before Reading

Molloy's text is taken from a book in which he investigates how men's clothing choices can impact how they are perceived. Take a close look at the kinds of outfits you wear on a typical day. How do these clothing choices reflect who you are—your values, your beliefs, your style? What do your clothing choices reveal about your social and economic status as well as conveys your sexual identity as a male or female? How do your clothes speak to your masculinity or femininity? What do your clothes say about your cultural background? How do these outfits reflect this cultural moment in the 2000s and where you live in the country?

The Proof: What Works and What Doesn't

Since I had very early on discovered that the socioeconomic value of a man's clothing is important in determining his credibility with certain groups, his ability to attract certain kinds of women and his acceptance to the business community, one of the first elements I undertook to research was the socioeconomic level of all items of clothing.

Take the raincoat, for example. Most raincoats sold in this country are either beige or black; those are the two standard colors. Intuitively I felt that the beige raincoat was worn generally by the upper-middle class and black by the lower-middle class.

First I visited several Fifth Avenue stores that cater almost exclusively to upper-middle-class customers and attempted to ascertain the number of beige raincoats versus black raincoats being sold. The statistical breakdown was approximately four to one in favor of beige. I then checked stores on the lower-middle-class level and found that almost the reverse statistic applied. They sold four black raincoats to each beige raincoat.

This indicated that in all probability my feeling was correct, but recognizing that there were many variables that could discredit such preliminary research, I set the second stage in motion. On rainy days, I hired responsible college students to stand outside subway stations in determinable lower-middle-class neighborhoods and outside determinable upper-middle-class suburban commuter-stations, all in the New York area. The students merely counted the number of black and beige raincoats. My statistics held up at approximately four to one in either case, and I could now say that in the New York area, the upper-middle class generally wore beige raincoats and the lower-middle class generally wore black ones.

My next step was to take a rainy-day count in the two different socioeconomic areas in Chicago, Los Angeles, Dallas, Atlanta and six equally widespread small towns. The research again held up; statistics came back from the cities at about four to one and from the small towns at about two-and-a-half to three to one. (The statistics were not quite that clear cut, but averaged out into those ranges.)

From these statistics I was able to state that in the United States, the beige raincoat is generally worn by members of the upper-middle class and the black raincoat generally worn by members of the lower-middle class. From this, I was able to hypothesize that since these raincoats were an intrinsic part of the American environment, they had in all probability conditioned people by their predominance in certain classes, and automatic (Pavlovian) reactions could be expected.

In short, when someone met a man in a beige raincoat, he was likely to think of him as a member of the upper-middle class, and when he met a man in a black raincoat, he was likely to think of him as a member of the lower-middle class. I then had to see if my hypothesis would hold up under testing.

My first test was conducted with 1362 people—a cross section of the general public. They were given an "extrasensory perception" test in which they were asked to guess the answers to a number of problems to which the solutions (they were told) could only be known through ESP. The percentage of correct answers would indicate their ESP quotient. Naturally, a participant in this type of test attempts to get the right answer every time and has no reason to lie, since he wants to score high.

In this test, among a group of other problems and questions, I inserted a set of almost identical "twin pictures." There was only one variable. The twin pictures showed the same man in the same pose dressed in the same suit, the same shirt, the same tie, the same shoes. The only difference was the raincoat—one black, one beige. Participants were told that the pictures were of twin brothers, and were asked to identify the most prestigious of the two. Over 87 percent, or 1118 people, chose the man in the beige raincoat.

I next ran a field test. Two friends and I wore beige raincoats for one month, then switched to black raincoats the following month. We attempted to duplicate our other clothing during both months. At the end of each month, we recorded the general attitude of people toward us—waiters, store clerks, business associates, etc. All three of us agreed that the beige raincoat created a distinctly better impression upon the people we met.

Finally, I conducted one additional experiment alone. Picking a group of business offices at random, I went into each office with a *Wall Street Journal* in a manila envelope and asked the receptionist or secretary to allow me to deliver it personally to the man in charge. When wearing a black raincoat, it took me a day and a half to deliver twenty-five papers. In a beige raincoat, I was able to deliver the same number in a single morning.

The impression transmitted to receptionists and secretaries by my black raincoat and a nondescript suit, shirt and tie clearly was that I was a glorified delivery boy, and so I had to wait or was never admitted. But their opinion of me was substantially altered by the beige raincoat worn with the same other clothes. They thought I might be an associate or friend of the boss because that is what I implied, and they had better let me in. In short, they re-acted to years of preconditioning and accepted the beige raincoat as a symbol of authority and status while they rejected the black raincoat as such.

This study was conducted in 1971. And although more and more lower-middle-class men are wearing beige raincoats each year (basically because of improved wash-and-wear methods that make them much less expensive to keep clean), the results of the study remain valid and will continue to be for years to come. You cannot wear a black raincoat, and you must wear a beige raincoat—if you wish to be accepted as a member of the upper-middle class and treated accordingly (among all other raincoat colors, only dark blue tests as acceptable).

I continue to test the beige raincoat each year in my multiple-item studies. In the field of clothing, multiple-item studies are those that incorporate an entire look: the upper-middle-class look, the lower-middle-class look, etc. These studies usually are not geared to test people's responses to specific items, but if a particular item is not consistent with the rest, it will destroy the effectiveness of the study because the incongruous item spoils the total look.

In one multiple-item study, I sent a twenty-five-year-old male college graduate from an upper-middle-class midwestern background to 100 offices. To fifty of them he wore an outfit made up entirely of garments that had been previously tested as having lower-middle-class characteristics; to the remaining fifty he wore an outfit of garments that had been previously tested as having upper-middle-class characteristics. Prior to his arrival at each office, I had arranged for the man in charge to tell his secretary that he had hired an assistant, and to instruct her to show the young man around. The executive also made sure that his secretary would not be going to lunch, would not be going home, and would not be overworked at the time of my man's arrival.

After being shown through the offices, which took anywhere from fifteen minutes to an hour, depending on the secretary and the office, the young man made a series of requests. He first asked for something simple like letterhead stationery or a pencil and pad. The responses of the secretaries to these requests had no statistical significance, although the young man did note that there was a substantial difference in attitude. In upper-middle-class garb, he received the requested item with no comment, but pejorative comments or quizzical looks were directed toward him at least one-third of the time when he wore lower-middle-class clothing.

Once the first request sequence was completed, the young man gave each secretary a standardized order. Before going to each office, he had been given the names of three people in the files of the office. These names were written on a card, and his procedure was always the same. Putting the card on the secretary's desk, he would say, "Miss (always using her name) Jones, please get these files for me; I will be at Mr. Smith's desk." He would then walk away, trying not to give the secretary a chance to answer him verbally. The results were quite significant.

In upper-middle-class garb, he received the files within ten minutes forty-two times. In lower-middle-class garb, he received the files only twelve times. Pejorative comments were directed at him twelve times while wearing upper-middle-class clothes, and eight times while wearing lower-middle-class clothes. This means that he received positive responses only four times out of fifty while wearing lower-middle-class garb; but he received positive responses thirty times out of fifty when he was wearing upper-middle-class garb.

From this experiment and many others like it, I was able to conclude that in upper-middle-class clothes, a young man will be more successful in giving orders to secretaries.

The experiment will give you an idea of why I have spent so many years and so much of my clients' money in determining what constitutes upper-middle-class dress. It is obvious from the experiment that secretaries, who generally were not members of the upper-middle class, did in fact recognize upper-middle class clothing, if not consciously then at least subconsciously, and they did react to it. The reactions of the secretaries indicate that dress is neither trivial nor frivolous, but an essential element in helping a man to function in the business world with maximum effectiveness.

But does everyone react as the secretaries did?

For years some companies have been attempting to increase the efficiency of employees by prescribing dress and establishing dress codes. Most of these schemes have proved ineffective because they have been created by amateurs who don't understand the effect clothing has on the work environment. Dress codes can work, but the assumption that clothing has a major, continuing impact on the wearer is erroneous. True, you may feel shabby when you wear shabby clothes, and your morale may perk up a bit when you splurge on an expensive tie. But clothing most significantly affects the people whom the wearer meets and, in the long run, affects the wearer only indirectly because it controls the reaction of the world to him. My research shows that in most business situations the wearer is not directly affected by his clothing, and that the effect of clothing on other people is mainly controlled by the socioeconomic level of the clothing.

Let me say it straight out: We all wear uniforms and our uniforms are clear and distinct signs of class. We react to them accordingly. In almost any situation where two men meet, one man's clothing is saying to the other man: "I am more important than you are, please show respect"; or "I am your equal and expect to be treated as such"; or "I am not your equal and I do not expect to be treated as such."

How 100 Top Executives Described Successful Dress

Over the years I have conducted literally thousands of studies, experiments and tests to aid my corporate and individual clients in using clothing better and as an indispensable tool of business life. Immediately prior to beginning this study, I asked several series of questions of 100 top executives in either medium-sized or major American corporations. The first series was to establish the most up-to-date attitudes on corporate dress.

I showed the executives five pictures of men, each of them wearing expensive, well-tailored, but high-fashion clothing. I asked if this was a proper look for the junior business executive. Ninety-two of the men said no, eight said yes.

I showed them five pictures of men neatly dressed in obvious lower-middle-class attire and asked if these men were dressed in proper attire for a young executive. Forty-six said yes, fifty-four said no.

I next showed them five pictures of men dressed in conservative upper-middle-class clothing and asked if they were dressed in proper attire for the young executive. All one hundred said yes.

I asked them whether they thought the men in the upper-middle-class garb would succeed better in corporate life than the men in the lower-middle-class uniform. Eighty-eight said yes, twelve said no.

I asked if they would choose one of the men in the lower-middle-class dress as their assistant. Ninety-two said no, eight said yes.

I next showed them pictures of four young men. The first had a very short haircut; the second had a moderate haircut with moderate sideburns; the third had a moderate haircut, but with fairly long sideburns; and the fourth had very long hair. I asked which haircut was the most profitable for a young man to wear. Eighty-two of them picked the moderate haircut with moderate sideburns; three picked the very short cut; and fifteen picked the moderate cut with long sideburns. No one picked the long hair.

I next asked if they would hire the man with long hair. Seventy-four said no.

To 100 other top executives of major corporations, I submitted the following written questions:

1. *Does your company have a written or an unwritten dress code?* Ninety-seven said yes. Three said no. Only two had a written dress code.
2. *Would a number of men at your firm have a much better chance of getting ahead if they knew how to dress?* Ninety-six said yes, four said no.
3. *If there were a course in how to dress for business, would you send your son?* All 100 said yes.
4. *Do you think employee dress affects the general tone of the office?* All 100 said yes.
5. *Do you think employee dress affects efficiency?* Fifty-two said yes, forty-eight said no.
6. *Would you hold up the promotion of a man who didn't dress properly?* Seventy-two said yes, twenty-eight said no.
7. *Would you tell a young man if his dress was holding him back?* Eighty said no, twenty said yes.
8. *Does your company at present turn down people who show up at job interviews improperly dressed on that basis alone?* Eighty-four said yes, sixteen said no.
9. *Would you take a young man who didn't know how to dress as your assistant?* Ninety-two said no, eight said yes.
10. *Do you think there is a need for a book that would explain to a young man how to dress?* Ninety-four said yes, six said no.
11. *Do you think there is a need for a book to tell people in business how to dress?* One hundred said yes.

Keep reading, fellows, you got it.

After Reading

Critical Perspective

1. Notice the differences between Molloy's argument and the others you have read thus far. How does Molloy use evidence differently? What effects might this have on his audience? What appeals to the audience's logos do you think Molloy makes? What evidence can you locate for this? Do you find this tactic persuasive?

Rhetoric and Argument

2. Trace Molloy's choice of rhetorical tactics—his use of audience, purpose, ethos, pathos, intertextuality, context, and constraints. Do you find these strategies effective? Why or why not?
3. What is Molloy's main claim and where does it appear in his text? Do you think that this is an effective place to make a claim in his argument? Why? Provide quotes to back up your thoughts.

4. How does Molloy support his claim? Do you find it persuasive? Why or why not? Try to furnish textual evidence to back up your views.

5. What assumptions does Molloy make in his text? Where and when do they surface? Do you believe that these are valid? Why or why not?

Analysis

6. Write a short argumentative response in which you tackle the following issues: Do you think that Molloy is advancing a cultural criticism about dress and how it functions in American culture? If yes, point to the places in his text that seem to support this hypothesis. If no, point to the places that seem to refute this idea. If he is making a cultural criticism, do you believe that it is a valuable one or not? Why? If he fails to offer a cultural criticism, what do you think about this choice and why? Make sure that you present a cogent argumentative claim and support it with close analyses and quotes from the text along with library and Internet sources.

Taking Action

In a small group, consider whether and how people's dress as well as the signs and codes dress conveys impact your impression of them. Select five people you can observe. Try to select people who you may not know well. Based on what they are wearing alone (include clothing, accessories, shoes, and the like), take notes on what cultural assumptions and stereotypes might dictate about their beliefs, ideals, values, and interests. Make a detailed list of what you imagine about those individuals based on dress, makeup, shoe choice, and hairstyle alone. When you are done, each small group should interview those people to see which of your assumptions were indeed correct.

Once you have completed the exercise, get back into the larger class group. Discuss to what degree you found that people's dress accurately reflects their interests or views of the world. To what degree did you discover that people's dress reveals and is also shaped by their social standing, cultural background, gender, or other social factors? Consult library and Internet sources as they are useful to your research.

Analysis

Take a look at the images on page 232 and page 233 from an October issue of *Martha Stewart Living* magazine, a magazine meant to convey a specific style. Describe the connotations that these various texts conjure up for you. Also, reflect upon the language used. What conventions about domesticity, femininity, ethnicity, and upper-class life do these images and words suggest? Based upon these texts, try to describe what Martha's goals for this magazine appear to be. How do they support particular ideas about women's roles in American culture? Do you think that this is positive (or, as Stewart has been known to say, a "good thing")?

MARGARET TALBOT

"Les Très Riches Heures de Martha Stewart"

Margaret Talbot is currently a contributing writer at The New York Times Magazine, *where she has published several cover stories. She has also been an editor at* Lingua Franca *and* The New Republic, *and has written for* The New Yorker, Salon, *and* The Atlantic Monthly. *Talbot was the recipient of a Whiting Writers' Award. Her work centers on identity politics; the future of mainstream feminism and of the sexual harassment regime; and the cultural meaning of privacy.*

EXERCISING YOUR SKILLS

Before Reading

Talbot examines the effects of Martha Stewart on women and style. Martha Stewart has been applauded for her domestic masterpieces as well as vilified for her conviction on charges of obstructing justice. She has built a vast media empire, resigned as director and chief creative officer of Martha Stewart Living Omnimedia as her television show *Living* was pulled from CBS, and then risen from the ashes to reestablish herself as a quintessential female icon.

Examine three media representations—advertisements, television shows, magazine articles, books—of Stewart (be sure to pick examples from both camps, those

who applaud her and those who criticize her).
What do these images of Stewart, ones that depict
her as a domestic goddess unfairly treated or a
perfect diva justly convicted, reveal about changes
in how various issues are viewed in American culture such as homemaking, femininity, ethnicity,
and class relations in American culture?

Every age gets the household goddess it deserves.
The '60s had Julia Child, the sophisticated French
chef who proved as permissive as Dr. Spock. She may
have proselytized for a refined foreign cuisine from
her perch at a Boston PBS station, but she was always an anti-snob, vowing to "take a lot of the la dee
dah out of French cooking." With her madras shirts
and her penumbra of curls, her 6′2″ frame and her
whinny of a voice, she exuded an air of Cambridge
eccentricity—faintly bohemian and a little tatty,
like a yellowing travel poster. She was messy and
forgiving. When Julia dropped an egg or collapsed
a soufflé, she shrugged and laughed. "You are alone
in the kitchen, nobody can see you, and cooking is
meant to be fun," she reminded her viewers. She
wielded lethal-looking kitchen knives with campy
abandon, dipped her fingers into creme anglaise and wiped her chocolate-smeared hands
on an apron tied carelessly at her waist. For Child was also something of a sensualist, a
celebrant of appetite as much as a pedant of cooking.

In the '90s, and well into the next century, we have Martha Stewart, corporate overachiever turned domestic superachiever, Mildred Pierce in earth-toned Armani. Martha is
the anti-Julia. Consider the extent of their respective powers. At the height of her success,
Child could boast a clutch of bestselling cookbooks and a *gemütlich* TV show shot on a
single set. At what may or may not be the height of her success, here's what Stewart can
claim: a 5-year-old magazine, *Martha Stewart Living,* with a circulation that has leapt
to 1.5 million; a popular cable TV show, also called "Martha Stewart Living" and filmed at
her luscious Connecticut and East Hampton estates; a dozen wildly successful gardening,
cooking and lifestyle books; a mail-order business, Martha-by-Mail; a nationally syndicated
newspaper column, "Ask Martha"; a regular Wednesday slot on the "Today" show; a line of
$110-a-gallon paints in colors inspired by the eggs her Araucana hens lay; plans to invade
cyberspace—in short, an empire.

Julia limited herself to cooking lessons, with the quiet implication that cooking was a
kind of synecdoche for the rest of bourgeois existence; but Martha's parish is vaster, her
field is all of life. Her expertise, as she recently explained to Mediaweek magazine, covers,
quite simply, "Beautiful soups and how to make them, beautiful houses and how to build
them, beautiful children and how to raise them." (From soups to little nuts.) She presides,

in fact, over a phenomenon that, in other realms, is quite familiar in American society and culture: a cult, devoted to her name and image.

In the distance between these two cynosures of domestic life lies a question: What does the cult of Martha mean? Or, to put it another way, what have we done, exactly, to deserve her?

If you have read the paper or turned on the television in the last year or so, you have probably caught a glimpse of the WASPy good looks, the affectless demeanor, the nacreous perfection of her world. You may even know the outlines of her story. Middle-class girl from a Polish-American family in Nutley, New Jersey, works her way through Barnard in the early '60s, modeling on the side. She becomes a stockbroker, a self-described workaholic and insomniac who by the '70s is making six figures on Wall Street, and who then boldly trades it all in . . . for life as a workaholic, insomniac evangelist for domesticity whose business now generates some $200 million in profits a year. (She herself, according to the *Wall Street Journal,* makes a salary of $400,000 a year from Time Inc., which generously supplements this figure with a $40,000 a year clothing allowance and other candies.) You may even have admired her magazine, with its art-book production values and spare design, every kitchen utensil photographed like an Imogen Cunningham nude, every plum or pepper rendered with the loving detail of an eighteenth-century botanical drawing, every page a gentle exhalation of High Class.

What you may not quite realize, if you have not delved deeper into Stewart's oeuvre, is the ambition of her design for living—the absurd, self-parodic dream of it. To read Martha Stewart is to know that there is no corner of your domestic life that cannot be beautified or improved under careful tutelage, none that should not be colonized by the rhetoric and the discipline of quality control. Work full time though you may, care for your family though you must, convenience should never be your watchword in what Stewart likes to call, in her own twee coinage, "homekeeping." Convenience is the enemy of excellence. "We do not pretend that these are 'convenience' foods," she writes loftily of the bread and preserves recipes in a 1991 issue of the magazine. "Some take days to make. But they are recipes that will produce the very best results, and we know that is what you want." Martha is a kitchen-sink idealist. She scorns utility in the name of beauty. But her idealism, of course, extends no further than surface appearances, which makes it a very particular form of idealism indeed.

To spend any length of time in Martha-land is to realize that it is not enough to serve your guests homemade pumpkin soup as a first course. You must present it in hollowed-out hand-gilded pumpkins as well. It will not do to serve an Easter ham unless you have baked it in a roasting pan lined with, of all things, "tender, young, organically-grown grass that has not yet been cut." And, when serving a "casual" lobster and corn dinner al fresco, you really ought to fashion dozens of cunning little bamboo brushes tied with raffia and adorned with a chive so that each of your guests may butter their corn with something pretty.

To be a Martha fan (or more precisely, a Martha adept) is to understand that a terracotta pot is just a terracotta pot until you have "aged" it, painstakingly rubbing yogurt into its dampened sides, then smearing it with plant food or "something you found in the woods" and patiently standing by while the mold sprouts. It is to think that maybe you could do this *kind* of thing, anyway—start a garden, say, in your scruffy backyard—and then to be brought up short by Martha's enumeration, in *Martha Stewart's Gardening,* of forty-nine "essential" gardening tools. These range from a "polesaw" to a "corn fiber broom" to three different kinds of pruning shears, one of which—the "loppers"— Martha says she has in three different sizes. You have, perhaps, a trowel. But then Martha's garden is a daunting thing to contemplate, what with its topiary mazes and state-of-the-art chicken coop; its "antique" flowers and geometric herb garden. It's half USDA station, half Sissinghurst. And you cannot imagine making anything remotely like it at your own house, not without legions of artisans and laborers and graduate students in landscape design, and a pot of money that perhaps you'll unearth when you dig up the yard.

In *The Culture of Narcissism,* Christopher Lasch describes the ways in which pleasure, in our age, has taken on "the qualities of work," allowing our leisure-time activities to be measured by the same standards of accomplishment that rule the workplace. It is a phenomenon that he memorably characterizes as "the invasion of play by the rhetoric of achievement." For Lasch, writing in the early '70s, the proliferation of sex-advice manuals offered a particularly poignant example. Today, though, you might just as easily point to the hundreds of products and texts, from unctuous home-furnishings catalogs to upscale "shelter" magazines to self-help books like *Meditations for Women Who Do Too Much,* that tell us exactly how to "nest" and "cocoon" and "nurture," how to "center" and "retreat," and how to measure our success at these eminently private pursuits. Just as late-nineteenth-century marketers and experts promised to bring Americans back in touch with the nature from which modern industrial life had alienated them, so today's "shelter" experts—the word is revealingly primal—promise to reconnect us with a similarly mystified home. The bourgeois home as lost paradise, retrievable through careful instruction.

Martha Stewart is the apotheosis of this particular cult of expertise, and its most resourceful entrepreneur. She imagines projects of which we would never have thought— gathering dewy grass for our Easter ham, say—and makes us feel the pressing need for training in them. And she exploits, brilliantly, a certain estrangement from home that many working women feel these days. For women who are working longer and longer hours at more and more demanding jobs, it's easy to think of home as the place where chaos reigns and their own competence is called into doubt: easy to regard the office, by comparison, as the bulwark of order. It is a reversal, of course, of the hoary concept of home as a refuge from the tempests of the marketplace. But these days, as the female executives in a recent study attested, the priority they most often let slide is housekeeping: they'll abide disorder at home that they wouldn't or couldn't abide at the office. No working couple's home is the oasis of tranquillity and Italian marble countertops that Marthaism seems to *promise. But could it be?* Should it be? Stewart plucks expertly at that chord of doubt.

In an era when it is not at all uncommon to be cut off from the traditional sources of motherwit and household lore—when many of us live far from the families into which we were born and have started our own families too late to benefit from the guidance of living parents or grandparents—domestic pedants like Martha Stewart rightly sense a big vacuum to fill. Stewart's books are saturated with nostalgia for lost tradition and old moldings, for her childhood in Nutley and for her mother's homemade preserves. In the magazine, her "Remembering" column pines moralistically for a simpler era, when beach vacations meant no television or video games, just digging for clams and napping in hammocks. Yet Stewart's message is that such simplicity can only be achieved now through strenuous effort and a flood of advice. We might be able to put on a picnic or a dinner party without her help, she seems to tell us, but we wouldn't do it properly, beautifully, in the spirit of excellence that we expect of ourselves at work.

It may be that Stewart's special appeal is to women who wouldn't want to take their mother's word anyway, to baby-boomer daughters who figure that their sensibilities are just too different from their stay-at-home moms', who can't throw themselves into housekeeping without thinking of their kitchen as a catering business and their backyards as a garden show. In fact, relatively few of Martha's fans are housewives—72 percent of the subscribers to *Martha Stewart Living* are employed outside the home as managers or professionals—and many of them profess to admire her precisely because she isn't one, either. As one such Martha acolyte, an account executive at a Christian radio station, effused on the Internet: "[Stewart] is my favorite independent woman and what an entrepreneur! She's got her own television show, magazine, books and even her own brand of latex paint. . . . Martha is a feisty woman who settles for nothing less than perfection."

For women such as these, the didactic faux-maternalism of Martha Stewart seems the perfect answer. She may dispense the kind of homekeeping advice that a mother would, but she does so in tones too chill and exacting to sound "maternal," singling out, for example, those "who will always be too lazy" to do her projects. She makes housekeeping safe for the professional woman by professionalizing housekeeping. And you never forget that Stewart is herself a mogul, even when she's baking rhubarb crisp and telling you, in her Shakeresque mantra, that "It's a Good Thing."

It is tempting to see the Martha cult purely as a symptom of anti-feminist backlash. Though she may not directly admonish women to abandon careers for hearth and home, Stewart certainly exalts a way of life that puts hearth and home at its center: one that would be virtually impossible to achieve without *somebody's* full-time devotion. (Camille Paglia has praised her as "someone who has done a tremendous service for ordinary women—women who identify with the roles of wife, mother, and homemaker.") Besides, in those alarming moments when Stewart slips into the social critic's mode, she can sound a wee bit like Phyllis Schlafly—less punitive and more patrician, maybe, but just as smug about the moral uplift of a well-ordered home. Her philosophy of cultivating your own walled garden while the world outside is condemned to squalor bears the hallmarks of Reagan's America—it would not be overreading to call it a variety of conservatism. "Amid the horrors of genocidal war in Bosnia and Rwanda, the AIDS epidemic and increasing crime in many cities," Stewart writes in a recent column, "there are those of us who desire positive reinforcement of some very basic tenets of good living." And those would be? "Good food, gardening, crafts, entertaining and home improvement." (Hollow out the pumpkins, they're starving in Rwanda.)

Yet it would, in the end, be too simplistic to regard her as a tool of the feminine mystique, or as some sort of spokesmodel for full-time mommies. For one thing, there is nothing especially June Cleaverish, or even motherly, about Stewart. She has taken a drubbing, in fact, for looking more convincing as a businesswoman than a dispenser of milk and cookies. (Remember the apocryphal tale that had Martha flattening a crate of baby chicks while backing out of a driveway in her Mercedes?) Her habitual prickliness and Scotchguard perfectionism are more like the badges of the striving good girl, still cut to the quick by her classmates' razzing when she asked for extra homework.

Despite the ritual obeisance that Martha pays to Family, moreover, she is not remotely interested in the messy contingencies of family life. In the enchanted world of Turkey Hill, there are no husbands (Stewart was divorced from hers in 1990), only loyal craftsmen, who clip hedges and force dogwood with self-effacing dedication. Children she makes use of as accessories, much like Parisian women deploy little dogs. The books and especially the magazine are often graced with photographic spreads of parties and teas where children pale as waxen angels somberly disport themselves, their fair hair shaped into tasteful blunt cuts, their slight figures clad in storybook velvet or lace. "If I had to choose one essential element for the success of an Easter brunch," she writes rather menacingly in her 1994 *Menus for Entertaining,* "it would be children." The homemade Halloween costumes modeled by wee lads and lasses in an October 1991 issue of *Martha Stewart Living* do look gorgeous—the Caravaggio colors, the themes drawn from nature. But it's kind of hard to imagine a 5-year-old boy happily agreeing to go as an acorn this year, instead of say, Batman. And why should he? In Marthaland, his boyhood would almost certainly be overridden in the name of taste.

If Stewart is a throwback, it's not so much to the 1950s as to the 1850s, when the doctrine of separate spheres did allow married or widowed women of the upper classes a kind of power—unchallenged dominion over the day-to-day functioning of the home and its servants, in exchange for ceding the public realm to men. At Turkey Hill, Stewart is the undisputed chatelaine, micromanaging her estate in splendid isolation. (This hermetic pastoral is slightly marred, of course, by the presence of cameras.) Here the domestic arts have become ends in themselves, unmoored from family values and indeed from family.

Stewart's peculiar brand of didacticism has another nineteenth-century precedent—in the domestic science or home economics movement. The domestic scientists' favorite recipes—"wholesome" concoctions of condensed milk and canned fruit, rivers of white sauce—would never have passed Martha's muster; but their commitment to painstakingly elegant presentation, their concern with the look of food even more than its taste, sound a lot like Stewart's. And, more importantly, so does their underlying philosophy. They emerged out of a tradition: the American preference for food writing of the prescriptive, not the descriptive, kind, for food books that told you, in M.F.K. Fisher's formulation, not about eating but about what to eat. But they took this spirit much further. Like Stewart, these brisk professional women of the 1880s and '90s believed that true culinary literacy could not be handed down or casually absorbed; it had to be carefully taught. (One of the movement's accomplishments, if it can be called that, was the home ec curriculum.)

Like Stewart, the domestic scientists were not bent on liberating intelligent women from housework. Their objective was to raise housework to a level worthy of intelligent women. They wished to apply rational method to the chaos and the drudgery of housework and, in so doing, to earn it the respect accorded men's stuff like science and business. Neither instinct, nor intuition, nor mother's rough-hewn words of advice would have a place in the scientifically managed home of the future. As Laura Shapiro observes in *Perfection Salad,* her lively and perceptive history of domestic science, the ideal new housewife was supposed to project, above all, "self-sufficiency, self-control, and a perfectly bland façade." Sound familiar?

It is in their understanding of gender roles, however, that the doyennes of home ec most closely prefigure Marthaism. Like Stewart, they cannot be classified either as feminists or traditionalists. Their model housewife was a pseudo-professional with little time for sublimating her ego to her husband's or tenderly ministering to his needs. She was more like a factory supervisor than either the Victorian angel of the home or what Shapiro calls the courtesan type, the postwar housewife who was supposed to zip through her chores so she could gussy herself up for her husband. In Martha's world, too, the managerial and aesthetic challenges of "homekeeping" always take priority, and their intricacy and ambition command a respect that mere wifely duties never could. Her husbandless hauteur is rich with the self-satisfaction of financial and emotional independence.

In the end, Stewart's fantasies have as much to do with class as with gender. The professional women who read her books might find themselves longing for a breadwinner, but a lifestyle this beautiful is easier to come by if you've never needed a breadwinner in the first place. Stewart's books are a dreamy advertisement for independent wealth—or, more accurately, for its facsimile. You may not have a posh pedigree, but with a little effort (okay, a lot) you can adopt its trappings. After all, Martha wasn't born to wealth either, but now she attends the weddings of people with names like Charles Booth-Clibborn (she went to his in London, the magazine tells us) and caters them for couples named Sissy and Kelsey (see her *Wedding Planner,* in which their yacht is decorated with a "Just Married" sign).

She is not an American aristocrat, but she plays one on TV. And you can play one, too, at least in your own home. Insist on cultivating only those particular yellow plums you tasted in the Dordogne, buy your copper cleaner only at Delherin in Paris, host lawn parties where guests come "attired in the garden dress of the Victorian era," and you begin to simulate the luster of lineage. Some of Stewart's status-augmenting suggestions must strike even her most faithful fans as ridiculous. For showers held after the baby is born, Martha "likes presenting the infant with engraved calling cards that the child can then slip into thank you notes and such for years to come." What a great idea. Maybe your baby can gum them for a while first, thoughtfully imprinting them with his signature drool.

The book that best exemplifies her class-consciousness is *Martha Stewart's New Old House,* a step-by-step account of refurbishing a Federal-style farmhouse in Westport, Connecticut. Like all her books, it contains many, many pictures of Martha; here she's frequently shown supervising the work of plasterers, carpenters and other "seemingly taciturn men." *New Old House* establishes Stewart's ideal audience: a demographic niche occupied by the kind of people who, like her, can afford to do their kitchen countertops in "mottled, gray-green, hand-honed slate from New York state, especially cut" for them. The cost of all this (and believe me, countertops are only the beginning) goes unmentioned. If you have to ask, maybe you're not a Martha kind of person after all.

In fact, Stewart never seems all that concerned with reassuring her readers of their ability to afford such luxuries or their right to enjoy them. She's more concerned with establishing her own claims. Her reasoning seems to go something like this: the houses that she buys and renovates belong to wealthy families who passed them down through generations. But these families did not properly care for their patrimony. The widowed Bulkeley sisters, erstwhile owners of Turkey Hill, had let the estate fall "into great disrepair. All the farms and outbuildings were gone. . . . The fields around had been sold off by the sisters in 2-acre building lots; suburbia encroached." The owner of the eponymous New Old House was a retired librarian named Miss Adams who "had little interest in the house other than as a roof over her head. Clearly a frugal spirit, she had no plans to restore the house, and she lived there until she could no longer cope with the maintenance and upkeep of the place. The house was in dire need of attention, and since no other family member wanted to assume responsibility, Miss Adams reluctantly decided to sell her family home. I wanted very much to save the Adams house, to put it to rights, to return its history to it, to make it livable once again."

It's a saga with overtones of Jamesian comedy: a family with bloodlines but no money is simultaneously rescued and eclipsed by an energetic upstart with money but no bloodlines. The important difference—besides the fact that Martha is marrying the house, not the son—is that she also has taste. And it's taste, far more than money, she implies, that gives her the right to these splendid, neglected piles of brick. Unlike the "frugal" Misses Bulkeley, she will keep suburbia at bay; unlike the careless Miss Adams, she would never resort to "hideous rugs" in (yuck) shades of brown. They don't understand their own houses; she does, and so she *deserves* to own their houses. But leave it to Martha to get all snippy about these people's aesthetic oversights while quietly celebrating their reversion to type. They're useful to her, and not only because their indifference to decor bolsters her claim to their property. Like the pumpkin pine floors and original fixtures, these quaintly cheeseparing New Englanders denote the property's authenticity.

The fantasy of vaulting into the upper crust that Martha Stewart fulfilled, and now piques in her readers, is about more than just money, of course. Among other things, it's about time, and the luxurious plenitude of it. Living the Martha way would mean enjoying a surfeit of that scarce commodity, cooking and crafting at the artisanal pace her projects require. Trouble is, none of us overworked Americans has time to spare these days—and least of all the upscale professional women whom Stewart targets. Martha herself seemed to acknowledge this when she told *Inside Media* that she attracts at least two classes of true believers: the "Be-Marthas," who have enough money and manic devotion to follow many of her lifestyle techniques, and the "Do-Marthas," who "are a little bit envious" and "don't have as much money as the Be-Marthas."

To those fulsome categories, you could surely add the "watch Marthas" or the "read Marthas," people who might consider, say, making their own rabbit-shaped wire topiary forms, but only consider it, who mostly just indulge in the fantasy of doing so, if only they had the time. There is something undeniably soothing about watching Martha at her absurdly time-consuming labors. A female "media executive" explained the appeal to Barbara Lippert in *New York* magazine: "I never liked Martha Stewart until I started watching her on Sunday mornings. I turn on the TV, and I'm in my pajamas, still in this place between sleep and reality. And she's showing you how to roll your tablecloths in parchment paper. She's like a character when she does her crafts. It reminds me of watching Mr. Green Jeans on Captain Kangaroo. I remember he had a shoebox he took out that was filled with craft things. There would be a close-up on his hands with his buffed nails. And then he would show you how to cut an oaktag with a scissor, or when he folded paper, he'd say: 'There you go, boys and girls,' and it was very quiet. It's like she brings out this great meditative focus and calm."

The show does seem strikingly unfrenetic. Unlike just about everything else on TV, including the "Our Home" show, which follows it on Lifetime, it eschews Kathy Lee-type banter, perky music, swooping studio shots and jittery handheld cameras. Instead there's just Martha, alone in her garden or kitchen, her teacherly tones blending with birdsong, her recipes cued to the seasons. Whimsical recorder music pipes along over the credits. Martha's crisply ironed denim shirts, pearl earrings, and honey-toned highlights bespeak the fabulousness of Connecticut. Her hands move slowly, deliberately over her yellow roses or her Depression glasses. Martha is a Puritan who prepares "sinful" foods—few of her recipes are low-fat or especially health-conscious—that are redeemed by the prodigious labors, the molasses afternoons, involved in serving them. (She preys upon our guilt about overindulgence, then hints at how to assuage it.) Here at Turkey Hill, time is as logy as a honey-sated bumblebee. Here on Lifetime, the cable channel aimed at baby-boom women, Martha's stately show floats along in a sea of stalker movies, Thighmaster commercials and "Weddings of a Lifetime" segments, and by comparison, I have to say, she looks rather dignified. Would that we all had these *très riches heures*.

But if we had the hours, if we had the circumstances, wouldn't we want to fill them with something of our own, with a domestic grace of our own devising? Well, maybe not anymore. For taste is no longer an expression of individuality. It is, more often, an instrument of conformism, a way to assure ourselves that we're living by the right codes, dictated or sanctioned by experts. Martha Stewart's "expertise" is really nothing but another name for the perplexity of her cowed consumers. A lifestyle cult as all-encompassing as hers could thrive only at a time when large numbers of Americans have lost confidence in their own judgment about the most ordinary things. For this reason, *Martha Stewart Living* isn't really living at all.

After Reading

Critical Perspective

1. Describe Talbot's tone throughout this text. Where and how does she use humor and sarcasm? In what ways might this aid her argument? In what ways might it undermine it?

Rhetoric and Argument

2. What interesting language choices and rhetorical appeals does Talbot make in this text? Give specific examples of audience, purpose, ethos, pathos, logos, intertextuality, context, and constraints. Are they convincing? Why or why not?
3. What is Talbot's main claim about Martha Stewart? How does she attempt to support it? Provide quotes from the text to back up your assertions.
4. Talbot describes the feminine stereotypes that Martha Stewart and her empire embody. What are they exactly? What do you think about them? Are there others that Talbot does not mention?

Analysis

5. Talbot claims that Martha's world is unreal—it offers a nearly impossible challenge to working women about how they ought to organize and systematize their leisure time. Of course, Stewart's public image also underwent a significant change in recent years, suggesting to her critics that her perfect world was not necessarily so perfect. In a short argumentative text, discuss the differences between positive and negative images of Stewart in the mainstream media. Consult library and Internet sources for additional evidence.

Taking Action

Get into a small group. Examine various parodies of Martha Stewart on television, in magazines, in the news, or in books. What precisely is being poked fun at? Try to provide evidence from actual examples as well as from your memory. Why would the audience find this humorous? What might this reveal about the function of Martha Stewart in American culture?

Now, consider whether there are other cultural figures who are involved in some of the same activities as Martha. The people you consider could include the following: Oprah Winfrey, Jamie Oliver, Emeril Lagasse, Ellen DeGeneres, the hosts of *The View*, Nigella Lawson, B. Smith, Alton Brown, Rachel Ray, Jeff Probst, and Donald Trump. How is Martha's image different from these peoples' images? Why do you think that this is the case? What does this imply to you about how issues of femininity and domesticity are treated in the mainstream media? Share your thoughts with the rest of the class.

WARREN ST. JOHN

"Metrosexuals Come Out"

Warren St. John is an Alabama native who writes for The New York Times. *He has also contributed extensively to the* New York Observer, The New Yorker, *and* Wired. *His most recent book is about the Alabama Crimson Tide,* Rammer Jammer Yellow Hammer: A Journey into the Heart of Fan Mania. *He attended Columbia University and lives in New York.*

EXERCISING YOUR SKILLS

Before Reading

St. John explores the style phenomenon of metrosexuality. What does the term "metrosexual" mean to you? If you have heard this term before, when did you first hear it and in what context? What specific products might you associate with the term?

By his own admission, 30-year-old Karru Martinson is not what you'd call a manly man. He uses a $40 face cream, wears Bruno Magli shoes and custom-tailored shirts. His hair is always just so, thanks to three brands of shampoo and the precise application of three hair grooming products: Textureline Smoothing Serum, got2b styling glue and Suave Rave hairspray. Mr. Martinson likes wine bars and enjoys shopping with his gal pals, who have come to trust his eye for color, his knack for seeing when a bag clashes with an outfit, and his understanding of why some women have 47 pairs of black shoes. ("Because they can!" he said.) He said his guy friends have long thought his consumer and grooming habits a little . . . different. But Mr. Martinson, who lives in Manhattan and works in finance, said he's not that different. "From a personal perspective there was never any doubt what my sexual orientation was," he said. "I'm straight as an arrow."

So it was with a mixture of relief and mild embarrassment that Mr. Martinson was recently asked by a friend in marketing to be part of a focus group of "metrosexuals"— straight urban men willing, even eager, to embrace their feminine sides. Convinced that these open-minded young men hold the secrets of tomorrow's consumer trends, the advertising giant Euro RSCG, with 233 offices worldwide, wanted to better understand their buying habits. So in a private room at the Manhattan restaurant Eleven Madison Park recently, Mr. Martinson answered the marketers' questions and schmoozed with 11 like-minded straight guys who were into Diesel jeans, interior design, yoga and Mini Coopers, and who would never think of ordering a vodka tonic without specifying Grey Goose or Ketel One. Before the focus group met, Mr. Martinson said he was suspicious that such a thing as a metrosexual existed. Afterward, he said, "I'm fully aware that I have those characteristics."

America may be on the verge of a metrosexual moment. Bravo now airs a popular makeover show, *Queer Eye for the Straight Guy,* in which a team of five gay men "transform a style-deficient and culture-deprived straight man from drab to fab." Conde Nast is developing a shopping magazine for men, modeled after *Lucky,* its successful women's magazine, which is largely a text-free catalog of clothes and shoes. There is no end to the curious new vanity products for young men, from a Maxim-magazine-branded hair coloring system to Axe, Unilever's all-over body deodorant for guys. And men are going in for self-improvement strategies traditionally associated with women. For example, the number of plastic surgery procedures on men in the United States has increased threefold since 1997, to 807,000, according to the American Society for Aesthetic Plastic Surgery.

"Their heightened sense of aesthetics is very, very pronounced," Marian Salzman, chief strategy officer at Euro RSCG, who organized the gathering at Eleven Madison Park, said of metrosexuals. "They're the style makers. It doesn't mean your average Joe American is going to copy everything they do," she added. "But unless you study these guys you don't know where Joe American is heading."

Paradoxically, the term metrosexual, which is now being embraced by marketers, was coined in the mid-90's to mock everything marketers stand for. The gay writer Mark Simpson used the word to satirize what he saw as consumerism's toll on traditional masculinity. Men didn't go to shopping malls, buy glossy magazines or load up on grooming products, Mr. Simpson argued, so consumer culture promoted the idea of a sensitive guy—who went to malls, bought magazines and spent freely to improve his personal appearance.

Within a few years, the term was picked up by British advertisers and newspapers. In 2001, Britain's Channel Four brought out a show about sensitive guys called *Metrosexuality.* And in recent years the European media found a metrosexual icon in David Beckham, the English soccer star, who paints his fingernails, braids his hair and poses for gay magazines, all while maintaining a manly profile on the pitch. Along with terms like "PoMosexual," "just gay enough" and "flaming heterosexuals," the word metrosexual is now gaining currency among American marketers who are fumbling for a term to describe this new type of feminized man.

America has a long tradition of sensitive guys. Alan Alda, John Lennon, even Al Gore all heard the arguments of the feminist movement and empathized. Likewise, there's a history of dashing men like Gary Grant and Humphrey Bogart who managed to affect a personal style with plenty of hair goop but without compromising their virility. Even Harrison Ford, whose favorite accessory was once a hammer, now poses proudly wearing an earring. But what separates the modern-day metrosexual from his touchy-feely forebears is a care-free attitude toward the inevitable suspicion that a man who dresses well, has good manners, understands thread counts or has opinions on women's fashion is gay.

"If someone's going to judge me on what kind of moisturizer I have on my shelf, whatever," said Marc d'Avignon, 28, a graduate student living in the East Village, who describes himself as "horrendously addicted to Diesel jeans" and living amid a chemistry lab's worth of Kiehl's lotions. "It doesn't bother me at all. Call it homosexual, feminine, hip, not hip—I don't care. I like drawing from all sorts of sources to create my own persona."

While some metrosexuals may simply be indulging in pursuits they had avoided for fear of being suspected as gay—like getting a pedicure or wearing brighter colors—others consciously appropriate tropes of gay culture the way white suburban teenagers have long cribbed from hip-hop culture, as *a* way of distinguishing themselves from the pack. Having others question their sexuality is all part of the game. "Wanting them to wonder and having them wonder is a wonderful thing," said Daniel Peres, the editor in chief of *Details,* a kind of metrosexual bible. "It gives you an air of mystery: could he be? It makes you stand out."

Standing out requires staying on top of which products are hip and which are not. Marketers refer to such style-obsessed shoppers as prosumers, or urban influentials— educated customers who are picky or just vain enough to spend more money or to make an extra effort in pursuit of their personal look. A man who wants to buy Clinique for Men, for example, has to want the stuff so badly that he will walk up to the women's cosmetics counter in a department store, where Clinique for Men is sold. A man who wants Diesel jeans has to be willing to pay $135 a pair. A man who insists on Grey Goose has to get comfortable with paying $14 for a martini. "The guy who drinks Grey Goose is willing to pay extra," said Lee Einsidler, executive vice president of Sydney Frank Importing, which owns Grey Goose. "He does it in all things in his life. He doesn't buy green beans, he buys haricots verts."

Other retailers hope to entice the man on the fence to get in touch with his metrosexual side. Oliver Sweatman, the chief executive of Sharps, a new line of grooming products aimed at young urban men, said that to lure manly men to buy his new-age shaving gels—which contain Roman chamomile, gotu kola and green tea—the packaging is a careful mixture of old and new imagery. The fonts recall the masculinity of an old barber shop, but a funny picture of a goat on the label implies, he said, something out of the ordinary.

In an effort to out closeted metrosexuals, Ms. Salzman and her marketing team at Euro RSCG are working at perfecting polling methods that will identify "metrosexual markers." One, she noted, is that metrosexuals like telling their friends about their new finds. Mr. Martinson, the Bruno Magli-wearing metrosexual, agreed. "I'm not in marketing," he said. "But when you take a step back, and say, 'Hey, I e-mailed my friends about a great vodka or a great Off Broadway show,' in essence I am a marketer and I'm doing it for free."

Most metrosexuals, though, see their approach to life as serving their own interests in the most important marketing contest of all: the battle for babes. Their pitch to women: you're getting the best of both worlds.

Some women seem to buy it. Alycia Oaklander, a 29-year-old fashion publicist from Manhattan, fell for John Kilpatrick, a Washington Redskins season ticket holder who loves Budweiser and grilling hot dogs, in part because of his passion for shopping and women's fashion shows. On their first dates, Mr. Kilpatrick brought champagne, cooked elaborate meals and talked the talk about Ms. Oaklander's shoes. They were married yesterday. "He loves sports and all the guy stuff," Ms. Oaklander said. "But on the other hand he loves to cook and he loves design. It balances out."

The proliferation of metrosexuals is even having an impact in gay circles. Peter Paige a gay actor who plays the character Emmett on the Showtime series *Queer as Folk,* frequently complains in interviews that he's having a harder time than ever telling straight men from gays. "They're all low-slung jeans and working out with six packs and more hair product than I've ever used in my life, and they smell better than your mother on Easter," he said. Mr. Paige said there was at least one significant difference between hitting on metrosexuals and their less evolved predecessors. "Before, you used to get punched," he said. "Now it's all, 'Gee thanks, I'm straight but I'm really flattered.'"

After Reading

Critical Perspective

1. Characterize how St. John begins his argument. Do you find this technique effective? Why or why not? Furnish evidence from the text to back up your assertions.

Rhetoric and Argument

2. Describe the organization of St. John's essay. Do you find the structure of this argument to be persuasive? Explain your views.
3. What does St. John assert about metrosexuals? Do you agree with his views? Why or why not? Offer evidence from this piece and thoughts from your own experiences to back up your thoughts.
4. St. John seems to provide support for the idea that metrosexuality is a marketing term used to describe a relatively new male demographic. In what ways might the term also describe a set of behaviors or attitudes? Find support from the text for your position.

Analysis

5. St. John suggests that women and gay men have a particular reaction to metrosexuals. What is that reaction? Do you think that St. John is accurate or not? Draw from your own experiences to support your perspective. Consult library and Internet sources as well.

Taking Action

Analyze an issue from a men's magazine such as *Maxim* or *Details*. Make note of all the ads in the magazine in terms of St. John's discussion of metrosexuality. In what specific ways are metrosexuals being targeted in these magazines? In what ways are they not being targeted? Then analyze an issue from a women's magazine such as *Vogue*, *Cosmo*, or *Glamour* that features ads depicting men to a female audience. Are metrosexuals being targeted similarly in these magazines?

When you are done, share your thoughts with the rest of the class. What have you all determined about the how metrosexuality is working as an advertising ploy to entice male consumers? Is this tactic being used differently on male and female audiences? Consult library and Internet sources as helpful.

RICHARD MAJORS AND JANET MANCINI BILLSON

"Cool Pose"

Richard Majors is a professor of psychology at the University of Wisconsin, Eau Claire. He has published a number of books about masculinity, African American culture, and education. Janet Mancini Billson is professor of sociology and women's studies at Rhode Island College. She has published a number of books on African American culture and women's lives. They cowrote Cool Pose: The Dilemmas of Black Manhood in America, *from which this essay comes.*

EXERCISING YOUR SKILLS

Before Reading

In their essay about style Majors and Billson offer some interesting analyses of how African American males are "supposed to act" and look in American culture. Think about your own home communities. What behaviors, activities, attitudes, habits, and clothes mark a person as distinctly masculine or feminine in such places? How do race, ethnicity, and class shift how we view what is masculine and what is feminine? Why is this the case?

> *The cat seeks through a harmonious combination of charm . . . the proper dedication to his "kick" and unrestrained generosity to make of his day to day life itself a gracious work of art.*[1]

For many African-American males, the character that best exemplifies the expressive life-style is the cool cat. Like other forms of cool pose, being a cool cat provides a way to accentuate the self. The cool cat is an exceptional artist of expressiveness and flamboyant style. He creates his unique identity by artfully dipping into a colorful palette of clothes and hairstyles that set him apart from the ordinary. His nonverbal gestures—his walk and handshakes, for example—are mixed with high verbal agility. He can be found "rapping it down to a woman" with a flair and virtuosity that others envy. He does not simply drive a car—he "leans" (drives with one arm) and sets his neighbors talking about his self-assured risk-taking. The cool cat is the consummate actor. His performance may also be characterized by deftly manipulative and deceptive strategies.

Black males put great emphasis on style and acting cool. Appearing suave, urbane, and charming is at the heart of being a cool cat. The black male is supremely skilled at utilizing cultural symbols in a way that stamps his personal mark on all encounters. This allows him to elevate his sense of pride and control. He can broadcast strength and masculinity or shore up flagging status and dignity.

Portrait of the Cool Cat

The portrait of a typical cool cat is usually that of a young black male found on the streets of American cities. He is probably unemployed, may be involved in drugs or alcohol, and has limited education. He is involved in some kind of hustling activity and is probably from a low-income, beleaguered family. Some embrace values of education and work and are marked by self-assurance. For example, in *Strategic Styles,* Mancini describes Hank as a "together guy" who exudes confidence and autonomy, as well as flamboyance; he states simply, "I got my own way in everything. I don't copy nothing from nobody."[2]

McCord and his colleagues in *Life Styles in the Black Ghetto* characterize the cool cat as a young man who spends his time on street corners, in pool halls, or in "running some type of racket." He has a distinctive style. Firestone defines the cool cat as a man who combines charm, dedication to his "kick," and unusual generosity to make everyday life a balanced and "gracious work of art" that contributes in some way to a pleasant, aesthetic life-style. The cool cat is unruffled, self-assured, and eminently cool in the face of emergencies.

Clothes and the Cool Cat

Few African-American males now wear the *dashikis* of the Black Revolution, but clothes are still used to make fashion and status statements. Clothes help the black male attract attention and enhance his self-image. After all, in a society that has kept blacks invisible, it is not surprising that seemingly flamboyant clothes might be worn to heighten visibility.

Clothes can also contribute to violence and fighting, even death, among young black males. For example, some gangs use baseball caps or colors to symbolize gang membership. Gangs have been known to kill youths for wearing the wrong colors or clothes. They have also fought, occasionally to death, over brand name clothes (such as Georgio and Gucci items), basketball sneakers, or gold chains. Black fraternities often use jackets to indicate membership and solidarity.

To style is the ultimate way hustlers attempt to act cool. Clothes are a portable and creative expression of styling. The interest in colorful male plumage begins in the early teens when attention-getting costumes earn the young cat his place on center stage. He begins to establish his own personal signature in dress, hairstyle, and language. To "style," "front off," "friend," "high sign," or "funk" all mean to show off or upstage others in a highly competitive war of masculine self-presentation. A young black woman describes how she compliments the cool cats in her life: "You all dressed up and you have your apple hat on, your flairs, and your boots and you walkin' down the street lookin' at all d' people, so you goin' style wid the lookin' good. Be more less flamboyant. . . . He's decked to kill! Da's what we [young women] tell 'em."[3]

Getting "clean" and dressing with style is an important way to get over in the world. Some teens see the world as a constant stage—a series of personal performances. They earn street applause for being clean and having style. Folb notes that because how you dress says so much about who you are, black males often resent wearing work-related uniforms. The uniform de-styles them. Folb quotes a youth who is contemplating quitting his job as groundskeeper aide for the County of Los Angeles: "I like to get clean and stay sharp."[4]

Hudson calls the attire of the hustler flashy and flamboyant and stresses that clothing is a central part of a hustler's front. In order to make money he must look like he already has money (somewhat akin to the Madison Avenue grey flannel suit or recent evocations for yuppies to "dress for success"). He cannot expect to "take off some fat suckers" if he looks like a "greaseball."

When a hustler starts making money, he immediately puts his wardrobe together in order to establish prestige with his audience. A monologue by well-known black recording artist Lou Rawls describes a popular young hustler on the South Side of Chicago who epitomizes the cool cat style:

Every Friday evening about 4:30 he would be standing there because his girl-friend works at Walgreen's . . . and on Friday, the eagle flies. He was wearing the very popular silk mohair wool worsted—continental to the bone—$250 hustler's suit . . . a pair of highly shined hustler's alligator shoes . . . white on white tab collar shirt, a very thin hustler's necktie . . . a very large artificial diamond stick pin in place . . . a hustler's hairdo . . . a process . . . hustler's shades on, cigarette in hand, a very broad smile on his face . . . staring hard and elated at what he saw . . . his automobile parked at the curb . . . white on white on white. The hustlers call them hogs, the trade name is Cadillac . . . (As the hustler is standing on the corner, he sees his wife approaching with a razor in hand, screaming at him): You no good jiving farmer . . . the rent's not paid and the baby is hungry and needs shoes and you're out here hustling and carrying on . . . (He says): Baby, you can have this car and anything you want. Just don't cut my new suit. I just got it out of the pawn shop and I've got to have my front so I can keep on making my game.[5]

Cool Wheels

Cars also underscore the significance of style and feature heavily in "making the game." Hustlers and others in the ghetto value and treasure their automobiles. The more expensive the automobile, the more valid is the hustler's claims to have made it. As the expression goes, "he is doing good in this town."

From an early age, black teens see cars as a status symbol. Many learn to pop the ignition so they can take joyrides—preparation perhaps for organized car theft later in life. Cars allow visible, conspicuous display of status—a perfect way for the cool cat to stage his performance literally throughout the community.

One stylized type of physical posturing noted by Folb is "leaning" or "low-riding," in which the driver (and sometimes the passenger) sits so low in his seat that only the top of his head is visible and his eyes peer out over the steering wheel. Low-riding is designed to draw attention to both driver and car—a performance that may be specifically directed toward females. Folb quotes a young woman's perception of these performances:

Leanin' that's when a dude be leanin' so hard like he's layin' down in d' car. Da's what they do in their cars. Lean like, "I'm jus' the man." But guys in low-ridin' cars lean and low ride 'cause they know they gotta be funky and they say, "Well, the car be lookin' good, I gotta look good."[6]

For the cool cat, driving a Cadillac (or other luxury car) is important for more than just transportation. Cadillac-type cars epitomize class because of their reputation and because they take up a great deal of physical space. They symbolize being seen—a critical experience for those who have been invisible in this country for so long. The cool cat feels, "If I can drive a stylish car like this, it proves to myself and others that I am as important as anyone else. I haven't given up. I am going to make it." The cool cat often sacrifices other economic goods in his life or his family's life to have a big luxury car as a way to make such a statement.

Lame to the Bone

If style is the ultimate way to act cool, cool cats must have definite beliefs as to what represents nonstylistic behavior. Being called "lame to the bone" or "uncool" is the ultimate insult in black teenage vernacular. Being lame means to be socially incompetent, disabled, or crippled—a sissy. The "lame brand" does not even know how to talk to females; he may appear frightened of them. Folb reports:

> Dudes be talkin' to d' young lady, he run aroun', shootin' marbles. Not too situ-
> ated . . . Dumb sucker have no girls, don't know where everything is . . . stone
> SUCKER! Sissy boy, hangin' 'round his momma all the time. Dedicated to d' home
> front. He don't know what's happ'nin'. He like a school book chump . . . stupid,
> ignorant, hide in d' books all d' time—like a bookworm. He square to d' wood! . . .
> Don't get high, don't smoke no weed. Show 'im a reefer, he wouldn't even know
> what it is! . . . Uncoordinated. He cain't fight or nothin'. Like he followin' you ever-
> place you go . . . wanna be wid everybody but don't do nothin' . . . They can't catch
> on to what's happ'nin'."[7]

For those who are lame, there is probably no hope of rehabilitation.

Half-stepping means to do something halfway and is a form of being lame or uncool. A person who is not appropriately dressed for an occasion is not mounting the correct performance. If he is giving a party, he should not dress the way he would for school or work, in off-brand tennis shoes or Levis, or wrinkled clothing: "Don't come half-steppin', come fiendish, righteously dap to a tee, silk to the bone. Or like a date. Like you dress yo'self up—some bad-boy bell bottom, nice shirt. Don't half step. Get yo'self together brother."[8]

Why Is Style So Important?

We might ask why style is so important to cool cats. Styling helps cool cats draw attention to the self and communicates creativity. The African-American man in this country has been "nobody" for generations. The purpose of styling, then, is to paint a self-portrait in colorful, vivid strokes that makes the black male "somebody."

The extravagant, flashy clothes often worn by cool cats, the blaring ghetto blasters playing earsplitting music as they walk or drive down the street, signify their need to be seen and heard. Styling is an antidote to invisibility and silence, a hope in a hopeless world, a defense against multiple attacks on cultural and personal integrity. It is proactive rather than defensive. Styling lets the black male show others that he is alive, and reminds himself as well.

The cool cat styles for the cosmetic effect (how he looks) and to symbolize the messages he wants to portray: "No matter how poor I am or what has happened to me in the past, this shows that I can still make it . . . and with class."

Irrespective of race or class, it is not enough to survive or just live from day to day in a social vacuum. Rather, individuals have a genuine need to know that they can make a contribution to their own welfare and personal growth and that they have control over their own destiny. That they can be noticed and can better their lives.

Perkins writes that black children internalize the roles that will allow them to perform on the only stage they know: the black ghetto colony. The cool cat and similar roles are adopted because they have great survival value, not just because they elicit applause from the immediate audience. Black children learn how to be cool under the most extenuating circumstances because being cool is a clear advantage. Perkins adds that when a situation is fraught with danger or anxiety (becomes "uptight"), the most sophisticated response is being cool, "hip," or "together." Cool stabilizes the situation and either minimizes or ignores threats that cannot be easily dealt with in other ways.

Firestone sees the "idea cat" as a person who is adequate to any situation. He adopts a cool image in order to deal with status and identity problems in a society that denies equal access. Foster hypothesizes that as the black man's drive for middle-class status in the North was thwarted by racism, a cool street-corner life-style evolved. White racism in urban areas both stimulates and perpetuates street-corner behavior. Whereas other ethnic groups have been allowed to assimilate after a period of initial bigotry, doors have remained impermeable to African-Americans. (Foster notes that where the doors have been opened for black males, a highly organized street life-style is not as likely to develop.) In most places in America, those doors remain at least partially closed.

The cool cat life-style has long functioned as a means to enhance the black male's ability to survive the harsh effects of racism and social oppression. Because of a lack of resources, services, goods, information, and jobs, lower-income blacks often have hours of free time on their hands. The cool cat life-style provides a kind of stimulation and entertainment. Something is always going on or being contemplated. Those who live in the ghetto often view cool cats as fashionable, hip, cool, and chic. This glamorized life-style helps the black male to achieve balance—entertainment and stimulation counter frustration and boredom.

Being a cool cat is one route toward creative masculinity, toward recognition. It helps black males to survive, to style and act cool, to show disdain for the white man and the Protestant work ethic, and to show pride and dignity. It enhances manhood, commands respect, vents bitterness and anger, establishes a sense of control, expresses artistry, accentuates the self, and provides a form of amusement.

Life on the Streets

For cool cats who like to style, the streets are the best place to hustle and earn a living. The streets are exhilarating, perilous, electric with possibilities, and lush with social meaning. As with some other groups, such as Hispanics, the streets are the main stage of daily life for black males. For whites and for middle-class blacks, the streets are just concrete pathways of neutrality and practicality, perhaps even of danger. For young blacks, especially those who live in impoverished inner-city neighborhoods, the streets become the community living room, the sports arena, the recreation hall, the marketplace, and the political forum. Drug deals, hanging out, love affairs, gang rivalries, and training in conventional wisdom all take place in the streets.

The streets are a school of life that easily competes with the dry, often irrelevant pap squeezed between pages of books in nearby school buildings. H. Rap Brown remembers his own early years in the ghetto. He says the streets are where "young bloods" seek and gain control and where they receive their most relevant education: "I learned how to talk in the streets, not from reading about Dick and Jane going to the zoo and all that simple shit. Sometimes I wonder why I ever bothered to go to school. Practically everything I know I learned on the corner."[9]

Phil talks about how the streets are his home and the place he learned to keep his true feelings to himself: "I am a street person. A street person will not tell The Man everything. Like you can't be too honest, man. Go ahead and be honest, you goin' wish you had not. You don't tell the truth all the time. You're screwing yourself up! I learned that shit from the white man."

Streets are where it happens—it being whatever holds emotional valence for the young black male. Streets are beyond parental control. Streets respond to the authority of youth and gangs, rather than of age, parents, teachers, or police. The streets train for criminality, not conventionality. For many, the streets become home for most of the day and night. Home (meaning house) becomes a place to catch a few hours of sleep and to dress for the next main stage (street) performance. For others, the streets become home, literally—or their coffin.

A young black boy raised by a prostitute mother and an alcoholic father remembers when he began to develop the street-smart ways of a cool cat liking the taste of cheap liquor, and meeting all the neighborhood's cats—the gamblers, pimps, bootleggers, and hustlers:

> I knew the ministers, teachers, and deacons of the church who came to the district to do no preaching or teaching. I knew the city and county officials who, in secret, slipped me quarters whenever they came for their share of the "dirty money" or just seeking the favor of the ladies. I remember the sharp gamblers who spent their spare time hanging around with my beautiful mother. They played with me and taught me the tricks of the trade. At nine, I knew how to ink and crimp the other guy's cards between my fingers. I remember the flashy clothes of the gamblers and pimps and sharp automobiles.[10]

The young boy's early training in such illegal activities as pimping, gambling, bootlegging, and prostitution prepared him for the fast life. He wanted to grow up to be just like these role models, reflecting the urgency of black males in the ghetto who are exposed to alternative life-styles and roles during their tenderest years. If they learn their lessons well, they can survive later as cool hustlers.

Hustling to Fill the Void

The cool cat life-style is a survival strategy par excellence because this role develops as a reaction to racism and social oppression. The art of hustling, expressed in various forms of deceptive and manipulative activities, is the cool cat's greatest weapon against poverty and social inequality. Hustling becomes the African-American male's original and indigenous means of waging a private war on poverty. Some believe that hustling is a more successful antipoverty weapon than the government has invented to date.

Foster writes that hustling, as a profession, is a way of life for many black men. It requires only a "degree from the streets." Horton asked some black males, "When a dude needs bread (money), how does he get it?" The universal response was "the hustle." Hustling, as the primary street activity, becomes the economic foundation for everyday life and sets the tone of social activities as well.

Hustling for the cool cat represents not only an alternative economic form, but an alternative form of masculinity. Black males have accepted the basic masculine goals, norms, and standards of our society (such as wanting to work and provide for a family), but unlike white males, they sometimes lack the means to achieve these masculine goals. Resolute attempts to work hard in legitimate jobs are, for many black males, met with being the last hired and first fired, low pay, insult, or lack of promotion. Playing the American game according to the standard rules does not necessarily lead to upward social or occupational mobility.

The constant pressure to prove his manhood without mainstream tools has left many black males feeling angry and bitter. They feel that they have been locked out of the American mainstream. The cool cat life-style is a way to mock whites and the Protestant work ethic by exploiting, rapping, conning, the "pimping game," and other hustling roles.

Hustling roles say to the white man: "Hustling makes me feel like a man and allows me to survive. But more important, I hustle, white man, because it is something you hate, and it therefore defies the principles you are most proud of . . . the Protestant work ethic. And even though I realize this life-style can potentially destroy me, at least I make a strong statement to you, white man, that no matter what happens by this hustling, I was in control, not you, and this is all that matters."

Hustling compensates for lack of income, goods and services, and status. It gives the cool cat a kit bag of identity tools for creating a sense of power, prestige, pride, and manhood. The road to mainstream American success is opened, at least for the moment or for the day. The oppressed man can use cool and hustling as his best chance to advance financially and socially and to feel important.

Foster believes that considerable talent is expended in pulling off the street-corner hustle. If racism and exploitation by whites had not pulled the plug on legitimate means for establishing masculinity, illegal outlets would not have thrived. He argues that countless young black males—cool cats and hustlers supreme—who have shown talent in their pursuit of the illegitimate game, would have shown extreme giftedness in the pursuit of mainstream avenues to success.

The street corner hustlers might have become more aggressive salesmen, businessmen, or politicians under more favorable conditions. But in the face of restricted opportunities, lack of middle-class black role models, and confronted with the successful models of the hustler and pimp, the young black male is tempted to take the street route to success. Ironically, the street man and the mainstream man both want the same thing. Both want to make it and to be seen by their families and friends as secure and successful—as somebody. But each sees a different road as the logical one to take.

Hudson offers an intriguing idea: although hustling might appear to be diametrically opposed to the Protestant ethic, it is actually an extension of it. He hypothesizes that the hustler's society may be deviant, but it is an adaptive, systematic form of deviance that struggles toward mainstream rewards and goals.

Survival dictates the cool cat's course. He accepts the expressive, cool path of the street because he quickly or eventually comes to believe that conventional routes are congested or closed off to him. For the cool cat who travels the road of hustling, conning, and gaming, pitfalls, as well as fame, may be around the corner.

Notes

1. H. Firestone, "Cats, Kicks and Color," *Social Problems* 1957, Vol. 5, p. 5.
2. J. K. Mancini, *Strategic Styles: Coping in the Inner City* (Hanover, N.H.: University Press of New England, 1981), p. 164.
3. E. Folb, *Runnin' Down Some Lines: The Language and Culture of Black Teenagers* (Cambridge, Mass.: Harvard University Press, 1980), pp. 109-10; see also M. L. Knapp, "The Field of Nonverbal Communication: An Overview," in *On Speech Communication,* ed. C. J. Stewart and B. Kendall (New York: Holt, Rinehart and Winston, 1978).
4. Ibid.
5. B. Dworkin and S. Dworkin, *Cool: Young Adults in the Negro Ghetto,* unpublished manuscript, Washington University, St. Louis, Mo.
6. Folb 1980, 112, 115.
7. Folb 1980, 38.
8. Folb 1980, 42.
9. H. R. Brown, *Die Nigger Die!* (New York: Dial Press, 1969).
10. W. J. McCord, et al., *Life Styles in the Black Ghetto* (New York: W. W. Norton, 1969), p. 129.

After Reading

Critical Perspective

1. How do you define the word "cool"? How do these authors define it? Do you agree with their definition? Where in their text do they describe it? What are its components? Furnish evidence from the text to back up your assertions.

Rhetoric and Argument

2. Describe the structure of Majors' and Billson's argument. Do you find the structure of this argument to be rhetorically effective? Why or why not? What format does it follow? What particular subclaims do these writers present? If you could offer suggestions to Majors and Billson about how to make their argument more effective, what would they be?

3. What do Majors and Billson claim about the "cool pose"? Do you agree with their perspectives? Why or why not? Point to their text and examples from your own life to support your thoughts.

4. Are there any faulty assumptions or warrants at work in this text? If yes, what are they and where do they appear in the text? Offer evidence from the essay.

Analysis

5. The feminist movement in American culture has made the poor treatment of women quite clear in American culture. However, many men from a wide range of backgrounds in American culture have restricted opportunities that may not be readily apparent. In a short essay, address the following concerns: What difficulties have the men you have known been through as a result of experiences related to their gender? How exactly did they deal with these problems? Did they find social support for their feelings of anger, pain, or marginalization? Consult library and Internet sources as well.

Taking Action

As music such as hip-hop and rap—as well as the cultural situations within which they were produced (urban street life)—become more popular and cross ethnic, race, and class lines, the young men (and sometimes young women) in other cultural groups have adopted their own versions of the cool pose.

In a short freewrite, describe your own personal experience and the experiences of those you know with the social pressures to adopt a cool pose in your community, the positives and negatives of this, and what you make of the cultural phenomenon. Consider how neighborhood groups, school cliques, and gang life reinforce these ideas. Write about specific media images in commercials, television, film, and in cyberspace that also rely upon and promote this cool pose.

When you are done, share your thoughts with the rest of the class. What have you determined about the cool pose, who adopts it and why, and what may be its effects on communities, neighborhoods, and American culture in general? Consult library and Internet sources as helpful. Consider finding ways to convey your findings to other groups both inside and outside the campus community.

ALISON LURIE

"The Language of Clothes"

Alison Lurie is a professor of American literature at Cornell University. Lurie is the author of numerous books, including the Pulitzer Prize–winning novel Foreign Affairs. *Lurie has also written* The Language of Clothes *and* Familiar Spirits: A Memoir of James Merrill and David Jackson.

EXERCISING YOUR SKILLS

Before Reading

Lurie writes about the history and language of fashion and style. Think about your own wardrobe. What do different outfits mean to you—your favorite ones, the ones you wear only for special occasions, and the ones that never see the light of day? What do these outfits say about who you are?

For thousands of years human beings have communicated with one another first in the language of dress. Long before I am near enough to talk to you on the street, in a meeting, or at a party, you announce your sex, age and class to me through what you are wearing—and very possibly give me important information (or misinformation) as to your occupation, origin, personality, opinions, tastes, sexual desires and current mood. I may not be able to put what I observe into words, but I register the information unconsciously; and you simultaneously do the same for me. By the time we meet and converse we have already spoken to each other in an older and more universal language.

The statement that clothing is a language, though made occasionally with the air of a man finding a flying saucer in his backyard, is not new. Balzac, in *Daughter of Eve* (1830), observed that dress is a "continual manifestation of intimate thoughts, a language, a symbol." Today, as semiotics becomes fashionable, sociologists tell us that fashion too is a language of signs, a nonverbal system of communication.

None of these theorists, however, has gone on to remark what seems obvious: that if clothing is a language, it must have a vocabulary and a grammar like other languages. Of course, as with human speech, there is not a single language of dress, but many: some (like Dutch and German) closely related and others (like Basque) almost unique. And within every language of clothes there are many different dialects and accents, some almost unintelligible to members of the mainstream culture. Moreover, as with speech, each individual has his own stock of words and employs personal variations of tone and meaning.

The vocabulary of dress includes not only items of clothing, but also hair styles, accessories, jewelry, make-up and body decoration. Theoretically at least this vocabulary is as large as or larger than that of any spoken tongue, since it includes every garment, hair style, and type of body decoration ever invented. In practice, of course, the sartorial resources of an individual may be very restricted. Those of a sharecropper, for instance, may be limited to five or ten "words" from which it is possible to create only a few "sentences" almost bare of decoration and expressing only the most basic concepts. A so-called fashion leader, on the other hand, may have several hundred "words" at his or her disposal, and thus be able to form thousands of different "sentences" that will express a wide range of meanings. Just as the average English-speaking person knows many more words than he or she will ever use in conversation, so all of us are able to understand the meaning of styles we will never wear.

Magical Clothing

Archaeologists digging up past civilizations and anthropologists studying primitive tribes have come to the conclusion that, as Rachel Kemper [*Costume*] puts it, "Paint, ornament, and rudimentary clothing were first employed to attract good animistic powers and to ward off evil." When Charles Darwin visited Tierra del Fuego, a cold, wet, disagreeable land plagued by constant winds, he found the natives naked except for feathers in their hair and symbolic designs painted on their bodies. Modern Australian bushmen, who may spend hours decorating themselves and their relatives with patterns in colored clay, often wear nothing else but an amulet or two.

However skimpy it may be, primitive dress almost everywhere, like primitive speech, is full of magic. A necklace of shark's teeth or a girdle of cowrie shells or feathers serves the same purpose as a prayer or spell, and may magically replace—or more often supplement—a spoken charm. In the first instance a form of *contagious* magic is at work: the shark's teeth are believed to endow their wearer with the qualities of a fierce and successful fisherman. The cowrie shells, on the other hand, work through *sympathetic* magic: since they resemble the female sexual parts, they are thought to increase or preserve fertility.

In civilized society today belief in the supernatural powers of clothing—like belief in prayers, spells and charms—remains widespread, though we denigrate it with the name "superstition." Advertisements announce that improbable and romantic events will follow the application of a particular sort of grease to our faces, hair or bodies; they claim that members of the opposite (or our own) sex will be drawn to us by the smell of a particular soap. Nobody believes those ads, you may say. Maybe not, but we behave as though we did: look in your bathroom cabinet.

The supernatural garments of European folk tales—the seven-league boots, the cloaks of invisibility and the magic rings—are not forgotten, merely transformed, so that today we have the track star who can only win a race in a particular hat or shoes, the plainclothes cop who feels no one can see him in his raincoat and the wife who takes off her wedding ring before going to a motel with her lover.

Sympathetic or symbolic magic is also often employed, as when we hang crosses, stars or one of the current symbols of female power and solidarity around our necks, thus silently involving the protection of Jesus, Jehovah or Astarte. Such amulets, of course, may be worn to announce our allegiance to some faith or cause rather than as a charm. Or they may serve both purposes simultaneously—or sequentially. The crucifix concealed below the parochial-school uniform speaks only to God until some devilish force persuades its wearer to remove his or her clothes; then it acts—or fails to act—as a warning against sin as well as a protective talisman.

Articles of clothing, too, may be treated as if they had mana, the impersonal supernatural force that tends to concentrate itself in objects. When I was in college it was common to wear a particular "lucky" sweater, shirt or hat to final examinations, and this practice continues today. Here it is usually contagious magic that is at work: the chosen garment has become lucky by being worn on the occasion of some earlier success, or has been given to its owner by some favored person. The wearing of such magical garments is especially common in sports, where they are often publicly credited with bringing their owners luck. Their loss or abandonment is thought to cause injury as well as defeat. Actors also believe ardently in the magic of clothes, possibly because they are so familiar with the near-magical transforming power of theatrical costume.

Fashion and Status

Clothing designed to show the social position of its wearer has a long history. Just as the oldest languages are full of elaborate titles and forms of address, so for thousands of years certain modes have indicated high or royal rank. Many societies passed decrees known as *sumptuary laws* to prescribe or forbid the wearing of specific styles by specific classes of persons. In ancient Egypt only those in high position could wear sandals; the Greeks and Romans controlled the type, color and number of garments worn and the sorts of embroidery with which they could be trimmed. During the Middle Ages almost every aspect of dress was regulated at some place or time—though not always with much success. The common features of all sumptuary laws—like that of edicts against the use of certain words—seem to be that they are difficult to enforce for very long.

Laws about what could be worn by whom continued to be passed in Europe until about 1700. But as class barriers weakened and wealth could be more easily and rapidly converted into gentility, the system by which color and shape indicated social status began to break down. What came to designate high rank instead was the evident cost of a costume: rich materials, superfluous trimmings and difficult-to-care-for styles, or as Thorstein Veblen later put it [in *The Theory of the Leisure Class*], Conspicuous Waste and Conspicuous Leisure. As a result, it was assumed that the people you met would be dressed as lavishly as their income permitted. In Fielding's *Tom Jones,* for instance, everyone judges strangers by their clothing and treats them accordingly; this is presented as natural. It is a world in which rank is very exactly indicated by costume, from the rags of Molly the gamekeeper's daughter to Sophia Western's riding habit "which was so very richly laced" that "Partridge and the postboy instantly started from their chairs, and my landlady fell to her curtsies, and her ladyships, with great eagerness." The elaborate wigs characteristic of this period conferred status partly because they were both expensive to buy and expensive to maintain.

By the early eighteenth century the social advantages of conspicuous dress were such that even those who could not afford it often spent their money on finery. This development was naturally deplored by supporters of the status quo. In Colonial America the Massachusetts General Court declared its "utter detestation and dislike, that men or women of mean condition, should take upon them the garb of Gentlemen, by wearing Gold or Silver lace, or Buttons, or Points at their knees, or to walk in great Boots; or Women of the same rank to wear Silk or Tiffiny hoods, or Scarfes. . . ." What "men or women of mean condition"—farmers or artisans—were supposed to wear were coarse linen or wool, leather aprons, deerskin jackets, flannel petticoats and the like.

To dress above one's station was considered not only foolishly extravagant, but deliberately deceptive. In 1878 an American etiquette book complained,

> *It is . . . unfortunately the fact that, in the United States, but too much attention is paid to dress by those who have neither the excuse of ample means nor of social claims. . . . We Americans are lavish, generous, and ostentatious. The wives of our wealthy men are glorious in garb as are princesses and queens. They have a right so to be. But when those who can ill afford to wear alpaca persist in arraying themselves in silk . . . the matter is a sad one.*

Color and Pattern

Certain sorts of information about other people can be communicated in spite of a language barrier. We may not be able to understand Welsh or the thick Southern dialect of the Mississippi delta, but when we hear a conversation in these tongues we can tell at once whether the speakers are excited or bored, cheerful or miserable, confident or frightened. In the same way, some aspects of the language of clothes can be read by almost anyone.

The first and most important of these signs, and the one that makes the greatest and most immediate impact, is color. Merely looking at different colors, psychologists have discovered, alters our blood pressure, heartbeat and rate of respiration, just as hearing a harsh noise or a harmonious musical chord does. When somebody approaches from a distance the first thing we see is the hue of his clothes; the closer he comes, the more space this hue occupies in our visual field and the greater its effect on our nervous system. Loud, clashing colors, like loud noises or loud voices, may actually hurt our eyes or give us a headache; soft, harmonious hues, like music and soft voices, thrill or soothe us. Color in dress is also like tone of voice in speech in that it can completely alter the meaning of what is "said" by other aspects of the costume: style, fabric and trimmings. Just as the words "Do you want to dance with me?" can be whispered shyly or flung as a challenge, so the effect of a white evening dress is very different from that of a scarlet one of identical fabric and pattern. In certain circumstances some hues, like some tones of voice, are beyond the bounds of polite discourse. A bride in a black wedding dress, or a stockbroker greeting his clients in a shocking-pink three-piece suit, would be like people screaming aloud.

Although color often indicates mood, it is not by any means an infallible guide. For one thing, convention may prescribe certain hues. The urban businessman must wear a navy blue, dark gray or (in certain regions) brown or tan suit, and can express his feelings only through his choice of shirt and tie, or tie alone; and even here the respectable possibilities may be very limited. Convention also alters the meaning of colors according to the place and time at which they are worn. Vermilion in the office is not the same as vermilion at a disco; and hot weather permits the wearing of pale hues that would make one look far more formal and fragile in midwinter.

There are other problems. Some people may avoid colors they like because of the belief or illusion that they are unbecoming, while others may wear colors they normally dislike for symbolic reason: because they are members or fans of a certain football team, for instance. In addition, some fashionable types may select certain hues merely because they are "in" that year.

Finally, it should be noted that the effect of any color in dress is modified by the colors that accompany it. In general, therefore, the following remarks should be taken as applying mainly to costumes composed entirely or almost entirely of a single hue.

The mood of a crowd, as well as that of an individual, can often be read in the colors of clothing. In the office of a large corporation, or at a professional convention, there is usually a predominance of conventional gray, navy, beige, tan and white—suggesting a general attitude of seriousness, hard work, neutrality, propriety and status. The same group of people at a picnic are a mass of lively, relaxed blue, red and brown, with touches of yellow and green. In the evening, at a disco, they shimmer under the rotating lights in dramatic combinations of purple, crimson, orange, turquoise, gold, silver and black.

Apart from the chameleon, man is the only animal who can change his skin to suit his background. Indeed, if he is to function successfully he must do so. The individual whose clothes do not fall within the recognized range of colors for a given situation attracts attention, usually (though not always) unfavorable attention. When a child puts its pet chameleon down on the earth and it does not turn brown, we know the creature is seriously ill. In the same way, men or women who begin to come to work in a conservative office wearing disco hues and a disco mood are regarded with anxiety and suspicion. If they do not blush a respectable beige, navy or gray within a reasonable length of time, their colleagues know that they will not be around for long.

After Reading

Critical Perspective

1. What is your general reaction to Lurie's text? What do you like about it? What elements might you change and why? Be specific in your answers.

Rhetoric and Argument

2. Describe the particular rhetorical tactics (audience, purpose, ethos, pathos, logos, intertextuality, context, and constraints) as well as the structure and arrangement of Lurie's essay. Do you find it persuasive? Why or why not?
3. What is Lurie's main claim? Where in her text does she offer it? Do you find it persuasive? Why or why not? Be sure to offer quotes to back up your views.
4. Lurie indicates that cultural conventions have often determined the sorts of clothing people wear in class-stratified societies. Do you agree with this claim? Why or why not? What does Lurie suggest about how color selection in clothing operates? What do you make of her ideas?
5. What evidence does Lurie employ to back up her assertions? Give examples. What kinds of warrants and assumptions are operating in her text? Be sure to provide evidence from the text to support your thoughts.

Analysis

6. Lurie asserts that clothes and speech are similar in various ways. How are they alike, according to Lurie? Do you find her examples persuasive? Why or why not? Write a short argumentative essay in which you advance a claim about these concerns and back it up with detailed readings of her text. Also, look at relevant library and Internet sources.

Taking Action

Get together in a small group and peruse a wide variety of fashion magazines targeting both women and men, looking specifically for those ads that advertise clothing. Choose a half dozen or so examples. Looking specifically at the colors featured, analyze each ad, explain what you know about the audience, how you know, and what ideas about identity, masculinity and femininity, clothes, and social status they promote.

    Then try to notice whether certain clothing ads targeting specific audience demographics use similar rhetorical tactics—or whether there are certain patterns or themes at work. Why might this be so, do you think? What does this imply about the language of clothes itself: the cultural and social significance of them as well as how they serve different audiences, class groups, ethnic or racial groups, or gender groups? Be sure to examine library and Internet sources to help support your position. Meet as a class and discuss what your research has revealed.

CHAPTER SIX

Playing Sports

INTRODUCTION

Considering Sports

In American culture much of our ritualized cultural activity occurs around sports. We watch our favorite teams—the Suns, the New England Patriots, the Spurs, the 49ers, the Nets, the Raiders, the Boston Red Sox, the Dolphins, the New York Yankees, the Arizona Diamondbacks—with our friends, laughing and eating pigs in blankets and Doritos until our stomachs ache. We go to the U.S. Open and comment on how Venus and Serena Williams' serves have improved this year. We watch the Tour de France stage by stage and listen to the commentators' perspectives. We witness Tiger Woods win the Masters. In these players we find heroes, people to admire and maybe to emulate. We watch basketball games, wear team colors, paint our faces, and yell our favorite players' names at the television at the top of our lungs. In spite of ourselves, my friends and I sometimes find ourselves talking back to the tube: If only Stephon Marbury of the New York Knicks could hear us, we tell ourselves, his playing would be all that much better.

Not only do we exhibit ritualized behavior around sports, of course. Sports themselves often have complicated rules and dynamics. And there are so many sports in which we can participate. In bowling we have frames, strikes, and spares. All the pins that are scored count. No frames or pins can be waived or conceded. The ball is to be rolled underarm and along the lane. In curling, we have the house, the tee, and the hacks. There is an umpire to oversee the measuring after each end, and to see that the rules are kept. Dress for the players is usually fairly informal, although rubber-soled shoes or boots are usually worn. Spiked shoes, or footwear which could damage the ice, are not allowed. In surfing we have making the wave, beating sections, tube rides, turns, cutbacks and reentries, as well as nose walking for longboarding. It is bad surfing etiquette to ride on someone else's wave, and it is against the rules in many competitions.

Overview of Selections: Rethinking Sports

In this chapter of *Pop Perspectives: Readings to Critique Contemporary Culture* you will examine many types of sports as well as the varied issues surrounding what ought to constitute "fair play" not only in the games themselves but in the politics of those games.

The first section is titled "Rethinking Sports," and it centers on how issues of masculinity and femininity are constructed through sports. This part of the chapter also addresses the ways in which gender, sexual orientation, and ethnic and racial discrimination operate within athletic arenas.

This section begins with an essay by Chris Rubio, a writer and teacher of English. She describes to us her personal journey as a young, athletic woman. Rubio poignantly yet humorously takes the reader through her struggle with the norms of heterosexuality, putting pressure upon standard cultural definitions of femininity allowable within American culture as well as allowable in women's athletics. Rubio exposes the importance of women's sports to their sense of confidence and self-empowerment. In the end Rubio celebrates her lesbian identity and reveals that she finds her most supportive community among a league of women softball players, a group that fights to resist women's typical roles in sports.

Then cultural critic Julio Rodriguez considers how American sportscasters talked about the 1998 home run race and what this revealed about the complex intersections of athletics, masculinity, race, and ethnicity. He traces the history of masculinity and race in baseball, exposing how biases and stereotypes about ethnicity and race have shaped "America's favorite pastime." Examining the careers of baseball greats such as Mark McGuire, Sammy Sosa, and Barry Bonds, Rodriguez reveals to us how the sports media creates caricatures of these players for its own interests. As such, Rodriguez's essay offers some crucial new directions for the cultural criticism of sports.

Finally, Abigail M. Feder-Kane, director of Corporate and Foundation Relations at Barnard College, examines how femininity is constructed in one of the traditionally female-dominated sports, ice skating. She observes the ways in which sports and other media coverage reinforce a sweet femininity—a "girl next door" image—in the representations of athletes such as Nancy Kerrigan and Kristi Yamaguchi while at the same time denigrating any behavior that seems bold, daring, or unfeminine. Supporting images of female ice skaters that are reminiscent of what feminist Naomi Wolf terms "beauty pornography," Feder-Kane argues that this sport risks reinforcing comfortable gender stereotypes in disturbing ways. In the end Feder-Kane shows that the sports world (including other female-dominated sports such as dance, ice dancing, gymnastics, and the like) as well as its marketers and financial supporters are perpetuating sexism.

Overview of Selections: Sporting Innovations and Celebrities

The second section in Chapter 6, "Sporting Innovations and Celebrities," centers on both new technological developments and recent sociocultural changes within sports culture. This part of the chapter reveals important new arenas with which athletes, coaches, and audience participants will have to contend in the years to come.

An essay by Evan Ratliff, who is a contributing editor for *Wired* magazine, begins this section. He takes us inside the world of sports video games and examines to what degree "real" sports culture—proffered by the NBA and NFL—can actually be maintained in the gaming world. What happens when sports no longer involve real players on a real field? How does the intersection of sports and computer gaming impact both televised sporting events as well as how video games operate? In what ways does videogaming alter the role of audience members, and do they become more accustomed to assuming "player" identities rather than "audience" identities?

Next is a piece by Monica Moorehead, a writer and managing editor for the socialist newspaper *Workers World*, who ran for president of the United States on the Workers World Party ticket in 1996 and 2000. Moorehead exposes the various ways in which "racist and class oppression" operate together within professional sports, suggesting that they are "more intense and omnipresent within the NBA than in other professional sports." Revealing how many white suburban fans resent black players getting paid millions of dollars, Moorehead contends that such fans "feel that because they help pay these salaries it is their 'right' to shout racist epithets as well as spit at them if they are from the opposing team." Moreover, the makeup of NBA teams is also impacted by classism. Despite the fact that 80 percent of the NBA players are African American and that the majority of these players come from the poorer inner cities, Moorehead indicates that "out of the 30 NBA teams, only a handful have African American head coaches." In the end, Moorehead suggests to us that analyzing the NBA situation carefully will entail considering how racism and class divisions are integrally connected.

Then Philip J. Deloria, history professor and well-known advocate for Native American rights, challenges us to consider the troubling stereotypes of Indian warriors as mascots for football teams. He reveals the ways in which the use of mascots—both in the past and in our present moment—perpetuates the oppression of Native peoples. Deloria asks us to consider how the aspects of sports that we often take for granted have long, complicated histories. Why do the cultural rituals as well as rules of various games exist? To what cultural histories are they responding? In what ways might these cultural histories silence certain people?

Next, Jay Nordlinger, managing editor of the long-standing conservative journal *National Review*, examines the effects that Tiger Woods has had on the game of golf and its spectators. Nordlinger observes and applauds Woods's resistance to being singled out as a "minority" as well as the word Woods has coined to describe his racial makeup (a mixture of Caucasian, black, American Indian, and Asian): "Cablinasian." Tracing how Woods has come under fire from many in the African

American community for not focusing on that identity to the exclusion of his other identities, Nordlinger maintains that while Woods refuses to be labeled a "hero," clearly he is one. In the end Nordlinger contends that Woods is a role model for our time—someone who accepts and embraces his varied cultural background without overemphasizing its importance.

Then, professor of justice studies, David Theo Goldberg, examines the intersection of sports, racism, classism, and radio programming. Concerned with contemporary legal issues and justice, he characterizes how sports and talk radio have changed over the years—particularly the ways in which discrimination and inequity operate. Goldberg describes how fan culture creates limited identities for sports viewers. Goldberg also exposes some of the crucial problems in sports coverage that currently exist and asks us to contemplate how we might tackle such issues in the future.

Finally, Amy Bass, a scholar and consultant to various sports television networks and professional organizations, examines the problematic ways in which America has historically dominated and colonized the world's sports arena. While the U.S. Women's Olympic Soccer Team succeeded in international competition despite the United States' cultural imperialism, they also recognized the real competition they faced globally. Many of today's teams do not. They fail to understand their competition outside the United States, instead operating according to the flawed assumption that American athletes will always win. In the end, Bass suggests that American sports will have to change in order for our teams to compete globally: We will have to overcome our history of cultural imperialism and its effects. Until we do, the main area in which Americans will dominate in the world of sports will not be in our athletic prowess but rather in our access to sports marketing, or what Bass calls the power of the "Swoosh."

As you work your way through this chapter, think about the roles that athletics and sports in general have played in your own life. Are sports—baseball, football, golf, softball, lacrosse, soccer, basketball, archery, hockey, running, or cycling—essential to how you view yourself as a man or a woman, as a person with your cultural heritage? What specific teams have you played on, how has your team performed, and how have your coaches functioned? Do you feel unable to compete in certain sports? If yes, for what reasons? Is being a spectator of certain sports a critical part of your leisure activities, and what do you gain from watching?

RETHINKING SPORTS

CHRIS RUBIO
"Throws Like the Girl She Is"

Chris Rubio has taught English at American River College in Sacramento, California since 1988. Her areas of expertise include women's literature, writing across the curriculum, and online education. Having served a two-year term as the director of a diversity project for the college, she helped develop and teach an online staff development course on "Understanding Diversity."

EXERCISING YOUR SKILLS

Before Reading

Rubio's essay charts the relationships between gender, sexuality, and sports. In mainstream American culture, what exactly does it mean to "throw like a girl"? Are there comparable insults for men who take on traditionally female-dominated sports? What do these phrases indicate about how gender and sports operate in American culture?

Although I was only twelve years old in 1972—too young to understand the significance of Title IX—I am thankful that I am one of the first generations to benefit from a society in which women's sports are more the rule than the exception. To those who know me, it's no secret that sports have played a major role in my life ever since I was old enough to hold a baseball bat. Growing up as a tomboy certainly had its drawbacks, but playing any of a wide variety of sports on a daily basis was pretty routine, considering that I had three older brothers to toss a ball around with and an older sister who often quarterbacked the opposing street football team.

For many reasons, I was one of the fortunate girls who not only loved sports but was encouraged to play them. Never once do I remember, for instance, either of my parents wincing when I flew out the door to play ball, embarrassed that their youngest daughter seemed more interested in sports than dolls. The idea of girls not playing sports—and not excelling at them—was quite foreign to me. And since my brother David taught me how to throw at a very young age, even the popular phrase she/he "throws like a girl," intended in most circles as an insult, meant only one thing in my household: that person obviously had a strong and accurate arm!

As I grew older, sports began to have even greater significance in my life. Although I mastered kickball and tetherball in my playground days, and as a teenager I quickly learned tennis and bowling (two of my parents' favorite sports), softball was clearly my favorite game. I loved baseball passionately, but as a woman, softball represented the closest I would get to baseball. That was just fine with me, for looking back, I realize I really grew up on a softball field, tasted some divine successes there, learned about teamwork and a sense of community. My closest friends in junior high and high school played softball with me, and I came to know and understand myself through this game. I found refuge for seven innings from feelings I did not comprehend, found a place to belong. Even then, I knew the softball diamond represented a safe place for me and other lesbians, a place where we could be different (even if we didn't understand how or why we were different) and yet belong.

Certainly, I realize not all women who play softball are lesbians, and I indeed hope all women find in their teams and games even a fraction of the sense of community lesbians enjoy on the softball diamond. But for me, I have come to realize that I cannot separate the two: I experience the sense of community I do on a softball diamond because I am a lesbian—not in spite of it. And for many lesbians my age (and older and younger ones, for that matter), the game of softball like no other has welcomed us with open arms, cradled us in our confusion and fear, and offered a home amidst the soft dirt and green grass. It helped us to no longer feel isolated in our youth and adulthood, providing us with a nurturing sense of community.

I'm not sure when I first became aware of the powerful connection between softball and my sexuality. Already by junior high, I was very much aware of feeling different, of not being interested in boys but having strong feelings for girls. Even in the mid-1970s, however, I knew better than to tell anyone about those feelings. As many gay teens still do, I kept my confusing feelings to myself for fear of somehow being discovered (and perhaps even reprimanded). That fear and caution stayed with me through high school, and though I had a few good friends and some special connections with some teachers, I hid my crushes on other girls and young women. It was difficult to feel safe with anyone in my young adult years, but I knew I felt the most comfortable hanging around the locker room and those memorable PE teachers, the women Meg Christian tributes in her classic song, "Ode to a Gym Teacher." No PE teacher who wanted to keep her job would ever acknowledge her lesbianism publicly, but I must admit that didn't matter to me at the time. I simply felt at ease with these strong, athletic women—more at ease than I felt anywhere else on campus—and I was drawn to them. And when the junior varsity softball coach asked me to come to softball tryouts after seeing me play the game during PE, and once I made the team, I knew I had found a home on the softball diamond and a new family and friends in my teammates.

As a loner throughout most of my pre-softball days in junior high and high school, imagine my elation at recognizing myself in the seemingly uninhibited athletes I met on my teams who unselfconsciously ran the bases and dove for line drives—and were rewarded for such behavior! But that was only part of the connection I felt to these young women and consequently this sport. Since so much of what I saw in them I recognized in myself—a love of the sport, a confidence on the diamond, even an independence from males (even at this young age)—how could I not bond with my new sisters? And after finally finding a group to connect with, after finally finding a place where it seemed I, too, belonged, how could I not recognize this group of women as my family?

It is important to note that I did not seek (consciously or unconsciously) a new "family" because my biological family had deserted me. Quite the contrary, I have always felt blessed by the love I have come to count on from my four older siblings and two parents who encouraged me to seek and become whatever I wanted. Some of my fondest memories in high school, for instance, involve my father coming to watch me play softball. Whenever we played our arch rivals in the next town (where my father also worked), my dad would make a point to stop by the diamond and catch a couple of innings. He always stayed long enough to at least watch me bat once, and his hello and goodbye kisses were the envy of even the toughest girls on my team. Even my mom caught a game or two—my mother who battled agoraphobia most of her adult life. No, I didn't long for a new family because I desired to trade in the one I had; I simply sought a connection with a group of people who I felt shared in my desire to belong—to shed our otherness, our fears—and seek comfort in a world in which we more often than not felt uncomfortable, sometimes unwelcomed. And on the softball field, we often found such a place.

A lifelong connection between softball, community, and my sexuality originated in junior high and high school, but the experience that provided the strongest sense of community I have ever experienced on a softball diamond happened a few years after high school when I moved from Antioch, California to Sacramento. In 1982, a group of lesbians who had long since graduated from high school and college but still had a tremendous love for fast pitch softball organized a league. Industrious and determined, they organized through the city parks and recreation department a Sunday softball league, complete with a single umpire and reserved field. Only four teams made up the Sunday fast-pitch women's softball league, but make no mistake about it: this wasn't just any league—it was a lesbian softball league. There was no guessing about who was or who wasn't a dyke in this league; lesbians played every position on every team. Former high school and college fast pitch softball players not yet ready to join a recreational, slow pitch team eagerly found a home on one of the four teams which also welcomed newcomers to the game of fast-pitch softball.

Two games were scheduled each Sunday; one at 10 am, one at noon. Regardless of whether your team played the first or second game—and even if you didn't even play the game of softball—dozens of lesbians gathered for both games. It was simply the place to be. The sense of community was that strong. You came out to visit with your own teammates, players of other teams, girlfriends of everyone, and the fans (including family members) who seemed enraptured by the sense of community as much as the players were.

At Curtis Park, we could be ourselves like in no other place. We got to play the game we loved the most, and our efforts were celebrated by fans of our community as much as fans of our sport. It simply never crossed our minds to not hug our girlfriends, current and former, or hold hands or snuggle close together on a blanket in foul territory in this park we inhabited. Homophobia, which seemed to peak during this Reagan era, had no place in this city park, and we grew strong as a group and as individuals. The softball diamond provided us the environment to build and foster the community and family that some experienced nowhere else. Though Monday through Saturday many of us hid our otherness from our co-workers and so-called friends, dressed in our mainstream attire and comformist attitudes, in this lesbian softball league we proudly wore our stylish baseball pants and custom-made, tattered tees.

In this sacred park ("our park," as we came to call it), we felt free to be ourselves and protected this "comfort zone" with zeal. Because of this, we guardedly welcomed outsiders to pay us a visit. Heck, it was a risk for many to invite someone into our culture. After all, this was our place, our day, our few hours in the week when we knew we could be ourselves in an all-too-often homophobic world. We knew we had a haven here, and some were reluctant, even scared, to let outsiders in. But for many of us, we knew the additional support from straight friends and family members further enriched these moments when they came into our world—not us into theirs—and they, too, became a part of the magic.

I was one of the Sunday regulars who invited outsiders to share in this experience, and I know my memories of this softball league are enriched because of the guests who accepted my invitations. How proudly did I introduce to my teammates my older brother, his wife, and his son, who all enthusiastically attended more than one game, regardless of the hour plus drive to Sacramento? My nephew considered me the best ballplayer he had ever seen, and he cheered for my team like we were the San Francisco Giants, not a group of softball-loving lesbians. For him, the sexuality—even the gender of the players—didn't matter. He just wanted to see a good ball game. But for those of us who had found a home and a kinship we knew no place else, our sexuality and gender mattered greatly. Because as lesbians living in the early 1980s, we didn't see our lives reflected in an *Ellen* sitcom or a *Desert Hearts* big screen movie. We found our lives mirrored in the other women in the batter's box, in the fans in the bleachers, and ultimately, in the extended families who confirmed that we belonged, that we mattered, that we were not "other"—we simply were another.

The "lesbian league" has been defunct for several years now, and many of us long ago traded in our fast-pitch cleats and aggressive play for multipurpose shoes and the arch and pace of slow pitch softball. Today, I still play softball at least one night a week for a team that happens to also field all lesbians, some even from the old fast pitch league. We still play in a city park, though this league caters to any and all women interested in softball. We are clearly still a family, too, this group of aging lesbians who are not ready to hang up our gloves, but it is the sense of community that continues to bring us out each week, the safety of this family that motivates us to stretch our now loose muscles (ok, maybe that's not muscle there anymore) and get together on a softball field once a week. For on a softball team, especially for lesbians young and old, one can feel a part of a greater whole, a place to belong, a community just waiting to be fostered.

After Reading

Critical Perspective

1. In her essay, Rubio redefines what it means to "throw like a girl." What does it mean in her family? What are your thoughts about this new definition?

Rhetoric and Argument

2. Discuss Rubio's tone and rhetorical choices in her essay—audience, purpose, ethos, pathos, logos, intertextuality, context, and constraints. Do you think her use of rhetoric helps or hinders her argument? Why do you think so? Be sure to provide quotes from the text to back up your views.
3. How does Rubio describe her relationship to softball? In what ways does softball offer her an important identity and protection from homophobia? In what ways does Rubio suggest that her softball functioned much like the positive representations of gay life offered on *Ellen* and *Desert Hearts?*
4. What does Rubio argue in her essay about the relationship between softball and lesbian community? Do you find her argument persuasive? Why or why not? In what ways might other sports function in similar ways, offering other "minority" groups a sense of community? Try to give specific examples.

Analysis

5. Think about the various sports you have played in your life. How have these sports supported or thwarted your relationships with those people who are most important to you? How and when can sports foster a sense of community that can provide people with important identities and experiences, ones that function almost like family? Drawing on these questions, make a short argument about a particular sport or sports' team and its importance in your life and your community. Consult the Internet and the library for sources.

Taking Action

Form a small group. Using library, magazine, and Internet sources, create an advertising campaign (including print ads, commercials, brochures, web sites) designed to convince people to attend the games played by a local sports team (it can be one on which you now play or have played in the past). In order to do this, you may want to contact the coach and members of the team for ideas and suggestions.

As you create your ad campaign for the team, make sure that you use all of the rhetorical tools at your disposal to make it persuasive—audience, purpose, ethos, pathos, logos, intertextuality, context, constraints, use of color, and arrangement. Depending on your access to technology, you may develop the campaign on the web, use color copies, and employ various multimedia computer programs with color visuals, video, and audio clips. Share your work with the rest of the class.

JULIO RODRIGUEZ

"Healing Power: *Sports Illustrated*, Masculinity, and the 1998 Home Run Race"

Julio Rodriguez teaches in the American Studies Department at Randolph-Macon Woman's College in Lynchburg, Virginia. He has published many articles on baseball, basketball, surfing, and boxing.

EXERCISING YOUR SKILLS

Before Reading

Rodriguez takes up concerns about sports coverage of male athletes. Look at images of men in sports that appear within print ads, commercials, television shows, and films. How is masculinity represented in these media images? Do you think that masculinity and its representation change when race and ethnicity issues are also foregrounded? If yes, how so? Be sure to give examples from visual texts. If not, explain why not and provide evidence from these media forms as well.

In her book *Stiffed,* Susan Faludi analyzes the perceived crisis in masculinity in the United States arguing that men have lost "a useful role in public life, a way of earning a decent and reliable living, appreciation in the home [and] respectful treatment in the culture" (40). Replacing these traditionally masculine prerogatives is the façade of masculinity. Masculinity has become a commodity constructed around celebrity and images without depth. Even though there are other sources mentioned, the main culprit for Faludi and the men she features is the inability of fathers to prepare their sons for the post–World War II world. Whether it is the biological fathers failing their sons, the industrial father downsizing its worker-sons, coaches not preparing their player-sons, or the military not protecting its warrior-sons, the father-son relationship is fractured and ineffectual. Rather than the idyllic world where fathers and sons were roughhousing and playing catch in the yard, boomer youths were presented with distant, authoritarian, oppressive, emotionally inaccessible fathers that gave them no skills to thrive in post-war America.

While Faludi's tone may seem extreme and bleak, she is far from alone in her assessment of besieged masculinity and paternal failure. The 1980s and 1990s were replete with books, magazine articles, movies, and television shows that, alternatively, bemoaned the death of effective masculinity or proposed a remedy. The 1990s also gave us men's movements led by figures like Robert Bly and Sam Keen. Self-help books for men pelted bookstores. Men's studies courses were added to college course offerings. Media took up the questions of men's changing roles in U.S. society. The crisis was in full swing and it suggested that it is predominantly White men who were trapped within traditional masculinities, and White men who needed extra help in learning how to change themselves for the better. Even the normally comforting spectacles of manhood, professional sports, were not above the crisis. Between 1987 and 1998 the three core sports, football, baseball and basketball all experienced a form of work stoppage. All three work stoppages sullied the relationship between players and fans, eroding the athlete's honorific position as masculine exemplar. However, the 1998 home run race brought an answer to nearly every question regarding the perceived crisis in masculinity.

Although there are a handful of other hitting records that have withstood the test of time—for runs batted in, hits and total bases—none of those feats approach the reverence fans have for home runs. The home run is grand and awe-inspiring. We gawk at it with the slack-jawed fascination of a child at a national monument. Hits, bases, and runs batted in are all integral to baseball and baseball lore, but none approach the mythic quality of the home run. It is clear that no other record approaches mythic qualities of masculinity either. Even 150 years after its creation, baseball remains an apt metaphor for America. The ballpark is a pasture placed in the middle of an urban setting, careful execution is countered by wild exuberance, relaxing spectators contrast with tense players, work masquerades as play and play as work. Baseball is located at the balance of boyhood and manhood and as such it becomes the perfect symbolic avenue to turn down when manhood is in peril. In particular we turn to the tales that surround those men that we deem masculine exemplars. These stories do not merely recount events; they reaffirm cultural beliefs and soothe social anxieties. They are one of the means by which we understand the world.

As the 1998 season began Major League Baseball was still suffering the ill effects of the 1994 players strike. League expansion had offset some of the bad blood, but attendance was not only still down, the low fan turnout had become a staple of baseball coverage.

The lone bright spot during the early going was the hope that Ken Griffey Jr. or Mark McGwire would begin flirting with the home run record. McGwire did not disappoint. He hit four home runs in the first four games and racked up eleven before the end of April. Even though the season was only a week old, Roger Maris' record of 61 in a season was in jeopardy and it appeared that baseball had bounced back. The emergence of Sammy Sosa provided a convenient foil for McGwire, and the excitement of a race *to* the record and not just *for* the record once again took baseball from the sport pages to the front pages, talk shows, and water coolers. The *Sports Illustrated* (*SI*) coverage of McGwire and Sosa retold the story about the sort of masculinity that displays awe inspiring power, creates runs, hits, and wins and most importantly, for a summer at least, saved fatherhood as a functional institution.

From the outset, McGwire's identity was unwittingly set as a cure-all for the ills be-setting contemporary masculinity. McGwire's preseason profile detailed his disdain for celebrity, notoriety, and masculine display. None of his numerous awards are visible in his home, the bulk of them in storage. He works out at an ordinary fitness center alongside mothers, toddlers, off-duty policemen and firemen. "[T]he old model of masculinity showed men how to be a part of a larger social system; it gave them a context and it promised them that their social contributions were the price of admission to the realm of adult manhood" (Faludi, 35). McGwire's comfort and association with these old models, policemen and firemen, locates him firmly within nostalgic notions of White masculinity. Men distinguish themselves as men through their purposeful function to the larger culture and are largely anonymous and duty-bound, the quintessential man in uniform. McGwire's lack of artifice places him firmly within this framework.

A given in this traditional notion of the masculine is power—physical, economic, and cultural. McGwire hob-knobbing with cops and firemen grants him cultural power. His economic power is beyond question due to his place among baseball's salary elite. His physical power is legendary and ever present. Scarcely an article is written that does not mention his awesome size—6′5″, 250 pounds, 20 inch biceps—and, of course, his home runs inspire awe. However, this form of masculinity—anonymous, societal, other-centered, purposeful, and ordinary—is said to be no longer viable in our culture. It is accused of creating the absentee father, the father who leaves the family to work long hours resulting in an emotional emptiness, a lack of a sense of self and an inability to relate to women. One solution to this form of manhood, this form of fathering, was therapy. Therapy is aimed at allowing men to get in touch with and express their feelings. The goal of this feelings-centered therapy was to create something of an androgynous man, one more feminine, more aware of his potential for nurturing, humility, and patience, less aggressive and obsessed with dominance. Here too, McGwire is presented as a fine example, seemingly both/and instead of either/or.

The *SI* preseason profile of McGwire begins poignantly with Mac (McGwire's nickname) relating how he began supporting programs that aid children from abusive families. Mac also cries at movies, *Philadelphia* and *Driving Miss Daisy* in particular. Mac is a poster boy for the new masculinity. In a later profile of McGwire, Mark spoke on the subject of feelings in his childhood home. "We didn't talk about stuff like that in our house. We just didn't. Anything I had like that, I always shoved inside." Of his life prior to therapy McGwire says, "I was kind of a wreck. I was having all kinds of relationship problems. I didn't know what love was all about. I had four brothers and no sisters. We never talked about it. You're never taught: These are how feelings are. It's like you're walking in a dark room and just feeling blindly around" (*Heroes,* 44).

Even though therapy played a role, the real cure for what ailed him and for what ails masculinity in the United States is fatherhood. In fatherhood McGwire is able to marry the old and new notions of masculinity. His maturation as a man and a father is paralleled to his maturation as a hitter. In the beginning of his career he spent a great deal of time on the disabled list. He lacked conditioning. He lacked focus. His 1998 manager, Tony LaRussa, credits the turnaround to an overall dedication to the game. *SI* credits the turnaround to Mac discovering a missing father, himself. McGwire offers, "Everything I do in life and in baseball now is for my son" (*Heroes,* 51). Matt, his son, is ever present. In pictures, as a batboy, on the team charter, McGwire is never far from his son. Correcting the error of Mac's childhood, he and his son talk all the time. "We talk so much that sometimes we don't even have to use words. We just look at each other and know what the other is thinking" (*Heroes,* 51).

Given the complexity of the masculine crisis and the multifaceted response that McGwire provided, the emergence of Sammy Sosa as a home run race competitor was most fortunate. Aside from providing drama and added media attention, Sosa provided a foil for Mac's mainstream masculinity. The framing of Sosa reminded readers and fans of the masculinity McGwire had moved beyond and, of course, provided a visible cultural and racial male other to contrast with McGwire.

Even though the comparison between McGwire and Sosa renders Sosa an example of Faludi's masculine façade, the reality is far more complex and part of a rich history of masculinity in Sosa's home culture of the Dominican Republic. Faludi argues that the shift in masculinity was ushered in by a corresponding shift in the American economy, the move from industry to service, or from production to consumption, which is symbolically a move from the traditional masculine to the traditional feminine. Where once masculinity was defined by utility, it is now defined by appearance, by display as opposed to deed. Curiously, both modes can be coded feminine, care taking and vanity. However, one is clearly more valued than the other, one selfless and the other selfish. In making that value judgment the coverage of Sosa proves to be shortsighted. There was more going on than self-centered vanity.

To understand the functional value of what Faludi terms "ornamental masculinity" as it applies to Sammy Sosa one needs to examine its role in Dominican public and political life. In the Dominican Republic maleness revolves around "five sets of ideas: notions (1) of *valentia* or courage; (2) of men's visibility in public spaces; (3) of the man as seducer and father; (4) of the power tied to a man's verbal skills; and (5) of a man's seriousness and sincerity" (Krohn-Hansen, 114). Together these ideas comprise the *tiguere* or tiger. Full of paradoxes and ambiguities, the elasticity of the term has allowed it to remain in popular parlance ever since the 1930s. The first notion is in accordance with the lost sense of masculinity as described by Faludi. This type of courage is based not on violence, but on a fearless defense when a man is set upon verbally, ideologically or physically. The other four strains are more in line with what Faludi terms "ornamental." Men's willingness to be seen is central to politics in the Dominican Republic and a key factor in definitions of masculinity. It speaks directly to successful interpersonal relationships. A man must be willing to partake of a community of men in order to achieve masculine legitimacy. An extension of this is the third characteristic of man as seducer and father. It corresponds to the idea of man as a womanizing nomad, even when married or in a stable relationship. Of course, he must also be a good provider for his family or families. It is a delicate balance, but one that must be struck. If a man leans too far to one side he loses a measure of credibility with those that value the opposite end of the scale. The fourth tenet also deals with relationship skills. Verbal excellence is valued, but more than that, the ability to persuade, to use speech as a source of power is closer to the ideal of masculinity. This leads us into the final notion, that of being serious. Serious, for Dominicans, describes a person of good faith, one who is sincere in their dealings with you. Again, it is a form of display, the way one is greeted and treated by the party in question and of course, the manner in which that person conducts himself or herself. The man who displays all of these characteristics is referred to as a *tiguere.*

The Dominican tiger mode of masculinity is clearly an ambiguous one. In the narrative that *Sports Illustrated* created, the more productive aspects of the form of masculinity displayed by Sosa took a back seat to the "ornamental" ones. In comparison to Mac, Sosa was repeatedly infantilized, caricatured and generally portrayed as a supporting character to Mac as leading man. Where Mac was framed as a panacea to what ailed America, Sosa was a spicy and short-lived invigorating tonic. These renderings of Sosa are in keeping with the stereotypical ideas of "other" masculinities. Generally, men in the "other" category are constructed as overcompensating for their marginalization by clinging to very narrow and strict definitions of masculinity—a distance from the feminine, economic dominance, emotional insularity and verbal and physical braggadocio. The Latin male suffers the additional burden of machismo, which renders him both more masculine and more feminine than his Anglo counterpart. On the one hand the term evokes images of virility, masculinity and sex appeal, but also negative attributes such as male dominance, authoritarianism, and spousal abuse. On the other, Latin machismo is also defined as warm, impulsive, emotional, and passionate. By contrast, white masculinity is associated with logic, reason and detachment. Since narratives are constructed to reflect the worldview of their assumed audience, it is no surprise that *Sports Illustrated* creates a familiar version of Latin masculinity through Sammy Sosa: One that is not without its charm, but like most charming things, lacking substance.

In a mid-season profile of Sammy Sosa, Tom Verducci characterizes Sosa's early career as empty, lacking discipline, reckless and irresponsible. The predominant metaphor on which he relies is a gold pendant that Sosa had commissioned after becoming the first Cub in history to hit 30 home runs and steal 30 bases in a single season:

> *It was a gold pendant approximately the size of a manhole cover, hung from a chain that seemed fashioned from a suspension-bridge cable. The bauble was*

inscribed with a drawing of two crossed bats and bore the numbers 30-30, inlaid with diamonds. The Chicago Cubs outfielder wore it when he drove to Wrigley Field in his sports car, the one with the SS 30-30 license plates. . . . What a piece of work! And the pendant, too—unintentional symbol of a vacuous career—was something to behold (Heroes, 22).

Clearly, Verducci has little regard for Sosa, at least prior to the season. Verducci grants that "at last" Sosa is maturing as a player, but not without the discipline and tutelage of Jim Riggleman and Jeff Pentland, the Cubs' manager and hitting coach. The pendant provides a fitting metaphor for the type of masculinity Verducci feels Sosa embodies; one that is fully in keeping with ornamental masculinity, but also one that fails to incorporate the functional aspects of the Dominican tiger.

The overriding ethos of the *tiguere* is to remain all right in any type of situation. Even as the pendant is condemned as a vacuous symbol according to contemporary American notions of masculinity, it can be seen as a functional part of the sign system of Dominican manhood. Superficially, in Sosa's case, it is a sign of a unique accomplishment, as is the personalized license plate. On a deeper level the pendant and the plate correlate with the necessity to be seen, to be visible among other men. It also speaks to the *tiguere*'s financial capacity. Part of this masculine visibility is a man's willingness to do others a favor, to give generously monetarily. While the pendant is not a form of outward generosity it is a robust symbol of financial health that addresses other facets of his masculinity, namely, a man's womanizing capacity.

That third tenet is plainly connected to his fiscal abilities and to the idea that a man should always be ready to party, to spend time out drinking and dancing with his buddies. In a later profile on Sosa, *SI* details the initial meeting between Sammy and his wife, Sonia. Predictably, it was at a dance club. Sammy had a waiter bring her a note: "If you will do me the honor of having one dance with me, it will be the start of a beautiful friendship. [She] looked at him and said, 'Oh wow—what a man'" (*Heroes,* 81). In the seven years since their meeting they have had four children. Sonia rarely sees Sammy play in person and never when he is traveling with the team. She watches on television, staying at home, caring for the children. By most modern measures their meeting and living arrangement appears dated, or at least nostalgic, but in the context of the *tiguere* it is ideal. The story acknowledges Sosa's womanizing roots and his successful domestic life.

The fourth and fifth notions of the *tiguere,* verbal acuity and seriousness, are clearly embodied by Sosa and detailed in the *SI* coverage. It is also the site where the identity of the *tiguere* shines the brightest in Sosa's case. Fairly early in his relationship with the media Sammy cracked the phrase, genuinely, "Baseball been berry, berry, good to me." *SI*, and every other media outlet, was quick to make the connection to the *Saturday Night Live* character, Chico Escuela (school boy). Like the Garret Morris character, Sosa was much older and wiser than a schoolboy, but the press eagerly cast him in the role of grateful infant and Sammy obliged. In response to the request to name his first love Sammy responded, "Cartoons." When asked why he seemed to be having a better time with the interviews than McGwire he answered, "I'm a little bit more Rico Suave than him." For a *tiguere* verbal skills are a source of power, a means to insure that he emerges well from any situation. Given his sidebar status in the home-run-race coverage, Sosa played the *tiguere* to a tee. Four days after McGuire hit his 62nd Sosa tied him with his own record breaking smash. McGuire had stalled at 62 and now, the crown baseball had handed to Mac was up for grabs. As if privy to some insider information, Gary Smith of *SI* articulated a version of the *tiguere* ethos, "Sammy loves the cool of Big Mac's shade. Don't dare blow his cover. He has drafted behind McGwire for nearly three months . . . making sure at all times to lean over Big Mac's shoulder and blow kisses and hosannas in his ear. . . . He applauded Mac. He hugged Mac. Then he ambushed Mac" (*Heroes,* 64). In retrospect Sosa was at his *tiguere* best toiling in McGwire's rear-view. He managed to deflect the majority of the pressure to break the record onto Mac. Even when Sosa briefly held the lead in the race, he deferred to McGwire.

In the above passage Smith mistakenly stumbles on the legitimacy of an alternative masculine construct. Rather than applaud it, he couches it within the negative trope of violence. The ambush is based on treachery, trickery, and surprise. The lovable clown becomes killer and thief, taking what rightfully belongs to another. The familiarity of the trope is heartbreaking and not isolated to the Latin male. The story of the loyal Other that betrays his trusting White master has a rich history. It is the bad variant of the good racial minority. (Sosa's 2003 corked bat incident was also framed as a betrayal.) The construct in Smith's article is not intended to lend credence to an alternate mode of masculinity. It is a familiar narrative that cements the Other's role as subservient and, as far as masculinity is concerned, ultimately unproductive. In this case and in accordance with the narrative surrounding Other masculinities, the lack of productivity stems solely from this racialized narrative. Though McGwire set the record at 70 (Sosa finished with 66), by all other significant measures Sosa had the more productive season and was able to lead his team to the National League playoffs, something McGwire failed to do. Yet, as a model of masculinity, it was only McGwire's that was celebrated and valorized. The Other alternative was never fully considered.

Much of the attention that the race received stemmed from the length of time the single-season home run record stood prior to McGwire and Sosa's onslaught: 37 years. McGwire's record would not last as long. In the 2001 season Barry Bonds set the record anew at 73. Bonds' setting of the record did not garner the amount of coverage as the 1998 record-breaking. One plausible explanation is that Bonds lacked a dramatic foil and dramatic finish. There was no race to the record, and his breaking of it was all but assured with weeks left in the season. The nation's somber mood post 9/11 surely affected the amount of coverage. Just as surely, however, Bonds could have been a healing figure in much the same way as McGwire had been a scant three years earlier. On the night Bonds broke the record his mother, wife, and daughters were all in the stands. They had been with him in much the same way Matt had been with Mac. Like Mac, Bonds suffers in the media spotlight. His rocky relationship with the press is nearly as well known as his on-field accomplishments. Unlike McGwire, Bonds has always had a good relationship with his father, former major leaguer Bobby Bonds. His uncle, Willie Mays, has also been a consistent presence throughout his career. Unlike McGwire, Bonds has been a consistent performer his entire career. Given the state of the nation in the months following the 9/11 attacks any one of these narrative strands could have framed his chase of the record. Bonds' unparalleled baseball pedigree should have invited such coverage. Instead the press was largely apathetic. *SI* columnist Rick Reilly went as far as saying fans should not root for Bonds because he was not a team player (118). Why the lack of coverage? Unlike Sosa, Bonds was unwilling to play a culturally prescribed role. He was not affable. He was not playful. He was not grateful. He was not second. The media had no ready-made script for an unapologetic Black man. Rather than draft one, to the extent that they could, the media largely ignored him.

Of course, none of this will age well. Two years after Bonds broke McGwire's record the Bay Area Laboratory Co-operative (BALCO) scandal broke Bonds' reputation. Many had suspected Bonds, McGwire, Sosa, and numerous other recent power hitters of steroid use. The scandal, in which Bonds' personal trainer was charged with supplying athletes with anabolic steroids, was taken as confirmation that Bonds was taking steroids even though he was never definitely named as one of the athletes in question. In the wake of the BALCO scandal, McGwire, Sosa, and several other major leaguers were called before a Congressional committee to testify on steroid use in baseball. McGwire refused to answer probing questions about steroid use replying simply, "I am not here to talk about the past." His non-answers were interpreted by the press and baseball fans as an admission of past steroid use. Though there is no smoking gun directly linking McGwire, Sosa, and Bonds to steroid use, the accusations cast a shadow of doubt on their accomplishments (as does the quickly forgotten and overshadowed Sosa corked bat incident). The entire era is rapidly becoming known as The Steroid Era and every accomplishment is seemingly marked with an asterisk. However, regardless of the extent of the use of performance enhancing drugs, the narratives surrounding the performances remain intact and instructive. Despite significant advances by men of color in the United States, racialized narratives of masculinity still delimit their behavior. For men who lack the clout of a Sosa or a Bonds, these narratives are at best constricting and at worst potentially deadly. For the benefit of all men, these narratives need to be challenged and transformed.

Works Cited

Faludi, Susan. *Stiffed: The Betrayal of the American Man.* New York: William Morrow and Company, 1999.

Krohn-Hansen, Christian. "Masculinity and the Political among Dominicans: 'The Dominican Tiger'," in Marit Melhuus and Kristi Anne Stolen, *Machos, Mistresses, Madonnas: Contesting the Power of Latin American Gender Imagery.* New York: Verso, 1996.

Noden, Merrell, ed. *Home Run Heroes: Mark McGwire, Sammy Sosa, and a Season for the Ages.* New York: Simon & Schuster, 1998.

Reilly, Rick. "The Life of Reilly: He loves himself Barry Much." *Sports Illustrated.* Aug. 27: 118.

After Reading

Critical Perspective

1. Characterize how Rodriguez frames his essay. Do you find this an effective approach? How does it encourage the reader to view him as a writer? Do you find him credible? Why or why not? Be sure to give quotes from the text to support your views.

Rhetoric and Argument

2. Describe the rhetorical features of this essay—audience, purpose, ethos, pathos, logos, intertextuality, context, and constraints. How and where does Rodriguez use these rhetorical tactics? Be sure to provide quotes from the text to back up your views. Does Rodriguez's use of these rhetorical tactics help to support or hinder his argument? Why do you think this is the case?

3. What is Rodriguez's main assertion in his essay? Where does it appear? Do you find that this is an effective claim and that it is well placed in the essay? Why or why not? Do you believe that Rodriguez's discussion about the history of masculinity in baseball backs up his main claim? Explain your views.

4. What are the major sections within Rodriguez's essay? How do you know? How do they work together? Do each of these pieces serve as support for Rodriguez's main claim? If yes, how so? If no, what might Rodriguez do to more fully support his claim?

5. Rodriguez makes a convincing case that the American media has treated McGuire, Sosa, and Bonds differently. Are there other similarities or differences in how specific baseball players are treated that Rodriguez does not mention but that you have noticed? Mention them in detail here and try to point to specific sources to back up your views.

Analysis

6. Think about how male athletes from various sports are represented in the American media. Write a short essay in which you tackle these issues: Do you think athletes' racial, ethnic, and cultural backgrounds shift how the sports media and celebrity media depict them? If yes, give some examples from other sports. If no, show how this is not operating or operates less than it used to. Do you think that women of color are represented in different ways as well? How so? Consult library and Internet sources for support.

Taking Action

Rodriguez's essay examines some major sporting events that occurred a number of years ago. However, his claims are still useful for examining most recent examples of sports in the media.

In a small group, decide upon another sporting event that has happened since this essay was published. Using newspapers, magazines, the library, and the Internet, research this event as well as how it was depicted in the media. Look especially for whether race, class, ethnicity, as well as gender issues played into how the event was represented. Examine the rhetorical tactics at work in these representations.

After you have conducted your research, answer the following questions: What kinds of argumentative claims could you make about how the media depicted this event? What became central to these representations? What was left out? Discuss why you think this may have been the case. Present your information to the rest of the class. Consider making your work accessible to other groups both inside and outside the campus community.

ABIGAIL M. FEDER-KANE

"'A Radiant Smile from the Lovely Lady': Overdetermined Femininity in 'Ladies' Figure Skating"

Abigail M. Feder-Kane is Barnard College Director of Corporate and Foundation Relations, responsible for all fundraising activity from private foundations, corporations, and government agencies. Prior to coming to Barnard in June 2005, Feder-Kane worked for two New York City cultural institutions: WNYC, New York Public Radio, and the Metropolitan Opera.

EXERCISING YOUR SKILLS

Before Reading

Feder-Kane suggests that ice skating and its media coverage are representative of a larger problem—the sexist roles women are required to adopt in sports. Do you think her claim is valid? What examples can you point to in order to support your views?

A casual observer of the figure skating coverage at the 1994 Olympics might have supposed that in the skating world Nancy Kerrigan had always been the princess and Tonya Harding the white trash whore. In a limited sense they would not have been wrong: Kerrigan and Harding were contrasted in figure skating coverage, especially television coverage, long before the attack on Kerrigan at the 1994 U.S. National Championships. But what might surprise some is that the contrast did not always favor Kerrigan. In the short-hand of figure skating identification, Kerrigan was the elegant lady, Harding the "tough cookie." The ubiquity of this short-hand identification was remarked on by Frank Deford: "everybody who makes reference to Harding, like her or not, is bound to say: 'a tough cookie.' It's like an official part of her name, a position, like: Tonya Harding, shortstop, or Tonya Harding, soprano; Tonya Harding, tough cookie" (52). White Kerrigan had more "telappeal" as a skating personality—the stereotypical "ice princess"—Harding had more legitimacy as an athlete, especially among sports writers who usually cover men's sports.

Femininity and athleticism have long been mutually exclusive concepts in American culture. Even in recent years, when the fitness craze extended to both sexes, women have been constantly reminded that all signs of their athleticism must be kept invisible. In our culture "it is assumed that sports success *is* success at being masculine. Physical achievement, and masculine activity, are taken to be the same" (Willis 123).

I became interested in exploring singles figure skating when I observed that, although the athletic requirements did not appear specifically gendered, the narrative surrounding the women's competition was sickly sweet in its presentation of the competitors' femininity. I discovered that in the original (short) program, for which the requirements are set by the International Skating Union (ISU), gender differences were built in. However in the free (long) program, for which the athletes choose their own material, there was little difference between the skills performed by men and women. Both were required to perform complex footwork and a variety of spins and jumps; no competitor would be taken seriously who did not perform several triple jumps, and for both men and women the triple Axel was the most difficult jump performed.[1] Judging ranged from the fairly objective to the extremely subjective: jumps were judged on height and clean take-offs and landings; skaters were judged on how well they "related" to their music. They were awarded two sets of marks, for technical merit and artistic impression.

When physical capabilities no longer distinguish men and women, femininity often has to be overdetermined to keep female athletes from being labeled as masculine or lesbian. "The more successful a female athlete, the more she tries to embody the culturally appropriate gender role [. . .] a role essentially at odds with her athleticism" (Faller 1987:154). As Susan Brownmiller has written, "Femininity must constantly reassure" (1984:15), reassure that, no matter their accomplishments, women athletes are still "just girls" underneath. Successful women athletes risk being labeled "mannish," with generally unspoken implications of lesbianism close to the surface. This connection between femininity and reassurance was made explicit in a 1982 *Sports Illustrated* article on glamorous professional golfer Jan Stephenson (who had posed for a Marilyn Monroe style pin-up poster). "Stephenson did a lot for the image of women's golf in 1981. That was the year in which Billie Jean King admitted she'd had a lesbian affair and almost knocked a wheel off the apple cart of women's sports. And all during that perilous time, there was Stephenson out front on the sports pages, looking good and playing better" (McDermott 1982:31). Women must precariously negotiate their societally contradictory roles of woman and athlete. Nancy Therberge summarizes one strategy, Jan Felshin's theory of the female apologetic in sports:

> *Felshin characterized the social dynamic of women in sport as an anomaly [. . .]. As an extension of this, women in sport advance an apologetic for their involvement. The apologetic affirms a woman's femininity despite her athletic endeavors and thus "legitimates the woman's role in sport by minimizing the anomaly." This legitimation is not complete, however, and social conflict over the contradictions inherent in women's sport activities persists. (1981:344)*

The anxiety about the success of women athletes is most obviously symbolized by the Olympic practice of sex-ID testing, which proves how closely sports success and masculine identity are connected in our culture.

---

[1] NB: the rules delineated herein, as well as the assumptions about the skills that the athletes performed, were applicable as of the original publication date of this article.

The idea of certifying female athletes as females originated more than 25 years ago. Athletic directors said they were trying to guard against male impostors, but a more subtle message was also being sent, said Alison Carlson, a member of the athletic federation's committee and a tennis coach. A successful female athlete "challenges society's notion of femininity," Ms. Carlson said, so both the athletic directors and the women themselves felt it important to prove they were real women. (Kolata 1992:E6)

In order to compete, women athletes must strive for strength, speed, and competitiveness—all those qualities which our society codes as masculine. "As an athlete becomes even more outstanding, she marks herself out as even more deviant [. . .]. To succeed as an athlete can be to fail as a woman, because she has, in certain profound symbolic ways, become a man" (Willis 1982:123). So in order to avoid being coded as overly masculine or a lesbian, the athlete will participate in her own construction as a hyperfeminine creature. This is more true in figure skating than in any other sport. Because of its element of theater, figure skating provides more opportunities for adornment and display, those familiar tropes of femininity with which the American public is comfortable. But even as they have become embraced as stars, female skaters have often been negated as athletes.

Figure skating's "apology" is actually incorporated into the competition, where costume, makeup, and gesture feminize and soften the athletic prowess required for executing triple jumps and flying sit-spins. The fact that the female competitors are still officially called 'Ladies' under U.S. and International Skating Union rules (a fact that even the typically unselfconscious U.S. television reporters felt the need to explain to its audience) is only the beginning. Television coverage is framed in vignettes featuring soft-focus lights, stars in little girls' eyes, glittery costumes, and flowers from adoring crowds. "A dream is a wish your heart makes when you're fast asleep" was the music accompanying shots of a little girl falling asleep surrounded by stuffed animals wearing skating medals which introduced ABC coverage of 1992 U.S. National Championship; "You look wonderful tonight" sang Eric Clapton over close-ups of the female Olympic medal hopefuls before the finals. In contrast, the framing device that introduced the men's finals played the percussive background to a Genesis song which has accompanying lyrics: "I can feel it coming in the air tonight," while computer animated lightning signaled each explosive editing cut. While the women were shown in flowing movement, in worried close-ups or applying makeup, the men were pictured doing their most difficult jumps, raising their hands in gestures of triumph. Spots publicizing the 1992 men's Olympic competition featured more explosive shots of men jumping or pumping their arms in triumph to rock music, while the voice-over punched out their names: "Boitano. Petrenko. Browning. Elvis. . . . The battle will be epic!" The teaser for the ladies final featured Frank Sinatra singing, "Yes, you're lovely, with your smile so warm, and your cheeks so soft, that there's nothing for me but to love you, and THE WAY YOU LOOK TONIGHT" over shots of the women spinning, smiling, bowing, waving and hand-kissing to the crowd.

There is always an emphasis on the women skaters' physical beauty (and a corresponding denigration of the sport), which is related to their exchange value and their commodification as the ultimate reward of Olympic victory. An insidious duality is established by labeling some women as athletic and others as artistic, with the artistry associated with physical beauty and a slender body type. Women in figure skating are caught in a trap that Naomi Wolf could have labeled "the bind of the Beauty Myth": a woman must live up to popular notions of beauty in order to compete successfully, both on the ice and in the commercial endorsement sweepstakes. The spectacle of their beauty is one factor in the fabulous popularity of women's figure skating, and why the women's competition is one of the few that is more popular than the men's equivalent. But the sport is taken less seriously precisely because its competitors are beautifully dressed and made-up women.

The concern with spectacle can be seen in the obsessive attention to women's costumes. Skating fashion has found its way from the sports pages to the "Living Arts" section of the *New York Times,* because top fashion designers, including French haute couture designer Christian LaCroix, make skaters' costumes. Vera Wang described the outfits she designed for Nancy Kerrigan: "Nancy wanted me to translate the look of couture evening wear to the ice" (Louie 1992:1). What was not pointed out is that all these costumes, in addition to sequins and tiny skirts, have some simulated nudity, whether it is a plunging neckline, a cutout back or "sheer illusion sleeves" (Louie 1992:1). "Appearance, not accomplishment, is the feminine demonstration of desirability and worth. [. . .] Feminine armor is never metal or muscle, but paradoxically, an exaggeration of physical vulnerability that is reassuring (unthreatening) to men" (Brownmiller 1984:51).

"So why do they play into it?" a male friend asked me. "What if they competed in full body coverings like the men?" As it turns out, both men and women are limited in their choice of costumes by the rules. Debi Thomas, who won the bronze medal at the 1988 Olympic games, skated her short program in a sequined body stocking rather than a short skirt. Although she skated her program "flawlessly," according to a Canadian magazine ([O'Hara 1988:49] which might be expected to be free from U.S. partisanship), she received low artistic impression marks. If, as speculated, artistic impression for women skaters is connected to a particular kind of unthreatening femininity, perhaps the scores were connected to her costume and to gold medalist Katarina Witt's, which made her look "like a member of the Rockette's chorus line" (O'Hara 1988:49). After this competition, the ISU adopted new rules on costuming which specified that "Costumes for Ladies cannot be theatrical in nature [?!]. They must have skirts [. . .] covering the hips and posterior. A 'unitard is not acceptable" (USFSA Rulebook 112). This rule eliminated the most sensible (and unisex) costume available to all skaters, the unitard.

In a lecture on sports photography, University of Washington professor Diane Hagaman emphasized the need for sports photos to be a "good quick read [. . .] eyecatching [. . . able to] entice readers to read the text" (1992). They must also reinforce the image conveyed by the text, be it winning or losing, endurance or conflict. Therefore, sports photography depends on "highly conventionalized images" (Hagaman 1992). For example, the narrative surrounding Nancy Kerrigan always emphasized her beauty and elegance; she could not step onto the ice without the commentators, male or female, remarking how "lovely-elegant-angelic-sophisticated" she was. Not surprisingly, therefore, many different newspapers and magazines caught her in the same arabesque pose (called a spiral in skating) from the end of her program, one long leg extended out behind her, arm extended out front, a very balletic pose.

Television editing can also manipulate our perception and lend credence to narrative. An impression of speed and choppiness can be emphasized by use of cuts, which instantaneously switch from one shot to another; while flow and grace can be emphasized by use of dissolves, which gradually replace one shot with another. Kerrigan's 1992 Olympic long program was broadcast with nine dissolves and eight cuts; in contrast the program of French skater Surya Bonaly, a former gymnast who is commonly described as a choppy skater and dynamic jumper, had only four dissolves to thirteen cuts.

In figure skating, despite the similarity in skills performed, certain poses and gestures are gendered female. The most obvious is the forward layback spin, a move meant to show the flexibility of female skaters. Back arched, eyes closed, mouth slightly open, arms extended as for an embrace—this is the same pose often used in fashion photography or "beauty pornography," as described by Naomi Wolf. "Beauty pornography looks like this: The perfected woman lies [. . .] pressing down her pelvis. Her back arches, her mouth is open, her eyes shut, [. . .] the position is female superior, the state of arousal, the plateau phase just preceding orgasm" (1991:132). In figure skating a layback spin is a requirement in the women's original program; men rarely perform this skill. There were more pictures of Yamaguchi in this position than in any other in 1992. The repetition of this image presents a disturbing convergence of racist and sexist images, playing into stereotypes of the sexually submissive Asian beauty. The virginal, elegant Kerrigan, in contrast, was rarely represented this way. In my review of two years' worth of skating articles in newpapers and magazines leading up to the 1992 Olympic games, I never saw one photograph of Kerrigan in this pose, although all the other top skaters (Harding, Ito, and Bonaly) were pictured this way at least twice. The notable exception was the picture of Kerrigan which was a prominent part of the cover montage for "*Life* Remembers '92." An irate reader wrote in response to that cover, "Did you guys forget Kristi Yamaguchi was the gold medal winner for the U.S.A.? 'Racist' is a very harsh word, but I can't think of any other word to explain this inexcusable slight." The editors replied, "All the cover images were chosen for their complementary shape, composition and perspective" (1993:30). My research indicates that *Life* would have had to pass over many representations of Yamaguchi in a layback spin in order to put an atypical Kerrigan photo on its cover.

It is not only the narrative surrounding skating which favors "feminine ladies." The rules and judging are also skewed to reward such skaters. Skating is judged in two categories, technical merit and artistic impression. A maximum technical merit score is predetermined by the difficulty of the program, and then deductions are made for each error. There is a range of possible deductions, making the technical merit score far from objective. By far the most straightforward part of the program to judge is the jumps, because the order of difficulty is agreed upon and the success or failure of a jump is usually obvious. In the original program, for which the requirements are set, the men are expected to do at least two and perhaps three triple jumps, while the women are only *allowed* to do one triple jump. This requirement reduces the most objective end of the scoring—how

difficult was the jump and was it landed cleanly—and gives far more emphasis to the more subjective areas of judgment that fall under "technical merit," along with the already nebulous category of "artistic impression."

One mark of Kerrigan's success as a skater was her ability to make the signs of her athleticism all but invisible. None of the stereotypical signs of the athlete—grunting, sweating, bulging muscles—ever seemed to disrupt the lady-like Kerrigan package. She was known not for her strong jumps (although, in fact, she was quite a strong jumper), but for her elegance and her line. In contrast Harding, with her huge jumps, speed and muscular body was aggressively athletic. Her incompetence as a woman, whether it was her choice of costumes, her hobbies (shooting pool, hunting, fixing cars and drag racing), or her controversial behavior (firing coaches, her rocky marriage, fighting with a fellow motorist on a Portand street) marked her as deviant. Because she was such a strong jumper, she threatened the very notions of sexual difference which to a large extent define masculinity. This 'deviance' reduced her value as a television entertainer and commercial spokeswoman long before she was connected to the Kerrigan attack.

What is always close to the surface, but rarely acknowledged, in the narrative of the artistry vs. athleticism debate is that for the women, artistry is indistinguishable from physical beauty. Why are artistry and athleticism considered mutually exclusive in ladies figure skating? A baseball player can be called poetry in motion; the balletic grace of Michael Jordan's jumps was admired without implying that he was less of an athlete. A woman's athleticism is belittled, often undercut in commentary which calls attention away from her athletic ability and right back to her physical appearance. For instance, after Kerrigan completed a difficult triple-double combination in the 1992 Olympics, Scott Hamilton commented, "Perfectly done!" and Verne Lundquist chimed in, "That brings a radiant smile from the lovely lady." After Yamaguchi's double Axel, Hamilton said, "Look at the height and flow," and Lundquist added, "And then look at the smile." Says Brownmiller: "A major purpose of femininity is to mystify or minimize the functional aspects of a woman's mind and body that are indistinguishable from a man's" (1984:84).

"I always tell my girls: think like a man, but act and look like a woman," said former skater turned coach Carol Heiss (in Deford 1992:6). But what does it mean to "think like a man"? Men are supposed to be competitive, focused, and ambitious. They can even be cocky, if they have the skill to back it. Proper masculinity is by definition ambitious and competitive. However, of Kristi Yamaguchi it was said, "she would skate even if they didn't give out medals." She was allowed ambitions as long as they were couched in terms of little girl dreams, creating a continuity with past champions such as 1976 gold medalist Dorothy Hamill. This connection was made by television interviewers who asked Yamaguchi, "Have you been dreaming of this moment?" and by television visuals which caught Yamaguchi talking to Hamill backstage before her free skate. It all seemed to lend credence to the "A dream is a wish your heart makes" framing device of the 1992 U.S. National Championships that I described above.

Women must be portrayed as emotional or in relationship to others; only men can thrive as lone individuals. And women will be punished for not being good girls. Coverage of Yamaguchi emphasized her steady, professional, but also close and loving working relationship with her choreographer and coach: "Says U.S. coach Don Laws: 'Kristi has the ideal temperament for a skater. She trusts her coach, her parents, and her program'" (Duffy 1992:49). Coverage of Kerrigan made her the perfect loving, obedient daughter and best friend of her blind mother. Harding was portrayed as recalcitrant and headstrong; she publicly regarded her coach as an employee rather than as a surrogate parent or friend; and she was "rightfully" punished for not "honoring her mother":

> *Harding's fourth-place finish in France was not surprising, given how erratically she had trained and her strong-willed decision to defy jet lag and travel fatigue by leaving Portland only three days before the competition began. [. . .] Teachman [her fired coach] said "I'm looking forward to working with other skaters who are hard workers, respectful of their coaches and are a joy to work with. I wish Tonya and her new 'employee' all the best." (Hersh 1992, sec.3:2)*

Harding's rough edges were admired when she was at the height of her success; later, these same qualities would be identified as the cause of her downfall. For a woman, strong-willed behavior is obviously wrong, and punishment is the "not surprising" outcome. Long before she became connected with any criminal behavior, Harding's rebellion was contained in the moral of her "punishment," her fourth-place finish in 1992; in contrast, quite similar erratic relationships with various coaches by U.S. skater Christopher Bowman (and more serious allegations of illegal drug use) were treated, at least among TV commentators, as just a part of his unconventional personality. Bowman laughed at his own bad boy reputation, nicknaming himself "Hans Brinker from Hell" and skating in exhibition to Buster Poindexter's "I'm Just a Bad Boy," mugging for the cameras with a showmanship that commentators treated with slightly exasperated but affectionate amusement.

In large measure, the Olympics are an audition for future commercial endorsements. One of the many ironies of being a successful woman athlete is that the most marketable and potentially lucrative images are those that are farthest removed in the public's mind from associations with filthy money. In 1994 Tonya Harding was repeatedly chastised for saying she had dollar signs in her eyes; meanwhile Kerrigan flew to California in the middle of her rehabilitation to film a Reebok commercial. Harding was condemned as a hotdog seeking the limelight, while Kerrigan was given sympathy because no one would leave her alone, despite the fact that Kerrigan was being paid by Seiko and Reebok to wear their products to each excessively photographed press briefing and Olympic practice. Kerrigan signed a multi-million dollar deal with Disney before the competition began and was featured in not one but three commercials which aired during the finals (adding yet another nail to the coffin of the concept of the Olympics as an "amateur" competition).

If Kerrigan and her agents took great advantage of her image as gallant lady athlete up until the Olympics, the post-Olympic backlash demonstrated how frail that image was. Beginning with her impatience before the medal ceremony, when she misinterpreted the delay in locating the Ukrainian national anthem as gold medalist Oksana Baiul redoing her makeup and snapped, "Oh, give me a break, she's just going to cry out there again. What's the difference?" to her endless comments of "I was perfect" in interviews about the competition to her "this is so corny" remark during the Disney parade in her honor, Kerrigan displayed an awkward streak that sent her image plummeting in the week following the competition. Her critics felt that she should have taken her money and shut her mouth; as her reputation worsened, the "brutal attack" of January was reduced to a "whack on the knee."

Arguing umpire calls is a respected skill in Major League Baseball, and postgame criticism of the officiating is accepted practice in the NBA. But being scrappy and pugnacious is one acceptable model of masculinity to which "ladies" do not have access. Allen Guttman writing on the history of women in sports noted that "advertisements are here to stay and that most advertisements will use physically attractive rather than unattractive models" (1991:263), ignoring the fact that advertisements not only reward but also determine what is attractive in our society. Frank Deford, in his preview of the 1992 games, predicted the possibility that a Yamaguchi win would touch off feelings of racism: "And now: what's a good ole boy to do if there's not only a Toyota in the driveway and a Sony in the bedroom and a Mitsubishi in the family room—but on the screen there, as the band plays the "Star-Spangled Banner," is the All-American girl of 1992, and her name is Yamaguchi?" (1992:53). An article in *BusinessWeek* after the Olympics stated that Yamaguchi was not getting the offers a white champion would have gotten ("The environment to 'max out' on her earning potential is not enhanced by the present mood of the country toward Japan," said one agent [1992:40]). Subsequently, Yamaguchi's agent denied the story, telling reporters that they simply had no time to sort through offers. Several months after the Olympics, E.M. Swift wrote in *Sports Illustrated* "Post-Olympic endorsements were down for all athletes in 1992, probably due to the sluggish economy. Still, Yamaguchi did pretty well. She signed lucrative deals with Hoechst Celanese Corporation, which makes acetate fabric for fashion designers, and DuraSoft contact lenses" (Swift 1992:75). Yamaguchi's television commercial for DuraSoft was especially interesting. She stated that since the Olympics, people had been encouraging her to change. A series of comic vignettes followed, with Kristi taking up tennis and hosting a talk show. But when she "really wants to change," she goes "blue, green, violet": in other words she changes the color of her eyes to colors an Asian woman would not normally have.

Post-1992-Olympic endorsements may have been down, but not for bronze medalist Nancy Kerrigan. Long before the attack which made her a household name, Kerrigan had been tagged by Campbell's Soup, Seiko, Reebok, Northwest Airlines, and Xerox to tout their products. Campbell's cited Kerrigan's "all-American charm and her grace and beauty on the ice" (Reisfeld 91) (was the implication all-American as opposed to Japanese American?). In naming Kerrigan one of the "50 Most Beautiful People in the World" in 1993, *People* magazine wrote, "Kristi Yamaguchi may have won the Olympic gold last year, but bronze-medal winner Nancy Kerrigan got the gasps for her Grace Kelly gleam." The article also confirmed that Kerrigan had six-figure endorsement contracts (1993:138).

The need for female athletes to also be conventionally feminine extends to sports other than figure skating. Speed skating gold medalist Bonnie Blair was shown a few mornings after she finished competing in 1992 being "made over." Her "wholesome image and nice smile" made her attractive as a possible product pitcher, but only with a "new do" and makeup, only when she could conform as closely as possible to societal norms of beauty. The female newscaster reporting the story observed, "I'm not sure if she liked that makeover" (CBS 19 February 1992). But like it or not, there she was, reassuring the public that despite her lightning speed, she's still "just a girl." The metaphor that Greg Faller uses to describe romance could also apply to commercial endorsement:

> *The promise of romantic union [or commercial success?] works like the three golden apples Melanion rolled in front of Atalanta. They will be seduced from their position of culturally unacceptable power and dominance in a masculine pastime to a culturally demanded position of submissive femininity within the patriarchal family. (1987:157)*

References

Brownmiller, Susan. 1984. *Femininity*. New York: Linden Press/Simon & Schuster.

BusinessWeek. 1992. "To Marketers, Kristi Yamaguchi Isn't As Good As Gold." *BusinessWeek*. (9 March).

Deford, Frank. 1992. "The Jewel of the Winter Games." *Newsweek*. (10 February).

Duffy, Martha. 1992. "When Dreams Come True." *Time*. 139, 9 (2 March).

Faller, Greg S. 1987. "The Function of Star-Image and Performance in the Hollywood Musical: Sonja Henie, Esther Williams, and Eleanor Powell." PhD dissertation, Northwestern University.

Guttman, Allen. 1991. *Women's Sports: A History.* New York: Columbia University Press.

Hagaman, Diane. 1992. "The Joy of Victory, The Agony of Defeat: Stereotypes in Newspaper Sports Feature Photography." CIRA lecture, Northwestern University, 6 March.

Hersh, Phil. 1992. "French Flip Stirs Tempest in Figure Skating's Teapot." *Chicago Tribune.* (21 February).

Kolata, Gina. 1992. "Who Is Female? Science Can't Say." *New York Times.* (16 February).

Life. 1993. "Letters to the Editor." 16, 3 (March).

Louie, Elaine. 1992. "Women's Figure Skating Puts Couture on the Ice." *New York Times.* (17 February).

McDermott, Barry. 1982. "More Than a Pretty Face." *Sports Illustrated.* 56, 2 (18 January).

O'Hara, Jane. 1988. "Stars in the Spotlight." *Maclean's.* (7 March).

People Weekly. 1993. "The 50 Most Beautiful People in the World 1993." (3 May).

Reisfeld, Randi. 1994. *The Kerrigan Courage: Nancy's Story.* New York: Ballantine Books.

Swift, E.M. 1992. "All That Glitters." *Sports Illustrated.* 77, 25 (14 December).

Therberge, Nancy. 1981. "A Critique of Critiques: Radical and Feminist Writings on Sport." *Social Forces.* 60, 2 (December).

United States Figure Skating Association. 1993. "The 1994 Official USFSA Rulebook." Colorado Springs, CO: The United States Figure Skating Association.

Willis, Paul. 1982. "Women in sport in ideology." In *Sport, Culture and Ideology.* Edited by Jennifer Hargreaves. London: Routledge and Kegan Paul.

Wolf, Naomi. 1991. *The Beauty Myth: How Images of Beauty Are Used Against Women.* New York: W. Morrow.

Television Coverage, "The Olympic Games" on CBS, February 1992.

After Reading

Critical Perspective

1. Look at the title of this essay. Why do you think Feder-Kane chose this particular title? What appeal to pathos is she trying to create? Do you think this helps or hinders her argument? Be sure to explain and support your views.

Rhetoric and Argument

2. Examine Feder-Kane's rhetorical choices in this essay in detail—audience, purpose, ethos, logos, intertextuality, context, and constraints. Do you believe that these strategies advance her argument? Explain why you think that this is the case, providing quotes from the text to support your assertions.

3. What kinds of evidence does Feder-Kane utilize in this essay? Do you find this support to be persuasive? Does Feder-Kane make any assumptions or warrants that you find questionable? Explain your assertions.

4. Feder-Kane points out that the role of the female athlete has never been an easy one—women have generally had few opportunities in professional sports, been neglected by the mainstream media, and tended to receive less compensation. Look at how Feder-Kane describes the media representations of skaters like Nancy Kerrigan and Kristi Yamaguchi. Do you agree with her assessment? If yes, give examples of other skaters or other female athletes who have been depicted similarly. If not, provide examples that undermine her claim.

Analysis

5. This essay ends with a quote by Greg Faller in which he states that women "will be seduced from their position of culturally unacceptable power and dominance in a masculine pastime to a culturally demanded position of submissive femininity within the patriarchal family." Why do you think that Feder-Kane ends her essay with this quote? What is the effect of concluding her essay in this way? Write a short response in which you support or refute the position Faller articulates. You may want to examine the ancient stories to which Faller refers to in his quotes as well. You can point to women's roles in sports or other arenas where they have gained increased visibility. Give evidence from the Internet, library, and your own experiences to back up your views.

Taking Action

Form a small group. Using Internet and library sources, research one high-profile female athlete of your choice. Examine her representation in the mainstream media, the various endorsements she receives, the companies and products she promotes, and how she claims she feels about her particular role in the sports world. Consider what you could claim about how representations of this female athlete function in American culture. In what ways does this support Feder-Kane's argument? In what ways might it challenge her claims? Present your findings to the rest of the class for large group discussion.

SPORTING INNOVATIONS AND CELEBRITIES

Evan Ratliff
"Sports Rule!"

Evan Ratliff is a freelance writer based in San Francisco and the coauthor of Safe: The Race to Protect Ourselves in a Newly Dangerous World. *As a contributing editor for* Wired *magazine, he has written on science, technology, terrorism, politics, crime, and culture. Ratliff's reporting and other writings have also appeared in* The New Yorker, Outside, Seed, Slate.com, *the* Los Angeles Times, *and the* The New York Times.

EXERCISING YOUR SKILLS

Before Reading

Ratliff looks at the popularity of sports video games. What sorts of video games do you play? Do any of them depict or emulate sports play? What images do you see, what sounds, and what kind of roles can you adopt as a player? Do you think that certain games are designed more for women than for men? What makes you think so? Consider a variety of examples.

It's a warm autumn day at the South Street Seaport in New York, and 500 men—most in their twenties and thirties and wearing baggy jeans, backward baseball caps, and football jerseys—are gathered inside the sort of huge white tent generally reserved for wedding receptions.

A quick glance seems to tell the story: armchair jocks elbowing for the best view of the big game, or any game at all. Jets–Giants, Eagles–Redskins, hell, even Bengals–Texans. They swarm around banks of TV sets, talking trash, bumping fists, and occasionally offering advice: "Play D, motherfucker!"

In the middle of one huddle stands Robert Hart, a 31-year-old barbershop owner from Philadelphia. "Come on, baby, let's go!" he shouts, pumping his fist in the air as a St. Louis Rams defensive back knocks down a pass. "That's what I'm talkin' about!" It's a scene out of any sports bar in America. But Hart isn't rooting; he's playing. Thanks to the controller in his hand and the game in the PlayStation 2 console—*Madden NFL 2003*—today Hart *is* the St. Louis Rams.

New York is the latest stop for the world's largest official football videogame tournament, the EA Sports Madden Challenge. The winner at this two-day, single-elimination competition gets a free trip to a Jamaican resort to compete against nine other city champs for the title of best *Madden* gamer in the country. Losers go home.

For Hart, a former high school football player, there's more than a free vacation on the line. "This is as close to the real thing as it gets for me," he says.

Videogames have always been about inhabiting a fantasy, and for old-school gamers that meant ogres and wizards and trolls. But today's gaming public resides squarely in mainstream America, and for them fantasy means Tigers and Kobes and Favres. With $4.6 billion in annual sales, software publishing is the largest part of the $9 billion video-game industry. The sports genre alone is worth $1 billion annually—and is growing on a hockey-stick curve. On the dominant console, the PlayStation 2, sports titles account for more than 30 percent of all sales. Most important, sports games are a gateway for non-gamers to join the club. First it's a few Sunday afternoons with *Madden,* then a couple of weeknights playing *Grand Theft Auto,* and all of a sudden you're spending three hours a day battling the Germans in *Medal of Honor.*

No game company has capitalized on the sports boom better than Electronic Arts. EA Sports, a division that accounted for nearly half the company's $1.5 billion in annual revenue last year, rules sports gaming. Credit its ability to create, better than anyone else, titles that are immersive and interactive. Yet there's more to EA's success than the products themselves. The company has crushed its competitors by figuring out how to market to a new class of gamers—Hart and every one of his goateed, official-merchandise-wearing, *SportsCenter*-talking peers. The bait is big-budget ad campaigns, teams of campus marketing guerrillas, traveling road shows, and a stream of trash-talking sports celebrities.

Games like *Madden,* which has sold more than 19 million units since 1989, are chasing "someone who has had the thrill of competition in their life and wants the closest thing to it," says Jeff Odiorne, creative director for Odiorne Wilde Narraway and Partners, EA's longtime advertising agency. EA Sports customers are less interested in getting lost in a sci-fi adventure and more into "looking at the guy next to them and saying, 'I'm going to kick your ass.'" From team-organized baseball, basketball, and soccer to NASCAR and golf, EA sells sports lovers the promise of living (and reliving) their passion through a console.

Of course, success breeds imitation, and as EA has grown, so too has its list of rivals. Activision has conquered non-mainstream sports with titles like *Kelly Slater's Pro Surfer* and *Tony Hawk's Pro Skater.* Midway and Konami have carved out smaller niches across the PS2, Xbox, and GameCube platforms. Sony's 989 Sports—which makes team sports titles for the PS2—and Microsoft—with football, basketball, and a forthcoming baseball game for the Xbox—do well on their own consoles. But EA's strongest challenge to date comes from Sega. Two years after ditching its failed Dreamcast console to focus on software, Sega has thrown its marketing heft behind its *2K3* line of sports games—most significantly basketball, where Sega outsold EA last year, and football, where, despite Sega's efforts, EA's *Madden* still dominates the way the Steelers ruled the NFL in the '70s. And now Sega Sports is taking a page from the EA playbook, spending $35 million on advertising for its new *2K3* football and basketball titles. The result: an EA-Sega branding war that will make the Nike–Reebok clash seem like a scrimmage.

For guys like Robert Hart, *Madden* is still clearly where the action is. By midday, the ranks of the tournament at Pier 17 are thinning, but Hart has become even more animated, his head bobbing to the hip hop music blaring through the tent, and his taunts have grown more aggressive. He breaks up a pass play to cap a dramatic comeback that puts him in the semifinals. "I've been holding my own," he says, in his version of a postgame locker room interview. "But now I'm just trying to maintain, stay focused, and play the type of game I'm capable of playing."

As Hart gets pumped for the semis, an EA Sports emcee cranks the volume, energizing the crowd and building the EA brand at the same time. "It's *Madden 2003,* playas," he booms. "Get yourself some! Who's gonna go all the way?" And then, for what seems like the thousandth time in two days, "EA Sports. It's in the game!"

If it's in the game, it's in the game. Sitting flat on the page like that, it seems like a New Age mantra—a string of words that's both meaningless and profound. Spoken with a voice that's half monster-truck rally, half boot camp, the decade-old EA Sports catchphrase has become as recognizable as almost any in popular culture. "That's mine," says Odiorne, who came up with the tagline for the brand's launch in 1992. "I had a bunch of them. One of the dogs that we threw out early was, 'The spittin' image of sports.' I'm not too proud of that.

"We ended up with the simple proposition that if these are real sports games for real sports fans, hell man, if it's in the *game,* then it's in the game."

The slogan's power reveals a deeper truth: Selling sports games is as much about communicating with consumers as it is about technology. With the release of every major title—timed to coincide with the start of the real season—EA unleashes a raft of commercials, print ads, and sponsorships to create an aura of cool. Over the past two years, that marketing machine has really started to hum. After a small loss in fiscal 2001—a transition year as the industry waited for a new round of consoles—EA rebounded, with $100 million in profits in fiscal 2002. Its stock has soared 30 percent over the past 12 months, even as the rest of the Nasdaq has tanked. EA's climb can be traced to the company's ability to expand its sports sales, thanks to the "annualized" revenue from gamers who return each year to plunk down $50 for the latest versions.

The key to bringing those customers back year after year is marketing. EA's commercials, like the games themselves, are designed to extend the notion of sports fantasy. Clearly, a TV spot would be a great place to demonstrate the superiority of an EA game—realistic graphics, the size of the player roster—but EA isn't selling products, it's selling an experience. Product drivel would only break the illusion. That's why you never see a TV, much less a console, in an EA Sports ad. Instead, you see one of EA's stable of pro athletes, like Ravens linebacker Ray Lewis, squinting at you, taunting you, daring you to get in the game. "As soon as you start bringing in things like controllers and pop-up bars that tell you what play to pick, you've reminded me, Oh, that's right, it's *only* a videogame," says Odiorne. "That's the cardinal rule for me: Never break the fantasy."

That means letting the athletes do the talking. Gaming consoles are a constant presence in the lives of mid-twenties pro athletes. The game of choice for Sacramento Kings point guard Mike Bibby, surprisingly, isn't basketball—it's *Madden,* in which he says he dominates family and friends on the Xbox. "Every football season we play a season of *Madden,*" he says. Each player drafts a fantasy team. "Out of 38 games," he says, "I won 35 in a row. I beat somebody 98–7." The secret of his success is simple experience: "I've played these games since I was a little kid."

In producing its sports games, EA ranks each onscreen player based on 20 or more categories, ranging from physical attributes like speed to tackling ability. The pros invariably want to check out their digital doppelgängers to see how they stack up. "The players get irate about their ratings," says John Schappert, former head of the *Madden* development team and now VP in charge of EA's Vancouver studio. "The guys who do them are listed in the credits, and they get calls from NFL athletes saying 'Why'd you screw me on speed this year?'" Mike Bibby's only problem with *NBA Live,* he says, after whipping New Jersey Net Jason Kidd online for a promotional event in Sacramento: "It won't let me dunk."

Athletes aren't the only celebrities jumping at the chance to work with EA. The company has been able to attract announcers as well as hip hop and alt-rock artists to score soundtracks for games. *NBA Live 2003,* EA's basketball game, features Snoop Dogg, Busta Rhymes, and Fabolous. Like the players, many of the artists are already part of the gaming culture. "When I came here five years ago, I was like, Shut up! I can't believe these guys are calling *us*," says Carolyn Feinstein, EA's vice president of marketing. Athletes and musicians call EA every year to try to get their hands on the latest version of titles like *Madden* before they hit the stores. "The whole model is reversed. Those guys want the game as much as we're interested in benefiting from a relationship with them."

The celebrity factor brings a certain cache to the EA Sports brand, which helps in the lower-budget guerrilla efforts to build street cred. The company signs up promoters at 50 colleges and universities, seeking out not hardcore gamers but students with a talent for networking. On-campus reps, working cheaply and often for course credit, are flown to EA's Redwood City, California, headquarters for a few days of training before fanning back out to organize tournaments, put games in the hands of fellow students, and spread the word about EA. The same tactics are applied to urban street teams, a concept that EA borrowed from the music industry. The formula works internationally, with on-the-ground promotion for global releases like *FIFA Soccer* (a title published in 15 languages that, in some seasons, tops *Madden* as EA's best-seller worldwide) rugby, and even Australian-rules football.

Based on the marketing success of titles like *Madden* and *NBA Live,* EA is rolling out an identical strategy for its nonsports titles. Under a new brand, called EA Games, *Harry Potter and the Sorcerer's Stone*—which sold 9 million units last year—assumes the position of franchise player. As with *Madden,* its popularity should help drive sales of lesser-known titles.

At a Sega production studio in San Rafael, California, Chicago Bulls rookie point guard Jay Williams demonstrates the tight ball handling and serious ups that made him 2002's number-two draft pick. In a skintight black motion-capture suit, the former Duke University star slams home dunk after dunk in front of a handful of approving producers and 16 infrared cameras. Sega staffers spent more than 300 hours watching college games on TV. Based on that, producers now call out a script of moves: *left-to-right crossover dribble ending in a right-handed jam.* The video feeds go straight to workstations used to incorporate Williams' best stuff into Sega's basketball games.

For companies like Sega and EA, motion-capture sessions with superstar athletes have become an important part of the effort to engineer real-life details into titles, making them as much a sports simulation as a videogame. After all, business textbooks bulge with the failures of crappy products backed by huge marketing machines (New Coke, *Waterworld,* the XFL). Solid games support the hype.

Building a quality title starts with the look. Publishers license player images from their respective leagues. Developers digitize faces and shape body types, then add in details like Allen Iverson's tattoos. Stadiums and arenas are meticulously reproduced down to the location of exit rows and the ads on each skybox. When the real-life Tampa Bay Buccaneers were constructing a new stadium, anyone playing the Bucs through a season in *Madden* saw the stadium going up in the background, each week one step closer to completion.

Then comes the tough part: making the players *act* realistically.

EA's player rating system provides a base for gamers to compare the raw skill of their digitized heroes. But then there are the intangible factors to consider. Star players are imbued with signature moves—Kobe Bryant demonstrates his obnoxious gape whenever he hits a big shot, Donovan McNabb has a great option fake. Reggie Miller is money with the game on the line. If Shaquille O'Neal tries to dribble up the court, he'll probably bounce the ball off his foot. The player's natural abilities are also combined with the gamer's skills. If you don't sub out for your star, he'll start dogging it. If you play him too much throughout a season—in 1998, *Madden* launched a Franchise mode, now standard in sports games, that lets you take one team all the way—he's liable to get injured.

The best sports games take a lot of coding. EA dedicates 25 programmers and 25 artists to the year-round development of *Madden;* it also employs people whose sole job is to watch thousands of hours of game films, noting players' habits, stadium conditions, and coaching strategies. "We're looking at tape for offensive and defensive tendencies, sets, formations, plays—something as specific as whether a quarterback throws sidearm," says Oge Young, manager of the five-man central production group at EA that examines NFL and NCAA film. "The guys here are dedicated to getting every minute detail correct, and they love football. You sort of have to." For its NASCAR game, EA sends out a team to visit racetracks nationwide, collect digital photos, record race conditions, and measure the width and banking angles of the track. For *Tiger Woods PGA Tour 2002,* the company mapped every last inch of Spyglass Hill, Cypress, and Pebble Beach by having employees walk the golf courses with GPS backpacks.

All of this fanatical detail serves to simulate not sports, exactly, but sports as fans know them: through the television lens. Both EA and Sega hire former television producers to incorporate TV camera angles. With its *2K3* series, Sega went further, licensing the ESPN brand and paying broadcasters to add *SportsCenter* pregame and highlight shows— *boo-ya!* EA now says it's moving beyond TV, adding field-level camera angles you won't see on *Monday Night Football.* "TV has been our guiding light for a long time," says Schappert. "At this point," he says, "I think TV might be taking some direction from us. We can do some things with our camera and our game that they simply can't do."

Capturing the minutiae serves a singular purpose: winning over an audience already obsessed with the intricacies of sports. In an era when 15 million Americans play in fantasy leagues, achieving ever-greater realism is critical to hooking new gamers and keeping the old ones. "People who appreciate the sport," says Kevin Wilkinson, senior producer for EA's *NBA Live* and *NCAA March Madness,* "are the people who can appreciate the level we've taken it to."

The elements of a good game are freely available to any publisher lured by the big dollars of the sports market. But as Sega discovered this fall, matching EA detail for detail doesn't guarantee matching them sale for sale. Last year—its first as a third-party publisher—Sega made headway in sports with its *2K* line, picking up 12 percent of football sales and a market-leading 30 percent of basketball. So far this year, EA has come back to punish Sega. Before the holiday season, *Madden* owned 85 percent of the football market to Sega's 10 percent. In NCAA games, EA was even more dominant, with a 95 percent share. In the weeks after release, *NBA Live* was rumored to be outselling *NBA 2K2* two to one.

Sega of America president Peter Moore knows what it's like to be the underdog. Moore came to the company in 1999 after seven years running Reebok, a company obsessed with Nike. Now he's trying to beat EA at its own game. Whereas EA has allotted $15 million each to push *Madden* and *NBA Live*—mostly during the all-important fourth quarter—Moore has allocated $35 million to promote two of Sega's *2K3* sports games. That's more than twice what Paramount spent to promote *Jackass the Movie.* Moore knows how hard it will be to take on the EA Sports machine, even with his own roster of big-name athletes. "Many people are critical of us for taking the dragon head-on," he says. "But quite frankly, it's the only way we know."

To Moore, winning over sports fans means more than making good games—just as taking on Nike meant far more than making quality shoes. "You need not only sports products but a brand above it," he says. In fact, he thinks the EA–Sega battle is precisely what he went through at Reebok. "Turn on an NFL game and you'll see Brian Urlacher and Warren Sapp and Jevon Kearse from Sega, and you'll see Shannon Sharpe and Randy Moss and Ray Lewis from EA, and *pshhhhhhh,*" he, says, making an exploding sound as he slams his fists together. "We're going head-to-head. It's very reminiscent of when I was at Reebok, with the Reebok–Nike wars. We had Shaq and Emmitt Smith and Frank Thomas. They had Jordan and just about everybody else. This is the shoe wars of the new millennium."

He also knows it will take a bit of time to erode EA's market share. "Are we going to beat them this year in football?" he says. "No."

"Are we going to start chipping away at their psyche and their sales? Yes. And that's what it's all about."

Sega better start chipping faster. Its stock was slumping as of early November, after company president Hideki Sato admitted "total defeat" in the battle against EA.

So why is EA Sports running away with the game? For one thing, the $30 million it allotted to push *Madden* and *NBA Live,* mostly during the fourth quarter. In basketball, EA revamped the engine beneath last year's *NBA Live,* which was much criticized for inferior graphics and gameplay. EA also employed some old-fashioned muscle, using its retail connections to flood the market and edge Sega off of store shelves.

To EA chair and CEO Larry Probst, there's no secret to why EA Sports is beating Sega. "They are both really high-quality games," he says of *Madden* and *NFL 2K3.* "But at the end of the day, the EA Sports brand is hugely powerful. You've got an installed base of people that have grown up and are accustomed to playing *Madden*. This year's product is very highly rated; it's got the EA Sports seal of approval on it. Why change?"

All of this demonstrates that in a world where sports games are racing toward parity, it's not about what's in the game, it's about what consumers *think* is in the game. Unfortunately for Sega, that gives EA Sports an unfair advantage—one that Odiorne is quick to point out. "We absolutely crushed them in marketing," he says. "If the games are even, we win."

As for Sega's long-term strategy: "Bring it on," says Probst, sounding like an athlete from one of his own commercials. "It will keep us on our toes, it will make us build better products. At the end of the day, the consumer benefits and the industry benefits."

About that, at least, there's little argument. Along with spending more on marketing in the fourth quarter than Nike and Reebok combined, EA and Sega are continually racing to improve their titles and broaden their appeal. EA programmers wanted *Tiger Woods 2002* to attract more nongolfing hardcore gamers, so they developed a number of new twitch features, like speed golf, where gamers pound buttons the way they would on a first-person shooter. The team sports will get increasingly complex Franchise modes each year, with all the arcane details that come with running a professional team. Both companies are adapting their entire line for the new online functionality of PS2 and the Xbox, allowing gamers to play live across the Net. And the next generation of hardware should further elevate play. "You'll start to see the emotions on the players' faces with animations that are 100 percent lifelike and realistic," says Probst.

For now, the finals at Pier 17 are real enough. Onlookers wince at the big hits and whoop at long runs just as though they're watching an NFL game. Playing a 19-year-old from New Jersey, Robert Hart runs away with the game. "He's beatin' him so bad," one fan shouts, "we're going to have to call the cops."

At the postgame trophy presentation, Hart humbly gives out props where they're due. He credits the new *Madden* online feature for his success; it allows him to play people outside his circle of friends. He also credits his own God-given ability to focus. "When I'm playing the game, it's just like me in the house practicing," he says. "I ain't worried about nobody else."

As he gathers up his trophy and heads for the exit, a kid no older than 10 in a red sweat suit timidly approaches the tent. With a push from a friend, he asks, "You play football?"

"That's right, boy," says Hart, stifling a smile. "I'm the best."

After Reading

Critical Perspective

1. Discuss how Ratliff begins his essay. What effect do his tactics have on the reader? Do you find this an effective approach? Why or why not?

Rhetoric and Argument

2. What kinds of rhetorical appeals are at work in Ratliff's essay—his use of audience, purpose, ethos, pathos, logos, intertextuality, context, and constraints? How does Ratliff's use of evidence tie into the rhetorical appeals he utilizes? Give specific examples from the text.

3. Describe Ratliff's tone in this essay. Is he supportive of these games, the technology, and the campaigns or not? What evidence leads you to conclude this? Are there any flawed assumptions or logical fallacies in his essay?

4. Why have sports video games sold so well, according to Ratliff? In addition, look at how the games are marketed. What ideas about sports and celebrity are being promoted through the advertising campaigns? In what ways have the EA Sports campaigns been more effective than Sega or other companies' campaigns? How are consumers being targeted specifically? What makes you think so? Provide evidence for your assertions.

Analysis

5. Ratliff's discussion of video sports reveals the extent to which "sports culture" is maintained in the gaming world. In a short argumentative paper, address the following questions: What behaviors, attitudes, and beliefs are associated with sports culture? Take a look at video games targeted to female consumers. What do you notice about how these games are different from those targeted to male consumers? Are there equivalent kinds of games available representing female athletes? If yes, how do they function? Do they operate similarly or differently from the ones that target men? Consult library and Internet sources if needed.

Taking Action

Form a small group with your classmates. Go to electronics stores that sell video games or examine them online. Survey the packaging—specifically the kinds of fonts used. In as much detail as possible, describe the rhetorical tools used to persuade customers to purchase these products. Examine audience, purpose, ethos, pathos, logos, intertextuality, context, constraints, use of color, and arrangement. What do you notice about the differences between packages aimed at male and female consumers? What do you notice about the differences between packages aimed at younger and older audiences? You may also want to consult library and Internet sources.

Once you have secured your information, present your findings to the rest of the class. Try to provide examples of the packaging from games you own or pictures from the Internet. Based upon what you discover as a class, what kind of argumentative claims about video games and packaging might you be able to make? How might you best support such assertions if you were to write a response?

MONICA MOOREHEAD

"Racism, Class and the NBA"

Monica Moorehead is a writer and managing editor for the socialist newspaper Workers World. *In 1996 and 2000 she ran for president of the United States on the Workers World Party ticket. She was a member of the 1998 Iraq Sanctions Challenge delegation, led by former U.S. Attorney General Ramsey Clark, that brought medicines to dying children in Baghdad suffering under U.N. sanctions. Moorehead graduated from historically African American college, Hampton Institute (now a university), in Hampton, Virginia.*

EXERCISING YOUR SKILLS

Before Reading

Moorehead considers the relationships between race, class, and basketball in American culture. Collect a series of images and news stories about some of your favorite basketball players from popular magazines. Jot down notes about how they are represented—what behaviors, postures, and attitudes are depicted. Then make note of whether race and ethnicity as well as economic issues are taken up in these images and discussed in these stories. If they are, how are they addressed? If they are not, why might this be the case?

For quite a while the fight at the Palace arena in suburban Michigan between members of the visiting Indiana Pacers basketball team and Detroit Pistons fans became the main topic of discussion in the National Basketball Association and U.S. sports in general.

On Nov. 19, 2004 Pacers forward Ron Artest committed a hard foul against Pistons center Ben Wallace on the court. Players from both teams reacted with a brief scuffle. As NBA referees were trying to sort out the various fouls to be called, a Pistons fan threw beer on Artest as he lay on top of the scorer's table. Artest went after this fan in the stands. Other male fans threw more beer, other debris and even a chair at the Pacers players, causing more fighting in the stands and on the court for 10 minutes.

A few days later, three Pacers players—Artest, Jermaine O'Neal and Stephen Jackson—and Wallace were suspended from playing multiple games by NBA commissioner David Stern. Artest has been suspended from playing for the rest of the 2004–2005 season. The NBA Players Association is filing grievances against the suspensions.

The three Pacers players could also face criminal charges following an investigation by the Auburn Hills police. Some fans have stated publicly that they plan to sue these players.

The sports media have had a field day covering this story, constantly replaying images of African American basketball players going after white fans. While some of the media have criticized the "drunken" behavior of the fans, many sports commentators have stated that the players must bear the overwhelming brunt of responsibility for the fight, especially Artest.

Is the Nov. 19 incident just an isolated situation? Is much of U.S. sports nothing more than supervised violence to make huge profits for sports owners? Opposing hockey players beating each other up on the ice while referees look on is seen as a normal aspect of that game.

There has been an increase in fights during Major League baseball games, with some fans running on the field to attack players and umpires, and players throwing chairs at taunting fans.

However, none of these incidents has come even close to getting the kind of national attention that the Palace incident received. This stems from the issues of both racist and class oppression, which are more intense and omnipresent within the NBA than in other professional sports.

Some 80 percent of the NBA players are African American. An increasing number are going into the NBA straight out of high school because of multi-million-dollar contracts being offered to them. The majority of these players come from the poorer inner cities.

Out of the 30 NBA teams, only a handful have African American head coaches. Black men still make up less than 1 percent of NBA owners and executives.

Who attends NBA games? The vast majority of the fans tend to be white and from the suburbs where the majority of NBA games are now played. For instance, the home games of the Pistons are played in the suburb of Auburn Hills, many miles from the predominantly Black city of Detroit.

A ticket for an NBA game is one of the most expensive in all of professional sports. Therefore, the players rarely see fans who look like them or who come from a similar social background. Many of the younger players, like Artest, relate to hip hop culture, which conjures up stereotypical images of violence and other anti-social behavior in the minds of older white suburbanites.

NBA games can be compared to the days of the Roman Empire. Today's gladiators, the players, perform before their "lords and masters," who pay a lot of money to be entertained.

Many of the white fans resent Black players getting paid millions of dollars. These fans feel that because they help pay these salaries it is their "right" to shout racist epithets as well as spit at them if they are from the opposing team.

It is not unusual to see white fans sporting Afro, dread-lock or corn-row wigs, which is a degrading slap in the face to the racial pride that many Black players express.

What happened on Nov. 19, 2004 cannot be separated from the larger problem endemic within U.S. society—that is, a heavy dose of racism which is integral to class divisions.

After Reading

Critical Perspective

1. Moorehead is concerned about how fans and the media respond to and represent the actions of Black basketball players. Can you point to recent examples in the news that might support or refute her perspectives? Provide evidence from her text, other texts, and from your own experiences to back up your position.

Rhetoric and Argument

2. Describe the rhetorical choices that Moorehead makes in her argument—how she addresses issues of audience, purpose, ethos, pathos, logos, intertextuality, context, and constraints. Do you think that her strategies are successful? Why or why not? Consider the organization of Moorehead's text. Do you think it is effective? Be sure to provide quotes from the text to support your views.

3. What is Moorehead's main claim in her essay? What kinds of evidence does Moorehead furnish in order to back up her claim? Do you find this evidence convincing? Give examples in the form of quotes to provide evidence for your views. Do you see any logical fallacies at work in her text? If yes, be sure to indicate where they occur in her text.

4. What connection does Moorehead suggest exists between the NBA basketball players and race as well as class inequities? Do you think that Moorehead's argument is credible? Why or why not?

5. Moorehead reveals that while a huge percentage of NBA players are Black, very few managers and businesspeople associated with the NBA are. Write down a few

ideas about why this may be the case and what it suggests to you about the inner workings of professional basketball.

Analysis

6. Some scholars—both from within and outside the African American community—have proposed that basketball as well as various forms of dance and music are specifically Black forms of cultural expression. What are the potential effects of making such a claim? Do you agree or disagree? Write a short essay that addresses these questions. Consult work by such scholars. Point to your own experiences if relevant as well as library and Internet texts to back up your perspectives.

Taking Action

Gather in a small group. Select a local high school or college sports team and interview their members about their experiences. Arrange meetings with players in small groups or one-on-one. Ask them to read Moorehead's article and to consider how it may or may not resonate with their own experiences. As part of your discussion about Moorehead's essay, inquire a bit about the team members' own backgrounds, where they grew up, as well as their neighborhood and life experiences. Be sure to take detailed notes about what you learn from each player, securing their anonymity if they wish.

Once your group has conducted a number of interviews, consider all of the materials you have gathered. Discuss the interviews in terms of patterns or themes that you believe are emerging. After you have some thoughts about how you might group, interpret, and analyze your interviews, report back to the class. What did you discover about these players based upon their reactions to Moorehead's essay? In what ways do racism and classism impact or fail to impact their lives? What do you make of what you have learned? In what ways may your findings be significant to understanding how high school or college sports teams operate?

PHILIP J. DELORIA
"I Am Not a Mascot"

Philip J. Deloria is a professor of history in the Department of History and the Program in American Culture at the University of Michigan where he works for Native American rights. He has published various essays as well as the book Playing Indian: Making American Identities From the Boston Tea Party to the New Age. *Most recently he has coedited* A Companion to American Indian History.

EXERCISING YOUR SKILLS

Before Reading

Deloria examines the role of mascots in sports. Consider your favorite sports teams. Are there any mascots associated with these teams? What do you know about the history of mascots and why they were selected? Were there other mascots used in the past? If yes, why were they abandoned? Then, think about how mascots function for sports teams. What are their purposes? To what specific evidence can you point in order to back up your views?

When the Florida State Seminoles football team rushes onto the field, it follows the university's mascot—a stereotyped Indian warrior with colored turkey feathers and a flaming spear, which is planted in the end zone with a whoop. Florida State's fans, many in Indian costumes themselves, then proceed to chant a faux-Indian melody, swinging their arms in a synchronized "tomahawk chop." The Florida State experience is a common one. "Indians"—in a variety of flavors ranging from warriors, red men, braves, and chiefs to "Fighting Sioux" and "Apaches" have been the most consistently popular mascot in American athletic history.

The University of Wisconsin at Lacrosse first named its teams Indians in 1909. In 1912. the Boston Braves baseball team followed suit, and three years later, Cleveland's baseball club also became the Indians. During the 1920s, many college and professional teams—including teams at Stanford, Dartmouth, and the University of Illinois, as well as the Chicago Black Hawks hockey club—adopted Indian names. The practice filtered down to thousands of high schools and junior high schools seeking institutional identities. Today, professional sports boast five major clubs that use "the Indian" as a name and mascot. In addition to Chicago and Cleveland, Atlanta has the Braves, Kansas City has the Chiefs, and Washington, D.C., has the Redskins. While some colleges and universities—including Stanford and Dartmouth—have dropped their Indian logos and mascots, many more continue to insist that their use of Indian stereotypes is harmless fun.

Americans' embrace of Indian mascots was only part of a broad, early-twentieth-century primitivist nostalgia that stamped Indian imagery on a nickel, positioned baskets and pottery in the "Indian corners" of arts-and-crafts revival homes, and permeated the rituals of Boy Scouts and Campfire Girls. At the turn of the century, many Americans perceived that the story they had been telling themselves about their origins and character—one of frontier struggle between bold adventurers and savage Indians—had lost much of its cultural power as historians and critics declared the frontier "closed." On the contemporary side of this closed frontier, Americans saw the modern world—a place of cities, immigrants, technology, lost innocence, and limited opportunity. Many Americans used a ritualized set of symbols—cowboys, Indians, scouts, and pioneers—to evoke the bygone "American" qualities of the frontier era: "authenticity," nature, community, and frontier hardiness. Through summer camp and wilderness outings in "nature," touristic contact with the "authenticity" of Indian primitivism in the southwestern deserts, and an increased emphasis on rugged, character-building athletic competition, they sought to reimagine "modern" compensatory experiences that might take the place of the now-lost "frontier struggle."

Bringing Indians—potent symbols both of a nostalgic, innocent past and of the frontier struggle itself—into the athletic stadium helped evoke the mythic narrative being metaphorically replayed on the field. It was no accident that many other mascots—mustangs, pioneers, and so on—were also prominent characters in the athletic rendering of the national story. Indian chiefs and braves represented the aggressiveness and fighting spirit that was supposed to characterize good athletic teams. This racial stereotyping justified an American history in which peaceable cowboys and settlers simply defended themselves against innately aggressive Indians in a defensive conquest of the continent. As mascots celebrated "Indian" ferocity and martial (read also athletic) skill, they were at the same time trophies of Euro-American colonial superiority: "Indians were tough opponents, but 'we' prevailed. Now we 'honor' them (and in doing so, celebrate ourselves)."

The performative aspects of mascot ritual bring this American narrative to life, and demonstrate to participants that their myths, enacted both on the athletic field and in the stands, remain valid. The virulent response to Indian protests against Indian mascots demonstrates the deep emotional investment many Americans have made both in their imagining of Indian people as ahistorical symbols and in their sports affiliations. In mass society, athletic spectacles have become a deeply ingrained tradition to which many Americans turn for personal and social identities. The Florida State Seminole, then, signifies not only the frontieresque American character sought by early-twentieth-century fans, but also a more contemporary longing for the relative purity, simplicity, and tradition of the early twentieth century itself.

Indian people have reacted to the use of Indian mascots differently. While many native people expressed dismay, others saw athletic rituals as truly honoring Indians. American Indian Movement (AIM) leader Dennis Banks, for example, has claimed that, until the late 1950s, Stanford and other schools promoted "positive, respectful images" of Indians. According to Banks, during the 1960s fans became more involved in a disrespectful, racist spectacle, and clubs expanded their mascot activities. In Atlanta, for example, "Chief Noc-a-homa" came out of a tipi and danced wildly each time the Braves hit a home run. So while some Indians have always found the very idea of mascots offensive, others do not find it so even today, and still others join Banks in being most concerned about the positive or negative quality of the stereotyping.

In 1972, Banks and other media-conscious Indian activists forcibly brought the mascot issue into public discussion. AIM's Russell Means threatened the Cleveland Indians and the Atlanta Braves baseball clubs with lawsuits, and delegations from AIM, Americans for Indian Opportunity, and the National Congress of American Indians met with Washington Redskins owner William Bennett to ask him to change the team's name. Aside from cosmetic changes to mascot rituals and team songs, however, these efforts proved unsuccessful. Although Indians continued to protest, the effort to eliminate Indian mascots lost momentum for almost twenty years.

Then, in October 1991, the Atlanta Braves played the Minnesota Twins in baseball's World Series. Just a few months later, in January 1992, the Washington Redskins competed in football's Super Bowl. Both events took place in Minneapolis, a city with a high concentration of Indian people in a state that had been attempting to eliminate Indian mascots at the college and high school levels. This convergence of place, people, and issue launched a series of protests and an often rancorous national dialogue about the appropriateness of Indian mascots in American sports. . . .

The continual use of Indianness as an important American symbol has raised serious questions and dilemmas for native people. Some Indians, for example, have left their communities and performed for white Americans a series of "positive" anti-modern roles—spiritual "teacher," eco-guru, community sage—in order to acquire political and economic power. While such performances indeed generate valuable cultural capital, they also force Indian people to define themselves around non-Indian criteria. For other native people, it has become increasingly apparent that, in an age of mass communication, Indians need to exert some control over—or, at the very least, constantly challenge—any and all ways they are represented in public discourse. As a result, many Indian people—in contrast to many non-Indians—have found struggles against the use of Indian mascots and against the activities of non-Indian countercultural and New Age spokespersons to be critical and significant in terms of social, cultural, and political survival.

After Reading

Critical Perspective

1. Deloria criticizes the use of "Indian names" for team mascots. Why is he concerned about this practice? Do you agree with his assessments or not? Provide evidence from his text or from your own experiences to back up your assertions.

Rhetoric and Argument

2. Characterize the specific rhetorical choices that Deloria makes in his argument—how he addresses issues of audience, purpose, ethos, pathos, logos, intertextuality, context, and constraints. Do you think that his strategies are successful? Why or why not? Be sure to provide quotes from the text to support your views.

3. What kinds of evidence does Deloria furnish in order to back up his claim? Do you find this evidence convincing? Why or why not? Give examples in the form of quotes to provide evidence for your views. Do you see any logical fallacies at work in his essay? If yes, be sure to indicate where they occur in his text.

4. How is Deloria suggesting that giving mascots "Indian names" operates? What American myths does it perpetuate? What analogies between these myths and American sports does this practice evoke? What evidence does Deloria offer to support his assertion? Do you think that his argument is valid? Why or why not?

5. In the conclusion to his essay, Deloria suggests two possibilities for how Native people might respond to this situation. Explain what they both are and which one you think Deloria supports more.

Analysis

6. Think about American sports of various kinds. Craft a short essay that tackles some of the following issues: In what ways do they challenge American mythologies about patriotism, individualism, and Eurocentrism? In what ways do they perpetuate them? Point to the rules and practices of specific games to back up your views as well as library and Internet texts.

Taking Action

Gather in a small group. Choose a particular local, national, or professional sports team that has a mascot. Using Internet and library sources, investigate the history of this sports team's mascot, why it was selected, whether there have been other mascots in the past, and the like. If the mascot was associated with a specific tribe, research that tribe and learn all you can about the tribe's history.

Next, interview other students on campus, asking them what they know about the mascot and the sports team. Record their responses. Then, tell them what you know about the tribe the mascot represents and outline Deloria's argument. Record their thoughts and responses.

Finally, share your research with the rest of the class. Then determine as a group whether you think students are concerned about this issue or not. Talk about why this might be the case. If students are not aware of this phenomenon, what could be done to raise student consciousness? Consider how you might launch a campuswide discussion.

JAY NORDLINGER

"Tiger Time: The Wonder of an American Hero"

Jay Nordlinger is managing editor of National Review. *He is also a reporter, essayist, and critic. He is music critic for* The New Criterion, *the* New York Sun, *and the* National Review. *Before joining* NR, *Nordlinger was an editor and writer at* The Weekly Standard. *Nordlinger has written for a variety of magazines and newspapers, and has been a guest on numerous TV and radio programs.*

EXERCISING YOUR SKILLS

Before Reading

Nordlinger writes about the Tiger Woods phenomenon. Watch a professional golf event in which Tiger Woods is playing. Take notes about how the commentators describe him, his life, and his accomplishments. Are these descriptions similar to or different from how other golfers are characterized? Also, make note of any commercials that air in between segments that feature Woods selling products. What thoughts do you have about Tiger Woods as a person, a golf player, and as a celebrity?

Sometime last season, I e-mailed a friend of mine, an ex-pro golfer and a keen student of the game. "Are we ready to concede that Tiger is the best ever?" I asked. His answer was slightly ambiguous; I couldn't tell whether he was being sincere or sarcastic. So I asked for a clarification. "Oh, let me be perfectly clear," he replied. "Nicklaus in his heyday couldn't carry Tiger's clubs. Really."

Now, my friend and I were Nicklaus worshipers from way back—we still are. When it comes to Nicklaus, we are dangerously close to violating the First Commandment. So acknowledging the truth about Tiger came hard. Jack Nicklaus—this is gospel in golf—

dominated his sport as no other athlete ever dominated any sport. I once began a piece about Nicklaus roughly this way: Boxing folks can talk about Louis versus Ali; baseball people can talk about Cobb and Ruth and Mays (or whomever); tennis people can have a high time about Laver and Sampras; but in golf, there's nothing to discuss.

What's more, no one else was ever supposed to dominate the game. Nicklaus was supposed to be the last giant, the last player ever to make the others quake, the last to win predictably. You see, "parity" had arrived: That was the big buzzword on Tour. There were now thirty, forty—maybe sixty guys who could win in any given week. Golf instruction—swing science—had equalized things. Advances in equipment had equalized things. Conditioning, nutrition, etc., had equalized things. If a guy won, say, three tournaments in a season, that would be practically a freak, and the fellow would be Player of the Year, for sure. We would never see anything close to Nicklaus again.

Furthermore, his mark of 18 professional majors—twenty majors, if you counted his two U.S. Amateurs (and most of us did, because we loved that round, awesome number)—was an inviolable record. It would stand forever. It was the most unapproachable record in golf.

All of this needs to be remembered, because people forget. I've seen this in my own (not terribly long) lifetime. When I was young, the greatest record in baseball—the one that would live unto eternity—was Lou Gehrig's 2,130 consecutive games. That, all the experts said, was the one mark no one would ever reach. But then, when Cal Ripken closed in on it, they changed. They cheated. Now they said it was Joe D's 56-game hitting streak that was numero uno. Ah, but I remember: I won't forget. Ripken's achievement must not be slighted—everyone said it was impossible.

And now Tiger: The non-golfer will simply have to trust me that no one was supposed to be able to do what Tiger has, in fact, done. His achievements are—or were—unimaginable. The question arises, Has Woods won the Grand Slam? I, for one, don't care: He has won something like it—four consecutive majors—and no one else has (forgetting Bobby Jones, in the "premodern" Slam). I vow not to forget—no matter how fuzzy the past becomes—that Woods has accomplished what was proclaimed by one and all unaccomplishable.

How to talk about Tiger Woods? I don't know. Start with this (a cliche, but a useful cliche): When Nicklaus first showed up at the Masters, Bob Jones said, "He plays a game with which I am not familiar." The same has to be said of Woods. Another friend of mine—a pro golfer and a genuine philosophe—made the following, arresting statement: "It's not just that Woods is the best ever to play the game; it is that he is the first ever to play it." Think about that for more than a second or two, and you grow dizzy. What does it mean? It means, I think, that Tiger is the first truly to exploit the possibilities of the game. That he is the first to swing the club as it ought to be swung. That he—this gets a bit mystical—sees a game that others have been blind to, or have caught only glimpses of.

In the last years of his life, I had lessons—and many long conversations—with Bill Strausbaugh Jr., the most decorated teacher in the history of the PGA. "Coach" was one of the wisest men I ever hope to meet in golf, or to meet, period. Speaking of Tiger—this was in 1998, I believe—he said, "That young man has the best golf motion ever." (Coach disdained the word "swing"—he thought it gave his students the wrong idea.) I replied, condescendingly, like an idiot, "Oh, Coach, you must mean that he has one of the best ever. You've seen Hogan, Snead—all of them." He fixed me with a look and said, "No, Jay, I meant what I said: Tiger has the best golf motion ever." I was tremendously impressed by this, because the old are usually afflicted with the vice of nostalgia: No one is ever as good now as then. Thus, in baseball, for example, you hear, "Yeah, Roger Clemens is okay, but Grover Alexander! There was a pitcher!" Right.

Bill Strausbaugh also said, "Tiger has three things: a great golf motion, a great golf mind, and a great golf body. [This last, Coach maintained, is grossly underrated.] He is ideal—I never thought I would see it."

Tiger Woods was a legend before he ever turned pro. He had, I would argue, the greatest amateur career ever. (Bobby Jones idolaters—of whom I am one, from the crib—should just sit still. There is an argument here. And Jones wasn't an "amateur" in our present sense.) In fact, it's unfortunate about Tiger's dazzling pro career that it has been allowed to overshadow, inevitably, his amateur career. Tiger Woods, starting when he was 15 years old, won three straight U.S. Junior Championships and three straight U.S. Amateur Championships. This achievement is positively stupefying. I could try to explain, but, again, I say: Trust me.

Tiger was the youngest ever to win the Junior—he was 15. No one had ever won twice, and he would win three times. He was the youngest ever to win the U.S. Amateur—he was 18. He would be the only player ever to win the Am three years in a row. This takes a discipline, a kind of genius, that is hard to fathom. I argued, quite seriously, that if, God forbid, Tiger died before he ever had a chance to tee it up as a pro, he would die as one of the finest players in history. And he would have.

(I should interject here that Tiger—it is almost an afterthought—won the NCAA championship. He attended college—Stanford—for two years. Condoleezza Rice once told me—she had been provost of Stanford—that it was a shame that Tiger left school, understandable as it was, because he "really enjoyed it.")

Then there is Tiger the pro. Once more, how to convey the uniqueness—the impossibility—of it all? Tiger is only 25—and he has won 27 tournaments, including six majors (nine, if you count the way we do for Nicklaus). To provide a little comparison, Curtis Strange, who was the best player in the world for several years, won 17 tournaments, and two majors. At one stage, Woods won six PGA events in a row: Farewell, parity. Indeed, before Woods, it was absurd to say, "I think so-and-so will win this golf tournament," or even, "So-and-so is the favorite." Golf is not a football game, in which one team or the other must win. Tiger has introduced a strange element: predictability.

Let's grapple with some victory margins: In 1997 (at age 21, but that's a different matter), Tiger won the Masters by twelve shots. I once heard the TV commentator Ken Venturi, in the pre-Tiger era, say of a guy who was leading some tournament by three shots—three shots—"He's lapping the field." And he was. When you win the Masters, you win it by one shot, two shots—three shots, maybe. Often, you're forced to win it in a sudden-death playoff. Tiger won the 1997 Masters by twelve shots: He could have made a 15 at the final par 4 and still won—could have made 16 to play off.

In 2000, he won the U.S. Open, at Pebble Beach, by fifteen shots. He won the British Open, at St. Andrews, by eight shots. (These are all records, but we can't possibly begin to go into the record book.) I argued—only half-jokingly, or a third jokingly—that Tiger should retire then and there, rather as Bobby Jones did, at age 28. What did he have left to prove? Sure, he had dreamed all his life of breaking Nicklaus's lifetime records, but that was just a matter of longevity, of hanging around, of staying uninjured, of keeping oneself interested. What is there left to do after winning the U.S. Open at Pebble (by fifteen) and the British at St. Andrews (by eight), and in the millennial year of 2000?

Well, you can go on to win a type of Slam, I guess. And Woods is still charging.

Of course, he is more than a golfer: He is an important American, not least because of the racial or ethnic question. There is probably no one in the country more refreshing, more resolute about race than Tiger Woods. He is a one-man army against cant and stupidity. One of the most thrilling television moments I have ever seen occurred at the Masters, when Tiger was playing as an amateur. Jim Nantz of CBS asked him one of those softball, standard, perfunctory questions: "Do you think you have an obligation to be a role model for minority kids?" Tiger answered, quick as a flash, "No." I almost fell out of my chair. He continued, "I have an obligation to be a role model for all kids."

After Tiger won the Masters in '97, President Clinton asked him, the morning after, to join him the following day, to participate in a Jackie Robinson ceremony at Shea Stadium. Tiger said . . . no, to the President of the United States. The invitation was last-minute, and Tiger was suspicious of its motives. He had long planned a vacation in Mexico with friends, and he wouldn't scrap or alter it. Many people criticized Tiger for this decision; but he told them, essentially, to get lost. Here was a firm, self-confident democratic citizen, not a serf, complying with the ruler's summons. The same mettle Woods shows on the golf course, he shows off it.

A good number of people don't like Tiger's attitude—don't like it at all. Larry King asked him, in 1998, "Do you feel that you're an influence on young blacks?" Tiger answered, calmly, unmovably, "Young children." An annoyed King shot back, "Just 'young children'? Don't you think you've attracted a lot more blacks to the game?" Replied Woods, "Yeah, I think I've attracted minorities to the game, but you know what? Why limit it to just that? I think you should be able to influence people in general, not just one race or social-economic background. Everybody should be in the fold." Again, I almost fell out of my chair. Tiger may be the most pointed universalist in public life.

Even Colin Powell, the [former] secretary of state, has gotten snippy with Tiger, or about him. Woods coined a word to describe his racial makeup: "Cablinasian." This is meant to stand for a mixture of Caucasian, black, Indian (American Indian), and Asian. Tiger's dad, a tough, no-nonsense career military man, is (to be disgustingly racial, but this is to make a point) half black, a quarter Chinese, and a quarter Indian; Tiger's mom is half Thai, a quarter Chinese, and a quarter white. Tiger is, in other words, 100 percent, pure American. Back to General Powell. On *Meet the Press* one Sunday in 1997, Tim Russert asked him (rather in the manner of Orval Faubus, actually), "If you have an ounce of black blood, aren't you black?" Powell responded that, like Tiger, he was of varied background, but "in order to not come up with a very strange word such as Tiger did, I consider myself black American. I'm very proud of it."

Well, despite his distaste for racial baloney, so is Woods: He is neither unaware nor unappreciative of the struggles of black people in this country. After winning the Masters that first time, he paid due homage to black players before him, including Charlie Sifford and Lee Elder (the first black to be allowed to play in the Masters, in 1975).

Yet Woods refuses to spend his life in obeisance to the race gods. At one point, he felt obliged to put out a "Media Statement," the purpose of which was "to explain my heritage." It would be—this is typical Tiger—"the final and only comment I will make regarding the issue":

> *My parents have taught me to always be proud of my ethnic background. Please rest assured that is, and always will be, the case. . . . On my father's side, I am African-American. On my mother's side, I am Thai. Truthfully, I feel very fortunate, and EQUALLY PROUD, to be both African-American and Asian!*
>
> *The critical and fundamental point is that ethnic background and/or composition should NOT make a difference. It does NOT make a difference to me. The bottom line is that I am an American . . . and proud of it! That is who I am and what I am. Now, with your cooperation, I hope I can just be a golfer and a human being.*

We're told that we shouldn't need heroes. Well, too bad: We got one.

Not every touring pro has been gracious about Tiger and what he means; envy and resentment run deep. But the Scottish champion Colin Montgomerie said a lot when he commented recently, "We never thought this would happen [Tiger's explosion] or that there was even a chance it would happen. We're fortunate to have the world's best athlete playing our game. We're all not bad. He's just better. He is magnificent in every department."

Yes, in every department. A rare spirit shoots through Tiger. Consider a few, disparate things. Every year at Augusta, the Champions Dinner is held, for which the previous year's winner selects the menu. In 1998, Tiger—age 22—chose hamburgers and milkshakes: the all-American meal. After he won the '97 Masters (remember, by a historic twelve shots), he took a look at the film and announced, "My swing stinks" (he didn't say "stinks," but I've cleaned it up a little). So he worked to make it even better—and it may become better yet. Woods is a perfect combination of the cool, self-contained golfer, à la Ben Hogan (or Nicklaus, for that matter), and the hot, impassioned golfer, à la Arnold Palmer, or Seve Ballesteros. And, finally, there is no better interview in sports: He handles himself superbly, and is not above displaying a contempt (usually sly) for dumb questions.

My golf friends and I have made our peace with Tiger, to say the least. Initially, I think we all had a fear of his displacing Nicklaus, which seemed . . . sacrilegious. It helped, however, that Woods is the biggest Nicklaus worshiper of all: He venerates him as Nicklaus venerated Jones, and as Nicklaus pledged to follow in Jones's footsteps, Tiger has pledged to follow in Nicklaus's. Said Nicklaus five years ago, "There isn't a flaw in [Tiger's] golf or in his makeup. He will win more majors than Arnold Palmer and me [Arnie was standing next to him] combined. Somebody is going to dust my records. It might as well be Tiger, because he's such a great kid."

Oh, it's a thrill to be alive in the Time of Tiger. Whether you give a hoot about golf or not, I ask you—a final time—to trust me: Rejoice.

After Reading

Critical Perspective

1. Consider how Nordlinger applauds Woods. What do you make of his thoughts?

Rhetoric and Argument

2. Describe the rhetorical choices Nordlinger makes throughout this piece—his use of audience, purpose, ethos, pathos, logos, intertextuality, context, and constraints? Do you find this to be a convincing strategy? Be sure to offer evidence to support your perspectives.
3. Nordlinger asserts that Woods is a tremendous golf player—that "he is the first to swing the club as it ought to be swung." What connections does Nordlinger make between Woods's aptitude for golf and his role as a person of color? Offer quotes from his text to back up your views.
4. Nordlinger makes mention of Larry King's as well as Colin Powell's comments about Tiger Woods. What does Nordlinger contend about these comments? Do you agree with his views? Why or why not?
5. Nordlinger offers a lengthy quote by Woods about his racial and ethnic heritage. What do you think about this statement? Offer evidence from your own life experiences and the text to back up your thoughts.

Analysis

6. Nordlinger states: "We're told that we shouldn't need heroes. Well, too bad: We got one." Write a short argumentative essay in which you define what it means to be a "hero" in our culture. In what ways does Woods fit this definition? In what ways might he challenge this definition? Point to various cultural examples as well as Internet and library sources to back up your assertions.

Taking Action

Form a small group. Think about a number of celebrities—sports figures in particular—who have been represented by the mainstream media as role models and who have argued that they did not want to be treated as such. Consulting the Internet as well as library sources in addition to your primary texts, write an argument in which you examine whether celebrities—and sports figures in particular—have a responsibility to be role models or not. What effects can and should such people in the public eye have on fans' (particularly impressionable people like children's) behavior? Discuss your findings with your classmates.

DAVID THEO GOLDBERG

"Call and Response: Sports, Talk Radio, and the Death of Democracy"

David Theo Goldberg is a professor of justice studies at Arizona State University. Most recently Goldberg was the coeditor of Between Law and Culture: Relocating Legal Studies *and* Relocating Postcolonialism.

EXERCISING YOUR SKILLS

Before Reading

Goldberg reflects on the role that talk radio (specifically sports talk radio) has in American culture. Listen to a series of popular talk radio shows such as *Howard Stern, Dr. Laura,* or *Rush Limbaugh.* What do you know about the person or people who run the talk show? What specifically about their use of language and rhetorical choices tells you this? In addition, what do you know about the guests and audience members? What particular claims of cultural criticism might you make about these shows in particular?

Sports talk radio, as talk radio generally, is all about entertainment. Yesteryear's sports radio was principally concerned with play-by-play, player and team stats, the season's progress. Radio days: Take me out to the ball game even if I can't actually go. This function has been taken over in any case by ESPN. For sports talk radio, the romance with numbers counts only superficially if at all. Today, sports talk radio concerns itself overwhelmingly, if not exclusively, as an arena for voicing opinion—about sports, of course, but about sports as a surrogate for almost anything. Sports talk radio is both symbol and expression of the "democratizing" of opinion, equal opportunity beliefs, evidence or its lack notwithstanding. Shout, shout, let it all out, these are the things we're thinking (and not thinking) about. If I can vent more entertainingly than the next guy, if I can shout louder and longer (and what better training than being a sports fan), I'm king not for a day but for my 15 seconds of self-elevated and self-promoting fame. Jim Rome, Mad Dog Russo, and Scott Ferrall have made their reputations on that stage, the kings of sports talk rap. Howard Stern meets The Last Poets, Rush reaching out to touch Geraldo. Good callers give good phone, imitating the style (if not the substance) of their hosts. Even if the unfed baby is screaming for food in the background. "It's a jungle out there, man." First-time callers be warned: Say something disagreeable, and you're radio-actively flushed down the toilet, thrown through shattering glass, subjected to a drug test, even shot. Click, you're off the air, baby. Life's over. Your 15-second soapbox just got swept away. Democratic consumption calls for public sphere police officers.

Talk radio is marked by class. Public radio in the talking head formats represents the intellectually inclined, upmarket, and somewhat more liberally oriented audience. Here, Diane Reams (in political reverse) is to public radio what Cornel West or Noam Chomsky are to C-Span, the exception that proves the rule. By contrast, AM talk radio reaches (out to) a more conservative, white male clientele. In 1960, only two radio stations—KABC in Los Angeles and KMOX in St. Louis—were devoted to talk formats. Through the 1960s, AM turned increasingly to talk as the explosion of rock and roll enabled the transmission muscle of FM to dominate music stations. Talk radio stations mushroomed in the 1980s, prompted by a confluence of inexpensive satellite capabilities, deregulation, sophisticated niche marketing, and dramatic localism spurred by growing antistatist sentiments. In a single decade, talk radio stations quadrupled remarkably to 800. This represents a new talk station every 4 or 5 days! That's a whole lot of jawing going on.

By 1996, more than 4,000 talk shows were on 1,200 stations and networks, a more than tenfold increase in less than two decades. Today, talk radio "captures" one fifth of the male audience over age 18, mainly middle and working class. In 1994, 20 million people were rushing each week to laugh along with Limbaugh on 659 stations. Talk radio listeners and participants are largely men who, in the midterm elections of 1994 (and probably still), tended (significantly more so than women listeners) to vote Republican, disaffected Reagan-Rush acolytes. Between 5% and 10% of the African American audience tune in to talk radio, mostly to shows offered on the 189 black-owned stations. Interestingly enough, white and black men listen to talk radio in roughly the same proportions (about 20% of each group), although listening to talk radio has no demonstrable bearing on African American male voting patterns in the ways it has on white male voting patterns (Coleman, 1996). Talk radio, to refashion William Rusher's (1995) characterization only slightly, has become a white male "conservative precinct" (Bolce, DeMaio, & Muzzio, 1996; Hutchby, 1992; Page & Tannenbaum, 1996).

Class of the '90s

Sports talk radio likewise is all about class formation, even as it represents itself as classless—as class blind or class transcendent. How could it escape class formation in a market where 7-year contracts run from $50m to $120m, where a 21-year-old golfer earns $40m on a promise before winning a professional tournament from a company able to pay him only because its product is made by those it barely pays at all. And yet, the audience for sports talk radio ranges from the un- or under- or lowly-employed at one end of contemporary class structure to the beeper/cellular phone/beamer generation at the other. By the mid-1990s, there were 100 24-hour sports talk stations: all sports talk, all the time. There are sports talk stations that serve sports franchises, cheerleading owners' commitments, apologists for "what it takes" for a franchise to get a city to subsidize its activities (a new stadium or arena, downtown revitalization, sales tax subsidy, selling the public on a trade of popular players). KMVP in Phoenix, the new CBS affiliate, for instance, is user friendly to Jerry Colangelo, mega sports overlord of the Phoenix Suns (basketball), the

Phoenix Coyotes (hockey, formerly the Winnipeg Jets), the Arizona Diamondbacks (the expansion baseball team), and the Arizona Rattlers (Arena football team).[1] Not only do these radio stations broadcast franchise games, but the likes of Al McCoy ("voice" of the Suns) and Greg Schulte ("voice" of the Diamondbacks) run regular daytime byline commentaries, homeboy Peter Vecseys or Frank Giffords. Radio callers here tend to be the cellular phone clientele, wishful clients or hopeful subcontractors, community partners or sky box inhabitants of their "home" teams.

Downmarket, by contrast, one finds (I think more interestingly) sports radio talking to and for, about and with, the little guy, sewing him into the seamless web of American consumptive practice, giving him a place he can call his own while dropping a buck in its name. The bleacher bums (Whoopi's whooping *Eddie*, the dawg pound masochists, collars and all), pooling resources for pay-per-view simulcasts where tickets for the game are out of reach. More vocally opinionated, more locally knowledgeable than the coach about the team's woes, longer suffering than anyone should be and still prepared to pay for it. The quintessential Cubs or Cleveland Browns fan. Upscale audio, down to earth radio; man in the car talking to himself on his car phone (never a moment alone), man in the street ranting at anyone who will listen (forced by circumstance to be alone); "good guy" radio, "bad dude" radio. Brent Musberger and Mad Dog.

Pamela Haag, nevertheless (or precisely consequently), thinks there is something inherently democratizing about sports talk radio, for she thinks it fashions civil talk in public space as an alternative to "hate radio," as well as giving local color to the all but hegemonic "corporate voice" of media representation: playful offense in the face of both hate speech and humorless homogenized commercialized blandness. Local living color rather than nationally syndicated sameness, civil disagreement rather than anarchic militia disobedience, playful projection rather than put-upon politics. Giving in to the thin romance of the local in the face of the homogeneity of the multinational, Haag concludes that sports talk radio fulfills people's desires to be "thrown together in unexpected, impassioned, even random social relations and communities."[2] They do? No segregation in this vision. Folks want "to mix with people they have nothing (but sports) in common with. They want to be *from* somewhere again, to be part of a heterogeneous tribe rather than a narrowly defined political cabal" (Haag, 1996, p. 467). Across class, irrespective of race, against the grain of gender. That's a different sports talk radio than the one I'm stuck with.

Haag's romantic longing suggests a telling point, although not quite the one she has in mind to project. Sports *is* productive of a sort of *uni*formity, and sports talk radio helps fashion it. Uniforms encourage, enable, establish sameness, identity, and identification. They throw together almost indistinguishably the large and small, fat and thin, dark and fair, large-chested and lanky, fat cats and working stiffs, high rollers and the tightfisted. The magnification of sports in our culture thus has massive ramifications for democracy, although otherwise than in the idealized sense Haag would have it. Public sphere exchange is mediated through the trading off of commitments to sports franchises, endless debates about who's better than whom, who should be MVP, who "belongs" in the Hall of Fame. In the end, it adds up now to little more than the commitment to purchase marketed merchandise, to root for the same team no matter how exploitative of fan sentimentality. The professional sports franchises in cities, owned by mega-capital conglomerate interests, establish their indispensability to civic life by fabricating the consciousness that they are "*your* Chicago Bulls/Phoenix Suns/New York Knicks/etc." This enacts at once a team loyalty exhibited through the purchase of a team T-shirt or baseball cap. We're all dancing to the same tune here, watching the same cheerleading dancers high-stepping, dressed *identically,* shouting in unison, "Let's go . . .!" "De-fense!" We're closer here to the mass psychology of fascism with a human face than to a democratic public sphere.

Sports talk radio plays a central role in producing this uniformity—a uniformity in style of expression, of opinion, of team support. Giving away team T-shirts and caps, tickets and corporate promotions. Getting fans to line up behind team players and chemistry, product development and consumption, trades and waivers, benchings and discipline, rationalization and exoneration through individualized charities that cover (up) for corporate profits. Something is abstractly ethno-nationalistic about the enterprise. Supporting one's team today has taken the place of what it was once like supporting one's country, right or wrong. Sports talk radio is the propaganda machine of the new fan-aticism.

The demographic and commercial makeup of professional sports in America has always reflected, as it has reified, prevailing social relations. Think of Jesse Owens or Joe Louis in 1936, the Negro League and the Women's League, Jackie Robinson and President Truman's desegregation of the military, free agency and deregulation, affirmative action and Al Campanis. Why should sports be any (in)different now? And why should sports talk radio make a social difference, rather than represent prevailing social relations? Sports reflects the divide between rich and poor; the stylized and improvisational; the incessant commercialized shifting of the fashionable required by commodified professionalism in the face of the necessary repetition of the everyday; the physically demanding, aggressive violence of daily life hidden behind the veneer of an exhilarating, breathtaking aesthetic beauty; the rule-bound, repetitive, task-oriented nature of so much in late modern life in the face of the entrepreneurial need to push the limits, break the bounds, defy regularity, the norm(al), the law(s of nature). Made for and imitative of, yet imitated by, television. Sport imitates life, which ironically has come to follow the lead of sports fashion.

We are encouraged by sports and sports talk to remember the winners and stars, and we forget all too quickly the role players and losers (this latter word itself drips pejoratively off the tongues of sports radio hosts: In a world where winner takes all, we couldn't be caught losing, now, could we?). The star phenomenon individualizes sport, hiding the collective efforts of producing competitiveness (even in the case of radically individualized giants like Muhammad Ali, or Carl Lewis, Michael Johnson or Michael Jordan, FloJo or Martina), elevating the pleasures of success while deriding the pains of their preparation, dismissing all too quickly the disappointments of their failures, blind to the hidden costs of life in retirement as the smile of the professional spotlight fades too often to a grimace of a life faced with physical suffering. Muhammad Ali has been resurrected in the public eye only now that his politics are deemed no longer relevant.

Men/to/Ring Boyz, Airing Race

Talk on sports radio ranges across the political, more than occasionally explicitly about race in sports, always implicitly about race in America. And it invariably represents men's interests. For example, the local sports talk downmarket station runs a weekly segment, "What's Your Beef?" encouraging callers to gripe, not just about sports and sports character concerns, but about "anything" and "anyone" in one's life one might want to chew or stew upon. This furnishes, in other words, a forum for letting off steam, for venting venom(ously). It effectively opens a channel for the performativity of angry white males (who are overwhelmingly its performers). "The worst thing a woman can have is lip hair." "Women should not be allowed to broadcast men's sports." "Women's professional basketball, what a joke. You wouldn't catch me dead watching it." Sports talk radio provides a covert political stage for those who think of themselves as nonpolitical or (what in the age of self-proclaimed political correctness amounts to the same thing) as politically disenfranchised. Like Limbaugh, though more discretely, sports talk radio enables white men to express themselves white and male.

David Roediger (1996) remarks, in an interesting read of Rush Limbaugh's cultural resonance in America, that "banality can carry much more social power than genius where white consciousness is concerned" (p. 42). Whiteness silently produces and reproduces itself behind the vocality of loudmouthed, flaccid ranting. Sports talk similarly enacts its whiteness through the banal, no longer through the micro details of sports statistics (in itself banal enough, though relatively harmless) but via the disputational and contentious, the licensed arrogance of self-opinionated expression where anything goes so long as one is heard to say it forcefully and angrily enough. Sports radio discussion overwhelmingly infantilized concerns raised about Fuzzy Zoeller's disparately arrogant references to Tiger Woods as "that little boy" likely to serve "fried chicken and collard greens" at the "green jacket dinner" in the wake of Woods's record-breaking win at the Augusta Masters, dismissing them as choices of the politically correct unable (once again) to take a joke. No surprise that no mention was made of the Internet appearance soon after of the call to boycott K-mart because, by dropping Zoeller as its spokesman in the wake of his remarks about Woods, the chain had chosen to cater to a "black clientele," thereby ignoring the interests of whites. By contrast, two local hosts on the sports station that for a while ran a daily segment of Howard Stern's morning show spent an hour talking about the virtues for men of tight-fitting but uncomfortable women's lingerie. Sports talk is to radio what the Wide World of Wrestling is to television. These are marriages made at the polls of the lowest common denominator of whitemaleness.

Men invest in mediated sports as a down payment on the (reproduced) pervasiveness of male domination. It is obviously not that all men are better than all women in sports, only that the best male athletes on the established physical criteria outstrip the best women. And this is the point: Men's investment in spectator sports accordingly becomes investment in their own projected superiority through the superiority of the best athletes (who "just happen to be" men) (Messner, 1989). Sports talk radio facilitates this (masculine) self-elevation, the ideological reproduction of hegemony—risk- and cost-free but for the price of the toll call.

A caller the other day to Jim Rome's "In the Jungle" trashed what he called "the Trail-gangsters"—referring to the off court criminal troubles of the Portland Trailblazers—for "all they can beat up is women." Notice the rhetorical force of *all* here, which effeminizes "the Trailgangsters" even as it demonizes them for physically assaulting women (as one of the team members was, in fact, accused). Another caller to another program positively gushed, "My estimation of Marv Albert [NBC basketball play-by-play analyst accused of assaulting a woman in a hotel room, biting her repeatedly, forcing her to commit fellatio, and then sodomizing her] just went up." The caller indicated in his remarks that he had hitherto assumed Albert sexually inept, a conclusion he had derived with impeccable logic from the "fact" of Albert's supposed (self-evident, it seems) toupee. Apparently, Albert hadn't heeded the exhortation, in this caller's estimate, of the ads run regularly on all sports talk radio stations to seek out (the presidency of) The Men's Hair Club. The charge of sexual abuse, its innuendo, is payment sufficient for white men to offset the sin of (covering up) baldness (black men apparently don't need to, as they "clearly" have no hair to speak of, as evidenced by the likes of Michael Jordan and Charles Barkley).

Behind the projection of masculinity here obviously lurks race. Many of the best, the most high-profile athletes in the most high-profile sports are—or at least are considered to be—people of color, as the euphemism would have it, whereas the players—hosts and callers alike—in sports talk radio are almost invariably white men. (The one very notable exception among sports talk hosts is the Fabulous Sports Babe, Nanci Donnellan, the dominatrix of sports talk; she who knows more and kicks butt harder than her competitors.) Here we find risk-free identification with the superiority of black men in sports—the action-at-a-distance of being born-to-it assumption—while rhetorically reenacting technologically and technophonically that segregating divide of black folk residentially, educationally, socioeconomically, and culturally marking America throughout the 20th century.

Sports talk has become a leading forum for expressing "whitemaleness." Whitemaleness traditionally has taken itself as the arbiter of rationality, of intelligence, reduced impotently to reflecting on and about what signifies overwhelmingly as physical activity. Sports talk manifests a peculiar version of this. Isaiah Thomas complained at the beginning of the 1990s about white basketball commentators gushing on about "the genius" of white players, whereas black talent was characterized merely as physically gifted. Everyone "knows" that "white men can't jump," so they must cut it through superior intelligence and work ethic. In this context, sports talk radio mediates the racialized gaze on the (black) body in and through sports. A colleague, a self-declared radical feminist, once blurted out in my company, "Oh, Shawn Kemp, he's gorgeous, from the neck down." Sports talk radio enables white men to imagine the black body in a sense without being in its presence, unthreatened by it racially or homoerotically, unchallenged by the sexuality projected onto it imaginatively by the racialized fantasies of ("their") white women. In that sense, Dennis Rodman's cross-dressing is radical, certainly more risky—as it is more risqué—than the safety of the reflexive metatalk about it on sports talk radio by the likes of Scott Ferrall. Rodman's performance in acting out or up expresses the audacity of speaking back, for which he inevitably gets endlessly spoken about—paraded and oddly parroted—by radio talkers and stalkers.

Interpellated Selves, Invisible Subjects

Sports has become not only big business but also the arbiter of fashion, and fashion increasingly has been set/led by black stylin'. The baggy shorts craze that has swept youthful America leapt first from the street of black youths into high fashion projected by the antics of Michigan Wolverines' Fab Five and kid rappers Kris Kross. Sports crosses over commercially with rap in the bank account of the Shaq Attack. The market meets the street, where "the street" floats signifyin'ly between the sign for the stock market ("Wall St.") and the culture of hip hop, the former an investment in being "up," the latter in being "down." Whitemaleness finds a place for self-expression through fandom, the market of youthful parents and their doted kids with disposable cash in hand and the mentorship of fan-aticism, through consumptive apparel. I recently sat next to a father and his 8-year-old son at a Phoenix Suns game. The child, sporting the mandatory Kevin Johnson vest, quietly sipped on a soft drink and munched tacos through much of the game, until late in the fourth quarter when, buoyed by his father's increasingly aggressive support for the team, he began screaming in tune with his dad. Here in the flesh, I thought, I was witnessing sports (talk radio's) interpellating power at work. Sports radio fashions a clientele, filling the unconscious with desires less and less of its own making. It molds subjects as seekers of spectatorial excitement, instantaneous gratification, consumers of newly fashioned and packaged merchandise, releasing expressions of commitment the force of which leave the cool reflectiveness of a thoughtful democracy in the public sphere quite chilled (out). Sport is the perfect medium for this fanatical consumptive power. It is all about winners and losers, excitability and excitement, releasing nervous energy that is at once manic yet for the most part socially controllable. It is unpredictable within predictable parameters, sensuously stimulating, open almost constantly to new configuration, therefore perfectly conducive to fashionable commodification and commodifiable fashion.

Beyond this, sport and sports talk radio have proved conducive also—a medium well fitted—to the "advancement" of the new racism over the past two decades: racist expression coded as race neutrality, racialized exclusions as color blindness, racist discrimination as market choices, as commodity preferences. If I fanatically support a team that is all black, how can I be racist in trashing welfare state policies? Indeed, my freedom to support that team is identical to my preference against welfare for anybody. It "just happens to be" that the racially marginalized lose out by welfare divestment. Racial neutrality is sustained only by historical amnesia, political erasure, and moral ignorance. The public disinvestment in the welfare state means I have more disposable cash in hand to spend on my team's merchandise, should I so choose. It's a win-win situation, only by virtue of rendering the losers invisible. We never hear their voices on democratically arranged sports talk radio.

Anne McClintock (1995, pp. 31–36) demonstrates the late 19th-century shift that emerged in dominant forms of racist expression from scientific racism to commodity racism. *Commodity racism* manifests in consumer spectacles: advertising, expositions, museum exhibitions. It could be added that today commodity racism finds its principal expression in and through the hyperconsumptive spectacle of sports. Sports sneakers like Nike promote their market superiority through the physical prowess of their overwhelmingly black sports superstars. The megasalaries associated with the racialized bodies of sports heroes hide from view the exploitative conditions marking racialized bodies elsewhere that precisely make such spectacular salaries possible. At the height of the controversy over Nike's exploitative labor practices in Indonesia and Vietnam, sports talk callers to a person dissed the concern: "Those countries should do something about it if they are so concerned, but they're getting good jobs. . . . It's not happening in America, so who cares." We might call this, without too much conceptual twisting, "commodity neo-colonialism." At the same time, the whiteness of sports talk radio is reflected in the music it advertises: Clapton, the Eagles, Country, as its class commitments are reflected in commercials for the likes of Sears and Home Depot.

Racialized commodity neo-colonialism hides in good part behind the feel-good color blindness of sports talk hosts: "We don't care whether someone is white, black, yellow, pink, or green." Color may not matter, but race surely does. So Scott Ferrall growls menacingly that Patrick Ewing's nostrils are wide enough for a basketball to fit. Sufficiently conscious that he has silently invoked the "r" word in a way that might get his radio balloon popped, he quickly adds, "This is not a race thing, it's a nose thing." Must be the nose thing that allows him to play so well, huh. Perhaps he can take in more air, thus allowing him to elevate more easily in the drive to the rim. I now understand that it's the aerodynamics of the nose, not the Nikes, that explain how black men get to jump so high. This is not so far a cry from the restaurant remarks about slavery and thigh bones that got Jimmy the Greek fired from CBS Sports.

Fan-Atic Communities

Talk radio creates new communities, or at the least the artifice of old communities anew. *Sports* talk radio re-creates the artifice of a whitemale community of like-minded, like-thinking souls, gated circles of virtual friends whose virtuality is reflected by the abstractness, the irreality of the friendships and the ephemerality, the ethereality, of the community. But irreality and ethereality notwithstanding, it reproduces the artifice, the sense of whitemaleness, by offering if only informally an apparatus of ideological interpellation, the hailing to be part of a subjectivity larger than oneself, a member of a body (politic) enactive of (self-)elevation and (social) mobility via racialized and (en)gendered exclusions.

This is, if only by indirection, the death of civil discourse, of a discourse of civility, as social control through fan-aticism takes over. It is prescient in this context to note that there is more on-field/on-court/on-ice violence in American sport than there is among fans. And noteworthy as well, the altogether white sport of ice hockey has shown such growth in fan and sports radio support. Against this icy uncool background, I end by emphasizing that "I love this game" reduces all too quickly to "Life is a game. Play hard." Life is sport, as (my) sport is life (on the whole, "I'd rather be . . ."). Winner takes all. No fear. As long as the Dow is climbing, my team's winning, my mutual funds are soaring. I can retire to . . . the living room to watch the next world final whatever. Drinking Miller Lite or Bud, eating nachos or tacos, my newest model Nikes thumping the couch, the fantasy of my leased Lexis or Nissan in the garage, the car audio and cellular phone safely out of reach of all those nonwhite vultures I see on *Cops* (when I'm watching sport of another kind), who if they didn't make it into professional sports are prowling my streets looking to commit a crime. And the homeless are not camped outside my suburban home, not selling their newspaper on my highway to work, not raiding my garbage can, not living off the taxes I'm no longer paying. Talk radio makes me just do it, at least in those intervals when television isn't gripping me.

Ahh, Our America. A commercial time-out for the dream (on) team. I believe I can fly, I believe I can touch the sky. Lite me up another. Life is good. Don't worry, be happy. I love what you do for me. Enjoy the ride.

As the game fades noisily to black. Welcome to the real terrordome.

Notes

1. KMVP recently took over sports from KTAR, now a 24-hour talk radio format, hiring many of the latter's sports personnel, no doubt, with the blessing of the father figure. KMVP has stations in major sports markets nationwide, the sports talk version of AutoNation, Wayne Huizenga's "blockbuster" new "discount" auto franchise. Huizenga owns the Miami Dolphins (football), the Florida Marlins (baseball), and the Florida Panthers (hockey) teams in three of the four major league professional sports covering the country's third largest television market. Colangelo and Huizenga are to sports perhaps what Turner and Murdoch are to broadcasting. They represent the new entrepreneurship in the rapidly expanding southern/southwestern demographic markets of Arizona and Florida, respectively. They offer to late modernity what Ford once made available to the immigrant *driven* expansion into the Midwest, or Mayer and Selznick to the movie industry, capturing the popular imagination of their times.

2. Cerullo, Ruane, and Chayko (1992) make out a similar line of argument regarding talk radio more generally—namely, that it offers "technological ties that bind," "time efficient ways to enjoy social interaction," a perfect form of community for the times. Similarly, Bolce, DeMaio, and Muzzio (1996) suggest the emergence of a "hyper-" version of "cyberdemocracy": "Talk radio can create instantaneous communities of coexistent interest and passion over continental distances."

References

Bolce, L., DeMaio, G., & Muzzio, D. (1996). Dial-in-democracy: Talk radio and the 1994 election. *Political Science Quarterly 111*(3), 457–481.

Cerullo, K., Ruane, J., & Chayko, M. (1992). Technological ties that bind: Media-generated primary groups. *Communication Research, 19*, 102–129.

Coleman, T. (1996). Black talk. *Emerge, 8*(2), 50–57.

Haag, P. (1996). "50,000 watt sports bar": Talk radio and the ethic of the fan. *South Atlantic Quarterly, 95*(2), 453–470.

Hutchby, I. (1992). The pursuit of controversy: Routine skepticism in talk on "talk radio." *Sociology, 26*(4), 673–694.

McClintock, A. (1995). *Imperial Leather: Race, Gender, and Sexuality in the Colonial Contest.* New York: Routledge.

Messner, M. (1989). Masculinities and atheletic careers. *Gender & Society, 3*, 71–88.

Page, B., & Tannenbaum, J. (1996). Populistic deliberation and talk radio. *Journal of Communication, 46*(2), 33–54.

Roediger, D. (1996). White Looks: Hairy Apes, True Stories, and Limbaugh's Laughs. *Minnesota Review, 47.*

Rusher, W. (1995). The importance of talk radio. *Newspaper Enterprise Association, 3.*

After Reading

Critical Perspective

1. Consider how reading this essay makes you feel and what it makes you think. What specifically about the essay created this impact on you? Be sure to point to particular quotes from the text.

Rhetoric and Argument

2. Describe the particular rhetorical choices Goldberg makes in the introduction to this essay—his use of audience, purpose, ethos, pathos, logos, intertextuality, context, and constraints? Do you find his strategies persuasive? Why or why not? Why do you think Goldberg makes these rhetorical choices?

3. How does Goldberg indicate that talk radio, and more specifically sports talk radio, are influenced by race, class, and gender relations? Why? Offer quotes from his text to back up your views.

4. What is Goldberg's main claim in this essay? How do you know? Where does he offer this assertion in his text? Do you find this claim persuasive? Why or why not?

5. How does Goldberg support this claim? Give examples of the kinds of evidence he furnishes and how this evidence functions in his essay. Do you find any logical fallacies or other problems in his text? If yes, be sure to locate where they are operating.

Analysis

6. Goldberg closes his essay with the ominous statement "As the game fades noisily to black. Welcome to the real terrordome." Write a short argumentative essay in which you address the following questions: What is Goldberg suggesting about the fate of American culture, consumption, and sports talk radio at this point in his essay? Do you agree with him? Why or why not? Point to various cultural examples as well as Internet and library sources to back up your assertions.

Taking Action

Select a popular talk radio show (perhaps a sports-related show). Listen to a number of episodes as well as order transcripts so that you can examine them in detail. Consulting the Internet as well as library sources in addition to your primary texts, write an argument in which answer the following questions: What cultural myths, values, ideals, beliefs, fears, and anxieties is this show responding to or perpetuating? What evidence can you point to in order to support your claim? What does this expose about how radio functions in American culture? How is this similar to as well as different from the ways in which radio has functioned during other historical moments? Share what you learn with your classmates.

AMY BASS

"We Don't Suck at Soccer: The Cultural Imperialism of Sports"

Amy Bass is the director of honors at the College of New Rochelle (in New York) and associate professor of history. She worked as a member of the NBC research team for the Atlanta Olympics in 1996, the Sydney Olympics in 2000, and the Salt Lake Olympic Winter Games in 2002. She has also published numerous books and journal articles, including Not the Triumph but the Struggle: The 1968 Olympics and the Making of the Black Athlete *and* In the Game: Race, Identity, and Sports in the Twentieth Century.

EXERCISING YOUR SKILLS

Before Reading

Bass writes about U.S. cultural imperialism and the role of sports. Sports are increasingly being associated with marketing specific brands. Watch a televised sports event of your own choosing and count how many brand names are featured in some way during the event. Consider the various effects that corporate advertising may be having on sports.

I hate it when people say that the U.S. sucks at soccer, because it ignores the feats of American women. After winning the inaugural Women's World Cup in 1991, the U.S. team kept pushing forward, understanding that they weren't alone out there. After Norway took its turn on top, the U.S. took Olympic gold in Atlanta and backed it up with victory at the 1999 World Cup. The dominance changed hands again, however, in Sydney, where the Americans gracefully sealed for silver, and then watched as Germany took the next world title in 2003. When the grand dames of U.S. soccer arrived in Athens, their mission was clear: win gold, which they did.

Now that's how you compete in an international arena.

During the Athens Olympics, where I worked for NBC, I fielded a call from an American reporter asking how the U.S. baseball team was faring. I let him in on a little secret: Team

USA, defending gold medalists, had not become licensed for these Games: the qualifying team had lost to Mexico, 2–1, in Panama City months earlier, paving the way for Cuba, Australia, and Japan to stand on the Olympic medal dais.

There's a perverse kind of cultural imperialism flying in the faces of Americans right now, as the mythology of American sports crumbles while we party it away. The Atlanta Olympics presented a great moment for U.S. women in terms of their collective effort: team gold in basketball, softball, soccer, and gymnastics. Much was made about this coming-of-age moment for those who had grown up under Title IX. Much was made about how the U.S. was the place to be for girls who liked to sweat, especially soccer players. But perhaps the most important lesson taught by the U.S. women's soccer team was how they understood that while they were first out of the gate, they were not alone, with teams from China, Norway, and Germany on their backs. They had a lot of work to do if they were going to reign supreme, and work they did. The elders—Mia, Julie, Brandi, Joy—ensured a legacy that hopefully makes for a smooth hand-off to the likes of Abby Wambach and Lindsay Tarpley. But elsewhere, such insight seems hard to come by, with an American refusal to comprehend that occasionally bringing a group of professionals to play together no longer works: the Dream Team model needs to be put to death.

The latest example? The World Baseball Classic, which saw the U.S. fall to Mexico once again. Pitching great Roger Clemens, with 341 career wins, had his hat handed to him by Grapefruit Leaguer Oliver Perez. Clemens gave up six hits and two runs. Perez? One hit in three scoreless innings, followed by seven (yes, seven) relievers from Mexico's bullpen who retired 12 straight batters. The score? A familiar 2–1.

So the Americans were out, leaving the final to Japan and Cuba, two teams familiar with one another in international play. Yet the Cubans seem to puzzle American media, despite their success in relatively rare international appearances. I saw them square off for the gold medal in Sydney against a Team USA that was having its last great moment, with Tommy Lasorda helming the ship, the Aussie fans stumbling through the words of "Take Me Out to the Ballgame," and rumors flying throughout the stadium that Castro was in the house. At the WBC, Castro's son was certainly in the house: Antonio Castro Soto del Valle, an orthopedic surgeon, serves as team doctor.

Of course, the fact that the Cuban team even was allowed to play is perhaps the most important part of all of this. While baseball is by far the island nation's most popular sport, the team's WBC status looked to be in peril when the U.S. Treasury Department's Office of Foreign Assets Control tried to impede its participation, citing 45-year-old sanctions that prevent U.S. currency being paid to Cuba. The U.S. State Department then took it a step further, arguing that Cuban spies could accompany the team to the tournament, which could be a threat—wait for it—to homeland security. But with other teams crying foul, and a Cuban promise to give any prize money won to victims of Hurricane Katrina (well done Cuba—not only have you bested most of the world's baseball elite, you're also one up on FEMA), the barricades disappeared, and Cuban fans watched their team on ESPN, because Cuban state television took the signal.

Apparently 45-year-old sanctions don't really apply to ESPN.

That sport is a ripe field for the exploration for such political operations shouldn't be a surprise, but it seems to keep startling us. The shortsightedness of American sports continues to assume that as long as the U.S. maintains the most visible, or at least most profitable, arena of professional sports, it will continue to enjoy global dominance, including in competition. This isn't by any means new: ideas of sports and global dominance have translated into various diplomatic battles since the early days of the Cold War. But the insistence by the United States, particularly in Olympic years, that sport doesn't exist in any kind of official capacity within American nation-state formation has prevented a solid understanding of how sports has played a codified, symbolic, and sanctioned role in constructing hegemonic ideas of democracy. Setting aside the obvious example of the NBA's Dream Team, designed to ensure gold medals in basketball (oh well), America historically has used sport to demonstrate how it operates as a racially sound, harmonious, and egalitarian nation. McCarthy's HUAC used Jackie Robinson to denounce Paul Robeson. The U.S. Information Service sent sports pages to Africa in an attempt to woo newly decolonized countries to "our side." Eisenhower pushed Congress to fund international tours of athletes, making someone like Wilma Rudolph a cultural ambassador, and then created the President's Council on Youth Fitness to ensure American youth were mentally and physically ready to be citizens. Shane McCarthy, the PCYF executive director (who could apparently rhyme as well as create patches for kids to sew on their jackets), urged the country to understand the importance of both, saying in 1956, "Perhaps as we consider the next Olympics, the theme should be not so much 'Win in Rome' as 'Win at Home' for if we succeed in getting our country off its seat and its feet, the victories in the field of international competition will inevitably follow."

Thus, American athletes became an official export, with assumptions that wherever they went, they would be adored. Yet today, as the faces in American professional sports, particularly in terms of increasing numbers of Asian and Latin players in baseball and approximately 25% of the NBA coming from abroad, these strategies need to be shaken, stirred, or tossed out completely. The oft-used example of the so-called World Series is a case in point: much of the rest of the world giggles at the moniker, as if the presence of a few Canadian teams makes it all okay. And why does no one ever seem to care that the ever-white NHL carries a huge non-American roster, and that its phenom, who happens to play in the nation's capital, is a 20-year-old Russian named Alex who doesn't seem to mind when folks mangle his last name?

But while most of the rest of the world still overwhelmingly prefers its own version of football over the American one, it does not preclude them from getting good at other things. Basketball, for example, demonstrates the increasing skill set of the globe while maintaining assumptions of the universal adoration of American superstars. In Athens, I watched the post-Dream Teamers take on Spain, seemingly ignoring the flack they had endured to knock in 12 three-pointers, break 100 points for the first time, and win. I saw Marbury set a U.S. Olympic men's record with 31 points, and Iverson add on 16 of his own. Surrounded by a sea of Spanish red and gold, I sat amid the booing that greeted each American basket, watching all seven feet of Pau Gasol, the Memphis Grizzlies' golden boy, try to rule the court. Only two years before, Gasol became the first European to win the NBA's Rookie of the Year award, and in his native country, he is an absolute rock star, evidenced by the frenzy of the Spanish fans every time he touched the ball. So much for anyone caring about Marbury's record.

Neither Spain nor the United States ended up pleased with their Olympic results in 2004. Unlike their female counterparts, the American men failed to defend their title: Argentina took home gold, Italy silver, and the U.S. settled for bronze. It marked the first time since 1988—or the first time since the creation of the Dream Team—that the men's title went to a nation other than the U.S.

But should that really have been as surprising as it seemed to be? The rest of the world has caught up, if not evidenced by Argentina's gold, then perhaps by the number of votes Yao Ming receives for the All-Star Game, proving that a billion Chinese people really can't be wrong. And while sports such as basketball and baseball are undeniably identified as American, such classification does not automatically translate to success. Further, the rest of the world's fixation on soccer, as well as other things that Americans—men and women—actually do suck at (such as cricket, field hockey, and rugby, not to mention badminton, whose stars adorn postage stamps in countries such as Indonesia) does not mean that they cannot be good at "our" sports. While the presence of cheerleaders (I'm not kidding) at the Winter Games in Torino indicates some sort of continued American influence, most of us who were there recoiled in horror as the dozen or so Italian women in traditional skirt and pom-pom costumes ran out to the center of the Oval Lingotto, attempting to silence the Dutch fans and their brass bands and orange feather boas.

It just seemed so wrong.

So it goes beyond U.S. baseball insisting on calling the World Series a world series. It goes beyond the likes of Clemens being handed a loss by Perez. The United States simply has to stop thinking of sports as its thing. Because when you think about it, are U.S. athletes—even ones like Michael Jordan—really that visible, or is it the Swoosh symbol on their chests that the rest of the world wants a part of? And if that's true, the real winners of this international exchange of athleticism are those in media and marketing, the masters of capital, the real professionals in the realm of professional sports.

After Reading

Critical Perspective

1. What does Bass mean when she says that "There's a perverse kind of cultural imperialism flying in the faces of Americans right now, as the mythology of American sports crumbles while we party it away"? How is she defining the term "cultural imperialism"? What is the "mythology of American sports" to which she refers? Offer textual evidence for your thoughts. Do you agree with her assessment? Why or why not?

Rhetoric and Argument

2. Describe the various rhetorical choices Bass makes in the introduction to this essay—her use of audience, purpose, ethos, pathos, logos, intertextuality, context, and constraints? Do you find this to be a credible strategy? Why or why not? Offer textual evidence to support your thoughts.

3. What is Bass's key assertion in this piece? Do you agree with her view? Why or why not? Provide quotes to back up your perspectives.

4. What sorts of evidence does Bass provide for her main claim? Do you find it persuasive? Why or why not? List the specific kinds of evidence she offers and how each piece of evidence functions in her text.

Analysis

5. Bass ends her essay with the following intriguing statements: "The United States simply has to stop thinking of sports as its thing. Because when you think about it, are U.S. athletes—even ones like Michael Jordan—really that visible, or is it the Swoosh symbol on their chests that the rest of the world wants a part of? And if that's true, the real winners of this international exchange of athleticism are those in media and marketing, the masters of capital, the real professionals in the realm of professional sports." Craft a short argumentative piece in which you take up the following questions: How do you think the American sports community could best address Bass's concerns? Then, consider Bass's own implicit as well as explicit suggestions. Do you agree with her? Why or why not? Point to various cultural examples as well as Internet and library sources to back up your ideas.

Taking Action

As a class, consider how you might transcend the colonizing impulses around American sports and the media. Create a public service announcement—using all of the media resources at your disposal—that argues for increased awareness of this problem. If you are able, be sure to create a voice over and appropriate visuals to accompany this spot. Utilize all of your rhetorical and argumentative skills. When you have completed your ad, consider sharing your announcement with other classes and communities across campus as well as organizing small discussion groups to address the issues you have raised.

Reading Visuals
and Other Media

CHAPTER 7

Analyzing Print Ads and Commercials

INTRODUCTION

Considering Advertising Culture, Images of Diversity, and Representations of Gender

Advertising is everywhere—on the buses we ride to work and school, in our elementary school classrooms, on our movie screens, in our magazines, on our radio and television stations, within our cafeterias, in our sports arenas, across our skies, on our beaches, and often in the bags and sales receipts we receive when we have purchased something at a store. It is so ubiquitous that in a typical day we might not be aware of how often advertising actually impacts our lives. Ads catch our eyes with bright colors, engaging sounds, provocative images, short and purposefully memorable tag lines, and attractive logos—sometimes as overt presences in our lives and sometimes just as background. Across an average day we may be exposed to as many as fifty advertising messages. Likewise, as cultural critic Sut Jhally tells us, advertising is "so attractive to us, so powerful, so seductive" because what it appears to offer are "images of the real sources of human happiness—family life, romance and love, sexuality and pleasure, friendship and sociability, leisure and relaxation, independence and control of life."[1] Ads appeal to many of our desires, anxieties, fears, beliefs, and values (i.e., our desire to be successful people, sexually attractive people, likeable people, respectable people, thoughtful and moral people, as well as intelligent people).

Advertising executives work hard to create needs in us, needs that the products they sell are meant to fill. These needs are often not actually related to the products being sold but instead for needs associated with these more basic human concerns. As a result, it is no surprise that we come to associate certain brands with certain

[1]See Sut Jhally. "Advertising at the Edge of the Apolcalypse." http://www.sutjhally.com/onlinepubs/apocalypse.html, p.6.

human qualities and none of us, including those of us who are cultural critics, are immune. If we eat Skittles we are told that we will taste a "rainbow of fruit flavors," and it should not be lost on us that the people shown in the commercial come from various ethnic, racial, gender, and class backgrounds. If we embrace one rainbow, it seems we are thought to simultaneously embrace another, one more affiliated with Jesse Jackson's "Rainbow Coalition" or "Rainbow" networks for gay, lesbian, bisexual, or transgender people—and the human qualities of trust, justice, equality, and peace—than candies or commercialism. Like you, I find myself watching far too many commercials for Geiko Auto Insurance and laughing as a white rapper performs in front of three African American studio executives. "I have good news," the studio producer tells the blatantly awful singer. The good news is not that this man has gotten a record deal, of course, but that the executive has just saved a lot of money on his auto insurance by switching to Geiko. And, even if he is not featured, immediately when we all see the company's name our minds conjure up the suave and green, animated gecko with the British accent.

We all examine the Got Milk? print ads and we see images of celebrities—people we know, admire, and respect—wearing silly milk moustaches and proclaiming the value of milk for healthy bones, teeth, and internal organs. If we drink milk, we are led to believe, we too can grow up to be strong, beautiful, and successful. We look at television commercials for Nike that sometimes tell us to "Just Do It!" and at other times these commercials play music, show images of athletic bodies (known and unknown), and leave behind only a swoosh. We need not even see the actual name of the company to be certain who is advertising: Nike has become such a well-known brand in American culture. Nike is one company among others—McDonald's, The Body Shop, Ralph Lauren being other examples—that is branding not just sneakers, sweat suits, and socks but a whole way of life, a Nike world in which we can live. Nike can be found everywhere, from the most exclusive boutique stores to the "hood" and everywhere in between.

Overview of Selections: Advertising Culture

In this chapter of *Pop Perspectives: Readings to Critique Contemporary Culture* you will learn a great deal about all kinds of advertising effects and approaches. You will read a number of very interesting essays about advertising as well as examine and analyze a number of compelling visual images in advertising.

The first section is titled "Advertising Culture." This phrase is meant to suggest the cultural world of advertising as well as the ways in which certain views about culture and our roles in it are being sold to us through advertisements.

The chapter commences with an intriguing essay that examines the advertising world according to Kalle Lasn, the founder of AdBusters, an internationally known watchdog group that creates spoof ad campaigns to challenge the role of advertising in our culture. Lasn exposes just how much of our world and how we view ourselves is shaped by products and advertising. Lasn contends that this has become a huge problem—our individual dreams are becoming subject to one dream, the dream sold to us through advertising about what a good life ought to be. Lasn leaves us wondering whether we can continue to be unique individuals in an advertising-saturated culture.

Next is a text by Wayne Dunn, a conservative critic who voices a completely different perspective on advertising for us. In this important essay Dunn argues that while advertising is often criticized for being manipulative, such advertising is critical for many companies, particularly those concerned with health care (e.g., drug companies). Using a logical model for argumentation, Dunn systematically refutes opposition to his views . Dunn challenges the notions that advertising raises product costs, that advertising is only about profits, and that drug companies are unnecessarily greedy and more interested in making money than in curing people.

Then Arthur Asa Berger, one of the most well-known scholars today in the area of advertising in magazines and television, presents some crucial examples as well as tips for us about how to read ads. Berger's first essay analyzes exactly how sexual appeals operate in fashion advertising. He shows the ways in which images and words work together to produce sometimes subtle but often powerful messages. Berger's two other pieces furnish concrete suggestions about how to usefully decode all sorts of rhetorical ploys (in both print ads and television commercials) so that we can become more savvy consumers—and produce better analyses. Berger's three essays are not just examples of cultural criticism in action but essential, practical tools for composing cultural criticisms themselves.

David Ogilvy, among the foremost ad executives as well as theorists and practitioners of advertising, next makes the claim that there is nothing inherently problematic about advertising itself or its cultural impacts. Instead, advertising is a pragmatic tool used to meet a reasonable goal: the selling of products to the appropriate audiences. Seeing ads as having any other purpose, value, or effect (including the role that some cultural critics assert advertising has—of creating detrimental desires in viewers), Ogilvy suggests to us, is to ignore the real and beneficial function of advertising. Ogilvy offers us many visual examples of advertisements, ones he has created. He also reveals some of the problems inherent in political advertising which he argues is an altogether different advertising genre.

The section closes with an influential essay by Naomi Klein, author of the best-selling exposé *No Logo*, in which she characterizes the global links between companies, assembly and manufacturing, labor conditions in sweatshops, and advertising. In this selection Klein traces the history of the idea of branding as a corporate strategy. She does so not just with a researcher's eye but with a journalist's sensibility—she has gone undercover and infiltrated a number of companies to reveal their practices from the inside. Klein reveals to us the larger social and political effects of corporate culture.

Overview of Selections: Images of Diversity

The second section is titled "Images of Diversity." In this section you will consider how ads represent cultural, racial, and ethnic differences.

The first essay is by cultural critic and visual theorist Matthew Reynolds. In this crucial piece Reynolds examines Pepsi's television commercials in detail, expounding the ways in which many of the ads have historically depended upon racist and sexist images, troubling lyrics in popular songs, as well as problematic assumptions about addiction. Reynolds calls upon us to rethink how seemingly benign and entertaining advertising campaigns can in fact send subtle messages that perpetuate the oppression of certain cultural groups over others.

Then Clint C. Wilson and Félix Gutiérrez, well-established critics of race and ethnicity relations in the mainstream media, reveal the history of how ads have represented people of color, particularly African Americans, Latinos/as, Asians, and Native Americans. This history suggests that while advertising has come some way in terms of addressing historically underrepresented groups positively, there is still much work to be done. In order to support their argument, Wilson and Gutiérrez's essay provides some examples of older ad campaigns. The principles that they use to analyze such ads can be important to us in our own cultural criticisms of today's ad campaigns.

The section ends with an essay by Gary R. Hicks, a professor of mass communications who used to work for the mass media industry. Hicks discusses how advertisers have failed to cater to a lucrative market—gay and lesbian readers and viewers. The industry has begun to try to address both heterosexual as well as gay and lesbian communities. Hicks analyzes a series of tactics used in contemporary ads. His essay includes visual images to support his argument. Hicks concludes his piece by asking us questions about whether such ad campaigns really do anything to help gay communities in America or instead further reinforce stereotypical and oppressive images about gay culture.

Overview of Selections: Representations of Gender

The final section of Chapter 7, "Representations of Gender," looks at representations of gender specifically. Considering how masculinity and femininity are constructed through advertisements, the writers in this part suggest, can be a very illuminating project.

The section begins with Carol Moog's famous essay from one of the first books that examined images of women in advertising. Here Moog studies the evolution of the Maidenform bra from the 1950s to the late 1980s and how images of women in advertising have shifted over time. Despite such drastic changes, Moog's text reveals the ways in which some trends have not ended but rather are being addressed in new ways. While Moog's essay was written a few years ago now it remains one of the best examples of cultural criticisms of advertising and gender issues.

Then Jackson Katz, a well-known antisexist, male activist, and the creator of various films on masculinity and the media, shares his thoughts about how the representation of the violent white male is one to which young men in American culture are constantly required to adhere. Katz examines images of violence and masculinity in advertising—the notions about genetically programmed male behavior, the use of military and sports symbolism to create masculine identification to sell products, the images of muscularity and masculinity, as well as equating heroic masculinity with male violence. Throughout his essay Katz encourages all readers—both male and female—to consider the high costs of sexism not only to women but to men as well. Katz maintains that images of men in advertising are reinforcing unrealistic standards for men as well as helping to create and perpetuate gender violence.

Finally, Wanda Coleman, a celebrated poet and fiction writer, writes about masculinity and the role of Joe Camel in American culture. Coleman outlines Joe Camel's connections to African American identity and image as well as the ways in which these representations are sold back to the African American community through the purchase of an unhealthy product, the Camel cigarette. Coleman encourages us to think about how young males are targeted by advertising companies and sold versions of adulthood, masculinity, and community that do not deliver what they promise. If we can be hypervigilant consumers of advertising culture, Coleman indicates, then we can change that culture and its effects.

Chapter 7 ends with a series of contemporary advertisements as well as Ad Analysis exercises. After you read through the chapter's essays, test your skills of critical thinking, reading and writing, rhetorical analysis, and argumentation by examining these ads in detail.

Likewise, as you scan this chapter, begin to consider all of the ad print campaigns and commercials that surround you. Look closely at their rhetorical features—use of color, design, arrangement, rhetorical appeals, font size, and so on. In what ways do you think that they represent the values, desires, anxieties, fears, needs, and ideologies held by people in American culture? In what ways do they fail to address them? Do you believe that these ads are just there to sell and entertain? Do you think that ads cater to our weaknesses and are therefore manipulative? Or, do you believe that some combination of these two possibilities is happening? How are issues of race, class, gender, ethnicity, sexual preference, disability, and age represented in ads? In what ways do ads both reflect the problems of our culture as well as help to produce and perpetuate them? What do you think can—and should—be done about the proliferation of advertising?

ADVERTISING CULTURE

KALLE LASN

"The Cult You're In"

Kalle Lasn founded the anticorporate AdBusters Media Foundation in 1989. For twenty years, he has produced documentaries for PBS and Canada's National Film Board. Along with numerous culture jam ad campaigns, Lasn has written Culture Jam: How to Reverse America's Suicidal Consumer Binge—and Why We Must.

EXERCISING YOUR SKILLS

Before Reading

Kalle Lasn is a well-known cultural critic, who is one of the founders of *AdBusters* magazine and created "culture jamming" campaigns such as "TV Turn-Off Week," "Buy Nothing Day," and "Free Car Day" (http://www.adbusters.com).

This essay describes the power advertising can have in our lives as consumers. Think about the products you purchase and the ads for those products. To what degree do you feel you have control over your purchases? To what extent do you think advertising is dictating what you purchase? Why?

A beeping truck, backing up in the alley, jolts you out of a scary dream—a mad midnight chase through a supermarket, ending with a savage beating at the hands of the Keebler elves. You sit up in a cold sweat, heart slamming in your chest. It was only a nightmare. Slowly, you reintegrate, remembering who and where you are. In your bed, in your little apartment, in the very town you grew up in.

It's a "This Is Your Life" moment—a time for mulling and stock-taking. You are still here. Just a few miles from the place you had your first kiss, got your first job (drive-through window at Wendy's), bought your first car ('73 Ford Torino), went nuts with the Wild Turkey on prom night and pulled that all-nighter at Kinko's, photocopying transcripts to send to the big schools back East.

Those big dreams of youth didn't quite pan out. You didn't get into Harvard, didn't get courted by the Bulls, didn't land a recording contract with EMI (or anyone else), didn't make a million by age twenty-five. And so you scaled down your hopes of embarrassing riches to reasonable expectations of adequate comfort—the modest condo downtown, the Visa card, the Braun shaver, the one good Armani suit.

Even this more modest star proved out of reach. The state college you graduated from left you with a $35,000 debt. The work you found hardly dented it: dreadful eight-to-six days in the circulation department of a bad lifestyle magazine. You learned to swallow hard and just do the job—until the cuts came and the junior people were cleared out with a week's severance pay and sober no-look nods from middle management. You began paying the rent with Visa advances. You got call-display to avoid the collection agency.

There remains only one thing no one has taken away, your only real equity. And you intend to enjoy fully that Fiat rustmaster this weekend. You can't run from your problems, but you may as well drive. Road Trip. Three days to forget it all. Three days of living like an animal (in the best possible sense), alert to sights and sounds and smells: Howard Stern on the morning radio, Slumber Lodge pools along the I-14. "You may find yourself behind the wheel of a large automobile," sings David Byrne from a tape labeled "Road Tunes One." The Fiat is, of course, only large at heart. "You know what FIAT stands for?" Liv said when she first saw it. "Fix It Again, Tony." You knew then that this was a girl you could travel to the ends of the Earth with. Or at least to New York City.

The itinerary is set. You will order clam chowder from the Soup Nazi, line up for standby Letterman tickets and wander around Times Square (Now cleaner! Safer!) with one eye on the Jumbotron. It's a place you've never been, though you live there in your mind. You will jog in Battery Park and sip Guinness at Michael's Pub on Monday night (Woody Allen's night), and you will dance with Liv in the Rainbow Room on her birthday. Ah Liv, who when you first saw her spraying Opium on her wrist at the cosmetics counter reminded you so much of Cindy Crawford—though of late she's put on a few pounds and now looks better when you close your eyes and imagine.

And so you'll drive. You'll fuel up with Ho Ho's and Pez and Evian and magazines and batteries for your Discman, and then you'll bury the pedal under your Converse All-

Stars—like the ones Kurt Cobain died in. Wayfarers on, needle climbing and the unspoken understanding that you and Liv will conduct the conversation entirely in movie catch-phrases.

"Mrs. Nixon would like you to pass the Doritos."

"You just keep thinking, Butch. That's what you're good at."

"It's over, Rock. Nothing on Earth's gonna save you now."

It occurs to you that you can't remember the last time Liv was just Liv and you were just you. You light up a Metro, a designer cigarette so obviously targeted at your demo-graphic . . . which is why you steered clear of them until one day you smoked one to be ironic, and now you can't stop.

You'll come back home in a week. Or maybe you won't. Why should you? What's there to come back *for?* On the other hand, why should you stay?

A long time ago, without even realizing it, just about all of us were recruited into a cult. At some indeterminate moment, maybe when we were feeling particularly adrift or vulner-able, a cult member showed up and made a beautiful presentation. "I believe I have some-thing to ease your pain." She made us feel welcome. We understood she was offering us something to give life meaning. She was wearing Nike sneakers and a Planet Hollywood cap.

Do *you feel* as if you're in a cult? Probably not. The atmosphere is quite un-Moonielike. We're free to roam and recreate. No one seems to be forcing us to do anything we don't want to do. In fact, we feel privileged to be here. The rules don't seem oppressive. But make no mistake: There are rules.

By consensus, cult members speak a kind of corporate Esperanto: words and ideas sucked up from TV and advertising. We wear uniforms—not white robes but, let's say, Tommy Hilfiger jackets or Airwalk sneakers (it depends on our particular subsect). We have been recruited into roles and behavior patterns *we did not consciously choose.*

Quite a few members ended up in the slacker camp. They're bunked in spartan huts on the periphery, well away from the others. There's no mistaking cult slackers for "down-shifters"—those folks who have *voluntarily* cashed out of their high-paying jobs and simplified their lives. Slackers are downshifters by necessity. They live frugally because they are poor. (Underemployed and often overeducated, they may never get out of the rent-and-loan-repayment cycle.)

There's really not much for the slackers to *do* from day to day. They hang out, never asking, never telling, just offering intermittent wry observations. They are postpolitical, postreligious. They don't define themselves by who they vote for or pray to (these things are pretty much prescribed in the cult anyway). They set themselves apart in the only way cult members can: by what they choose to wear and drive and listen to. The only things to which they confidently ascribe value are things other people have already scouted, deemed worthy and embraced.

Cult members aren't really citizens. The notions of citizenship and nationhood make little sense in this world. We're not fathers and mothers and brothers: We're consumers. We care about sneakers, music and Jeeps. The only *Life, Freedom, Wonder* and *Joy* in our lives are the brands on our supermarket shelves.

Are we happy? Not really. Cults promise a kind of boundless contentment—punctuated by moments of bliss—but never quite deliver on that promise. They fill the void, but only with a different kind of void. Disillusionment eventually sets in—or it would if we were allowed to think much about it. Hence the first commandment of a cult: *Thou shall not think*. Free thinking will break the trance and introduce competing perspectives. Which leads to doubt. Which leads to contemplation of the nearest exit.

How did all this happen in the first place? Why have we no memory of it? When were we recruited?

The first solicitations began when we were very young. If you close your eyes and think back, you may remember some of them.

You are four years old, tugging on your mother's sleeve in the supermarket. There are products down here at eye level that she cannot see. Cool products with cartoon faces on them. Toys familiar from Saturday morning television. You want them. She keeps pushing her cart. You cry. She doesn't understand.

You are eight. You have allowance money. You savor the buying experience. A Coke here, a Snickers bar there. Each little fix means not just getting what you want, but *power*. For a few moments *you* are the center of attention. *You* call the shots. People smile and scurry around serving you.

Michael Jordan goes up on your bedroom door. He is your first hero, throwing a glow around the first brand in your life—Nike. You wanna be like Mike.

Other heroes follow. Sometimes they contradict each other. Michael Jackson drinks Pepsi but Michael Jordan drinks Coke. Who is the false prophet? Your friends reinforce the brandhunting. Wearing the same stuff and hearing the same music makes you a fraternity, united in soul and form.

You watch TV. It's your sanctuary. You feel neither loneliness nor solitude here.

You enter the rebel years. You strut the malls, brandishing a Dr Pepper can full of Scotch, which you drink right under the noses of the surveillance guards. One day you act drunk and trick them into "arresting" you—only this time it actually *is* soda in the can. You are immensely pleased with yourself.

You go to college, invest in a Powerbook, ride a Vespa scooter, don Doc Martens. In your town, a new sports complex and performing arts center name themselves after a car manufacturer and a software company. You have moved so far into the consumer maze that you can smell the cheese.

After graduating you begin to make a little money, and it's quite seductive. The more you have, the more you think about it.

You buy a house with three bathrooms. You park your BMW outside the double garage. When you grow depressed you go shopping.

The cult rituals spread themselves evenly over the calendar: Christmas, Super Bowl, Easter, pay-per-view boxing match, summer Olympics, Mother's Day, Father's Day, Thanksgiving, Halloween. Each has its own imperatives—stuff you have to buy, things you have to do.

You're a lifer now. You're locked and loaded. On the go, trying to generate more income to buy more things and then, feeling dissatisfied but not quite sure why, setting your sights on even greater income and more acquisitions. When "consumer confidence is down," spending is "stagnant," the "retail sector" is "hurting" and "stingy consumers are giving stores the blues," you do your bit for the economy. You are a star.

Always, always you have been free to dream. The motivational speakers you watched on late-night TV preached that even the most sorry schleppers can achieve their goals if they visualize daily and stay committed. *Think and grow rich.*

Dreams, by definition, are supposed to be unique and imaginative. Yet the bulk of the population is dreaming the same dream. It's a dream of wealth, power, fame, plenty of sex and exciting recreational opportunities.

What does it mean when a whole culture dreams the same dream?

After Reading

Critical Perspective

1. How does Lasn begin his text? Why do you think he makes this choice, and how does it make you feel? Do you find this to be a persuasive tactic? Why or why not?

Rhetoric and Argument

2. Describe Lasn's rhetorical strategies—his use of audience, purpose, ethos, pathos, logos, intertextuality, context, and constraints. Then describe his particular use of tone and the second person "you." Does he establish a convincing persona for his audience? Where and how? Be sure to point to specific examples from the text to support your thoughts.
3. List all of the product and brand names Lasn uses throughout his essay. Are these effective in making his argument persuasive or not? Explain your views in detail.
4. At what point in Lasn's text does he make a major shift in his approach? How does this shift relate to the main argumentative claim and the structure of Lasn's essay? Give textual examples.
5. What kind of support does Lasn provide for his claims? Do you find this support persuasive? Why or why not? Do you see any flaws in Lasn's logic that undermine his assertions? If yes, how so?

Analysis

6. According to Lasn, what is the difference between a "cult member" and a "citizen"? Write a short argumentative essay in which you address the following questions: What do you think Americans need to do to become more "citizenlike" and less "cultlike?" What specific activities, actions, or events might encourage this? Consult library and Internet sources to flesh out your perspectives.

Taking Action

Get together in a small group. Your task is to create an ad or commercial campaign that encourages consumers to consider the negative impacts (social, ethical, political, environmental, and cultural) of purchasing specific products or services. You can use websites, print ads, video clips, or brochures to accomplish this. Be sure to utilize all of the rhetorical tools at your disposal—including author and producer, context, purpose, structure, constraints, intertextuality, ethos, pathos, and logos, composition, visuals, sound, camera positioning, and cultural narratives, codes, and conventions. Of course, you can spoof an existing ad campaign if this helps you to best get your points across. Be sure to examine relevant library and Internet sources.

Share your ad campaigns with the rest of the class. Be sure to explain the rhetorical choices you made and what you hoped to convey to your audience. Learn from your peers about how successful you were as well as the specific ways in which you can improve the campaign so that it is even more persuasive. Revise the project based on this feedback. Consider making your work accessible to other groups both inside and outside the campus community.

WAYNE DUNN

"Advertising Is Good Medicine"

Wayne Dunn is a former Army officer who is also a freelance writer, activist, and resident of Nashville, Tennessee. Dunn writes about political and cultural events from what he terms an Objectivist perspective. His work has been published in Capitalism Magazine *and* The Tennessean. *Visit his website at http://www.rationalview.com.*

EXERCISING YOUR SKILLS

Before Reading

Dunn examines the role of advertising and the medical profession. In contrast to cultural critics who focus on the negative aspects of advertising, Wayne Dunn contends that some advertising can have positive benefits. Create a list of advertising campaigns—for products, services, or concepts—that you think are valuable for the public and describe why. How do the tactics used in these ads differ from the ones used in other kinds of ads?

Imagine that you spent years of research and millions of investors' dollars developing an idea that could save or prolong hundreds of thousands of lives. You put your product on the market and advertise.

But a few weeks later, various columnists and "talking heads" begin deriding you for it. Advertising, they say, harms consumers by raising the cost of the product they so desperately need (a product which wouldn't exist had you not created it). Soon there's a movement afoot to prevent you from advertising—in the name of "the public good," of course.

Unfair? That's exactly what's currently happening to drug companies.

The main fallacy of the anti-drug-advertising crowd is based on the premise that an individual (or group of individuals, i.e., a company) has a moral obligation to be charitable. Well, if your moral code demands charity, fine. Go invent a new lifesaving drug and simply give it away. No one will stop you. You certainly have the right to be generous with your own goods, but not with your neighbor's—even if he's the CEO of a pharmaceutical corporation.

Another fallacy lies in not recognizing advertising for what it is: a form of speech. If you judge that it's to your self-interest to spend money to promote the product of your mind, so be it. No one should be able to forcibly compel you to act contrary to your own judgment—or to use the power of government to do so.

This is not some complicated medical issue requiring months of exhaustive analysis of the intricate details of how drugs are made; it's a basic issue of individual rights requiring a firm grasp of the concept "freedom." Freedom means that each individual is at liberty to chart his own course in life and reap the effects of his own actions. And that includes individuals who run drug companies and whose job it is to increase their companies' profitability.

At this point, this article could end. One is either for free speech or one is not. One either believes in individual liberties or one does not. But there are a few ancillary falsehoods I will address:

"Advertising raises a product's cost." The expense of advertising actually *lowers* the product's cost, in the long run, just as the expense of electricity and machines used in the product's manufacture results in the finished good being more, not less, affordable. Would a handmade car be less or more expensive than one mass produced, even though the costs associated with operating a modern automobile factory, i.e., the raw materials, utility costs, labor, etc., are reflected in the latter car's price? Obviously, a handmade car, such as the ostentatious Morgan, which one never sees advertised, is far costlier than the typical car that rolls off an assembly line and is advertised heavily.

Certainly the cost of advertising drugs is passed on to the drugs' consumers, just as the cost of advertising cars is passed on to the cars' buyers. But the purpose of advertising is to expand the customer base by informing more people of a product's existence and virtues. The more consumers a company attracts to its goods, the more it sells. The more it sells, the less money it must make per unit sold in order to become profitable. Advertising generally attracts more customers, which might allow the company to charge less in anticipation of making more money through increased volume.

Regardless, there shouldn't be a law that restricts a company from charging anything it wishes, even if it slaps a million-dollar price tag per tiny vial of much needed medicine. If the price proved too prohibitive, the company would go broke waiting on its first sale. Reality would demand the business lower the drug's price to accommodate at least enough consumers to allow it to turn a profit.

"Corporations advertise drugs solely to increase their profits." Absolutely! The fallacy is not in that statement, but in the ethical implications commonly attached to such a statement. It's true that drug companies seek profits. All companies do. That's how they remain in existence. But how do they *earn* profits? By producing goods or providing services that people wish to purchase. If a drug that a company makes had no value, people would eventually stop buying it (or never start).

But it's untrue that prescription drug advertising *solely* benefits the drug companies, even if that's the advertisers' sole purpose. Advertising is a way of making people aware of a product. And this awareness can have a positive impact not only on the company's bottom line, but also, in the case of medicines, on those suffering illness. One who views a commercial and believes the drug advertised there could relieve his ailment may then decide to make a doctor's appointment to obtain a prescription. The doctor, of course, can then make a diagnosis and determine whether the desired drug is appropriate. In fact, those who might otherwise suffer in silence might be spurred, after seeing such an ad, to seek medical attention that results in saving their lives.

"Even some *doctors* think drug advertisements should be banned." So what? No one, no matter how many degrees he has, has a right to restrict someone else's freedom of speech. Perhaps these doctors, due to the government only recently easing restrictions of prescription drug advertising, are disconcerted by the recent influx of patients inquiring about some new pill they saw on TV. Again, so what? If a drug is unsuitable for a patient, then the doctor simply shouldn't prescribe it to him. But it's generally better that a patient investigate a potentially effective drug now than languish until his doctor reads about it weeks or months later in a medical journal.

"Medicine is so expensive because drug companies are so greedy." Wrong. A new drug is so expensive for some of the same reasons that any new invention may be: because its maker is trying to recoup the initial investment, i.e., the cost of years or decades of research and development that led to its creation. If investors—the ones who made the new drug possible in the first place—aren't convinced the company is striving to promote the drug, they're less likely to support the company's future endeavors.

But apart from the above, the fact that the government is so active in the area of medicine actually makes drugs and privately-funded medical research of all natures more expensive to consumers by making it riskier for investors. What "greedy," "money-grubbing" capitalist would want to sink millions of dollars into such a long-term undertaking as developing a new disease-curing drug, when at any moment the government could arbitrarily declare the entire field off-limits or impose some regulation that throws a monkey-wrench into the whole works? Once a drug has been approved for market, companies have learned from experience to get their profits quickly, before some pressure group tries to have the drug yanked off the shelves—or, as has recently been the case, tries to restrict advertising. Therefore, the possibility or reality of government intervention, not corporate "greed," is fundamentally what increases the cost to consumers.

"Drug companies are more concerned with short-term profits than they are with curing diseases." Huh? Talk about a false dichotomy. The absolute surest way for a company to shower itself with short-term (and long-term) profits is to cure a disease! But the idea that corporations tend to be short-ranged *does* contain a modicum of validity only because the government's interloping into every aspect of medicine has made long-range thinking and planning next to impossible. Why attempt to project ten years out when the government might sink your plans next quarter?

"More government programs are needed to help people pay for prescription drugs." The government already undermines market forces and thereby raises the cost of medicine with existing programs such as Medicare and Medicaid. New or expanded programs would only make things worse.

Understand that a drug company is a seller out to make as much money as possible on the drugs it creates while a patient is a buyer who hopes to pay as little as possible for the drugs he needs. Along comes the government as a "disinterested" third party, playing stand-in for the buyer, the consumer. It pays for all (or a significant portion), let's say, of the drugs that participants in the government program require.

Now in this situation the consumer needs medicine but is less concerned with its price than he would be if he were paying out of his own pocket; thus, he has much less interest (if any) in economizing. In fact, he's probably permitted to purchase medicine only from certain providers, regardless of whether a cheaper option is available. Moreover, the seller knows that the buyer isn't as price-conscious as he would be if he, not the government, were picking up the tab. Well, if the buyer isn't worried about getting a good value for his money, you can bet the seller isn't worried about giving him one.

In a free market a seller is constantly under pressure to reduce his prices; he certainly cannot price his goods or services so high that no one can afford them. But when the government guarantees payment, a seller then has every incentive to *increase* his prices, while the buyer has no incentive to get him to decrease them.

"A drug company has a monopoly on any new drug it creates and thus may charge anything it wants." This is a half-truth conjoined with a false premise. The false premise is that such a "monopoly" is immoral and should somehow be prohibited. A creator does and should have patent protection on his creation. Without patenting, a company would never spend time and money developing a drug only to be "rewarded" by everyone else cashing in on its hard work. Each company would wait for someone else to complete the onerous task of researching and testing a drug, and then all would pounce on the formula. Thus, without patent protection, there would be little incentive to invent or create anything new and complex.

The half-truth of the assertion is that drug companies are able to charge anything they want. As previously discussed, in a free market they could charge no more than a profitable number of consumers could pay. The statement does, however, contain a smattering of truth only because of the Welfare State's usurpation of the free market. In our current system, to the degree the government acts as a third party, drug companies are able to charge higher prices than they would under a completely market-driven system. And with the government ever-poised to goose-step into the health care industry at the whim of the latest squealing pressure group or rhetoric-spouting politician, companies understand they must grab as much profits as possible as quickly as possible.

***

Advertising, of prescription drugs or anything else, is a form of free speech that should never be restricted, unless it's fraudulent. And the cost of advertising, which apparently miffs so many, is a pittance compared to the cost stemming from the government's short-circuiting of the free market by asserting itself into the health care system in a thousand ways, both great and small. The right answer is not to ban advertising, but to recognize that every individual has a right to his own life and may set whatever terms he desires upon the creations of his own mind and the products of his own efforts.

After Reading

Critical Perspective

1. What is your general reaction to Dunn's essay? What about the essay leads you to feel this way? Try to point to aspects of the essay that make you react as you do.

Rhetoric and Argument

2. Describe Dunn's rhetoric in this essay—his particular use of audience, purpose, ethos, pathos, logos, intertextuality, context, and constraints. Then characterize his tone. Do you think these choices are likely to persuade readers to his position or not? What suggestions do you have for making his argument more persuasive? Be specific in your thoughts.
3. What is Dunn's main claim in this essay? What argument is he refuting in order to make his own? Provide evidence from the text to support your views.
4. Dunn is careful to map out the logical fallacies inherent in the arguments he is debunking. Where and how does he accomplish this in his essay? Do you think his characterizations of these arguments are fair or not? Provide quotes to back up your points.
5. Dunn's argument moves quickly and is sometimes critical of others' positions. Do you see any logical fallacies at work in Dunn's own argument? If yes, which ones? Give textual support for your assertions.
6. What type of evidence does Dunn utilize to back up his views? Do you think that this evidence is sufficient to support his views? What, if any, counterarguments could be made against his positions?

Analysis

7. Dunn concludes his essay by proposing that advertising is a "form of free speech that should not be restricted." Write a short argumentative essay in which you address the following question: Do you think that all advertising—on television, in magazines and newspapers, on the web, in schools, on the roads, on beaches, in sporting events—should be protected in this way? Why or why not? Supply examples from your own experiences as well as library and Internet sources to back up your views.

Taking Action

Dunn's assertion that advertising should be protected under the First Amendment raises the issue of what rights should be available to the consumer and corporations.

Form two debate teams within your class. One group will make a case that advertising of all kinds should be protected under the right of free speech. The other group will argue that advertising should be regulated and sanctioned in certain ways. Each group should prepare positions ahead of time, drawing on library and Internet sources as well as personal experiences to back up their views. Begin with short position statements from each group. Give each group several five-minute opportunities for rebuttal and for making closing arguments.

After the debate, form the larger class group again. Confer about what people's positions were prior to the debate. Have people's thoughts shifted or changed? What would each of you argue now—the pro view, the con view, or something in between? Consider making your work accessible to other groups both inside and outside the campus community.

ARTHUR ASA BERGER

"Sex as Symbol in Fashion Advertising," "Checklist for Analyzing Print Advertisements," and "A Primer on Analyzing Television Commercials"

Arthur Asa Berger is a famous writer and professor of broadcast and electronic communication arts at San Francisco State University. He has written many articles and book chapters. His books include Cultural Criticism: A Primer of Key Concepts, Media and Communication Research, *and* Ads, Fads, and Consumer Culture. *The selections provided here are meant to contribute additional tools for reading advertisements and commercials as well as act as models for cultural criticism and analysis.*

EXERCISING YOUR SKILLS

Before Reading

Berger's three texts offer tools for reading advertisements and commercials critically. Take a look at several magazines. Try to select ones that target audiences from different class backgrounds, ages, as well as of different genders, races, or ethnicities. Reflect upon some of the ads inside these magazines. Which kinds of ads stand out to you as a viewer and why? How do these ads play on the viewer's anxieties, values, desires, fears, and beliefs?

Now reflect upon the ads one more time. What kind of ethos do these ads construct for the viewer? How is this ethos based on narratives in American culture that focus upon valuing money, luxury, leisure, and other upper-class ideals? Point to specific rhetorical features in the ads to back up your views.

While reading an issue of *Vogue* recently, I noticed that I was, somehow, taken by a number of the advertisements for fashions and cosmetics. Many of these advertisements contained striking photographs and suggestive (and in some cases rather overt) copy. I found myself absorbed by the advertisements. They had a remarkable power over me—to seize my attention and to stimulate, if only for a moment, fantasies of an erotic nature. It was not only the physical characteristics of the models that affected me; it was a kind of gestalt effect. There was the element of graphic design, of color, of light, and a host of other matters that "conspired" to excite me.

"What's going on?" I asked myself. That question led me to consider how magazine advertising works to stimulate desire and sell clothes, cosmetics, and everything else that is connected with beauty (in this case) or any product.

In analyzing an advertisement there are a number of factors that we must consider, such as the ambience, the design, the use of white space, the significant images and symbols, the use of language, the type faces [employed], and the item itself (and its role and function in society). We can also consider how the advertisement attempts to "sell" us and what roles it offers us to imitate, as well as examine how social phenomena might be reflected, indirectly. (Here I'm thinking about such things as alienation, boredom, conformism, generational conflict, and so on.) We can use whatever concepts we have at our command from history, psychology, sociology, anthropology, and any other disciplines to help us "dissect" the advertisement. In applying all of the above it is important to keep one cardinal principle in mind: The creators of any advertisement are trying to generate some kind of an effect or emotional response. So we must start with the effect and work backwards. What is the fantasy? And how is it induced?

Selling Magic

I will answer these questions by examining some of the advertisements in the April 1978 issue of *Vogue* magazine. I've selected advertisements that, for some reason, caught my attention for a moment and that I think are interesting and worth examining closely.

Let me start with a double-page advertisement by Revlon for its Formula 2 cleanser and moisturizer. The left-hand page of the advertisement is devoted to an extreme close-up of a woman's face, but the face is rendered by using quarter-inch squares of various colors. We are, in fact, given an optical illusion. If we squint, or place the magazine fifteen feet away from us, the squares merge together and form a face. But at arm's length, the face is somewhat distorted and out of focus. It is also larger than life in size. From there we move over to the right-hand page, which has a great deal of white space and is formally designed, approximating axial balance. Generally speaking, large amounts of white space and axial balance (and formality) are associated with quality and "class" in most people's mind.

The copy of the ad stresses science and technology as opposed to nature. We find the following suggestive words and phrases in the advertisement:

Revlon Research Group
skincare system
natural electricity
formula
skincare that's simple, scientific
precision tip
beauty technology
hygiene
principle

All of these terms are signifiers for science and technology; we are led to think of scientists in laboratories discovering remarkable things that lead to "the New-Face Hygiene" and "beautiful life for your skin." A smaller photograph on this page shows two medicinal-looking bottles, in which the future-age Formula 2 cleanser and moisturizer are packaged.

Though this is something of a generalization, there seems to be a polar opposition in the public's mind that posits a world divided between culture (and with it science and technology) and nature. Thus the people who created the Revlon advertisement had two possibilities: to stress nature and all that's suggested by it, or to stress culture, in this case, science and technology. They chose the latter course and offered their readers a minicourse in science and technology: *This* principle leads to *those* results.

Ultimately what is being sold here—and what is being sold in most cosmetics ads—is magic, and that is where the large rendering of the woman's face comes in. It is an optical illusion that has two functions: First, it catches our attention because when we look at the face we see that it is really only a huge patchwork of squares. At first glance it seems out of focus and strange. But, if we squint or stare at it, magically it becomes a face, just the same way that Revlon Formula 2's "beauty technology of the future" gives you the gift of "life" (for your skin). Just as the law of closure forces us to complete that which is unfinished, we find ourselves obliged to make sense of the picture, and we visualize the woman's face even more completely than we find it. This act of visualization is what is asked of patrons or purchasers of the product. From the bits and pieces of their old faces they are asked (almost forced) to envision the new faces they will have with Formula 2.

Now that the face is taken care of, let us "finish off" the job (the law of closure once again) and take care of the entire body. For this we can use Benandré, which says it "will do for your body what a facial does for your face." This single-page advertisement has, like the Revlon advertisement, axial balance and a considerable amount of white space. It shows a woman in a glass bathtub bathing herself in "Mediterranean blue" water. A bit of greenery signifies the Mediterranean here. The woman's face is clearly shown, in profile, but her body is not. We see only a diffused figure in blue-green water. Benandré promises that its special form of collagen (a protein contained in the connective tissues and bones, which yields gelatin on boiling) helps the body retain moisture and helps it to restore moisture it loses during the day.

This matter of keeping the skin (and body) moist is interesting. A great deal of cosmetic advertising stresses wetness, moisture, and related concepts, as if the body were in danger of becoming an arid desert, devoid of life, dry, uninteresting, and infertile. These ads suggest that women fear, or should fear, losing their body fluids, which becomes the equivalent of losing their capacity to reproduce. This, in turn, is connected with sexuality and desirability. Anxiety over the body as a kind of wasteland is implicit in appeals in advertisements about retaining and restoring moisture. Dehydration is a metaphor for loss of sexual attractiveness and capacity, that is, desexualization.

Dry skin becomes, then, a sign of a woman who is all dried up and who is not sexually responsive—and who may also be sterile. This is because water is connected, in our psyches, with birth. It is also tied to purity, as in baptismal rites when sin is cleansed from a person. All of this suggests that words and images that picture a body of a woman as being dehydrated and losing water have great resonance.

In *Man and His Symbols*, Carl Jung (1968: 29) writes:

> *Every concept in our conscious mind, in short, has its own psychic associations. While such associations may vary in intensity . . . they are capable of changing the "normal" character of that concept. It may even become something quite different as it drifts below the level of consciousness.*
>
> *These subliminal aspects of everything that happens to us may seem to play very little part in our daily lives. But in dream analysis, where the psychologist is dealing with expressions of the unconscious, they are very relevant, for they are the almost invisible roots of our conscious thoughts. That is why commonplace objects or ideas can assume such powerful psychic significance in a dream.*

If we substitute "advertisements" for "dreams" in the above quotation, we can understand why and how we are affected so profoundly by images and words.

The copy in the Benandré ad is full of purple prose indicating power and luxury. Some of the more interesting words and phrases appear below:

lavished
unique
expensive
luxury
rare oils
prefer
enriching
treat yourself
beneficial
beauty treatment

This product is sold as a kind of indulgence for women. The copy hints at sex ("You'll make the skin of your body as nice to touch as the skin on your face. Just ask the one who touches you most."), which is always a strong selling point for beauty aids. But the pictorial element is connected with symbols of innocence—baptism, cleanliness, and so on. And the towel in the lower right-hand corner of the ad is a chaste white. From a psychoanalytic perspective, there is also something regressive about all this. It is almost as if the woman emerges with the skin of a baby. She also is quite undefined sexually; we are certain we are seeing a woman, but her sexuality has been subdued a great deal, which is in keeping with "class" as we have been taught to think of it.

Next let us move on to some clothes for our moist and soft-skinned beauty: Danskins. The advertisement for Danskins shows three female bodies lying down on a blue-green piece of fabric that may also be water—it is hard to say. What is interesting is the arrangement of the bodies, all horizontal and jammed together. Two of the models are lying with heads on the left and the third is between them with her head to the right side of the picture. Although they touch one another, each seems unaware of any of the others—they all stare off into space in separate directions.

The Danskin ad is extremely simple and formal. It has three elements: a headline, the photograph of the three women, and an element containing six lines of copy, all in capitals. The product advertised is a "freestyle" leotard/swimsuit that comes in various "sensuous styles and colors." The large element of white space contrasts with the crowding in the photograph, a crowding that a Marxist would say reflects a diffuse alienation among the women, who are touching one another but do not seem to be aware of each other. They are all, we must assume, pursuing their private fantasies.

Finally, let us move on to an ad depicting a fully dressed woman in Calvin Klein separates. Here we find a model with her right hand on her hip, her left hand behind her head, and her left knee bent (in the "bashful knee pose") and prominently displayed. The background is gray and there is hardly any text. The shirt the model wears has a plunging neckline, but there is no cleavage showing, and there is a slit in the skirt, which enables her to splay her knee.

We are given little textual information: the designer, Calvin Klein; the store where the outfit can be purchased, I. Magnin; and the fabric manufacturer, the Ideacomo group.

The model has long, curly hair. She has a rather cold look on her face, a look that is commonly seen in high-fashion advertising. And she is posed in a way that emphasizes her arms and legs rather than her breasts and hips. Thus attention is focused on her append-ages, which are sexually undifferentiated. Yet there is something of a sexually alluring quality about this pose, which shows a lot of upper leg. It may have something to do with the tilt of the hips, the twist of the torso, and the neckline. Perhaps the unnaturalness of the pose is important, also.

Breaking the Advertising Code

The codes of simplicity, white space and formality, appear in the Calvin Klein advertise-ment just as they did in all the other advertisements discussed to this point. These "cou-ture" codes are learned by people, who are taught, by advertisers, to associate simplicity, spaciousness, and formal structure with "class." In the same manner, we are taught the "meanings" of various typefaces and kinds of images. Soft focus signifies dream-like states, formal structure or design implies "classic" (whatever that means), and so on. All of these associations are carried around in our heads, so that all the advertiser has to do is "activate" us by striking the appropriate responsive chord. As Tony Schwartz (1974: 24–25) writes in *The Responsive Chord*:

> *The critical task is to design our package of stimuli so that it resonates with information already stored with the individual and thereby induces the desired learning or behavioral effect. Resonance takes place when the stimuli put into our communication evoke meaning in a listener or viewer. That which we put into the communication has no meaning in itself. The meaning of our communication*

*is what a listener or viewer **gets out** of his experience with the communicator's stimulus.*

Culture, and "couture," which is part of culture, is a collection of codes we learn that provide us with meaning in the world. But how, specifically, do these codes work and how do we find meaning in advertisements (as well as other forms of communication)?

In a magazine (or other form of print) advertisement there are two ways that information is communicated—through the text and through pictorial and design elements. We can examine the text to determine what appeals are being pressed forward and what means are used to lead the reader/viewer to desire the product. Anxiety may be provoked. There may be inducements to self-gratifications of varying natures. Snobbery may be invoked. Any number of techniques of persuasion can be used here. And in the pictorial material there is also a "language" that may be employed to generate the desired feelings and fantasies. I have mentioned some of these techniques: design, size, color, grain, focus, and so on. And I have suggested that we learn to associate certain kinds of advertisements with certain kinds of fashions.

Can we take matters a step further? Can we explain how these associations are made and how the various signs and symbols generate the meanings they do? In some cases, yes. To do so we must expand our vocabulary of analysis. I would like to reintroduce some terms from semiology at this point:

> metaphor: relationship by analogy (example: my love is a red rose)
> metonymy: relationship by association (example: rich people and mansions)
> icon: relationship by resemblance (example: photograph of an object)
> index: relationship by implication (example: smoke implies fire)
> symbol: relationship by convention (example: Star of David and Jews)

There is a problem in differentiating between metonymy and symbol that I find hard to solve. Neither are motivated or natural, but relationships by association seem to be stronger than relationships by convention. Anything can be a symbol once people learn to accept it as such. But the association between wealth and large mansions seems quite logical. Wealthy people, people with "class," tend to live in large houses, have a great deal of land and space for themselves, and are powerful. Thus spatiality becomes associated with wealth and class indirectly, through the matter of living space found in large homes.

In metonymy, then, the relationships are stronger than in symbols. One important form of metonymy is synecdoche, in which a part stands for a whole or vice versa. Monoco (1977: 135) in *How to Read a Film* suggests that in film "close shots of marching feet to represent an army" is synecdochic and "falling calendar pages" to indicate the passing of time are metonymic, and that it is through metonymy and synecdoche that Hollywood and films in general are able to communicate with people so quickly and powerfully. Thus, for example, sweat is an index of body heat (or nervous anxiety) that functions metonymically since "associated details invoke an abstract idea."

Magazine advertisements function in much the same way, using whatever devices they can to signify "abstract ideas"—what we call signifields—such as passion, love, romance, and so on. Because these advertisements can use language, they can use metaphor, but more often they also wish to imply or suggest things (fantasies of exotic love, hopes for beauty) through pictorial elements that make use of the devices described above in various combinations.

With these terms we can do more than simply say that signs and symbols work on the basis of associations that people learn and that become codes by which they interpret the world and function in it. For example, let us consider our first advertisement, the one for Revlon's Formula 2 cleanser and moisturizer. Although there are many things going on in this advertisement it seems to me that the most important thing in the ad is the way it forces the reader to turn the optical illusion into a face, which suggests, perhaps subliminally, *magic*. Most cosmetic advertisements involve a belief in magic, but usually the appeals are verbal. In this advertisement, however, we are forced to do a great deal of work that "convinces" us that it is logical to believe in magic. Why not? We've just done something magical. We've seen that magic works, with our own eyes.

I see this process as indexical. The Revlon products promise beauty by magic just the way the square patches hold the promise of a face, once we learn how to see the patches correctly. The implication is that Revlon is magic and it will work for you the way your eyes work to figure out the optical illusion. There may also be an element of suggesting that beauty is an illusion and is attainable by all who can employ the correct magic. The picture of the woman in the ad is indexical, but the bottles are symbolic and rely upon the conventional look of medicinal products for their power. The stylishness of the advertisement, with its use of white space and simplicity, is also symbolic. There is nothing natural or logical about our associating white space and simplicity with "class." It is historical, part of our culture, and something that most of us learn.

In the Revlon advertisement and in all advertisements we find a kind of chain reaction taking place. The verbal and pictorial elements in the advertisement function as signifiers that generate feelings and beliefs or signifieds for those who look at and read the advertisement. These feelings and beliefs (and, we might add, hopes, fantasies, and the like) are based on codes (structured belief systems), which, in turn, operate via metaphor, metonymy, icon, index, and symbols in various combinations. Thus, in order to determine how advertisements and other forms of visual-verbal communication generate meaning, we can move beyond the notion of codes and see how the codes themselves function.

It is a fascinating business taking advertisements apart to see how they function and determining what they reflect about society. It is also a perilous business, for there is always the possibility that we are not examining society's fantasies, or those of the creators of the advertisements, but our own. In *The Strategy of Desire*, Ernest Dichter (1960: 11), one of the founding fathers of motivation research, writes:

> *Human desire is the raw material we are working with. The strategy of desire is the tool of shaping the human factor, the most important aspect of our worldly arsenal. Human progress is a conquest of the animal within us. No conquest is possible without strategy.*

Whether or not advertising and other tools of persuasion are leading us to higher levels of development is questionable. One thing seems quite evident—knowing the strategies used by the people who work at creating and shaping our desire is important, for then we can make more rational decisions and avoid manipulation. The person who is a slave to fashion is often also a slave to his or her own emotions—emotions that can be manipulated by the fashion advertising industry. But escape is possible.

References

Dichter, E. (1960). *The Strategy of Desire.* London: Boardman.
Jung, C. (1968). *Man and His Symbols.* New York: Dell.
Monoco, J. (1977). *How to Read a Film.* New York: Oxford University Press.
Schwartz, T. (1974). *The Responsive Chord.* Garden City, NY: Doubleday.

Checklist for Analyzing Print Advertisements

There is a distinction between commercials, which are broadcast on television, radio, and other electronic media, and advertisements, which are found in the various print media, such as magazines, newspapers, billboards, and posters. (On the Internet, the many static advertisements are, I would suggest, best seen as electronically disseminated print advertisements.) The following checklist focuses on print advertisements:

The Mood

1. What is the general ambience of the advertisement—the mood that is created, the feelings it stimulates?

The Design

2. What is the basic design of the advertisement? Does it use axial balance, or are the fundamental units arranged in an asymmetrical manner?
3. What relationship exists between the pictorial aspects of the advertisement and the copy, or written material?
4. How is spatiality used in the advertisement? Is there lots of white (blank) space, or is the advertisement crowded—full of written and graphic material?
5. Is there a photograph used in the advertisement? If so, what kind of shot is it? What angle is it taken from? What is the lighting like? How is color used?

The Context and Content

6. If there are figures in the advertisement (people, animals), what are they like? Consider factors (to the extent that you can) such as facial expressions, hairstyles and hair color, body shape and body language, clothes, age, sex, race, ethnicity, education, occupation, relationships, and so on.

7. What does the background of the figures suggest? Where is the action taking place, and how does the background relate to this action?
8. What is going on in the advertisement, and what significance does this action have? Assuming that the advertisement represents part of a narrative, what can we conclude about what has led to this particular moment in time? That is, what is the plot?

Signs and Symbols

9. What symbols and signs appear in the advertisement? What role do they play in stimulating positive feelings about or desire for the product or service being advertised?

Language and Typefaces

10. How is language used in the advertisement? What linguistic devices provide information or generate some hoped for emotional response? Does the advertisement use metaphor? Metonomy? Repetition? Alliteration? Comparision and contrast? Sexual innuendo? Definitions?
11. What typefaces are used, and what messages do these typefaces convey?

Themes

12. What are the basic themes in the advertisement? What is the advertisement about? (For example, the plot may involve a man and a woman drinking, and the theme may be jealousy.)
13. What product or service is being advertised? What role does it play in American society and culture?
14. What political, economic, social, and cultural attitudes are reflected in the advertisement—such as alienation, sexism, conformity, anxiety, stereotyped thinking, generational conflict, obsession, elitism, loneliness, and so on?
15. What information do you need to make sense of the advertisement? Does it allude to certain beliefs? Is it a reflection of a certain lifestyle? Does it assume information and knowledge on the part of the person looking at the advertisement?

A Primer on Analyzing Television Commercials

Here I would like to consider some of the more important aspects of television commercials. We must remember that a television commercial is a special kind of work of art—one which is created to persuade, to shape behavior in specific ways. But it still is a work of art and therefore can be analyzed much the same way a film or television program can be understood: in terms of its various components and the role they play in the production.

A. *The Narrative Structure.* What happens in the commercial and what significance do the various actions and events have? How might the actions and events affect viewers and what meaning do they have for people? In this area we focus on the story-line of the commercial and its symbolic significance.

B. *Dialogue and Language.* What do the characters say to one another and, in some cases, what are they saying to us? What devices do they use to gain our attention or affection and to persuade us? What rhetorical techniques, such as alliteration or metaphor or metonymy, are used? What kind of language is used? What use is made of phenomena such as humor, comparisons, associations, exaggeration, praise, and logic?

C. *Actors and Actresses.* Sometimes we forget that when we watch commercials we are seeing actors and actresses plying their trade. But rather than trying to convince us they are Hamlet or Ophelia, they try to convince us they are housewives who love this or that product or rugged he-men who love this or that brand of light beer. Do we feel attracted to them and empathize with them? What kinds of symbolic figures are used as characters in the commercial? What use do the performers make of facial expression, body language and their voices? What about the clothes they wear? How old are they, and what significance do their ages have? What's interesting about the setting in which they are found?

D. *Technical Matters: Lighting, Color, Editing and Music.* Here we concern ourselves with how lighting, cutting and shot selection impact upon viewers. For instance, close-ups lead to a different feeling about things than longshots and shots from below convey different attitudes toward power than shots from above. Does the commercial have many quick cuts in it? If so, what impact does this have? How are things lighted and what kind of use is made of color? All of these matters are kinds of "messages" and must be included in any analysis of a television commercial.

E. *Sound and Music.* We are profoundly affected by sound and music, which seem to have the power to work directly on our psyches. What use is made of sound effects? Is there music used? If so, what kind and for what purposes? How does it affect us?

F. *Signs, Symbols and Intertextual Devices.* Signs and symbols are phenomena which represent other things: a cross can represent Christianity, the sacred, religion, and so on. Intertextuality refers to the process by which we interpret one text in terms of another. Thus parody, for example, is based upon ridiculing a text (which must be known in order for the parody to work). The associative power of texts can be used to suggest things or ideas connected with the original text. This means that commercials can take advantage of what people already know—about history, literature, the arts, and popular culture—in getting their messages across.

In short, every aspect of a commercial—from the typefaces used in captioning to the hairstyles of the performers—can be considered as potentially important. Commercials are complex and "rich" works of art that demand a great deal of attention if one is to discover the mechanisms by which they achieve their aims.

After Reading

Critical Perspective

1. Now that you have read through all three of Berger's texts, compose a short free-write. Describe the particular issues about advertising that Berger raises that surprise or interest you the most. Point to where this occurs in his writing. Then explain your reactions.

Rhetoric and Argument

2. Reflect on Berger's use of audience, purpose, ethos, pathos, logos, intertextuality, context, and constraints throughout his own essays. Do you think he employs rhetorical tactics successfully? Why or why not? Be sure to present evidence for your perspectives.
3. Berger supplies a specific claim about how ads for beauty care products operate in "Sex as Symbol in Fashion Advertising." What is this claim? Where does he make it? Do you agree with him? Why or why not? Draw from your own experiences inspecting magazines, particularly those aimed at women, to back up your thoughts.
4. What kind of evidence does Berger use in "Sex as Symbol in Fashion Advertising" to support his claim? Do you think that he might have used other kinds of evidence to make his argument more convincing? If yes, what kinds?
5. Are there any logical fallacies or assumptions in any of Berger's texts that you find less than persuasive? If yes, where do they appear? Why do you feel this way? What counterarguments might you make to dismantle his assertions?
6. Berger originally wrote about ads that appeared in women's magazines in the late 1970s. Do you think ads for women's beauty products have changed since then? Look at a series of ads from the late 1970s in women's magazines and compare them to contemporary ads. Are there different kinds of techniques being used to persuade women to be consumers? If yes, what are they and how do they work? Be sure to point to specific examples to back up your thoughts.

Analysis

7. Reexamine all of Berger's texts. Write a short argumentative essay in which you consider the following questions: Why does Berger suggest that female viewers of these ads are drawn to be consumers of the products advertised? Do ads promoting male beauty products such as men's aftershave operate in similar ways? How yes and how no? Be sure to scrutinize the different kinds of techniques that may be operating in advertisements for men's cologne, deodorant, or hair care products. When these ads are geared toward women who might purchase this product for a male, how do the rhetorical tactics of these ads differ? Why do you think that this might be the case? Consult library and Internet sources to support your perspectives.

Taking Action

Take a look at Berger's proposals for how to "read" the rhetoric of print advertisements and television commercials. Gather several issues of one of your favorite magazines. Apply Berger's tools for analysis to several ads that appear in this magazine. Record all of your thoughts and impressions.

In preparation for large class discussion, bring your chosen ads to class and jot down informal responses to the following questions: What did you learn about how advertisers view you, a person who reads this magazine regularly, from this exercise? Do you perceive yourself in those terms? How yes, and how no? Be sure to point to the specific rhetorical features of the ads that make you respond this way. Consult library and Internet sources if helpful.

Ad Analysis

Examine several ads from popular magazines that you would not typically read. As you would with any rhetorical analysis, write about the setting that is depicted in each of the ads, the colors used, the arrangement of the images, the audience to which the ads appeal, the multiple purposes of the ads, and the specific rhetorical appeals made to ethos, pathos, and logos. Also consider the implicit as well as explicit claims being offered by the ads, the evidence presented, and the warrants utilized.

Now contemplate the following more specifically: How exactly do they represent issues of sexuality and gender? What stereotypes do these images depend upon and why? What stereotypes do these images challenge and how? What claims of cultural criticism would you propose about these ads? What support could you use to back up your thoughts?

DAVID OGILVY

"What's Wrong with Advertising?"

David Ogilvy is considered one of the founders of contemporary advertising theory and practice. He has written many books and articles on the subject including Confessions of an Advertising Man, Blood, Brains & Beer, *and* Ogilvy on Advertising. *He also founded his own advertising agency and produced many well-known ad and commercial campaigns.*

EXERCISING YOUR SKILLS

Before Reading

As an advertising theorist, Ogilvy's essay offers a middle-of-the-road, pragmatic position on advertising—advertising does not force people to purchase products but it is not an altogether innocent force in our lives either. He states, "My view is that advertising is no more and no less than a reasonably efficient way to sell." Scrutinize a specific ad campaign designed to sell a particular product. Reflect upon this campaign in light of Ogilvy's perspective. What do Ogilvy's views allow you to say about these ads? What do they fail to address?

In my *Confessions* I quoted the classic denunciations of advertising by Arnold Toynbee, John Kenneth Galbraith and a galaxy or earlier economists, and wheeled up Franklin Roosevelt and Winston Churchill as witnesses for the defense.

Twenty years later the dons are still tilting at their old windmill. Thus a professor at the New School of Social Research in New York teaches his students that "advertising is a profoundly subversive force in American life. It is intellectual and moral pollution. It trivializes, manipulates, is insincere and vulgarizes. It is undermining our faith in our nation and in ourselves."

Holy smoke, is *that* what I do for a living?

Some of the defenders of advertising are equally guilty of overstating their case. Said Leo Burnett, the great Chicago advertising man; "Advertising is not the noblest creation of man's mind, as so many of its advocates would like the public to think. It does not, single-handedly, sustain the whole structure of capitalism and democracy and the Free World. It is just as nonsensical to suggest that we are superhuman as to accept the indictment that we are subhuman. We are merely human, trying to do a necessary human job with dignity, with decency and with competence."

My view is that advertising is no more and no less than a reasonably efficient way to sell. Procter & Gamble spends more than $600,000,000 a year on advertising. Howard Morgens, their former president, is quoted as saying, "We believe that advertising is the most effective and efficient way to sell to the consumer. If we should ever find better methods of selling our type of products to the consumer, we'll leave advertising and turn to these other methods."

Few of us ad men lie awake nights feeling guilty about the way we earn our living. We don't feel "subversive" when we write advertisements for toothpaste. If we do it well, children may not have to go to the dentist so often.

I did not feel "evil" when I wrote advertisements for Puerto Rico. They helped attract industry and tourists to a country which had been living on the edge of starvation for 400 years.

I do not think, that I am "trivializing" when I write advertisements for the World Wildlife Fund.

My children were grateful when I wrote an advertisement which recovered their dog Teddy from dognappers.

Nobody suggests that the printing press is evil because it is used to print pornography. It is also used to print the Bible. Advertising is only evil when it advertises evil things. Nobody I know in advertising would advertise a brothel, and some refuse to advertise booze or cigarettes.

Left-wing economists, ever eager to snatch the scourge from the hand of God, hold that advertising tempts people to squander money on things they don't need. Who are these elitists to decide what you need? Do you *need* a dishwasher? Do you *need* deodorant? Do

Pablo Casals is coming home
– to Puerto Rico

THIS SIMPLE ROOM is in his mother's home at Mayaguez. The first concert Casals ever gave in Puerto Rico was from the balcony of this house last year—just beyond that fanlight.

While his mother's kinsmen listened from the street, Casals played her lullaby, smoked his pipe and wept.

The back of that armchair bears an inscription in Casals' own handwriting. "Este es mi sillón." This is my rocking chair.

Here are gentle thoughts from the world's greatest cellist—on Puerto Rico, the sea and himself:

"The first time I was aware that I was alive, I heard the sound of the sea. Before, I would have said that the most beautiful sea was the one I had in front of my Spanish house. But now I must confess that the sea I am looking at this moment is even more beautiful."

Of his plans for the future, Pablo Casals had this to say:

"The natural thing that occurs to me, is to come back to Puerto Rico and to do for this country everything within my power. I will be back for the festival I have planned for this coming Spring."

PUERTO RICO'S GREAT NEW MUSIC FESTIVAL IN SAN JUAN

The Casals Festival in San Juan opens on April 22nd and will continue through May 8th. Pablo Casals will conduct or perform at each of twelve concerts.

The Festival Orchestra brings together fifty-four of the world's most talented musicians. Principal performers include: Mieczyslaw Horszowski, Eugene Istomin, Milton Katims,

Jesus Maria Sanromá, Alexander Schneider, Rudolf Serkin, Gérard Souzay, Maria Stader, Isaac Stern, Joseph Szigeti.

Two chamber music concerts will feature the Budapest String Quartet.

For further details, write Festival Casals, P. O. Box 2672, San Juan, Puerto Rico; or to 15 West 44th Street, New York 17, N. Y.

© 1957 Commonwealth of Puerto Rico, 579 Fifth Avenue, New York 17, N. Y.

Living room of the house where Casals' mother was born—in Mayaguez, Puerto Rico's third largest city. Photograph by Elliott Erwitt.

LOST DOG

Our dog Teddy lost
on 84th street
(Manhattan)

looks like Lassie

Telephone LE5-1053

Reward $100.00

My children were grateful when I wrote this advertisement. It recovered their dog Teddy from dognappers.

---

you *need* a trip to Rome? I feel no qualms of conscience about persuading you that you do. What the Calvinistic dons don't seem to know is that buying things can be one of life's more innocent pleasures, whether you need them or not. Remember your euphoria when you bought your first car? Most people enjoy window-shopping the ads, whether for bargains or for luxuries. For 40 years I shopped the ads for country houses, and finally saved up enough money to buy one.

It is not unknown for an advertisement in a newspaper to be read by more people than any news item. When all the New York newspapers went on strike for several weeks in 1963, research showed that it was the advertisements which readers missed most.

If advertising were abolished, what would be done with the money? Would it be spent on public works? Or distributed to stock-holders in the form of extra dividends? Or given to the media to compensate them for the loss of their largest source of revenue? Perhaps it could be used to reduce prices to the consumer—*by about 3 per cent.**

---

*Automobile manufacturers spend 1 per cent of their revenue on advertising. Appliance manufacturers 2 per cent. Soft drinks 4 per cent. Food manufacturers and brewers 5 per cent.

Is Advertising a Pack of Lies?

Introducing me at an Asian Advertising Congress in New Delhi the other day, the Vice-President and former Chief Justice of India said that I had "mastered what Stephen Leacock called the art of arresting the human intelligence long enough to get money from it."

If there are still any natural-born liars in advertising, we are under control. Every advertisement we write is scrutinized by lawyers, by the National Association of Broadcasters and other such bodies. The Better Business Bureau and the National Advertising Review Board (in Britain, the Advertising Standards Authority) review suspected violations of the various codes, and the Federal Trade Commission stands ready to prosecute us for deception. *Caveat emptor* has given way to *caveat vendor*.

But how odd that the Commission does not monitor the advertising put out by departments of the U.S. Government. Writes Milton Friedman, "Anyone who has bought government bonds over the past decade has been taken to the cleaners. The amount he received on maturity would buy less in goods and services than the amount he paid for the bond, and he has to pay taxes on the mislabeled 'interest.' Yet the Treasury continues to advertise the bonds as "building personal security," and a "gift that keeps on growing."[†]

"The Dirge of Our Times"

While very little advertising can be convicted of crimes against humanity, exposure to 30,000 TV commercials every year—the average dosage in American homes—suggests that Wilfrid Sheed had a point when he wrote that "the sound of selling is the dirge of our times." When I lived in New York, I did not notice it, either because I was too busy to watch for more than half an hour a day (Walter Cronkite), or because I was corrupted by familiarity. But when I went to live in Europe, I grew accustomed to smaller doses of advertising. Today, when I return to the United States, I am enraged by the barrage to which I am subjected. And this does not apply only to television. On Sundays, the *New York Times* often carries 350 pages of advertisements, and some of the radio stations devote 40 minutes in every hour to commercials. I don't know how all this clutter can ever be brought under control; the profit motive is too strong in those who own the media.

In the average American home, the TV is turned on, if not watched, for five hours a day, which adds up to 25 years in the average life. But don't blame the *commercials* for this addiction.

Manipulation?

You may have heard it said that advertising is "manipulation." I know of only two examples, and neither of them actually happened. In 1957 a market researcher called James Vicary hypothesized that it might be possible to flash commands on television screens so

[†]*Free to Choose*, Harcourt Brace, 1980.

HOW DARE THEY!

If you see an advertisement in the press, in print, on posters or a cinema commercial which makes you angry, write to us at the address below. (TV and radio commercials are dealt with by the I.B.A.)

The Advertising Standards Authority.
If an advertisement is wrong, we're here to put it right.

ASA Ltd, Brook House, Torrington Place, London WC1E 7HN.

The Advertising Standards Authority is the watchdog on British advertising.

fast that the viewer would not be conscious of seeing them, but his *unconscious* would see them—and obey them. He called this gimmick "subliminal" advertising, but he never even got around to testing it, and no advertiser has ever used it. Unfortunately word of his hypothesis found its way into the public prints, and provided grist for the mills of the anti-advertising brigade. The British Institute of Practitioners in Advertising solemnly banned the use of subliminal advertising—which did not exist.

My only other example of manipulation will make you shudder. I myself once came near to doing something so diabolical that I hesitate to confess it even now, 30 years later. Suspecting that *hypnotism* might be an element in successful advertising, I engaged a professional hypnotist to make a commercial. When I saw it in the projection room, it was so powerful that I had visions of millions of suggestible consumers getting up from their armchairs and rushing like zombies through the traffic on their way to buy the product at the nearest store. Had I invented the *ultimate* advertisement? I burned it, and never told my client how close I had come to landing him in a national scandal.

One way and another, the odds against your being manipulated by advertising are now very long indeed. Even if I wanted to manipulate you, I wouldn't know how to circumvent the legal regulations.

Hold your horses—I almost forgot. There is one category of advertising which is totally uncontrolled and flagrantly dishonest: the television commercials for candidates in Presidential elections.

Governer Dewey, a *scientific* demagogue.

Political Chicanery

While statesmen in England, France and Persia have sometimes consulted me, I have never taken political parties as clients of Ogilvy & Mather. First, because they would preoccupy the best brains of the agency, to the detriment of its permanent clients. Second, because they are bad credit risks. Third, because it would be unfair to those people in the agency who pray for the victory of the opposing party. And finally, because it would be difficult to avoid the chicanery which is endemic in all political campaigns.

The first politician to use television was Governor Dewey in his 1950 campaign for the governorship of New York. On one program, Happy Felton, the entertainer, interviewed passers-by under the marquee of the Astor Hotel on 7th Avenue. They would say what

The bally-hoo of American politics. Should American political advertising have to pass the same scrutiny as commercial advertising?

interested them in the campaign, and ask questions of the Governor. Dewey watched them on a monitor in the studio, and answered their questions. The day before, his staff had carefully *selected* the passers-by. They had *told* them what they were interested in, and rehearsed their questions. On the last day of the campaign, Dewey was on television from 6 am to midnight. People could telephone the studio. Four women on camera answered the calls and passed along the questions for Dewey to answer. A member of his staff was in a phone booth at the corner drug-store with a pile of nickels.

Dewey, the ex-District Attorney, the battler against corruption, the Governor of the State, thought of himself as an honorable man. It never occurred to him that he was involved in deception. I doubt that it would occur to anyone, honorable or dishonorable, to pull such a play today, [many] years later. Times change.

Dewey was a *scientific* demagogue. Before speaking on major issues, he used research to find out which policies had the widest popular support and then put them forward as if he believed in them.

In his book *The Duping of the American Voter** my colleague Robert Spero analyzed the commercials used by Kennedy, Johnson, Nixon, Ford and Carter. He concluded that they were "the most deceptive, misleading, unfair and untruthful of all advertising . . . the sky is the limit with regard to what can be said, what can be promised, what accusations can be made, what lies can be told."

The nine Federal agencies which regulate advertising for products have no say in political advertising. The broadcasting networks, which turn down half the commercials for products submitted to them because they violate their codes, do not apply any code whatever to political commercials. Why not? Because political advertising is considered "protected speech" under the First Amendment of the U.S. Constitution. The networks are obliged to broadcast every political commercial submitted to them, however dishonest.

In 1964, Johnson's commercials disparaged Senator Goldwater with a cynical dishon-esty which would never be tolerated in commercials for toothpaste. They gave voters to understand that Goldwater was an irresponsible, trigger-happy ogre who would start nuclear wars at the drop of a hat. Johnson was presented as a dove of peace.

What had happened was this. Goldwater, one of the most decent men in public life, had been asked by an interviewer to differentiate between the *reliability* and the *accuracy* of

*The Duping of the American Voter. Copyright © 1980 by Robert Spero, Harper & Row, NY.

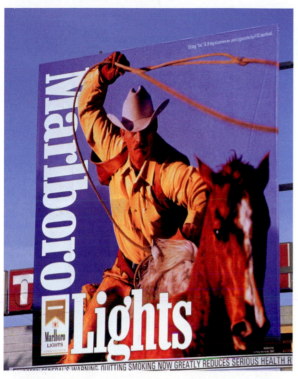

Here are two billboards—one advertising Marlboro Lights cigarettes and the other offering a cultural criticism of cigarette smoking. Characterize the argumentative claims and warrants or assumptions operating in both texts. Describe their visual features (composition and layout, written text, cultural narratives, codes and conventions, as well as other visual elements such as patterns, colors, arrangement, and harmony). Then, determine how their other rhetorical tactics are operating (audience, purpose, ethos, pathos, logos, intertextuality, context, and constraints).

- What argumentative claims or claims of cultural criticism would you make about each of these billboards?
- What particular evidence could you point to in order to substantiate your views?

Take a look at these texts—one advertising Armani Code perfume and the other providing a political commentary from the Guerrilla Girls, a group of anonymous women who seek to "expose sexism and racism in politics, the art world, film, and the culture at large" (see http://www.guerrillagirls.com).

- What argumentative claims, warrants, or assumptions does each text makes about femininity and women's roles in American culture? How does each text support these assertions?
- How does the Guerrilla Girls image offer a cultural criticism of the Armani ad? Point to the specific visual and other rhetorical features that back up your ideas.

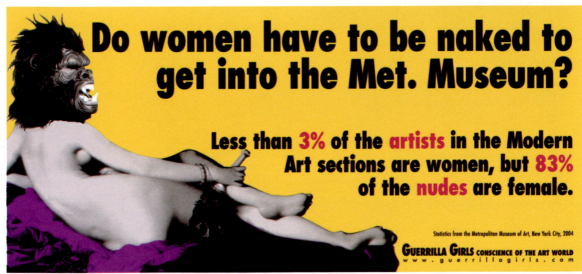

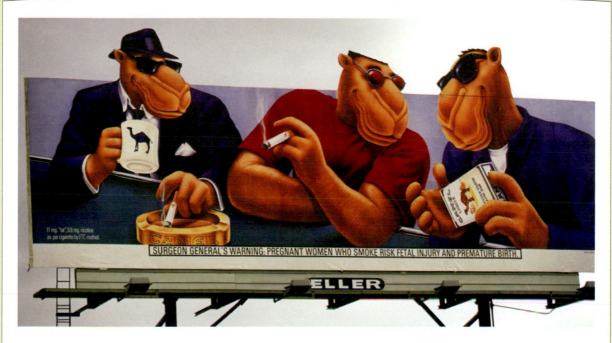

Many advertising campaigns, even those not aimed at children as their primary audience, utilize cartoon images to sell their products. Consider a billboard for Camel cigarettes alongside an AdBusters spoof featuring Joe Chemo.

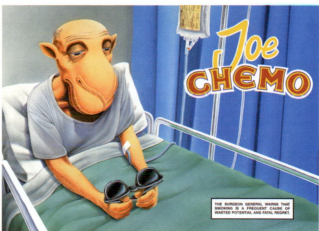

- What cultural narratives about "coolness" or masculinity does this ad present to boys and men?
- How does the spoof ad's visual (composition and layout, written text, cultural narratives, codes and conventions, and as other visual elements such as patterns, colors, arrangement, and harmony) and other rhetorical features (audience, purpose, ethos, pathos, logos, intertextuality, context, and constraints) undermine the original ad's argument?
- Do you think that such a strategy is persuasive? Offer examples from both texts as evidence.

Consider the two billboards on this page.

- What particular argumentative claims do these texts advance about sports, race, ethnicity, class status, and disability?
- What warrants or assumptions as well as support do they each use? What visual and other rhetorical features are at work here?
- Do you find these techniques effective? Why or why not?

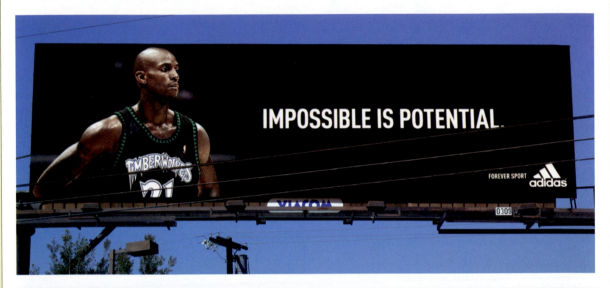

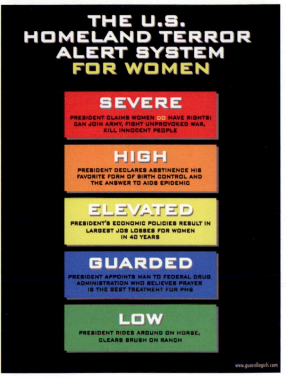

Consider these two texts—one advertising Cover Girl makeup and the other offering a cultural criticism titled "The Women's Homeland Security System."

- What argumentative claims are they each advancing? What warrants or assumptions to they depend upon? What evidence do they furnish?

- How do these two texts employ visual (composition and layout, written text, cultural narratives, codes and conventions, as well as other visual elements such as patterns, colors, arrangement, and harmony) and other rhetorical strategies (audience, purpose, ethos, pathos, logos, intertextuality, context, and constraints)?

- What claims of cultural criticism might you make about these two texts? Provide examples from both texts to back up your views.

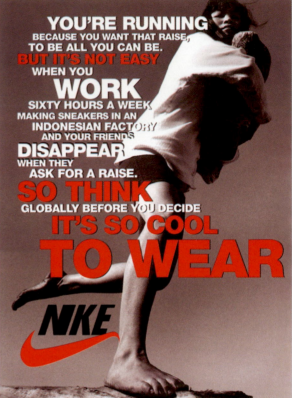

Most advertisements foreground their products' most positive aspects. However, sometimes the production of these goods can be a far less positive experience—including poor pay and hard working conditions for those who make those products.

Look at a Nike billboard alongside a Nike spoof from an AdBusters spoof of Nike.

- Consider the visual and other rhetorical features of the Nike ad. What notions about athleticism, strength, femininity, sports, and class status does the ad depend upon?
- Describe how the spoof utilizes tactics used by the original ad in order to make an altogether different argument about Nike and its products. What visual and other rhetorical strategies does the spoof use?

Think about drugstores such as CVS and Walgreens aside a public service ad.

- What claims of cultural criticism might you make about how drugstores operate as cultural spaces? What do you notice about how they are organized or how their various products are packaged and featured?

- What claims of cultural criticism might you make about how anti-drug campaigns function in American culture? What specific rhetorical features do they rely upon?

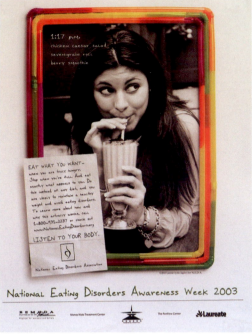

Here are two texts—one advertising Sisley and the other offering a public service announcement about eating disorders.

- What are the argumentative claims and the warrants or assumptions contained within both texts?
- Compare and contrast their visual features. How do they utilize composition and layout, written text, cultural narratives, codes and conventions, and other visual elements such as patterns, colors, arrangement, and harmony?
- What might the juxtaposition of these texts suggest about cultural views surrounding eating and femininity? What argumentative claims might you make about these texts? Give examples from both texts to back up your views.

In 1964, Barry Goldwater's presidential campaign was effectively scuppered by unscrupulous commercials put out by his opponent, Lyndon Johnson.

guided missiles. He had replied that they were accurate enough "to lob one into the men's room at the Kremlin." And he had told another interviewer that it would *be possible* to destroy the forests in North Vietnam by using low-yield atomic weapons. These were no more than theoretical answers to speculative questions. Goldwater did not *recommend* the use of atomic weapons, and Johnson knew this perfectly well.

Nixon's campaigns against Hubert Humphrey and George McGovern were less dishonest, but they too violated the network code for product advertising.

Jimmy Carter's commercials pictured him as an innocent newcomer to politics, with no politics, with no political organization—a poor farmer with no money. Nothing could have been further from the truth, but the voting public swallowed it. Gerald Ford, his Republican opponent, used commercials which were relatively honest—and lost the election.

The Kennedys and the Rockefellers have proved that it helps a politician to be *rich*. In his campaign for election to a second term as Democratic Governor of West Virginia, Jay Rockefeller spent $11,000,000 of his own money and defeated his Republican opponent, who spent only $800,000. Rockefeller's commercials were unusually statesmanlike, and a survey found that the people of West Virginia were not shocked by his expenditure. Even his uncle Nelson Rockefeller had not spent so much in his re-election campaign for Governor of New York.

The "down-home" image of Jimmy Carter's campaign belied the reality—a highly professional, and costly, publicity machine.

In a period when television commercials are often the decisive factor in deciding who shall be the next President of the United States, dishonest advertising is as evil as stuffing the ballot box. Perhaps the advertising people who have allowed their talents to be prostituted for this villainy are too naive to understand the complexity of the issues.

The United States is almost the only country which allows political candidates to *buy* commercial time. In England, France and other democracies, the networks allot free time to serious discussion of the issues.

Could political commercials be banned in the United States? Not without violating the U.S. Constitution. Could they be regulated, like every other kind of advertising? That too would be illegal.

Can you imagine Abraham Lincoln hiring an agency to produce 30-second commercials about slavery?

Down with Billboards

Highways with billboards have three times as many accidents as highways without billboards. President Eisenhower said, "I am against those billboards that mar our scenery, but I don't know what I can do about it." In California, Governor Pat Brown said, "When a man throws an empty cigarette package from an automobile, he is liable to a fine of $50. When a man throws a billboard across a view, he is richly rewarded."

When President Johnson sent the Highway Beautification Bill to Congress, the head of one billboard company claimed that "There are times when most people would rather look at posters than scenery."

Bob Moses, the illustrious Parks Commissioner of New York State, said that "effrontery and impudence can go no further. The time for compromise with these stubborn and ruthless people is over." But the majority of legislators are still ready to compromise with them. Here is how a State Senator explains it:

> The billboard lobby shrewdly puts many legislators in its debt by giving them free space during election time. The lobby is savage against the legislator who dares oppose it by favoring anti-billboard laws. It subsidizes his opposition, foments political trouble in his home district, donates billboards to his opponents and sends agents to spread rumours among his constituents.

Says the *New York Times*, "the forces of uglification are rampant. The Illinois Democrat and the Florida Republican are united in their determination to protect the financial welfare of the billboard industry at the expense of millions of ordinary tourists who would like to see some scenery as they drive."

The Highway Beautification Act actually states that it is the purpose of Congress to *promote* outdoor advertising. Some departments of the Federal Government are *users* of billboards. The Internal Revenue Service once accepted the free gift of 4,000 empty billboards and used them to urge taxpayers to make honest returns.

One day Monty Spaght, then President of Shell, asked me, "We get a lot of letters protesting against our use of billboards. Do we *need* billboards?" I replied, "If you give up billboards, you can still use newspapers and magazines and radio and television. That ought to be enough." Shell gave up billboards.

Billboards represent less than 2 per cent of total advertising in the United States. I cannot believe that the free-enterprise system would be irreparably damaged if they were abolished. Who is *in favor* of them? Only the people who make money out of them. What kind of people are they? When President Johnson sent the Highway Beautification Bill to Congress, the head of one billboard company protested that Johnson had "taken a stand in favor of an abstract concept—*beauty*. Some people like scenery and are interested in it. Others can take it or leave it. *There are times when most people would rather look at posters than scenery!*"

The Roadside Business Association has said, "We do not believe that everyone is for beauty in all things."

On a Sunday morning in 1958, vigilantes sawed down seven billboards along a highway in New Mexico. Citizens of surrounding areas expressed support for them. One telephone call complained that the vigilantes had not cut down *enough* billboards, and another that they had frustrated the plan of a large group of citizens who had scheduled a mass burning of billboards for later in the month. The vigilantes were never arrested.

In 1961 the Quebec government sent hundreds of men with axes to chop down billboards. In 1963 the head of the New York State Thruway Authority knocked down 53 billboards in a dawn raid; he was sick of legal bickering. But in June 1982, a judge in Oregon overturned an ordinance that required the removal of billboards on the ground that it was *a denial of free speech*. The battle goes on.

Can Advertising Sell Bad Products?

It is often charged that advertising can persuade people to buy inferior products. So it can—*once*. But the consumer perceives that the product is inferior and never buys it again. This causes grave financial loss to the manufacturer, whose profits come from *repeat* purchases.

The best way to increase the sale of a product is to *improve the product*. This is particularly true of food products; the consumer is amazingly quick to notice an improvement in taste and buy the product more often. I have always been irritated by the lack of interest brand managers take in improving their products. One client warned me, "You are too prone to criticize our products. We could find it easier to accept criticism of our wives."

Not Enough Information

Do you think advertising gives you enough information about products? I don't.

Recently, I smashed my car beyond repair and had to buy a new one. For six months I read all the car ads in search of *information*. All I found was fatuous slogans and flatulent generalities. Car manufacturers assume that you are not interested in facts. Indeed, their advertising is not aimed at consumers. Its purpose is to win an ovation when it is projected on the screen at hoopla conventions of dealers. Show-biz commercials have that effect. Sober, factual advertising does not. If their engineering was as incompetent as their advertising, their cars would not run ten miles without a breakdown.

When I advertised Rolls-Royce, I gave the *facts*—no hot air, no adjectives. Later, my partner Hank Bernhard used equally factual advertising for Mercedes. In every case sales went up dramatically—on peppercorn budgets.

I have written factual advertising for a bank, for gasoline, for a stockbroker, margarine, foreign travel and many other products. It *always* sells better than empty advertising.

Before I started writing advertisements, I spent three years selling Aga cooking stoves to Scottish housewives, door to door. All I did was give my customers the facts. It took me 40 minutes to make a sale; about 3,000 words. If the people who write Detroit advertising had started *their* careers as door-to-door salesmen, you and I would be able to find the facts we need in their advertisements.

After Reading

Critical Perspective

1. Describe Ogilvy's tone at the beginning of this essay. What do you think about it? Do you believe that it is a successful tactic given his argument? Why or why not?

Rhetoric and Argument

2. How would you characterize Ogilvy's ethos in this text? What appeals to pathos does he make? Do you find his use of logical appeals convincing? You may also want to consider his audience, purpose, use of intertextuality, context, and constraints. Be sure to furnish examples from the text to support your thoughts.
3. Outline the organization or structure of Ogilvy's piece. Do you think that this approach is successful? Explain your position and back it up with textual evidence.
4. What sorts of evidence does Ogilvy utilize to substantiate his main claim? Do you find this evidence convincing? How yes or how no? What other kinds of support might he have used to bolster his assertions?

Analysis

5. Ogilvy seems to anticipate countercharges to his assertions. Present a short argumentative response in which you trace what these charges are, exactly where and how Ogilvy attempts to refute these charges, and whether he accomplishes this successfully. In addition, are there any logical fallacies or unwarranted assumptions in his essay? Give quotes as well as examine library and Internet sources to back up your opinions.

Taking Action

Recall Ogilvy's notion that advertising is "no more no less than a reasonably efficient way to sell." One could take Ogilvy's statement in a number of different directions. Perhaps companies and advertisers have little to no social or cultural responsibility for the effects of their ads on consumers.

Form two debate teams within your class. One group will argue that advertisers should not be responsible for the effects of advertising. The other group will assert that advertising is more than just a reasonable way to sell products, and that advertisers should be held responsible for the effects of their campaigns. Each group should construct positions ahead of time, consulting library and Internet sources as well as personal experiences to back up their views. Begin with short position statements from each group. Give each group several five-minute opportunities for rebuttal and to make closing arguments.

After the debate, form a large classroom group again. Discuss what arguments were most convincing and why. Talk about what is important to each of you about this debate, whether you argued a position you believed or not, and how this impacted you. Consider making your work accessible to other groups both inside and outside the campus community.

Naomi Klein

"No Logo"

Naomi Klein is a journalist and anticorporate activist. She writes for the Globe and Mail, *a national newspaper in Canada, the* Guardian *in Britain, and the U.S. publication* In These Times. *She has written several books, including* Fences and Windows: Dispatches from the Front Lines of the Globalization Debate. *Her book* No Logo: No Space, No Choice, No Jobs *from which this essay comes examines the function of multinational corporations, their practices, and global activism.*

EXERCISING YOUR SKILLS

Before Reading

Klein is interested in the local and global impacts of logos and advertising. How do companies, using advertising and promotion, develop "brand loyalty" in consumers? To what brands are you loyal? (If you have trouble coming up with ideas, reflect on the purchases you often make.) Why is this the case? Think back upon your own experiences. How did your interest in this brand begin? How old were you, where were you, and how did the brand make you feel? How has your allegiance been sustained and strengthened?

> *As a private person, I have a passion for landscape, and I have never seen one improved by a billboard. Where every prospect pleases, man is at his vilest when he erects a billboard. When I retire from Madison Avenue, I am going to start a secret society of masked vigilantes who will travel around the world on silent motor bicycles, chopping down posters at the dark of the moon. How many juries will convict us when we are caught in these acts of beneficent citizenship?*
> —David Ogilvy, *founder of the Ogilvy & Mather advertising agency,*
> *in* Confessions of an Advertising Man, *1963*

The astronomical growth in the wealth and cultural influence of multinational corporations over the last fifteen years can arguably be traced back to a single, seemingly innocuous idea developed by management theorists in the mid-1980s: that successful corporations must primarily produce brands, as opposed to products.

Until that time, although it was understood in the corporate world that bolstering one's brand name was important, the primary concern of every solid manufacturer was the production of goods. This idea was the very gospel of the machine age. An editorial that appeared in *Fortune* magazine in 1938, for instance, argued that the reason the American economy had yet to recover from the Depression was that America had lost sight of the importance of making *things*:

> *This is the proposition that the basic and irreversible function of an industrial economy is* the making of things; *that the more things it makes the bigger will be the income, whether dollar or real; and hence that the key to those lost recuperative powers lies in the factory where the lathes and the drills and the fires and the hammers are. It is in the factory and on the land and under the land that purchasing power* originates.

And for the longest time, the making of things remained, at least in principle, the heart of all industrialized economies. But by the eighties, pushed along by that decade's recession, some of the most powerful manufacturers in the world had begun to falter. A consensus emerged that corporations were bloated, oversized; they owned too much, employed too many people and were weighed down with *too many things*. The very process of producing—running one's own factories, being responsible for tens of thousands of full-time, permanent employees—began to look less like the route to success and more like a clunky liability.

At around this same time a new kind of corporation began to rival the traditional all-American manufacturers for market share; these were the Nikes and Microsofts, and later, the Tommy Hilfigers and Intels. These pioneers made the bold claim that producing goods was only an incidental part of their operations, and that thanks to recent victories in trade liberalization and labor-law reform, they were able to have their products made for them by contractors, many of them overseas. What these companies produced primarily were not things, they said, but *images* of their brands. Their real work lay not in manufacturing but in marketing. This formula, needless to say, has proved enormously profitable, and its success has companies competing in a race toward weightlessness whoever owns the least, has the fewest employees on the payroll and produces the most powerful images, as opposed to products, wins the race.

And so the wave of mergers in the corporate world over the last few years is a deceptive phenomenon: it only looks as if the giants, by joining forces, are getting bigger and bigger. The true key to understanding these shifts is to realize that in several crucial ways—not their profits, of course—these merged companies are actually shrinking. Their apparent bigness is simply the most effective route toward their real goal, divestment of the world of things.

Since many of today's best-known manufacturers no longer produce products and advertise them, but rather buy products and "brand" them, these companies are forever on the prowl for creative new ways to build and strengthen their brand images. Manufacturing products may require drills, furnaces, hammers and the like, but creating a brand calls for a completely different set of tools and materials. It requires an endless parade of brand extensions, continuously renewed imagery for marketing and, most of all, fresh new spaces to disseminate the brand's idea of itself. In this section I'll look at how, in ways both insidious and overt, this corporate obsession with brand identity is waging a war on public and individual space: on public institutions such as schools, on youthful identities, on the concept of nationality and on the possibilities for unmarketed space.

The Beginning of the Brand

It's helpful to go back briefly and look at where the idea of branding first began. Though the words are often used interchangeably, branding and advertising are not the same process. Advertising any given product is only one part of branding's grand plan, as are sponsorship and logo licensing. Think of the brand as the core meaning of the modern corporation, and of the advertisement as one vehicle used to convey that meaning to the world.

The first mass-marketing campaigns, starting in the second half of the nineteenth century, had more to do with advertising than with branding as we understand it today. Faced with a range of recently invented products—the radio, phonograph, car, light bulb and so on—advertisers had more pressing tasks than creating a brand identity for any given corporation; first, they had to change the way people lived their lives. Ads had to inform consumers about the existence of some new invention, then convince them that their lives would be better if they used, for example, cars instead of wagons, telephones instead of mail and electric light instead of oil lamps. Many of these new products bore brand names—some of which are still around today—but these were almost incidental. These products were themselves news, and that was almost advertisement enough.

The first brand-based products appeared at around the same time as the invention-based ads, largely because of another relatively recent innovation: the factory. When goods began to be produced in factories, not only were entirely new products being introduced but old products—even basic staples—were appearing in strikingly new forms. What made early branding efforts different from more straightforward salesmanship was that the market was now being flooded with uniform mass-produced products that were virtually indistinguishable from one another. Competitive branding became a necessity of the machine age—within a context of manufactured sameness, image-based difference had to be manufactured along with the product.

So the role of advertising changed from delivering product news bulletins to building an image around a particular brand-name version of a product. The first task of branding was to bestow proper names on generic goods such as sugar, flour, soap and cereal, which had previously been scooped out of barrels by local shopkeepers. In the 1880s, corporate logos were introduced to mass-produced products like Campbell's Soup, H.J. Heinz pickles and Quaker Oats cereal. As design historians and theorists Ellen Lupton and J. Abbott Miller note, logos were tailored to evoke familiarity and folksiness, in an effort to counteract the new and unsettling anonymity of packaged goods. "Familiar personalities such as Dr. Brown, Uncle Ben, Aunt Jemima, and Old Grand-Dad came to replace the shopkeeper, who was traditionally responsible for measuring bulk foods for customers and acting as an advocate for products . . . a nationwide vocabulary of brand names replaced the small local shopkeeper as the interface between consumer and product." After the product names and characters had been established, advertising gave them a venue to speak directly to would-be consumers. The corporate "personality," uniquely named, packaged and advertised, had arrived.

For the most part, the ad campaigns at the end of the nineteenth century and the start of the twentieth used a set of rigid, pseudoscientific formulas. Rivals were never mentioned, ad copy used declarative statements only, and headlines had to be large, with lots of white space—according to one turn-of-the-century adman, "an advertisement should be big enough to make an impression but not any bigger than the thing advertised."

But there were those in the industry who understood that advertising wasn't just scientific, it was also spiritual. Brands could conjure a feeling—think of Aunt Jemima's comforting presence—but not only that, entire corporations could themselves embody a meaning of their own. In the early twenties, legendary adman Bruce Barton turned General Motors into a metaphor for the American family, "something personal, warm and human," while GE was not so much the name of the faceless General Electric Company as, in Barton's words, "the initials of a friend." In 1923 Barton said that the role of advertising was to help corporations find their soul. The son of a preacher, he drew on his religious upbringing for uplifting messages. "I like to think of advertising as something big, something splendid, something which goes deep down into an institution and gets hold of the soul of it. . . . Institutions have souls, just as men and nations have souls," he told GM president Pierre du Pont. General Motors ads began to tell stories about the people who drove its cars—the preacher, the pharmacist or the country doctor who, thanks to his trusty GM, arrived "at the bedside of a dying child" just in time "to bring him back to life."

By the end of the 1940s, there was a burgeoning awareness that a brand wasn't just a mascot or a catchphrase or a picture printed on the label of a company's product; the company as a whole could have a brand identity or a "corporate consciousness," as this ephemeral quality was termed at the time. As this idea evolved, the adman ceased to see himself as a pitchman and instead saw himself as "the philosopher-king of commercial culture," in the words of ad critic Randall Rothberg. The search for the true meaning of brands—or the "brand essence," as it is often called—gradually took the agencies away from individual products and their attributes and toward a psychological/anthropological examination of what brands mean to the culture and to people's lives. This was seen to be of crucial importance, since corporations may manufacture products, but what consumers buy are brands.

It took several decades for the manufacturing world to adjust to this shift. It clung to the idea that its core business was still production and that branding was an important add-on. Then came the brand equity mania of the eighties, the defining moment of which arrived in 1988 when Philip Morris purchased Kraft for $12.6 billion—six times what the company was worth on paper. The price difference, apparently, was the cost of the word "Kraft." Of course Wall Street was aware that decades of marketing and brand bolstering added value to a company over and above its assets and total annual sales. But with the Kraft purchase, a huge dollar value had been assigned to something that had previously been abstract and unquantifiable—a brand name. This was spectacular news for the ad world, which was now able to make the claim that advertising spending was more than just a sales strategy: it was an investment in cold, hard equity. The more you spend, the more your company is worth. Not surprisingly, this led to a considerable increase in spending on advertising. More important, it sparked a renewed interest in puffing up brand identities, a project that involved far more than a few billboards and TV spots. It was about pushing the envelope in sponsorship deals, dreaming up new areas in which to "extend" the brand, as well as perpetually probing the zeitgeist to ensure that the "essence" selected for one's brand would resonate karmically with its target market. For reasons that will be explored in the remainder of this essay, this radical shift in corporate philosophy has sent manufacturers on a cultural feeding frenzy as they seize upon every corner of unmarketed landscape in search of the oxygen needed to inflate their brands. In the process, virtually nothing has been left unbranded. That's quite an impressive feat, considering that as recently as 1993 Wall Street had pronounced the brand dead, or as good as dead.

The Brand's Death (Rumors of Which Had Been Greatly Exaggerated)

On April 2, 1993, advertising itself was called into question by the very brands the industry had been building, in some cases, for over two centuries. That day is known in marketing circles as "Marlboro Friday," and it refers to a sudden announcement from Philip Morris that it would slash the price of Marlboro cigarettes by 20 percent in an attempt to compete with bargain brands that were eating into its market. The pundits went nuts, announcing in frenzied unison that not only was Marlboro dead, all brand names were dead. The reasoning was that if a "prestige" brand like Marlboro, whose image had been carefully groomed, preened and enhanced with more than a billion advertising dollars, was desperate enough to compete with no-names, then clearly the whole concept of branding had lost its currency. The public had seen the advertising, and the public didn't care. The Marlboro Man, after all, was not any old campaign, launched in 1954; it was the longest-running ad campaign in history. It was a legend. If the Marlboro Man had crashed, well, then, brand equity had crashed as well. The implication that Americans were suddenly thinking for themselves en masse reverberated through Wall Street. The same day Philip Morris announced its price cut, stock prices nose-dived for all the household brands: Heinz; Quaker Oats, Coca-Cola, PepsiCo, Procter and Gamble and RJR Nabisco. Philip Morris's own stock took the worst beating.

Bob Stanojev, national director of consumer products marketing for Ernst and Young, explained the logic behind Wall Street's panic: "If one or two powerhouse consumer products companies start to cut prices for good, there's going to be an avalanche. Welcome to the value generation."

Yes, it was one of those moments of overstated instant consensus, but it was not entirely without cause. Marlboro had always sold itself on the strength of its iconic image marketing, not on anything so prosaic as its price. As we now know, the Marlboro Man survived the price wars without sustaining too much damage. At the time, however, Wall Street saw Philip Morris's decision as symbolic of a sea change. The price cut was an admission that Marlboro's name was no longer sufficient to sustain the flagship position, which in a context where image is equity meant that Marlboro had blinked. And when Marlboro—one of the quintessential global brands—blinks, it raises questions about branding that reach beyond Wall Street, and way beyond Philip Morris.

The panic of Marlboro Friday was not a reaction to a single incident. Rather, it was the culmination of years of escalating anxiety in the face of some rather dramatic shifts in consumer habits that were seen to be eroding the market share of household-name brands, from Tide to Kraft. Bargain-conscious shoppers, hit hard by the recession, were starting to pay more attention to price than to the prestige bestowed on their products by the yuppie ad campaigns of the 1980s. The public was suffering from a bad case of what is known in the industry as "brand blindness."

Study after study showed that baby boomers, blind to the alluring images of advertising and deaf to the empty promises of celebrity spokespersons, were breaking their lifelong brand loyalties and choosing to feed their families with private-label brands from the supermarket—claiming, heretically, that they couldn't tell the difference. From the beginning of the recession to 1993, Loblaw's President's Choice line, Wal-Mart's Great Value, and Marks and Spencer's St. Michael prepared foods had nearly doubled their market share in North America and Europe. The computer market, meanwhile, was flooded by inexpensive clones, causing IBM to slash its prices and otherwise impale itself. It appeared to be a return to the proverbial shopkeeper dishing out generic goods from the barrel in a prebranded era.

The Brands Bounce Back

There were some brands that were watching from the sidelines as Wall Street declared the death of the brand. Funny, they must have thought, we don't feel dead.

Just as the admen had predicted at the beginning of the recession, the companies that exited the downturn running were the ones who opted for marketing over value every time: Nike, Apple, the Body Shop, Calvin Klein, Disney, Levi's and Starbucks. Not only were these brands doing just fine, thank you very much, but the act of branding was becoming a larger and larger focus of their businesses. For these companies, the ostensible product was mere filler for the real production: the brand. They integrated the idea of branding into the very fabric of their companies. Their corporate cultures were so tight and cloistered that to outsiders they appeared to be a cross between fraternity house, religious cult and sanitarium. Everything was an ad for the brand: bizarre lexicons for describing employees (partners, baristas, team players, crew members), company chants, superstar CEOs, fanatical attention to design consistency, a propensity for monument-building, and New Age mission statements. Unlike classic household brand names, such as Tide and Marlboro, these logos weren't losing their currency. They were in the midst of breaking every barrier in the marketing world—becoming cultural accessories and lifestyle philosophers. These companies didn't wear their image like a cheap shirt—their image was so integrated with their business that other people wore it as *their* shirt. And when the brands crashed, these companies didn't even notice—they were branded to the bone.

So the real legacy of Marlboro Friday is that it simultaneously brought the two most significant developments in nineties marketing and consumerism into sharp focus: the deeply unhip big-box bargain stores that provide the essentials of life and monopolize a disproportionate share of the market (Wal-Mart *et al.*) and the extra-premium "attitude" brands that provide the essentials of lifestyle and monopolize ever-expanding stretches of cultural space (Nike *et al.*). The way these two tiers of consumerism developed would have a profound impact on the economy in the years to come. When overall ad expenditures took a nosedive in 1991, Nike and Reebok were busy playing advertising chicken, with each company increasing its budget to outspend the other. In 1991 alone, Reebok upped its ad spending by 71.9 percent, while Nike pumped an extra 24.6 percent into its already soaring ad budget, bringing the company's total spending on marketing to a staggering $250 million annually. Far from worrying about competing on price, the sneaker pimps were designing ever more intricate and pseudoscientific air pockets, and driving up prices by signing star athletes to colossal sponsorship deals. The fetish strategy seemed to be working fine: in the six years prior to 1993, Nike had gone from a $750 million company to a $4 billion one and Phil Knight's Beaverton, Oregon, company emerged from the recession with profits 900 percent higher than when it began.

Benetton and Calvin Klein, meanwhile, were also upping their spending on lifestyle marketing, using ads to associate their lines with risque art and progressive politics. Clothes barely appeared in these high-concept advertisements, let alone prices. Even more abstract was Absolut Vodka, which for some years now had been developing a marketing strategy in which its product disappeared and its brand was nothing but a blank bottle-shaped space that could be filled with whatever content a particular audience most wanted from its brands: intellectual in *Harper*'s, futuristic in *Wired*, alternative in *Spin*, loud and proud in *Out*, and "Absolut Centerfold" in *Playboy*. The brand reinvented itself as a cultural sponge, soaking up and morphing to its surroundings.

Saturn, too, came out of nowhere in October 1990 when GM launched a car built not out of steel and rubber but out of New Age spirituality and seventies feminism. After the car had been on the market a few years, the company held a "homecoming" weekend for Saturn owners, during which they could visit the auto plant and have a cookout with the people who made their cars. As the Saturn ads boasted at the time, "44,000 people spent their vacations with us, at a car plant." It was as if Aunt Jemima had come to life and invited you over to her house for dinner.

In 1993, the year the Marlboro Man was temporarily hobbled by "brand-blind" consumers, Microsoft made its striking debut on *Advertising Age*'s list of the top 200 ad spenders—the very same year that Apple computer increased its marketing budget by 30 percent after already making branding history with its Orwellian takeoff ad launch during the 1984 Super Bowl. Like Saturn, both companies were selling a hip new relationship to the machine that left Big Blue IBM looking as clunky and menacing as the now-dead Cold War.

And then there were the companies that had always understood that they were selling brands before product. Coke, Pepsi, McDonald's, Burger King and Disney weren't fazed by the brand crisis, opting instead to escalate the brand war, especially since they had their eyes firmly fixed on global expansion. They were joined in this project by a wave of sophisticated producer/retailers who hit full stride in the late eighties and early nineties. The Gap, Ikea, and the Body Shop were spreading like wildfire during this period, masterfully transforming the generic into the brand-specific, largely through bold, carefully branded packaging and the promotion of an "experiential" shopping environment. The Body Shop had been a presence in Britain since the seventies, but it wasn't until 1988 that it began sprouting like a green weed on every street corner in the U.S. Even during the darkest years of the recession, the company opened between forty and fifty American stores a year. Most baffling of all to Wall Street, it pulled off the expansion without spending a dime on advertising. Who needed billboards and magazine ads when retail outlets were three-dimensional advertisements for an ethical and ecological approach to cosmetics? The Body Shop was all brand.

The Starbucks coffee chain, meanwhile, was also expanding during this period without laying out much in advertising; instead, it was spinning off its name into a wide range of branded projects: Starbucks airline coffee, office coffee, coffee ice cream, coffee beer. Starbucks seemed to understand brand names at a level even deeper than Madison Avenue, incorporating marketing into every fiber of its corporate concept—from the chain's strategic association with books, blues and jazz to its Euro-latte lingo. What the success of both the Body Shop and Starbucks showed was how far the branding project had come in moving beyond splashing one's logo on a billboard. Here were two companies that had fostered powerful identities by making their brand concept into a virus and sending it out into the culture via a variety of channels: cultural sponsorship, political controversy, the consumer experience, and brand extensions. Direct advertising, in this context, was viewed as a rather clumsy intrusion into a much more organic approach to image building.

Scott Bedbury, Starbucks' Vice President of marketing, openly recognized that "consumers don't truly believe there's a huge difference between products," which is why brands must "establish emotional ties" with their customers through "the Starbucks Experience." The people who line up for Starbucks, writes CEO Howard Shultz, aren't just there for the coffee. "It's the romance of the coffee experience, the feeling of warmth and community people get in Starbucks stores."

Interestingly, before moving to Starbucks, Bedbury was head of marketing at Nike, where he oversaw the launch of the "Just Do It!" slogan, among other watershed branding moments. In the following passage, he explains the common techniques used to infuse the two very different brands with meaning:

Nike, for example, is leveraging the deep emotional connection that people have with sports and fitness. With Starbucks, we see how coffee has woven itself into the fabric of people's lives, and that's our opportunity for emotional leverage. . . . A great brand raises the bar—it adds a greater sense of purpose to the experience, whether it's the challenge to do your best in sports and fitness or the affirmation that the cup of coffee you're drinking really matters.

This was the secret, it seemed, of all the success stories of the late eighties and early nineties. The lesson of Marlboro Friday was that there never really was a brand crisis—only brands that had crises of confidence. The brands would be okay, Wall Street concluded, so long as they believed fervently in the principles of branding and never, ever blinked. Overnight, "Brands, not products!" became the rallying cry for a marketing renaissance led by a new breed of companies that saw themselves as "meaning brokers" instead of product producers. What was changing was the idea of what—in both advertising and branding—was being sold. The old paradigm had it that all marketing was selling a product. In the new model, however, the product always takes a back seat to the real product, the brand, and the selling of the brand acquired an extra component that can only be described as spiritual. Advertising is about hawking product. Branding, in its truest and most advanced incarnations, is about corporate transcendence.

It may sound flaky, but that's precisely the point. On Marlboro Friday, a line was drawn in the sand between the lowly price slashers and the high-concept brand builders. The brand builders conquered and a new consensus was born: the products that will flourish in the future will be the ones presented not as "commodities" but as concepts: the brand as experience, as lifestyle.

Ever since, a select group of corporations has been attempting to free itself from the corporeal world of commodities, manufacturing and products to exist on another plane. Anyone can manufacture a product, they reason (and as the success of private-label brands during the recession proved, anyone did). Such menial tasks, therefore, can and should be farmed out to contractors and subcontractors whose only concern is filling the order on time and under budget (ideally in the Third World, where labor is dirt cheap, laws are lax and tax breaks come by the bushel). Headquarters, meanwhile, is free to focus on the real business at hand—creating a corporate mythology powerful enough to infuse meaning into these raw objects just by signing its name.

The corporate world has always had a deep New Age streak, fed—it has become clear—by a profound need that could not be met simply by trading widgets for cash. But when branding captured the corporate imagination, New Age vision quests took center stage. As Nike CEO Phil Knight explains, "For years we thought of ourselves as a production-oriented company, meaning we put all our emphasis on designing and manufacturing the product. But now we understand that the most important thing we do is market the product. We've come around to saying that Nike is a marketing-oriented company, and the product is our most important marketing tool." This project has since been taken to an even more advanced level with the emergence of on-line corporate giants such as Amazon.com. It is on-line that the purest brands are being built: liberated from the real-world burdens of stores and product manufacturing, these brands are free to soar, less as the disseminators of goods or services than as collective hallucinations.

Tom Peters, who has long coddled the inner flake in many a hard-nosed CEO, latched on to the branding craze as the secret to financial success, separating the transcendental logos and the earthbound products into two distinct categories of companies. "The top half—Coca-Cola, Microsoft, Disney, and so on—are pure 'players' in brainware. The bottom half [Ford and GM] are still lumpy-object purveyors, though automobiles are much 'smarter' than they used to be," Peters writes in *The Circle of Innovation* (1997), an ode to the power of marketing over production.

When Levi's began to lose market share in the late nineties, the trend was widely attributed to the company's failure—despite lavish ad spending—to transcend its products and become a free-standing meaning. "Maybe one of Levi's problems is that it has no Cola," speculated Jennifer Steinhauer in *The New York Times*. "It has no denim-toned house paint. Levi's makes what is essentially a commodity: blue jeans. Its ads may evoke rugged outdoorsmanship, but Levi's hasn't promoted any particular life style to sell other products."

In this high-stakes new context, the cutting-edge ad agencies no longer sold companies on individual campaigns but on their ability to act as "brand stewards": identifying, articulating and protecting the corporate soul. Not surprisingly, this spelled good news for the U.S. advertising industry, which in 1994 saw a spending increase of 8.6 percent over the previous year. In one year, the ad industry went from a near crisis to another "best year yet." And that was only the beginning of triumphs to come. By 1997, corporate advertising, defined as "ads that position a corporation, its values, its personality and character" were up 18 percent from the year before.

With this wave of brand mania has come a new breed of businessman, one who will proudly inform you that Brand X is not a product but a way of life, an attitude, a set of values, a look, an idea. And it sounds really great—way better than that Brand X is a screwdriver, or a hamburger chain, or a pair of jeans, or even a very successful line of running shoes. Nike, Phil Knight announced in the late eighties, is "a sports company"; its mission is not to sell shoes but to "enhance people's lives through sports and fitness" and to keep "the magic of sports alive." Company president-cum-sneaker-shaman Tom Clark explains that "the inspiration of sports allows us to rebirth ourselves constantly."

Reports of such "brand vision" epiphanies began surfacing from all corners. "Polaroid's problem," diagnosed the chairman of its advertising agency, John Hegarty, "was that they kept thinking of themselves as a camera. But the ' [brand] vision' process taught us something: Polaroid is not a camera—it's a social lubricant." IBM isn't selling computers, it's selling business "solutions." Swatch is not about watches, it is about the idea of time. At Diesel Jeans, owner Renzo Rosso told *Paper* magazine, "We don't sell a product, we sell a style of life. I think we have created a movement. . . . The Diesel concept is everything. It's the way to live, it's the way to wear, it's the way to do something." And as Body Shop founder Anita Roddick explained to me, her stores aren't about what they sell, they are the conveyers of a grand idea—a political philosophy about women, the environment, and ethical business. "I just use the company that I surprisingly created as a success—it shouldn't have been like this, it wasn't meant to be like this—to stand on the products, to shout out on these issues," Roddick says.

The famous late graphic designer Tibor Kalman summed up the shifting role of the brand this way: "The original notion of the brand was quality, but now brand is a stylistic badge of courage."

The idea of selling the courageous message of a brand, as opposed to a product, intoxicated these CEOs, providing as it did an opportunity for seemingly limitless expansion. After all, if a brand was not a product, it could be anything! And nobody embraced branding theory with more evangelical zeal than Richard Branson, whose Virgin Group has branded joint ventures in everything from music to bridal gowns to airlines to cola to financial services. Branson refers derisively to the "stilted Anglo-Saxon view of consumers," which holds that a name should be associated with a product like sneakers or soft drinks, and opts instead for "the Asian 'trick'" of the *keiretsus* (a Japanese term meaning a network of linked corporations). The idea, he explains, is to "build brands not around products but around reputation. The great Asian names imply quality, price and innovation rather than a specific item. I call these 'attribute' brands: They do not relate directly to one product—such as a Mars bar or a Coca-Cola—but instead to a set of values."

Tommy Hilfiger, meanwhile, is less in the business of manufacturing clothes than he is in the business of signing his name. The company is run entirely through licensing agreements, with Hilfiger commissioning all its products from a group of other companies: Jockey International makes Hilfiger underwear, Pepe Jeans London makes Hilfiger jeans, Oxford Industries make Tommy shirts, the Stride Rite Corporation makes its footwear. What does Tommy Hilfiger manufacture? Nothing at all.

So passé had products become in the age of lifestyle branding that by the late nineties, newer companies like Lush cosmetics and Old Navy clothing began playing with the idea of old-style commodities as a source of retro marketing imagery. The Lush chain serves up its face masks and moisturizers out of refrigerated stainless-steel bowls, spooned into plastic containers with grocery-store labels. Old Navy showcases its shrink-wrapped T-shirts and sweatshirts in deli-style chrome refrigerators, as if they were meat or cheese. When you are a pure, concept-driven brand, the aesthetics of raw product can prove as "authentic" as loft living.

And lest the branding business be dismissed as the playground of trendy consumer items such as sneakers, jeans and New Age beverages, think again. Caterpillar, best known for building tractors and busting unions, has barreled into the branding business, launching the Cat accessories line: boots, back-packs, hats, and anything else calling out for a postindustrial *je ne sais quoi*. Intel Corp., which makes computer parts no one sees and few understand, transformed its processors into a fetish brand with TV ads featuring line workers in funky metallic space suits dancing to "Shake Your Groove Thing." The Intel mascots proved so popular that the company has sold hundreds of thousands of bean-filled dolls modeled on the shimmery dancing technicians. Little wonder, then, that when asked about the company's decision to diversify its products, the senior vice president for sales and marketing, Paul S. Otellini, replied that Intel is "like Coke. One brand, many different products."

And if Caterpillar and Intel can brand, surely anyone can.

There is, in fact, a new strain in marketing theory that holds that even the lowliest natural resources, barely processed, can develop brand identities, thus giving way to hefty premium-price markups. In an essay appropriately titled "How to Brand Sand," advertising executives Sam Hill, Jack McGrath and Sandeep Dayal team up to tell the corporate world that with the right marketing plan, nobody has to stay stuck in the stuff business. "Based on extensive research, we would argue that you can indeed brand not only sand, but also wheat, beef, brick, metals, concrete, chemicals, corn grits and an endless variety of commodities traditionally considered immune to the process."

Over the past six years, spooked by the near-death experience of Marlboro Friday, global corporations have leapt on the brand-wagon with what can only be described as a religious fervor. Never again would the corporate world stoop to praying at the altar of the commodity market. From now on they would worship only graven media images. Or to quote Tom Peters, the brand man himself: "Brand! Brand!! Brand!!! That's the message . . . for the late '90s and beyond."

After Reading

Critical Perspective

1. Why do you think that Klein begins this chapter with the particular quote she selects? In what ways did it prepare you for Klein's argument? Explain your responses.

Rhetoric and Argument

2. Consider Klein's use of rhetorical tactics, specifically audience, purpose, ethos, pathos, logos, intertextuality, context, and constraints. Do you think that her text is rhetorically effective? Why or why not?

3. What does Klein mean when she contends that "branding" is the latest corporate strategy? According to Klein, what problems and possibilities does branding pose? Do you agree with her or not? Why? Be sure to give examples from the text as well as your own experiences to back up your assertions.

4. Klein advances her argument by using a great deal of historical information as support. What is her main claim? Do you think that it is adequately supported by this kind of evidence? Why or why not? Is there any other type of evidence she might use that would additionally support her thoughts?

5. Was there anything about Klein's argument—the evidence she uses, the facts she cites, or her position—that surprised you in particular? Why or why not? Give quotes from her essay. In the end, do you agree with her argument or not? Explain your perspective. Are there any logical fallacies in her argument? If yes, pinpoint where they are in her text. If there are no flaws, draw from her text to back up your opinions.

6. Think about a specific company—one that Klein does not mention—that is also using branding in successful or perhaps unsuccessful ways. Explain the various places, events, ideas, and concepts that are incorporated into what constitutes

"the brand." What feelings, worldviews, and images are these brands conveying? Who might want to purchase these products as a result?

Analysis

7. Write an informal argumentative response in which you either support or refute Klein's thesis or use of rhetorical tactics. Draw your evidence from a close analysis of her text. In addition, be sure to consult library and Internet sources to back up your assertions.

Taking Action

Form a small group with classmates. Your task is to create your own fake company, to develop a set of product ideas, and to fashion a brand, logo, and slogan. There is only one restriction: Your company's main consumer for its products is young children—ages 6 to 10. Write up your insights and thoughts. When you have developed the necessary fake product as well as ad campaign copy and visuals, imagine you are in a business meeting. As clearly and articulately as you can, pitch your company, product, and brand to the rest of the class. Be sure to use all of your rhetorical and argumentative skills to accomplish this. Seek out library and Internet sources as well.

Once everyone has had a chance to share and discuss their ideas, have a large group discussion in which you address some of the following concerns: How might companies that market to children create brand visibility? Are there more ethical ways to create brand loyalty than others? Draw evidence from your own experiences with products when you were a child as well as from the ideas shared in class. Consider making your work accessible to other groups both inside and outside the campus community.

IMAGES OF DIVERSITY

MATTHEW REYNOLDS

"Pepsi's Nasty Habits?: Commercializing Rock, Race, and Addiction"

Matthew Reynolds completed his dissertation, "Soft Focus: Glamour and the Hollywood Redevelopment Project," in the Visual and Cultural Studies Program at the University of Rochester. He is currently visiting assistant professor in the History of Art Department at UC Riverside and works as a programming coordinator at the Getty Research Institute.

EXERCISING YOUR SKILLS

Before Reading

Reynolds analyzes Pepsi's ad campaigns in detail. Watch a series of contemporary commercials and notice the particular songs used to sell products. Make note of who sings the song, when it was written, and what it is about. How are the lyrics to the song and the jingle being used differently than when the song was created originally? What connotations does the song have on its own? Does it have different or similar connotations when it is applied to the product? Explain your view.

> *"Brown sugar, how come you taste so good?*
> *Brown sugar, just like a black girl should."*
> —The Rolling Stones, "Brown Sugar," 1971

Introduction

In late 2003, a commercial appeared on America's television screens featuring a new treatment of the age-old boy-meets-girl scenario: a young man dressed as a giant can of Pepsi stands on a corner passing out flyers for a fast food restaurant. Across the street, a girl in an enormous hot-dog suit does the same. The two spot each other and exchange a flirtatious glance. As the familiar strains of Blind Melon's decade-old hit song "No Rain" reverberate over the soundtrack, the can and the hot-dog meet in the middle of the street, clasp hands, and walk off into the sunset; two great tastes that taste great together (to quote another famous advertising campaign). At first glance the ad, entitled "Summer Job," is a clever riff on finding fun and love amidst the low-paid drudgery of seasonal employment. On another level, an argument might be made that the commercial is promoting a vision of diversity. After all, these are two separate species—soda and hot dog, food and drink—falling in love with one another despite their obvious differences. But many who recognize the rock song used on the commercial's soundtrack will sense yet another, perhaps unintended level of meaning. Ten years earlier Blind Melon, whose name is an homage to the 1920s-era African-American blues legend Blind Lemon Jefferson, scored a massive hit with "No Rain." The song was a catchy, melancholy tune about watching the rain gather in puddles and sleeping the day away. It was pushed up the charts by a video that featured home movie footage of a young girl dancing in a giant bee costume. Shortly after the song peaked, rumors surfaced about lead singer Shannon Hoon's drug problem. In 1995, Hoon was found dead from an overdose of heroin, an event that prompted fans to look back over the band's lyrics for references to the pain and torment of his addictions. After Hoon's death, "No Rain" took on a different set of connotations. Instead of a simple song about lying in bed on a rainy day, it became to many a tune about the euphoric, pain-numbing haze one experiences while high on heroin. In light of this new interpretation and the facts surrounding the lead singer's death, one has to ask: just what was Pepsi buying when they purchased the rights to this song for their "Summer Job" commercial? How does this particular song help them sell soda? What, if anything, are they trying to say about diversity and racial integration by pairing a hot dog with a can of Pepsi? And, finally, is the use of a tune that may or may not be about drug use and addiction a "habit" that Pepsi finds hard to break?

The answer to such questions might be discovered in another Pepsi ad that predates "Summer Job" by nearly five years. In 1998, Pepsi launched its then-new can and "Globe" logo during Super Bowl XXX with a commercial featuring a gnat singing the classic Rolling Stones song "Brown Sugar." But less than a week later and with little fanfare, Pepsi pulled the commercial from the airwaves. Why? Again, sifting back through layers of time and meaning, the reason is most likely found in a 1971 review of the song written by rock music critic Greil Marcus. Marcus began his assessment of The Rolling Stones album *Sticky Fingers* with a harsh indictment of the band's chart-topping single "Brown Sugar." "[The song] was racist and sexist. It threw me and a lot of other people and took the fun out of listening just as if the Stones had done 'The Ballad of the Green Berets' and meant it."[1] "Brown Sugar" and its lyrics about "slave ships," "houseboys," and whipping women caused a storm of protest that placed it among the racial and feminist debates of the era. Later in the review, however, Marcus admits to misjudging the song. He states that "Brown Sugar" had "two sides to it"; that it was a "spectacular and definitive parody and reversal of the anti-woman currency the Stones have used for money all these years, shot through with a weird admission of the racial ambivalence of their own music."[2]

The conjunction of rock-and-roll and advertising can be understood as a relatively new phenomenon. The use of recognizable rock songs has become an increasingly common practice over the last decade. Classic rock hits like The Who's "Happy Jack" and Led Zeppelin's "Rock and Roll" have been used to sell Hummers and Cadillacs, respectively. Likewise, other bands and performers from David Bowie to Iggy Pop have gotten in on the act, hawking everything from computer software to vacation getaways. In the process, the continuing collision between rock songs and consumer products is constructing a new language, one that is defined by the juxtaposition of two very different systems of meaning. This language is dependent on one product (the song) being used to sell another product, creating both a tension and fusion between two distinct systems of meaning. The use of this particular song—"Brown Sugar"—to sell this particular product—Pepsi—can be seen to take on a symbolic significance. What happens when a song about slavery, addiction, and exploitation is used to sell soda pop? This issue foregrounds the debate in rock music over its status as an artistic form capable of provoking cultural change or merely a tool of capitalism and consumption.

Marketing "Brown Sugar"

The "Brown Sugar" commercial begins with a computer-animated gnat buzzing around a table at which a casually dressed young man is sitting. After landing on the table, the bug spies a drop of Pepsi that has spilled and takes a drink. The sip causes an immediate metamorphosis. The bug stands upright, sprouts enormous red lips, grabs a nearby match to use as stand-in for a microphone and proceeds to sing "Brown sugar, how come you taste so good? Brown sugar just like I knew you would." To many viewers, the catchy guitar riff, the lyrics, and the big red lips are a recognizable representation of The Rolling Stones song "Brown Sugar" as sung by their iconic lead singer, Mick Jagger. The song

---

[1]Greil Marcus, "Sticky Fingers," *The Rolling Stones: An Unauthorized Biography*, David Dalton, ed. (Amsco Music Publishing, Co., New York, 1972), p. 342.

[2]Ibid., p. 343.

was and is a staple of classic rock radio stations around the nation and The Rolling Stones, with their frequent touring and popular videos, remain positioned in the public spotlight to this day. As the commercial progresses the bug continues to dance and sing, frequently framed with the new Pepsi can and logo in the background. As the song reaches its climax there is a close shot of the insect repeating Jagger's cries of "yeah . . . yeah . . . yeah." Before finishing the song, the can is slammed onto the table (with the new logo prominently displayed), crushing the gnat, and eliciting an "oooooooh" from the squashed insect. The final shot shows the young man taking another drink from the can with the bug stuck to the bottom. As the crushed but still-living pest drops the match, a voice-over states: "Watch out for the new Pepsi can."

Since 2000, Pepsi has targeted a younger market in their ad campaigns by featuring famous pop artists Britney Spears, Shakira, and Beyoncé Knowles. Like the "Brown Sugar" commercial, the ads featuring Pepsi's "women of pop" were all high profile campaigns that, underneath the surface, mobilized race and sex in highly problematic ways; all three performers arguably employ racial ambiguities in order to cross-over into mainstream chart successes. But these ads were aimed directly at an under-20 crowd. In contrast, the "Brown Sugar" spot's target audience was more ambiguous. It contains all of the elements by which Pepsi commercials have come to be identified. There is a young person, drinking the soda in a vibrant, kinetic environment, surrounded by bright, flashy colors. Like other Pepsi commercials, the ad is characterized by energetic music and features a likeable protagonist whose consumption of the soda transforms him/her from something ordinary into someone (or something) that is "lively," "exuberant," and "fun."

But despite these common visual signifiers, the conclusion of the "Brown Sugar" commercial, along with the music used to elicit viewer interest, allows for a somewhat confusing interpretation. The Rolling Stones are a band primarily associated with an era (the 1960's and 1970's) foreign to the young audiences who make up the next generation of Pepsi drinkers and to whom these ads are presumably directed. The crushing of the Jagger-esque bug and the use of this song raised a series of questions when it first appeared in 1998: did the "Brown Sugar" commercial signal a new direction for Pepsi advertising? Did Pepsi intend to capitalize on the nostalgic association baby-boomers have for the song and the band? Or was the crushing of the fly meant to dissociate Pepsi from the nostalgia represented by The Rolling Stones? And lastly, as in the Blind Melon "Summer Job" commercial, how will those familiar with the song's racial and sexual references interpret the ad?

The history of Pepsi's marketing strategy can be understood largely as a response to the soft drink's main competitor, and the number one selling cola manufacturer in the world, Coke. Pepsi has continuously sought to "differentiate" itself from Coca-Cola by attempting to appeal to a broader range of social and economic groups. In its own advertising campaigns, Coke consistently sold an image of nostalgia, order, and traditional American values. Their commercials proclaimed "Things go better with Coke," "It's the Real Thing," and "Coke Is It." Capitalizing on the social and political turmoil of the late 1960's, Pepsi would reach out to an emerging youth market by appealing to their desire for change and their rebellion against the status-quo. The company would seek to align its product with the dissenting attitudes of the time. As a means of tapping into the youthful mores of the era, Pepsi began using a rock-and-roll sound (as opposed to specific, recognizable rock songs) as a means of differentiating itself from Coke.[3] The success of their advertising campaigns catapulted Pepsi into a position through which they were able to challenge Coke's dominance in the soft-drink market. The resulting competition between the two companies was labeled "the cola wars," a tag which would thereafter define the companies and their products in relation to each other.

Made in the late 1990's, the "Brown Sugar" commercial would initially seem to meet Pepsi's criteria for establishing and maintaining a product image consistent with the advertising strategies developed in the 1960's. This song, and the Stones themselves, are invariably associated with cultural dissent, rebellion, and the desire to challenge the status-quo. But Pepsi's appeal to youth, the commercial's use of visual imagery, and the attempt to capitalize on "Brown Sugar's" recognizability, are all problematized by the shifting interpretations of the song and the band's on-going public evolution. In its effort to construct a new image for its product, Pepsi's appropriation of this song has inevitably created a strange collision between meaning-making systems. In order to understand this collision, it is necessary to explore the collective images of The Rolling Stones and their notorious song. As musicians dependent on the mechanizations of capitalism and consumerism to sustain their careers, The Rolling Stones can also be seen as a product. As a band, they constructed (and were constructed as) a specific image in order to differentiate themselves from other products (rock bands). As a product of a product, the song "Brown Sugar" is one of the ways in which this image is constructed. These images must be examined in order to understand the layers of meaning created in this commercial.

The Rolling Stones—Sex, Drugs, and Rock-and-Roll

During the 1960's and 1970's The Rolling Stones proclaimed themselves "The World's Greatest Rock-and-Roll Band." Their albums and singles consistently topped the charts and their concerts became cultural events. The core members of the band emerged from working and middle-class backgrounds in England. Like other British bands of the early 1960's, The Rolling Stones appropriated the musical style of American blues and R&B. But while other bands sought to combine blues music with a mainstream, middle-class subject matter, the Stones spiked their music with numerous (and for the time explicit) references to sex and drugs. Second to The Beatles in terms of popularity and record sales, the two bands, like Coke and Pepsi, sought to define themselves in opposition to each other. Where The Beatles could be wholesome and good-natured, The Stones were "ugly, raunchy, and surly."[4] Where The Beatles were psychedelic, The Stones were bluesy. If all The Beatles needed was love, then The Stones were street-fighting men. The Rolling Stones frequently seemed to embrace the seamier sides of life in both their personal affairs and their music and their career has been characterized by a seemingly unending series of sex or drug-related scandals. During a ten-year period from 1965 to 1975, the band endured the mysterious death of one of its founding members (Brian Jones), drug-related arrests, sexual

[3]Thomas Frank, *The Conquest of Cool* (University of Chicago Press, Chicago, 1997), p. 173.
[4]David Dalton, op. cit., p. 106.

affairs within the group, and accusations of Satanism and occultism. In addition, the band presided over what is commonly thought to be the defining moment in which the 1960's, the so-called era of peace and love, died. Their free concert at the Altamont Speedway in Northern California (immortalized in the Maysles Bros.' film *Gimme Shelter*) was marred by the stabbing death of a young black man at the hands of Hell's Angels who were hired to serve as security for the event. As a result of such associations, the band helped to define an era marked by the Vietnam war, student protests, urban riots, and general political and social unrest.

It is this period that is widely regarded as The Rolling Stones most creatively fertile. It was during this decade that the band set about rediscovering the bluesy roots of rock-and-roll and recorded the album *Sticky Fingers,* from which "Brown Sugar" became the first single. Frequently cited as one of the band's best records, it can easily be interpreted as an allegory of the dangers and pleasures of addiction in its many forms. At the time of its release, the album cover (designed by Andy Warhol) featured a photograph of a pair of tight jeans hugging the outline of a noticeably visible semi-flaccid penis. In addition, the cover featured a real zipper which provided a not-so-subtle allusion to the suggestively masturbatory title of the record and the band's well-earned reputation as "cocksmen." Every track contains a reference to longing, addiction, or temptation. "Can't You Hear Me Knockin'" is about a guy with "cocaine eyes" and a "speed-freak jive" who "prowls," stalks and voyeuristically spies on a former lover. "Sister Morphine's" title is an obvious and explicit reference to drugs. The song was written with singer Marianne Faithfull who had tried to kill herself by over-dosing on heroin after she and Jagger ended their tumultuous relationship. But it is "Brown Sugar" that introduces these thematic motifs to the listener and sets the stage for the songs to come. The lyrics are as follows:

Gold coast slave ship bound for cotton fields
Sold in a market down in New Orleans
Scarred old slaver knows he's doing all right
Hear him whip the women just around midnight

Brown sugar how come you taste so good
Brown sugar just like a young girl should

Drums beating, cold English blood runs hot
Lady of the house wonderin' where it's gonna' stop
House boy knows that he's doing all right
You shoulda' heard him just about midnight

(chorus—"young" is substituted with "black")

I bet your mama was a tent show queen
And all her boyfriends were sweet sixteen
I'm no schoolboy but I know what I like
You shoulda' heard me just around midnight

(chorus—fade out)

Like advertisements, products, and other texts, "Brown Sugar" is a signifying system with a number of different possible meanings. At one level, the song's first two verses indicate that the narrative, with its references to slavery, Southern culture, and sexuality is about white men who cannot resist their urge for sexual relations with black (or mulatto) women. For Marcus the song seemed to imply a desire on The Stones' part to enjoy the company of young, black women, hence its "racist, sexist" meaning. However, his further interpretation indicated The Stones' willingness to point out the power relations at work within the song. The fact that the black woman/women who serve as the object/s of desire have no control over their own exploitation allows the listener to understand the strange relationship between desire and its prohibition, especially in regards to traditional relations of race and gender. "We always want what we can't have, or what is forbidden to us," Marcus and the Stones seem to be saying.

Since the time when "Brown Sugar" was a hit, The Stones' image has continued its steady transformation. While the band will forever be associated with rock-and-roll's bad side, they are now bad-gone-gray. The Rolling Stones are currently a symbol of the past; anti-heroes become legitimate heroes of the baby-boomer generation. Their message of non-conformity and rebellion has been channeled into the mainstream. The Rolling Stones were one of the first bands to use corporate sponsorship for their tours. In addition, their 1998 tour was sponsored by Pepsi and the band has played several exclusive concerts for Pepsi bottlers. Thus, the "Brown Sugar" commercial, like Marcus' interpretation of the two-sides of the song, seems to have two sides itself.

Reading "Brown Sugar"

Pepsi's "Brown Sugar" commercial seems at first glance to reinforce the company's tried-and-true advertising strategy. At the same time, the company's use of a nearly forty-year-old song to market its new can and logo potentially undermines that strategy and ultimately illuminates a dilemma faced by the company. How does it appeal to new cola drinkers while keeping the ones it converted back in the 1960s? In other words, how does Pepsi market to "GenerationNext" and Generation "Then" at the same time? The resolution of the commercial may provide a clue. Pepsi tries to have it both ways when the bug singing the out-of-date tune is crushed by the young hipster drinking from the new can. But while the young drinker crushes the Jagger-bug, it doesn't really die. The youth can squash the past without the act becoming too threatening to those boomers who still want to "think young" and for whom the Stones will always represent rebellion.

For those who remember the lyrical content of the song and the political and social position it occupied, the act of interpretation and the intent of the advertiser is further complicated. There are doubtless those who were offended by the chorus—"How come you taste so good . . . just like a *black* girl should"—despite the fact that these lines were excised from the commercial. In addition, there are those who will associate the song with the images of exploitation, aggression, racial unrest, and sexism that it invariably recalls, whether parody of those social forces or not. Such reasons may account for the fact that the commercial was pulled from rotation almost immediately after it aired. There are also those who will remember and associate none of these things with the song, the commercial, the band, or the product itself. But just because viewers (or listeners) do not recognize these elements, does that mean they don't exist?

Perhaps there is a final meaning contained within the commercial that begs examination; the ad's appeal to addiction. Pepsi's goal as a soft-drink manufacturer and a major world-wide corporation is to get consumers to drink their cola and to keep them drinking as much as they can. The success of Pepsi-Co is dependent on "hooking" as many drinkers as possible and keeping those drinkers "addicted" to their product. The ultimate intent of the "Brown Sugar" commercial is to associate Pepsi with the iconography of temptation, excess, appropriation, and addiction. These elements are embodied by The Rolling Stones and their song. The commercial contains several references to drugs. There is a suggestive moment when the bug drinks the Pepsi, dipping its needle-like mouth into the fluid, that brings to mind images of junkies shooting up. Furthermore, after drinking the cola the gnat is "transformed," having clearly ingested a mind and body altering substance. That this message fits in neatly with the references to drugs and addiction in The Rolling Stones song "Brown Sugar," and with the lyrical imagery of the album from which it came, is perhaps more than coincidence. Such an association is only reinforced in the Blind Melon "Summer Job" ad. Ultimately, the producers of both commercials, knowingly or not, have incorporated these levels of meaning into their ads through the use of these songs.

Conclusion

The use of rock-and-roll in commercials is constantly housed within debates of "selling out" and authenticity. For a band to allow a song to be used to sell a product has, until very recently, been seen as a debasement of their music. Fans constantly decry the corruption of their memories, their past, their spirit when a hit song is used to sell soda, or shoes, or cars. Lawrence Grossberg writes in "The Framing of Rock: Rock and the New Conservatism":

> [Rock] . . . has been "colonized" by the economic interests of capitalism, and incorporated into the routinized daily life of capitalist, patriarchal and racist relations. It is all over television; it provides the background music for advertising, films and even shopping. The result, according to many critics and fans, is that rock is losing its cutting edge, its ability to encapsulate and articulate resistance, even its marginality. It has become "establishment culture."[5]

Perhaps this is all true. But it is also reasonable to assume that this process of homogenization is inevitable to a mode of music and expression dependent on, and exploitative of, temptation, addiction, and exploitation. That The Rolling Stones can and should be

[5]Tony Bennett, Simon Frith, Lawrence Grossberg, John Shepherd, Graeme Turner, eds., *Rock and Popular Music* (Routledge, New York, 1993), p. 194.

used for this process should not be lost on consumers, and was hopefully not lost on the producers of this particular commercial.

Like rock-and-roll itself (and like Blind Melon or any reasonably successful band for that matter), The Rolling Stones are themselves dependent—"hooked"—on appropriation, exploitation, temptation, and addiction. They used the musical style of another era and lifestyle for their own purposes, just as they used their knowledge and experience of addiction as an important factor for their success as artists. Their song about appropriation, exploitation, addiction, temptation, and the slavery iconography on which it is based, is itself a potent metaphor about the tools and power relations inherent within capitalism and consumerism. The fact that it is being used to sell a product—that a song about exploitation and addiction from a band that itself appropriated its sound to gain success in a musical form dependent on appropriation—seems ultimately, and ironically, appropriate. What is finally symbolic about the "Brown Sugar" commercial is that it is an ad that, at last and explicitly, exposes rock's value to advertisers.

After Reading

Critical Perspective

1. What is Reynolds's main claim about how the Rolling Stones' song "Brown Sugar" is being used in Pepsi's advertising campaign? Do you find this claim viable? Why or why not? Be sure to point to the text for evidence to support your views.

Rhetoric and Argument

2. Offer a rhetorical analysis of Reynolds's essay. How does he employ the rhetorical appeals—ethos, pathos, and logos? You may also examine his use of audience, intertextuality, context, and constraints. Do you find his approach persuasive? Why or why not? Give textual examples to back up your claims.
3. Describe the arrangement of Reynolds's essay. Chart the movement of the essay and explain the differences between certain sections. Do you find this structure effective in supporting his argument? Why or why not?
4. Examine the kinds of evidence that Reynolds uses to support his assertions in detail. Why does he use certain kinds of evidence at certain points in his essay and other kinds at other points? Do you find that Reynolds's evidence backs up his main assertion? Why or why not? Give textual evidence to back up your thoughts.
5. Look at the lyrics of "Brown Sugar" that Reynolds cites. How does Reynolds analyze these lyrics? Do you find his analyses convincing? If yes, why? If no, why not? Be sure to clarify your thoughts by pointing to his essay as well as the song.

Analysis

6. Reynolds exposes some of the sexism and racism inherent in the Rolling Stones' song "Brown Sugar." At the same time Reynolds also reveals how much their music relies upon exploitation and appropriation. In a short argumentative text, consider several contemporary songs from the rock-and-roll, hip-hop, rap, or similar genres. What examples can you find of songs that evoke sexist and racist images? Be sure

to find the lyrics for these songs as well as watch their music videos. Do you think that the way such images are depicted has changed? If yes, how so? Try to point to very detailed examples to back up your ideas. Consult library and Internet sources.

Taking Action

Gather as a small group. You are going to act as detectives. Each group should interview ten people on campus (or people that you know from other areas of your life). They should include people of various ages, cultural and ethnic backgrounds, class allegiances, regional backgrounds, political beliefs, and of both genders. Ask them the following questions (feel free to add to this general list): Do you think that there is still racism in advertising? Do you think that advertising still promotes and fosters addictions? Can you give specific examples? Do you think that advertising has a responsibility to not promote racist stereotypes? Why or why not? What do you think the major role of advertising should be in American culture? Why do you think that this is the case? Seek out library and Internet sources if useful.

When you have compiled your information (broken down in a table by the interviewee's demographics listed above), share your findings with the rest of the class. Based upon this brief exercise, discuss what your evidence seems to suggest. Did you learn what you expected to learn or not? Explain your thoughts.

CLINT C. WILSON AND FÉLIX GUTIÉRREZ

"Advertising and People of Color"

Clint C. Wilson and Félix Gutiérrez have published many articles and books about multiculturalism, race, ethnicity, and the media. Along with Lena Chao they most recently have published the book Racism, Sexism, and the Media: The Rise of Class Communication in Multicultural America.

EXERCISING YOUR SKILLS

Before Reading

Wilson and Gutiérrez trace the history of racism in advertising. Go to the library or surf the Internet, seeking out a series of advertisements from older magazines that feature "minorities" over time. What major changes do you see in the kinds of products being advertised, the context and content of the ads, the rhetorical tactics employed, and the ways in which representations of people of color are being used to sell products? Based on the evidence you find, what do you think this says about race in the United States?

Given the social and legal restrictions on the participation of racial minorities in the society of the United States during much of this country's history, it is not hard to see how the desire to cater to the perceived views of the mass audience desired by advertisers resulted in entertainment and news content that largely ignored people of color, treated them stereotypically when they were recognized, and largely avoided grappling with such issues as segregation, discriminatory immigration laws, land rights, and other controversial issues that affected certain minority groups more than they did the White majority. Although the entertainment and editorial portrayal of non-Whites is amply analyzed elsewhere [in our work], it important to recognize that those portrayals were, to a large extent, supported by a system of advertising that required the media to cater to the perceived attitudes and prejudices of the White majority and that also reinforced such images in its own commercial messages. For years advertisers in the United States reflected the place of non-Whites in the social fabric of the nation either by ignoring them or, when they were included in advertisements for the mass audience, processing and presenting them in a way that would make them palatable salespersons for the products being advertised. These processed portrayals largely mirrored the stereotypic images of minorities in the entertainment media that, in turn, were designed to reflect the perceived values and norms of the White majority. In this way, non-White portrayals in advertising paralleled and reinforced their entertainment and journalistic images in the media.

The history of advertising in the United States is replete with characterizations that, like the Frito Bandito, responded to and reinforced the preconceived image that many White Americans apparently had of Blacks, Latinos, Asians, and Native Americans. Over the years advertisers have employed Latin spitfires like Chiquita Banana, Black mammies like Aunt Jemima, and noble savages like the Santa Fe Railroad's Super Chief to pitch their products to a predominately White mass audience of consumers. In 1984 the Balch Institute for Ethnic Studies in Philadelphia sponsored an exhibit of more than 300 examples of racial and ethnic images used by corporations in magazines, posters, trade cards, and storyboards. In an interview with the advertising trade *Advertising Age*, institute director Mark Stolarik quoted the catalog for the exhibit, which capsulized the evolution of images of people of color and how they have changed.

"Some of these advertisements were based on stereotypes of various ethnic groups. In the early years, they were usually crude and condescending images that appealed to largely Anglo-American audiences who found it difficult to reconcile their own visions of beauty, order and behavior with that of non-Anglo-Americans," said Stolarik. "Later, these images were softened because of complaints from the ethnic groups involved and the growing sophistication of the advertising industry."[1]

The advertising examples in the exhibit include positive White ethnic stereotypes, such as the wholesome and pure image of Quakers in an early Quaker Oats advertisement and the cleanliness of the Dutch in a turn-of-the century advertisement for Colgate soaps. But they also featured a late 19th century advertisement showing an Irish matron threatening to hit her husband over the head with a rolling pin because he didn't smoke the right brand of tobacco. Like Quaker Oats, some products even incorporated a stereotypical image on the package or product line being advertised.

"Lawsee! Folks sho' whoops with joy over AUNT JEMIMA PANCAKES," shouted a bandanna-wearing Black mammy in a magazine advertisement for Aunt Jemima pancake mix, which featured a plump Aunt Jemima on the box. Over the years, Aunt Jemima has lost some weight, but the stereotyped face of the Black servant continues to be featured on the box. Earlier advertisements for Cream of Wheat featured Rastus, the Black servant

on the box, in a series of magazine cartoons with a group of cute but ill-dressed Black children. Some of the advertisements played on stereotypes ridiculing Blacks, such as an advertisement in which a Black school teacher standing behind a makeshift lectern made out of a boldly lettered Cream of Wheat box, asks the class "How do you spell Cream of Wheat?" Others appeared to promote racial integration, such as a magazine advertisement captioned "Putting it down in Black and White," which showed Rastus serving bowls of the breakfast cereal to Black and White youngsters sitting at the same table.

Racial imagery was also integrated into the naming of trains by the Santa Fe railroad, which named one of its passenger lines the Super Chief and featured highly detailed portraits of the noble Indian in promoting its service through the Southwestern United States. In another series of advertisements, the railroad used cartoons of Native American children to show the service and sights passengers could expect when they traveled the Santa Fe line.

These and other portrayals catered to the mass audience mentality by either neutralizing or making humor of the negative perceptions that many Whites may have had of racial minorities. The advertising images, rather than showing people of color as they really were, portrayed them as filtered through Anglo eyes. This presented an out-of-focus image of racial minorities, but one that was palatable, and even persuasive, to the White majority to which it was directed. In the mid-1960s Black civil rights groups targeted the advertising industry for special attention, protesting both the lack of integrated advertisements including Blacks and the stereotyped images that the advertisers continued to use. The effort, accompanied by support from federal officials, resulted in the overnight inclusion of Blacks as models in television advertising in 1967 and a downplaying of the images that many Blacks found objectionable.

"Black America is becoming visible in America's biggest national advertising medium," reported the *New York Times* in 1968. "Not in a big way yet, but it is a beginning and men in high places give assurances that there will be a lot more visibility."[2]

But the advertising industry did not generalize the concerns of Blacks, or the concessions made in response to them, to other groups. At the same time that some Black concerns were being addressed with integrated advertising, other groups were being ignored or singled out for continued stereotyped treatment in such commercials as those featuring the Frito Bandito.

Among the Latino advertising stereotypes cited in a 1969 article[3] by sociologist Tomás Martínez were commercials for Granny Goose chips featuring fat gun-toting Mexicans, an advertisement for Arid underarm deodorant showing a dusty Mexican bandito spraying his underarms after a hard ride as the announcer intones, "If it works for him it will work for you," and a magazine advertisement featuring a stereotypical Mexican sleeping under his sombrero as he leans against a Philco television set. Especially offensive to Martínez was a Liggett & Meyers commercial for L&M cigarettes that featured Paco, a lazy Latino who never "feenishes" anything, not even the revolution he is supposed to be fighting. In response to a letter complaining about the commercial, the director of public relations for the tobacco firm defended the commercial's use of Latino stereotypes.

"'Paco' is a warm, sympathetic and lovable character with whom most of us can identify because he has a little of all of us in him, that is, our tendency to procrastinate at times," wrote the Liggett & Meyers executive. "He seeks to escape the violence of war and to enjoy the pleasure of the moment, in this case, the good flavor of an L&M cigarette."[4] Although the company spokesman claimed that the character had been tested without negative reactions from Latinos (a similar claim was made by Frito-Lay regarding the Frito Bandito), Martínez roundly criticized the advertising images and contrasted them to what he saw as the gains Blacks were then making in the advertising field.

"Today, no major advertiser would attempt to display a black man or woman over the media in a prejudiced, stereotyped fashion," Martínez wrote.

> *Complaints would be forthcoming from black associations and perhaps the FCC. Yet, these same advertisers, who dare not show "step'n fetch it" characters, uninhibitedly depict a Mexican counterpart, with additional traits of stinking and stealing. Perhaps the white hatred for blacks, which cannot find adequate expression in today's ads, is being transferred upon their brown brothers.*[5]

In 1970 a Brown Position Paper prepared by Latino media activists Armando Rendón and Domingo Nick Reyes charged that the media had transferred the negative stereotypes it once reserved for Blacks to Latinos, who had become "the media's new nigger."[6] The protests of Latinos soon made the nation's advertisers more conscious of the portrayals that Latinos found offensive. But, as in the case of the Blacks, the advertising industry failed to apply the lessons learned from one group to other racial minorities.

Although national advertisers withdrew much of the advertising that negatively stereotyped Blacks and Latinos, sometimes replacing them with affluent, successful images that were as far removed from reality as the negative portrayals of the past, the advances made by those groups were not shared with Native Americans and Asians. Native Americans' names and images, no longer depicted either as the noble savage or as cute cartoon characters, have all but disappeared from broadcast commercials and print advertising. The major exceptions are advertising for automobiles and trucks that bear names such as Pontiac, Dakota, and Navajo and sports teams with racial nicknames such as the Kansas City Chiefs, Washington Redskins, Florida State University Seminoles, Atlanta Braves, and Cleveland Indians. Native Americans and others have protested these racial team names and images, as well as the pseudo-Native American pageantry and souvenirs that accompany many of them but with no success in getting them changed.

Asians, particularly Japanese, continue to be dealt more than their share of commercials depicting them in stereotypes that cater to the fears and stereotypes of White America. As was the case with Blacks and Latinos, it took organized protests from Asian American groups to get the message across to the corporations and their advertising agencies. In the mid-1970s, a Southern California supermarket chain agreed to remove a television campaign in which a young Asian karate-chopped his way down the store's aisles cutting prices. Nationally, several firms whose industries have been hard-hit by Japanese imports fought back through commercials, if not in the quality or prices of their products. One automobile company featured an Asian family carefully looking over a new car and commenting on its attributes in heavily accented English. Only after they bought it did they learn it was made in the United States, not Japan. Another automobile company that markets cars manufactured in Japan under an English-language name showed a parking lot attendant opening the doors of the car, only to find the car speaking to him in Japanese. For several years Sylvania television ran a commercial boasting that its television picture had repeatedly been selected over competing brands as an off-screen voice with a Japanese accent repeatedly asked, "What about Sony?" When the announcer responded that the Sylvania picture had also been selected over Sony's, the off-screen voice ran off shouting what sounded like a string of Japanese expletives. A 1982 *Newsweek* article observed that "attacking Japan has become something of a fashion in corporate ads" because of resentment over Japanese trade policies and sales of Japanese products in the United States, but quoted Motorola's advertising manager as saying, "We've been as careful as we can be" not to be racially offensive.[7]

But many of the television and print advertisements featuring Asians featured images that were racially insensitive, if not offensive. A commercial for a laundry product featured a Chinese family that used an "ancient Chinese laundry secret" to get their customer's clothes clean. Naturally, the Chinese secret turned out to be the packaged product paying for the advertisement. Companies pitching everything from pantyhose to airlines featured Asian women coiffed and costumed as seductive China dolls or exotic Polynesian natives to pitch and promote their products, some of them cast in Asian settings and others attentively caring for the needs of the Anglo men in the advertisement. One airline boasted that those who flew with it would be under the care of the Singapore Girl.

Asian women appearing in commercials were often featured as China dolls with the small, darkened eyes, straight hair with bangs, and a narrow, slit skirt. Another common portrayal featured the exotic, tropical Pacific Islands look, complete with flowers in the hair, a sarong or grass skirt, and shell ornament. Asian women hoping to become models sometimes found that they must conform to these stereotypes or lose assignments. Leslie Kawai, the 1981 Tournament of Roses Queen, was told to cut her hair with bangs by hairstylists when she auditioned for a beer advertisement. When she refused, the beer company decided to hire another model with shorter hair cut in bangs.[8]

The lack of a sizable Asian community, or market, in the United States was earlier cited as the reason that Asians are still stereotyped in advertising and, except for children's advertising, are rarely presented in integrated settings. The growth rate and income of Asians living in the United States in the 1980s and 1990s, however, reinforced the economic potential of Asian Americans to overcome the stereotyping and lack of visibility that Blacks and Latinos challenged with some success. By the mid-1980s there were a few signs that advertising was beginning to integrate Asian Americans into crossover advertisements that, like the Tostitos campaign, were designed to have a broad appeal. In one commercial, television actor Robert Ito was featured telling how he loves to call his relatives in Japan because the calls make them think that he is rich, as well as successful, in the United States. Of course, he adds, it is only because the rates of his long distance carrier were so low that he was able to call Japan so often.

In the 1970s mass audience advertising in the United States became more racially integrated than at any time in the nation's history. Blacks, and to a much lesser extent Latinos and Asians, could be seen in television commercials spread across the broadcast week and in major magazines. In fact, the advertisements on network television often appeared to be more fully integrated than the television programs they supported. Like television, general circulation magazines also experienced an increase in the use of Blacks, although studies of both media showed that most of the percentage increase had come by the early 1970s. By the early 1970s the percentage of prime-time television commercials featuring Blacks had apparently leveled off at about 10%. Blacks were featured in between only 2% and 3% of magazine advertisements as late as 1978. That percentage, however small, was a sharp increase from the 0.06% of news magazine advertisements reported in 1960.[9]

The gains were also socially significant, because they demonstrated that Blacks could be integrated into advertisements without triggering a White backlash among potential customers in the White majority. Both sales figures and research conducted since the late 1960s have shown that the integration of Black models into television and print advertising does not adversely affect sales or the image of the product. Instead, [as a] study by the American Newspaper Publishers Association showed, the most important influences on sales were the merchandise and the advertisement itself. In fact, while triggering no adverse affect among the majority of Whites, integrated advertisements were found to be useful in swaying Black consumers, who responded favorably to positive Black role models in print advertisements.[10] Studies conducted in the early 1970s also showed that White consumers did not respond negatively to advertising featuring Black models, although their response was more often neutral than positive.[11] One 1972 study examining White backlash, however, did show that an advertisement prominently featuring darker-skinned Blacks was less acceptable to Whites than those featuring lighter-skinned Blacks as background models.[12] Perhaps such findings help explain why research conducted later in the 1970s revealed that, for the most part, Blacks appearing in magazine and television advertisements were often featured as part of an integrated group.[13]

Although research findings have shown that integrated advertisements do not adversely affect sales, the percentage of Blacks and other minorities in general audience advertising did not increase significantly after the numerical gains made through the mid-1970s. Those minorities who did appear in advertisements were often depicted in upscale or integrated settings, an image that the Balch Institute's Stolarik criticized as taking advertising "too far in the other direction and created stereotypes of 'successful' ethnic group members that are as unrealistic as those of the past."[14] Equally unwise, from a business sense, was the low numbers of Blacks appearing in advertisements.

> *Advertisers and their ad agencies must evaluate the direct economic consequences of alternative strategies on the firm. If it is believed that the presence of Black models in advertisements decreases the effectiveness of advertising messages, only token numbers of Black models will be used,*

wrote marketing professor Lawrence Soley at the conclusion of a 1983 study.

> *Previous studies have found that advertisements portraying Black models do not elicit negative affective or conative responses from consumers. . . . Given the consistency of the research findings, more Blacks should be portrayed in advertisements. If Blacks continue to be under-represented in advertising portrayals, it can be said that this is an indication of prejudice on the part of the advertising industry, not consumers.*[15]

Notes

1. "Using Ethnic Images," p. 9.
2. Cited in Philip H. Dougherty, "Frequency of Blacks in TV Ads," *New York Times*, May 27, 1982, p. D19.
3. Martínez, "How Advertisers Promote," p. 10.
4. Martínez, "How Advertisers Promote," p. 11.
5. Martínez, "How Advertisers Promote," pp. 9–10.
6. Domingo Nick Reyes and Armando Rendón, *Chicanos and the Mass Media* (Washington, DC: The National Mexican American Anti-Defamation Committee, 1971).
7. Joseph Treen. "Madison Ave. vs. Japan. Inc.," *Newsweek* (April 12, 1982), p. 69.
8. Ada Kan, *Asian Models in the Media*, unpublished term paper, Journalism 466: Minority and the Media, University of Southern California, December 14, 1983, p. 5.
9. Studies on increase of Blacks in magazine and television commercials cited in James D. Culley and Rex Bennett, "Selling Blacks, Selling Women," *Journal of Communication* (Autumn 1976, Vol. 26, No. 4), pp. 160–174; Lawrence Soley, "The Effect of Black Models on Magazine Ad Readership," *Journalism Quarterly* (Winter 1983, Vol. 60.

No. 4), p. 686; and Leonard N. Reid and Bruce G. Vanden Bergh, "Blacks in Introductory Ads," *Journalism Quarterly* (Autumn 1980, Vol. 57, No. 3), pp. 485–486.

10. Cited in D. Parke Gibson, *$70 Billion in the Black* (New York: Macmillan, 1979), pp. 83–84.

11. Laboratory studies on White reactions to Blacks in advertising cited in Soley, "The Effect of Black Models," pp. 585–587.

12. Carl E. Block, "White Backlash to Negro Ads: Fact or Fantasy?" *Journalism Quarterly* (Autumn 1980, Vol. 49, No. 2), pp. 258–262.

13. James D. Culley and Rex Bennett, "Selling Blacks, Selling Women."

14. "Using Ethnic Images," p. 9.

15. Soley, *The Effect of Black Models*, p. 690.

After Reading

Critical Perspective

1. Wilson and Gutiérrez cover a great deal of historical ground in their essay. After reading their text, which particular examples of racism in advertising stick with you in particular? Why do you think that this might be?

Rhetoric and Argument

2. Consider the writers' use of tone, audience, purpose, ethos, pathos, logos, intertextuality, context, and constraints. Which of their rhetorical tactics are most as well as least effective and why? Give textual support for your perspectives.

3. What is Wilson and Gutiérrez's main claim about the history of how people of color have been depicted in mainstream American advertising? What comments do they seem to be making about contemporary advertising campaigns? What evidence can you point to in their text to back up your assertions? Do you agree with their views? Why or why not?

4. Consider whether this essay's argument might be made more effectively. Are there any logical fallacies or assumptions at work that strike you as important to consider? If you were rewriting this essay, what would you add? What might you remove? Why?

5. Choose one cultural group that Wilson and Gutiérrez focus upon in their essay. Think about how advertisers use packaging, print advertisements, and the commercials that feature this cultural group. Are any of the stereotypes that the authors mention in their essay still being associated with certain products? Can you recall any attempts by advertisers to undermine the history of stereotypes associated with these products? If yes, how so?

Taking Action

Wilson and Gutierrez's argument centers upon how race and ethnicity have been treated historically in print advertisements. Consider the history of an ad campaign for one particular product that has represented these issues. In a short essay, chart the ways in which this campaign has changed over the years and how these changes reflect broader cultural shifts. Offer a claim of cultural criticism about what this history reveals about rhetoric and advertising as well as whether race and ethnicity depictions have "developed" or simply become more covert over time. Consult relevant library and Internet sources. Share your response with your classmates.

Analysis

6. Examine how people of color are depicted in the latest popular magazines, specifically those magazines targeting specific racial or ethnic groups. What differences do you see between the advertisements that appear in these kinds of publications and the ones that appear for the same products in other kinds of magazines? If you do notice some important differences, indicate what they are. If you do not, reflect on why there may be few differences. Write a short essay in response to these concerns. Consult library and Internet sources.

GARY R. HICKS

"Media at the Margins: Homoerotic Appeals to the Gay and Lesbian Community"

Gary R. Hicks is an associate professor and director of Graduate Studies in the Department of Mass Communications at Southern Illinois University, Edwardsville. His research interest centers on the media's portrayal of marginalized people and has focused largely on media depictions of the lesbian, gay, bisexual, and transgender communities. Hicks's work includes an article in the Journal of Mass Media Ethics, *chapters in* Desperately Seeking Ethics *by Howard Good and the book in which this essay appears,* Sex in Advertising, *edited by Tom Reichert and Jacqueline Lambiase.*

EXERCISING YOUR SKILLS

Before Reading

Hicks examines the ways in which some advertisements cater to both straight and gay audiences suggesting some of the problems and possibilities associated with this phenomenon. Examine an ad campaign—print ads as well as commercials—that you think could accomplish something similar. How might these ads manage to use sexual appeal to persuade both straight and gay audiences? In what ways do you think that they are successful? In what ways do you think that they may fail to address the needs of both groups?

Contemporary advertising abounds with sexually ambiguous images. Who's to say that the perfume ad that features a near-naked woman is designed to appeal only to men? And whereas a straight audience can see the image of handsome young men playing touch football in a Tommy Hilfiger ad as a symbol of American manhood and, on a quite different level, the joys of consumerism, gay readers might see a lightly veiled homoerotic scene. For years, mainstream advertisers have utilized what Lukenbill (1999) called social, sexual, and image *codes* to sell products to mainstream markets while making gays and lesbians feel connected. This form of "doublespeak" uses innuendo and images that can be decoded by people "in the know."

The subtlety with which advertisers insert homoerotic images into ads targeted at mainstream audiences can be viewed as nothing short of an art form. Ads that employ these dual messaging images—attractive to both heterosexuals and gays—have been used successfully for years to sell products such as clothing, alcohol, and tobacco. When these same advertisers began using more overt sexual imagery to reach out to a lesbian and gay market, the codes took on a different role. In recent years, mainstream advertisers have begun placing their ads with more blatantly homoerotic images in the gay press to attract the gay and lesbian community, and, more specifically, its money. This attention to the gay consumer is not unwarranted. Although common myths about large disposable incomes among gays have mostly been debunked, the lesbian and gay community does represent a potential market of millions. A 1997 ad by the National Gay Newspaper Guild noted that gays and lesbians make up a $35 billion market and that they are 11.7 times more likely to be in a professional work position and 8 times more likely to own a computer notebook than heterosexuals.

This essay examines the "mainstream" sexual advertising that now frequently appears in such gay and lesbian publications as *The Advocate*, *Out*, and *Instinct*. By means of textual analysis, these ads may be studied not only to see both their blatant and hidden sexual images and innuendo, but also to consider their images and messages within the larger issue of gay and lesbian politics and its place within society.

Mass Media and the Construction of Sexuality

Postmodern scholars have argued that sexuality is socially constructed, created through the continuous interplay among individuals, society, and those institutions that make up culture (Foucault, 1978). Among these institutions, media have been cited as the most important contemporary factor in the socialization of gay men and lesbians. The media influence not only how nongay society views gays, but also how lesbians and gay men see themselves. The frequent lack of positive gay images within other institutions of society—family, church, school—make media an even more important source of information about gay and lesbian issues and identities. A 1984 study indicated that self-identification by gays is not even possible until an identity is acknowledged by the media (O'Neil, 1984). Gay people, like all people, define themselves in relation to their environment. In a mediated world, this environment is in turn shaped by media images. As Kellner (1994) wrote, the power of the mass media cannot be underestimated when it comes to helping us define where we as individuals fit within the grand scheme of things. This scheme, it can be argued, has been historically heterosexist and injuriously homophobic.

The mass media provide, as Gross (1994) suggested, a "common ground" from which members of a diverse culture can derive shared meanings and basic understandings of how the world works, of how things are. Power in its truest sense comes not only from the ability to facilitate a shared awareness of the gay experience, but also from actually *creating* this common understanding of what it means to be gay or lesbian in society.

Some who hold this immense power include those who run television networks, publish magazines, direct advertising agencies, and manage Fortune 500 companies. Much of what constitutes gay identity today has been created, or at the least modified, by corporate and media organizations—institutions that are generally conservative and mostly white, male, middle-aged and heterosexual.

A Marginal Community

The emergence of the homosexual as a minority figure occurred at mid-20th century through the convergence of politics and science. World War II provided social and sexual contacts never before available to millions of gays and lesbians. The release in 1948 of Alfred Kinsey's *Sexual Behavior in the Human Male* (followed in 1953 by a book focusing on women's sexuality) acknowledged that upwards of 10% of the population is at any time homosexual. Armed with scientific validation and the presence of large numbers of gay people who transplanted themselves to major American cities after the war, early gay-rights leaders such as Harry Hay made the first tentative steps toward formulating the idea of being gay into an identity. During this time in American history, ". . . every move a homosexual made was fraught with the danger of self-disclosure and subsequent persecution" (Hay, 1996). Although the liberating forces unleashed by these political and social phenomena would be kept covert during much of the 1950s (including a complete absence of homosexual images in advertising), they provided the springbed from which the consciousness movement of the 1960s and 1970s would arise (Miller, 1995).

Heterosexual America of the 1950s was settling into the post-war economic expansion with little regard for homosexuals. While advertisers zeroed in on the emerging middle class with pitches for products that would help make the American dream a reality, homosexual America remained invisible. Worse than invisibility, homosexuals maintained their own cover for threat of prosecution. "Every evening spent in a gay setting, every contact with another homosexual or lesbian, every sexual intimacy carried a reminder of the criminal penalties that could be exacted at any moment" (D'Emilio, 1983).

If the 1950s represented "a period of wintry despair for homosexuals in the United States" (Gross, 1993), the 1960s were not much better. Although Americans were consumed with new societal and sexual freedoms, concerns over the needs of gay America did not register on most people's radars. At a time when basic civil rights were still being sought and the anti-Vietnam war movement was overshadowing many other concerns, homosexual rights "were the last priority on an already overburdened national agenda" (Herdt & Boxer, 1993). When the media did pay attention to gays and lesbians, their portrayals were anything but flattering.

In a 1964 *Life* magazine article titled "Homosexuality in America: The 'Gay' World Takes to the City Streets," the writers concluded that homosexuals had been "rejected by the 'straight' world," and made reference to "fluffy-sweatered young men," who wear the "attention-calling clothes that the 'gay' world likes." The article continued to reference issues of male prostitution and cross dressing (Mardi, Sanders, & Mormor, 1994). This is one example of how the media saw gay life in the 1960s.

Throughout the 1970s, as women, people of color, and other marginalized members of society became more vocal in their demands for equality and societal benefits, gays and lesbians also took a more visible, more political stance. "Out of the Closets and Into the Streets!" became the slogan for a new more open way of "being" gay. Sizable numbers of lesbians and gay men were finding their way out of the closet, and insisting that others find the courage to do the same. In 1973 the American Psychiatric Association finally deleted homosexuality as a category of mental illness. Being "out" was the new imperative of the gay liberation movement, an imperative that not only "transformed the meaning of 'coming out'" (D'Emilio, 1983), but was responsible for changing the very nature of the movement itself. Although not as militant and in-your-face as the 1980s rallying cry used by Queer Nation—"We're Here, We're Queer, Get Used to It"—the demand by gays for gays to be open about their identities represented a monumental shift from earlier ideas about gay life, gay community, and gay responsibility. American television, particularly situation comedies, discovered gays in the 1970s but typified them as sources of comic relief, further marginalizing the community. The advertising industry, long credited with staying on top of—if not initiating—cultural shifts, was nowhere to be seen as the gay community took its first tenuous steps toward visibility.

By 1980, the work of the past decade seemed about to pay off. More than 100 of the nation's largest companies had adopted personnel policies that prohibited discrimination on the basis of sexual orientation, and 40 cities across the country had passed similar laws (Kaiser, 1997). The political power of the gay community was at an all-time high. The time to safely come out of the closet, it seemed, had come. By the end of 1981, fear of another kind of enemy pushed many gay men back in. It was in the media that most people first heard of AIDS, an illness that at first seemed to be affecting only gay men. As the 1980s progressed, media coverage helped to merge the gay identity with an AIDS identity. Television dramas about AIDS either made gays appear as promiscuous deviants or portrayed them as objects to be pitied.

By the 1990s, a generation of young gay males had come of age with no memory of sex before AIDS. For them, ". . . sex, love, queerness, and AIDS have all been inextricably linked from the very beginning" (Kaiser, 1997). The impact of the illness on gay society actually served to lead many community-minded people out of the closet and led to the reappropriation of words and symbols that were once used to denigrate gays and lesbians. An example can be seen in activists' use of the word *queer* as almost a mantra of empowerment.

Media and Gay Visibility

It is undeniable that gay men and lesbians have become more visible in society than at any time in the past, and that much of that visibility can be seen as positive. More openly lesbian women and gay men hold political office than at any time in the nation's history, television programs that revolve around the multi-dimensional lives of gay characters have topped the ratings charts, and queer theory courses have multiplied within university curricula. But what is the gay *identity* here at the beginning of the 21st century? What role have media played in forming it? To what end are advertisers using that identity to market their products, and in what ways are these advertisements themselves further defining what it means to be gay or lesbian? Are gays and lesbians portrayed as normal, law-abiding citizens who happen to be attracted to the same sex, or as outcasts who participate in risky, deviant sex acts? What do sexually suggestive advertisements teach gay people about themselves? Much of what emerges depends on a mediated definition. When it comes to media images, few are as powerful as advertisements, and few have been so off-limits to the representation of gay and lesbian people and issues. In a media environment where one mainstream newsmagazine, *Time*, can run a cover story on an openly lesbian comedian ("Roll Over," 1997) and a year later question how tolerant Americans are of gay people ("For Better or Worse," 1998), the world of advertising to lesbians and gay men has, until recently, remained a bastion of conservative messages and no-risk images.

The earliest gay publications can be traced to the 1960s. They contained little advertising overall, and none that could be considered mainstream. Some advertisers pointed to the presence in the early gay magazines of ads for pornography, gay bars, and escort services as the reason they kept their distance. As some national gay and lesbian publications, such as the *Advocate*, matured into respectability, and new magazines were launched, mainstream advertisers rethought their position in the 1990s. Major corporations such as IBM, United Airlines, R. J. Reynolds, and Absolut Vodka became regular advertisers in the gay press. Most of their ads, however, were the same ones that were placed in mainstream publications. When the advertising became more obviously targeted to the gay market, the images remained the same as in the "straight" advertisements, only the gender of the models changed. For example, an ad for Safeco Insurance that ran in a 2001 *Advocate* features two men sitting on a floor surrounded by boxes and drinking coffee. Having just purchased a home, as the ad implies, this couple can rest easy because they are covered by Safeco insurance.

From "Safe" Sexuality to Homoerotic Explicitness

Selling with sex or the suggested promise of sex is nothing new in advertising. Although it has became a truism that sex sells, a review of the past century of advertising shows that the kind of sex that sells is of the "red-blooded, all-American, heterosexual variety." The sight of Brooke Shields contorting in tight jeans while declaring, "Nothing comes between me and my Calvins," might have raised some eyebrows for pushing the envelope of advertising standards a few decades back, but it was still well within the socially sanctioned boy-meets-girl brand of sexual image. Of course, no one in the 1970s seriously viewed the Calvin Klein ads as an example of lesbian eroticism. But when Anheuser-Busch in 1999 ran an ad in gay media showing two male arms with hands intertwined and the slogan, "Be Yourself and Make It a Bud Light," right-wing religious groups mounted a boycott of Anheuser-Busch products. Before ultimately deciding to stand by its campaign, the company set up phone numbers that people could call to voice their support or opposition to the ad.

"Be yourself and make it a Bud Light." Ads like this contributed to a boycott of Anheuser-Busch product[s].

Although the image of two people of either gender simply holding hands can hardly constitute blatant sexual imagery, the beer ad was among the first for a mainstream product to use same-sex models with flesh touching flesh. Subsequent ads from both Anheuser-Busch and other companies have continued to push the boundaries of advertising proprieties.

Among the first, and most surprising, ads to feature a same-sex image was a Coors beer ad that appeared in gay magazines in 2000. What makes it surprising is that the Adolph Coors Company was the target of a boycott by gay consumers in the 1970s. At the time, gay rights groups had accused the company, controlled by a family deeply involved in right-wing politics, of discriminating against its gay and lesbian employees. Anti-Coors sentiment was so strong among gay beer drinkers that a research analyst for Coors wrote about how company employees were encouraged not to mention for whom they worked during business trips to San Francisco (Burgess, 1993).

The Coors ad campaign shows how much society has progressed in 20 years. In 2000, an advertisement for Coors Light beer appeared in an issue of *Instinct*, a gay male lifestyle magazine, that featured two hunky male models in an idyllic country scene, posed beside a bicycle built for two with food and a six-pack of Coors Light in a picnic basket. One model has his hand around the other's shoulder as they both gaze outward from the page. Except for both models being of the same gender, this image has been used countless times by advertisers to sell products like clothing and perfume. In the same issue an Anheuser-Busch ad occupies the back cover. The image is of an empty beer glass sitting on a counter in what appears to be a gay bar. Above the glass is the slogan, "You're Out!" It is important to note that *Instinct*, like all of the magazines mentioned in this chapter, is not pornographic. However, this issue, which attracted advertisements from two of the world's largest brewers, contained articles with titles such as, "Loosen Up! Get Your Man to Sexperiment," and "Slut or Stud? Another Night, Another Notch." Although major mainstream corporations such as Coors and Anheuser-Busch definitely do not advertise in pornographic magazines, it is important to note that the editorial content of these magazines is not necessarily bland, either.

Although many of the mainstream advertisers limit the sexual nature of their ads to romance, such as in the Coors Light ad, more are becoming bolder in both sexual innuendo and image. In a 2000 issue of the *Advocate* a Miller Lite ad asks for reader participation in bringing two handsome gay men together. In a bar scene, one model is posed on the far left of the ad while the other is on the far right. The model of the left has a line marked "A" next to him, while the model on the right has one marked "B" next to him. The ad's copy reads, "Connect A to B and Celebrate with Miller Lite." The reader who actually goes so far as to follow these directions ends up making the models touch bodies, one model's hand rubbing against the other's.

Phallocentric Appeals

Almost an entire genre of ads has emerged around the tilted or exploding image of a bottle. A 1995 Bud Light ad showed a beer bottle jutting from the page at an angle so reminiscent of an erect penis that mere coincidence is hardly believable. While the use of sexual images in ads targeted to heterosexual male audiences has long been a staple for the beer industry, the provocative nature of those ads seems somehow diminished by the ordinariness attached by society to heterosexual imagery. To a general audience, the image of a bottle positioned to resemble an erect penis appears more threatening when it is known that the intended target is another male. A Slates Clothing ad takes the image one step further with an ad in a 1999 *Advocate* featuring a bottle at the same exact angle as the bottle in the beer advertisement. In the Slates ad, the cap has been removed and the contents of the bottle are spewing out and filling the page. Although the similarity of this image to male ejaculation is striking, a more interesting question is just what this has to do with selling clothing.

Another clothing company, Diesel, appropriated homoerotic fantasies of uniformed sailors in an ad featuring a naval ship full of young attractive men coming home to port. In the foreground are two hunky men in their sailor whites, lips locked in a passionate kiss. Like the Slates ad, there is no presence in the ad of any Diesel clothing. A 2001 Bud Light ad shows a black-and-white photograph of a muscular man's body wearing only a pair of cut-off blue-jean shorts and combat boots. His hand holds a beer bottle, but his head has been completely cropped out of the picture. The cut-offs, the boots, and the anonymity provided by the headless, faceless torso is reminiscent of much gay male erotica.

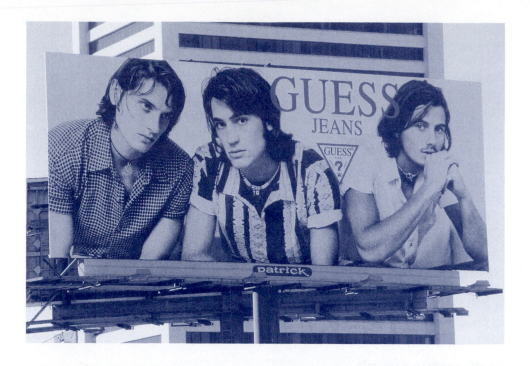

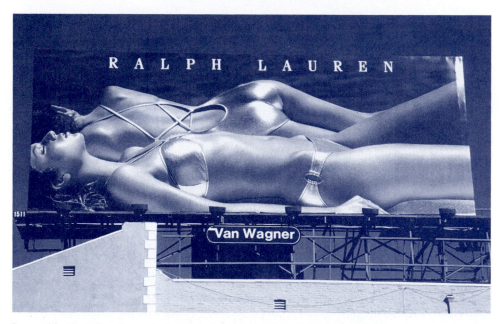

Images like these have been staples in contemporary ad campaigns.

An advertisement by Interflora that promotes sending flowers for Valentine's Day has appeared in both the British gay lifestyle magazine *AXM* and U.S. publications. The romantic image is of three red rose blooms connected by a single long stem. One of the blooms is at the top of the stem while the other two are snuggled together at the bottom. The image by itself appears to be a portrayal of male genitalia, but once the caption "FloralSex" is read the intent of the advertiser become unmistakable.

One of the most sexually bold ads appeared in a 2000 issue of the *Advocate*. Again from Anheuser-Busch, this Bud Light ad is photographed from beneath a glass-top table. Visible through the glass are the bottoms of Bud Light bottles, along with the removed metal caps. At the top of the ad are the words, "Tops and Bottles." There is no overt message nor any hint of nudity in this ad, but for the gay reader, the innuendo is clear. Men who are the penetrators in anal sex are called tops; those who are penetrated are called bottoms. Can this ad be viewed as simply a clever play on words, or is there a more profound message? Does it reinforce or create an identity for a gay reader? If so, what identity? Another Bud Light ad features the simple picture of a six-pack of Bud Light bottles. The caption reads "Nice Package." Again, the sexual innuendo is clear to the gay reader. When Anheuser-Busch advertises to heterosexual audiences, it uses proudly stepping Clydesdale horses, wise-cracking frogs, and the ubiquitous sports figure. For the gay market, the image is one-dimensional, focusing on sexuality, and in the case of this ad, notions of blatant sexual activity.

Lesbian Images

If sexual images are the way mainstream advertisers reach out to gay men, what about appeals to lesbians? Most advertising targeting lesbians in the gay press contains images of attractive women, mostly fully clothed, and rarely doing anything more erotic than embracing. A very romantic ad specifically targeting lesbians—although it might indeed appeal to heterosexual males—is for Disaronno Originale Amaretto. Against the backdrop of Florence, two young women are shown on the cover of a matchbox. While they are embracing, one woman's head is on the other's shoulder and they are fully clothed. At the bottom of the ad is the image of a lit match and the words "Light A Fire." In what may be the most provocative of lesbian-themed ads, the Prada clothing company ran an ad featuring two women facing each other lying together in a hammock with their legs spread wide in a 2001 issue of *The New York Times*' monthly magazine *The Fashion of the Times*.

Despite these ads, those featuring women present more subtle representations of sexuality than in ads focused on gay men, leaving how the ad is construed up to reader's imagination and sexual orientation. A study of advertising directed to heterosexual audiences found a significant increase in the explicitness of images of both female and male models from the early 1980s to the early 1990s. However, whereas 11% of male models were found to be dressed provocatively in 1993 advertisements, 40% of women were (Reichert, Lambiase, Morgan, Carstarphen, & Zavoina, 1999). Is society simply more accustomed to seeing women in sexual roles? Is it that these images, popular in their extreme form in men's pornography, are really not much different from those that regularly appear in magazines such as *Cosmopolitan* and *Glamour*? In her book, *The Beauty Myth*, Naomi Wolf compared the advertising content of ordinary women's magazines with pornographic images and found very little difference outside of the degree of explicitness (Wolf, 1991).

Of course, another reason why suggestive ads with women are viewed differently from those with men could be reflective of women's perceived place in society's power hierarchy. The notion of women portrayed sexually with other women is not as threatening to a male-centered culture in which male homosexuality is often viewed as an affront to male privilege. "One of the most effective ways to demean a man in many societies continues to be to question his masculinity, and allude to the possibility that he may be homosexual" (Dubin, 1992, p. 435).

Buying In or Selling Out?

In a society where the government imposes a "Don't Ask, Don't Tell" policy on gays in the military, in which AIDS activists chant "Silence Equals Death," and where state legislatures are tripping over themselves to enact laws to deny lesbian and gay couples many of the privileges that heterosexuals take for granted, it would seem that visibility at any cost would be the mantra of the gay movement. But does visibility in mass media serve gay and lesbian causes? The mainstream media often present gay life as one-dimensional, usually revolving around sex. This is the same image painted in many of these "gay" advertisements. Are these advertisements, and the corporate lust for gay dollars that make them possible, proof that lesbians and gay men have further entered mainstream life, or are they just another example of how popular culture and commerce work together to keep minority groups marginalized and powerless? Is the advertising industry, long given credit for both reflecting American culture and moving it forward, serving as a harbinger of changes to come in society as a whole? Is the willingness of advertisers to use sexually suggestive gay-themed images an indication of progressive thinking, or simply an effective means to tap into a lucrative market? If so, will these ads actually produce the brand loyalty that the advertisers expect? A recent study showed that the majority of gays and lesbians feels that companies are reaching out to them through advertising for financial gain, and not as a way to enhance the community's stature in society (Gardyn & Fetto, 2001). And so, these questions are not easily answered. Certainly it is unwise to give powerful advertisers too much credit for progressive thinking or to underestimate their propensity for confusing people for markets and for manipulating communities for monetary gain.

References

Burgess, R. J. (1993). *Silver bullets: A soldier's story of how Coors bombed in the beer wars*. New York: St. Martin's Press.

D'Emilio, J. (1983). *Sexual politics, sexual communities: The making of a homosexual minority in the United States*, 1940–1970. Chicago: University of Chicago Press.

Dubin, S. C. (1992). Gay images and the social construction of acceptability. In P. Nardi & B. Schneider (Eds.), *Social perspectives in lesbian and gay studies: A reader* (pp. 434–466). London: Routledge.

For better or worse: In Hawaii, a showdown over marriage tests the limits of gay activism. (1998, October 26). *Time, 152*(17), 43–44.

Foucault, M. (1978). *The history of sexuality.* New York: Random House.

Gardyn, R., & Fetto, J. (2001). In broad daylight: Marketers who want to target homosexuals may have better luck using mass media than gay-specific venues. *American Demographics, 23*(2), 16.

Gross, L. (1993). *Contested closets: The politics and ethics of outing.* Minneapolis: University of Minnesota Press.

Gross, L. (1994). What is wrong with this picture? Lesbian women and gay men on television. In J. Ringer (Ed.), *Queer words, queer images: Communication and the construction of homosexuality* (pp. 143–156). New York: New York University Press.

Hay, H. (1996). *Radically gay: Gay liberation in the words of its founder.* Boston: Beacon Press.

Herdt, G., & Boxer, A. (1993). *Children of horizons: How gay and lesbian teens are leading a new way out of the closet.* Boston: Beacon Press.

Kaiser, C. (1997). *The gay metropolis: 1940–1996.* Boston: Houghton Mifflin.

Kellner, D. (1994). *Media culture: Cultural studies, identity, and politics between the modern and the postmodern.* London: Routledge.

Kinsey, A. (1948). *Sexual behavior in the human male.* Philadelphia: Saunders.

Kinsey, A. (1953). *Sexual behavior in the human female.* Philadelphia: Saunders.

Lukenbill, G. (1999). *Untold millions: Secret truths about marketing to gay and lesbian consumers.* New York: Harrington Park Press.

Mardi, P. M., Sanders, D., & Mormor, J. (1994). *Growing up before stonewall: Life stories of some gay men.* London: Routledge.

Miller, N. (1995). *Out of the past: Gay and lesbian history from 1869 to the present.* New York: Vintage Books.

O'Neil, S. (1984). The role of the mass media and other socialization agents in the identity formation of gay males. In S. Thomas (Ed.), *Studies in Communication, Vol. 1: Studies in Mass Communication and Technology* (p. 201). Norwood, NJ: Ablex.

Reichert, T., Lambiase, J., Morgan, S., Carstarphen, M., & Zavoina, S. (1999). Cheesecake and beefcake: No matter how you slice it, sexual explicitness in advertising continues to increase. *Journalism & Mass Communication Quarterly, 76*(1), 7–20.

Roll over, Ward Cleaver and tell Ozzie Nelson the news: Ellen Degeneres is poised to become TV's first openly gay star. Is America ready or not? (1997, April 14). *Time, 149*(15), 78–85.

Wolf, N. (1991). *The beauty myth: How images of beauty are used against women.* New York: Doubleday.

After Reading

Critical Perspective

1. Hicks's essay charts a part of advertising history that often goes unrecognized. Describe your reaction to his text. What did you learn from Hicks's essay that was particularly interesting, insightful, or new to you? Why do you think that you had this reaction? Be sure to quote from his text to support your thoughts.

Rhetoric and Argument

2. Characterize Hicks's rhetorical strategies throughout his piece. How does he deal with audience, purpose, ethos, pathos, logos, intertextuality, context, and constraints? Give quotes to back up your ideas.
3. What is Hicks's main claim in his text? Where does it appear? Do you agree with his thesis? Why or why not?
4. What does Hicks mean when he says that "sexuality is socially constructed"? Paraphrase this concept in your own words. What do you think about this idea? Can you point to examples of this concept from your own life and experiences?
5. Hicks provides detailed descriptions of the ads he analyzes in his text. Why do you think that Hicks makes this choice? Would you argue that including these descriptions helps support his argument? If yes, how so? If no, explain.

Analysis

6. In a short argumentative essay, address the following concerns. You will make a claim about the effectivity of Hicks's essay—whether it is persuasive or not. Be sure to characterize the structure of Hicks's argument. Why do you think he sets up his argument in this way? Do you find this arrangement effective? Why or why not? Be sure to offer textual evidence to support your views as well as consult library and Internet sources.

Taking Action

Hicks offers an important caution concerning the growing number of ads targeting gay consumers. He asks us to consider whether representations of gay people in ads further the gay rights movement or exist only for monetary gain. Consider an image of homosexuality in the mainstream media from ads, television, magazines, or film that Hicks does not mention. For ads, you may want to consult The Commercial Closet at http://www.commercialcloset.org/cgi-bin/iowa/index.html. Be sure to take very detailed notes on the text you select, examine it multiple times, and begin to formulate a claim of cultural criticism about it.

After you have completed this exercise, form a small group. Analyze the ways in which these particular images further gay rights, fail to address them, or even impede them. Support your answers by providing primary evidence from the media form you discuss as well as secondary sources from the library and Internet. Share your findings with the rest of the class.

REPRESENTATIONS OF GENDER

CAROL MOOG

"Media Mirrors"

Carol Moog is a writer and cultural critic who has published numerous articles as well as Are They Selling Her Lips? Advertising and Identity, *where this essay can be found.*

EXERCISING YOUR SKILLS

Before Reading

Moog writes about the history of Maidenform's advertising and how women's needs and desires have changed over time. In what ways do media images shape how we view masculinity and femininity? Do you think that consumers shape how the media depicts masculinity and femininity? Or, is something else going on?

Try to think of a long-term advertising campaign for a product geared specifically toward men or women. What rhetorical tactics does this ad campaign employ to draw in its viewers? How do the advertisers utilize stereotypes about what it means to be masculine or feminine to get consumers interested in buying the products? What views, anxieties, fears, beliefs, values and desires does this ad campaign draw upon? What evidence can you point to in order to support this?

> *Breasts.*
> *Philip Roth yearned for them.*
> *He built an empire on them.*
> *But Maidenform made the fortune from them.*

Sharon, the forty-seven-year-old wife of a dentist with two grown children, is telling me about the dream she had three nights before:

> *Richard and I were in a restaurant. I think it was the Citadel, where we ate about a month ago—I don't know. But it was different. There were all these men around, and I felt uncomfortable. But they weren't alone. They were there with some old women—like their mothers or grandmothers or something. And I was very angry at Richard. I remember fighting with him there before too. He kept telling me to shut up, that I was drinking too much. Suddenly, I realized I didn't have anything on and he was mad at me because everyone was staring. I thought, I've got to get out of here. I panicked. But I couldn't move. No one at the other tables seemed to pay any attention. And here's where it got really strange. I started to relax. I felt beautiful. And Richard smiled.*

Sharon's dream has triggered a thought in my mind that starts to crystallize into an image that helps me understand what she's thinking about. I'm imagining Bea Coleman and her mother, Ida Rosenthal, and the brilliant campaign they launched more than thirty years ago. A campaign so brilliant that it touched the most potent fantasies of a woman's dreams.

It was the Maidenform fantasy. The "I dreamed I was . . . in my Maidenform bra" campaign ran for twenty years and made Bea Coleman and Ida Rosenthal rich beyond their wildest dreams.

The original Maidenform ads were created by the agency of Norman, Craig and Kummel Advertising, and showed women acting out fantasies (frequently controversial fantasies), that fully displayed their Maidenform bras. Ads like the lady lawyer who "dreamed I swayed the jury in my Maidenform bra" unleashed and exposed the secret fantasies of traditional women of the fifties and invited them to step brazenly into dreams of power and influence. What the ads had women "dream" was that they could go ahead and be exhibitionistic, but not just about their bodies; about their capabilities. Clearly, a psychological chord was struck with this campaign. Women sent scores of unsolicited photos of themselves in endless scenes of "I dreamed I was . . . in my Maidenform bra." In terms of how the campaign portrayed women, it was a real set-breaker. The campaign put the company on the map and gave cultural approval to powerful wishes women certainly harbored but rarely advertised.

What was going on in the women who responded so positively to the Maidenform campaign? This was pre-women's lib, when gender roles were still plainly spelled out: Females were Devoted Housewives and males were Preoccupied Breadwinners. Then along comes Maidenform with full-color photos of poised, clear-eyed, confident women unabashedly exposing their fantasies along with their chests. They're not in the least self-conscious. They're relaxed and composed. The campaign offered a sensational subconscious release for the duty-bound women of that period. It was enormously gratifying to identify with the courage of the Maidenform woman daring to show herself as fully developed to anyone interested in looking. Interested persons included parents, husbands, clergymen, and teachers. The fifties woman got to vicariously thumb her nose at all the right people. She got to break out of the socially appropriate straitjacket she'd willingly donned—ostensibly for the good of family and cultural stability—and try on a new identity.

Psychologically, that's what dreams are about anyway. They're what the unconscious produces, busily fulfilling wishes that our rational selves have deemed too outrageous to express in real life. There's something else about dreams. They show us images of ourselves that we've already accepted internally but that we haven't risked trying out yet.

I see the "I dreamed . . ." campaign as a kind of emotional road map for the women's lib activities that came to the surface in the seventies. Phyllis is the only woman I know who actually, ceremoniously, *burned* a bra—and if I told her that she could thank Maidenform for helping her get a picture of herself as an independent person, she'd have been furious. But like it or not, the campaign set the stage for Phyllis and the other women of her generation. Women interacted with the ads in spite of themselves because they were already gearing up for the kind of real-life dreams they made happen when the feminist movement took hold.

The "I dreamed I took the cue in my Maidenform bra" ad is a prime example of the kind of ad that could get to Phyllis, regardless of her conscious protests. When a woman already fantasizing about being less inhibited reads the line "I dreamed I took the cue . . .," she's already projecting herself into the picture. She's already hooked into seeing herself taking charge in what was traditionally a male-dominated situation. Not only does she take the cue stick, but she proceeds to handle it in a deft behind-the-back maneuver, all without losing a trace of her sultry femininity. The fantasy was powerful but safe. Although Phyllis would never admit it, it was perfectly congruent with women's needs at that time to stay feminine while getting strong. At the same time, the campaign helped women picture having power and control far outside the domestic domain.

Here was a landmark campaign that came at precisely the right time to rivet women's attention. A piece of anatomical support empowered their dreams, permitting them to become "Maidenform women," in control of themselves, their circumstances, and their futures. The Maidenform campaign was a strong one, largely because it reflected one advertiser's personal convictions. Bea Coleman, Maidenform's dynamic CEO, always admired her entrepreneurial mother, Ida Rosenthal, who founded the company with her physician-husband William. Ida was a powerhouse. Mother and daughter both dared to dream big and do more. The "I dreamed . . ." concept was turned down by another lingerie company but embraced by Maidenform perhaps because it was consistent with both Bea's and Ida's perceptions of women. Bea seemed to use her mother as a positive role model, and Ida may have unintentionally modeled aspects of herself through the endless permutations of the dream campaign. She persuaded women not just to buy $100 million worth of underwear, but to see themselves as more capable people.

But the dream campaign hit social forces beyond its control—and turned with the tide of change. By the late sixties, the younger women who should have been buying Maidenform bras had begun to associate "I dreamed . . ." images with their mothers—and bras themselves with the constraints of traditional female roles and functions. When young women started ditching their bras along with their mothers' ideas as they reached for autonomy, the advertiser responded to the psychological climate by ditching the "I dreamed . . ." campaign. (Interestingly, Bea Coleman's own story runs a close parallel to the course of the campaign—this was just about the time that she shocked the male-dominated intimate-apparel industry in 1968 by taking over the company as president after her husband's death.)

What happened? Like Bea Coleman herself, women weren't just acknowledging their dreams of power, they were out there making them happen. The dream campaign symbolized the exciting but frustrated longings of the past. These were fantasy ads meant for the women they were trying to escape in their mothers and in themselves. The ads no longer had their initial freeing effect. Instead, they waved a red flag. Women like my old friend Phyllis were burning their bras, not dreaming about showing them off.

The Maidenform woman was mothballed for eleven years. When she reappeared, she launched the greatest controversy in bra history. In a reincarnation created by the Daniel & Charles advertising agency, she was still depicted doing active, even aggressive things, like commuting to work, reading *The Wall Street Journal*, going to the theater, or being a lawyer. She was daringly clad in her matching bra and panties. But now *there were men in the picture!* They appeared disinterested, oblivious to the delectable spectacle of "The Maidenform Woman. You never know where she'll turn up." The men were shot slightly out of focus. They were deeply absorbed, eyes discreetly everywhere else but you-know-where.

Here was a real twist, and the campaign ended up generating the kind of hot attention that left feminists seething and Maidenform sales soaring. Completely unanticipated! Maidenform didn't intend (as many advertisers do) to create a potentially explosive campaign. The agency just thought it had a great new approach for a new age. Advertiser and agency were equally surprised when the campaign got scorching reviews from angered members of women's movements. It also put Maidenform in the painful position of having to reevaluate the "success" of a campaign that, without question, was a success in terms of sales.

What ticked off women when Maidenform tried to turn them on? As the advertiser sees it, the campaign was inadvertently suggesting that the Maidenform woman had achieved her enviable position, such as tiger tamer, strictly on the basis of her sexuality rather than her actual competence. The most noteworthy clunker, the one that finally deep-sixed the "You never know where she'll turn up" campaign, was the white-coated lady doctor piece. Everyone (male or female) who had ever worn a white coat—nurses, lab technicians, beauticians, the American Medical Association—bombarded Maidenform with calls and letters of protest.

As the mail indicated, there were some obvious reasons why this campaign caused the uproar it did. With a female doctor exposing herself in a patient's hospital room, women's lib took a giant step backward. "Strip off the professional cover," these ads seemed to be saying, "and what you'll find is just another sex object."

At the time this campaign got started, however, I thought it would have upset people for an entirely different unconscious reason. I showed the ad to some of my colleagues and just asked their opinions of it. Mark, a Ph.D. psychologist who's been practicing about as long as I have, came up with what turned out to be the consensus:

"That's going to be one angry lady!"

"Okay," I asked, "why?"

Mark pointed to the two samples I'd shown him—the woman in the tiger cage and the doctor ad—and noted, "Look at the men in the pictures. Here's a woman with her clothes off, and they aren't paying any attention to her at all."

Mark and the others confirmed my own sense of the underlying problem. The most insulting thing about the ads was not that the woman had exposed herself—even in a professional role. That might have been intellectually offensive—yes, it could be demeaning to women who were rising in their professions—but it didn't explain the strength of the emotional reactions women had to the ads.

What was really most offensive were the self-indulgent, narcissistic posturings of the *men* in the picture. For the woman wearing the Maidenform bra, the experience was no longer a good dream. It was bad dream. It is humiliating on the deepest levels, where our feelings of self-worth are most fragile, for any of us to expose ourselves at our most naked and vulnerable . . . and make no impact whatsoever. Women can easily identify with the Maidenform image in the ads, put themselves in her position and feel the angry confusion of someone who dolls herself up but still gets ignored.

There's more. Despite being pictured in the trappings of power, this Maidenform woman ended up looking weak and vulnerable. Look at the contrast between the unblinking confidence and forward thrusting body posture of the lady pool-shark and check out the demure, downcast glance and tight-kneed toe-tipped stance of the tiger tamer. Maidenform tried to tell women that it was listening, that it respected their hard-won accomplishments, but it sent some subtle messages that undercut the communication. Women bought the bras but were left with images of themselves as "sweet nothings"—ironically the name of one of Maidenform's best-selling lines.

After four years of profitable (although sometimes uncomfortable) campaigning, Maidenform pulled back from its big-strong-pretty-young-things-turning-up-half-naked-in-front-of-self-involved-men approach. Romance, Maidenform perceived, was coming back. It was time to turn from power to syrup. Women were beginning to gag on advertisers' endless portraits of them as superhuman jugglers of kids, career, hubby, and housework.

Stripped of any power cues, the next Maidenform Woman was one who "Dares to Dream." And what are her daring dreams about now? Sitting around wearing underwear and a wistful, vacant expression, she boldly fantasizes about going out on a date. Here is a woman with no pretensions of being anything other than the lovely, compliant, and ever-so-feminine creature her mother modeled in the fifties. She's straight out of the whistle-clean Harlequin Romance series, right down to the quasi-book-jacket logo in the corner. And like these little stories, Maidenform declares that its "Delectables" will "make your life as soft and smooth as your dreams."

At this stage of the game, all of us, women especially, have gotten to be fairly sophisticated cynics. We know that advertisers run various images of us to see whether they can stir a ripple of salesworthy responses. The "Dares to Dream" campaign reached out to women who had been feeling like miserable failures for fantasizing about guys. While everybody else was out there self-actualizing into steel-plated CEOs, Maidenform gave the "new romantics" permission to go ahead and dream the dreams of adolescent girls if they wanted.

Sales proved that many women wanted just that. Enough battling against male indifference and resistance. Maidenform was tired of trying to tickle the fancies of feminists; the campaign regressed to the lowest-risk imagery for the masses—woman as a glowworm for love.

While it clearly qualifies as a fluff piece, Wyse Advertising's "Dares to Dream" campaign is surpassed in regressiveness by its next series of "lifestyle" ads. "The Maidenform Woman. Today she's playful," whisks our heroine backward in time until she's a prepubescent who gets kind of emotional, but that's okay, because Maidenform will "fit" her "every move and mood" so she can stay just as cute as she is now. She's not even old enough to think about guys—"frisky as a kitten," "Today she's playful."

Now, no angry letters spewed forth on the heels of "Today she's playful." Whom *did* this appeal to? Well, there's Liz. She's very bright and possesses an MBA, which she sometimes waves over a conversation like a silk scarf—something to be admired but not used. She's surrounded by working friends, but she's filled her life with tennis and shopping and lunches. I like Liz, and it's over one of these lunches that she says to me, "I feel like having a temper tantrum."

I can't help thinking about how Liz creates herself in the image of the "Today she's playful" ad—defining herself not in terms of what she's accomplishing, but by her moods. Does Liz know what she's doing? I don't think so. Did the agency know what it was doing? I don't think so. Both are just creating what they hope are pretty pictures.

Where do you go with this? Unfortunately, Liz will probably just continue to be the subject of her moods. Maidenform wasn't quite so stuck—it changed agencies.

Following this purely saccharine retreat from Maidenform's gutsy heritage, the sixty-five-year-old lingerie company set out in pursuit of the Holy Grail of advertising—a new image. After a grueling selection process, Levine, Huntley, Schmidt & Beaver won the account—and the opportunity to sweat its way toward a singularly brilliant advertising idea.

What Levine, Huntley, Schmidt & Beaver created, and what the advertiser had the courage to appreciate, is a radical departure for lingerie ads.

No women, no product—just male movie-star-types like Omar Sharif, Michael York, and Corbin Bernsen. The campaign has been noticed by the media, by competitors, and apparently by women, who've written comments to the advertiser like "I don't normally watch commercials—however, your Michael York commercial is fantastic! So much so I've switched to Maidenform." "Your commercial will be shown at our annual meeting . . . as a prime example of excellent advertising. It appeals to women as adults, not children . . . keep up the good work." And "This is the type of commercial that instills a need in me to purchase your product."

Now just what is driving these ads? What happens when women see someone like Omar Sharif shot in deep shadows, murmuring, "Lingerie says a lot about a woman. I listen as often as possible"? There's an edge of the forbidden, the dangerous, to Sharif's exotic, rakish seductiveness that is a psychological turn-on to the dainty dreamers of Maidenform's recent past. They can rebel against the sweet-young-thing image, and run away (in their fantasies) with a sexy devil. No one has to take the modesty of a woman publicly displayed in her underwear. Sharif's appeal is also clearly to a mature market; he's not exactly the current heartthrob of younger women. So the advertiser moved away from charming vignettes of moody little models and is effectively hooking grown-ups with male bait.

With Corbin Bernsen of *L.A. Law*, the psychological lure isn't just juicy evil. Here's a recognizably competent lady-killer, who enters the mysterious realm of a lingerie department and finds it "a little embarrassing. A little intimidating." What a gift to the female ego! If Maidenform can give women a way to embarrass and intimidate the likes of Mr. Bernsen, even "a little," it's not just underwear anymore—it's personal power.

The story of women's relationship with Maidenform's images reflects the complex interactions we all have with advertising. Advertisers have to communicate with as large a group of us consumers as possible, but in reality, the communication is always one-to-one. Maidenform's first "I dreamed I . . ." campaign was a success because the fantasy it promoted matched the underlying aspirations of enough individuals to make up a mass market. The advertiser gave a big push to a hoop already rolling out the kitchen door of convention, but things changed when the fantasy of sexual power turned to the reality of political and social power.

Then Maidenform held up concrete images of strong women to try to keep up with all the changes. The trouble came when the advertiser unwittingly introduced doubts and insecurities with its "You never know where she'll turn up" series and women felt a bit as though they'd bought a measure of male indifference along with Maidenform's dream images. The advertiser responded by attempting to soothe its buyers with pictures of romantic security. And finally it courts its market with its latest put-yourself-in-the-picture invitations offered by dashing male sex objects.

The promise is still largely romance. But a woman isn't just faced with relating to an image of herself; now, she's asked to relate to her idea of a man's image of her. For this to work for Maidenform, a woman has to have enough self-confidence to imagine that she is the object of these lingerie lovers' underwear fantasies. It would work for Liz, but not for Ann. Ann's a nice woman who feels fat and unattractive and prefers to undress in the dark. These ads make her feel worse because she *can't* imagine herself in them. She flunks the fantasy test.

Maidenform's current strategy works for one other important reason—it sidesteps the question faced by all lingerie advertisers: How can you show a woman in her underwear without making her look either like an idiot or a slut? Most answers bomb. . . .

Advertisers don't deliberately insult the people they are trying to seduce; they're basically family-oriented, intelligent, profit-minded sorts who often take really lousy pictures that they think are great shots of their subject. Even more interesting is that we may like how we look in a picture at one point in our lives, and later on feel disgusted or embarrassed by the same photo. What we identified with in an ad five years ago may be completely out of sync with who we are now. And we form these conclusions almost immediately—not from logical deliberation, but by unconsciously weighing all the subtle verbal cues that make up an advertising message. If some of the pieces don't fit, don't ring true—if we don't like how we see ourselves now or how we'd like to see ourselves in the future—we can end up feeling insulted, misunderstood, or confused . . .

The trouble with the advertising mirror is that we never really see ourselves reflected; we only see reflections of what advertisers want us to think their products will do for us. If the image of who we might be if we used the advertiser's product resonates with where we secretly, or not so secretly, wish we were—then there we are, consciously or unconsciously, measuring up to Madison Avenue. Sometimes that's not such a bad thing, but sometimes whatever insecurities we have get exacerbated by advertisers' image-making and by our own intense desires to make it—to win first prize in Madison Avenue's perpetual lookalike contest.

After Reading

Critical Perspective

1. How did you react to reading Moog's essay? Why do you think you felt this way about it? Is there anything in Moog's text about which you were not aware? If yes, what? Why do you believe that Moog organizes her text in the way she does? Do you think this is an effective technique or not?

Rhetoric and Argument

2. Reflect upon Moog's rhetorical choices in her text—her tone, audience, purpose, ethos, pathos, logos, intertextuality, context, and constraints. In what ways is her essay rhetorically persuasive? In what ways may it not be? Be sure to provide textual evidence to support your claims.

3. What is Moog's main claim in her text and where does it appear? What kind of claim does she utilize? How does Moog support this main claim? Does she do so persuasively? Explain your perspective by offering support from the essay.

4. What kinds of warrants or assumptions does Moog make in her text? Where does she make them? Do you find these assumptions valid? Why or why not?

5. Do you see any logical fallacies at work in Moog's text? If yes, where do they appear? How do you think they impact the effectiveness of her argument?

Analysis

6. Moog's essay was written over fifteen years ago. Have the issues that she mentions changed significantly since then? Write a short argument in which you update and extend Moog's argument, providing a similar analysis of a contemporary lingerie ad campaign. Draw in relevant rhetorical analyses of this ad campaign in addition to library and Internet sources to support your perspectives.

Taking Action

In a recent interview with the journal *Current Health 2* Moog offered some additional thoughts on the issues she raises in her essay. Moog said the following: "Teens are coming up with an identity based on the images they see in advertising. . . . Teens are more vulnerable every year, as the ability of parents to be around and provide a mature presence at home is eroded by the economic picture. There's no place [for teens] to pull back to. You have increasingly rootless, disconnected young people, and advertising is growing in power because too often, nothing much else of value is happening in many kids' lives."

Form a small group and consider the validity of Moog's comment. Do you agree with her assertion? Why or why not? Examine various media forms that target teens and offer rhetorical analyses to support your views. Also consider your own experiences as a teenager to back up your thoughts. Consult library and Internet sources as well. Then present your findings to the class. Consider making your work accessible to other groups both inside and outside the campus community.

JACKSON KATZ

"Advertising and the Construction of Violent White Masculinity"

Jackson Katz is a well-known antisexist, male activist. In 1993 he founded the multiracial, mixed-gender Mentors in Violence Prevention (MVP) Program, at Northeastern University's Center for the Study of Sport in Society, to prevent gender violence in college athletics. Katz is the creator of an award-winning educational video for college and high school students titled Tough Guise: Violence, Media, and the Crisis in Masculinity *as well as the videos* Wrestling With Manhood *and* Spin the Bottle: Sex, Lies, and Alcohol. *Katz has appeared on TV programs such as* The Oprah Winfrey Show, Good Morning America, The Montel Williams Show, CBS Evening News, ABC News, 20/20, *and on MSNBC and Lifetime Television.*

EXERCISING YOUR SKILLS

Before Reading

Katz's text examines how masculinity is represented in the mainstream media, particularly in advertising. He suggests that advertising tends to depict men in terms of military and sports symbolism, muscularity, and heroism. Now consider what the term "sexual violence" might mean and its connections to these representations of men in advertising. How would you define it? What are some examples to which you might point—from your own life or the lives of people you know? In what ways do both men and women suffer as a result of sexual violence? Is there anything that can be done to solve this problem? Make note of your thoughts and ideas.

Violence is one of the most pervasive and serious problems we face in the United States. Increasingly, academics, community activists, and politicians have been paying attention to the role of the mass media in producing, reproducing and legitimating this violence.[1]

Unfortunately, however, much of the mainstream debate about the effects of media violence on violence in the "real" world fails to include an analysis of gender. Although, according to the Federal Bureau of Investigation, approximately 90% of violent crime is committed by males, magazine headline writers talk about "youth" violence and "kids'" love affair with guns. It is unusual even to hear mention of "masculinity" or "manhood" in these discussions, much less a thorough deconstruction of the gender order and the way that cultural definitions of masculinity and femininity might be implicated. Under these conditions, a class-conscious discussion of masculine gender construction is even less likely.

---

1. *Violence* refers to immediate or chronic situations that result in injury to the psychological, social or physical well-being of individuals or groups. For the purpose of this chapter, I will use the American Psychological Association's (APA) more specific definition of interpersonal violence. Although acknowledging the multidimensional nature of violence, the APA Commission on Violence and Youth defines interpersonal violence as "behavior by persons against persons that threatens, attempts, or completes intentional infliction of physical or psychological harm" (APA, 1993, p. 1).

There is a glaring absence of a thorough body of research into the power of cultural images of masculinity. But this is not surprising. It is in fact consistent with the lack of attention paid to other dominant groups. Discussions about racial representation in media, for example, tend to focus on African Americans, Asians or Hispanics, and not on Anglo Whites.[2] Writing about the representation of Whiteness as an ethnic category in mainstream film, Richard Dyer (cited in Hanke) argues that "white power secures its dominance by seeming not to be anything in particular." "Whiteness" is constructed as the norm against which nondominant groups are defined as "other." Robert Hanke, in an article about hegemonic masculinity in transition, argues that masculinity, like Whiteness, "does not appear to be a cultural/historical category at all, thus rendering invisible the privileged position from which (white) men in general are able to articulate their interests to the exclusion of the interests of women, men and women of color, and children" (186).

There has been some discussion, since the mid-1970s, of the ways in which cultural definitions of White manhood have been shaped by stereotypical representations in advertising. One area of research has looked at the creation of modern masculine arche-types such as the Marlboro Man. But there has been little attention, in scholarship or antiviolence activism, paid to the relationship between the construction of violent mascu-linity in what Sut Jhally refers to as the "commodity image-system" of advertising and the pandemic of violence committed by boys and men in the homes and streets of the United States.

This essay is an attempt to sketch out some of the ways in which hegemonic con-structions of masculinity in mainstream magazine advertising normalize male violence. Theorists and researchers in profeminist sociology and men's studies in recent years have developed the concept of *masculinities*, as opposed to *masculinity*, to more adequately describe the complexities of male social position, identity, and experience. At any given time, the class structure and gender order produce numerous masculinities stratified by socioeconomic class, racial and ethnic difference, and sexual orientation. The central delineation is between the hegemonic, or dominant, masculinity (generally, White and middle-class) and the subordinated masculinities.

But although there are significant differences between the various masculinities, in patriarchal culture, violent behavior is typically gendered male. This doesn't mean that all men are violent but that violent behavior is considered masculine (as opposed to feminine) behavior. This masculine gendering of violence in part explains why the movie *Thelma and Louise* touched such a chord: Women had appropriated, however briefly, the male prerogative for, and identification with, violence.

One need not look very closely to see how pervasive is the cultural imagery linking various masculinities to the potential for violence. One key source of constructions of dom-inant masculinity is the movie industry, which has introduced into the culture a seemingly

2. Although hegemonic constructions of masculinity affect men of all races, there are important variables due to racial differences. Because it is not practical to do justice to these variables in an essay of this length, and because the vast majority of images of men in mainstream magazine adver-tisements are of White men, for the purpose of this piece, I will focus on the constructions of various White masculinities.

endless stream of violent male icons. Tens of millions of people, disproportionately male and young, flock to theaters and rent videocassettes of the "action-adventure" (a Hollywood euphemism for *violent*) films of Arnold Schwarzenegger, Sylvester Stallone, Bruce Willis, et al.

These cultural heroes rose to prominence in an era, the mid-to-late 1970s into the 1980s, in which working-class White males had to contend with increasing economic instability and dislocation, the perception of gains by people of color at the expense of the White working class, and a women's movement that overtly challenged male hegemony. In the face of these pressures, then, it is not surprising that White men (especially but not exclusively working-class) would latch onto big, muscular, violent men as cinematic heroes. For many males who were experiencing unsettling changes, one area of masculine power remained attainable: physical size and strength and the ability to use violence successfully.

Harry Brod and other theorists have argued that macro changes in postindustrial capitalism have created deep tensions in the various masculinities. For example, according to Brod,

> *Persisting images of masculinity hold that "real men" are physically strong, aggressive, and in control of their work. Yet the structural dichotomy between manual and mental labor under capitalism means that no one's work fulfills all these conditions.*
>
> *Manual laborers work for others at the low end of the class spectrum, while management sits at a desk. Consequently, while the insecurities generated by these contradictions are personally dissatisfying to men, these insecurities also impel them to cling all the more tightly to sources of masculine identity validation offered by the system. (14)*

One way that the system allows working-class men (of various races) the opportunity for what Brod refers to as "masculine identity validation" is through the use of their bodies as instruments of power, dominance and control. For working-class males, who have less access to more abstract forms of masculinity-validating power (economic power, workplace authority), the physical body and its potential for violence provide a concrete means of achieving and asserting "manhood."

At any given time, individual as well as groups of men are engaged in an ongoing process of creating and maintaining their own masculine identities. Advertising, in a commodity-driven consumer culture, is an omnipresent and rich source of gender ideology. Contemporary ads are filled with images of "dangerous"-looking men. Men's magazines and mainstream newsweeklies are rife with ads featuring violent male icons, such as uniformed football players, big-fisted boxers, and leather-clad bikers. Sports magazines aimed at men, and televised sporting events, carry millions' dollars' worth of military ads. In the past decade, there have been hundreds of ads for products designed to help men develop muscular physiques, such as weight training machines and nutritional supplements.

Historically, use of gender in advertising has stressed difference, implicitly and even explicitly reaffirming the "natural" dissimilarity of males and females. In late 20th century U.S. culture, advertising that targets young White males (with the exception of fashion advertising, which often features more of an androgynous male look) has the difficult task of stressing gender difference in an era characterized by a loosening of rigid gender distinctions. Stressing gender difference in this context means defining masculinity in opposition to femininity. This requires constantly reasserting what is masculine and what is feminine. One of the ways this is accomplished, in the image system, is to equate masculinity with violence (and femininity with passivity).

The need to differentiate from the feminine by asserting masculinity in the form of power and aggression might at least partially account for the high degree of male violence in contemporary advertising, as well as in video games, children's toys, cartoons, Hollywood film and the sports culture.

By helping to differentiate masculinity from femininity, images of masculine aggression and violence—including violence against women—afford young males across classes a degree of self-respect and security (however illusory) within the more socially valued masculine role.

Violent **White** Masculinity in Advertising

The appeal of violent behavior for men, including its rewards, is coded into mainstream advertising in numerous ways: from violent male icons (such as particularly aggressive athletes or superheroes) overtly threatening consumers to buy products, to ads that exploit men's feelings of not being big, strong or violent enough by promising to provide them with products that will enhance those qualities. These codes are present in television and radio commercials as well, but this essay focuses on mainstream American magazine ads (*Newsweek, People, Sports Illustrated,* etc.), from the early 1990s.

Several recurring themes in magazine advertising targeting men help support the equation of White masculinity and violence. Among them are violence as genetically programmed male behavior, the use of military and sports symbolism to enhance the masculine appeal and identification of products, the association of muscularity with ideal masculinity, and the equation of heroic masculinity with violent masculinity. Let us now consider, briefly, each of these themes.

Violence as Genetically Programmed Male Behavior

One way that advertisers demonstrate the "masculinity" of a product or service is through the use of violent male icons or types from popular history. This helps to associate the product with manly needs and pursuits that presumably have existed from time immemorial. It also furthers the ideological premise, disguised as common sense, that men have always been aggressive and brutal, and that their dominance over women is biologically based. "Historical" proof for this is shown in a multitude of ways.

An ad for the Chicago Mercantile Exchange, an elite financial institution, depicts a medieval battlefield where muscle-bound toy figurines, accompanied by paradoxically muscular skeleton men, prepare to engage in a sword fight. They might wear formal suits and sit behind desks, the ad implies, but the men in high finance (and those whose money they manage) are actually rugged warriors. Beneath the veneer of wealth and class privilege, *all* men are really brutes. The text reads: "How the Masters of the Universe Overcame the Attack of the Deutschmarks."

An ad for Trojan condoms features a giant-sized Roman centurion, in full uniform, muscles rippling, holding a package of condoms as he towers over the buildings of a modern city. Condom manufacturers know that the purchase and use of condoms by men can be stressful, partially because penis size, in popular Western folklore, is supposedly linked to virility. One way to assuage the anxieties of male consumers is to link the product with a recognizably violent (read: masculine) male archetype. It is no coincidence that the two leading brands of condoms in the United States are named for ancient warriors and kings (Trojan and Ramses).

Sometimes products with no immediately apparent connection to gender or violence nonetheless make the leap. An ad for Dell computers, for example, shows a painting of a group of White cowboys on horseback shooting at mounted Indians who are chasing them. The copy reads "Being Able to Run Faster Could Come in Real Handy." The cowboys are foregrounded and the viewers are positioned to identify with them against the Indian "other." The cowboys' violence is depicted as defensive, a construction that was historically used to justify genocide. The ad explains that "you never know when somebody (read: Indians, Japanese business competitors) is going to come around the corner and surprise you." It thus masculinizes the White middle-class world of the computer business by using the violent historical metaphor of cowboys versus Indians.

An even more sinister use of historical representations involves portraying violence that would not be acceptable if shown in contemporary settings. Norwegian Cruise Line, for example, in an ad that ran in major newsweekly magazines, depicted a colorful painting of a scene on a ship's deck, set sometime in the pirate era, where men, swords drawn, appear simultaneously to be fighting each other while a couple of them are carrying off women. The headline informs us that Norwegian is the "first cruise line whose entertainment doesn't revolve around the bar."

It is highly doubtful that the cruise line could have set what is clearly a rape or gang rape scenario on a modern ship. It would no doubt have prompted feminist protests about the company's glorification of the rape of women. Controversy is avoided by depicting the scene as historical.[3] But Norwegian Cruise Line, which calls itself "The Pleasure Ships," in this ad reinforces the idea that rape is a desirable male pastime. Whether intentional or not, the underlying message is that real men (pirates, swashbucklers) have always enjoyed it.

3. Some feminist groups did protest the ad, such as the Cambridge, Massachusetts–based group Challenging Media Images of Women. But the protests never reached a wide audience and had no discernible effect. [Author's note]

The Use of Military and Sports Symbolism to Enhance the Masculine Identification and Appeal of Products

Advertisers who want to demonstrate the unquestioned manliness of their products can do so by using one of the two key subsets in the symbolic image system of violent masculinity: the military and sports. Uniformed soldiers and players, as well as their weapons and gear, appear frequently in ads of all sorts. Many of the Camel Smooth Character cartoon ads, for example, display submarines surfacing or fighter jets streaking by as Joe Camel stands confidently in the foreground. One ad features Joe Camel himself wearing an air force bomber pilot's jacket. The message to the young boys and adolescent males targeted by the campaign is obvious: Violence (as signified by the military vehicles) is cool and suave. The sexy blond woman gazing provocatively at the James Bond-like camel provides female ratification of Joe's masculinity.

Ads for the military itself also show the linkage between masculinity and force. The U.S. military spends more than $100 million annually on advertising. Not surprisingly, armed services advertisements appear disproportionately on televised sporting events and in sports and so-called men's magazines. Military ads are characterized by exciting outdoor action scenes with accompanying text replete with references to "leadership," "respect," and "pride." Although these ads sometimes promote the educational and financial benefits of military service, what they're really selling to young working-class males is a vision of masculinity—adventurous, aggressive and violent—that provides men of all classes with a standard of "real manhood" against which to judge themselves.

Boxers and football players appear in ads regularly, promoting products from underwear to deodorants. Sometimes the players are positioned simply to sanction the masculinity of a product. For example, an ad for Bugle Boy clothing depicts a clean-cut young White man, dressed in Bugle Boy jeans and posed in a crouching position, kneeling on a football. Standing behind him, inexplicably, is a large, uniformed football player flexing his muscles. The only copy says, in bold letters, "Bugle Boy Men." It seems reasonable to infer that the goal of this ad was to shore up the masculine image of a product whose name (Bugle Boy) subverts its macho image. The uniformed football player, a signifier of violent masculinity, achieves this task by visually transmitting the message: Real men wear Bugle Boy.

Advertisers know that using high-profile violent male athletes can help to sell products, such as yogurt and light beer, that have historically been gendered female. Because violence establishes masculinity, if these guys (athletes) use traditionally "female" products, they don't lose their masculinity. Rather, the masculinity of the product—and hence the size of the potential market—increases. Miller Brewing Company proved the efficacy of this approach in their long-running television ad campaign for Lite beer. The Miller Lite campaign, which first appeared in the early 1970s, helped bring Miller to the top of the burgeoning light beer market and is often referred to as the most successful TV ad campaign in history.

The Association of Muscularity with Ideal Masculinity

Men across socioeconomic class and race might feel insecure in their masculinity, relatively powerless or vulnerable in the economic sphere and uncertain about how to respond to the challenges of women in many areas of social relations. But, in general, males continue to have an advantage over females in the area of physical size and strength. Because one function of the image system is to legitimate and reinforce existing power relations, representations that equate masculinity with the qualities of size, strength, and violence thus become more prevalent.

The anthropologist Alan Klein[4] has looked at how the rise in popularity of bodybuilding is linked to male insecurity. "Muscles," he argues, "are about more than just the functional ability of men to defend home and hearth or perform heavy labor. Muscles are markers that separate men from each other and, most important perhaps, from women. And while he may not realize it, every man—every accountant, science nerd, clergyman, or cop—is engaged in a dialogue with muscles" (16).

Advertising is one area of the popular culture that helps feed this "dialogue." Sports and other magazines with a large male readership are filled with ads offering men products and services to enhance their muscles. Often these ads explicitly equate muscles with violent power, as in an ad for a Marcy weight machine that tells men to "Arm Yourself" under a black and white photograph of a toned, muscular White man, biceps and forearms straining, in the middle of a weight lifting workout. The military, too, offers to help men enhance their bodily prowess. An ad for the Army National Guard shows three slender young men, Black and White, working out, over copy that reads "Get a Part-Time Job in Our Body Shop."

The discourse around muscles as signifiers of masculine power involves not only working-class men but also middle- and upper-class males. This is apparent in the male sports subculture, where size and strength are valued by men across class and racial boundaries. But muscularity as masculinity is also a theme in advertisements aimed at upper-income males. Many advertisers use images of physically rugged or muscular male bodies to masculinize products and services geared to elite male consumers. An ad for the business insurance firm Brewer and Lord uses a powerful male body as a metaphor for the more abstract form of (financial) power. The ad shows the torso of a muscular man curling a barbell, accompanied by a headline that reads "the benefits of muscle defined." The text states that "the slow building of strength and definition is no small feat. In fact, that training has shaped the authority that others see in you, as well."

Saab, targeting an upscale, educated market, bills itself as "the most intelligent car ever built." But in one ad, they call their APC Turbo "the muscle car with a social conscience"—which signals to wealthy men that by driving a Saab they can appropriate the working-class tough guy image associated with the concept of a "muscle car" while making clear their more privileged class position.

4. The article cited here was excerpted from Klein's book *Little Big Men: Bodybuilding Subculture and Gender Construction* (Albany: State University of New York Press, 1993).

The Equation of Heroic Masculinity with Violent Masculinity

The cultural power of Hollywood film in the construction of violent masculinity is not limited to the movies themselves. In fact, many more people see the advertising for a given film than see the film itself.

Advertising budgets for major Hollywood releases typically run in the millions of dollars. Larger-than-life billboards enhance the heroic stature of the icons. Movie ads appear frequently on prime time TV and daily in newspapers and magazines. Not surprisingly, these ads highlight the movies' most violent and sexually titillating scenes.

Violence on-screen, like that in real life, is perpetrated overwhelmingly by males. Males constitute the majority of the audience for violent films, as well as violent sports such as football and hockey. It is important to note, then, that what is being sold is not just "violence," but rather a glamorized form of violent masculinity.

Guns are an important signifier of virility and power and hence are an important part of the way violent masculinity is constructed and then sold to audiences. In fact, the presence of guns in magazine and newspaper ads is crucial in communicating the extent of a movie's violent content. Because so many films contain explicit violence, images of gun-toting macho males (police detectives, old west gunslingers, futuristic killing machines) pervade the visual landscape.

Conclusion

Recent research in sociology, media, and cultural studies strongly suggests that we need to develop a much more sophisticated approach to understanding cultural constructions of masculinity. Feminists, who have been at the forefront in studying the social construction of gender, have, historically, focused on images and representations of women. Clearly we need a similarly intensive examination of the representation of men—particularly in light of the crisis of men's violence in our society.

This essay focuses attention on constructions of violent White masculinity in mainstream magazine advertising. But we need also to examine critically a number of other areas where violent masculinities are produced and legitimated: comic books, toys, the sports culture, comedy, interactive video, music video, pornography. This will help us to understand more fully the links between the construction of gender and the prevalence of violence, which might then lead to effective antiviolence interventions.

References

American Psychological Association. (1993). *Violence and youth: Psychology's response*. Washington, DC: Author.

Brod, H. (Ed.). (1987). *The making of masculinities: The new men's studies*. Boston: Allen & Unwin.

Federal Bureau of Investigation. (1992). *Uniform crime reports*. Washington, DC: Author.

Hanke, R. (1992). Redesigning men: Hegemonic masculinity in transition. In S. Craig (Ed.), *Men, masculinity and the media* (pp. 185–198). Newbury Park, CA: Sage.

Jhally, S. (1990, July). Image-based culture: Advertising and popular culture. *The World and I*, pp. 508–519.

Klein, A. (1993, January). Little big men. *Northeastern University Magazine*, p. 14–19.

After Reading

Critical Perspective

1. What does Katz mean when he states that "hegemonic constructions of masculinity in mainstream magazine advertising normalize male violence"? How does this statement relate to Katz's purposes or goals in writing this piece? How do you know?

Rhetoric and Argument

2. Think about Katz's rhetorical choices in his text—his tone, audience, purpose, ethos, pathos, logos, intertextuality, context, and constraints. In what ways is Katz's essay rhetorically persuasive? In what ways may it not be? Be sure to provide textual evidence to support your claims.
3. What sorts of support does Katz provide in order to back up his main assertion? Do you find this evidence convincing? Find quotes from the essay to back up your views.
4. What kinds of warrants or assumptions does Katz make in his text? Where does he evidence them? Do you find these assumptions valid? Why or why not?
5. Are there any logical fallacies or faulty assumptions at work in Katz's text? If yes, where do they appear, and how do you think they impact the effectiveness of his argument?

Analysis

6. Katz closes the essay by asserting that he has only begun to analyze masculinities in the media and that now we need to look to other areas where "violent masculinities are produced and legitimated." Among the cultural texts he mentions, Katz includes comic books, toys, the sports culture, comedy, and the like. In what ways do these other cultural texts also reinforce violent masculinities? Write a short argument in which you choose a cultural text from one of these genres listed above and advance a similar analysis of the advertising and cultural phenomenon around it. Be sure to reference library and Internet sources to support your perspectives.

Taking Action

Watch Katz's film *Tough Guise* as a class. Make sure to take careful notes about the images of masculinity in this film and the ways in which they are troubling.

After you have watched the film, create a safe space to discuss your reactions. How did watching this film impact you personally and why? In what ways might men and women both be effectively educated about the violence of masculinity and its impacts on men as well as women? Reflect on how you might share your impressions of this film—and thoughts about the representations of violent masculinity altogether—to creating an education program for students and/or boys and girls in elementary, middle school, or high school environments. Consider sharing your work with other groups both inside and outside the campus community.

WANDA COLEMAN

"Say It Ain't Cool, Joe"

Wanda Coleman has held a position as a Guggenheim fellow in poetry. She is also an Emmy Award-winning television writer and poet. Coleman has authored several books of poetry, fiction, and critical essays.

EXERCISING YOUR SKILLS

Before Reading

Coleman writes about the phenomenon of "Joe Camel" in contemporary advertising. Consider how notions of "coolness" are sold to us through advertising. Where have you seen images of Joe Camel, the illustrated character in Camel cigarettes' advertising campaign? In what context has he appeared, what activities has he been involved in, and what has he been wearing? Make a list of his main traits. What views of race, ethnicity, and masculinity does Joe Camel promote? In what ways has he become so interesting to young male children?

Boy, oh boy, there's Joe, sportin' those Polaroid peepers, looking rakishly Mediterranean with hot babes and hotter cars. His hair looks like Moammar Kadafi's. The tuxedoed dome-nose has all the sleek arrogance of a shah exiled to Malibu.

I like Joe Camel. And I don't smoke. Not out of the closet anyway. And Camels? Never. But . . .

In Afro-American street parlance, Joe the Camel is a player. Life is a game and he's winning it. He runs in the fast lane. And he's about as gangsterish as it comes. The cat—er, dromedary—is too cool Old School. (Consult your Digital Underground[1] on TNT Recordings.)

If I didn't know better, I'd say Joe was patterned after one of my father's old cronies. Doc was the original "crip," meaning physically challenged. But that didn't stop any action. He hustled his way around South-Central with one crutch on his best days, a wheelchair on his worst. According to his own legend, he had lost one leg in World War II, but rumor was that he'd sacrificed the gam in some unsavory back-alley adventure.

In spite of his cop-and-blow existence, Doc always sported highly polished wingtip kicks, though one shoe was always curiously devoid of mass. As Mama would say, he was "sharp as a tack." And generous. One of his philanthropic pleasures was formal-dress tea parties, where he gave us munchkins a crash course on etiquette, Perle Mesta–style. He

---

1. **Digital Underground:** A rap group.

paid polite attention to me and charmed my little socks off—the adult who takes a child seriously is always an attraction.

Doc smoked. He carried the first gold cigarette case I ever saw. It was impressive to watch him slip it from the pocket of his pin-striped vest. Thing about Doc was that, no matter how vulnerable he might've been, he was not to be pitied or messed with. A gat[2] was concealed in the creases of his threads.

And therein lies the appeal of Joe Camel as a clever selling gizmo and tobacco kingpin's dream.

Underneath Joe's Cheshire cat–smug macho is a deeper message. Joe's not just another lung-collapse peddler. He's a self-respect maven. In rural bottoms and urban ghettos nationwide, rife with runaways and bored, unemployed youth, there's a serious shortage of self-esteem. Like Doc or Joe, you can fire up a coffin nail for instant attitude, the easiest way to strike a pose.

Face it. Joe Camel has life-style appeal. He's rich and he's infamous. And he runs with the pack. There's Joe the suave, white-on-white betuxed academic. If you ain't got it, you can fake his "smooth philosophy" by lighting up. Or you can rack 'em up for Pool Shark Joe cuz he's about to run the table.

In his stingy fedora, Hard Pack Joe and his Wide cousins have all the Hollywood charisma of William Bendix breathing down Robert Mitchum's neck in *The Big Steal* or Brando in *The Godfather*.

Beachcomber Joe has done his share of Venice Beach schmoozing, no doubt sipping Long Island iced tea on the volleyball court. Calypso Joe opens the doors of Club Camel on some tiny Caribbean isle where the cane grows tall and the money laundering is easy.

Joe's crimey, Eddie Camel, was a bead-wearing, apple-capped, paintbrush-totin', long-haired flower child in the sixties. But today he's a loose-lipped, slack-collared, tam-topped, neo-bebop jazz drummer. Bustah (note the idiomatic black spelling) Camel undergoes a similar transformation, and only his electric guitar remains the same.

I can't resist poking fun at ol' Joe. But underneath the fun, the birth of his cool is linked to the birth of survival strategies that have allowed the black male to withstand the relentlessness of racism. It is the cool personified by Malcolm X, Miles Davis, Willie Brown, and Ice Cube. To be cool is to be laid-back black.

But Joe Camel is offensive. Not only because cigarettes can be addictive and debilitating but because, at root, old Joe's shtick is plain-and-simple racist. He's a composite of little-understood cultural traits designed to sucker in youngsters, especially black children. And that ain't cool.

You dig?

---

2. **gat:** A gun.

After Reading

Critical Perspective

1. Describe Coleman's tone and approach in this piece. How does she attempt to draw in her reader? Do you find this approach useful given her subject matter? Why or why not? Give textual evidence to support your views.

Rhetoric and Argument

2. Discuss Coleman's use of audience, purpose, ethos, pathos, logos, intertextuality, context, and constraints. Do you think that her rhetorical techniques are effective or not? Explain your position.
3. Do you find Coleman's claim persuasive? Why does she indicate that Joe Camel is so interesting to young male viewers? What does he represent to Coleman?
4. What sorts of evidence does Coleman provide for her assertion? Do you find this support convincing? If not, how might Coleman make this even more persuasive? What other examples might you mention that could bolster her claims?
5. Coleman mentions Joe Camel as promoting a kind of coolness that young males find attractive. Are there other characters in advertising as well as in television generally that function in similar ways? Be sure to give support to back up your thoughts.

Analysis

6. Consider what Coleman's text indicates about how gender roles for young children are formed by advertising. Look at how girls are being targeted through advertising—though often in radically different ways from boys. Then try to recall how specific images, advertising campaigns, and packaging of products shaped your ideas about gender roles at a young age. Give as many examples as you can and explain how these cultural texts impacted you. Provide a short argumentative response that addresses these concerns. Consult additional library and Internet sources.

Taking Action

Watch a set of television shows created for young children such as cartoons. Pay particular attention to the commercials for toys that air during these programs. Offering a careful rhetorical analysis of several such ads, create an argument in which you make a claim about how gender is represented and constructed through these ads. Be sure to support your views with close analyses of the texts as well as library and Internet sources. After you have made your argument, consider why your findings are significant and exactly how advertising may be shaping the identities, values, anxieties, fears, and desires of young children. Share your thoughts with the rest of the class group.

CHAPTER 8

Watching Television

INTRODUCTION

Considering Reality Television, Popular Television Images, and News and Infomercials

We all have our guilty pleasures when it comes to television watching. Some of us will not miss our morning shows—*The Today Show, Good Morning America, The CBS Morning Show, The View*, or shows specific to the region where we live such as *Good Morning Arizona*. For years *The Today Show's* Katie Couric (and more recently Meredith Vieira), Matt Lauer, Ann Curry, and Al Roker have been fixtures in American viewers' lives, so much so that on occasion they are asked by producers to offer revealing stories about their own lives and personal experiences. American viewers don't want to just know about news and events—they want to know about the television personalities' lives—their families, their hardships, and their thoughts. Some of us will not miss our favorite soap operas: *One Life to Live, Guiding Light, The Young and the Restless*, or *General Hospital*. We can get wrapped up in who is dating whom, who is whose real father, and who has had amnesia and forgotten who she is. Or perhaps we are drawn in by some of the daytime reality shows such as *Ambush Makeover* or *Starting Over*. Others of us will sneak a peek at television talk shows—*The Jerry Springer Show, Dr. Phil, Ellen, Oprah*, or *Maury*. Here the cast of characters is changing moment to moment. The only constant is the talk show host—often offering her or his own perspectives on what appropriate behaviors, relationships, and attitudes should be and sometimes showering lucky audience members with lavish gifts. Those of us who want racier, late night versions of the morning variety show will turn to *The Tonight Show with Jay Leno, Late Night with Conan O'Brien, Late Show with David Letterman*, or *Last Call with Carson Daly*. Others of us are looking for a comedic slant on world events and may turn to *The Daily Show* with Jon Stewart, *The Colbert Report*, *Mind of Mencia*, or *Real Time with Bill Maher*. And then some of us cannot miss our entertainment television shows. My own secret vices include *Entertainment Tonight*, *Access Hollywood*, *Extra*, and the E! television network, those sources for mundane, gossipy details about celebrities as well as the latest television shows and movie releases.

If that is not enough, there is always another episode of *Real World* or *Road Rules*, *American Idol*, *Deal or No Deal*, *The Apprentice*, *Survivor*, *Big Brother*, *Beauty and the Geek*, *Dancing with the Stars*, or *The Bachelor*. Here we can imagine ourselves trying to survive in the corporate jungle or the Amazon jungle, the world of music and entertainment or the world of high-stakes romance, sexuality, and love. Others have to be home to watch (or at least able to TiVo) *The Gilmore Girls*, *Scrubs*, *Ugly Betty*, *The Wire*, *24*, *South Park*, *Grey's Anatomy*, *The Office*, *Veronica Mars*, *My Name Is Earl*, *CSI*, *Extreme Makeover: Home Edition*, *Men in Trees*, *Lost*, or *Desperate Housewives*. We need to know what is happening with Lorelai and Rory and who they are dating now in the town of Stars Hollow or what strange things Dwight might be up to on *The Office*. And finally, as if that were not enough, there are all of those other networks on cable that we might watch—Comedy Central, Nickelodeon, the Food Network, the CW, LINK television, the various versions of MTV, QVC, the History Channel, the Game Show Network, TV Land, Bravo, Showtime, HBO, and the Independent Movie Channel.

Overview of Selections: Reality Television

In this chapter of *Pop Perspectives: Readings to Critique Contemporary Culture* you will read about television of all kinds: from reality television to popular television to the kinds of television that often go unanalyzed such as newscasts, homeshopping segments, and infomercials.

The first section is titled "Reality Television." Here the authors analyze what has become perhaps the most popular genre on television today—"reality" shows, or those television shows that take snippets of the real lives of real people and strategically rearrange and reproduce them for consumption by the American viewing public.

In the first essay Erin Aubry Kaplan offers her intriguing thoughts on the phenomenon of Oprah. Kaplan briefly touches on the ways in which Winfrey's very successful television talk show and *O* magazine have had major impacts on our culture. However, Kaplan dedicates the majority of her essay to Winfrey's celebrity status and the ever growing importance of Oprah's Book Club on her talk show for the publishing industry as well as American readers. As Kaplan suggests, what has made the book club so popular is Winfrey's "ability to align worthy ideals with canny marketing." Kaplan also examines the ways in which Winfrey herself works hard to create a sympathetic, confessional persona, to come across as a person who has survived great hardships and has risen from the ashes. Kaplan also traces the ways in which Winfrey plays the role of the "ignorant reader" in order to draw in her audiences. In the end, Kaplan concludes that Winfrey's persona—on and off her talk show—is exactly what makes her and many others buy the books Winfrey endorses. In effect, everyone hopes to tap into what her show promises as well as to be "saved by books" just as Winfrey herself claims to have been.

Next Amanda A. Putnam, a cultural critic who has traced *Survivor* episodes from their earliest to their latest incarnations, convincingly contends that the show represents gender hierarchies in troubling ways. Putnam argues that the show effectively maintains unequal power relations between men and women, depicting men who ask for what they want as proactive and women who ask for what they want as unfeminine and aggressive. Though the show has gone through many changes over the years—with different casts, different deserted locations, and different plot twists—Putnam reveals to us that the reality show structure of *Survivor* still depends in large part upon reproducing limiting roles for women.

Then an essay written by writer and historian Bob Batchelor relies on comedy and sarcasm to adeptly describe his perspective as a male viewer while watching the show *The Bachelor* as well as its various spin-offs. Batchelor makes note of how the show depicts masculinity and femininity as well as the fairy-tale myths about romance that *The Bachelor* depends upon. Batchelor also explains to us why these tactics have made the show so absorbing. Finally, Batchelor reflects upon how the concept of celebrity itself has changed radically as a result of such reality shows. Now, he suggests, people who are not a part of the celebrity machine are given the idea that they too are on constant display, perpetuating the false belief that if they look and act the parts, they also can be stars.

The final essay is by Anita Creamer, a lifestyle columnist for the *Sacramento Bee*. In this compelling piece, Creamer examines a recent trend in reality television—the serious makeover. Observing how plastic surgery shows such as *I Want a Famous Face*, *The Swan*, and *Extreme Makeover* make people look different through numerous nips, tucks, and injections, Creamer contends that "surgery has become entertainment." She maintains that this is part of a larger phenomenon in American culture that involves constantly being dissatisfied with and reinventing ourselves. Creamer argues that such makeovers are not about the creation of a new self as it would first appear, but rather the "annihilation of the self in the name of self-improvement." In closing, Creamer points to real people's experiences on the show to expose the ways in which participants are so "made over" that they cease to look natural.

Overview of Selections: Popular Television Images

The next section is titled "Popular Television Images." In this part of the chapter authors investigate how popular television shows—prime-time and otherwise featured programs—take up issues of race, gender, class, ethnicity, age, and environment.

The first essay by Ariel Gore, an author who teaches creative writing classes at The Attic Writers' Workshop in Oregon, offers an amusing and yet significant challenge to the idea that television is necessarily negative. Drawing upon her own experiences as a television watcher and mother, Gore explains to us the ways in which television can be a potentially positive parenting tool. Gore indicates that critics who find television troubling ought not to dismiss it out-of-hand but rather consider its potential benefits.

Busy women who work and raise children, she asserts, need to feel good about using television to be the beneficial parenting tool that it can be. People of privilege may feel that they can take the moral high ground, Gore maintains, but people trying to make ends meet know that television is among the better possible alternatives.

Next there is an important statement provided for the NAACP's Hollywood Bureau by Vic Bulluck on the question of diversity on contemporary network television. The organization criticizes the cancellation of television programs such as the *Bernie Mac Show*, contending that while there are an increasing number of situation comedies appearing on television, they fail to adequately represent black families, stating that "African Americans are missing in action." The piece also asserts that the recent merger of UPN and the WB has made the situation still "more bleak for the hundreds of African Americans and minorities who have made their careers working on television comedies." Bulluck also contends that any attempts to criticize Hollywood's practices of failing to hire adequate numbers of minorities have been met with the response that networks "have little or no control over who is hired on the staff of the show." Bulluck makes note of some important television shows that feature more diverse casts including *The Unit*, *American Idol*, and *America's Next Top Model*. Quoting Dr. Martin Luther King Jr.'s words, Bulluck concludes his essay by asserting that television network executives have a responsibility to include more people of color at every level of the production process.

Then Paul A. Cantor, a professor of English at the University of Virginia and a noted scholar of Elizabethan and Romantic English literature, offers an interesting, somewhat unusual essay about the long-running animated series *The Simpsons*. He claims that neither conservative nor liberal critics' assertions—that the show presents the American family in a negative light or that the show challenges traditionally oppressive social institutions—are altogether accurate. Instead, Cantor maintains that this show satirizes and mocks some of the key social issues of our time—religion, the media, politics, and the family—while at the same time reinforcing their cultural importance. Arguing that the show is neither presenting an immoral view of contemporary life nor a moral one, Cantor maintains that while *The Simpsons* may appear to "many people as trying to subvert the American family or to undermine its authority, in fact, it reminds us that antiauthoritarianism is itself an American tradition and that the family authority has always been problematic in democratic America." As a result, Cantor indicates to us that this hip, postmodern show "ends up weirdly celebrating the old ideal of small-town America" in ways that have been often overlooked.

Finally, media critic Eric Deggans examines the increased representation of Hispanics on network television for the *St. Petersburg Times*. In this significant essay, Deggans considers television shows that have emerged in recent years, tracing how Hispanics have been depicted. Quoting Hispanic actors and actresses as well as television network producers, Deggans shows how the growing power of the Hispanic watching public is driving these important changes. While Deggans is heartened by the recent trend toward increased representations of Latinos/as, he also reveals the extent to which troubling stereotypes still sometimes shape those depictions. Deggans also considers the complexities of increased representation itself—especially the fact that Hispanic actors and actresses are still being called upon to act in non-Hispanic roles and non-Hispanic actors and actresses are still being cast in Hispanic roles. In the end, Deggans indicates to us that while there are some positive representations of Hispanics on contemporary television, the trend must continue and develop further.

Overview of Selections: News and Infomercials

The final section of Chapter 8 is titled "News and Infomercials." Here writers explore exactly how news programs and infomercials produce certain behaviors, beliefs, attitudes, values, desires, and needs in their viewers. The authors ask whether this is valuable or not and what the repercussions may be.

This section begins with a well recognized essay about news as entertainment written by two authors—the late Neil Postman, an internationally famous social critic who wrote many books about popular culture and technology, and Steve Powers, a radio and television journalist and news reporter. The writers analyze the specific sections of a typical television newscast and detail how television news repackages events in particular ways for audiences, ones that maximize dramatic tension and minimize coherent explanations of events. Tracing the use of dramatic visuals and musical themes, Postman and Powers encourage us to be more careful and conscious news viewers. No news program, they argue, is truly just news but a highly choreographed and carefully selected version of what is happening in the world around us.

Next is an important essay from the British weekly news and international affairs publication, *The Economist*, about homeshopping from catalogs and on television. The collective authors of the essay consider the new function of television networks such as QVC and HSN and their online spin-offs, iQVC and ISN, which are following in the tracks of the multilayered, user-friendly approaches offered by companies such as Amazon.com. The authors investigate both the positive and negative possibilities offered by increased consumer options available on television and on the Internet. They reveal why televison shopping networks seem unable to gain the consumers that catalogs and on-line shopping outlets have. While consumers want to have ready access to goods through the media, television does not offer them round-the-clock access to a wide range of goods. *The Economist*'s writers tell us that television shopping will need to better mimic these other shopping forms if it is to finally catch on.

In conclusion, Mark Kingwell, a well-known Canadian-born philosopher and cultural theorist who is a professor at the University of Toronto, provides a piece for us about television infomercials. He describes the predictable formula for these spots— and the hawking of pasta makers and rotisseries (the Ron Popeil empire), Ab-Roller pulses, and Sophist-O-Twist hair accessories. With wittiness, Kingwell describes the ways in which television infomercials mimic television talk shows and carnival midways, always with the idea of pretending that what is really only about sales is in fact about "real life." Kingwell's fear is that soon television programming will offer little more than "selling things, selling things, selling things." While television has certainly been involved in advertising since its inception, today's infomercials create a seamlessness between television programming for education and entertainment purposes and advertising for the purposes of getting television viewers to buy products.

As you read this chapter, take a closer look at your favorite television programs. Like all media forms, television is not just about entertainment. It may make us laugh, wince, or cry—but its effects are far broader than simple appeals to our emotions. Television aims to entertain us toward certain ends and with specific effects. What ideals, myths, ideologies, and worldviews do these television shows promote? What desires and values do they inculcate and reinforce in us as viewers? How are issues of race, gender, class, ethnicity, age, sexuality, and disability depicted on these shows? Are these shows offering useful views of such relations, detrimental depictions, or some combination? Finally, how do these shows construct our ethos as viewers—instruct us about who we should be, the identities and desires we ought to have?

REALITY TELEVISION

ERIN AUBRY KAPLAN

"The Oprah Effect"

Erin Aubry Kaplan has worked as a writer for the Los Angeles Times *and* LA Weekly. *Kaplan's articles have appeared in the* London Independent, The Crisis, Newsday, *the* Utne Reader, Black Enterprise, *and on* Salon.com. *She has completed a first book, an essay collection titled* Views and Blues from the Edge: Dispatches from a Black Journalista.

EXERCISING YOUR SKILLS

Before Reading

Kaplan's essay centers on the phenomenon of Oprah Winfrey, the queen of today's television talk show genre. Watch several episodes of *The Oprah Winfrey Show*. Consider the sorts of topics that Oprah covers. In what ways is this show similar to as well as different from other talk shows with which you are familiar? Are there topics that *Oprah* discusses that you might not see on other talk shows? Why do you think that this might be the case?

An author friend confides his fondest career wishes: scoring a film deal for his first book, publishing a second by summer—and "getting my book on the Oprah Book Club. That would be . . ."

The ellipsis is appropriate. It's hard to exaggerate the impact that Oprah's Book Club has had on the book world. Each month, when she recommends a favorite work to her viewers worldwide, they buy and, presumably, read in staggering numbers. All 15 Oprah picks, which range from the quirky (Wally Lamb's *She's Come Undone*) to the highbrow (Toni Morrison's *Song of Solomon* and *Paradise*), have rocketed onto best-seller lists; books that might otherwise not have cracked 100,000 in sales easily sell in the millions. Oprah's Book Club has transformed the publishing monde so quickly and profoundly that the industry has given it a name, as scientists give those celestial phenomena they can predict but can't quite explain: the Oprah effect.

Watching the reader roundtables with authors on Oprah makes it abundantly clear that the Book Club's largest purpose is to humanize books, to pluck them out of the cloistered circles of letters and make them as fundamental to good, lusty living as the crab cakes and biscuits Oprah and company chow down on. At the roundtables with Maya Angelou and Toni Morrison, dissection of the books wasn't the point: The gatherings functioned as a kind of jury duty, where people of various ethnic backgrounds and stations who would otherwise never give each other a glance were not only talking, but freely sharing long-held secrets, tears, tales of how reading the book shifted their lives monumentally. One woman who described herself in her letter as "Little Miss White Woman" and had resisted reading Angelou had, in the end, the greatest catharsis of anyone.

Oprah's power resides in the intimacy with her audience that she established in her earliest days on television. What is a book club, after all, but a latter-day sewing circle, a reason for a bunch of people to get together and talk? Her unflagging sincerity has taken the notoriously fickle beast of public opinion and focused it on books. More remarkably, she has convinced her cozy circle of millions not simply that books are cool, but literary books are cool, which in a national climate hostile to deep thinking is like convincing a kid to eat peas.

Perhaps the secret of Oprah's success lies in her ability to align worthy ideals with canny marketing. There are those who balk at the fact that she is the world's most influential book critic, that Toni Morrison landed on the mass-culture map not because of her Nobel Prize but because Oprah coronated two of her books. That Morrison might be, at least for a moment, as hot a commodity as a Beanie Baby is an irony, but even the mustiest academic has to admit it's a sweet one. Perhaps because pop-icon status is so often accorded to people of slight or dubious achievement, we become suspicious when achievers like Morrison get what they deserve from us. If a rhapsodic review from Oprah can help to untie that Gordian knot of reasoning, so much the better.

Some would say that Oprah's effusions occasionally border on a kind of intellectual genuflection that pumps up the writers plenty, but doesn't always serve viewers looking to engage in serious literary discussions of the works. When Oprah and a group of readers gathered with Maya Angelou for dinner and chatted about club pick *The Heart of a Woman*, English teacher Yvonne Divans Hutchinson, who watched the show, was put off by the pajama-party atmosphere, in which enraptured guests listened at the feet of the author as she read. Oprah was similarly wide-eyed in her discussion with Morrison. "It wasn't about the book," says Hutchinson, who teaches honors courses at Markham Middle School in Watts. "It was more about adulation than about works of fiction. It was a little syrupy. With Toni, Oprah confessed to a lot of ignorance about the complexity of *Paradise*, to the point where Toni seemed a bit impatient. Oprah was identifying with the masses who may not have understood, but whether she was playing that up or whether she really didn't understand, I don't know."

There may be some "just folks" orchestration on Oprah's part, but the star has never really been about asking hard questions, at least not on the air. Precisely because she knows hardship—she survived a harrowing childhood, and her defining TV moment came when she admitted to the world in 1985 that she had been sexually abused at the age of 9—she is primarily a validator, an affirmer of good. It's no surprise, then, that Oprah's Book Club choices tend toward the confessional, the crucible-of-the-female-experience revelational—not sop, but tough, ambitious narratives like those of Morrison, Ursula Hegi or Wally Lamb. Oprah does encourage redemption, though she doesn't pretend that it comes easy. She often cautions her audience against expecting a quick read. Stick with the 500-page *Stones From the River*, she told them, and the rewards will be many.

All in all, I'd rather have Oprah than, say, Howard Stern or Jerry Springer gush and play tastemaker. Her Book Club may not advance the cause of literary analysis, but it may do something greater in advancing her conviction that people ought to read more. Oprah has never been brazenly liberal, but neither has she been afraid to be moral, to let her social conscience show. She refused to have Bob Dole or Dennis Rodman (after the publication of his instantly infamous *As Bad as I Wanna Be*) as a guest. And there's a reason why Starbucks Coffee, eager to be a good corporate citizen, now sells Book Club picks in stores and donates the net proceeds to literacy programs. "With Oprah, there's a purity of intention there," says Starbucks marketing director John Williams. "Her titles reflect a real appreciation for great literary work. It was important for her to hear what our commitment would be."

Some say that Oprah's Book Club doesn't do enough to promote black authors, which someone as powerful as she should feel charged to do. Yet she has showcased a good number of them—Morrison, Ernest J. Gaines, Angelou, Bill Cosby—and claims them as her touchstones. (She has said that Morrison is her heroine, and that Angelou saved her life.) Those who still question her soul-sister credentials might consider that her television and film projects have been taken largely from black literature, from Gloria Naylor to Walter Mosley to Harlem Renaissance survivor Dorothy West. "Whatever else we think of her, she's affiliated with projects that are related to black literature, and that's an important pattern," says Richard Yarborough, English professor and acting director of UCLA's Center for African American Studies. "Oprah's doing what we always wish empowered people, especially empowered black people, would do more of."

James Fugate, co-owner of Eso Won Books in Baldwin Hills, says that the boost Oprah has provided to sales more than qualifies as social responsibility. "We sold 27 copies of *Paradise* the first weekend it was out, then 70 the weekend after Oprah made it a Book Club pick," says Fugate, who carries all of Oprah's picks in his store, including those by nonblack authors. "Since Oprah, we've sold over 200. She revitalized books."

Race may be a prevailing force in the Oprah Club books, but it is incidental to the stories that move her most—those that chronicle the often tortured search for the geography of one's own soul. As remarkable as the book renaissance is, what's more remarkable is the fact that it is fostered by a black woman who is also an individualist, whose eclectic tastes embrace hardscrabble Southern roots but aren't bound by them, who is as easily transported to a contemporary suburb or life in Nazi Germany as she is to a plantation. Oprah says that the vision fueled by books helped her survive, and I believe her, because I, too, have been saved by books, and by writers wholly unlike myself. The best books renew a belief in self and possibility by realigning the outlook of the reader. With its clamor of voices that sound different to every ear, fiction inspires a kind of wonder that the group activities of television and movies never can. Oprah, by the way, says she never watches TV.

After Reading

Critical Perspective

1. Kaplan maintains that Winfrey's television talk show and the Oprah Book Club have had major impacts on the publishing market. Do you concur with this claim? Why or why not? Provide quotes from the text and your own experiences to back up your views.

Rhetoric and Argument

2. Describe Kaplan's use of rhetorical tactics such as audience, purpose, ethos, pathos, logos, intertextuality, context, and constraints. Do you think that her language choices are persuasive? Be sure to furnish evidence from the essay.
3. Why does Kaplan think that Winfrey has been so successful? What does this imply about Winfrey and the persona she projects? What does it indicate about the beliefs and values of Winfrey's viewers? Be sure to furnish particular examples from your experiences and her show to back up your assertions.
4. What role, if any, does race play in "the Oprah effect," according to Kaplan? Do you agree with her position? Why or why not? Cite textual examples as evidence.
5. How does Kaplan support her claim? Is this evidence adequate? Why or why not? Do you see any logical fallacies at work in Kaplan's essay? Do you think that the structure of Kaplan's essay is effective in advancing her argument? Explain your views.

Analysis

6. Kaplan ends her essay by stating that Winfrey says she has been "saved by books"—and that Kaplan has as well. Write a short essay in which you explain what they both mean by this and whether you think that this is possible. Offer support from *Oprah*, library sources, and the Internet to back up your opinion.

Taking Action

Examine several issues of *O* magazine and take detailed notes. Now compose a freewrite about the following questions: What sorts of stories and advertisements do you notice? Why do you think that this is the case? What does this imply about the cultural impacts of Oprah? What does this reveal about Oprah, her audience, and American culture? Then read through your notes and freewrite, considering what argumentative claims you might make about the magazine and how it supports Winfrey's show as well as her Book Club. Consult library and Internet sources as necessary.

AMANDA A. PUTNAM

"Vote the Bitch Off!"

Amanda A. Putnam is an associate professor at Roosevelt University in Chicago. Along with her interests in examining gender and race in reality television, Putnam is also intrigued by other signs of contemporary popular culture, including African American pop fiction, gendered issues in sci-fi series television (like *Star Trek*), and contemporary museum rhetoric.

EXERCISING YOUR SKILLS

Before Reading

Putnam writes about the reality television show "Survivor." Watch several episodes. What do you think about how the characters treat one another, how and why alliances are formed, and the ways in which people are "voted off"? What ideas about masculinity and femininity contribute to how characters on this show are represented? Try to point to particular examples from the show. Do you believe that masculinity and femininity have operated differently on different seasons of the show? If yes, how so? Are we witnessing any additional changes as new versions of *Survivor* emerge?

Think about the different players a bit. How do their behaviors mark them as distinctly masculine or feminine? When have male bodies been made to appear feminine and female bodies masculine? How have these issues been impacted by concerns of race, class, ethnicity, and sexual preference? In what ways do these issues impact how we as audience members are asked to view them?

Survivor, CBS's best-known and longest running reality show, has brought a whole new dimension to assertive women being called "bitches." From trash-talking ambushes by previously scorned jury members in the final season episodes to unanimous oustings of allegedly-traitorous women along the way, players, critics, and viewers alike can't stand the women who will do anything to win.

Ironically, that's exactly what some of the men are doing too—without the incessant name-calling and liability attached. Richard Hatch, the diabolical schemer, mastermind, and ultimate winner of the first season, had viewers cheering him on every manipulative step of the way. In fact, Sean Kenniff, the dopey doc of that season, said he voted for Rich to win because even though he was "an out-and-out scoundrel," Sean "liked him, in some bizarre manner" ("Episode 13," *Survivor*). The second season, shot in the Outback, hailed Jeff Varner (the wanna-be schemer of Kucha tribe) who delighted in voting off victims. In that same season, smiling and sexy Colby Donaldson of Ogakor tribe was also quietly deceptive, pretending to align with various factions depending on the good he could gain from each temporary alliance. In the African season, temperamental Brandon Quinton played members of his own alliance several times, and even nice guy and eventual winner of that third season, Ethan Zohn, suggested throwing a crucial immunity challenge simply to vote off someone who could have been a threat to his own physical dominance in competitions. Ultimate winners, Brian "this is business" Heidik of the Thailand season (which was season five) and Chris Daugherty of the Vanuatu (season nine), as well as both third place runner-ups Rob Cesternino of the Amazon season (six) and Jon Dalton of the Pearl Islands season (seven), proved worthy of the original surviving schemer, Richard, by aligning with each and every one of their tribe mates in separate secret alliances. Jon even swore on his very-much-alive grandmother's "grave" to help persuade his teammates he was trustworthy. While not always liked, none of these guys were branded anything but a survivor, trying to win the game.

So why are the devious women so hated? Why was original season's Kelly Wiglesworth vehemently attacked by her teammates when they realized she was maneuvering more tribal members than originally thought? Her teammate Susan Hawk said Kelly was "two-faced and manipulative"; likewise Sean said she was "more deceptive" than Rich; and even Colleen Haskell mentioned as she voted for "wishy-washy" Kelly to win the million-dollar prize that she hoped the money would "make [Kelly] be nice or something" ("Episode 13," *Survivor*).

Similarly, in season two, why did Jerri Manthey evoke such anger as she influenced group sentiment against the alleged beef jerky eater, Kel Gleason, orchestrating his early exit from the game? (Didn't male player Colby stage the same trick six days later when he influenced his tribe members to vote off lanky 7-ft tall Mitchell Olson? Isn't the point of the game to control your position so as to "outlast" others?) In fact, the entire merged second season Outback tribe of Barramundi agreed with seemingly unskilled chef, Keith Famie, that "the wicked witch [was] gone" when Jerri won a food reward challenge and left camp for the evening ("Episode 8"). Clearly, no one liked women playing to win in these early seasons.

In that same Outback season, viewers saw similar plots hatching to dispatch any "bitchy" female. While personal trainer Alicia Calaway's show of assertiveness by railing on vegen Kimmi Kappenberg seemed to work to her advantage initially, her tough girl appearance earned her one of the first votes out of the merged tribe. Farmer, teacher, and all-around nice guy, Rodger Bingham said his tribe had contemplated voting Alicia out before the merger, considering keeping low-key Kimmi instead of head-bobbing, finger-wagging Alicia. Thinking of Alicia's confrontational manner, Rodger added "We would miss her . . . she's athletic . . . but there might be a little more harm in her around now too" ("Episode 5"). Of course, the infamous Jerri also received her comeuppance after a merger, when her temper, outspoken personality, and treacherous nature became more frequently a topic of individual Barramundi confessionals. But even the quiet Amber Brkich suffered a stigma that season simply by being associated with someone considered a bitch: Keith said, "Amber is a big girl; she made her decision early on to be close to Jerri, and there is nothing that can be done about it now" (Episode 11").[1] Apparently, the stain from the scarlet letter of bitchiness is impossible to scrub clean.

Amusingly, during the same season that found several women despised for their bitchiness, Colby plotted, lied, and influenced his way through the game without earning similar resentment. He ingratiated himself by bringing shells and trinkets back for his fellow tribe members after reluctantly co-winning the reward challenge of snorkeling near the Great Barrier Reef with persona non grata Jerri. No one seemed to notice or care that he was quietly setting the scene so that he would end up the sole Survivor as well as the most liked. Colby was fickle and opportunistic—making and breaking alliances as needed—yet nobody noticed once receiving one of his stunning smiles.

However it was both Brian Heidik from the fifth season (Thailand) and Chris Daugherty in the ninth season (Vanuatu) who took being wily to a level reminiscent of the original Survivor, Richard Hatch, and ultimately, won their games. By noticeably working hard in camp, pulling more than his own weight in tribal challenges, and befriending nearly everyone in his tribe, Brian managed to manipulate an entire host of people who had no idea how smart he really was. Likewise, even though Chris "single-handedly" lost the first team Challenge for his male-only tribe, he somehow persuaded a majority of them to keep him around ("Stunned")—and Chris continued to work within whichever tribe he was in until he was—literally—the last man standing in an otherwise all-female alliance. Similarly, Jon Dalton, self-dubbed "Johnny Fairplay, the guy who *never* plays fair," said his goal during the seventh season (Pearl Islands) was to "take home the title of 'dirtiest player to ever play this game' ("Jon"). He did just that and managed to remain in the game until the final three contestants were left, regardless of his spectacular weaseling.

As this game show continues to evolve, most players assume others—regardless of gender—are scheming heavily. Nonetheless, in most seasons, the women still carry the heavier burden of needing to seem more truthful than the men. Initially, the third season's African tribes appeared to evolve in their gender politics by voting out some men if they schemed too obviously without important voting pacts in place. For example, young Silas Gaither was quickly voted out when he lost access to an important alliance after the two tribes exchanged members unexpectedly mid-game. Isolated within a tribe whose players didn't trust him due to his earlier conniving, Silas couldn't recover quickly enough to save himself, and thus it seemed *Survivor*'s gendered rules were bending to include men.

Likewise, the fourth season, filmed in Marqueses, showed more gender equity initially, when two overly manipulative men were ejected from the game early on. Rob Mariano, who liked to compare the game to *The Godfather*, ruled the original Maraamu tribe like Don Corleone, whacking surprised tribe mates at will for challenging his order. Nonetheless, upon arrival in merged tribe Soliantu and left with few members that trusted him, Rob was treated more like pathetic Fredo Corleone—done in when his usefulness was over.[2] In that same season, overly confident John Carroll also mistakenly believed himself impervious to the vote due to his four-way strategic alliance but found himself strangely vulnerable when rival alliances banded against him en masse. Tenth season's young dolphin trainer Ian Rosenberger was practically tarred and feathered in Palau for his dishonesty; in fact, he finally gave up a coveted spot in the final two simply to regain the respect of his tribe. Clearly, the game looked like it was leveling the gendered playing field and men were also being held accountable for the lies they told.

However, across the seasons of *Survivor*, women who even *appeared* to be untrustworthy have been quickly dismissed from the game, banished for seeming deceptive.

It was the unfortunate Kelly Goldsmith who was deemed the ultimate betrayer in the African season when it only looked like she might be untrustworthy. Having received an unexpected vote at tribal council that maddened him due to his inability to determine by whom it was cast, heavily tattooed Lex Van Den Berghe played McCarthy in Kelly's witch-hunt, ironically blacklisting her, a fellow member of his own alliance, when in actuality, a different player had written down his name. Thus, just the appearance of deviousness in a female is enough to rid the tribe of a possible "Linda Tripp."

Likewise, Christa Hastie from the seventh season (Pearl Islands) and Janet Koth from the sixth season (Amazon) were also ousted because of supposedly bitchy actions, which may or may not have been theirs. Christa was accused—falsely it turned out—of spitefully dumping the tribe's anticipated fish dinner after a tribal council unexpectedly voted out her friend (and primary tribal fisherman) Rupert Boneham. One season earlier, Janet had been accused by her all-female tribe of smuggling in granola bar contraband, and worse, eating it without sharing with her tribe mates. Christa and Janet both pleaded that they had not done the terrible deeds, but no one believed them. Interestingly, no one saw these women commit either of their crimes, but the guilt hung around their necks like albatrosses and they were summarily voted off the islands as soon as possible.

Do women have to play by different rules than men in these games of *Survivor*? Should they hide assertive and deceptive qualities, traits that are necessary to stay in the game, so as not to annoy their tribal members with their similar unbridled lust for the cold, hard cash?

It seems so! Women who initially appear virtuous or noble, but then are caught by tribe mates spinning webs of intrigue get targeted very quickly. First season's Kelly Wiglesworth was dangerous because even with the large tattoo sprawled across her lower back, she looked and seemed like the girl next door, but she didn't act accordingly. Slender and pretty, Kelly was, as her eventual nemesis Susan said, "sweeter than me" and appeared to be easily led ("Episode 13," *Survivor*). At one point, Susan even indicated that she would never turn on Kelly, their friendship was so strong. But Kelly told the camera she wasn't there to make friends, and trouble started. It seemed good girl Kelly was lying to everyone.

But in the end, Kelly's deceptiveness worked against her, in ways that the men's deceit and disloyalty did not. In the final moments of the jury that decided who won the million dollars, Susan publicly condemned Kelly as a liar—but said almost nothing about Richard's strategic handlings, which were far more obvious and wide-spread. In fact, Susan spent almost her entire jury speaking time explaining that Rich's maneuvering was okay because he had "approached" the game that way from the beginning, never claiming to be friends with anyone ("Episode 13," *Survivor*). Susan even admitted she admired his "frankness" ("Episode 13," *Survivor*). Susan felt duped by Kelly because she had believed her. Thus Kelly was a bitch—and unworthy of winning the money.

In that first season, only Gervase Peterson seemed to understand that while Kelly may have "played both sides of the fence" during the game ("Episode 13," *Survivor*), outwitting others *was* the game! By the end of Susan's pretentious speech, Susan theatrically asked the jury to permit "Mother Nature" to end the contest by allowing "Richard the snake, who knowingly went after prey" to eat "Kelly the rat" ("Episode 13," *Survivor*). After all, while scheming Rich was clearly a smooth operator, Kelly was a woman—and supposedly a nice one. She wasn't expected to want to win that badly.

Interestingly, both Vecepia Towery and Nelah Dennis, the last two survivors standing in Marqueses (season four) as well as being two outspoken, Scripture-quoting Christians, dealt with their own image problems at their final tribal council. Deemed "good girls" like Kelly from the first season, both had to justify their deviousness later, with Nelah taking the brunt of the juried anger. Striking chords resonating of Susan Hawk's ambush of Kelly Wiglesworth in the original season's last episode, juror Tammy Leitner gave Nelah and Vecepia a vicious tongue-lashing because they had the audacity to be more strategic than the good girls they appeared to be:

> *I have always been up front about the way I was going to play this game. I was going to lie. I was going to cheat. I was going to do whatever it took to win the game . . . [and you both said] "I'm not going to lie. . . . Let's take this game to a new level. Let's play it with ethics and morals and integrity." Well, you guys are hypocrites . . . and you may have been the two biggest liars out on the island. ("Episode 13,"* Survivor Marquesas)

So while Tammy believed it necessary to lie to stay in the game, in fact mandatory to win the game, she did *not* think it was fair for either Nelah or Vecepia to fib since they did not admit they were liars up front. In other words, only those who got caught lying or those who would be stupid enough to confess to lying, i.e. *bad* liars, should be allowed to lie.

Similarly, three female runner-ups from seasons seven (Pearl Islands), nine (Vanuatu), and eleven (Guatamala) had to contend with upset jury members who felt the women had been unfairly dishonest. Lill, from the Pearl Islands season, had the misfortune of wearing a Boy Scout troop leader's uniform upon arrival in the game (and the survivors were abandoned with no other clothes), so several people thought Lill shouldn't lie, cheat, or steal to win. After all, in an interesting gendered flip-flop, the woman was a Boy Scout! Like self-confessed liar Tammy who scorched Nelah and Vecepia for their duplicity, Chicago attorney Andrew Savage theorized as he compared Lill to other players in the game who deceived that "the true Lill in the game should be upholding the Scout's honor . . . and Ryno [Ryan Opray] is an electrician—he didn't have a Scout's uniform on—so he can lie as much as he wants" ("Survivor: Pearl Islands Reunion"). Even bronzed and pretty Stephenie LaGrossa, deemed "America's Sweetheart" by host Jeff Probst when she played the game in Palua (season ten), was unable to preserve that beloved image when she began ruthlessly voting out fellow teammates in her surprise return season in Guatemala (season eleven).[3]

Likewise, Twila Tanner's downfall in the ninth season (Vanuatu) was that she appeared not only dishonest, but worse, unmotherly (gasp!). Laughing slyly behind the other women's backs, Twila told the cameras that she "swore . . . on [her] son's name that [she] was with them one hundred percent. But maybe if I win a million dollars, God will forgive me" ("On"). However, once the other women realized she had invoked her son's name fraudulently, Twila could not salvage her reputation regardless of the sins the double-crossing eventual winner Chris committed. Leading this charge was "queen" Ami Cusack, but others joined in, repeatedly reminding Twila she had crossed a line by vowing on her son's name to prove her word was good. So even though Chris lied more frequently, to more people, throughout most of the game, Twila's one *Mommie Dearest* fib became a million dollar mistake.

With these confusing bits of logic guiding players during the game as well as the final jury voting, all of these amateur philosophers determined Nelah, Lill, Stephenie, and Twila far too treacherous to be worthy of the million dollar prize. Tammy curiously added that only Kathy Vavrick-O'Brien—someone who had believed "integrity is critical" to the game of *Survivor* ("Episode 13," *Survivor Marquesas*)—had truly earned the rights to a million of those new big-face greenbacks. In essence, all four of these women had their characters questioned because, like Kelly on the original season, they seemed honorable—and thus were not expected to deceive to get those last coveted spots.

So far, the winners of *Survivor* have been equally split in gender.[4] However, six of the eight men—Richard (winner), Colby, Ethan (winner), Clay Jordan, Brian (winner), and Chris (winner)—who made it to final tribal councils were either openly or quietly deceptive, but none of them were made responsible for that quality by the jury. In fact, four of those men—half of those with the opportunity—won the game.[5] Even more interestingly, two of the men who made it to the final three were exceptionally deceitful or corrupt. Sixth season's Rob Cesternino—dubbed by host Jeff Probst during the "Survivor: Amazon Reunion" show as "the smartest player to play the game and *not* win"—and "grandmother-killing" Jon Dalton from the seventh season, both took scheming to new levels of corruption. And yet, the majority of the jury for Rob's season said they would have voted for him had he made it to the final two. Similarly, only four out of seven hands went up to vote for Lill in a hypothetical decision between the female Boy Scout leader and dastardly villain Jon, had Lill chosen him as her competitor in the final two instead of winner Sandra Diaz-Twine. Even against a confirmed snake in the grass like "Johnny Rotten," who had lied to almost everyone multiple times, hard-working troop leader Lill could just barely overcome her double-dealing image to beat him.

In contrast to the men's numbers, at least eight of the eleven women who made it to the final judgment acted deceptively. However, instead of half of them winning the cash like the men did, two-thirds of them—Kelly Wiglesworth, Vecepia, Nelah, Lill, Twila, and Stephenie LaGrossa from the Guatemalan season—were harshly condemned by the jury because of those behaviors.[6] In fact, only two of the sneaky seven females—Tina Wesson and Vecepia—claimed the million dollar prize, and it's significant that Vecepia's competition—Nelah—was completely browbeaten by jury members for showing insincere qualities, indicating that the jury still chose the woman they perceived to be the lesser of two Eve-ils. As juror Tammy said, she had to decide "which one screwed [her] less in the game" ("Episode 13," *Survivor Marquesas*). Likewise, while almost all *Survivor* male "villains" have gained enormous popularity with audiences, the only "villain" ever booed off a reunion show was Jerry Manthey, notably the most prominent (and possibly only) female villain ("Reunion").

In contrast to all the other winners—male or female, Tina Wesson, as the ultimate winner of the second season in the Outback, seems to epitomize the balance of what women need to embody to win: deceptive, without appearing overly manipulative, ruthless, while suggesting friendliness; Tina took strategy to new heights. Being bold while couching her methods in southern charm, Tina avoided being dubbed a bitch by anyone.

Several fundamental incidents positioned Tina as an honorable player. Early on in that season viewers witnessed her magnanimity when she politely gave Keith a much-needed immunity win when he asked her for it—"I need this one," Keith had said ("Episode 7"). As well, she gave Elisabeth Filarski the means to get an extra food award, when times were especially tough, building a careful friendship that would come in handy later when Elisabeth voted for the ultimate Survivor. Tribe members and viewers alike also beheld Tina's tenacity when she helped rescue one of the much-needed lost tins of rice from a fast-moving river, after a flood wiped out the tribe's camp.

However, there were times of incredible deceptiveness too—many of which went unnoticed, and more importantly, undissected by either tribe members or host Jeff Probst. One of the moments most evident was the episode in which Rodger is voted out. As Rodger reported it, Tina asked him "which one . . . needed the money the worst: [him] or Elisabeth" ("Episode 12"). Not surprisingly, Rodger responded that "Elisabeth probably does . . . and [Rodger] just decided that [he] would take the out first for Elisabeth" ("Episode 12"). Playing on Rodger's often-communicated paternal affection for Elisabeth, Tina lets him think *he* is choosing the next person voted out—but of course, it is *Tina* who gently moves this puppet's strings. Similarly, Tina ensured a different tribe member's early conclusion, orchestrating Amber's elimination when Tina realized Amber's presence as a potential threat. As Tina put it, "Amber can't survive by just flying below the radar. . . . She has proved to me that she's a tougher girl than I thought" ("Episode 11"). Wary of Amber's comparable aura of nice girl on the outside, but strategist on the inside, Tina gets her alliance to remove the menace as soon as possible by reminding her voting bloc of Amber's relationship with Jerri, the scorned bitch of all Survivors.

But Tina's biggest coup was befriending Colby enough to get him to choose her as his competitor for the final tribal council. Ironically Colby entered the game indicating in true Texan style that in "the game of *Survivor*, you've got to switch hats a lot. You've got to wear a white hat part of the time, and sometimes you gotta put on the black hat. . . . You've got to be a little bit selfish" ("Episode 14"). Thinking this way, many thought he'd choose to contend with Keith in the final vote, as Keith didn't have as many clear-cut fans as Tina did, but instead Colby chose someone who he didn't "know that [he] even [had] a 50–50 shot against" ("Episode 14"). Why?

Colby said he chose Tina because the game "changed" for him ("Survivor: The Reunion 2"). He felt they became "close" and that he was "able to sleep every night since then" knowing he had made the right decision ("Survivor: The Reunion 2"). Ironically, though, had he followed his own advice, he might have won the million dollars: "trust in people in this game will get you in trouble . . . so if you trust somebody, it's your own fault. You're a fool for not playing the game" ("Episode 14"). But Colby also chose Tina because she presented an important balance between manipulation and kindness, which eventually won him over. Host Bryant Gumbel asked the female Outback survivor in "Survivor: The Reunion 2" whether she was "the sweet motherly Tina . . . [or] the one who was described as . . . ruthless." Tina answered truthfully that she was "a little of both." Able to balance her decency (and even more importantly, her *appearance* of decency) with the necessary trickery needed to win the game, Tina was not only able to outwit her fellow players, but also the dangerous female labels that have been so prevalent in this game.

Winners Sandra Diaz-Twine from the Pearl Islands season, Jenna Morasca from the Amazon season, and Danni Boatwright from the Guatemalan season also made sure they weren't considered bitchy as they went into their final votes. Both Sandra and Danni realized that the reason they made it to the final two was because, as Sandra said, other players "had other agendas—they had bigger fish to fry" and thus they were able to continue in the game without being blamed for voting out people or strategizing—their tactics were to be available and yet invisible. Likewise, just as fortunate Vecepia was matched with a jury-demolished Nelah, Sandra looked great in comparison to Lill, the untrustworthy Boy Scout leader, and Danni shined next to the manipulative Stephenie.

Jenna, who started the memorable Amazon season in a female-only tribe, was part of the "younger, cuter girls" who sequestered themselves apart from the older, harder-working women. Even host Probst indicated on that season's reunion show that Jenna had behaved like a "spoiled rotten brat" ("Survivor: Amazon Reunion"). However, Jenna was able to overcome her initially bitchy persona by being the clear underdog to the remaining powerful alliance, and winning four immunity challenges in a row which precluded anyone voting her off. Finally, she made a key statement when she chose Matthew Von Ertfelda instead of scheming Rob Cesternino to accompany her to the coveted final two spots: she said she was choosing the "most deserving" player ("Episode 13," *Survivor: Amazon*). When asked later about that remark, Jenna admitted, that "it was strategy. I wanted the jury to think I was taking the most deserving person to the final two . . . that I *believed* I was" ("Survivor: Amazon Reunion"). Spinning her decision in this manner kept her from appearing bitchy to the jurors and solidified their opinion of her as an honorable player.

In any season of *Survivor*, women deemed "bitchy" are voted off first, unlike many of their male "bitchy" counterparts who just might win the game. Likewise, "nice girls" have to be careful to keep their goodness as they become wilier in the closing episodes. If they can balance the overly naive nature of original season's Jenna Lewis—"I'm actually very happy I got out [of the game] when I did . . . I can't even lie!" ("Episode 13," *Survivor*),[7] with the obviousness of treachery that second season's Jerri had—"when did this game start being *fair*?!"("Episode 9"), or the arrogance of third season's Lindsay Richter and her young-person-only alliance—"Don't mess with me. Don't underestimate my people!" ("Changing"), a woman can win the game as easily as Tina or Sandra or Jenna did. However, if they step over the "wholesome line" (and that line is none-too-stable for women), and appear even slightly conniving, they are goners, voted off for playing the "outwit" part of the game without ladylike restraint.

All in all, *Survivor* is not just about outwitting, outplaying, and outlasting; for female players, it's about wanting to win without appearing that way. It's about being sly without getting caught. *Survivor*'s men outlast each other by being shrewd and cunning, and they do so because it is okay for men to want to win and okay for men to do anything to succeed. *Survivor*'s women, on the other hand, may not face a typical glass ceiling, but the tribal councils and juries can act in similar ways, subtly modifying the rules for what surviving women must do to win the game, and ultimately, win the cash. Thus, it's pretty clear: while a man, like Richard Hatch, can be obviously conniving and manipulative to become the sole Survivor, when a woman survives the last vote, she sure can't be a bitch.

Notes

[1]Interestingly, Amber's alliance with a prominent male cut-throat, Rob Mariano, in the later *Survivor: All-Stars* (season #8, which showed beloved players returning for a second try in the game) did not stigmatize her in similar ways. This difference suggests a contrast in being associated with a merciless male player rather than a ruthless female participant, both of whom might use comparable strategies.

[2]In the later *Survivor: All-Stars* season, Rob Mariano showed he had learned from his earlier mistakes, and manipulated others only from within strong alliances; however, in a true alteration of *Survivor* gendered politics, that season, which presented returning players using different and more evolved strategies, revealed that playing hard-ball with players who knew the game, could actually cost him the winning spot, regardless of his gender.

[3]It would have been interesting to see the results of a final vote between Stephenie LaGrossa and third-place runner-up Rafe Judkins, since he and Stephenie manipulated (and voted out) the same people—even those within their own alliance. With those same people on the jury choosing between her and Danni Boatwright, Stephenie only managed to garner a single vote in her favor (from Rafe). The final voting tally between a male and a female who had essentially made the same devious calculations would have been fascinating.

[4]Not including the *All-Stars* season, which portrayed returning players using very different strategies than they used in their first attempt in *Survivor*, men and women are tied at 5–5 overall within the other ten seasons.

[5]This calculation does not include the "Robfather's" (Rob Mariano) unsuccessful attempt to win the million in the *All-Stars* season due to the drastically different methods that were used when players were competing a second time. However, to continue the point that men were still not held as responsible for their conniving, we need only review "America's Tribal Council"—a surprise second reunion show after the *All-Stars*, which allowed viewers to cast their votes for the most-deserving Survivor to win a second million dollars. While Rupert Boneham won this viewers' contest—and he is notably very well liked by many, the other candidates significantly were three other men, including two of the most double-dealing men, Mariano and Colby Donaldson ("America's Tribal Council"). No women—and certainly none deemed dishonest—were selected.

[6]Again, this calculation does not include Amber Brkich's win in the *All-Stars* season. See note #4.

[7]For what it's worth, Jenna overcame her inability to lie by the time she competed in the *All-Stars* season, making it to the final three.

Works Cited

"America's Tribal Council." *Survivor: All-Stars*. Producer Mark Burnett. Host Jeff Probst. CBS. 13 May 2004.

"Changing of the Guard." *Survivor: Africa*. 1 November 2001. CBS.com. 5 January 2004. <http://www.cbs.com/primetime/survivor3/show/episode04/story.shtml>.

"Episode 5." *Survivor 2: The Australian Outback*. Producer Mark Burnett. Host Jeff Probst. CBS. 22 February 2001.

"Episode 7." *Survivor 2: The Australian Outback*. Producer Mark Burnett. Host Jeff Probst. CBS. 8 March 2001.

"Episode 8." *Survivor 2: The Australian Outback*. Producer Mark Burnett. Host Jeff Probst. CBS. 29 March 2001.

"Episode 9." *Survivor 2: The Australian Outback*. Producer Mark Burnett. Host Jeff Probst. CBS. 14 March 2001.

"Episode 11." *Survivor 2: The Australian Outback*. Producer Mark Burnett. Host Jeff Probst. CBS. 12 April 2001.

"Episode 12." *Survivor 2: The Australian Outback*. Producer Mark Burnett. Host Jeff Probst. CBS. 19 April 2001.

"Episode 13." *Survivor*. Producer Mark Burnett. Host Jeff Probst. CBS. August 2000.

"Episode 13." *Survivor Marquesas*. Producer Mark Burnett. Host Jeff Probst. CBS. May 2002.

"Episode 13." *Survivor: Amazon*. Producer Mark Burnett. Host Jeff Probst. CBS. 11 May 2003.

"Episode 14." *Survivor 2: The Australian Outback*. Producer Mark Burnett. Host Jeff Probst. CBS. 3 May 2001.

"Jon Explains His Devious Lie." *Survivor: Pearl Islands*. 2003. CBS.com. 5 January 2004. <http://www.cbs.com/primetime/survivor7/show/episode11/s7story.shtml>.

"On My Son's Life." *Survivor: Vanuatu*. 2005. CBS.com. 13 September 2005. <http://www.cbs.com/primetime/survivor9/show/ep11/index02.shtml>.

"Reunion." *Survivor All-Stars*. Producer Mark Burnett. Host Jeff Probst. CBS. 9 May 2004.

"Stunned at Tribal Council: Brook Eaten Alive." *Survivor: Vanuatu*. 2005. CBS.com. 12 September 2005. <http://www.cbs.com/primetime/survivor9/show/ep01/index.shtml>.

"Survivor: Amazon Reunion." Producer Mark Burnett. Host Jeff Probst. CBS. 11 May 2003.

"Survivor: Pearl Islands Reunion." Producer Mark Burnett. Host Jeff Probst. CBS. 14 December 2003.

"Survivor: The Reunion 2." Producer Mark Burnett. Host Bryant Gumbel. CBS. 3 May 2001.

After Reading

Critical Perspective

1. What is your main reaction to Putnam's text? Why do you think that the text evokes these feelings for you?

Rhetoric and Argument

2. What uses of ethos, pathos, and logos do you see at work in Putnam's essay? Are these rhetorical tactics helpful to her argument? Do they seem to undermine it in particular ways? Also reflect upon Putnam's use of audience, purpose, intertextuality, context, and constraints. Give textual evidence to support your views.
3. Putnam employs a rather unique tone, approach, and argumentative structure in this essay. Do you think that this is an effective approach for examining a well-watched television show like *Survivor*? Why or why not? In what ways do Putnam's rhetorical choices mirror those of the show? Offer evidence from the text and the show to back up your assertions.
4. What is Putnam's main claim about "Survivor"? Do you agree with her, disagree, or find that you take a position somewhere in between? Explain your thoughts. Do you find Putnam's argument and the structure of her essay persuasive? Why or why not? Be sure to provide examples as evidence for your claims.
5. How does Putnam provide support for her main claim? Do you believe that this kind of evidence is convincing? Are there counterarguments you might draw from to refute her claims? Try to be as specific as you can.
6. Are there any logical fallacies at work in Putnam's text? What assumptions or warrants does Putnam's text depend upon? Do you think that they are sound? Why or why not?

Analysis

7. Watch an episode from the most recent version of the show *Survivor*. Write a short argumentative essay in which you address the following concerns: Do you think that Putnam's claim about how the show perpetuates stereotypes about masculinity and femininity continues to be valid? Has it changed at all from the beginning of the show, to the last episodes Putnam analyzes, and now to the most recent episodes? If you think so, why do you believe that this is the case? If you don't, why not? Provide evidence from the show itself to support your ideas. In addition, consult library and Internet sources.

Taking Action

Your class has been instructed to create a new reality television show, a show that has one main goal: To challenge traditional gender dynamics as they exist among young men and women on college campuses. Form small working groups that will take on the following tasks: (1) Decide the rules of the game, (2) consider how contestants will be selected, (3) think about what kind of camera coverage the contestants will experience, and (4) determine the potential pitfalls that might be encountered along the way. Consult relevant library and Internet sources. Your class group can then discuss why you made the choices you did, what significance they have, and why such a show does not currently exist on mainstream television.

Alternatively, your class might choose to go through with your plan—interview contestants, have them play the game, and videotape the entire process. If this option is selected, perhaps the show could be screened by a campus-wide group of students. The people from class could then lead a discussion about why they made the rhetorical choices that they did.

BOB BATCHELOR

"Is This Reality?: *The Bachelor* Feeds Our Desire for Fame"

Bob Batchelor (http://www.bobbatchelor.com) is a writer and historian. He lives in northern California with his wife Katherine, a teacher. Batchelor is the author of The 1900s *and editor of* Basketball in America: From the Playgrounds to Jordan's Game. *Batchelor wrote this piece because he felt that too few critics were discussing* The Bachelor *from a male perspective.*

EXERCISING YOUR SKILLS

Before Reading

Batchelor's essay centers on the reality television show, *The Bachelor*. Have you seen reality television shows such as *The Bachelor, The Bachelorette,* or *Average Joe*? Oftentimes these shows depict one eligible male or female who has to choose between many women or men in order to decide who will become his or her future love interest. The particular person judges who is attractive and who is not, as well as who is marriage material and who is not.

What thoughts do you have about the premises of such shows? Why do you think people tune in? If you watch these types of shows, what do we hope to see and why? Do you think this is a positive thing? Why or why not? What do such shows reveal about how masculinity and femininity are represented? What do they expose about the myths, dreams, and beliefs inherent in contemporary American culture about what it means to be a man or what it means to be a woman? What do these shows suggest about the cultural narratives of romantic love, seduction, and marriage?

Reality television has cruised right through fad status and emerged as an international phenomenon. The numbers don't lie. Each new installment seems to deliver record-shattering ratings, whether it is 19 million viewers tuned into the debut of *Joe Millionaire* or the second season of Fox's *American Idol* posting the network's highest ratings ever for a non-sports show. Despite highbrow critics who grumble about the genre being proof of western civilization's collapse, reality television is exactly what viewers want to watch, whether serving as handy escapism from a faltering economy and war in the Middle East or as a voyeuristic peek into other people's lives. Like all obsessions, the reality television craze will end someday, but the fascination has revealed quite a bit about the American psyche in the early twenty-first century.

At the same time the public speaks with its remote control, the media and television networks weigh in with their pocketbooks. As long as television viewers continue to demonstrate an insatiable thirst for reality-based programs, thus generating easy money for the networks, old shows will be repackaged and new programs will appear—despite the eventual saturation of the airwaves.

Television executives love the genre because shows like *Fear Factor* and *High School Reunion* are cheap to produce and reap big-time advertising dollars. Looking back, it is easy to trace early successes, such as *The Jerry Springer Show* and *Survivor*, which beget countless imitators and knockoffs, like *Dog Eat Dog* and *The Mole*. Throughout the maturation (then saturation) of a television genre there are countless hands in the kitty, each taking a handsome cut of the money pouring into network coffers. Next, adding their considerable heft to promote reality-based programming, mainstream and entertainment media outlets jumped on the bandwagon, presenting the latest information about reality shows as real news and then treating the contestants/participants as celebrities. From *People* magazine and *US Weekly* to *Entertainment Tonight* and *Good Morning America*, these newfound stars entered the illusory world of American celebrity culture.

Survivor is arguably the grandfather of reality television programming, particularly if talk shows and game shows are considered a different beast. I contend, however, that ABC's *The Bachelor* (currently in its third incarnation, *The Bachelorette*) was the genre's "crossover" hit. In other words, *The Bachelor* served as the show, like in the music industry—think Shania Twain or Jay-Z—that gained momentum from a initial large fan base among reality show enthusiasts and then crossed over to a broader audience.

The crossover audience included the hordes of people that suddenly gathered around the water cooler the next morning, analyzing each move, and then theorizing about future installments. As the show's popularity increased, it also roped in many highly-educated, pro-capitalist, proto-hippie viewers who naturally felt superior to the stereotypical television-lobotomized couch potatoes of the world, the people David Brooks so accurately labeled "bourgeois bohemians" in his best-selling book, *Bobos in Paradise: The New Upper Class and How They Got There*.

Part of ABC's brilliance was choosing a successful, Harvard-educated guy to be the first bachelor (appealing to Bobo tastes), while ensuring that his looks and personality were sufficiently vanilla so that neither would be a total turnoff to normal viewers. While *The Bachelor* did not post *Joe Millionaire* ratings from the start, it gradually lured in a broad audience from up and down the socio-economic ladder. Because of its power to ensnare this type of viewer, no examination of reality television is complete without a look at the first season of *The Bachelor*.

Alex Michel: Bobo Prince

I admit that I was one of the 10 million viewers watching *The Bachelor*. But to be honest, I have to push the blame for this onto my wife. She was instantly mesmerized by the show, labeling it "car crash television." Like a roadside accident, once you see it, you just can't turn away, even if you don't really want to see under the white sheet.

Mondays at 9 p.m. we watched in fascination as 25 women vied for the attention of— and reportedly, a life-long commitment from—Alex Michel, a 31-year-old management consultant. During the show, we engaged in an hour-long therapy session, trying to figure out what possessed seemingly normal women to submit to this kind of publicized public flogging. Routinely, the next morning in the office, a group of us compared notes: How many women did Alex grope last night? Doesn't he look like Jack Nicholson as the Joker with the turned up smirk? Could this guy be more of a player? And so on.

Early media criticism blasted *The Bachelor* from a feminist perspective. Surprisingly, given the cash reward precedent on other reality shows, no money changed hands on *The Bachelor* (although ABC admitted that the finalist would get a small remuneration). At least the contestants on *Fear Factor* received a shot at $50,000 for eating cow brains; women selected for *The Bachelor* risked public humiliation for a blueblood Harvard grad with peninsula hair and a rather dorky demeanor. As criticism of the show intensified (at the same time more viewers tuned in), I was disappointed that a male-oriented critique did not materialize, particularly an assessment of Alex's proto-male personality and the way he treated the women.

Many critics questioned the collective intelligence of the females who continued to claim what a great catch he was, despite having to endure his endless banal and empty-headed questions. For example, he once asked a woman's parents what their daughter liked to do in her spare time. My first thought was that the question of intelligence should be pointed at Alex, not just the women on the show.

Furthermore, despite all the on-air discussion about his being a "nice guy" and "sweet," he came across as superficial (in both his actions and reasons for choosing which women to keep). In my eyes, Alex was a total player; his dates included kissing and groping, and although the women were plainly uncomfortable with this kind of "sharing," he did not back off. For all Alex's education and wealthy rearing, our television hero was not the kind of guy I wanted as a representative of my gender or age group.

On the day Alex ventured to meet Trista's family, for example, he asked her (despite her coolness toward him from the start) to consider them dating, as he put it, "exclusively." This took place just before he left to visit the two other remaining "dates" and meet their families. When she told him she could not consider them exclusive because that would mean he was cheating on her with the others, he balked and later (speaking alone to the camera, when he didn't have to face the women) insinuated that it could hurt her chances of moving on.

Worse, Alex bullied his way through the first season. The most flagrant example hap-pened while he was with Shannon (who deliciously spent more time playing with her dog than doting on him, which led to Alex's scowl being caught on camera more than one occasion). While in the limousine, the sweet, wonderful bachelor tried to force Shannon into talking about sex—the whole time firmly gripping her knee.

Not only would he not let the issue die when it was clear she was uncomfortable, but he kept badgering her until she broke down in tears. He wanted her to speak to him as if they were in private, but she blurted out, "We're not alone" and gestured to the camera. She asked him to imagine that her mother and grandmother were sitting there with them. He scoffed at the notion, insisting they were alone, even though every moment was taped for a national television audience.

Amazingly, Shannon's parents were the only ones who appeared concerned with the dating arrangement. They seemed dumbfounded after he left and were quick to question their daughter's actions. Their concerns about the compatibility between the two flustered Shannon to the point that she protested the "grilling" she was getting and fled the house. Finally, I thought, someone on this program has shown some commonsense.

To be blunt, I simply didn't like Alex and wouldn't want any female I care about to be associated with a guy like him. Though the other parents seem to think he'd make a great "catch" for their daughter, viewers privy to his interactions with each of the women could not help but feel that Alex enjoyed manipulating the women and lording over them, like some kind of pimp-daddy guarding his "ladies."

Throughout the show, I thought that if this guy's the cream of the crop in the dating world, I felt sorry for single women (an egotistic, goofy-looking, inauthentic player—what a catch!). Each week after watching *The Bachelor*, I questioned why these women didn't decline the rose. Instead, why didn't they look directly into the camera, smirk, and kick Alex in the family jewels? That would be an "accident" worth watching.

Alex's artificiality only increased when he chose Amanda Marsh, a 23-year-old surgically enhanced buxom blonde with stars in her eyes every time Alex entered the room. Instead of asking her to marry him, the stated goal of the program, Alex said he wanted to get to know her better. Sure enough, the two appeared together for the cameras and to publicize *Bachelor II*, but it soon became apparent that their relationship was a sham, her living in Kansas and him shopping television scripts in Los Angeles.

Aaron Buerge: The Anti-Alex

With a southern drawl and twinkle in his eyes, 28-year-old Missouri banking executive Aaron Buerge spent most of the second season proving that he wasn't like Alex—never overtly criticizing the first bachelor, but making it clear that he would treat the women with more respect and chivalry. Aaron struggled mightily to keep his lips to himself, the groping to a minimum, and rarely let even the faintest clue about which woman he favored slip out.

The differences between Alex and Aaron did not end at their personalities. For the second season, ABC went with a younger, seemingly more successful, better-looking bachelor. Sporting more than looks and muscles, Aaron served up his credentials as American Heartthrob, playing classical piano, touting his dream of becoming a restaurateur, and strutting his stuff as a pilot.

The contrasts between Alex and Aaron paid off for ABC. The less Aaron revealed about himself and about whom his potential choice might be, the higher ratings surged (bolstered by the catty infighting among the competitors). When Aaron finally picked 27-year-old Jersey girl Helene Eksterowicz over 22-year-old college belle Brooke Smith in the season finale, 26 million viewers tuned in. Stunningly, the cliffhanger gave ABC a victory over a parade of nearly naked, overtly thin supermodels on CBS's *Victoria's Secret Fashion Show*. On the strength of *The Bachelor*, ABC placed second in the November 2002 sweeps race. The show drew heavily on the prized 18–49-year-old demographic and consistently beat NBC's critically acclaimed *West Wing*.

Despite the nationally televised proposal and millions of viewers, Aaron and Helene did not set a wedding date or even move closer to one another—he firmly rooted in Missouri, and her in New Jersey. The couple maintained that they were taking time to get to know one another better before hitching up.

Trista Rehn: Hunted Becomes Hunter

The outcry of public disapproval concerning Alex's choice of Amanda over Trista Rehn caused ABC to do what many television enthusiasts thought unthinkable: launch *The Bachelorette*, with 25 men vying for Trista's hand. The audacious move, twisting traditional gender roles by giving the female ultimate power, probably would have never been attempted if reality shows had begun to fade.

Before the show debuted, many observers thought the American public would not stand for a woman dating so many men concurrently. The networks are so anxious to air reality-based programming, however, that *The Bachelorette* does not seem like much of a risk anymore.

Maybe the fact that neither of the first two bachelors actually walked down the aisle had softened the audience. It's one thing for our hero or heroine to go on television looking for a soul mate; it's an entirely different story to really get married. Instead of thinking about how a bachelor or bachelorette may have to spend the rest of his/her life with someone he/she met eight weeks ago, the audience can focus on how cute or studly the love interests are and how wonderful or pathetic the contestants prove to be.

Terry O'Neill, a vice president of the National Organization of Women, summed up the public's response to *The Bachelor* series as the first show began heating up, saying, "Getting married is something you win? It's extremely creepy." The true genius of *The Bachelor* is that it has taken a situation that is steeply cemented in reality ('til death do us part) and reduced it to yet another competition in which there are clearly defined winners and losers who can be cheered or booed, just like the home team in the sports world.

The Warhol Addendum

Over the last 20 years, cable television, global satellite communications, the proliferation of movie theaters, cell phones, instant messaging, email, and the Internet have combined to swamp us with information. As a result, Andy Warhol's statement, "in the future everybody will be famous for 15 minutes" is more prescient now than at any other point in American history. Today the world is awash in information. In response, I offer a codicil to Warhol's proclamation. Let's call it the Warhol Addendum.

The Warhol Addendum asserts that as the numbers of media outlets multiply, total fame time decreases proportionately, but burns more intensely, until the next sensationalist event occurs to push it out of favor. So, in other words, Warhol's original 15 minutes of fame is now reduced to about five minutes. For those in the spotlight, those five minutes are going to be frenzied, but will end quickly as the next sensationalized event heats up to replace it.

For instance, look at Richard Hatch's circuitous route to fame. First, *Survivor* gains a large national audience, and goes on to set ratings records. The media frenzy turns Richard, the show's first victor, into a celebrity. In his five minutes, Richard appears on a bunch of television shows, gets a book deal, and participates in the pre-publicity mania leading up to the next *Survivor* series. As that cast replaces the first, his fame peters out. As a result, Richard basically floats in second tier celebrity status (or lower), while the spotlight shifts to the next subject.

In modern American popular culture, nothing defines celebrity more than television. It is this need to grasp at a moment's fame that prompts hundreds of people to wait outside Rockefeller Center in New York City on a daily basis, hoping that the *Today* show camera will highlight them, regardless of bone-chilling temperatures or debilitating humidity. A national yearning for fame, however short-lived, causes people to do or say just about anything to appear on *The Jerry Springer Show, Dr. Phil*, or the many other talk shows.

We are a nation addicted to our own self-importance. Do you want your shot at fame? Just wait for the call-in number to flash. You may very well win a spot as the next contestant on *The Bachelor, Survivor, Temptation Island*, [*Beauty and the Geek*] or the next round of reality programs. Go ahead . . . let decorum fall by the wayside. Don't you deserve your moment in the sun?

After Reading

Critical Perspective

1. What is your reaction to these types of reality shows? What about them makes you feel this way? Do you think that Batchelor adequately captures how these shows work? Why or why not?

Rhetoric and Argument

2. How would you describe Batchelor's rhetoric in this piece—his use of audience, purpose, ethos, pathos, logos, intertextuality, context, and constraints? Characterize his tone and approach. Do you believe that he employs effective strategies to reach his audience? Why or why not? What other suggestions might you have for extending or further developing this argument?

3. What does Batchelor assert about *The Bachelor* (a show that echos his own name) and similar shows? What is the author's own relationship to the show, and how did he come to have this relationship to it? Do you think that this adds to his credibility and ethos as a writer or not? Be sure to provide examples from the text to support your views.

4. Would you argue that Batchelor provides enough evidence to support his assertions? Why or why not? Give quotes from the essay to back up your ideas.

5. What does Batchelor indicate about how masculinity and femininity are portrayed on the show? What might he imply about how romantic love and seduction operate on *The Bachelor*?

Analysis

6. Watch the newest versions of the shows *The Bachelor* or *The Bachelorette*. Write a short argumentative essay in which you address the following questions: Does the bachelor or bachelorette operate in much the same ways as Batchelor describes here? Is the audience having a greater say in what happens on the show than they initially did? Do you think masculinity and femininity work in similar or different ways within these new shows? Be sure to present evidence from the visual texts as well as library and Internet sources to support your thoughts.

Taking Action

One of Batchelor's main contentions in his essay is that reality television fulfills a cultural need: people's desire for fame. Examine another popular reality show such as *Fear Factor, The Apprentice,* or *American Idol,* providing a rhetorical analysis of its main features.

Then form a small group in which you discuss the following: What lengths are people willing to go to in order to secure this fame? What do they have to gain? What do they have to lose? How are racial, class, ethnic, age, religious, regional, environmental, disability, and gender issues represented on this show? Why is this significant, and what does it say about American culture's reality obsession? Seek out library and Internet sources. Share your results with the larger class group.

ANITA CREAMER

"Reality TV Meets Plastic Surgery: An Ugly Shame"

Anita Creamer has been the Sacramento Bee's *lifestyle columnist since 1990. A New Orleans native and journalism graduate of Southern Methodist University, she began her career in Texas. She was a features reporter and part-time columnist at* The Dallas Times Herald *and* The Dallas Morning News. *An award-winning reporter, Creamer has also written for numerous regional publications and national magazines, including* Self, New Woman, *and others.*

EXERCISING YOUR SKILLS

Before Reading

Creamer's text examines how the focus on plastic surgery in American culture is shaping reality television. Plastic surgery has been very beneficial in helping people function who might not otherwise be able to—those who have been hurt in accidents or who have suffered as a result of disease. However, it also has another popular connotation. Plastic surgery has become an option many women as well as men turn to as they age to maintain the appearance of youthfulness. Consider examples of celebrities as well as people you might know who have considered or received such surgery. What was achieved by making this choice? What was lost? After you have considered these questions, make a list of the various plastic surgery operations today that are available to people. How do they support traditional American ideals about femininity and masculinity?

On MTV, a baby-faced blonde named Sha is talking about her life's ambition, which is to look like Pamela Anderson and become a *Playboy* centerfold. Sha—pronounced Shay— already looks cute, but that's not enough. She's collected stacks of old *Playboys*, and she pores over them as if they're how-to manuals.

She's 19, but the older you get, the younger that sounds. So: Should Sha really make such an important decision, to undergo major surgery and have her double chin suctioned and her lips and breasts augmented, when she's so deluded in her aspirations?

Ethics aren't MTV's deal.

But the moral of *I Want a Famous Face* seems to be that tragically insecure people make bad decisions about their lives—and not surprisingly, their families, who should've raised them with better values and bigger ambitions, aren't of any help at all. The eternal American habit of reinvention has come to this—remaking our faces and bodies instead of our lives; the annihilation of the self in the name of self-improvement. And all for TV ratings.

Surgery has become entertainment. Making a name for yourself—once the product of education, achievement and providing something of worth in the world—now involves allowing a voyeuristic nation to watch the transformation of your looks.

Your inner life doesn't matter.

"The new wave of plastic surgery reality television"—now there's a fabulous phrase—"is a serious cause for concern," Dr. Rod Rohrich, president of the American Society of Plastic Surgeons, has said in a press release. "Some patients on these shows have unrealistic and frankly unhealthy expectations about what plastic surgery can do for them."

What gave it away, *Famous Face's* seriously misguided 20-year-old-twins who underwent surgery to look like Brad Pitt? Telling them to grow up, grow into their faces and appreciate their uniqueness doesn't exactly make for good TV.

While plastic surgeons may be alarmed about cosmetic surgery reality TV, they're still taking advantage of the trend. Americans are spending more money than ever on Botox injections and brow lifts, according to ASPS, with 8.7 million cosmetic procedures performed in 2003. That number represents a 33 percent jump over 2002 figures. Elective plastic surgery has become routine.

Yet the reality TV programs showcasing it could just as easily serve as cautionary tales instead of success stories. The fact is, for example, that many of the folks on *Extreme Makeover*, ABC's entry in the genre, end up looking nothing at all like themselves. At best, they look attractive in a bland and homogeneous way; at worst, they look like transvestites with orange makeup and badly styled hair. Now *The Swan*—Fox's appalling show, in which 17 so-called ugly ducklings undergo an array of cosmetic surgery procedures, then compete in a beauty contest—is drawing mediocre ratings.

It would be nice to think this lack of audience enthusiasm is proof that we find a TV show that takes advantage of women's body dysmorphia to be cruel beyond words. But the problem with *The Swan*, according to critics, is less its utter lack of sensitivity than its lack of TV-friendly dramatic moments.

So. Perhaps enlightenment remains on hold.

By the end of Sha's *I Want a Famous Face* episode, a *Playboy* scout is telling her that the magazine prefers a more natural look, instead of the obviously phony va-voom of those Andersonesque implants. Sha doesn't look like a cute little blonde any more. She has duck lips, and her breast augmentation makes her look overstuffed instead of sexy. But she got her wish. She's on TV, a flash-in-the-pan star, just like Pamela Anderson.

And for the impressionable and unassured, that may be all that matters.

After Reading

CRITICAL PERSPECTIVE

1. Examine how Creamer commences her essay. Why do you think she makes this particular choice? Do you find this approach persuasive? How does this decision impact her potential choices for concluding her essay?

Rhetoric and Argument

2. How would you describe Creamer's rhetorical tactics in this piece—her use of audience, purpose, ethos, pathos, logos, intertextuality, context, and constraints? Characterize her tone and the ways in which she addresses her audience. Do you believe that Creamer employs effective strategies to reach her audience? Why or why not? Be sure to provide support for your views.
3. Summarize Creamer's key points in your own words—including her thoughts about the "American habit of reinvention." How do you know that these are her main claims? Where do they appear in her text? Quote from the essay to back up your assertions.
4. Does Creamer furnish enough evidence to support her thesis? Why yes? Why no? What warrants or assumptions does Creamer make in this essay? Do you think that they are valid? Why or why not? Give evidence from the essay to back up your ideas.
5. Reread Creamer's conclusion. How does her ending for the piece mirror her introduction? Do you find this approach persuasive or not? Why? Offer textual support.

Analysis

6. Creamer describes the fact that "surgery has become entertainment." Write a short argumentative essay in which you consider the veracity of this statement and what this may reveal about trends in American culture. You will want to consult Creamer's essay as well as library and Internet sources to back up your thoughts.

Taking Action

Form several small teams in your class. Your roles are to act as investigative reporters in order to answer the following questions: How do students on your college campus feel about the prospect of getting plastic surgery for cosmetic purposes? Why do they feel the ways that they do about it? Each small group should be sure to interview both male and female students ranging from first-year students through seniors. You may want to audiotape or videotape your conversations if participants are willing.

When you have spoken to a number of students in each of these age categories, present your findings to the other students in your class. Then, form a larger group to consider the significance of what you have all learned. What recurring themes or patterns did you notice? What were you surprised to discover? What do you think this reveals about how college students' desires to be more attractive, more youthful, or even just different impacts their thoughts about plastic surgery?

POPULAR TELEVISION IMAGES

ARIEL GORE

"TV Can Be a Good Parent"

Ariel Gore teaches creative writing classes at The Attic Writers' Workshop in Portland, Oregon. She has written a novel, The Death and Resurrection Show *and* The Essential Hip Mama: Writing from the Cutting Edge of Parenting, *a text that brings together essays from the first decade of her popular 'zine* Hip Mama. *This essay is taken from her book* The Hip Mama Survival Guide.

EXERCISING YOUR SKILLS

Before Reading

Gore writes about the value of television as a parenting tool. Think about some of the television shows that you watched (or were forbidden from watching) as a child or a tweenager. Recall some of the main characters, the story lines, and the lessons or morals. What times of day did you watch these shows? What did you like about them and why? What do you think that they were teaching you about yourself, your family, and your place in the world? Looking back on your experiences, what positive or negative things do you feel like you learned from watching those shows?

Let me get this straight.

The corporations have shipped all the living-wage jobs off to the developing world, the federal government has "ended welfare" and sent poor women into sub-minimum wage "training programs" while offering virtually no child-care assistance, the rent on my one-bedroom apartment just went up to $850 a month, the newspapers have convinced us that our kids can't play outside by themselves until they're 21 and now the American Academy of Pediatrics wants my television?

I don't think so.

Earlier this month, the AAP released new guidelines for parents recommending that kids under the age of 2 not watch TV. They say the box is bad for babies' brains and not much better for older kids. Well, no duh.

When I was a young mom on welfare, sometimes I needed a break. I needed time to myself. I needed to mellow out to avoid killing my daughter for pouring bleach on the Salvation Army couch. And when I was at my wits' end, Barney the Dinosaur and Big Bird were better parents than I was. My daughter knows that I went to college when she was a baby and preschooler. She knows that I work. And, truth be told, our television set has been a helpful co-parent on rainy days when I've been on deadline. Because I'm the mother of a fourth-grader, Nickelodeon is my trusted friend.

There was no TV in our house when I was a kid. My mother called them "boob tubes." But that was in the 1970s. My mother and all of her friends were poor—they were artists—but the rent she paid for our house on the Monterey (Calif.) Peninsula was $175 a month and my mother and her friends helped each other with the kids. The child care was communal. So they could afford to be poor, to stay home, to kill their televisions. I, on the other hand, cannot.

Now the AAP is saying I'm doing my daughter an injustice every time I let her watch TV. The official policy states that "Although certain television programs may be promoted to [young children], research on early brain development shows that babies and toddlers have a critical need for direct interactions with parents and other significant caregivers for healthy brain growth and the development of appropriate social, emotional, and cognitive skills. Therefore, exposing such young children to television programs should be discouraged."

Maybe my brain has been warped by all my post-childhood TV watching, but I'm having a little trouble getting from point A to point B here. Babies and toddlers have a critical need for direct interactions with actual people. I'm with them on this. "Therefore, exposing such young children to television programs should be discouraged." This is where they lose me. I can see "Therefore, sticking them in front of the TV all day and all night should be discouraged." But the assumption that TV-watching kids don't interact with their parents or caregivers is silly. Watching TV and having one-on-one interactions with our kids aren't mutually exclusive.

I've been careful to teach my daughter critical thinking in my one-woman "mind over media" campaign. It started with fairytales: "What's make-believe?" and "How would you like to stay home and cook for all those dwarves?" Later we moved on to the news: "Why was it presented in this way?" and "What's a stereotype?" But if you think I was reading "Winnie the Pooh" to my toddler when I thought up these questions, think again. I was relaxing with a cup of coffee and a book on feminist theory while Maia was riveted to PBS.

I read to my daughter when she was little. We still read together. But even a thoughtful mama needs an electronic baby sitter every now and again. Maybe *especially* a thoughtful mama.

Not surprisingly, the television executives feel there's plenty of innocuous programming on television to entertain young kids without frying their brains. "It's a bunch of malarkey," said Kenn Viselman, president of the Itsy Bitsy Entertainment Co., about the new policy. Itsy Bitsy distributes the British show "Teletubbies," which is broadcast on PBS. While I prefer Big Bird to Tinky Winky, I have to agree with him when he says, "Instead of attacking shows that try to help children, the pediatricians should warn parents that they shouldn't watch *The Jerry Springer Show* when kids are in the room."

The AAP's policy refers to all television, of course, but it's hard not to feel like they're picking on PBS. "Teletubbies" is the only program currently shown on non-cable television marketed toward babies and toddlers. Just two weeks ago, the station announced a $40 million investment to develop six animated programs for preschoolers. The timing of the AAP's report is unfortunate.

Cable stations offer a wider variety of kid programming. Take for example Nick Jr., an offshoot of the popular Nickelodeon channel. On weekdays from 9 a.m. to 2 p.m., the programming is geared specifically toward the preschool set. "Our slogan for Nick Jr. is 'Play to Learn'," Nickelodeon's New York publicity manager, Karen Reynolds, told me. "A child is using cognitive skills in a fun setting. It's interactive. With something like 'Blues Clues,' kids are talking back to the TV. They are not just sitting there."

Still, the station has no beef with the new AAP policy on toddlers. "Nick Jr. programs to preschool children ages 2 to 5, but we are aware that children younger than 2 may be watching television," said Brown Johnson, senior vice president of Nick Jr. "We welcome a study of this kind because it encourages parents to spend more time bonding and playing with their children."

In addition to telling parents that young children shouldn't watch television at all and that older kids shouldn't have sets in their bedrooms, the AAP is recommending that pediatricians ask questions about media consumption at annual checkups. The difference between recommending less TV-watching and actually mandating that it be monitored by the medical community is where this could become a game of hardball with parents. What would this "media file" compiled by our doctors be used for? Maybe television placement in the home will become grounds for deciding child custody. ("I'm sorry, your honor, I'll move the set into the bathroom immediately.") Or maybe two decades from now Harvard will add TV abstention to their ideal candidate profile. ("'Teletubbies' viewers need not apply.") Better yet, Kaiser could just imprint "Poor White Trash" directly onto my family's medical ID cards. Not that those cards work at the moment. I'm a little behind on my bill.

I called around, but I was hard-pressed to find a pediatrician who disagreed with the academy's new policy. Instead, doctors seemed to want their kids to watch *less* TV, and they're glad to have the AAP's perhaps over-the-top guidelines behind them. "If all your kids did was an hour of Barney and 'Sesame Street' a day, I don't think that the academy would have come out with that statement," said a pediatrician at La Clinica de la Raza in Oakland, Calif., who asked not to be named. "It's not the best learning tool." And he scoffs at the notion of "interactive" TV. "It's not a real human interaction. When you're dealing with babies and toddlers, this screen is an integral part of their reality. You want kids to be able to understand interaction as an interaction. It's like the Internet. We're getting to a place where all of your relationships are virtual relationships."

Fair enough.

I'm not going to say that TV is the greatest thing in the world for little kids—or for anyone. I'm not especially proud of the hours I spend watching "Xena: Warrior Princess," "The Awful Truth" and "Ally McBeal." Mostly I think American television is a string of insipid shows aired for the sole purpose of rounding up an audience to buy tennis shoes made in Indonesian sweatshops.

But it seems that there is a heavy middle-class assumption at work in the AAP's new policy—that all of us can be stay-at-home moms, or at least that we all have partners or other supportive people who will come in and nurture our kids when we can't.

I say that before we need a policy like this one, we need more—and better—educational programming on TV. We need to end the culture of war and the media's glorification of violence. We need living-wage jobs. We need government salaries for stay-at-home moms so that all women have a real career choice. We do not need "media files" in our pediatricians' offices or more guilt about being bad parents. Give me a $175 a month house on the Monterey Peninsula and a commune of artists to share parenting responsibilities, and I'll kill my TV without any provocation from the AAP at all. Until then, long live Big Bird, "The Brady Bunch" and all their very special friends!

After Reading

Critical Perspective

1. Gore offers a different perspective on the role of television in the American home. How do you respond to her views? What specifically can you point to in this essay that caused you to have this reaction?

Rhetoric and Argument

2. Describe Gore's tone. Do you think it's likely to create a stronger bond with her audience or not? What about the text makes you think this? What kinds of rhetorical choices—use of audience, purpose, ethos, pathos, logos, intertextuality, context, and constraints—does her essay rely on? Back up your assertions with quotes.
3. What is Gore's main claim in this essay? Is this claim developed clearly or not? Be sure to present examples from the text to back up your thoughts.

4. How does Gore support her main claim? What kinds of evidence does she employ? Do you find her tactics persuasive? Why or why not?

5. Does Gore make any assumptions, warrants, or logical fallacies that undermine her argument? If you were writing Gore's argument, what might you do to make your argument even more persuasive?

Analysis

6. Write a short argumentative essay in which you address the following: Do you think that Gore's argument is valid, convincing, and rhetorically effective? Why or why not? What countercharges might be made against her claims? Do you think Gore adequately anticipates her opposition? Back up your views by offering quotes from her essay as well as consulting library and Internet sources.

Taking Action

Gather in a small group. Choose a particular television show that targets young children. After watching episodes of the show and taking detailed notes, consider the cultural criticism you might make about the program. Then put together a cultural criticism of this show, explaining how the characters, the plots, the narratives, and the lessons or morals offered are likely to have positive and/or negative effects on their audience. Support your views by offering a close rhetorical analysis of the text as well as additional library and Internet sources. When you are ready, present your findings to the class.

Vɪᴄ Bᴜʟʟᴜᴄᴋ

"NAACP Takes a Closer Look at Television Diversity—Diversity: No Laughing Matter"

Vic Bulluck is Executive Director of the Hollywood Bureau of the National Association for the Advancement of Colored People. The NAACP provides this very useful overview of its history and goals at http://www.naacp.org/about/about_index.html:

> *Since its inception the National Association for the Advancement of Colored People (NAACP) was poised for a long, tumultuous and rewarding history. Although it may be possible to chronicle the challenging and harrowing legacy of the NAACP, the real story of the nation's most significant civil rights organization lies in the hearts and minds of the people who would not stand still while the rights of some of America's darker citizens were denied . . .*
>
> *The history of the NAACP, is one of blood sweat and tears. From bold investigations of mob brutality, protests of mass murders, segregation and discrimination, to testimony before congressional committees on the vicious tactics used to bar African Americans from the ballot box, it was the talent and tenacity of NAACP members that saved lives and changed many negative aspects of American society. While much of its history is chronicled in books, articles, pamphlets and*

magazines, the true movement lies in the faces—black, white, yellow, red, and brown—united to awaken the conscientiousness of a people, and a nation. This is the legacy of the NAACP!

EXERCISING YOUR SKILLS

Before Reading

Vic Bulluck's text reveals the NAACP's views about today's popular televison. Take a few minutes to surf the NAACP's main web page at http://www.naacp.org/. Jot down some notes about the sorts of stories that appear there, the aims of the NAACP, the accomplishments of the NAACP, and the future goals of the NAACP. What specific issues is the organization addressing right now and how? Consider how you might help the NAACP to reach its goals by getting involved in its programs or other related outreach programs.

Diversity on broadcast network television has been an issue for years. In 1999 the networks joined the NAACP and other minority groups in an initiative that promised to diversify the entertainment industry workforce not only in front of the camera, but also behind the scenes. The goal was to create programming that better reflects the American viewing audience. While there has been some progress, everyone recognizes that there is still much to be done.

Employment numbers for actors, directors and writers on staff for the 2006 fall season will not be available until November/December. It is important to comment on the announced fall line up now because these shows could be indicative of what is to come.

One very disconcerting fact is that, with the cancellation of the *Bernie Mac Show*, for the first time in recent history, there is not a comedy with an African-American lead character left on the big four networks. When it comes to returning sitcoms and the announced new comedies, African Americans are missing in action. While the genre is not as popular as it once was, there is not a shortage of sitcoms on the schedule: ABC: *Big Day, Help Me Help You, Ugly Betty, Notes from the Underbelly, According to Jim, What About Brian, George Lopez.* CBS: *The Class, Two and Half Men, How I Met Your Mother, New Adventures of Old Christine.* NBC: *20 Good Years, 30 Rock, My Name Is Earl, The Office.* FOX: *The Loop, The War at Home, 'Til Death.* Out of the nearly twenty sitcoms on network television this fall, it is unconscionable that there is not an African American lead among them.

When you take into account the recent merger of UPN and the WB, the television landscape becomes even more bleak for the hundreds of African Americans and minorities who have made their careers working on television comedies. It is unfair to put the burden of diversity on television on the new CW. At least there you can find a Sunday night block of African American comedies. UPN was the only network to actively program for an African American audience. The detrimental impact of the CW's formation is indisputable. Five of the eight African-American comedies UPN aired (*One On One, Half & Half, Eve, Cuts,* and *Love Inc.*) did not make the CW fall line up.

Many of the UPN shows had African American show runners and predominantly black casts. They also employed many minority writers, directors, technicians and crafts people. The harsh reality is that with each canceled show upwards of two hundred people may lose their jobs. Now that those shows are canceled, the NAACP is concerned not only about where people will find work, but how long it will take to recover lost ground. If these writers, actors, directors and crafts persons were considered equally for other industry jobs and opportunities, then we would have no issue. But, regrettably, this is not the way it works in Hollywood.

The 2006 Diversity Report by the Directors Guild of America offers a glimpse into the state of ethnic representation at the networks. After examining all episodes of last season's top 40 network dramas and sitcoms, the guild found that 83 percent of the shows were directed by white men, 10 percent by white women, 5 percent by minority men and 2 percent by minority women.

In 1999 when the NAACP diversity initiative was first started in Hollywood there were seven African American show runners. In 2005 there were thirteen African American show runners. It is anticipated that in 2006 there will be eight. This is due in large part to the loss of UPN shows.

When we question employment practices in Hollywood we are continually told that the networks have little or no control over who is hired on the staff of a show; that those decisions are made by the show runner. They hire [whomever] they trust to get the job done. Everyone is acutely aware of this inherent discriminatory "it's who you know" hiring practice but no one takes responsibility. The NAACP recognizes two groups who can directly affect this practice and, because of the enormous power and influence that they wield and the top down pressure they can exert, must be held accountable; the WGA, of which many if not all of the show runners are members, and the network executives who employ the show runners and empower them to hire.

The news is not all bad. On the one hour dramatic front, bolstered by the success of series like *ER*, *CSI*, *Law and Order*, *Grey's Anatomy* and *Lost*, every network can point to shows on their schedule and count diverse roles. When it comes to one hour dramas the emphasis is principally on multiethnic ensemble casts.

ABC continues to be a progressive leader when it comes to diversity in dramatic programming. However, there is some consternation in our community over the way the Applewhites' story line ended on *Desperate Housewives*—murderous young black man hiding out in suburbia. Launching the largest number of new scripted shows, ABC continues to build on its successful line up that includes *Lost* and *Grey's Anatomy*. *Ugly Betty* is executive produced by Salma Hayek and has Vanessa Williams as a series regular. *Men in Trees*, with series regular John Amos, takes place in Alaska and seems to provide an organic opportunity to include Native Americans. *The Nine* features Chi McBride. *Six Degrees*, with Jay Hernandez, has a diverse cast and a theme that demonstrates how all our lives are interconnected. *Day Break* is a mid-season replacement with a young diverse cast starring Taye Diggs.

We applaud CBS and its hit series *The Unit*, starring Dennis Haysbert. This is currently the only one hour drama starring an African American male lead on a major network in the fall line up. While minorities are increasingly being cast as ensemble players in one hour dramatic series, *The Unit* is an ensemble show which promotes Haysbert as its star. Spike Lee directed the new James Woods courtroom drama, *Shark*. *Jericho*, is a one hour drama about the survivors of a nuclear holocaust. It takes place in a small town in Kansas. Lennie James is a series regular. We hope he is not the only minority survivor and that we will see Native Americans, Hispanics and African Americans alive and well in Kansas. Building on its popular CSI franchise, at least on the dramatic front, CBS continues its commitment to diversity on television.

NBC builds on its hugely successful *Law and Order* franchise. All of its new dramas have diverse casts [such as] *Kidnapped* starring Delroy Lindo along with Mykelti Williamson and Carmen Ejogo. Another encouraging show to watch for includes *Heroes*; this one-hour drama chronicles the lives of a multiethnic group of ordinary people who find out they have some extraordinary abilities. There is also the sports drama based on the film *Friday Night Lights*. The highly anticipated *Studio 60 on the Sunset Strip* has DL Hughley as a series regular.

FOX has the most popular and most diverse show on television, *American Idol*. FOX continues the successful formula it found in having a diverse ensemble cast on shows like *Prison Break* and *House*. This fall they are launching *Vanished* starring Ming Na, one of the few Asian series regulars on network television this season. Tim Story directed the pilot and will executive produce *Standoff*. *Justice*, a courtroom drama from Jerry Bruckheimer features Eamonn Walker as one of four disparate lawyers who are the "dream team" that tackle the most controversial and newsworthy cases. FOX's strong commitment to diversity programming is seemingly undermined by their continuing support for the *O.C.* and *The Loop,* however. These two shows, targeted at young adults, do not have diverse casts for unknown purely creative reasons.

On the dramatic side, the CW has the Tyra Banks' hit reality series *America's Next Top Model*. It must be noted that "Reality TV" seems to inherently better reflect the diversity of our culture. NAACP leadership has met with the CW executives and are encouraged that they are committed to diversity and will be launching new programs to reflect that commitment. They were also asked to take a close look at the casting on its shows *One Tree Hill* and *Smallville*. Again, these are two shows, targeted at young adults, that do not have diverse casts for creative reasons.

The network executives have come to recognize that minority viewers have a tremendous impact on a network's overall rating. Nearly one third of the viewing audience is diverse. Removing minority numbers from the viewing audience overall would cause ratings to drop considerably. One could argue that one third of all those working in Hollywood should be minorities. It is important to continually remind the entertainment industry and network decision makers that diversity is not only good for our shared society. It is good business.

We urge the networks along with the WGA and all network show runners to look closely at those who are being hired on all scripted shows before the launch of the new fall season. We ask them to pay close attention to those working on their writing staffs as well as the actors, directors, craftspeople and technicians.

Paraphrasing the words of Martin Luther King, no one wants to be "*judged by the color of their skin but by the content of their character.*" We profoundly hope that the entertainment community will continue to use these words as inspiration.

After Reading

Critical Perspective

1. Consider your gut reaction to this text. How did reading this essay from the NAACP make you feel? Why do you think that you had this reaction? Provide evidence from the text to support your thoughts.

Rhetoric and Argument

2. What sorts of rhetorical tactics—context, intertextuality, constraints, ethos, pathos, and logos—does Bulluck utilize to convince his audience? How would you describe his use of tone, in particular? Be sure to provide detailed examples from the text.
3. What does Bulluck claim about today's television shows—particularly situation comedies? Where in his argument does he make this claim? Offer quotes from the essay.
4. What kinds of evidence does Bulluck employ to back up his assertions? Do you find these different sorts of evidence persuasive? Why or why not? Provide textual evidence to support your views.
5. Map the structure of Bulluck's argument. What are the key features of his argument? Do you think that this organizational format helps to support Bulluck's argument or not? Be sure to cite detailed examples to back up your ideas.

Analysis

6. In a short response, analyze this essay and offer your own argumentative claim about its use of rhetoric and argument. Be sure to present details from specific television shows, quotes from the text, as well as library and Internet resources to support your views.

Taking Action

This essay ends with a paraphrase from Dr. Martin Luther King Jr.: no one wants to be "judged by the color of their skin but by the content of their character." This reference comes from King's famous speech, "I Have A Dream."

Form small groups and examine the official Dr. Martin Luther King Jr. website at http://www.thekingcenter.org/. Consider the mission and efforts of this center. In order to listen to an audio or watch a video version of this speech accompanied by a transcript you can do a web search or see http://www.historychannel.com.

After you have learned more about this speech, consider its content in light of Vic Bulluck's essay for the NAACP. What connections do you see between the two documents? What does this intertextual reference allow Bulluck to accomplish rhetorically? If useful, include library and Internet sources to support your assertions. When you are done, share your work with other groups in your class.

Paul A. Cantor

"The Simpsons: Atomistic Politics and the Nuclear Family"

Paul A. Cantor is a professor of English at the University of Virginia, a member of the National Council on the Humanities, and a noted scholar of Elizabethan and Romantic English literature. This essay comes from his book-length work Gilligan Unbound.

EXERCISING YOUR SKILLS

Before Reading

Cantor's piece examines the television show *The Simpsons* in detail. Watch several episodes of *The Simpsons*. Who are the main characters in this show—and what are their key personality traits? Which specific images, plot lines, or dialogue make you laugh and why? Describe some of the main narrative in the show, and think about what they might reveal about American culture. Then consider how this show is similar to as well as different from other situation comedies as well as cartoons.

When Senator Charles Schumer (D-N.Y.) visited a high school in upstate New York in May 1999, he received an unexpected civics lesson from an unexpected source. Speaking on the timely subject of school violence, Senator Schumer praised the Brady Bill, which he helped sponsor, for its role in preventing crime. Rising to question the effectiveness of this effort at gun control, a student named Kevin Davis cited an example no doubt familiar to his classmates but unknown to the senator from New York:

> *It reminds me of a* Simpsons *episode. Homer wanted to get a gun but he had been in jail twice and in a mental institution. They label him as "potentially dangerous." So Homer asks what that means and the gun dealer says: "It just means you need an extra week before you can get the gun."*[1]

Without going into the pros and cons of gun control legislation, one can recognize in this incident how the Fox Network's cartoon series *The Simpsons* shapes the way Americans think, particularly the younger generation. It may therefore be worthwhile to take a look at the television program to see what sort of political lessons it is teaching. *The Simpsons* may seem like mindless entertainment to many, but in fact, it offers some of the most sophisticated comedy and satire ever to appear on American television. Over the years, the show has taken on many serious issues: nuclear power safety, environmentalism, immigration, gay rights, women in the military, and so on. Paradoxically, it is the farcical nature of the show that allows it to be serious in ways that many other television shows are not.[2]

I will not, however, dwell on the question of the show's politics in the narrowly partisan sense. *The Simpsons* satirizes both Republicans and Democrats. The local politician who appears most frequently in the show, Mayor Quimby, speaks with a heavy Kennedy accent[3] and generally acts like a Democratic urban-machine politician. By the same token, the most sinister political force in the series, the cabal that seems to run the town of Springfield from behind the scenes, is invariably portrayed as Republican. On balance, it is fair to say that *The Simpsons*, like most of what comes out of Hollywood, is pro-Democrat and anti-Republican. One whole episode was a gratuitously vicious portrait of ex-President Bush,[4] whereas the show has been surprisingly slow to satirize President Clinton.[5] Nevertheless, perhaps the single funniest political line in the history of *The Simpsons* came at the expense of the Democrats. When Grandpa Abraham Simpson receives money in the mail really meant for his grandchildren, Bart asks him, "Didn't you wonder why you were getting checks for absolutely nothing?" Abe replies, "I figured 'cause the Democrats were in power again."[6] Unwilling to forego any opportunity for humor, the show's creators have been generally evenhanded over the years in making fun of both parties, and of both the Right and the Left.[7]

Setting aside the surface issue of political partisanship, I am interested in the deep politics of *The Simpsons*, what the show most fundamentally suggests about political life in the United States. The show broaches the question of politics through the question of the family, and this in itself is a political statement. By dealing centrally with the family, *The Simpsons* takes up real human issues everybody can recognize and thus ends up in many respects less "cartoonish" than other television programs. Its cartoon characters are more human, more fully rounded, than the supposedly real human beings in many situation comedies. Above all, the show has created a believable human community: Springfield, USA. *The Simpsons* shows the family as part of a larger community and in effect affirms the kind of community that can sustain the family. That is at one and the same time the secret of the show's popularity with the American public and the most interesting political statement it has to make.

The Simpsons indeed offers one of the most important images of the family in contemporary American culture and, in particular, an image of the nuclear family. With the names taken from creator Matt Groening's own childhood home, *The Simpsons* portrays the average American family: father (Homer), mother (Marge), and 2.2 children (Bart, Lisa, and little Maggie). Many commentators have lamented the fact that *The Simpsons* now serves as one of the representative images of American family life, claiming that the show provides horrible role models for parents and children. The popularity of the show is often cited as evidence of the decline of family values in the United States. But critics of *The Simpsons* need to take a closer look at the show and view it in the context of television history. For all its slapstick nature and its mocking of certain aspects of family life, *The Simpsons* has an affirmative side and ends up celebrating the nuclear family as an institution. For television, this is no minor achievement. For decades, American television has tended to downplay the importance of the nuclear family and offer various one-parent families or other nontraditional arrangements as alternatives to it. The one-parent situation comedy actually dates back almost to the beginning of network television, at least as early as *My Little Margie* (1952–1955). But the classic one-parent situation comedies, like *The Andy Griffith Show* (1960–1968) or *My Three Sons* (1960–1972), generally found ways to reconstitute the nuclear family in one form or another (often through the presence of an aunt or uncle) and thus still presented it as the norm (sometimes the story line actually moved in the direction of the widower getting remarried, as happened to Steve Douglas, the Fred MacMurray character, in *My Three Sons*).

But starting with shows in the 1970s like *Alice* (1976–1985), American television genuinely began to move away from the nuclear family as the norm and suggest that other patterns of child rearing might be equally valid or perhaps even superior. Television in the 1980s and 1990s experimented with all sorts of permutations on the theme of the non-nuclear family, in shows such as *Love, Sidney* (1981–1983), *Punky Brewster* (1984–1986), and *My Two Dads* (1987–1990). This development partly resulted from the standard Hollywood procedure of generating new series by simply varying successful formulas.[8] But the trend toward nonnuclear families also expressed the ideological bent of Hollywood and its impulse to call traditional family values into question. Above all, though television shows usually traced the absence of one or more parents to deaths in the family, the trend away from the nuclear family obviously reflected the reality of divorce in American life (and especially in Hollywood). Wanting to be progressive, television producers set out to endorse contemporary social trends away from the stable, traditional, nuclear family. With the typical momentum of the entertainment industry, Hollywood eventually took this development to its logical conclusion: the no-parent family. Another popular Fox program, *Party of Five*, shows a family of children gallantly raising themselves after both their parents were killed in an automobile accident.

Party of Five cleverly conveys a message some television producers evidently think their contemporary audience wants to hear—that children can do quite well without one parent and preferably without both. The children in the audience want to hear this message because it flatters their sense of independence. The parents want to hear this message because it soothes their sense of guilt, either about abandoning their children completely (as sometimes happens in cases of divorce) or just not devoting enough "quality time" to them. Absent or negligent parents can console themselves with the thought that their children really are better off without them, "just like those cool—and incredibly good-looking—kids on *Party of Five*." In short, for roughly the past two decades, much of American television has been suggesting that the breakdown of the American family does not constitute a social crisis or even a serious problem. In fact, it should be regarded as a form of liberation from an image of the family that may have been good enough for the 1950s but is no longer valid in the 1990s. It is against this historical background that the statement *The Simpsons* has to make about the nuclear family has to be appreciated.

Of course television never completely abandoned the nuclear family, even in the 1980s, as shown by the success of such shows as *All in the Family* (1971–1983), *Family Ties* (1982–1989), and *The Cosby Show* (1984–1992). And when *The Simpsons* debuted as a regular series in 1989, it was by no means unique in its reaffirmation of the value of the nuclear family. Several other shows took the same path in the past decade, reflecting larger social and political trends in society, in particular the reassertion of family values that has by now been adopted as a program by both political parties in the United States. Fox's own *Married with Children* (1987–1998) preceded *The Simpsons,* portraying an amusingly dysfunctional nuclear family. Another interesting portrayal of the nuclear family can be found in ABC's *Home Improvement* (1991–1999), which tries to recuperate traditional family values and even gender roles within a postmodern television context. But *The Simpsons* is in many respects the most interesting example of this return to the nuclear family. Though it strikes many people as trying to subvert the American family or to undermine its authority, in fact, it reminds us that antiauthoritarianism is itself an American tradition and that family authority has always been problematic in democratic America. What makes *The Simpsons* so interesting is the way it combines traditionalism with antitraditionalism. It continually makes fun of the traditional American family. But it continually offers an enduring image of the nuclear family in the very act of satirizing it. Many of the traditional values of the American family survive this satire, above all the value of the nuclear family itself.

As I have suggested, one can understand this point partly in terms of television history. *The Simpsons* is a hip, postmodern, self-aware show.[9] But its self-awareness focuses on the traditional representation of the American family on television. It therefore presents the paradox of an untraditional show that is deeply rooted in television tradition. *The Simpsons* can be traced back to earlier television cartoons that dealt with families, such as *The Flintstones* or *The Jetsons*. But these cartoons must themselves be traced back to the famous nuclear-family sitcoms of the 1950s: *I Love Lucy*, *The Adventures of Ozzie and Harriet, Father Knows Best*, and *Leave It to Beaver*. *The Simpsons* is a postmodern re-creation of the first generation of family sitcoms on television. Looking back on those shows, we easily see the transformations and discontinuities *The Simpsons* has brought about. In *The Simpsons*, father emphatically does not know best. And it clearly is more dangerous to leave it to Bart than to Beaver. Obviously, *The Simpsons* does not offer a simple return to the family shows of the 1950s. But even in the act of recreation and transformation, the show provides elements of continuity that make *The Simpsons* more traditional than may at first appear.

The Simpsons has indeed found its own odd way to defend the nuclear family. In effect, the show says, "Take the worst-case scenario—the Simpsons—and even that family is better than no family." In fact, the Simpson family is not all that bad. Some people are appalled at the idea of young boys imitating Bart, in particular his disrespect for authority and especially for his teachers. These critics of *The Simpsons* forget that Bart's rebelliousness conforms to a venerable American archetype and that this country was founded on disrespect for authority and an act of rebellion. Bart is an American icon, an updated version of Tom Sawyer and Huck Finn rolled into one. For all his troublemaking—precisely because of his troublemaking—Bart behaves just the way a young boy is supposed to in American mythology, from *Dennis the Menace* comics to the *Our Gang* comedies.[10]

As for the mother and daughter in *The Simpsons*, Marge and Lisa are not bad role models at all. Marge Simpson is very much the devoted mother and housekeeper; she also often displays a feminist streak, particularly in the episode in which she goes off on a jaunt a la *Thelma and Louise*.[11] Indeed, she is very modern in her attempts to combine certain feminist impulses with the traditional role of a mother. Lisa is in many ways the ideal child in contemporary terms. She is an overachiever in school, and as a feminist, a vegetarian, and an environmentalist, she is politically correct across the spectrum.

The real issue, then, is Homer. Many people have criticized *The Simpsons* for its portrayal of the father as dumb, uneducated, weak in character, and morally unprincipled. Homer is all those things, but at least he is there. He fulfills the bare minimum of a father: he is present for his wife and above all his children. To be sure, he lacks many of the qualities we would like to see in the ideal father. He is selfish, often putting his own interest above that of his family. As we learn in one of the Halloween episodes, Homer would sell his soul to the devil for a donut (though fortunately it turns out that Marge already owned his soul and therefore it was not Homer's to sell).[12] Homer is undeniably crass, vulgar, and incapable of appreciating the finer things in life. He has a hard time sharing interests with Lisa, except when she develops a remarkable knack for predicting the outcome of pro football games and allows her father to become a big winner in the betting pool at Moe's Tavern.[13] Moreover, Homer gets angry easily and takes his anger out on his children, as his many attempts to strangle Bart attest.

In all these respects, Homer fails as a father. But upon reflection, it is surprising to realize how many decent qualities he has. First and foremost, he is attached to his own—he loves his family because it is his. His motto basically is, "My family, right or wrong." This is hardly a philosophic position, but it may well provide the bedrock of the family as an institution, which is why Plato's *Republic* must subvert the power of the family. Homer Simpson is the opposite of a philosopher-king; he is devoted not to what is best but to what is his own. That position has its problems, but it does help explain how the seemingly dysfunctional Simpson family manages to function.

For example, Homer is willing to work to support his family, even in the dangerous job of nuclear power plant safety supervisor, a job made all the more dangerous by the fact that he is the one doing it. In the episode in which Lisa comes to want a pony desperately, Homer even takes a second job working for Apu Nahasapeemapetilon at the Kwik-E-Mart to earn the money for the pony's upkeep and nearly kills himself in the process.[14] In such actions, Homer manifests his genuine concern for his family, and as he repeatedly proves, he will defend them if necessary, sometimes at great personal risk. Often, Homer is not effective in such actions, but that makes his devotion to his family in some ways all the more touching. Homer is the distillation of pure fatherhood. Take away all the qualities that make for a genuinely good father—wisdom, compassion, even temper, selflessness—and what you have left is Homer Simpson with his pure, mindless, dogged devotion to his family. That is why for all his stupidity, bigotry, and self-centered quality, we cannot hate Homer. He continually fails at being a good father, but he never gives up trying, and in some basic and important sense that makes him a good father.

The most effective defense of the family in the series comes in the episode in which the Simpsons are actually broken up as a unit.[15] This episode pointedly begins with an image of Marge as a good mother, preparing breakfast and school lunches simultaneously for her children. She even gives Bart and Lisa careful instructions about their sandwiches: "Keep the lettuce separate until 11:30." But after this promising parental beginning, a series of mishaps occurs. Homer and Marge go off to the Mingled Waters Health Spa for a well-deserved afternoon of relaxation. In their haste, they leave their house dirty, especially a pile of unwashed dishes in the kitchen sink. Meanwhile, things are unfortunately not going well for the children at school. Bart has accidentally picked up lice from the monkey of his best friend Milhouse, prompting Principal Skinner to ask, "What kind of parents would permit such a lapse in scalpal hygiene?" The evidence against the Simpson parents mounts when Skinner sends for Bart's sister. With her prescription shoes stolen by her classmates and her feet accordingly covered with mud, Lisa looks like some street urchin straight out of Dickens.

Faced with all this evidence of parental neglect, the horrified principal alerts the Child Welfare Board, who are themselves shocked when they take Bart and Lisa home and explore the premises. The officials completely misinterpret the situation. Confronted by a pile of old newspapers, they assume that Marge is a bad housekeeper, when in fact she had assembled the documents to help Lisa with a history project. Jumping to conclusions, the bureaucrats decide that Marge and Homer are unfit parents and lodge specific charges that the Simpson household is a "squalid hellhole and the toilet paper is hung in improper overhand fashion." The authorities determine that the Simpson children must be given to foster parents. Bart, Lisa, and Maggie are accordingly handed over to the family next door, presided over by the patriarchal Ned Flanders. Throughout the series, the Flanders family serves as the doppelganger of the Simpsons. Flanders and his brood are in fact the perfect family according to old-style morality and religion. In marked contrast to Bart, the Flanders boys, Rod and Todd, are well behaved and obedient. Above all, the Flanders family is pious, devoted to activities like Bible reading, and more zealous than even the local Reverend Lovejoy. When Ned offers to play "bombardment" with Bart and Lisa, what he has in mind is bombardment with questions about the Bible. The Flanders family is shocked to learn that their neighbors do not know of the serpent of Rehoboam, not to mention the Well of Zahassadar or the bridal feast of Beth Chadruharazzeb.

Exploring the question of whether the Simpson family really is dysfunctional, the foster parent episode offers two alternatives to it: on one hand, the old-style moral/religious family; on the other, the therapeutic state, what is often now called the nanny state. Who is best able to raise the Simpson children? The civil authorities intervene, claiming that Homer and Marge are unfit as parents. They must be reeducated and are sent off to a "family skills class" based on the premise that experts know better how to raise children. Child rearing is a matter of a certain kind of expertise, which can be taught. This is the modern answer: the family is inadequate as an institution and hence the state must intervene to make it function. At the same time, the episode offers the old-style moral/religious answer: what children need is God-fearing parents in order to make them God-fearing themselves. Indeed, Ned Flanders does everything he can to get Bart and Lisa to reform and behave with the piety of his own children.

But the answer the show offers is that the Simpson children are better off with their real parents—not because they are more intelligent or learned in child rearing, and not because they are superior in morality or piety, but simply because Homer and Marge are the people most genuinely attached to Bart, Lisa, and Maggie, since the children are their own offspring. The episode works particularly well to show the horror of the supposedly omniscient and omnicompetent state intruding in every aspect of family life. When Homer desperately tries to call up Bart and Lisa, he hears the official message: "The number you have dialed can no longer be reached from this phone, you negligent monster."

At the same time, we see the defects of the old-style religion. The Flanders may be righteous as parents but they are also self-righteous. Mrs. Flanders says, "I don't judge Homer and Marge; that's for a vengeful God to do." Ned's piety is so extreme that he eventually exasperates even Reverend Lovejoy, who at one point asks him, "Have you thought of one of the other major religions? They're all pretty much the same."

In the end, Bart, Lisa, and Maggie are joyously reunited with Homer and Marge. Despite charges of being dysfunctional, the Simpson family functions quite well because the children are attached to their parents and the parents are attached to their children. The premise of those who tried to take the Simpson children away is that there is a principle external to the family by which it can be judged dysfunctional, whether the principle of contemporary child-rearing theories or that of the old-style religion. The foster parent episode suggests the contrary—that the family contains its own principle of legitimacy. The family knows best. This episode thus illustrates the strange combination of traditionalism and antitraditionalism in *The Simpsons*. Even as the show rejects the idea of a simple return to the traditional moral/religious idea of the family, it refuses to accept contemporary statist attempts to subvert the family completely and reasserts the enduring value of the family as an institution.

As the importance of Ned Flanders in this episode reminds us, another way in which the show is unusual is that religion plays a significant role in *The Simpsons*. Religion is a regular part of the life of the Simpson family. We often see them going to church, and several episodes revolve around churchgoing, including one in which God even speaks directly to Homer.[16] Moreover, religion is a regular part of life in general in Springfield. In addition to Ned Flanders, the Reverend Lovejoy is featured in several episodes, including one in which no less than Meryl Streep provides the voice for his daughter.[17]

This attention to religion is atypical of American television [today]. Indeed, judging by most [contemporary] television programs, one would never guess that Americans are by and large a religious and even a churchgoing people. Television generally acts as if religion played little or no role in the daily lives of Americans, even though the evidence points to exactly the opposite conclusion. Many reasons have been offered to explain why television generally avoids the subject of religion. Producers are afraid that if they raise religious issues, they will offend orthodox viewers and soon be embroiled in controversy; television executives are particularly worried about having the sponsors of their shows boycotted by powerful religious groups. Moreover, the television community itself is largely secular in its outlook and thus generally uninterested in religious questions. Indeed, much of Hollywood is often outright antireligious, and especially opposed to anything labeled religious fundamentalism (and it tends to label anything to the right of Unitarianism as "religious fundamentalism").

Religion has, however, been making a comeback on television in the past decade, in part because producers have discovered that an audience niche exists for shows like *Touched by an Angel*.[18] Still, the entertainment community has a hard time understanding what religion really means to the American public, and it especially cannot deal with the idea that religion could be an everyday, normal part of American life. Religious figures in both movies and television tend to be miraculously good and pure or monstrously evil and hypocritical. While there are exceptions to this rule,[19] generally Hollywood religious figures must be either saints or sinners, either laboring against all odds and all reason for good or religious fanatics, full of bigotry, warped by sexual repression, laboring to destroy innocent lives in one way or another.[20]

But *The Simpsons* accepts religion as a normal part of life in Springfield, USA. If the show makes fun of piety in the person of Ned Flanders, in Homer Simpson it also suggests that one can go to church and not be either a religious fanatic or a saint. One episode devoted to Reverend Lovejoy deals realistically and rather sympathetically with the problem of pastoral burnout.[21] The overburdened minister has just listened to too many problems from his parishioners and has to turn the job over to Marge Simpson as the "listen lady." The treatment of religion in *The Simpsons* is parallel to and connected with its treatment of the family. *The Simpsons* is not proreligion—it is too hip, cynical, and iconoclastic for that. Indeed, on the surface, the show appears to be antireligious, with a good deal of its satire directed against Ned Flanders and other pious characters. But once again, we see the principle at work that when *The Simpsons* satirizes something, it acknowledges its importance. Even when it seems to be ridiculing religion, it recognizes, as few other television shows do, the genuine role that religion plays in American life.

It is here that the treatment of the family in *The Simpsons* links up with its treatment of politics. Although the show focuses on the nuclear family, it relates the family to larger institutions in American life, like the church, the school, and even political institutions themselves, like city government. In all these cases, *The Simpsons* satirizes these institutions, making them look laughable and often even hollow. But at the same time, the show acknowledges their importance and especially their importance for the family. Over the past few decades, television has increasingly tended to isolate the family—to show it largely removed from any larger institutional framework or context. This is another trend to which *The Simpsons* runs counter, partly as a result of its being a postmodern re-creation of 1950s sitcoms. Shows like *Father Knows Best* or *Leave It to Beaver* tended to be set in small-town America, with all the intricate web of institutions into which family life was woven. In re-creating this world, even while mocking it, *The Simpsons* cannot help recreating its ambience and even at times its ethos.

Springfield is decidedly an American small town. In several episodes, it is contrasted with Capitol City, a metropolis the Simpsons approach with fear and trepidation. Obviously, the show makes fun of small-town life—it makes fun of everything—but it simultaneously celebrates the virtues of the traditional American small town. One of the principal reasons why the dysfunctional Simpsons family functions as well as it does is that they live in a traditional American small town. The institutions that govern their lives are not remote from them or alien to them. The Simpson children go to a neighborhood school (though they are bussed to it by the ex-hippie driver, Otto). Their friends in school are largely the same as their friends in their neighborhood. The Simpsons are not confronted by an elaborate, unapproachable, and uncaring educational bureaucracy. Principal Skinner and Mrs. Krabappel may not be perfect educators, but when Homer and Marge need to talk to them, they are readily accessible. The same is true of the Springfield police force. Chief Wiggum is not a great crime fighter, but he is well known to the citizens of Springfield, as they are to him. The police in Springfield still have neighborhood beats and have even been known to share a donut or two with Homer.

Similarly, politics in Springfield is largely a local matter, including town meetings in which the citizens of Springfield get to influence decisions on important matters of local concern, such as whether gambling should be legalized or a monorail built. As his Kennedy accent suggests, Mayor Quimby is a demagogue, but at least he is Springfield's own demagogue. When he buys votes, he buys them directly from the citizens of Springfield. If Quimby wants Grandpa Simpson to support a freeway he wishes to build through town, he must name the road after Abe's favorite television character, Matlock. Everywhere one looks in Springfield, one sees a surprising degree of local control and autonomy. The nuclear power plant is a source of pollution and constant danger, but at least it is locally owned by Springfield's own slave-driving industrial tyrant and tycoon, Montgomery Burns, and not by some remote multinational corporation (indeed, in an exception that proves the rule, when the plant is sold to German investors, Burns soon buys it back to restore his ego).[22]

In sum, for all its postmodern hipness, *The Simpsons* is profoundly anachronistic in the way it harks back to an earlier age when Americans felt more in contact with their governing institutions and family life was solidly anchored in a larger but still local community. The federal government rarely makes its presence felt in *The Simpsons*, and when it does it generally takes a quirky form like former President Bush moving next door to Homer, an arrangement that does not work out. The long tentacles of the IRS have occasionally crept their way into Springfield, but its stranglehold on America is of course all-pervasive and inescapable.[23] Generally speaking, government is much more likely to take local forms on the show. When sinister forces from the Republican Party conspire to unseat Mayor Quimby by running exconvict Sideshow Bob against him, it is local sinister forces who do the conspiring, led by Mr. Burns and including Rainer Wolfcastle (the Arnold Schwarzenegger lookalike who plays McBain in the movies) and a Rush Limbaugh lookalike named Burch Barlow.[24]

Here is one respect in which the portrayal of the local community in *The Simpsons* is unrealistic. In Springfield, even the media forces are local. There is of course nothing strange about having a local television station in Springfield. It is perfectly plausible that the Simpsons get their news from a man, Kent Brockman, who actually lives in their midst. It is also quite believable that the kiddie show on Springfield television is local, and that its host, Krusty the Klown, not only lives in town but also is available for local functions like supermarket openings and birthday parties. But what are authentic movie stars like Rainer Wolfcastle doing living in Springfield? And what about the fact that the world-famous *Itchy & Scratchy* cartoons are produced in Springfield? Indeed, the entire *Itchy & Scratchy* empire is apparently headquartered in Springfield. This is not a trivial fact. It means that when Marge campaigns against cartoon violence, she can picket *Itchy & Scratchy* headquarters without leaving her hometown.[25] The citizens of Springfield are fortunate to be able to have a direct impact on the forces that shape their lives and especially their family lives. In short, *The Simpsons* takes the phenomenon that has in fact done more than anything else to subvert the power of the local in American politics and American life in general—namely, the media—and in effect brings it within the orbit of Springfield, thereby placing the force at least partially under local control.[26]

The unrealistic portrayal of the media as local helps highlight the overall tendency of *The Simpsons* to present Springfield as a kind of classical polis; it is just about as self-contained and autonomous as a community can be in the modern world. This once again reflects the postmodern nostalgia of *The Simpsons*; with its self-conscious re-creation of the 1950s sitcom, it ends up weirdly celebrating the old ideal of small-town America.[27] Again, I do not mean to deny that the first impulse of *The Simpsons* is to make fun of small-town life. But in that very process, it reminds us of what the old ideal was and what was so attractive about it, above all the fact that average Americans somehow felt in touch with the forces that influenced their lives and maybe even in control of them. In a presentation before the American Society of Newspaper Editors on April 12, 1991 (broadcast on C-SPAN), Matt Groening said that the subtext of *The Simpsons* is "the people in power don't always have your best interests in mind."[28] This is a view of politics that cuts across the normal distinctions between Left and Right and explains why the show can be relatively evenhanded in its treatment of both political parties and has something to offer to both liberals and conservatives. *The Simpsons* is based on distrust of power and especially of power remote from ordinary people. The show celebrates genuine community, a community in which everybody more or less knows everybody else (even if they do not necessarily like each other). By recreating this older sense of community, the show manages to generate a kind of warmth out of its postmodern coolness, a warmth that is largely responsible for its success with the American public. This view of community may be the most profound comment *The Simpsons* has to make on family life in particular and politics in general in America today. No matter how dysfunctional it may seem, the nuclear family is an institution worth preserving. And the way to preserve it is not by the offices of a distant, supposedly expert, therapeutic state but by restoring its links to a series of local institutions that reflect and foster the same principle that makes the Simpson family itself work—the attachment to one's own, the principle that we best care for something when it belongs to us.

The celebration of the local in *The Simpsons* was confirmed in an episode that aired May 9, 1999, which for once explored in detail the possibility of a Utopian alternative to politics as usual in Springfield. The episode begins with Lisa disgusted by a gross-out contest sponsored by a local radio station, which, among other things, results in the burning of a travelling Van Gogh exhibition. With the indignation typical of youth, Lisa fires off an angry letter to the Springfield newspaper, charging, "Today our town lost what remained of its fragile civility." Outraged by the cultural limitations of Springfield, Lisa complains, "We have eight malls, but no symphony; thirty-two bars but no alternative theater." Lisa's spirited outburst catches the attention of the local chapter of Mensa, and the few high-IQ citizens of Springfield (including Dr. Hibbert, Principal Skinner, the Comic Book Guy, and Professor Frink) invite her to join the organization (once they have determined that she has brought a pie and not a quiche to their meeting). Inspired by Lisa's courageous speaking out against the cultural parochialism of Springfield, Dr. Hibbert challenges the city's way of life: "Why do we live in a town where the smartest have no power and the stupidest run everything?" Forming "a council of learned citizens," or what reporter Kent Brockman later refers to as an "intellectual junta," the Mensa members set out to create the cartoon equivalent of Plato's *Republic* in Springfield. Naturally, they begin by ousting Mayor Quimby, who in fact leaves town rather abruptly once the little matter of some missing lottery funds comes up.

Taking advantage of an obscure provision in the Springfield charter, the Mensa members step into the power vacuum created by Quimby's sudden abdication. Lisa sees no limit to what the Platonic rule of the wise might accomplish: "With our superior intellects, we could rebuild this city on a foundation of reason and enlightenment; we could turn Springfield into a utopia." Principal Skinner holds out hope for "a new Athens," while another Mensa member thinks in terms of B. R. Skinner's "Walden II." The new rulers immediately set out to bring their Utopia into existence, redesigning traffic patterns and abolishing all sports that involve violence. But in a variant of the dialectic of enlightenment, the abstract rationality and benevolent universalism of the intellectual junta soon prove to be a fraud. The Mensa members begin to disagree among themselves, and it becomes evident that their claim to represent the public interest masks a number of private agendas. At the climax of the episode, the Comic Book Guy comes forward to proclaim, "Inspired by the most logical race in the galaxy, the Vulcans, breeding will be permitted once every seven years; for many of you this will mean much less breeding; for me, much much more." This reference to *Star Trek* appropriately elicits from Groundskeeper Willie a response in his native accent that calls to mind the *Enterprise*'s Chief Engineer Scotty: "You cannot do that, sir, you don't have the power." The Mensa regime's self-interested attempt to imitate the *Republic* by regulating breeding in the city is just too much for the ordinary citizens of Springfield to bear.

With the Platonic revolution in Springfield degenerating into petty squabbling and violence, a *deus ex machina* arrives in the form of physicist Stephen Hawking, proclaimed as "the world's smartest man." When Hawking voices his disappointment with the Mensa regime, he ends up in a fight with Principal Skinner. Seizing the opportunity created by the division among the intelligentsia, Homer leads a counterrevolution of the stupid with the rallying cry: "C'mon you idiots, we're taking back this town." Thus, the attempt to bring about a rule of philosopher-kings in Springfield ends ignominiously, leaving Hawking to pronounce its epitaph: "Sometimes the smartest of us can be the most childish." Theory fails when translated into practice in this episode of *The Simpsons* and must be relegated once more to the confines of the contemplative life. The episode ends with Hawking and Homer drinking beer together in Moe's Tavern and discussing Homer's theory of a donut-shaped universe.

The Utopia episode offers an epitome of what *The Simpsons* does so well. It can be enjoyed on two levels—as both broad farce and intellectual satire. The episode contains some of the grossest humor in the long history of *The Simpsons* (I have not even mentioned the subplot concerning Homer's encounter with a pornographic photographer). But at the same time, it is filled with subtle cultural allusions; for example, the Mensa members convene in what is obviously a Frank Lloyd Wright prairie house. In the end, then, the Utopia episode embodies the strange mixture of intellectualism and anti-intellectualism characteristic of *The Simpsons*. In Lisa's challenge to Springfield, the show calls attention to the cultural limitations of small-town America, but it also reminds us that intellectual disdain for the common man can be carried too far and that theory can all too easily lose touch with common sense. Ultimately, *The Simpsons* seems to offer a kind of intellectual defense of the common man against intellectuals, which helps explain its popularity and broad appeal. Very few people have found *The Critique of Pure Reason* funny, but in *The Gay Science*, Nietzsche felt that he had put his finger on Kant's joke:

> Kant wanted to prove in a way that would puzzle all the world that all the world was right—that was the private joke of this soul. He wrote against the learned on behalf of the prejudice of the common people, but for the learned and not for the common people.[29]

In Nietzsche's terms, *The Simpsons* goes *The Critique of Pure Reason* one better: it defends the common man against the intellectual but in a way that both the common man and the intellectual can understand and enjoy.

Notes

[1]As reported in Ed Henry's "Heard on the Hill" column in *Roll Call*, 44, no. 81 (May 13, 1999). His source was the *Albany Times-Union*.
[2]This essay is a substantial revision of a paper originally delivered at the Annual Meeting of the American Political Science Association in Boston, September 1998. All *Simpsons* episodes are cited by title, number, and original broadcast date, using the information supplied in the invaluable reference work *The Simpsons: A Complete Guide to Our Favorite Family*, ed. Ray Richmond and Antonia Coffman (New York: HarperCollins, 1997). I cite episodes that aired subsequent to the publication of this book simply by broadcast date.
[3]The identification is made complete when Quimby says, "Ich bin ein Springfielder" in "Burns Verkaufen der Kraftwerk," #8F09, 12/5/91.
[4]"Two Bad Neighbors," #3F09, 1/4/96.
[5]For the reluctance to go after Clinton, see the rather tame satire of the 1996 presidential campaign in the "Citizen Kang" segment of the Halloween episode, "Treehouse of Horror VII," #4F02, 10/27/96. Finally in the 1998–1999 season, faced with the mounting scandals in the Clinton administration, the creators of *The Simpsons* decided to take off the kid

gloves in their treatment of the president, especially in the February 7, 1999, episode
(in which Homer legally changes his name to Max Power). Hustled by Clinton at a party,
Marge Simpson is forced to ask, "Are you sure it's a federal law that I have to dance with
you?" Reassuring Marge that she is good enough for a man of his stature, Clinton tells her,
"Hell, I've done it with pigs—real no foolin' pigs."

[6]"The Front," #9616, 4/15/93.

[7]An amusing debate developed in the *Wall Street Journal* over the politics of *The Simpsons*. It began with an Op-Ed piece by Benjamin Stein titled "TV Land: From Mao to Dow" (February 5, 1997), in which he argued that the show has no politics. This piece was answered by a letter from John McGrew given the title "The Simpsons Bash Familiar Values" (March 19, 1997), in which he argued that the show is political and consistently left-wing. On March 12, 1997, letters by Deroy Murdock and H. B. Johnson Jr. argued that the show attacks left-wing targets as well and often supports traditional values. Johnson's conclusion that the show is "politically ambiguous" and thus appeals "to conservatives as well as to liberals" is supported by the evidence of this debate itself.

[8]Perhaps the most famous example is the creation of *Green Acres* (1965–1971) by inverting *The Beverly Hillbillies* (1962–1971)—if a family of hicks moving from the country to the city was funny, television executives concluded that a couple of sophisticates moving from the city to the country should be a hit as well. And it was.

[9]On the self-reflexive character of *The Simpsons*, see my essay "The Greatest TV Show Ever," *American Enterprise*, 8, no. 5 (September/October 1997), 34–37.

[10]"Oddly enough, Bart's creator, Matt Groening, has now joined the chorus condemning the Simpson boy. Earlier this year, a wire-service report quoted Groening as saying to those who call Bart a bad role model, "I now have a 7-year-old boy and a 9-year-old boy so all I can say is I apologize. Now I know what you were talking about."

[11]"Marge on the Lam," #1F12, 11/4/93.

[12]"The Devil and Homer Simpson" in "Treehouse of Horror IV," #1F04, 10/30/93.

[13]"Lisa the Greek," #8F12, 1/23/92.

[14]"Lisa's Pony," #8F06, 11/7/91.

[15]"Home Sweet Homediddly-Dum-Doodily," #3F01, 10/1/95.

[16]"Homer the Heretic," #9F01, 10/8/92.

[17]"Bart's Girlfriend," #2F04, 11/6/94.

[18]I would like to comment on this show, but it is scheduled at the same time as *The Simpsons,* and I have never seen it.

[19]Consider, for example, the minister played by Tom Skerritt in Robert Redford's film of Norman Maclean's *A River Runs Through It.*

[20]A good example of this stereotyping can be found in the film *Contact*, with its contrasting religious figures played by Matthew McConaughey (good) and Jake Busey (evil).

[21]"In Marge We Trust," #4F18, 4/27/97.

[22]"Burns Verkaufen der Kraftwerk," #8F09, 12/5/91.

[23]See, for example, "Bart the Fink," #3F12, 2/11/96.

[24]"Sideshow Bob Roberts," #2F02, 10/9/94.

[25]"Itchy & Scratchy & Marge," #7F09, 12/20/90.

[26]The episode called "Radioactive Man" (#2517, 9/24/95) provides an amusing reversal of the usual relationship between the big-time media and small-town life. A Hollywood film company comes to Springfield to make a movie featuring the comic book hero, Radioactive Man. The Springfield locals take advantage of the naive moviemakers, raising prices all over town and imposing all sorts of new taxes on the film crew. Forced to return to California penniless, the moviemakers are greeted like small-town heroes by their caring neighbors in the Hollywood community.

[27]In his review of *The Simpsons: A Complete Guide to Our Favorite Family*, Michael Dirda aptly characterizes the show as "a wickedly funny yet oddly affectionate satire of American life at the end of the 20th century. Imagine the unholy offspring of *Mad* magazine, Mel Brooks's movies, and 'Our Town.'" See the *Washington Post*, Book World, January 11, 1998, p. 5.

[28]Oddly enough, this theme is also at the heart of [another] Fox television series, *The X-Files*.

[29]See *Die frohliche Wissenschaft*, sec. 193 (my translation) in Friedrich Nietzsche, *Samtliche Werke: Kritische Studienausgabe*, ed. Giorgio Colli and Mazzino Montinari, vol. 3 (Berlin: de Gruyter, 1967–1977), 504.

After Reading

Critical Perspective

1. Describe your response to reading Cantor's essay. Compare it to other essays about television that you have read thus far. In what ways is it similar? In what ways is it different?

Rhetoric and Argument

2. What sorts of rhetorical tactics—context, intertextuality, constraints, ethos, pathos, and logos—does Cantor utilize to draw in his audience? Do you think that he is successful? Why or why not? Be sure to provide detailed examples from the text.

3. Describe Cantor's tone in his essay, referencing specific examples of his language choices. Do you think that his decision to employ this tone was a good one? Why or why not?

4. What does Cantor claim about *The Simpsons* in relationship to both other contemporary family situation comedies as well as past ones? What is Cantor's main argumentative claim about how the show itself functions? Where does Cantor make this claim in his text? Do you agree with this claim? Why or why not? Be sure to include quotes from the text to back up your views as well as specific examples from the episodes.

5. What kinds of evidence does Cantor employ to support his assertions? Do you find this evidence convincing? Why or why not? Also, reflect upon whether you find any

logical fallacies in his text. Present evidence from the text that substantiates your thoughts.

6. How would you describe the organization of Cantor's text? Draw a map or outline of the structure he employs. Be sure to give detailed examples to support your views.

Analysis

7. In a short argumentative response, address the following questions: Do you find Cantor's argument about *The Simpsons* persuasive? Why or why not? If you do, provide examples of his argument's positive features to back up your assertions. If not, offer examples of his argument's negative features to back up your ideas. Consider Cantor's use of rhetoric, tone, structure, logical fallacies, and warrants. Be sure to mention details and quotes from the text as well as library and Internet resources to support your views.

Taking Action

As a class, watch one specific episode of *The Simpsons* that is mentioned in Cantor's text. Interrupt your viewing repeatedly to discuss the features that you notice: What is the structure of the show? What are the roles of the main characters? How do the peripheral characters function? What kinds of commercials air in between the show's segments? What do these ads reveal about how the producers of the show and the advertisers themselves understand their audience? How are the particulars of this show and its commercials different from and similar to other situation comedies and other cartoons? What crucial roles might audience and purpose play in establishing these differences?

After you have talked about these concerns as a class, reflect upon what kinds of claims of cultural criticism—other than those Cantor advances—you might make about *The Simpsons*. How might you support them given the evidence you have just examined? Which specific examples from the televisual text might you point to in order to back up your thoughts? Consult library and Internet sources as needed to back up your assertions.

ERIC DEGGANS

"Grading Hispanic Gains on TV? Start with ABC"

Eric Deggans is a full-time media critic employed by the St. Petersburg Times. *Before taking the media critic job in August 2005, Eric worked as an editorial writer and columnist for the newspaper, specializing in race issues, pop culture, media, and national affairs. Deggans has been a guest lecturer and adjunct professor at many universities and worked as a professional drummer in the 1980s, touring and performing with Motown recording artists* The Voyage Band *throughout the Midwest and in Osaka, Japan. He continues to perform with area bands and recording artists as a drummer, bassist, and vocalist.*

EXERCISING YOUR SKILLS

Before Reading

In this essay Deggans focuses on representations of Hispanics in popular television. Watch one of your favorite television programs that features Hispanics. Think about which characters or ideas are featured and how they interact. Consider what kind of plot lines dominate the show as well as how humor works. Determine what you think this show accomplishes in terms of representations of race and ethnicity, and what sorts of claims of cultural criticism you could make about it. What do you appreciate about the show? What do you not like about it? Why do you have these reactions?

A few months ago, I asked ABC entertainment president Stephen McPherson a question: Given the huge increase in Hispanic actors on its fall lineup, was the network deliberately trying to make its casts more diverse?

"We're not out there trying to actively hire more Hispanics," said McPherson, still high on his reputation as the guy who saved the alphabet network with hits such as *Lost* and *Desperate Housewives*. "We try to be colorblind and get the best actor or actress for any role."

I figured it was the typical head fake by a network executive: Pretend you're not doing something you clearly are doing, with full knowledge the media will give you credit for something you fear may upset viewers if you actually admitted it.

But McPherson was more explicit with the *New York Post*, telling the newspaper in a Nov. 21 story, "I think it's been part of our initiative for a couple of years and it's something that's important to me. . . . I look at it as a business decision. There's a gigantic Hispanic audience out there."

To this, I say just one thing: It's about time.

For many years, Hispanics have been the most under-represented minority on television, with a 2000 study revealing that the country's largest ethnic minority—about 14 percent of the population—filled about 2 percent of roles in prime time.

But years of steady increases in population (35.3 million in 2000 to 41.3 million in 2004, according to the U.S. Census) and buying power ($404 billion in 2000 to $686 billion in 2004, according to the Selig Center for Economic Growth) have brought a new reality in network TV, particularly at ABC.

The National Latino Media Council recognized the network TV industry's success last week in its annual report card for 2005, handing high marks to most networks for strides in casting, program development and hiring among writers and producers.

It was a striking change from fall 1999, when the council joined other groups to complain that no people of color were featured in the casts of new series at the top four TV networks.

"The diversity programs that were begun four and five years ago are now bearing fruit," NLMC president Alex Nogales said in a statement. "What (Latinos) contribute to our nation has to be more clear, so this perception counters the view of the bigots among us."

On ABC, there's Freddie Prinze Jr.'s hit sitcom *Freddie, Lost*'s latest take-charge leader Michelle Rodriguez, Eddie Cibrian's grown-up Cuban immigrant on *Invasion* and new *Grey's Anatomy* cast member Sara Ramirez; ABC has moved aggressively this season to ensure nearly every show has a Hispanic actor in its core cast.

The network's news department followed suit this week, naming Elizabeth Vargas co-anchor of *World News Tonight*, making her the first Hispanic to reach the top job in network TV evening news.

It's what you might expect from the network that also was the first to feature subtitles or secondary audio programs offering Spanish translations for all its prime-time shows. They also offered the first regular series character who only speaks Spanish with English subtitles: the character of Prinze's grandmother, who appears on a show featuring *four* Hispanic actors.

And it's not just ABC that has finally awakened to the reality of diversity. Look to NBC and see Benjamin Bratt on NBC's *E-Ring* (okay, he does play a guy named J.T. Tisnewski—with no explanation of the guy's heritage), John Leguizamo in a high-profile turn on *ER*, Miguel Sandoval as a down-to-earth district attorney on *Medium* and Jimmy Smits running for president on *The West Wing*.

Behind the scenes, Greg Garcia (whose great-grandfather was Mexican entertainer Cantinflas) is producing NBC's only comedy hit, *My Name Is Earl*, while Jennifer Lopez's Nuyorican Films production company is developing the night-time soap opera *South Beach* for UPN.

Considering that last season there were only three new TV series prominently featuring Hispanics—*Lost*, *Housewives* and UPN's ill-fated *Jonny Zero*—this year's surge in new characters feels like a virtual avalanche.

"I'm the youngest executive producer ABC has ever had, and I'm the only Puerto Rican," Prinze said. "You think about the number of Hispanics who have led their own (successful sitcoms), and you've got something like four in the history of this business."

Five years ago, *Freddie* executive producer Bruce Helford quizzed ABC executives on whether they were serious about airing a sitcom pilot featuring an up-and-coming Mexican comic named George Lopez. Now that Lopez's self-titled sitcom is a hit, Helford sees the network taking the next logical step.

"It's a huge financial risk—each pilot costs a couple million—and until George's show, there had been no successful (Hispanic cast) shows," Helford said. "They believed in George's show, believed in more Hispanic representation, and now, for everybody, it makes sense to take more risk."

Indeed, statistics show Hispanics watch an average four more hours of prime-time TV each week and have a median age nearly 10 years younger than the general population. Why wouldn't a smart network go after a wealthier, younger segment of the population that the TV industry has traditionally ignored?

"We know that the Hispanic audience has a very powerful voice," said CBS entertainment president Nina Tassler, whose self-described "Russia-rican" heritage (Russian father, Puerto Rican mother) likely makes her the most powerful Hispanic woman in network TV.

"This year, we really tried to increase the numbers of Hispanics in our existing shows and our new shows. It is increasingly important to our advertisers."

A look at the top-rated English-language TV shows in Hispanic households shows the strategy may be paying off.

Just a couple of years ago, that roster was topped by shows such as *American Idol* and *Fear Factor*; during the week of Nov. 14, it included four ABC series featuring Hispanics in prominent roles: *Desperate Housewives*, *Lost*, *George Lopez* and *Freddie*.

Already, viewers have reaped benefits with more complex and varied characters, from Eva Longoria and Ricardo Chavira's bickering couple on to *Desperate Housewives* to Cibrian's grown-up Cuban orphan on *Invasion*. Such characters are a welcome relief from the parade of gang-bangers, gardeners and maids Hispanic actors were often forced to play.

Still, such close counting sometimes feels awkward, even to Hispanic actors who would like to see more diversity in the industry.

Actor Kiele Sanchez, whose blond hair and blue eyes belie her Puerto Rican and French heritage, has never played a Latina on screen, and is currently cast as an Italian woman on the WB drama series *Related*. She often jokes about such issues with co-star Jennifer Esposito, a New York-born Italian who is often cast as a Hispanic woman—most recently in the hit film, *Crash*.

"I've never played a Hispanic, because people don't believe that I am," Sanchez said. "The image people still have in the industry is that Latinas have to have dark hair, dark eyes and dark skin. It's like, have you turned on Telemundo lately?"

Meanwhile, other ethnic minorities, particularly Asian-Americans, have criticized stagnant hiring levels for their groups. And former *NYPD Blue* star Esai Morales remains wary the current hiring boom will fade.

"We live in a world that is so media saturated, if the media doesn't show it, the public doesn't know it," Morales said in an interview earlier this year. "And if people of ethnicity are not allowed to express their own reality, then they are being suppressed."

After Reading

Critical Perspective

1. What do you think Deggans hopes to show by writing this essay? What about his text indicates this?

Rhetoric Argument

2. What sorts of rhetorical tactics—context, intertextuality, constraints, ethos, pathos, and logos—does Deggans employ to persuade his audience? How would you describe his use of quotes throughout his essay to both support his argumentative assertions as well as to convey his own thoughts? Be sure to provide detailed examples from the text.

3. Deggans indicates that network television is making some significant strides in terms of representing Hispanics in positive ways. What sorts of support does

Deggans employ to back up his assertions? Do you find this evidence persuasive? Why or why not? Provide quotes from the text to back up your views.

4. Deggans exposes some of the complexities surrounding representations of Hispanics as well as Hispanic and non-Hispanic actors and actresses in the media. Explain where and how he does this. What do you make of these complexities? What do you think this reveals about issues of race and ethnicity in television? Be sure to present detailed examples to support your perspectives.

Analysis

5. Deggans ends his essay with a quote from former *NYPD Blue* star Esai Morales who is concerned that Hispanics are underrepresented in the media. He states, "We live in a world that is so media saturated, if the media doesn't show it, the public doesn't know it. And if people of ethnicity are not allowed to express their own reality, then they are being suppressed." Do you agree or disagree with this statement? Explain your position. In a short argumentative response, consider some specific negative stereotypes of Latinos/as in the media. What problems do they pose and why? Then mention some positive images that you have witnessed. What possibilities do they proffer and why? Consult library and Internet resources to support your analyses.

Taking Action

Form a small group. Visit several websites (such as "Hispanic Foundations" at http://www.hispanicfoundations.org/; "Hispanic Tips" at http://hispanictips.com/index.php; *Latina Style Magazine* at http://www.latinastyle.com/currentissue/v11-5/publisher.html; "Hispanic Business" at http://www.hispanicbusiness.com/; or others) associated with empowerment for specific groups of Latin people living in the United States. Discuss what you find on these sites and how the efforts of these groups may help to create better cultural awareness about various aspects of Latin culture. Share your information and thoughts with the rest of the class.

NEWS AND INFOMERCIALS

Neil Postman and Steve Powers

"The Bias of Language, The Bias of Pictures"

Neil Postman was the chair of the Department of Culture and Communications at New York University until he passed away in 2003. He was a renowned scholar and cultural critic who wrote a series of books during his lifetime including Marshall McLuhan: The Medium and the Messenger: A Biography, Post-Intellectualism and the Decline of Democracy, The End of Education: Redefining the Value of School, Technopoly: The Surrender of Culture to Technology, *and* Conscientious Objections: Stirring Up Trouble About Language, Technology, and Education, *among others. The essay here was taken from* How to Watch TV News. *His most recent works included* Building a Bridge to the 18th Century: How the Past Can Improve Our Future. *Steve Powers is a newscaster as well as a radio and television journalist.*

EXERCISING YOUR SKILLS

Before Reading

Postman and Powers describe the function of television news in American culture. Watch a number of newscasts—local newscasts as well as national newscasts, network newscasts as well as tabloid news shows and cable news channels such as CNN, MSN, CSPAN, and HeadLine News. What similarities and differences in show format, information, and newscasters do you notice? What do you make of these similarities and differences, and why might they be significant? How do these newscasts differ from the newscasts of the past? What do today's newscasts imply about the values, fears, and anxieties we have at this particular historical moment?

When a television news show distorts the truth by altering or manufacturing facts (through re-creations), a television viewer is defenseless even if a re-creation is properly labeled. Viewers are still vulnerable to misinformation since they will not know (at least in the case of docudramas) what parts are fiction and what parts are not. But the problems of verisimilitude posed by re-creations pale to insignificance when compared to the problems viewers face when encountering a straight (no-monkey-business) show. All news shows, in a sense, are re-creations in that what we hear and see on them are attempts to re-present actual events, and are not the events themselves. Perhaps, to avoid ambiguity, we might call all news shows "re-presentations" instead of "re-creations." These re-presentations come to us in two forms: language and pictures. The question then arises: what do viewers have to know about language and pictures in order to be properly armed to defend themselves against the seductions of eloquence (to use Bertrand Russell's apt phrase)?

Let us take language first. Below are three principles that, in our opinion, are an essential part of the analytical equipment a viewer must bring to any encounter with a news show.

1. Whatever anyone says something is, it isn't.

This sounds more complex—and maybe more pretentious—than it actually is. What it means is that there is a difference between the world of events and the world of words about events. The job of an honest reporter is to try to find words and the appropriate tone in presenting them that will come as close to evoking the event as possible. But since no two people will use exactly the same words to describe an event, we must acknowledge that for every verbal description of an event, there are multiple possible alternatives. You may demonstrate this to your own satisfaction by writing a two-paragraph description of a dinner you had with at least two other people, then asking the others who were present if each of them would also write, independently, a two-paragraph description of the "same" dinner. We should be very surprised if all of the descriptions include the same words, in the same order, emphasize the same things, and express the same feelings. In other words, "the dinner itself" is largely a nonverbal event. The words people use to describe this event are not the event itself and are only abstracted re-presentations of the event. What does this mean for a television viewer? It means that the viewer must never assume that the words spoken on a television news show are exactly what happened. Since there are so many alternative ways of describing what happened, the viewer must be on guard against assuming that he or she has heard "the absolute truth."

2. Language operates at various levels of abstraction.

This means that there is a level of language whose purpose is to *describe* an event. There is also a level of language whose purpose is to *evaluate* an event. Even more, there is a level of language whose purpose is to *infer* what is unknown on the basis of what is known. The usual way to make these distinctions clear is through sentences such as the following three:

> Manny Freebus is 5'8" and weighs 235 pounds.
> Manny Freebus is grossly fat.
> Manny Freebus eats too much.

The first sentence may be said to be language as pure decription. It involves no judgments and no inferences. The second sentence is a description of sorts, but is mainly a judgment that the speaker makes of the "event" known as Manny Freebus. The third sentence is an inference based on observations the speaker has made. It is, in fact, a statement about the unknown based on the known. As it happens, we know Manny Freebus and can tell you that he eats no more than the average person but suffers from a glandular condition which keeps him overweight. Therefore, anyone who concluded from observing Manny's shape that he eats too much has made a false inference. A good guess, but false nonetheless.

You can watch television news programs from now until doomsday and never come across any statement about Manny Freebus. But you will constantly come across the three kinds of statements we have been discussing—descriptions, judgments, and inferences. And it is important for a viewer to distinguish among them. For example, you might hear an anchor introduce a story by saying: "Today Congress ordered an investigation of the explosive issue of whether Ronald Reagan's presidential campaign made a deal with Iran in 1980 to delay the release of American hostages until after the election." This statement is, of course, largely descriptive, but includes the judgmental word "explosive" as part of the report. We need hardly point out that what is explosive to one person may seem trivial to another. We do not say that the news writer has no business to include his or her judgment of this investigation. We do say that the viewer has to be aware that a judgment has been made. In fact, even the phrase "made a deal" (why not "arranged with Iran"?) has a somewhat sleazy connotation that implies a judgment of sorts. If, in the same news report, we are told that the evidence for such a secret deal is weak and that only an investigation with subpoena power can establish the truth, we must know that we have left the arena of factual language and have moved into the land of inference. An investigation with subpoena power may be a good idea but whether or not it can establish the truth is a guess on the journalist's part, and a viewer ought to know that.

3. Almost all words have connotative meanings.

This suggests that even when attempting to use purely descriptive language, a journalist cannot avoid expressing an attitude about what he or she is saying. For example, here is the opening sentence of an anchor's report about national examinations: "For the first time in the nation's history, high-level education policymakers have designed the elements for a national examination system similar to the one advocated by President Bush." This sentence certainly looks like it is pure description although it is filled with ambiguities. Is this the first time in our history that this has been done? Or only the first time that high-level education policymakers have done it? Or is it the first time something has been designed that is similar to what the President has advocated? But let us put those questions aside. (After all, there are limits to how analytical one ought to be.) Instead, we might concentrate on such words as "high-level," "policymakers," and "designed." Speaking for ourselves, we are by no means sure that we know what a "high-level policymaker" is, although it sounds awfully impressive. It is certainly better than a "low-level policymaker," although how one would distinguish between the two is a bit of a mystery. Come to think of it, a low-level "policymaker" must be pretty good, too, since anyone who makes policy must be important. It comes as no surprise, therefore, that what was done was "designed." To design something usually implies careful thought, preparation, organization, and coherence. People design buildings, bridges, and furniture. If your experience has been anything like ours, you will know that reports are almost never designed; they are usually "thrown together," and it is quite a compliment to say that a report was designed. The journalist who paid this compliment was certainly entitled to do it even though he may not have been aware of what he was doing. He probably thought he had made a simple description, avoiding any words that would imply favor or disfavor. But if so, he was defeated in his effort because language tends to be emotion-laden. Because it is people who do the talking, the talk almost always includes a feeling, an attitude, a judgment. In a sense, every language contains the history of a people's feelings about the world. Our words are baskets of emotion. Smart journalists, of course, know this. And so do smart audiences. Smart audiences don't blame anyone for this state of affairs. They are, however, prepared for it.

It is not our intention to provide here a mini-course in semantics. Even if we could, we are well aware that no viewer could apply analytic principles all the time or even much of the time. Anchors and reporters talk too fast and too continuously for any of us to monitor most of their sentences. Besides, who would want to do that for most of the stories on a news show? If you have a sense of what is important, you will probably judge most news stories to be fluff, or nonsense, or irrelevancies, not worthy of your analytic weaponry. But there are times when stories appear that are of major significance from your point of view. These are the times when your level of attention will reach a peak and you must call upon your best powers of interpretation. In those moments, you need to draw on whatever you know about the relationship between language and reality; about the distinctions among statements of fact, judgment, and inference; about the connotative meanings of words. When this is done properly, viewers are no longer passive consumers of news but active participants in a kind of dialogue between a news show and themselves. A viewer may even find that he or she is "talking back to the television set" (which is the title of a book by former FCC commissioner Nicholas Johnson). In our view, nothing could be healthier for the sanity, and well-being of our nation than to have ninety million viewers talking back to their television news shows every night and twice on Sunday.

Now we must turn to the problem of pictures. It is often said that a picture is worth a thousand words. Maybe so. But it is probably equally true that one word is worth a thousand pictures, at least sometimes—for example, when it comes to understanding the world we live in. Indeed, the whole problem with news on television comes down to this; all the words uttered in an hour of news coverage could be printed on one page of a newspaper. And the world cannot be understood in one page. Of course, there is a compensation: television offers pictures, and the pictures move. Moving pictures are a kind of language in themselves, but the language of pictures differs radically from oral and written language, and the differences are crucial for understanding television news.

To begin with, pictures, especially single pictures, speak only in particularities. Their vocabulary is limited to concrete representation. Unlike words and sentences, a picture does not present to us an idea or concept about the world, except as we use language itself to convert the image to idea. By itself, a picture cannot deal with the unseen, the remote, the internal, the abstract. It does not speak of "man," only of *a* man; not of "tree," only of *a* tree. You cannot produce an image of "nature," any more than an image of "the sea." You can only show a particular fragment of the here-and-now—a cliff of a certain terrain, in a certain condition of light; a wave at a moment in time, from a particular point of view. And just as "nature" and "the sea" cannot be photographed, such larger abstractions as truth, honor, love, and falsehood cannot be talked about in the lexicon of individual pictures. For "showing of" and "talking about" are two very different kinds of processes: individual pictures give us the world as object; language, the world as idea. There is no such thing in nature as "man" or "tree." The universe offers no such categories or simplifications; only flux and infinite variety. The picture documents and celebrates the particularities of the universe's infinite variety. Language makes them comprehensible.

Of course, moving pictures, video with sound, may bridge the gap by juxtaposing images, symbols, sound, and music. Such images can present emotions and rudimentary ideas. They can suggest the panorama of nature and the joys and miseries of humankind.

Picture—smoke pouring from the window, cut to people coughing, an ambulance racing to a hospital, a tombstone in a cemetery.

Picture—jet planes firing rockets, explosions, lines of foreign soldiers surrendering, the American flag waving in the wind.

Nonetheless, keep in mind that when terrorists want to prove to the world that their kidnap victims are still alive, they photograph them holding a copy of a recent newspaper.

The dateline on the newspaper provides the proof that the photograph was taken on or after that date. Without the help of the written word, film and videotape cannot portray temporal dimensions with any precision. Consider a film clip showing an aircraft carrier at sea. One might be able to identify the ship as Soviet or American, but there would be no way of telling where in the world the carrier was, where it was headed, or when the pictures were taken. It is only through language—words spoken over the pictures or reproduced in them—that the image of the aircraft carrier takes on specific meaning.

Still, it is possible to enjoy the image of the carrier for its own sake. One might find the hugeness of the vessel interesting; it signifies military power on the move. There is a certain drama in watching the planes come in at high speeds and skid to a stop on the deck. Suppose the ship were burning: that would be even more interesting. This leads to an important point about the language of pictures: Moving pictures favor images that change. That is why violence and dynamic destruction find their way onto television so often. When something is destroyed violently it is altered in a highly visible way; hence the entrancing power of fire. Fire gives visual form to the ideas of consumption, disappearance, death—the thing that burned is actually taken away by fire. It is at this very basic level that fires make a good subject for television news. Something was here, now it's gone, and the change is recorded on film.

Earthquakes and typhoons have the same power. Before the viewer's eyes the world is taken apart. If a television viewer has relatives in Mexico City and an earthquake occurs there, then he or she may take a special interest in the images of destruction as a report from a specific place and time; that is, one may look at television pictures for information about an important event. But film of an earthquake can be interesting even if the viewer cares nothing about the event itself. Which is only to say, as we noted earlier, that there is another way of participating in the news—as a spectator who desires to be entertained. Actually to see buildings topple is exciting, no matter where the buildings are. The world turns to dust before our eyes.

Those who produce television news in America know that their medium favors images that move. That is why they are wary of "talking heads," people who simply appear in front of a camera and speak. When talking heads appear on television, there is nothing to record or document, no change in process. In the cinema the situation is somewhat different. On a movie screen, close-ups of a good actor speaking dramatically can sometimes be interesting to watch. When Clint Eastwood narrows his eyes and challenges his rival to shoot first, the spectator sees the cool rage of the Eastwood character take visual, form, and the narrowing of the eyes is dramatic. But much of the effect of this small movement depends on the size of the movie screen and the darkness of the theater, which make Eastwood and his every action "larger than life."

The television screen is smaller than life. It occupies about 15 percent of the viewer's visual field (compared to about 70 percent for the movie screen). It is not set in a darkened theater closed off from the world but in the viewer's ordinary living space. This means that visual changes must be more extreme and more dramatic to be interesting on television. A narrowing of the eyes will not do. A car crash, an earthquake, a burning factory are much better.

With these principles in mind, let us examine more closely the structure of a typical newscast, and here we will include in the discussion not only the pictures but all the non-linguistic symbols that make up a television news show. For example, in America, almost all news shows begin with music, the tone of which suggests important events about to unfold. The music is very important, for it equates the news with various forms of drama and ritual—the opera, for example, or a wedding procession—in which musical themes underscore the meaning of the event. Music takes us immediately into the realm of the symbolic, a world that is not to be taken literally. After all, when events unfold in the real world, they do so without musical accompaniment. More symbolism follows. The sound of teletype machines can be heard in the studio, not because it is impossible to screen this noise out, but because the sound is a kind of music in itself. It tells us that data are pouring in from all corners of the globe, a sensation reinforced by the world map in the background (or clocks noting the time on different continents). The fact is that teletype machines are rarely used in TV news rooms, having been replaced by silent computer terminals. When seen, they have only a symbolic function.

Already, then, before a single news item is introduced, a great deal has been communicated. We know that we are in the presence of a symbolic event, a form of theater in which the day's events are to be dramatized. This theater takes the entire globe as its subject, although it may look at the world from the perspective of a single nation. A certain tension is present, like the atmosphere in a theater just before the curtain goes up. The tension is represented by the music, the staccato beat of the teletype machines, and often the sight of news workers scurrying around typing reports and answering phones. As a technical matter, it would be no problem to build a set in which the newsroom staff remained off camera, invisible to the viewer, but an important theatrical effect would be lost. By being busy on camera, the workers help communicate urgency about the events at hand, which suggests that situations are changing so rapidly that constant revision of the news is necessary.

The staff in the background also helps signal the importance of the person in the center, the anchor, "in command" of both the staff and the news. The anchor plays the role of host. He or she welcomes us to the newscast and welcomes us back from the different locations we visit during the filmed reports.

Many features of the newscast help the anchor to establish the impression of control. These are usually equated with production values in broadcasting. They include such things as graphics that tell the viewer what is being shown, or maps and charts that suddenly appear on the screen and disappear on cue, or the orderly progression from story to story. They also include the absence of gaps, or "dead time," during the broadcast, even the simple fact that the news starts and ends at a certain hour. These common features are thought of as purely technical matters, which a professional crew handles as a matter of course. But they are also symbols of a dominant theme of television news: the imposition of an orderly world—called "the news"—upon the disorderly flow of events.

While the form of a news broadcast emphasizes tidiness and control, its content can best be described as fragmented. Because time is so precious on television, because the nature of the medium favors dynamic visual images, and because the pressures of a commercial structure require the news to hold its audience above all else, there is rarely any attempt to explain issues in depth or place events in their próper context. The news moves nervously from a warehouse fire to a court decision, from a guerrilla war to a World Cup match, the quality of the film most often determining the length of the story. Certain stories show up only because they offer dramatic pictures. Bleachers collapse in South America: hundreds of people are crushed—a perfect television news story, for the cameras can record the face of disaster in all its anguish. Back in Washington, a new budget is approved by Congress. Here there is nothing to photograph because a budget is not a physical event; it is a document full of language and numbers. So the producers of the news will show a photo of the document itself, focusing on the cover where it says "Budget of the United States of America." Or sometimes they will send a camera crew to the government printing plant where copies of the budget are produced. That evening, while the contents of the budget are summarized by a voice-over, the viewer sees stacks of documents being loaded into boxes at the government printing plant. Then a few of the budget's more important provisions will be flashed on the screen in written form, but this is such a time-consuming process—using television as a printed page—that the producers keep it to a minimum. In short, the budget is not televisable, and for that reason its time on the news must be brief. The bleacher collapse will get more time that evening.

While appearing somewhat chaotic, these disparate stories are not just dropped in the news program helter-skelter. The appearance of a scattershot story order is really orchestrated to draw the audience from one story to the next—from one section to the next—through the commercial breaks to the end of the show. The story order is constructed to hold and build the viewership rather than place events in context or explain issues in depth.

Of course, it is a tendency of journalism in general to concentrate on the surface of events rather than underlying conditions; this is as true for the newspaper as it is for the newscast. But several features of television undermine whatever efforts journalists may make to give sense to the world. One is that a television broadcast is a series of events that occur in sequence, and the sequence is the same for all viewers. This is not true for a newspaper page, which displays many items simultaneously, allowing readers to choose the order in which they read them. If newspaper readers want only a summary of the latest tax bill, they can read the headline and the first paragraph of an article, and if they want more, they can keep reading. In a sense, then, everyone reads a different newspaper, for no two readers will read (or ignore) the same items.

But all television viewers see the same broadcast. They have no choices. A report is either in the broadcast or out, which means that anything which is of narrow interest is unlikely to be included. As NBC News executive Reuven Frank once explained:

> *A newspaper, for example, can easily afford to print an item of conceivable interest to only a fraction of its readers. A television news program must be put together with the assumption that each item will be of some interest to everyone that watches. Every time a newspaper includes a feature which will attract a specialized group it can assume it is adding at least a little bit to its circulation. To the*

degree a television news program includes an item of this sort, . . . it must assume that its audience will diminish.

The need to "include everyone," an identifying feature of commercial television in all its forms, prevents journalists from offering lengthy or complex explanations, or from tracing the sequence of events leading up to today's headlines. One of the ironies of political life in modern democracies is that many problems which concern the "general welfare" are of interest only to specialized groups. Arms control, for example, is an issue that literally concerns everyone in the world, and yet the language of arms control and the complexity of the subject are so daunting that only a minority of people can actually follow the issue from week to week and month to month. If it wants to act responsibly, a newspaper can at least make available more information about arms control than most people want. Commercial television cannot afford to do so.

But even if commercial television could afford to do so, it wouldn't. The fact that television news is principally made up of moving pictures prevents it from offering lengthy, coherent explanations of events. A television news show reveals the world as a series of unrelated, fragmentary moments. It does not—and cannot be expected to—offer a sense of coherence or meaning. What does this suggest to a TV viewer? That the viewer must come with a prepared mind—information, opinions, a sense of proportion, an articulate value system. To the TV viewer lacking such mental equipment, a news program is only a kind of rousing light show. Here a falling building, there a five-alarm fire, everywhere the world as an object, much without meaning, connections, or continuity.

After Reading

Critical Perspective

1. What are your thoughts about this essay? Do you find Postman and Powers's essay to be helpful in terms of how you might analyze news programs? If yes, in what ways? If no, why not?

Rhetoric and Argument

2. Do you think that this argument is rhetorically effective? How do the authors appeal to our ethos, pathos, and logos? Offer specific examples of each. What kinds of identifications do the writers want us to have with their text and why? Also examine use of audience, purpose, intertextuality, context, and constraints where relevant.
3. What do Postman and Powers claim about the differences between stationary pictures, moving pictures, and language? How is this important to their larger point in the essay? What is the writers' main claim about today's newscasts? Do you agree with them? Present quotes to support your thoughts.
4. Consider Postman and Powers's detailed description of the "structure of a typical newscast." Does offering this thorough explanation help to support their main claim? In what ways? Is there any other important aspect of contemporary news programs that you have noticed that the writers do not mention? If yes, what might this be?

5. Given the state of today's newscasts, what must be the role of the viewer, according to Postman and Powers? Make a list of what viewers might do to come to every newscast "with a prepared mind." What specific aspects of television newscasts make it hard to discern what is important about the information conveyed?

Analysis

6. Recall a time when you watched several hours of CNN or another national newscast during a national crisis. Then, address the following concerns in a short essay: What bits of information did you learn during this newscast? How did the structure of the newscast, the music used, the role of the anchor, and other features create feelings of fear, anxiety, concern, or the like in you as a viewer? Be as detailed as you can about the rhetorical tactics employed by the news program to achieve this. Consult library and Internet sources to back up your views.

Taking Action

Now that you have read Postman & Powers's essay, your task as a class is to create a plan to produce a news program of your own—one that is designed to challenge how news programs typically function today. You might consider Comedy Central's *The Daily Show* or *The Colbert Report*—with their use of humor, unusual stories, and unlikely visuals—as models for how to do this.

Using Postman and Powers's essay as a guide for what to avoid, deliberate about all of the changes you will make to the rhetorical tactics operating on these shows. Seek out relevant library and Internet sources as well. One group in the class might consider the kinds of stories that will appear on the news program. Another should reflect on the role of the anchor. Yet another might think about how sound will work. Another could focus on visuals.

Once you have made your decisions in small groups, get back together as a whole class to decide how you would implement them and how they might work. If you have access to video equipment, once you have written up your plans, you might tape the entire fake news show. After you have produced your show, get together with the rest of your class. Discuss why each of the groups made the choices it did, how you specifically tried to challenge the typical rhetoric and format of such shows, and what you hope to have proven through taking this approach. Consider screening the show with other groups both inside and outside the campus community.

The Economist

"Home Alone?"

The Economist is a weekly paper first published in 1843 by The Economist Newspaper Limited in London. The Economist focuses on world politics and business, science and technology, as well as the arts. Articles are generally written without a byline.

EXERCISING YOUR SKILLS

Before Reading

This essay examines the phenomenon of shopping on television in comparison to shopping from catalogs and online. How do you most frequently shop for things you want and need? Do you go to stores, shop from television shows, shop from catalogs, or shop online? Why do you think that you choose to purchase specific products via certain means and not others? Think about the infomercials and television homeshopping programs you have watched. How do they operate? What do you notice about them and the ways in which they function? Have they ever convinced you to buy or not buy a product? Why or why not? Explain your experiences.

The idea of doing your shopping from home, rather than visiting a store, spans over a century of American commerce. In 1893 Sears, Roebuck mailed out the first edition of its catalogue, from which the country's farmers were able to [outfit] themselves with everything from guns to Sunday-best suits. Pioneers could even find themselves a wife in a catalogue. Yet the idea still has a futuristic feel to it: the 21st-century couple lounging on their shiny bubble chairs and dictating orders to a sonorously deferential computer.

Despite all the hype about multimedia, old-fashioned catalogues still dominate the home-shopping industry. They clocked up sales of almost $70 billion in America in 1995, according to the Direct Marketing Association (DMA), an industry group. Of that, some $43 billion was spent by consumers, the rest by businesses. In contrast, sales through infomercials or direct-response ads on television totalled $4.5 billion, $2.6 billion of which came from dedicated home-shopping channels. Sales of goods over the Internet and other online services were worth a mere $518 million, estimates Forrester Research, a consultancy in Cambridge, Massachusetts.

Catalogue shopping has been on a roll for the past decade and a half. The number of catalogues mailed in America rose from 8.7 billion in 1983 to 13.2 billion last year. The DMA forecasts that the industry's revenue will continue to grow at almost 7% a year for the rest of the decade, as it has since 1990. This growth is mostly driven by a large group of people spending increasing amounts on mail-order goods, rather than more people starting to buy them—59% of adult Americans already order from catalogues, and three-quarters of them spend more than $100 a year.

Clothing remains the most popular item sold through catalogues, followed closely by home furnishings. Computers and the software for them are also a big chunk of the business. Five of the top ten catalogue groups ranked by revenues are computer sellers. The biggest general catalogue retailer, J. C. Penney, which also has a chain of department stores, depends mostly on clothing and furnishings.

There are hitches. Last year, for example, the two main expenses of the catalogue business—postal charges and the cost of paper—both increased at the same time. But catalogue shopping still seems to have a number of things in its favor:

- Various social changes, such as more women in work and greater worries about violence on the streets, have boosted home shopping.

- State tax regulations mean that goods bought from a company in another state do not incur sales tax.
- New computer technology allows retailers to target their customers with more precision, sorting through databases of names and addresses to work out who is likely to want, say, golf clubs and who would prefer china figurines.
- As more companies shed central purchasing teams in bouts of downsizing, leaving individual departments to buy their own supplies independently, time-strapped managers are increasingly turning to catalogues. As a result, sales to businesses are growing rapidly; the DMA predicts that they will represent 39% of all catalogue sales in 2001.

In theory, all of these advantages should particularly benefit more modern forms of home shopping. But the TV-based version seems stuck in something of a rut. Sales of Home Shopping Network (HSN), one of America's two leading networks, have been stuck at a little over $1 billion a year for the past five years. Those of QVC, its big rival, have risen from $1.2 billion in 1993 to $1.5 billion in 1995.

Most of the pressure is now on HSN, which reported an operating loss in 1995 of $80 million. Its owner, Barry Diller, a Hollywood mogul who used to run QVC, has restructured the company: in the past year about 300 jobs have gone from HSN's headquarters in St Petersburg, Florida, where 1,800 telephonists and a large computer system can answer up to 50,000 calls an hour. Mr. Diller has also brought in a new chief executive, James Held, who has ditched many of HSN's clothing lines and focused the network around jewelry and cosmetics.

This reflects TV shopping's narrow audience. Some 85% of the shoppers are women, and the most popular category of goods is jewelry, which accounts for nearly 40% of the business. Other items include clothes, cosmetics and complicated fitness machines that are demonstrated by lots of healthy-looking presenters.

One reason that TV shopping has not prospered more is that, in a sense, it is a step backward from catalogues. The format—goods paraded past the camera one after another—favors impulse buying rather than a search for something particular; it also attracts people with enough time on their hands to sit watching until something appealing flickers by. The average length of time spent watching QVC before the first purchase is made is 36 hours. The network tried to move up market in 1994 with Q2, a second channel that sold more expensive goods, but its failure to catch on with yuppies led the firm to recast Q2 simply as a "best of QVC" channel, showing repeats of successes from the main channel.

The thought of avoiding TV shopping's defects is what makes online shopping so exciting to people such as Mr. Diller. Computers let customers navigate their way to the goods that they want when they want them. And their users certainly do not resemble stereotypical TV shoppers.

At present, the biggest part of the online market (around 25–30% of it) is made up of computer goods—hardware, software and books about them. Travel (20–25%) is the next biggest category. Forrester predicts that this mixture will stay much the same over the next four years. The value of goods and services sold will grow to $6.6 billion. Other forecasters think the figure could be ten times this amount.

The Search for Net Profits

Both QVC and HSN have started online enterprises—iQVC and the Internet Shopping Network (ISN), respectively. ISN is selling about $1 million-worth of goods a month, vying with Amazon.com, a bookshop based in Washington state, and others as the most popular online merchant. At the moment ISN sells only computer goods, but Mr. Diller intends to change that. Interactive searching, he argues, is worthwhile only if there is a wide range of goods to forage through. Amazon lists over one million titles, more than any of its rivals, online or off. For its part, iQVC outdoes its television parent in the breadth of its stock, offering everything from power tools to pajamas.

If offering a broader range of goods than your rivals is one big competitive advantage in online shopping, another is excellence in what traditional retailers like to call "supply-chain management." Taking an order online will be easier—customers will do most of the data-entry work that firms' telephone operators currently have to do with catalogue or TV sales. But the warehousing and delivery of these goods will be fiendishly complex to organize.

Mr. Diller argues that this favors firms with experience in TV home shopping: fulfilling orders fast and accurately is what HSN and QVC are geared up to do. But there is an important difference. The TV-shopping channels can broadly control the time when products are sold (most sales happen either while or soon after the infomercial is shown): this means that they can buy job-lots of goods. With interactivity, orders may flow in over a much longer period. Rather than stock their warehouses with small runs of countless products, ISN and iQVC may be wiser to relay some orders directly to the manufacturer.

Amazon is an excellent example of why, even on the Internet, the intermediary still has a role. It distributes books for some 20,000 publishers, and guarantees its customers that it can deliver any book in print in the United States: 18 of its 106 staff deal with rare books (nearly a third are in warehousing and distribution). It keeps minimal stocks, at most a two-day supply of its 500 bestsellers in its warehouse; the rest it orders from publishers on demand. Some publishers say privately that they prefer selling through Amazon than through their own direct-sales operations. Unlike its slightly stale televisual rivals, Amazon offers interviews with authors. In short, it tries to make buying books easier for both consumers and manufacturers.

A century ago, Richard Sears, a station telegrapher, used his country's new railways to distribute goods and build up his business. But Sears and Roebuck's strength was its range of merchandise and a solid reputation for quality, bolstered by generous guarantees. Even in today's online world, that is still a winning formula.

After Reading

Critical Perspective

1. Reflect upon how you might describe the goals of this essay to someone who had not read it. Write a short summary of its main ideas. Do you agree with the argument? Why or why not?

Rhetoric and Argument

2. What kinds of rhetorical choices—use of audience, purpose, ethos, pathos, logos, intertextuality, context, and constraints—do the authors of this text offer? Include quotes to substantiate your assertions.
3. What is the main claim of this piece? What sort of claim is it? Do you believe it is as persuasive as it could be? Where does the author make this claim? Why or why not? Be sure to support your thoughts with textual evidence.
4. What support do the authors offer for this claim? Where does the claim appear in the text? Do you think the support backs up the claim? Why or why not? Give quotes from the text to evidence your views.
5. Describe the structure of this argument. Is the organization effective? Why or why not? Are there any logical fallacies or faulty assumptions at work in this argument? What specific suggestions could you give the author that might make it more effective?

Analysis

6. After reading this piece, write a short argumentative essay in which you tackle the following questions: What do you think the "winning formula" is for businesses in America trying to find a market for their products? Why might QVC and ISN not have seen the revenues they hoped for? In what way might web sales guarantee a higher captive audience than television has thus far? Try to give examples from your own experiences with websites as well as from library and Internet sources.

Taking Action

In a small group watch some television shopping channels and check out various websites for products and services. Make note of the specific similarities and differences between the two rhetorical forms (television and the Internet) as well as how companies selling the same types of products in different media approach their tasks. Consult library and Internet sources as helpful.

Report your findings to the larger class group. As a class, consider what kinds of claims of cultural criticism you might be able to support about the differences between television and Internet shopping given the evidence you have found.

MARK KINGWELL

"Not Available in Stores"

Mark Kingwell is professor of philosophy at the University of Toronto and a contribu-
tor editor of Harper's Magazine. *He is the author of nine books of political and cultural*
theory, including his most recent title Empire State Building, Nearest Thing to Heaven.
His essays and reviews have appeared in many leading academic journals as well as
more than forty mainstream publications, including Harper's, The New York Times
Magazine, *and* AdBusters.

EXERCISING YOUR SKILLS

Before Reading

Kingwell's essay focuses on the growth and effects of television infomercials. Consider
which television infomercials you have seen recently. Are there any that have struck
you as particularly humorous, interesting, disturbing, or trite? Examining a number
of these in detail, present a close rhetorical analysis of them while providing quotes
from these texts to back up your assertions. What sorts of claims of cultural criticism might you make about television infomercials and why? What might this reveal
about today's consumers and our values, desires, myths, dreams, ideals, and fears?

It begins like one of those cozy Women's Television Network chat shows, complete with
bad lighting, fuzzy lenses, and warm looks. The host is an attractive, soft-spoken woman of
a certain age. She purrs at the camera. She and her guests are here to tell you about what
she chucklingly calls "Hollywood's breast-kept secret." Yes, it's true: Accents, the Plasti-
cine bust enhancers favored by movie stars and models alike, are now available to you, the
lowly viewer. No surgery. No hideous contraptions. You don't even have to leave home to
get them.

And what a difference they make! Soon a line-up of gorgeous but slightly flat-chested
women are being transformed before your eyes into jiggly supermodels or *Baywatch*
lifeguards. These flesh-colored slabs of silicone gel that "fit into any underwire bra" and
"within minutes warm to your natural body temperature" can actually be used in the
swimming pool! At the end of the half-hour, the ever-smiling host and her guests admit
that they are all wearing Accents themselves! Well, shut my mouth.

"Accents" is only the most outrageous of the current crop of television infomercials:
those over-the-top attempts to hawk make-up, cleaning products, and ab-flexers under the
guise of a genial talk show (*Kathie Lee Talks*) or breathless science program (*Amazing*
Discoveries!). Turn on your television late at night or on a weekend afternoon—even,
these days, at midmorning—and the good-natured hosts, a has-been actress (Ali McGraw)
or never-was celeb (Ed McMahon), are touting cosmetics or miracle car wax as if they are
doing us a public service. Information + commercial = infomercial. Line up the word, and
the phenomenon, next to those long advertising features in newspapers and magazines,
often slyly imitating the publications' actual typeface and design, known as "advertorials."

Patently absurd, maybe, but if emerging trends continue, infomercials will not remain what they have been so far—a marginal and benign, if irritating, television presence. With the loosening of CRTC [Canadian Radio-Television and Telecommunications Commission] regulations, the explosion of cable channels, and the crude economics that can make them more lucrative than regular programming for network affiliates, infomercials are showing up in more and more places on the TV schedule, elbowing aside such popular quality fare as Sunday-afternoon sports, syndicated comedies, and old movies. They are also getting more and more sophisticated, as big-name companies with mainstream products—Ford Motor Co., Procter & Gamble, Apple Canada—enter the infomercial market.

And if, as enthusiasts in the business press insist, this is the future of TV advertising, then that is very bad news indeed for television and its viewers. But not because there is anything inherently wrong with infomercials, at least not as they have existed until now. The delicate pact between ads and shows that makes television possible has always been able to withstand the amateurish, ad-becomes-show genre they represent. But when infomercials are everywhere, and especially when they go high market, that pact is in danger of being overturned, and the thin line between entertainment and pitch may be erased for good.

Blame Ron Popeil. Blame him a lot, and at length. Blame him until his smiling, trout-like face is imprinted on your mind as the fount of all evil. Because Popeil is the one who started the sort of television hard sell that reaches its tacky terminus in today's infomercials. Founder of Ronco, restless inventor of the Popeil Pocket Fisherman, the Patti-Stacker, and other cheesy "labor-saving" devices too numerous to mention, Popeil is the guy who all but invented television shopping. In the 1970s he discovered that people got very excited, and very willing to spend, at the thought that you need never leave your couch to have the entire Ronco or K-Tel product line delivered to your home. His favorite author was the guy who came up with "Call this toll-free number now."

Popeil has recently come out from behind the camera to appear in his own convection-oven and pasta-machine infomercials. Looking like an also-ran from a professional tanning competition, he slops flour and water into slowly spinning machines that disgorge brightly colored goo for thirty minutes. Your own fresh pasta every night! Operators are standing by!

It isn't hard to decipher what makes these and other low-end infomercials so successful. Potential buyers are never made to feel bad, even as their baser desires are being pandered to. For example, we are told at least four times that Accents "are shipped confidentially" and arrive at your door in (get this) "a beautiful designer chest that will look great on your vanity." The Accents people even muster expert opinion, the sine qua non of the TV hard sell. In this case, it's a panel of Hollywood make-up artists and photographers. "I tried everything," says one. "Foam pads, wires, push-up bras, duct tape. Nothing works like Accents." (Duct tape?)

The same forms of reassurance are visible on all the successful infomercials now airing, from The Stimulator to the Ab-Roller Plus. The Stimulator—a small syringe-like device that is supposed to kill pain by means of mild electric shock, a sort of mini stun gun—also produces what has to be the funniest infomercial moment of all time. Evel Knievel, the all-but-forgotten daredevil of the 1970s, shares, over footage of his famous Caesars Palace motorcycle crash, his belief in the pain-relieving properties of The Stimulator. "If it hepped me," Knievel twangs, "it can hep you." Now that's expert opinion.

This is so silly that it is easy to imagine a kind of self-parody operating, of the sort in the hilarious *Money Show* spots on CBC's "This Hour Has 22 Minutes," "Gus, I want to pay less in taxes, but I'm not sure how," "Marsha, it couldn't be easier; stop filing your returns!" But that would misread the intentions of the makers—and the attitudes of the audience, whose response to infomercials has been wholehearted. Canadians spent $100 million on infomercial products in 1995, up thirty-four per cent from 1994. One Ontario company, Iona Appliances Inc., quadrupled annual sales of its "dual-cyclonic" vacuum cleaner when it started marketing via infomercial.

In fact, the point of infomercials has so far been their lack of sophistication. The niche is still dominated by the charmingly inept likes of Quality Special Products, the Canadian company responsible for such thoroughly trailer-park items as the Sweepa ("The last broom you'll ever have to buy!") and the Sophist-O-Twist hair accessory ("French braids made easy!").

Most current efforts eschew the cleverness and quality visible on more traditional commercial spots in favor of the lowball aesthetic of public-access cable. Instead of competing with shows for our attention—and therefore being pushed to find better writing, multimillion-dollar budgets, and gilt-edged directorial talent—infomercials become the shows. Yet they do so in ways so obviously half-hearted that nobody, not even the quintessential couch-potato viewer, could actually be fooled. The talk-show cover story is really nothing more than a tacit agreement between marketer and viewer that they're going to spend half an hour in each other's company, working over a deal.

And this is what many critics miss: most infomercials, as they now appear, aren't really trying to dupe the viewer. They are instead the bottom-feeding equivalent of the irony observable in many regular commercials. Bargain-basement infomercials offer a simpler form of customer complicity than the crafty self-mockery and self-reference that appeals to young, kitsch-hungry viewers. Infomercials are a pure game of "let's pretend," taken straight from the carnival midway.

That's why the entry of high-end marketers into the field is so alarming. Big-money companies are not content to maintain the artless facade that now surrounds infomercials. They break the carny-style spell of cheap infomercials, where we know what we see is fake, but we go along anyway, and offer instead the high production quality, narrative structure, and decent acting of actual shows.

A recent Apple Canada effort, for example, which aired last year in Toronto, Calgary, and Vancouver, is set up as a saccharine half-hour sitcom about a whitebread family deciding to buy a home computer ("The Marinettis Bring Home a Computer"). It is reminiscent of *Leave It to Beaver* or *The Wonder Years*, complete with Mom, Pop, Gramps, the family dog, and an annoying pre-teen narrator named T.J. Gramps buys the computer, then bets grumpy Pop that the family will use it enough to justify the expense. Soon TJ is bringing up his slumping math grades, Mom is designing greeting cards for profit, and Gramps is e-mailing fellow opera buffs. It's nauseating, but effective. Heather Hutchison, marketing communications manager for Apple Canada, explains the company's decision to enter the infomercial universe this way: "Having produced something of higher quality," she says, "there's a recognition at—I hesitate to use the word 'subconscious,' but at a lower level— that it says something about the quality of the product. The Canadian market responds well to this kind of softer sell."

We all know that television, as it now operates, is primarily a vehicle for the delivery of advertising. That is, we know that if it weren't for ads, nobody would get to spend a million dollars on a single episode of an hour-long drama or employ some of the best dramatic writers and directors now working. True, this symbiosis is uneasy at best, with good shows all but free-riding on the masses of dreck that keep the advertisers happily reaching their targets. That's fine or at least not apocalyptic. We can accept that advertising is the price we have to pay (every seven minutes) for good television.

But slick infomercials, unlike their cheapo forebears, threaten to destroy this shaky covenant. Only a moron could mistake a low-end infomercial for a real show. (And only a condescending jerk could think that all people who buy Sweepas and Abdomenizers are, in fact, morons.) Up-market infomercials have a much greater potential to muddy the waters between advertising and programming. It may be that, without the cheesy aesthetics and side-show barker style, these new infomercials won't find an audience. But it's more likely that big companies with big budgets and top advertising talent will be able to suck even non-morons into these narrative ads that masquerade as entertainment. The new corporate offerings, in other words, may actually do what Ron Popeil couldn't: strip TV of extraneous effects like quality programming so that it finally reveals its essential nature— selling things, selling things, and selling things.

When that's true, maybe it's time to turn the damn thing off for good.

After Reading

Critical Perspective

1. What do you notice about this text, its rhetorical appeals (ethos, pathos, logos), argumentative structure, as well as its arrangement? Explain your thoughts.

Rhetoric and Argument

2. Describe how Kingwell begins his text. What language choices does he make? How would you describe his tone? Do you think Kingwell's use of audience, purpose, intertextuality, context, and constraints is effective? Be sure to provide examples from the text to back up your views.
3. What is Kingwell's main claim about infomercials? Where does he make this assertion in his text? Do you find his ideas convincing? Why or why not?
4. Why does Kingwell indicate that we should "blame Ron Popeil" for the current ascendance of the infomercial? Do you concur with him or not? Do you think King-

well is really "blaming" Popeil or just using him as an example to support his claim? How do you know?

5. What evidence does Kingwell use to support his assertions? Point to the examples he relies on and explain how they either support or don't support his argumentative claims.

Analysis

6. Write a short argumentative essay in which you address the following concerns: What is Kingwell's greatest fear about infomercials and their potential effects? Where in his essay does he articulate this concern? Do you agree with it? Why or why not? Draw from particular infomercials that you have watched to support your thoughts. Use relevant library and Internet sources to back up your perspectives.

Taking Action

As a class, choose a product that is very unlikely to ever have an infomercial created to promote it. Using all of the rhetorical tactics at your disposal, construct a fake infomercial designed to promote the product to a particular audience. Form small groups to tackle the various parts of the infomercial (the opening, the use of the product, the role of the studio audience, the role of the pitch person). Remember, you are creating a visual and aural text that is meant to be a cultural criticism of infomercials themselves. Seek out relevant library and Internet sources.

Be sure to use colorful visuals as well as follow the typical formats of most infomercials. Feel free to satirize what you believe are the more humorous elements of infomercials as you do this. Once you have decided as a group how you will structure the infomercial, the narrative you will use, as well as what the various segments will look like, write up your plan.

Now you have a number of options. Act out the infomercial as a class and then discuss why you made the choices you did, what you hoped to foreground by making them, what kind of cultural criticism of infomercials you hoped to create, and why. Alternatively, you can create and videotape a fake infomercial and show it to a larger audience. After seeing it, talk about your choices with your audience.

CHAPTER 9

Seeing Movies and Listening to Music

INTRODUCTION

Considering Films and Music

Many of us take pleasure in the experience of going to the movies—the lights dimming in the theater as the screen is illuminated; the hot, buttered popcorn; the junior mints. More and more we can have this same experience in the comfort of our own homes with videotapes and DVDs that offer us new windows into filmic production—never-before-seen clips that have been cut from the finished production, exclusive interviews with casts and directors, and detailed glimpses into the entire production process including sound, costumes, and special effects. In addition, there are Pay-Per-View as well as cable channels such as HBO, Cinemax, Bravo, and the Independent Film Network that provide us ready access to films of all kind. Who among us has not spent an evening curled up on the couch with good friends or family, ordered a pizza, and watched a film that we have not had the chance to see yet? This weekend I finally watched "Little Miss Sunshine," with Greg Kinnear, Toni Collette, Steve Carrell, Alan Arkin, and Abigail Breslin, a film I had been hoping to see for months.

What are your favorite movies? Are you partial to series films such as *The Godfather* trilogy, the Tolkien Trilogy, *Star Wars*, *Charlie's Angels*, the *Scream* trilogy, the *Dumb and Dumber* films, the "Jackass" movies, or *Harry Potter*? Do you prefer single-feature films such as *Bourne Supremacy*, *Confessions of a Teenage Drama Queen*, *Elephant*, *Mission Impossible*, *Passion of the Christ*, *Supersize Me!*, *Bend It Like Beckham*, *Spiderman*, *Riding Giants*, *Shrek*, or *Barbershop*? Are you a fan of *Save the Last Dance*, *Love and Basketball*, *The Notebook*, *Mean Girls*, *Crash*, *Napolean Dynamite*, or *Clerks*? Or do you prefer older films such as *American History X*, *Dead Poet's Society*, *Breakfast Club*, *Pretty in Pink*, *Fast Times at Ridgemont High* or *Ferris Bueller's Day Off*? Do you favor action and adventure films, comedies, documentaries, "chic flicks," or dramatic productions? What specifically do you like about them—the characters, the plots, the images, the sound?

Much like movies, music plays an important function in our everyday lives. A sound track can accompany nearly everything we do. So often we are "plugged in" with our Sirius and XM satellite radio, Sony Discmen, iPods and iTunes, as well as personal car and home sound systems. We can listen to our music privately as it is playing into our own ears, drowning out the world around us. Or, we can hear music at parties, clubs, raves, stadiums—music we jump around to, dance to, and sing along to with friends. What is your favorite type of music? Do you prefer punk music, Latin pop music, country music, hip-hop, mainstream pop, hard rock, or rap? What are your favorite musical groups and artists—the White Stripes, Fergie, Simple Plan, Ashlee Simpson, Evanescence, Queens of the Stone Age, Britney Spears, Incubus, Faith Hill, 50 cent, System of a Down, Foo Fighters, Green Day, Seether, OutKast, Usher, John Mayer, Good Charlotte, My Chemical Romance, Coldplay, AFI, Interpol, Eminem, or various independent, lesser-known artists? When I listen to the melodic Joss Stone on my iPod this says something very different about me, my mood, and how I view myself in the world than when I blast the pulsating alt beat of 30 Seconds to Mars, for instance. What do your musical choices reveal about who you are—your ideals, values, beliefs, and tastes? What does the music you like to listen to say about your identity, how you view yourself, as well as how you want to be viewed by others?

Overview of Selections: Films

In this chapter of *Pop Perspectives: Readings to Critique Contemporary Culture* you will read about different films and various kinds of music—from various popular films to independent art films and from popular music to alternative music.

The first section is titled "Films." Here you will reflect on a series of movies from different genres. Each essay presents a window into the world of film, our responses to film, and what films reveal about the desires, values, anxieties, and fears that dominate our culture.

The chapter begins with an intriguing essay by cultural critic Susan Pell. She traces for us how cultural perspectives about and representations of masculinity have changed in movies during the 1990s and into the 2000s—from what she contends is a Dirty Harry or John Wayne masculinity to a masculinity that is more fluid and actually attainable for real men. Looking specifically at the films *As Good As It Gets*, *Good Will Hunting*, and *Magnolia*, Pell maintains that men are now depicted with more flexible, productive understandings of masculinity and therefore male viewers are no longer locked into specific roles about what it means to be a man in American culture. Pell remains concerned, however, that while this makes more masculine identities available to male viewers, it does little to challenge patriarchal institutions in our culture.

Then, media and speech communication theorists Brian L. Ott and Eric Aoki advance an important, scholarly analysis of the movie *Rush Hour*, a film in the buddy-cop/action-comedy genre. Drawing upon contemporary cultural theory, they unravel how this particular film as well as other contemporary American movies privilege a white, male European perspective, making little room for positive depictions of African American and Asian American men. Ott and Aoki examine dialogue in the film as well as the use of music and images, revealing how they contribute to the stereotyping and exoticizing of cultural difference in the film. Contextualizing the film's production within the beating of Rodney King and the O.J. Simpson trial, Ott and Aoki call upon us to create more detailed analyses of race, ethnicity, and masculinity in contemporary film.

Next, feminist critic Meredith A. Love provides a compelling cultural criticism about the eccentric art-house film *Being John Malkovich*. She struggles honestly with the film and asks questions about how well it takes up the representation of lesbian relationships. While Love acknowledges to us that she is not sure finally how she feels about the film, one of its most positive effects, Love suggests, is forcing the viewer to confront her or his assumptions about romance and sexuality and the ways in which they may depend greatly upon narrow categories of gender. Love investigates how Malkovich's body becomes a cultural space through which definitions of what constitute masculinity and femininity become unhinged and finally revealed as always in flux.

Then Todd Boyd, a professor of critical studies in the School of Cinema-Television at the University of Southern California, offers an innovative historical argument, examining the move from the "gangster" movies of the past to the "gangsta" movies of today. He asserts that this genre has always been a "renegade space" in which powerful voices often repressed in typical social environments have sometimes had more free play and impact but at other times have been devoid of political messages. Beginning with the Italian gangsters of *Scarface* and the *Godfather* films, Boyd views how race and ethnicity issues are treated. He also explores the emergence of "sexploitation" films in the 1960s and 1970s, observing the role of Latino and African American males as gangsta. Boyd then examines *Boyz N the Hood* and *Menace II Society*, making note of some of their important political images as well as the ways in which they reinforce some notions that result in further racial and class oppression.

The essay that follows investigates the interesting phenomenon of the "teen movie." With rich descriptions of stock characters and plot lines, David Denby of *The New Yorker* questions whether or not these films depict students' everyday high school realities. He concludes that these films are often about those outside the popular cliques finally outshining those in the in-crowd. While this might seem to be a "veiled strike at the entire abs-hair advertising culture," Denby argues that such films oftentimes offer no sustained criticisms of consumerism. Instead, most of the genre might be aptly called "Portrait of the Filmmaker as a Young Nerd." Denby also details for us the "menacing subgenre, in which the desire for revenge turns bloody." In this twist on the standard plot, when the outsiders cannot become part of the popular crowd, the outsiders eliminate them. Toward the end of his essay, however, Denby contends that not all teen films need fall into these two categories, pointing instead to a new and positive approach to the teen film as seen in *Clueless*, *Romy and Michele's High School Reunion*, *Election*, and others.

The last critic, Jill Fields, analyzes the film *Nurse Betty*, examining how race, gender, and ethnicity operate in troubling ways within this film. In this captivating piece, Fields states that there is a "shared social space occupied by black men and white women"; one that relegates them both to the margins of American culture. However, this film, Fields contends, never allows these two oppressed groups to mutually support each other, instead "buying off the white housewife by providing her with the job and the educational opportunities." As a result, while at first glance the film seems to complicate race and gender issues, it only reaffirms them. In conclusion Fields asserts that increasingly filmic depictions of gender, race, and ethnicity have to present more empowering perspectives for a wider range of viewers.

Overview of Selections: Music

The second section of Chapter 9, "Music," considers various musical genres and how they impact us. The essays cover a wide range of artists and topics, leading you through the landscape of sounds on radio, CDs, iPods, and MP3 players as well as the world of music videos.

This section begins with an innovative essay by Josh Delmar Zimmerman, a critic of popular culture, rhetoric, and representations of Chicanos. Zimmerman takes us through his own very personal journey within the punk subculture in the Southwest, describing the ways in which he and his friends were labeled and discriminated against. Showing how punk culture furnished a space where race and class boundaries became blurred and problems within mainstream American society could be openly criticized, Zimmerman's essay uses some of the very same rhetorical techniques and attitudes rampant in punk lyrics to draw his readers into his text. Zimmerman calls upon us to see the punk music scene as not just about youth or anger but about questioning and changing the status quo.

Next, Jamilah Evelyn, who is known for her publications with *The Chronicle of Higher Education* and her research on race and ethnicity in institutional settings, provides a compelling essay for us about hip-hop. She interviews various students and teachers to get their perceptions about hip-hop culture's influence on university campuses. Evelyn asks whether poor student retention rates can be linked to musical choices, whether university officials don't understand today's students, or whether there is actually a link between musical choice and academic performance. Though Evelyn does not pose any ready answers to these questions, she does reveal that hip-hop culture's enormous popularity means that professors and students alike need to make the effort to understand and support as well as criticize its lyrics and behavior. Evelyn also indicates that teachers would do well to make efforts to understand this student culture and find ways to bring it into their teaching.

Then a media critic whose internationally famous novels feature the incredible race and class diversity within Latin culture, Alisa Valdes-Rodriguez, presents a crucial piece for us. She notes that Latino and Latina pop stars such as Ricky Martin, Shakira, Marc Anthony, and Jennifer Lopez are too often characterized in the media according to sexualized stereotypes—represented as "spicy"—rather than described according to their musical talents. She also notes that such artists are too often lumped together in one group or wrongly placed in other groups. Artists from Puerto Rico are falsely labeled "foreigners," for instance, revealing a lack of familiarity with geography but also with complexities and differences within Latin culture. Valdes-Rodriguez contends that the desire of the media to categorize such artists according to only one racial or ethnic group often means that their full, diverse identities and ethnic heritages are rarely exposed or understood.

Next Gavin James Campbell, a critic of American popular culture who lives and teaches abroad, writes about pop artist Britney Spears. He takes us on an unanticipated journey, detailing his investigative work about Spears and her life, tracing everything from her earliest to her most recent work. Campbell travels back to Spears' hometown in Kentwood, Louisiana, interviews people who knew her, and investigates the town's own checkered history. Using sources as varied as local histories of Kentwood and Spears's biographies as well as *Teen People*, Campbell reveals how mainstream stories about Britney Spears's religious allegiances, overt sexuality, and "Southern belle" persona may obscure a more critical concern—the racial and class conflicts underlying her success and crucial to the town in which she grew up.

Then, central Texas writer and musician Lindsey Eck provides a crucial piece about country music. Eck begins by defining country music then describes its move from the South and West to pop mainstream and tackles the newly emerging criticism that most country music today is "all hat, no tractors." Eck makes the claim that while much country music emanates from several regions of the country, country music is also largely representative of one ethnic group—American Anglo-Celtics. Eck examines the phenomenon of Garth Brooks and his alter rock-n-roll ego, Chris Gaines. Eck exposes why Gaines failed to gain a substantial rock audience and yet might also be rejected by country fans. In the end, Eck shows the critical influences this ethnic group has had on country music and provides insights about the future of country music.

The next essay is by Londoner and accomplished writer about American culture, Nathan D. Abrams. In this important text Abrams considers rap music's history, cultural resistance to rap, and rap's use of technology. Abrams discusses the detractors of such music and the ways in which they maintain that rap is now selling out. Instead Abrams counters that the success of rap reveals not the extent to which rap artists have bought into the trappings of consumerism. Rather, he argues that they have "actively shaped, reshaped, and even destroyed the commodities of consumer culture. They hijacked the technology to voice their opposition." Abrams points to specific rap groups' lyrics and their creative use of technology as evidence. For Abrams the bling-bling of rap is proof positive that its political messages are now being heard.

The final essay presents us with a unique perspective on the effects of music television. David Laskin, a journalist and cultural critic, argues that he hates MTV not only because his daughters cannot stop watching it but also because of its lurid content, imagery, and situations. Music television, he contends, is a form of pornography. Rather than simply supporting his argument and ending there, Laskin makes the interesting choice to reconsider the accuracy of his claim, instead consulting several experts about their views—his daughters. Laskin includes his three daughters' different views on MTV with his readers. His essay closes with his eldest daughter Emily's thoughts: "Perfect channel indeed! I assume you know that MTV stands for Music Television, but I say that's false advertising. Where's the music?" While Emily agrees with her father about MTV's content, she also states, "But really, do you think my sisters and I can't tell the difference between a Britney Spears video and real life? Do you think we don't realize that exploitation (of men and women) is MTV's big selling point? And if we realize that it's exploitation we can't be numb to it or in favor of it. Please, father, be reasonable." In the end, while Laskin remains skeptical of MTV he is convinced that his daughters are not just blindly absorbing what MTV promotes—they are using it for their own ends and, to some degree, they are also applying their critical thinking and logical reasoning skills to consider its effects.

As you study this chapter, deliberate about what kinds of social and political messages the movies you watch are sending. What worldviews and ideologies do films offer us, and what are their impacts? What do contemporary films expose about gender relations, class relations, and race as well as ethnicity? What identities do they construct for us as viewers? Likewise, as you continue to listen to various forms of music, consider whether what you are listening to advances a particular perspective on politics, power, sexuality, or relationships. What views about sexuality, race, class, ethnicity, and age are these artists putting forward, and what might be the potential effects on their listeners? How do music videos serve to reinforce such perspectives and how might they undermine them? What stories and narratives about American culture do these images promote?

FILMS

SUSAN PELL

"Anxiously Entering into the 21st Century: Watching for Changing Masculinities in Film"

Susan Pell is currently working on her Ph.D. at Simon Fraser University in British Columbia, where she focuses on interdisciplinary studies in the Department of Humanities. Her research interests include issues of political participation, media representations, and public space. She is also a research assistant for SFU's Centre for Canadian Studies.

EXERCISING YOUR SKILLS

Before Reading

Pell writes about how constructions of masculinity in the movies are changing. While some writers may argue that in the late 1990s and 2000s we saw a return to traditional masculinities within television and film, Pell contends that masculinity in the movies is changing and become more "sensitive," usefully expanding the roles available to men in today's society. What are your thoughts about how masculinity operates in media images today? Think about your favorite contemporary television shows and movies. In what ways are the roles that men are being asked to adopt becoming broader? In what ways do we see a return to traditional conceptions of what Pell calls "hypermasculinity" as embodied by the John Wayne's and Dirty Harry's of yesteryear? In what ways do we see kinder and gentler, more fluid understandings of masculinity?

Representations of masculinity have been changing in popular culture. Men are less often seen today in the fashions of Dirty Harry or John Wayne. This traditional form of masculinity has been expanded upon as a response to the social, economic, and political changes that have accompanied social and activist movements since the '60s. Just as women are increasingly seen in the workplace, within films, the reverse is the true of men, who are now portrayed more often within the family. Consequently, the heterosexual couple has also increased in importance for this new type of man. Being the corporate climber or hero is no longer the sole desire. Instead, men are being responsible to those they love. The lesson learned is that money, alone, is not enough. A man still does need the affection of a woman.

Many of the films produced in Hollywood focus on this metamorphosis of the male lead. Susan Jeffords points out that in films, "a changed image of U.S. masculinity is being presented, an image that suggests that the hard-bodied male action heroes of the eighties have given way to a 'kinder, gentler' U.S. manhood, one that is sensitive, generous, caring, and perhaps most importantly, capable of change" (197). These new men are being changed through romance and the desire for committed relationships. There is a new image of men wanting intimacy and love that had previously only been seen as a desirable virtue for women. Television characters, such as Ross from *Friends*, have shown audiences that men too want to be loved unconditionally and that the women in their lives do take priority.

This is especially seen in film. Men have been increasingly shown as needing to overcome obstacles and transform themselves in order to obtain romance and love. These men are no longer able to get women solely with their brawn, but instead must embrace their more sensitive and nurturing side. As Jeffords claims, "Many nineties Hollywood men get doors slammed in their faces, or they are forced to stand patiently outside them while the women inside decide whether to see them or not" (198). She continues to assert that, "in these films, families provide both the motivation for and the resolution of changing masculine heroisms. . . . Retroactively, the men of the eighties are being given feelings, feelings that were, presumably, hidden behind their confrontational violence" (200). Male characters in the early nineties had to divorce their form of masculinity from the violence and aggression of their eighties counterparts.

In late nineties films, there [was] more of an emphasis on healing the emotional scares of the past and of the psyche. Being able to heal oneself emotionally [is] a response to the altered roles of men in North American society. The economy of the late nineties hit white men particularly hard. As blue-collar jobs disappeared, what once seemed like a concrete livelihood gave way to a fluid job market. Being a group that was traditionally dominant, the new economy became seemingly indifferent to past privileges and weeded out those who were incapable of flexibility. These modifications have necessitated an expansion of the definition of masculinity. As Jeffords suggests, "These new transformations happen only to men. More specifically, heterosexual white men, the men whose profit from traditional masculinities seems most threatened by the changing economic and social marketplace that typifies U.S. culture of the nineties" (205). Flexibility and cooperation have become established and inescapable. The lone and rigid individual was no longer able to survive and thrive in the nineties economy.

The nineties were also a time when it became increasingly acceptable to "pop a pill" when life was seen as overwhelming. Depression and anxiety became common ailments, whose mention no longer caused a stir. As a result, the heroes of the late nineties, in particular, needed to be able to fight their own inner demons, not solely external ones. These new men battled through their depression and neuroticisms, instead of alien invaders or communists—not alone, but with assistance. They sought the help of male friends or an older male mentor. Men were working together to heal themselves and these forms of relationships became central in their lives. However, to ward off any allusions to homosexuality, changes that occurred [often] actualized a romantic relationship with a woman.

Two films that stand out as examples of men trying to change their emotional patterns and form new committed relationships are *As Good As It Gets* (Tri-Star Pictures, 1997) and *Good Will Hunting* (Miramax, 1997). Both lead characters, Melvin and Will respectively, have to confront their pasts in order to progress and change. A woman is the catalyst that leads both characters to seek this help. However, while both of these films reflect an expanded role of masculinity, neither questions the privilege that continues to be structurally allotted to men.

Healing Masculinity: Two Cases

In *As Good As It Gets*, writer Melvin Udall (Jack Nicholson) has obsessive/compulsive disorder. In the beginning of the film, he must closely follow a set routine in order to survive the day. Nothing can vary for him. He embodies the old, static form of masculinity with no concept of flexibility. He also has no close human relationships, nor does he want any. The lack of relationships allows Melvin to remain fixed and unresponsive to changes occurring outside of him.

Inescapable social interaction, though, forces Melvin to alter his daily patterns. After his next-door neighbor, Simon (Greg Kinnear), is badly beaten and robbed, Melvin is coerced into looking after Verdell, his dog. Verdell is the first being ever to be in Melvin's apartment. Verdell imposes change into Melvin's routine. At the same time, Carol Connelly (Helen Hunt), the waitress who has always served Melvin his breakfast, begins to miss work because of her son's illness. These two events [create] disruption and chaos in Melvin's life. He can no longer hide in his secluded and self-centered world. Verdell metaphorically opens up Melvin and provides the catalyst for him to form relations with Carol and Simon.

Slowly, Melvin begins to look to others for support. He is willing to open himself to Simon, who is gay, when before he only verbally abused him. Melvin even seeks help from his former psychiatrist. However, even though Melvin is developing relationships, he still lacks proper social skills and etiquette. His self-absorption leads to distant and retarded relationships. Melvin's doctor points out to Melvin that he has no interest in changes taking place within others; it is only himself about which he is concerned. However, in acknowledging his desire for relationships with others, Melvin also begins to transform his actions towards them. As a result, these changes of pattern [encourage] Melvin to extend his financial stability to Carol. He sets up a permanent doctor to assist in the treatment of her son's illness. Upon helping Carol, Melvin is subsequently helping himself. He is able to start giving to others, and they will reciprocate.

Further patterns are broken in Melvin's life and all contribute to his metamorphosis. While at first Melvin is an unsympathetic character, the audience begins to relate to his social awkwardness. The inappropriate comments that Melvin makes make him appear flustered or awkward, but not necessarily cruel. He also begins to take medication to assist him in treating his obsessive-compulsive disorder. His willingness to change and the desire to heal himself leads Melvin to his ultimate goal of "getting the girl." Carol, who is initially hostile and cold, begins to view Melvin as a kind, and even sexy, man. Melvin has, in the course of the story, been transformed into a compassionate and generous man.

Initial comments that were heard from Melvin, such as "I think of a man and take away reason and accountability" (in response to how he creates such believable female characters in his writing) and "No need to stop being a lady, you'll be back on your knees in no time" (commenting on Simon's depression), have morphed into statements like, "You make me want to be a better man" (said to Carol). People now see Melvin's insides, his internal goodness, and respond to his vulnerability. Simon tells Melvin, "You overwhelm me," and Carol relates, "extraordinary kindness did take place."

Contrary to Jeffords' assertions that, "[Nineties men] are not called upon to repair the damage they've done. . . . They have only to become *aware, of* themselves and their needs to change" (204), Melvin makes an effort to rectify his past actions. He was the only person to come to the aid of Simon when he lost everything and he helped to heal Carol's son. Melvin was punished, through his disrupted patterns, and he repented through amendments to those he hurt the most.

Similar to *As Good As It Gets*, *Good Will Hunting* focuses on the emotional journey into new masculinity, through the life of a young mathematical genius, Will Hunting (Matt Damon). Will is from the working class area of South Boston. He suffered parental abandonment and a cruel upbringing within abusive foster homes, yet he has a close-knit group of male friends. Will also has a long history of violence. In one of the opening scenes of the film, Will and his friends initiate a fight with a person who had beaten him in kindergarten. This act places him in court facing a jail sentence. Around the same time, however, Will was also discovered solving an advanced mathematical theorem at MIT. Will's exceptional brilliance keeps him out of jail. However, this time it is under the supervision of Professor Lambough (Stellan Skarsgård), with whom Will is required to meet regularly to work on math problems and theories. As well, Will has to have psychological therapy.

A dominant theme in *Good Will Hunting* is Will's fragmented identity. He is unwilling to reveal himself in totality to anyone. Instead, he hides his intellectual abilities and also his inner vulnerabilities. While the math is easy for Will, he is resistant and manipulative within therapy. He puts up walls and toys with therapists. Will's poor attitude finally leads him to the only therapist who is willing to continuously see him, Sean (Robin Williams).

Sean was the university roommate of Professor Lambough, whom Will is working with on mathematics, and has a background similar to Will's, as he is also from South Boston. A mentorship becomes established between Sean and Will. Though Will is initially defensive towards the therapy, they form an intimate relationship. In fact, the problems Will and Sean personally face parallel each other. They are both scared of intimacy, loss and new experiences: Sean because of the death of his wife, and Will because of his fear of losing control.

It is Will's involvement with a woman, however, that forces him to confront his past. Skylar (Minnie Driver) and Will meet at a Harvard bar. Will impresses her with his intelligence and lack of pretension. Skylar is a smart and engaging woman, unlike the previous women in Will's life. He does not hide his brilliance from her, yet he is unable to reveal his past. Will lies about his family, saying he has twelve older brothers and strong familial relations. Will is incapable of giving himself fully to Skylar. He is frightened that she too would leave him if she were to learn the truth of his upbringing. Nevertheless, their relationship continues to grow and develop. A barrier is created when Skylar has to leave for California. She wants Will to go with her, yet he feels it will be a mistake and that she will regret the offer. They fight and Will unconsciously reveals his past experiences with abuse and rushes away from her sympathy.

The relationship's breakup, however, is a source of regret and an impetus for Will to emotionally change. Will does not want to be alone. Through Sean's help he comes to terms with his fears of commitment and intimacy. [By] challenging Will, Sean makes him confront his imperfections. Sean forces Will to face his fears and enter the unknown. Through Sean's guidance and support Will is able to accept his intellectual talents and aspire to fulfill his potential. More importantly, though, Will is able to leave his friends and the stability and certainty of his life to chase after Skylar in California.

Other men in Will's life similarly encourage him to aspire for change. His best friend, Chuckie (Ben Affleck), wants nothing more for Will than to see him use his abilities to leave the blue-collar existence that he cannot. Chuckie tells Will that it is shameful for him to be a demolitioner when he has the intellectual capabilities to do something that is more satisfying than manual labor. He tells Will that he is sitting on a winning lottery ticket and it will be an insult to him if he does not cash it in. Chuckie ultimately gives Will the incentive and excuse to leave Boston.

Because of the different men in Will's life he is able to embrace his genius and confront his vulnerability. Skylar was his motivation to change and through relationships with men he is given the courage to do it. Like Melvin, Will must face his fears in order to create and sustain a relationship with a woman. Likewise, Will too must pay for his past violence and defensiveness. He has to expose his abilities and weaknesses to avoid prison. Similarly, Will is thrown into new experiences and challenges, which he fears more than anything.

Will's and Melvin's personal developments and alterations, however, conform to Jeffords' conclusion that nineties men's transformations are limited. She states that, "Their histories as men are limited to their personal sufferings at the hands of traditional codes of masculinity, and their messages of change remain at the level of individualized experience within the interpersonal realm" (207). Though Melvin must rectify past actions, he does not confront the social structures that have privileged him, such as class, race and gender. Will, on the other hand, does challenge class issues and the authority that education affords people. Though he is aware of inequalities, Will does not systematically confront class discrimination. Criticism of class is less of a focus in the film once Will is integrated into the work of university professors. Will becomes incorporated within the institution and is only able to leave the blue-collar world because of his individual gift of genius.

Further, these films correspond to Jeffords's observations that the future of masculine transformations is left vague. Though both Will and Melvin change, the film's endings are ambiguous [as to whether] these transformations are permanent. Near the conclusion of *As Good As It Gets*, Carol still is unable to tell if Melvin is being "cute" or "crazy." Though they begin a romantic relationship, it is new and uncertain. Melvin states that the pills he is taking gradually build in their effectiveness, yet it is unknown if he will be permanently transformed. *Good Will Hunting* ends with Will driving alone to California to reconcile the relationship with Skylar. The audience never finds out what happens, though it is assumed that the two will end up together. Similarly, it is unknown if Will will continue to confront his past or whether he will again be violent.

Overall, *As Good As It Gets* and *Good Will Hunting* coincide with Jeffords' findings about early nineties men. Will and Melvin both undergo changes in order to sustain a romantic relationship with a woman. These transformations are at a personal level and do not challenge social, economic and political inequalities. Jeffords quotes Donna Haraway's opinion that, "the image of the sensitive man calls up, for me, the male person who, while enjoying the position of unbelievable privilege, also has the privilege of gentleness" (pp. 206–207). Men in the late nineties, as seen in these films, continue to parallel the conclusions Jeffords made in the early nineties. While representations of masculinity have expanded to include men who are sensitive and want to heal emotionally, the systematic privilege that men have is left unaddressed.

Masculinity into a New Century

While this essay is intended to understand the representations of masculinity in the late nineties, it is important to speculate how films in the early 2000s have challenged or continued this pattern. Has the image of the sensitive man changed? Have films moved beyond the personal to begin to address systematic male privilege? Though it is not possible to make any conclusive statements about overall representations of masculinity in the new century, it can be proposed that there is at least some continuity in Jeffords's claim regarding a "'kinder, gentler' U.S. manhood, one that is sensitive, generous, caring, and perhaps most importantly, capable of change" (197). However, the representations of masculinity where "[Nineties men] are not called upon to repair the damage they've done. . . . They have only to become *aware, of* themselves and their needs to change" (204) also appears to be continuing. In order to explore these two veins of masculinity, a few comments will be offered regarding the film, *Magnolia* (1999).

Magnolia is richly layered and complex, with multiple storylines being woven together throughout the course of the film. The dominant theme regarding masculinity, however, is much simpler: the way in which masculinity has been acted out needs to be rethought. Two of the male characters will be considered briefly: Frank T. J. Mackey (Tom Cruise)[1] and his dying father Earl Partridge (Jason Robards). Within these two characters, masculinity is seen as problematic; yet, the conclusion about men's roles in society continues to be ambiguous.

The character of Frank Mackey can be seen as a response to the "new" sensitive man. Instead of embracing his emotions, being flexible, and receptive to women, he takes the opposite approach. Frank holds women in contempt and sees them as the source of men's woes. Accordingly, Frank, a well-known motivational speaker and author of a self-help book for men, makes the message clear, as he booms, "tame the pussy, love the cock." Frank's estranged father, Earl, is no better in his treatment of women. On his deathbed, Earl confesses the pain that he caused his family through his continuous adultery and his absence while his wife died of cancer. From this statement, it can be inferred that he saw women as subordinate to men and primarily as sexual objects.

The film, however, suggests that these men are deeply troubled, much of which stems from their masculinity. Earl is deeply distressed by what he has done (and has not done) to his family. In order to make amends, Earl wants to see his son before he dies and Frank reluctantly comes to his side. While Earl is passing in and out of consciousness, Frank expresses his hatred for his father. Frank asserts that Earl does not deserve his sympathy since he had abandoned his family, which left him responsible for the care of his mother as she died. Frank was not going to cry for him. But he does. Frank breaks down and weeps over the pain and suffering that he has lived with due to the lack of caring and responsibility of his father. Both of these men, therefore, are faced with the problems of their masculinity—Earl with the pain he has caused his family and Frank in the repression of this pain.

While the film does challenge the emotional feasibility of traditional masculinity as these two men represent it, *Magnolia* does not question the privilege that is afforded socially through it. Both of these men can be seen as successes in the careers they have chosen and neither are held responsible to those whom they have hurt. Frank is not made accountable nor forced to apologize to the women and men he hurts in propagating a sexist form of masculinity. Earl is not even cognizant of his son's complaints. Frank and Earl are thus seen as hurtful and hurting, but are not forced to face those people they have offended or address the privilege that has enabled them to be irresponsible to others.

Earl's dying words, therefore, sum up the lesson that is learned in a life led according to the dictates of traditional masculinity, regret. He says, "I wanted to be a man and I didn't want her to be a woman . . . so stupid that fucking mind. . . . The two I had and I lost, this is the regret that you make." Out of this statement it becomes apparent that mistakes are made in life, that regret is inevitable. This is a limited lesson though. Expanding mascu-

---

[1]Tom Cruise was nominated for the Best Supporting Actor at the 2000 Academy Awards for this role.

linity is confined to simply being aware of one's personal faults. By confessing "regret," the need to be a different type of man is nullified, as altering masculinity is presented as [an] individualized [process,] and not requiring examination of systematic male privilege. So, while these characters are able to open themselves to their failures and faults, they are not held accountable for their actions, not given the opportunity to rectify them, and do not have to entertain political and social change that would actually promote better ways to be a man.

Representations of masculinity in the new century will most likely continue in a similar pattern as seen in these three films. *Magnolia*, along with *Good Will Hunting* and *As Good As It Gets*, all support Jeffords' statements of early nineties cinematic portrayals of masculinity. [These representations] propose a path that probes the problems of traditional male roles, yet they offer no way to change such roles. Consequently, the degree to which these films move past the personal to criticisms of societal power afforded to these types of masculinity is debatable. Without the questioning of privilege that traditional masculinity holds, the ability to offer a diversity of representations will continue to be restricted, and the result will be marginalization for those who depict a wider range of masculine identities in film and in the real world.

Bibliography

"*As Good As It Gets.*" James L. Brooks. TriStar Pictures, 1997.

"*Good Will Hunting.*" Gus Van Sant. Miramax Films, 1997.

"*Magnolia.*" Paul Thomas Anderson. New Line Cinema, 1999.

Jeffords, Susan. "The Big Switch: Hollywood Masculinity in the 90s." *Film Theory Goes to the Movies*. Eds. J. Collins, H. Radner, and A.P. Collins. Routledge, 1993: 196–208.

After Reading

Critical Perspective

1. What are your general thoughts and reactions to this essay? How did it make you feel and why?

Rhetoric and Argument

2. Discuss Pell's rhetorical choices in her text—use of audience, purpose, ethos, pathos, logos, intertextuality, context, and constraints. Is Pell's text as rhetorically effective as it could be? Try to provide some suggestions for rhetorical choices she might have made that could have made her text more persuasive.

3. Pell argues that we see images of "the new man" on television but that we have seen even more in film. She points to the example of Ross from *Friends* as a man who "wants intimacy and love." Are there other visible characters on contemporary television that function in similar ways? Provide evidence from television shows as well as quotes from the essay to support your thoughts.

4. Pell contends that these newly emerging understandings of masculinity are occurring because of critical changes in American culture. What are these changes? In

the end, what is Pell claiming about them? Do you find her accounts persuasive? Why or why not?

5. Pell presents a close reading of three films as evidence for her claims. How would you describe the genre of these films? Are the primary viewers men or women, do you think? How might audience factor into the emergence of new masculinities in the media as well as how we analyze them?

6. Do you find Pell's evidence convincing? Are there any problematic assumptions or logical fallacies in her text? Provide other textual examples from the films that might further support Pell's assertions. In addition, offer specific examples that you think might pose a challenge to Pell's claims.

Analysis

7. Pell indicates that Melvin in *As Good As It Gets* does less to challenge social structures than Will does in *Good Will Hunting*. However, Pell suggests that both characters undergo transformations only at a "personal level" and do not challenge existing social relations. In a short argumentative essay address the following questions: Do you agree with Pell's assessment of these two films? Why or why not? Try to provide textual evidence from these films to back up your views as well as consult library and Internet sources.

Taking Action

As a class, select several recent films. Watch them and look specifically for examples of the different kinds of masculinities that Pell outlines. Take detailed notes about what you notice. You may also want to gather relevant library and Internet sources about the films as well.

Then, in a large class discussion, consider the following issues: How do masculinities operate in these films? Are there any new versions of masculinity at work? If yes, do you think that such different or new versions of masculinity offer significant challenges to the personae that men in American culture were forced to adopt in the past? How so? How might these changes or lack of changes impact today's male viewers? How do you think new gender roles might be offered to men in film, ones that are less limited and constraining? What sorts of recent examples of masculinities in film could you point to that resist traditional "male" behaviors and attitudes?

BRIAN L. OTT AND ERIC AOKI

"The Colonization and Commodification of Racial Identities: Stereotyping and Exoticizing Cultural Difference in *Rush Hour*"

Brian L. Ott (Ph.D., Pennsylvania State University) and Eric Aoki (Ph.D., University of Washington) are Associate Professors in the Department of Speech Communication at Colorado State University. Ott's scholarship has appeared in journals such as Critical Studies, Cultural Studies = Critical Methodologies, The Journal of Popular

Culture, Rhetoric and Public Affairs, *and* Women's Studies in Communication. *His book,*
The Small Screen: How Television Equips Us to Live in the Information Age, *is forthcoming from Blackwell. Aoki's scholarship has appeared in the* Western Journal of Communication, the Journal of GLBT Family Studies, Women's Studies in Communication, *and* The Howard Journal of Communications. *He serves on the President's Commission for Gender Equity, the University Commission on Campus Climate, and as the Media Reviews for the* Journal of GLBT Family Studies.

EXERCISING YOUR SKILLS

Before Reading

Ott and Aoki expose some key problems concerning how people of color are depicted in film. Think about representations of men who are Native American, Asian American, African American, Latino, or from other minority groups in television, film, advertising, or other cultural texts. Consider how these men and their masculine identities are represented. Which stereotypes about their masculinity are challenged in these cultural texts and which ones are supported? Are there any particular television shows, films, or advertising campaigns that you believe provide empowering representations of minority masculinities? If yes, what are they and how do they function?

During the 1990s, the "politics of race" in the United States became increasingly visible and unsettling. One key event shaping this new political landscape was a short home video, whose startling images of White LAPD officers beating Black motorist Rodney King played again and again on the evening news. Another key, if less public, factor in the racial politics of the 90s was the overwhelming evidence in support of George Gerbner's "symbolic annihilation" hypothesis, which held that racial minorities were grossly and consistently under-represented in mainstream U.S. media. Although seemingly disparate, both events involve the complex intersection of race, violence, and representation. While the Rodney King video highlighted the connection between institutional racism (in the LAPD) and *physical* violence, media research on exclusionary casting practices highlighted the connection between institutional racism (in Hollywood) and *symbolic* violence. Thus, both events functioned to significantly undercut the nation's ability to maintain a national image of racial justice, harmony, and equality.

Since, as English Professor David Blakesley (2003) notes, "Hollywood films reflect their times . . . functioning as both symptom and (proposed) cure [for social and public anxieties]" (p. 125), we read Brett Ratner's film, *Rush Hour* (1998), near the close of the millennium as an attempt both to refurbish the nation's tarnished image regarding race and as an articulation of deep-seated racial ideologies. The film, after all, is set in Los Angeles and its heroes are Black LAPD detective James Carter (Chris Tucker) and Hong Kong Inspector Lee (Jackie Chan). That *Rush Hour* is the first big-budget, mainstream Hollywood film in the buddy-cop/action-comedy genre to feature non-White actors in both leading protagonist roles suggests that it attempts to "repair" the national image regarding race through a racial "(re)pairing" of the main characters. Although we regard the film's multiracial, multinational cast to be a positive and progressive step in the race-related representational practices of the media, we contend that *Rush Hour* ultimately colonizes and commodifies the central characters' racial identities through the stereotyping and exoticizing of cultural difference. But before turning to our analysis of this process, we offer a brief synopsis of the plot.

The film *Rush Hour* opens in Hong Kong on the last day before the end of British colonial rule, where Inspector Lee (Jackie Chan) has just single-handedly broken up a smuggling ring. But the ring's mastermind, Juntao (Tom Wilkinson), narrowly escapes to the United States and kidnaps Soo Yung (Julia Hsu)—the young daughter of the Chinese consul. As the FBI begins investigating the kidnapping and $50 million ransom request, Consul Han (Tzi Ma) insists that his close family friend, Inspector Lee, be brought from Hong Kong to assist with the investigation. The territorial and xenophobic FBI agents are opposed to any outside help and privately devise a plan to distract Lee from the investigation upon his arrival in Los Angeles. The plan involves using local troublemaker and LAPD detective James Carter (Chris Tucker) as an unwitting "baby-sitter" for Inspector Lee. As both Carter and Lee prefer to work alone, there is tension (mostly comic) in their relationship from the outset. In the tradition of the buddy-cop genre, however, the two ultimately recognize that if they combine their talents and resources, then they can rescue the consul's daughter.

Stereotyping Cultural Difference

In this portion of the essay, we examine how the film perpetuates a series of damaging racial *stereotypes*, or misleading and reductionistic representations of a cultural group. It is vital that media consumers and critics interrogate stereotypes because they imply value judgments about an entire cultural group and thus function to shape attitudes and behaviors toward that group (Casas & Dixon, 2003). In today's media saturated environment, the marketing strategy for nearly all big-budget Hollywood films involves a tag line—a short, memorable phrase that is endlessly repeated on movie posters and in TV commercials. In the case of *Rush Hour*, the tag line—"The fastest hands in the East meet the biggest mouth in the West"—embodies the film's two central stereotypes.

The phrase, "The fastest hands in the East," immediately marks the identity of Jackie Chan's character as "foreign" (from the East) and reduces that foreign identity to the crude stereotype of the martial arts master. In Chan's first appearance in the film, he is moving "ninja-like," veiled in darkness, through a ship docked in a Hong Kong port, silently but effectively incapacitating everyone aboard. The scene, which draws on a long cinematic tradition of representing "Asian" characters as martial arts experts who can successfully defeat multiple opponents at once, marks Lee's "Eastern" fighting abilities as the defining element of his identity. As the narrative unfolds, this core identity is subsequently layered with a series of other racial stereotypes. Lee is further constructed, for instance, as the silent and reserved Asian. For nearly the first third of the film, Chan's character has almost no dialogue and when he first meets and interacts with Tucker's character, he does not speak, leading Carter to incorrectly conclude that Lee cannot speak English:

CARTER: Please tell me you speak English. (in a slow and exaggerated tone) I'm Detective Carter. Do you speaka any English? Do you understan the words that are comin' outta my mouf? (Lee just smiles) I cannot believe this shit! First, I get a bullshit assignment. Now, Mr. Ricearoni don't even speak 'merican.

That Lee *can* speak English but *chooses* not to, reinforces the stereotype of Asians as silent and reserved, and exaggerates the difference between he and Carter, who as we demonstrate shortly is stereotyped as the loud, obnoxious, overbearing Black man. Chan's character also reaffirms the common image of the Asian man as deeply honorable—a defender of tradition. At one point in the story, for example, Lee tells Carter, "You are devoted only to yourself. You're a shame of being a police officer. You dishonor your father's name." This statement, like so many in the film, functions simultaneously to highlight the cultural differences between the two characters and to reduce their identities to opposing stereotypes. Finally, Lee is (re)presented as intensely asexual in contrast to the hypersexual Carter, who sexually harasses virtually every female in the film. Lee is portrayed without sexual desire; his actions being defined, instead, entirely in terms of a sense of duty and honor.

In stark contrast to Lee, Carter is, as the film's tag line suggests, "the biggest mouth in the West." The stereotypical construction of Detective Carter as an obnoxious, loudmouth, jive-talking Black man occurs in Tucker's first screen appearance. He enters the frame driving a shiny black Corvette convertible, cutting erratically across four lanes of traffic, and shouting insults at other drivers. In this scene, Carter is working undercover to bust an illegal explosives dealer in Los Angeles. His behavior, which is hypercoded as wild and unpredictable, results in two LAPD police officers being shot and a car with C4 in its trunk exploding on a busy LA boulevard. In response to the explosion, Carter begins breakdancing and striking poses in the street as hip-hop music plays in the background. The importance of the scene lies in the way it associates Carter's obnoxious and unpredictable behavior with violence and danger, suggesting in effect that he is violent and dangerous. In Carter's second screen appearance, he has returned to LAPD headquarters, where he is dramatically relaying the events of the bust and exaggerating and bragging about his role in it. Both scenes indicate Carter is far more concerned with image and appearance than, for instance, duty and honor. What Carter brings to the buddy-cop pairing, then, is his fast-talking skills. Later in the film, he uses these "skills" in an attempt to arrange a meeting with the elusive Mr. Juntao at a Chinese restaurant:

WAITRESS: [Table] For one?

CARTER: No, for two. I'm here for a meeting with Mr. Juntao.

WAITRESS: I'm sorry I do not know Mr. Juntao.

CARTER: Look, maybe you don't understand. I'm Mr. Juntao's lawyer, legal advisor. He got into some shit again and he told me to come down here and I'm a very busy man, ain't got time to be down here this late but I'm down here. My wife want me to come home, my baby is shittin' all over the house, he needs diapers. Would you please go get Mr. Juntao?

The capacity of virtually every other character in the film to "see-through" Carter's fast-talking jive constructs him as a relatively ineffectual (i.e., powerless) figure and feminizes him in relationship to Lee, who must repeatedly use his (masculine) fighting skills to rescue Carter.

At the same time, the film is careful not to overtly homoeroticize Carter and Lee's relationship, and thus, Carter is both hyper- and hetero-sexualized in relation to the film's female characters. Perpetuating the "Black-buck" stereotype, Carter responds to a female officer's criticism of his unpredictable behavior with the remark, "First of all, if you want to go out on a date with me, you gonna have to wait on the list like every other woman." As bell hooks (2004) has noted,

> *Undoubtedly, sexuality has been the site of many a black male's fall from grace. Irrespective of class, status, income, or level of education, for many black men sexuality remains the place where dysfunctional behavior first rears its head. This is in part because of the convergence of racist sexist thinking about the black body, which has always projected onto the black body a hypersexuality. (p. 67)*

The characterizations of both Lee and Carter, then, would suggest that *Rush Hour*'s racial re-pairing of the buddy-cop formula relies upon and reproduces a long history of racial and ethnic stereotypes.

Exoticizing Cultural Difference

In addition to stereotyping, we argue that *Rush Hour* also engages in a practice of exoticizing cultural difference. Whereas stereotypes reduce racial identities to flat, one-dimensional (and often derogatory) caricatures, *exoticism* treats cultural difference as stimulating or exciting, and thereby positions it as an "object" of voyeuristic intrigue and fascination (Ott & Aoki, 2004, pp. 155–157). To view someone voyeuristically is to exercise power over him/her through surveillance. It is to transform a some*one* into a some*thing* and to dominate that object through looking, since the looked-at object cannot return the gaze, and indeed, does not even know it is the object of a dominating gaze. In the film *Rush Hour*, we suggest that Chan and Tucker's racial identities are consistently constructed as the "exotic Other," meaning they are made to appear "foreign" and "alien" (Berger, 2005, p. 121). But foreign and alien from what? Their racial identities are "exotic" *only* when viewed from a White European-centered perspective, which the film silently and unreflectively privileges. To illustrate how *Rush Hour* does this, we turn again to the characters of Lee and Carter.

Throughout the film, the "Orient" is treated both visually and narratively as an object of intrigue and fascination. From the film's opening scene in Hong Kong to the search for Soo Yung in the Chinatown district of LA, the film works to heighten viewers's fascination with the character of Lee by associating him with an exotic and distant world. This world is constructed as culturally "different" (from European culture) on a number of key levels, ranging from language and music to tradition and art. In the Hong Kong scene, for instance, the characters are speaking Chinese, as the underlying soundtrack furnishes Asian-sounding music complete with stereotypical gong riffs. What is interesting about this and similar scenes is the symbolic function performed by the language and the music. That English is one of two official languages in Hong Kong, a mandatory subject in government-run schools, used widely in public domains such as business, government, and law, and included on the majority of signs in the city, suggests that the use of Chinese in the scene functions as more than *merely* an appeal to authenticity. It works to code Lee, who audiences later learn speaks English, as first and foremost a foreigner. Similarly, the overly traditional Asian-sounding music appeals to a popular image of the Orient as ancient and mystical—a land and people steeped in strange, but wondrous traditions. The consistent portrayal of the Orient as an ancient and mysterious land *across* U.S. media functions both to secure it in the past and to primitivize it in relation to the "modern" and "civilized" West. Viewers are invited, then, to see Lee, at least in part, as a cultural curiosity, as an ultimately unknowable object. As Lee himself tells Carter at one point, "Leave me alone. A man like you could never understand [me]." Presumably, the audience can never fully understand Lee either, so instead it adopts a voyeuristic gaze.

Carter, like Lee, is also constructed in the film as an object of cultural fascination. But in the case of Carter, difference is structured around a Black/White dualism as opposed to an East/West dualism. As with Lee, language is central to how Carter is represented as culturally exotic. Over the course of the film, Tucker speaks in an exaggerated Ebonics stereotype that is portrayed as more difficult to understand than Chan (whose is a non-native English speaker). So, when Carter asks Lee, "Do you understan the words that are comin' outta my mouf," early in the narrative, the audience is invited to laugh at the irony of the question—at the fact that Carter's English is more "different" (from "standard" English) than is Lee's. Music is also a site for the structuring of Carter's cultural difference. Shortly after Carter and Lee team-up, the pair has the following interchange over music in Carter's car:

LEE: (changing the radio station) Ah! Beach Boys!

CARTER: Oh, hell no! You didn't just touch my goddam radio! (tuning the radio back to a hip hop station)

LEE: [But] The Beach Boys are great American music.

CARTER: The Beach Boys gonna get you a great ass whuppin'. Don't you ever touch a Black man's radio, boy! You can do that in China, but you can get your ass killed out here, man!

In addition to perpetuating the stereotype of the quick to anger (and potentially violent) Black man, the scene contrasts The Beach Boys, which are represented as "great American music" generally, with an unidentified (nameless) hip-hop artist, who is coded as (sub)culturally specific. Imagine how the message of this scene would have been altered, for instance, had Lee changed the station *from* The Beach Boys *to* a prominent hip-hop artist and been similarly scolded. It would be more difficult, then, for Carter's musical preferences to mark him as culturally different. But the exaggeration of his cultural difference (from the invisible norm of Whiteness) is precisely how the film creates and encourages the audience's fascination with him. Viewers are invited to stare in amazement at Tucker's character because he looks, sounds, and behaves so "different." The net effect of the visual and narrative exoticizing of Lee and Carter's racial identities is objectification and the pleasure that comes with consumption.

Colonization and Commodification

To *colonize* something is to invade it and to take control of it. To *commodify* something is to package it for easy and palatable consumption. How, then, do these concepts relate to Brett Ratner's 1998 film *Rush Hour*? In the introduction to this essay, we suggested that this film emerged at a particularly challenging and racially charged moment in U.S. history. Due in large part to the Rodney King video (not to mention the handling of evidence in the O.J. Simpson case), the image of the LAPD was in need of serious repair—a point obviously not lost on the film's writers, who have Carter telling Lee at one point, "This is the LAPD. We're the most hated cops in all the free world. My own mama's ashamed of me. She tells everybody I'm a drug dealer." Like the LAPD, Hollywood also came under heavy attack during the nineties for its exclusionary casting practices and subsequent dramatic under-representation of racial minorities. On the surface, *Rush Hour* responds to both of these concerns with its racial (re)pairing of the central characters. Viewers encounter a film that is both racially diverse and one in which much of the heroism centers on a Black LAPD detective. But as we have shown, the film's racial diversity is made safe, comfortable, and unthreatening by stereotyping and exoticizing cultural difference.

By treating Chan and Tucker's characters as one-dimensional and exotic, the film colonizes their racial identities. It invades the very categories of "race," takes them over, and defines "Asianness" and "Blackness" from an invisible European/White perspective. But it also does much more. The film invites audiences to laugh at cultural differences in an unreflective manner—a point echoed by columnist Jamie Malanowski (2002) in the *New York Times*. In *Rush Hour*, not only do Lee and Carter *embody* racial stereotypes, they uncritically treat each other and the secondary characters *as* racial stereotypes. While ordering Chinese food, for example, Carter asks the restaurant attendant, "Damn, Chin, this some greasy shit. You ain't got no better food, like some chicken wings, some baby back ribs, some fries or something?" to which the attendant responds, "Chinese food, no soul food here!" In another scene, Carter informs one of the Asian characters, "I've been lookin' for your sweet and sour chicken ass." Lee, like Carter, also makes numerous racially charged statements, such as when he asks a bartender, "Whassup, my nigga?" In these and countless other scenes, racial difference is played for comic effect. So, rather than teaching audiences about how racial difference is culturally constructed and the ways it is implicated in relationships of power, the film de-politicizes racial difference—making it one big, long cinematic joke. In this way, *Rush Hour* transforms racial difference into a commodity that promises viewer pleasure in its consumption. Far from healing the deep racial wounds that surfaced in the 1990s, the film masks them behind a façade of multiculturalism.

The ongoing danger of the representational practices described in this essay could not have more timely implications than in the post-9/11 political landscape of the twenty-first century, for "the discourse of Orientalism persists into the present, particularly in the West's relationship with 'Islam'" (Ashcroft, Griffiths, & Tiffin, 2001, p. 168). Today, the "Middle East" rather than the "East" supplies the principal geographic region for constructing cultural difference in a manner that affirms the "rightness" of U.S. national identity, and "Middle Easterners" are the "foreigners" upon which much of the West projects racial stereotypes of violence, primitiveness, and terrorism. Such stereotyping has led not simply to prejudice and discrimination, but has fundamentally shaped national foreign policy, justifying everything from war to occupation. It is our hope, therefore, that our analysis of the film *Rush Hour* serves not only as a model for understanding the "politics of race" nationally in the 1990s, but also for critically viewing the "politics of race" globally in the present.

References

Ashcroft, B., Griffiths, G., & Tiffin, H. (2001). *Post-colonial studies: The key concepts* (2nd ed.). New York: Routledge.

Berger, A. (2005). *Media analysis techniques* (3rd ed.). Thousand Oaks, CA: Sage Publications.

Blakesley, D. (Ed.). (2003). *The terministic screen: Rhetorical perspectives on film.* Carbondale, IL: Southern Illinois University Press.

Casas, M., & Dixon, T. (2003). The impact of stereotypical and counter-stereotypical news on viewer perceptions of Blacks and Latinos: An exploratory study. In A. Valdivia (Ed.), *A companion to media studies* (pp. 480–492). Malden, MA: Blackwell Publishing.

hooks, b. (2004). *We real cool: Black men and masculinity*. New York: Routledge.

Malanowski, J. (2002, November 10). Colorblind buddies in black and white. *New York Times*. Late Edition. Section 2, p. 1.

Ott, B. L., & Aoki, E. (2004). Counter-imagination as interpretive practice: Futuristic fantasy and *The Fifth Element. Women's Studies in Communication, 27*(2), 149–176.

After Reading

Critical Perspective

1. Before you read this essay, did you ever think about this film (or others that may have emerged since) in terms of race and ethnicity issues? Explain why or why not. Drawing on your own experiences, detail explicitly why this may be the case.

Rhetoric and Argument

2. Do you find the way in which Aoki and Ott use rhetorical strategies helps or hinders their argument? What kinds of rhetorical choices—use of audience, purpose, ethos, pathos, logos, intertextuality, context, and constraints—does their text offer? Provide textual examples that support your position.

3. Where in their text do the writers place their main claim? Do you find the claim itself to be persuasive? Explain your perspectives. Describe how the structure of their argument supports their claim. Be specific in your use of examples.

4. Do you agree with Aoki and Ott's contention about this film (or other recent representations of Asian American and African American men in the media)? Do you think that their evidence adequately supports their claim? Why or why not? Consider whether there may be some contemporary examples of media representations that do not privilege a White European perspective.

5. Though Aoki and Ott are discussing complicated theoretical ideas about race, ethnicity, and masculinity, they choose to define their terms thoroughly and carefully. How does this impact the effectiveness of their argument?

Analysis

6. Like all writers, Aoki and Ott are open to countercharges by readers who oppose their views. Some might contend, for instance, that this film should be read only as a parody of the buddy-cop genre. Looked at in this view, the film might actually offer a challenge to racist stereotypes. In a short argumentative response, discuss whether this is indeed the case or not—whether you agree with the authors, take the opposition's perspective, or a combination of the two. As part of this exercise, be sure to consider how you might support either claim, what counterarguments you might need to refute, and how you would challenge them. Provide quotes from the text in addition to library and Internet sources to back up your ideas.

Taking Action

In a small group discuss other buddy-cop films from the 1970s to the present. Do you think that there have been any major changes in this genre and how it operates during this period? What racial, class, ethnic, and gender stereotypes have these sorts of films promoted in the past? What, if any, new understandings are being promoted now? How so? Consult library and Internet sources as needed. When you have considered these issues, share what you have discussed with the rest of the class.

MEREDITH A. LOVE

"Gazing Through Malkovich: Identity and Lesbian Desire in *Being John Malkovich*"

Meredith A. Love is a professor of English at Francis Marion University, in South Carolina, where she teaches first-year composition, advanced writing, composition theory, and business communication. She has written and published various essays about other issues in popular culture, including rape in daytime drama and the feminist 'zine culture. Love's most recent research centers on performance studies and the teaching of writing, focusing on the relationships between actors and orators, contemporary approaches to acting, and how students might benefit from thinking about their writing as performance.

EXERCISING YOUR SKILLS

Before Reading

Love writes about the ways in which gender representations of identity operate in film and how too often they are narrowly prescribed. While *Being John Malkovich* was an artsy, modestly budgeted film, over time it developed a large following. Watch the film and think about how gender roles work in the narrative. When people can inhabit another person's body, a number of questions are raised: What does it mean to be "female"? What does it mean to be "male"? How do we make sense of what is "masculine" and what is "feminine"? What might it mean to be female but inhabit a male body? Does this film play with gender stereotypes and try to dismantle them? Or, does it work to produce such stereotypes?

A film's title, trailers, posters, and all other modes of publicity work together to create what Stephen Heath calls the "narrative image" of a film (de Lauretis 225). While the title of Spike Jonze's 1999 film *Being John Malkovich* might suggest an autobiography of the great American stage and film actor John Malkovich (*Dangerous Liasons*, *In the Line of Fire*), the posters lead the potential viewer in an entirely different direction, away from the actor's life and towards larger questions of identity. Both posters use the tagline "Have you ever wanted to be someone else?" One poster features a theater full of people, all covering their faces with masks of John Malkovich's face. A second poster, featured on the cover for the video and DVD, uses the outline John Malkovich's head as a frame, and inside the frame John Cusack and Cameron Diaz are crouching on the floor of an office, looking into a small doorway, into the head of Malkovich and out at you. A barely visible Catherine Keener sits behind them in a chair, with her legs crossed, looking at the camera as if to say "Can you believe they are doing this?" Or maybe she's asking "Wanna give it a try?"

The box of the DVD and video edition features an extra line of text, reading "Have you ever wanted to be someone else? Now you can." This question and promise raise questions about the nature of identity itself: Can we choose our identities? If not, who chooses and controls our identities? Can we ever *be* someone else? How *are* we ourselves? While these promotional visuals lead the spectator to think about larger questions of identity, the film narrows our attention even further, drawing the spectator to inquire specifically about gender and sexual identity. In this movie where men become other men, women become men, and women desire women who become men, the characters Lotte and Maxine encourage the spectator to question traditional categories and consider the possibilities of gender and sexual fluidity.

Being John Malkovich is a movie about people who want to escape the identities conferred upon them on the basis of their class, sex, occupation, race, or sexual preference. When Craig (John Cusack) moves a file cabinet and haplessly discovers a portal into the head of John Malkovich, he shares the news with his coworker Maxine (Catherine Keener). Eager to please her, Craig goes into business with Maxine, placing an ad in the paper and offering people the chance to "be John Malkovich," for a price. Their partnership, and Craig's attempts to seduce Maxine, are complicated when Craig's wife Lotte (Cameron Diaz) goes through the portal and, as Malkovich, shares a romance with Maxine.

Lotte, played by a very glamed-down Cameron Diaz, assumes the identity of Malkovich to escape the limitations imposed on her as a woman. Lotte is usually shot in a dark, half-light, her silhouette recognizable only by her big, frizzy hair which usually hides her face. Her body is covered with many layers of clothing, and her *self* seems to be hidden as well. In fact, she seems fairly invisible to Craig who barely looks at her. Although she is the primary breadwinner for the household and the caregiver for Craig and their many pets, Lotte is virtually ignored. After Craig is assaulted in the street for performing near-pornographic puppet shows, Lotte takes him into her arms and cares for him. Later, we see her cradling their pet chimpanzee Elijah and asking Craig if he's thought anymore about their having a baby. He brushes her off with a comment about their economic instability, and the conversation is over.

But Lotte undergoes a surprising change after visiting the Malkovich body. Her reaction is shockingly different from what we might expect from this quiet, caring woman. Upon exiting Malkovich's head, she breathlessly exclaims, "Being inside did something to me. I knew who I was. Everything made sense . . . I was John-Fucking-Malkovich. Take me back, Craig!" The very next day Lotte tells Craig, "I think I'm a transsexual" and angrily warns him, "Don't stand in the way of my actualization as a man." Later, in a moment of anger, Lotte tells Craig to "Suck my dick!" It's pretty clear that Lotte identifies differently after being Malkovich. She is aware that she is a woman, yet she also claims the male sex. Craig also recognizes her as a man, as he confronts Lotte with her affair with Maxine, saying, "You stuck your dick in Maxine, Lotte." She is biologically marked "woman," and Lotte and the people around her see her and read her as a woman. But, after being Malkovich she speaks as though she is a man, she talks about having a penis, and Craig even acknowledges her possession of a penis.

During her second time in Malkovich we hear Lotte thinking/saying, "Strong. I want that voice." When she is in Malkovich she does have strength, and she *does* have a voice, unlike her female role as "Lotte Schwartz, wife of Craig Schwartz," a performance for which she doesn't garner much attention or respect. This seems reason enough to want to *be* someone else entirely. In fact, we sympathize with her desire so much that it's no surprise when Lotte tells Craig that she wants gender re-assignment surgery. Craig is (surprisingly) astute when he says to Lotte, "You shouldn't be so quick to assume that switching bodies is going to be the answer to all of your problems." He's right. The problem is not Lotte's body, as she seems to think, but the way in which her identity as "woman" and "wife" and "mother" (to Craig and all of the animals in her home) has been constrained and dictated by society. This mandated identity is not allowing her to achieve self-actualization, and she sees *being* John Malkovich as one route to obtain strength, respect, love, and voice.

Although it would be easy to attribute Lotte's motives for wanting to be Malkovich as directly related to her desire for Maxine, it is important to note that Lotte claims that "everything made sense" when she was in Malkovich's body comes *before* she even meets Maxine. Also, her conversation with Craig about gender reassignment surgery occurs only within minutes of meeting Maxine and before having any real contact with her. However, *after* Lotte meets Maxine, Lotte's desire to be in the body of Malkovich does directly relate to her desire for Maxine. Upon meeting Maxine for the first time, Lotte asks Craig, "Is this your partner? She's pretty." Lotte smiles at Maxine. Maxine smiles back and watches her leave the office. Maxine then proceeds to set up a rendezvous with Malkovich when she knows that Lotte will be inside of his head. At "their" date, we see, through the eyes of Malkovich, Maxine sitting across the table, and we hear Lotte's voice say, "You're so beautiful. And the way you're looking at me, at us, I've never been looked at like this by a woman before. I think I'm sweating." Later, when Craig and Lotte have Maxine over for dinner, Lotte tries to kiss her. Maxine responds, "Lotte, I'm smitten with you, but only when you're in Malkovich. I could feel you peering out. I sensed your feminine longing." From this point on, Lotte wants to be in Malkovich so that she can be with Maxine.

Maxine is the one major character who does not want to enter the body of Malkovich. While she has several opportunities to do so, we never see her enter Malkovich except when Lotte chases her into his subconscious near the end of the film. Why does Maxine *not* want to *be* John Malkovich? Perhaps it is because Maxine can get what she wants without taking on the identity of another person and without taking on the identity of a man, in particular. Maxine's body fits the standard for Hollywood's notion of the conventionally attractive woman, and the camera certainly emphasizes her femininity and sexuality. Throughout most of the film, she is dressed in rather provocative clothing: her skirts are tight, her shirts are usually transparent or stretched tightly over her breasts. Not only does the camera gaze upon her body, but Craig and John Malkovich also participate in looking at her. However, Maxine does not allow the men in the film to get away with gazing upon her body; instead, she confronts them with their own desire. For example, Craig meets Maxine in a bar and they have the following conversation:

Craig: I like you. I don't know what it is about you.

Maxine: My tits?

Craig: No, it's your energy, your attitude, you know, the way you carry yourself.

Maxine: You're not a fag are you?

Craig: No. I *am* really attracted to you.

Maxine knows that she is desired, and she makes Craig admit it. One could say that Maxine is resisting the feminine position as "castrated," as it is articulated within the framework of the Oedipal narrative. Rather than assume the position of the "lacking" woman, Maxine resists any association with a weaker sex and retains a position of power by exposing Craig's desire rather than merely succumbing to it.

But, as many feminist critics have noted, when women in film resist traditional femininity, they are seen as negative or destructive, and Maxine's manipulative behavior certainly casts her in a negative light. Although she is a strong character, the male character, Craig, occupies the center of the narrative. Craig is featured in the opening shot of the film, he finds the portal into Malkovich, and the film follows his desire—his quest for Maxine and for notoriety as a puppeteer through the commandeering of John Malkovich's body. Craig gains the affection of Maxine as she realizes that she can gain money and power through controlling Craig and Malkovich, and Maxine seems to fit a recognizable portrait of the manipulative woman. And, it is Craig's fixation on Maxine, his desire for her, that causes his downfall. At the end of the film Craig has lost Maxine to Lotte and is trapped, power-less, in the unconscious mind of Maxine and Lotte's little girl. In *Alice Doesn't: Femi-nism, Semiotics, Cinema*, Teresa de Lauretis notes that many mainstream Hollywood films follow this typical Oedipal structure, charting the male's journey where women are either the object of desire or irritating stumbling blocks that hinder him from his pur-poseful action. De Lauretis notes that the Oedipal scheme only allows women to be the castrated figure, and "if she survives," writes de Lauretis, "her reward is motherhood" (*Alice* 131–2).

In some ways, the narrative of *Being John Malkovich* adheres to the Oedipal scheme. While Maxine resists acting as the subservient object of affection for the majority of the film, she seems to change after she realizes that she can control Craig in the body of Malkovich. Immediately following the scene where Malkovich/Craig and Maxine meet with Malkovich's publicist and tell him that Malkovich wants to make a career move into puppeteering, the narrative shifts to "eight months later." The next shot is of Maxine gingerly hanging a mobile over a baby crib. She is quite pregnant and has shed her more provocative clothing for a cotton shirt and skirt. We see her place a puppet in the blankets of the crib as she says, "I'm so sorry Lotte." Then we see her on the floor of the apartment with head phones wrapped around her belly. She says, "Like that little girl? I love you." This is a new Maxine. She is sweet, maternal, soft, and contemplative. While we are not given the story of what has happened in those eight months, except through part of a television biography on Malkovich, we are left to assume that her new role as "mother" has in some way transformed her. She has survived, and "her reward is motherhood" (*Alice* 132).

Thinking about Maxine and Lotte in terms of identity is productive because it opens up the opportunity to think about it in complicated ways, to consider the alternatives to the binary thinking about sexuality and identity promoted by our culture. In other words, we cannot say with certainty that Maxine is gay or straight. Nor can we definitely say that Lotte is a man or a woman. Within the reality constructed by the film we can say that Lotte is a wife and a father—she has sperm; after all, Maxine *does* consider Lotte to be the father of her child. The visualization of these multi-faceted identities breaks open the bi-nary of our constructed and naturalized notions of man, woman, lesbian, straight, mother, and father. It makes it impossible for us to identify these two women in any of the provided categories.

I'd like to end this [essay] by returning to the love relationship between Maxine and Lotte. In conventional terms Lotte seems to identify in a more "lesbian" way than Max-ine—she desires Maxine when she *is* woman and when she *is* man. In contrast, Maxine seems to identify "straight" as she only desires Lotte when Lotte is Malkovich. But at the end of the film, the relationship between Lotte and Maxine as coupled women is realized. When they are expelled from the unconscious of Malkovich onto the side of the New Jersey Turnpike, Maxine says to Lotte, "I'm sorry, Lotte. I loved you too, in my own way. . . . It's your baby, okay?" Although conceived "biologically" through her sexual relations with the body of Malkovich, Maxine considers the child to be Lotte's. She continues, "I got pregnant when you were in Malkovich. I kept it because you were the father, or the mother, whatever. Because it was yours."

Yet I also think that *Being John Malkovich* is problematic in its overall portrayal of Maxine and Lotte's relationship. In writing about the film *She Must Be Seeing Things* in her article "Film and the Visible" De Lauretis observes that

> *Unlike women in most of the movies we have seen (with very few exceptions, and those mostly in avant-garde or independent women's cinema), Catalina does not die or get married. . . . Nor does Catalina end up surviving, even victorious, but alone, like Scarlett O'Hara. . . . Instead, she escapes with the other woman, whom she does not hate, compete with, or prove herself 'better' than, but whom she . . desires? loves? Is fascinated by? ("Film" 227)*

De Lauretis goes on to say that this film creates a "new position of seeing in the movies, a new place of the look" because the women in the film look at each other with desire and that look is projected on the screen for the spectator to see ("Film" 227). In light of this assessment, it seems that *Being John Malkovich* fails to create this "new position." After all, the desire of Maxine *for* Lotte is mediated by the Malkovich body until the very end of the film. While we see Lotte's desiring of Maxine, most of their contact with one another is over the phone and then through Malkovich. Therefore, the spectator does not *see* this look of desire or any physical signs of intimacy between the two women until that very short scene at the very end of the film. While Jonze visualizes the sex between Malkovich and Maxine, we never see Lotte and Maxine physically expressing their desire for one another.

I have to admit that I feel differently about this film every time I see it. Sometimes I think that the relationship between Lotte and Maxine is not risky enough. I want lesbian desire to be acknowledged positively in mainstream film, and I think that *Being John Malkovich* diminishes the reality of lesbian desire by creating a love affair between two women who only make love while one of them is a man. But, at the end of the film we do see two women, in two bodies marked as "female" together, poolside, enjoying the day and their daughter—presenting the spectator with lesbian characters who are able to fulfill their desire and not be punished for it. Although I am ambivalent about the portrayal of lesbian desire in this film, I remain fascinated by its provocative questioning of identity. One thing is for certain—*Being John Malkovich* makes it very clear that we have such narrow, suffocating categories to describe who we are and who we want to be.

Works Cited

Being John Malkovich. Dir. Spike Jonze. Perf. John Cusack, Cameron Diaz, and Orson Bean. 1999. Videocassette. USA Home Entertainment, 2000.

De Lauretis, Teresa. *Alice Doesn't: Feminism, Semiotics, Cinema*. Bloomington, IN: Indiana University Press, 1984.

—. "Film and the Visible." *How Do I Look? Queer Film and Video*. Ed. Bad Object-Choices. Seattle: Bay Press, 1991. 223–264.

After Reading

Critical Perspective

1. Reflect upon several independent or art-house films you have watched recently. Select one that challenges the traditional genre conventions of film. In what ways might it undermine stereotypes about race, ethnicity, class, age, region, sexuality, ability, religion, or environment? Point to your own experiences to support your thoughts.

Rhetoric and Argument

2. Discuss how Love opens her essay. Do you think that her rhetorical strategies—use of audience, purpose, pathos, logos, intertextuality, context, and constraints—are persuasive and help her to back up her argument? Present evidence from the text to support your thoughts.

3. What assertion does Love make about identities early in her text? Why is this important to the rest of her argument? Do you agree with her perspective? Why or why not?

4. Love's main claim in this text is a bit complicated. What is Love's thesis? Where and how does she make it? Is it or is it not effective for her main claim to appear at this point in the argument? Be sure to furnish evidence from the text to substantiate your thoughts.

5. What outside sources or experts does Love draw from in her argument? Do you find these to be credible sources? How do they establish her ethos as a writer? How might they undermine her credibility? Be sure to provide textual evidence to support your claims.

6. What warrants or assumptions does Love make in her argument? Do you find them effective? Why or why not? Provide evidence to support your views.

Analysis

7. Love closes her essay by indicating that it is not often in mainstream movies that we see images of lesbian desire. In a short argumentative essay, discuss the following: What other significant representations of lesbian and homosexual relationships have you seen in the movies? In what ways do these images support the claim Love makes? In what ways might they refute such a claim? Be sure to point to examples from your own experiences viewing such visual texts as well as library and Internet sources.

Taking Action

Gather in a small group. Choose one film or television show that features openly gay characters. Screen the film or show as a group, making note of how images, words, tone, visuals, sound, and narrative structure operate.

Based upon your research, write a detailed cultural criticism about this text. Consult additional library and Internet sources. Imagine that you are sending your review to the "Entertainment" section of a local newspaper.

Once you have created your group's response, make copies of your review for the other groups. Present your review to your classmates, lead them through your cultural criticisms, and take up any comments, suggestions, or countercharges they might offer. In addition, consider making your work accessible to other groups both inside and outside the campus community—such as actual newspaper audiences.

Todd Boyd

"So You Wanna Be a Gangsta?"

Todd Boyd is a professor of critical studies in the School of Cinema-Television at the University of Southern California. He is coeditor of Out of Bounds: Sports, Media, and the Politics of Identity *(with Aaron Baker) and* Basketball Jones: America Above the Rim *(with Kenneth Shropshire). Boyd has written for various journals, including* Wide Angle, Film-Forum, *and* Public Culture. *His most recent book is* Young, Black, Rich, and Famous: The Rise of the NBA, the Hip Hop Invasion, and the Transformation of American Culture.

EXERCISING YOUR SKILLS

Before Reading

Boyd describes the history of gangster and gangsta movies as well as the ways in which they have appealed to male viewers. Watch one of the *Godfather* films. Then view *Boyz N the Hood*. Make a list of the similarities as well as differences in the films's character development (particularly the role of the gangster/gangsta) as well as plot lines and structure. What do the films seem to share in common? In what ways are they different?

The gangster film and the Western are two of the most important genres in the history of Hollywood, especially with respect to articulation of the discourse of American history and masculinity. Whereas the Western concentrated on the mythic settling of the West and a perceived notion of progression, it was primarily concerned with the frontier mentality of the eighteenth through the late nineteenth century. The gangster genre, on the other hand, is about the evolution of American society in the twentieth century into a legitimate entity in the world economy.

Though the Western covertly articulated the politics of oppression against Native Americans during the settling of the West, the gangster genre focused on questions of ethnicity—e.g., Italian, Irish—and how these are transformed over time into questions of race—Black, Latino, etc. This ideological shift provided an interesting representation of the significant position that race has come to occupy in the discourse of American society. We must look at the transformation of the linguistic sign "gangster" and its slow transition to its most recent embodiment as "gangsta" as an instructive historical metaphor. . . .

Americans have always had a fascination with the underworld society populated by those who openly resisted the laws of dominant society and instead created their own world, living by their own rules. Gangsters have in many ways been our version of revolutionaries throughout history. Whereas Europe has always had real-life political revolutionaries, twentieth-century American discourse, upheld by police and government activity, seems to have found ways of perverting for the public the political voices that exist outside the narrow traditions of allowed political expression.

The displacement of these political voices by the forces of oppression has created a renegade space within American culture that allows for the expression of gangster culture. Gangsters indeed function as somewhat revolutionary in comparison to the rest of society, as demonstrated by their open defiance of accepted societal norms and laws, existence in their own environment, and circulation of their own alternative capital. This allows them to remain part of the larger society but to fully exist in their own communities at the same time. This lifestyle has been a consistent media staple throughout the twentieth century, particularly in film.

From as early as D. W. Griffith's *Musketeers of Pig Alley* (1912) and the celebrated studio films of the 1930s—e.g., *Little Caesar* (1930), *Public Enemy* (1931), and *Scarface* (1932)—through the epic treatment rendered in the first two *Godfather* films (1972, 1974), the gangster has enjoyed a vivid screen life. What is important here is that these criminals, as they are deemed by the dominant society, are defined as deviant primarily because of issues of ethnicity, as opposed to issues of race, though to some extent all definitions of ethnicity in this context are inevitably influenced by a subtle definition of race.

This emphasis on ethnicity as it functions in opposition to the standard "white Anglo-Saxon Protestant" is summarized in the first two *Godfather* films. As the United States, both at and immediately after the turn of the century, increasingly became a nation of European immigrants, incoming Italians were consigned to the bottom of the social ladder. In the opening segment of *Godfather II*, Michael Corleone is berated and verbally abused by Senator Geery of Nevada because of his Italian heritage. The word "Italian" is set in opposition to "American" constantly in this segment so as to highlight the ethnic hierarchy which remains a foundational issue in this film. Corleone's ascension to power is complicated by his inability to fully surmount this societal obstacle, at least at this point in the film, and by extension that point in American history—the early 1950s.

It is Francis Ford Coppola's argument that such oppression forced these Italian immigrants into a subversive lifestyle and economy much like that practiced throughout southern Italy, especially in Sicily. Borrowing from their own cultural tradition, some of these new Americans used the underground economy as a vital means of sustenance in the face of ethnic, religious, and cultural oppression. And though their desire, being heavily influenced by the discourse of an "American dream," was to ultimately be fully assimilated into American society, the achievement of this desire was revealed to be at the cost of losing their ethnic and cultural heritage. . . .

At a larger level, the film's historical themes indicate the assimilation of ethnicity into a homogeneous American society, yet foreground the continued rejection of race as a component of the metaphoric "melting pot"—because it is the challenge of race that accelerates the assimilative process of ethnicity.

In the first *Godfather* film, we see this same social dynamic at play regarding ethnicity over race. Near the film's conclusion, we witness the memorable meeting of the "heads of the five families," where the dilemmas of drug trafficking are being discussed by the various Mafia leaders. Vito Corleone is characterized as opposing this potentially lucrative venture for moral reasons, while many of the other members are excited about the possible financial benefits. The chieftain from Kansas City suggests that the Mafia should engage in selling drugs, but only at a distance, leaving the underside of this environment to be experienced by what he describes as the "dark people" because, as he adds, "they're animals anyway, let them lose their souls." His use of the phrase "dark people" and his labeling of them as "animals" clearly reference African Americans, and by extension racialized others in general. This line of dialogue is viewed by many African Americans as prophetic, seeing that the release of *The Godfather* in the early 1970s closely paralleled the upsurge in underworld drug activity throughout African American ghetto communities.

In relation to the assimilation of ethnicity at the expense of race, this line also signifies the way in which the previously mentioned structural hierarchy exists aside from the racial hierarchy, which many African Americans have been unable to transcend because of the difference in skin color. Though Italians through this perverted formulation could be considered inferior to "wasps," those traits that make them different can be easily subsumed when contrasted with the obvious difference of skin color and the history that goes along with being darker. It is in this context that the thematic progression of the *Godfather* films signals the end of the public fascination with the Italian gangster and his ethnically rich underworld.

Furthermore, this line indicates that the drug culture would be an important turning point in the historical discourse specific to the question of race as time moved forward. This line of reasoning has been pursued in numerous texts, [particularly] through Bill Duke's film *Deep Cover* (1992), which comments on the conspiracy involved in both furnishing and addicting segments of the Black community with drugs as a political maneuver by the government to keep these individuals sedated and oppressed so as to quell any potential political resistance. Mario Van Peebles's film *Panther* (1995) asserts the same theory in connection with the attempted destruction of the Black Panther Party by J. Edgar Hoover and the FBI. In both cases, crime can be seen as affirming capitalism, yet in specifically racial terms.

With this assimilation of ethnicity as signified through the Coppola films, America finds the need to fulfill this otherwise empty space with the next logical descending step on the social ladder, that being race.[1] Two other films from the 1980s effectively mark the

---

1. The popular 1990 Martin Scorsese film *Goodfellas* is different from the gangster films which preceded it. At the conclusion of this film, the main character, Henry Hill, turns state's evidence on his former colleagues, thus violating one of the most stringent codes of the gangster lifestyle. And though some would argue that this film is a revisionist gangster film, it is sufficiently separated from other examples of the genre so as not to be confused. Scorsese's *Casino* (1995) continues this move to a contemporary gangster epic.

Another example of this revisionist trend would be Barry Levinson's fictional account of the life of Benjamin "Bugsy" Siegel, with its emphasis on Siegel's mistress, Virginia Hill, and the way in which

shift away from the ethnic gangster to the racialized gangsta. Brian De Palma's remake of *Scarface* (1983) is an obvious rewriting of the genre from the perspective of race. Whereas the main character in the 1932 film was an Italian, in the De Palma version we deal with a racialized Cuban.

Drawing from real political events, De Palma's film begins with the Mariel boat lift of Cuban refugees into south Florida during the latter part of the 1970s, an event which many still consider a lingering legacy of Jimmy Carter's presidency. The film's main character, Tony Montana, is clearly foregrounded as a racialized other. His Cuban identity, broken accent, penchant for garishness, and overall ruthless approach to wealth and human life served as the basis for the popular media representation of Latin American drug dealers that came to dominate the 1980s.

With an increase in drug paranoia from the conservative Reagan and Bush administrations, this form of representation would nearly erase past images of Italian mob figures from the popular memory. While John Gotti was a celebrated folk hero for his stylish media-friendly disposition, individuals such as Carlos Lader Rivas, Pablo Escobar, and Manuel Noriega, who became common sights on the evening news and network news magazine programs, were depicted as threats to the very fabric of our society. To add to this popular form of representation, NBC's series *Miami Vice* drew many of its story lines and criminal figures from this newly accepted version of racialized representation.[2] . . . .

The other major filmic event that reflected this obsession with the drug culture and the question of race was Dennis Hopper's *Colors* (1988). Hopper's film offered an intricate look at the gang culture that existed in both South Central and East Los Angeles. Its main characters were two white Los Angeles police officers who were commissioned with the monumental task of eliminating the urban crime being perpetrated by African American and Latino youth. This film tied in neatly with the increasing commentary presented by national news programs about what had begun as a regional situation and was later argued to have spread throughout the country. Using the police, and by extension the rest of white society, as its victims, the film endorsed the racial paranoia concerning criminality that at this time was in full swing.

Colors, for all intents and purposes, made the gangbanger America's contemporary criminal of choice, turning a localized problem into a national epidemic that once again linked crime with specific notions of race. In many ways, *Colors* served the same function for gangsta culture that *Birth of a Nation* served for the early stages of African American cinema. Both films, through their overt racial paranoia, and in both cases using

---

her influence can be read as substantial, though detrimental, to Siegel in the financial decisions that he makes. *Bugsy* (1991) presents a sentimental underworld figure who has been "softened" by this female presence, which goes against the masculinist approach normally associated with the gangster. This rereading of the central character, with an emphasis on the female, adds to my notion of a revisionist trend in the genre, though in this case it is gender, not race, that is the point of transition.

2. For a detailed discussion of the drug trade in Los Angeles, see Mike Davis, "The Political Economy of Crack," in *City of Quartz* (New York: Verso, 1990), and for a larger discussion of the role played by the media, the politics of Reagan/Bush, and the drug culture of the 1980s, see Jimmie Reeves and Richard Campbell, *Cracked Coverage* (Durham: Duke Univ. Press, 1994).

armed militia as an answer to the perceived Black threat—in one case the Ku Klux Klan, in the other a racist police department—inspired a series of African American cinematic responses. This regressive film engendered a public fascination with the newly defined "gangsta."

With the traditional white ethnic gangster film having all but disappeared, the way was clear for the entrance of a new popular villain to be screened across the mind of American society. The ideological link between crime and race would be made worse, and the image of the African American gangbanger would become not only popular in the sense of repeated representation, but financially lucrative as well. In addition to the changing history of the Hollywood gangster film, several other historical factors specific to African American culture would contribute to the emergence and eventual proliferation of the African American "gangsta."

From the Black Godfather to the Black Guerrilla Family

The late 1960s and early 1970s saw an increase in underworld activity, especially involving drugs, throughout many lower-class Black communities. In many ways more important than the drugs themselves was the culture that accompanied this underworld lifestyle and the way in which it was represented visually. The garish fashions popularized by Eleganza and Flag Brothers, heavily adorned, ornament-laden Cadillacs, and other materialistic excesses helped to define this cultural terrain as "cool" during this period. . . .

In several of the films that define this period, eventually known as the "Sexploitation" era of Hollywood (1970–73), the Black protagonist was presented in opposition to a stereotypical white menace who was bent on destroying the African American community, primarily through the influx of drugs and the accompanying culture of violence. For the most part, evil in the films was personified in the form of a corrupt police or mafia figure, if not both at the same time. Thus much of the narrative action appeared in battles between some faction of the white mafia, who had traditionally been in control of the ghetto, albeit from a distance, and the emerging Black underworld figures who were striving to wrest control of this alternative economy from their white counterparts.

It was as if the loosening of societal restrictions gained during the civil rights movement permitted exploitation of the community through control of underworld vices, though the actual control was in the hands of manipulative outsiders, who used the Black gangster as their foil. The Black gangster, whether he was a pimp, dope dealer, or hustler, through these films became a prominent example of what it meant to be an entrepreneur. The tension between outside influence and inside control is represented in many of the films of the period, most notably *Cotton Comes to Harlem, Across 110th Street, Superfly,* and *The Mack*. The African American gangster had become a media staple by the mid-1970s. . . .

Many of the films of this period were based on the dynamics of an African American underworld existence (e.g., *Sweetsweetback's Badass Song, The Mack, Willie Dynamite, Coffy, Cleopatra Jones*), and in conjunction with the popular ghetto literature of Iceberg Slim and Donald Goines, as well as the more esoteric works of author Chester

Himes and playwright Charles Gordone, this form of representation remained viable long after this period had passed. In line with Nelson George's argument that "Sexploitation movies are crucial to the current '70's retro-nuevo phase" (149), this historical period left a series of low-budget films which would eventually be perfect for transfer to the home video format. The "Sexploitation" films would leave an indelible imprint on African American popular culture as the "gangsta" continued to rise in prominence and position.

A Small Introduction to the "G" Funk Era

With the historical antecedents of the Hollywood gangster film and 1970s Sexploitation films, along with popular African American literature that explored the culture, the stage was set for the flowering of gangsta culture in the late 1980s and early 1990s. The contemporary manifestation continued to appear in the form of cinema, but also gained increasing visibility in the world of rap music, to the point of establishing its own genre and forming a solid cultural movement. This transition from genre to cultural movement included representations in film, music, and literature, and involved multiple layers of society: communal, political, and corporate. From the regular individuals whose personal narratives drew heavily from gangster culture, to rap artists whose real-life antics coincided with the fictional rhetoric of their lyrics, and finally to the highest levels of government, where questions of moral integrity, community debasement, and freedom of speech were constantly being posed, this cultural movement had a great deal of currency with respect to African Americans in society, especially the African American male. . . .

Though there are glimpses of the gangster lifestyle in a number of films that appeared throughout the late 1980s and especially in the early 1990s, the two films most relevant to an understanding of gangsta culture are John Singleton's *Boyz N the Hood* (1991) and Allen and Albert Hughes's *Menace II Society* (1993). Not to ignore such a popular film as Mario Van Peebles's *New Jack City* (1991) or Abel Ferrara's cult video classic *The King of New York* (1990), but these texts are more directly influenced by the traditional gangster paradigm, in addition to being set in New York City. The filmic representation of gangsta culture draws many of its influences from rap music, and in turn rap music assumes a great deal of identity within the work of Singleton and the Hughes brothers. Contemporary gangsta culture is undoubtedly a West Coast phenomenon.

The other film that holds a vital position in the representation of gangsta culture is Edward James Olmos's *American Me* (1992). This film addresses the culture from a Latino perspective as opposed to an African American one. This is of utmost importance, for while gangsta culture is publicly regarded an African American entity, much of the culture derives from the close proximity in which African Americans and Latinos coexist in racialized Los Angeles. . . .

Hispanics Causin' Panic

American Me demonstrates that aspects of African American gangsta life and Mexican American gangsta culture are in dialogue with one another, though it can at times be a highly contested dialogue. There are two distinct instances in the film where a potential clash between the races is openly criticized as being counterproductive to someone's coming to consciousness and ultimate cultural empowerment. As the Mexican mafia (La Eme) smuggles drugs into the prison, we witness a Black inmate who steals the cocaine intended for another inmate. Upon revelation of the culprit, Santana, the leader of La Eme, instructs his soldiers to burn the man as an act of punishment. This triggers a cell-block confrontation that borders on a riot between La Eme and the Black Guerrilla Family (BGF). As the prison guards descend, the riot is aborted, but not without critical commentary. Santana informs the leader of the BGF that the situation was not racially motivated, but simply an action of retribution to forestall any future attempts at hindering their drug-trafficking efforts in prison. In other words, "business, never personal." This is a case in which the interest of underground capitalism supersedes any specific racial agenda.

Yet this scene is important as the setup for a similar situation that occurs later in the film. When La Eme attempts to sever its tie with the traditional Italian Mafia, the move is met with much resistance. Scagnelli, the mob boss, refuses to relinquish his end of the drug business in East L.A.. As a result, several members of La Eme rape and murder Scagnelli's son while he is in prison. In response, Scagnelli sends uncut heroin into the barrio, causing several overdoses. This creates a chain reaction of retribution, which eventually culminates in Santana's death at the hands of his own men. At a certain point during this series of events, J.D., the only white member of La Eme, who slowly attempts to wrest control of the gang from Santana, orders a hit on the BGF by using the Aryan Brotherhood, the white gang represented in the film. Santana objects to this action and criticizes J.D. for "sending out the wrong message."

Santana's objection is based on his increasing awareness of racial and social consciousness, which has been facilitated by the politically empowered female character Julie. Julie, like the female character of Ronnie in *Menace*, helps Santana to realize the error of his misguided ways. On several occasions she criticizes his violent philosophy in ways that other characters cannot for fear of death. In a pivotal scene late in the film, Julie exposes Santana's position in all its limitations. After a series of extremely critical remarks about Santana's hypocritical use of crime as a way of arguing for *la raza*, he tells her, "If you were a man, I'd . . ." His incomplete sentence is cut short by Julie's own completion of it: "You'd kill me; no, you'd fuck me in the ass." Having witnessed several scenes in which men were raped because of Santana's power over them, in addition to his rape of Julie, we can feel the magnitude of her statement. She not only criticizes his politics, she has criticized his masculinity by alluding to the latent homosexuality of his supposed gestures of power.

Ultimately, she forces Santana to understand that the power struggles which often take place between those who are marginalized permit the continued oppression of their voices by those in power. Santana even says to J.D., "We spend all our time dealing with the miatas [their slang term for Blacks], and the Aryan Brotherhood, only to be dealing with ourselves." In other words, ideological distractions ultimately leave us in the same place, with no advancement in consciousness or power.

These ideas eventually separate Santana's newfound political consciousness from J.D.'s "business as usual" approach to crime and the underlying destruction of the community.

It is not coincidental that J.D.'s whiteness, which is endorsed by Santana early in the film, looms as the final authority once he has ordered the killing of Santana and presumably taken control of the gang. At the beginning of the film, as expressed through the American military oppression of the Mexican American citizens, and at the conclusion, with J.D.'s murdering of Santana, thus destroying any possibility for an overall group consciousness, we can see that racism and white supremacy are the root causes of the chaos that permeates much of the present-day urban landscape. It is this fundamental understanding of race, racism, and complicity in one's own oppression that substantiates the importance of *American Me. American Me* engages history and politics to subtly yet convincingly argue that the real root of evil in American society as it relates to oppressed minorities is the bondage of systemic and institutionalized racism. This understanding also distinguishes it as a political statement from the rather limited bourgeois politics of *Boyz N the Hood* and the nihilistically apolitical *Menace II Society*.

Boyz Will Be Boyz

Either they don't know, won't show, or don't care what's going on in the hood.

—DOUGHBOY, *Boyz N the Hood*

While *American Me* serves as an "objective third party" against which to evaluate *Boyz* and *Menace*, the similarities notwithstanding, to engage the culturally specific tenets of Black popular culture we must look at texts which are firmly situated in the domain of African American cinema in order to study the class politics of each film. In this regard, the political position of *Boyz N the Hood* can be defined as either a bourgeois Black nationalist or an Afrocentric model that focuses on the "disappearing" Black male, yet also fits easily into the perceived pathology of the culture in a modernized version of the legendary Moynihan report of the late 1960s. This report regarded the typically broken African American family as a cause of societal dysfunction at the highest level.

Singleton's film was integral to the politically charged period of resurgent Black nationalism in the late 1980s and early 1990s. This cultural resurgence of Black nationalism, most closely associated with the work of Public Enemy, KRS-One, and Sister Souljah, also set the tone for the discourse that informed *Do the Right Thing*, as well as many of the debates that emerged after the film's release.

From the outset it is obvious that Singleton's film is conversant with the Afrocentric discourse that permeates much of Black intellectual and cultural life. The film opens by establishing South Central Los Angeles as its geographical, cultural, and political center. Yet the landscape of Los Angeles is a historically specific one. The film begins in 1984, as we quickly spot several campaign posters that support the re-election of President Ronald Reagan—the obvious contradiction of this image being seen in a community such as South Central, which is the type of community most victimized by the racial and class politics of Reagan's first term. Another contradiction is signaled as a young Black male, while looking at an abandoned dead body lying in an alley, gives this political image "the finger." This young character is identified as being closely associated with gang culture. He declares that both of his brothers have been shot, and in turn they are heroic in his mind because they have yet to be killed. His marginal status allows him to recognize at some level that this supreme image of white male authority is in stark contrast to his own existence.

As we enter the classroom, we are presented with another contradiction. The camera pans the student drawings that cover the wall. These pictures contain images of people being shot, police brutality, and other acts that emphasize the daily violence that defines many of the lives in this poor Black community. These images are contradicted by the speech being delivered by the white teacher about the historical importance of the first European "settlers" or "pilgrims" on American soil. Her lecture is on the reasons this country celebrates the Thanksgiving holiday, yet by implication it also articulates the exploitation of America and Native Americans and the ensuing colonization, which was a helpful instrument in establishing the societal hierarchy that we inhabit today.

The ideology that is being discussed is being put into practice through the attitudes and policies of Ronald Reagan. Reagan clearly felt the need to return to some form of these earlier examples of oppression in the course of his presidential career, as his repeated attacks on affirmative action, his support of states' rights, and his overall embrace of positions consistent with right-wing conservatism about race clearly indicated. In a sense, the actions of those who are being celebrated by the teacher, the "pilgrims," have contributed to the conditions of the people depicted in the children's drawings. The film sets up a binary opposition between the conservative politics of America and African Americans' rejection of these oppressive policies. This scene is one of the few in the film in which racism and white supremacy are directly critiqued.

As the scene develops, Tre, the film's main character, confronts his elementary school teacher, asserting that humankind originated in Africa and not in Europe. Yet in his presentation, Tre is criticized not only by his teacher, but by other students as well. The same student who gave Reagan "the finger" completely dissociates himself from Tre's Afrocentric assertion, "We're all from Africa." In response, this child declares, "I ain't from Africa. I'm from Crenshaw Mafia," further linking himself to gang culture through his identification with the set known as "Crenshaw Mafia." The obvious irony of this scene is that gang affiliation is set in direct conflict with one's racial and cultural identity. It is as if being a gangsta supersedes race, as opposed to being a result of racial and class hierarchies in America.

In this same exchange, we can also hear echoes of Tre's father, Furious, and his lessons on life that recur throughout the film. This is once again set in opposition to the words of the aspiring gangsta's older brothers. This exchange leads to a fight between the two children, underscoring the incompatibility of progressive politics and existence in gangsta culture. Yet through the setting of gangsta culture in opposition to nationalist politics, it becomes clear that this bourgeois understanding ignores the fact that gangsters historically are easily transformed into revolutionaries because of their marginal status in society.

Remarks about the plight of the "Black man" dominate much of Furious's commentary in the film. As critic Michael Dyson has alluded, these comments fit well with the male-centered Afrocentric ideals of thinkers such as Jawanza Kanjufu, Haki Madhabuti, and Molefi Asante. *Boyz* uses gangsta culture as an alluring spectacle, which is underscored by the film's exaggeratedly violent trailer, but this spectacle is used to engage an Afrocentric critique that denounces the routine slaying of Black men, whether by other gang members or by the police. *Boyz* makes interesting use of many of the icons of gangsta culture while conducting its Black nationalist critique. The film straddles both areas, opening the door to the ensuing onslaught of gangsta imagery.

In this sense, *Boyz* is much like the imagery connected with one of its co-stars, Ice Cube. As a rapper, Ice Cube has consistently combined signs of gangsta culture with an ideological perspective that emphasizes a perverted Black nationalist agenda, borrowed primarily from the Nation of Islam. Similarly, *Boyz* combines gangsta icons with Afrocentrism, ultimately privileging the ideological critique over the iconography. This strain of political discourse was popular during the late 1980s and early 1990s, with *Boyz* providing a cinematic counterpart to rap music. Singleton's film, though visualizing gangsta culture on a mass scale, is really more acceptable as a political text than as a thesis on the complex gangsta mentality. In many ways, *Boyz* represents the culmination of this politically resurgent period, as the theme of Black nationalism slowly disappeared from most popular forms shortly thereafter.

Though the film is overtly political, it reflects a bourgeois sense of politics. At the conclusion of the film we see a didactic scroll which tells us that Tre and Brandi, the one utopic Black male/female relationship presented in the film, have ventured off to Morehouse and Spelman College in Atlanta, respectively, to pursue their middle-class dreams far away from South Central L.A.. Morehouse and Spelman have often been thought of as the Black equivalent of Harvard or Yale, the historical breeding ground for bourgeois Blackness. The fact that the two colleges are located in Atlanta, the current "mecca" of Black America, underscores the film's flimsy political position. *Boyz N the Hood* demonizes the landscape of Los Angeles while uncritically offering middle-class Atlanta as a metaphoric space where future generations of African Americans can exist free of the obstacles that are depicted in this film.

After Reading

Critical Perspective

1. Why do you think that Boyd asserts that the "gangster film and the Western are two of the most important genres in the history of Hollywood, especially with respect to articulation of the discourse of American history and masculinity"? Do you agree with this statement? Explain your response.

Rhetoric and Argument

2. Reflect upon Boyd's use of rhetorical tactics, specifically audience, purpose, ethos, pathos, logos, intertextuality, context, and constraints. Do you think that his text is rhetorically effective? Why or why not?

3. What does Boyd hope to establish by investigating the history of the gangster/gang-sta film genre? How can you tell? Be sure to furnish examples from the text as well as your own experiences to back up your assertions.

4. Boyd makes his argument by using various film depictions as support. Do you think that his claim is adequately supported by this kind of evidence? Why or why not? Are there any other types of evidence he might use that would additionally support his thoughts?

5. Boyd concentrates upon how both ethnicity and race are represented in film within his piece. Provide support with quotes from the essay. Examine his critique of *Boyz N the Hood.* What is Boyd asserting about the politics of this film? Do you agree with his views?

6. Are there any logical flaws or faulty assumptions in Boyd's argument? If yes, pinpoint where they are in his text. If there are no flaws, draw from the text to back up your opinions.

Analysis

7. Write an informal argumentative response in which you either support or refute Boyd's major argument or his use of rhetorical tactics. Draw your evidence from a close analysis of his text. In addition, be sure to consult library and Internet sources to back up your assertions.

Taking Action

Form a small group. Reflect upon whether there are additional gangsta movies (as Boyd defines them) that have been released since Boyd wrote his essay. Select one that you would like to watch. Arrange a time to watch it together and take detailed notes. After you have finished, compare your thoughts. What claims of cultural criticism could you offer about this film? What evidence might you use to support your views? Seek out library and Internet sources as well. Together create a polished draft of your cultural criticism.

Get back into the larger class group and share your cultural criticisms. Then discuss whether you are noticing any patterns or themes. Have films in this genre changed since Boyd wrote his essay or not? Why might this be significant?

David Denby

"High-School Confidential: Notes on Teen Movies"

David Denby has been a staff writer and film critic at The New Yorker *since 1998. His writing has also appeared in* The Atlantic Monthly, The New York Review of Books, *and* The New Republic. *Denby is also the editor of* Awake in the Dark: An Anthology of Film Criticism from 1915 to the Present *and author of* The Great Books: My Adventures with Homer, Rousseau, Woolf, and Other Indestructible Writers of the Western World *and* American Sucker.

EXERCISING YOUR SKILLS

Before Reading

Denby's essay investigates the genre of teen films. Watch several of the most recent and popular high school or teen movies. Make note of the characters and the plot lines. What sorts of themes or patterns do you notice in these films? Why do you think that these themes and patterns are so popular with teen audiences?

The most hated young woman in America is a blonde—well, sometimes a redhead or a brunette, but usually a blonde. She has big hair flipped into a swirl of gold at one side of her face or arrayed in a sultry mane, like the magnificent pile of a forties movie star. She's tall and slender, with a waist as supple as a willow, but she's dressed in awful, spangled taste: her outfits could have been put together by warring catalogues. And she has a mouth on her, a low, slatternly tongue that devastates other kids with such insults as "You're vapor, you're Spam!" and "Do I look like Mother Teresa? If I did, I probably wouldn't mind talking to the geek squad." She has two or three friends exactly like her, and together they dominate their realm—the American high school as it appears in recent teen movies. They are like wicked princesses, who enjoy the misery of their subjects. Her coronation, of course, is the senior prom, when she expects to be voted "most popular" by her class. But, though she may be popular, she is certainly not liked, so her power is something of a mystery. She is beautiful and rich, yet in the end she is preeminent because . . . she is preeminent, a position she works to maintain with Joan Crawford-like tenacity. Everyone is afraid of her; that's why she's popular.

She has a male counterpart. He's usually a football player, muscular but dumb, with a face like a beer mug and only two ways of speaking—in a conspiratorial whisper, to a friend; or in a drill sergeant's sudden bellow. If her weapon is the snub, his is the lame but infuriating prank—the can of Sprite emptied into a knapsack, or something sticky, creamy, or adhesive deposited in a locker. Sprawling and dull in class, he comes alive in the halls and in the cafeteria. He hurls people against lockers; he spits, pours, and sprays; he has a projectile relationship with food. As the crown prince, he claims the best-looking girl for himself, though in a perverse display of power he may invite an outsider or an awkward girl—a "dog"—to the prom, setting her up for some special humiliation. When we first see him, he is riding high, and virtually the entire school colludes in his tyranny. No authority figure—no teacher or administrator—dares correct him.

Thus are the villains of the recent high-school movies. Not every American teen movie has these two characters, and not every social queen or jock shares all the attributes I've mentioned. (Occasionally, a handsome, dark-haired athlete can be converted to sweetness and light.) But as genre figures these two types are hugely familiar; that is, they are a common memory, a collective trauma, or at least a social and erotic fantasy. Such movies as *Disturbing Behavior*, *She's All That*, *Ten Things I Hate about You*, and *Never Been Kissed* depend on them as stock figures. And they may have been figures in the minds of the Littleton shooters, Eric Harris and Dylan Klebold, who imagined they were living in a school like the one in so many of these movies—a poisonous system of status, snobbery, and exclusion.

Do genre films reflect reality? Or are they merely a set of conventions that refer to other films? Obviously, they wouldn't survive if they didn't provide emotional satisfaction to the people who make them and to the audiences who watch them. A half century ago, we didn't need to see ten Westerns a year in order to learn that the West got settled. We needed to see it settled ten times a year in order to provide ourselves with the emotional gratifications of righteous violence. By drawing his gun only when he was provoked, and in the service of the good, the classic Western hero transformed the gross tangibles of the expansionist drive (land, cattle, gold) into a principle of moral order. The gangster, by contrast, is a figure of chaos, a modern, urban person, and in the critic Robert Warshow's formulation he functions as a discordant element in an American society devoted to a compulsively "positive" outlook. When the gangster dies, he cleanses viewers of their own negative feelings.

High school movies are also full of unease and odd, mixed-up emotions. They may be flimsy in conception; they may be shot in lollipop colors, garlanded with mediocre pop scores, and cast with goofy young actors trying to make an impression. Yet this most commercial and frivolous of genres harbors a grievance against the world. It's a very specific grievance, quite different from the restless anger of such fifties adolescent-rebellion movies as *The Wild One*, in which someone asks Marlon Brando's biker "What are you rebelling against?" and the biker replies "What have you got?" The fifties teen outlaw was against anything that adults considered sacred. But no movie teenager now revolts against adult authority, for the simple reason that adults have no authority. Teachers are rarely more than a minimal, exasperated presence, administrators get turned into a joke, and parents are either absent or distantly benevolent. It's a teen world, bounded by school, mall, and car, with occasional moments set in the fast-food outlets where the kids work, or in the kids' upstairs bedrooms, with their pinups and rack stereo systems. The enemy is not authority; the enemy is other teens and the social system that they impose on one another.

The bad feeling in these movies may strike grownups as peculiar. After all, from a distance American kids appear to be having it easy these days. The teen audience is facing a healthy job market; at home, their parents are stuffing the den with computers and the garage with a bulky SUV. But most teens aren't thinking about the future job market. Lost in the eternal swoon of late adolescence, they're thinking about their identity, their friends, and their clothes. Adolescence is the present-tense moment in American life. Identity and status are fluid: abrupt, devastating reversals are always possible. (In a teen movie, a guy who swallows a bucket of cafeteria coleslaw can make himself a hero in an instant.) In these movies, accordingly, the senior prom is the equivalent of the shoot-out at the O.K. Corral; it's the moment when one's worth as a human being is settled at last. In the rather pedestrian comedy *Never Been Kissed*, Drew Barrymore, as a twenty-five-year-old newspaper reporter, goes back to high school pretending to be a student, and immediately falls into her old, humiliating pattern of trying to impress the goodlooking rich kids. Helplessly, she pushes for approval, and even gets herself chosen prom queen before finally coming to her senses. She finds it nearly impossible to let go.

Genre films dramatize not what happens but how things feel—the emotional coloring of memory. They fix subjectivity into fable. At actual schools, there is no unitary system of status; there are many groups to be a part of, many places to excel (or fail to excel), many avenues of escape and self-definition. And often the movies, too, revel in the arcana of high-school cliques. In *Disturbing Behavior*, a veteran student lays out the cafeteria ethnography for a newcomer: Motorheads, Blue Ribbons, Skaters, Micro-geeks ("drug of choice: Stephen Hawking's *A Brief History of Time* and a cup of jasmine tea on Saturday night"). Subjectively, though, the social system in *Disturbing Behavior* (a high-school version of *The Stepford Wives*) and in the other movies still feels coercive and claustrophobic: humiliation is the most vivid emotion of youth, so in memory it becomes the norm.

The movies try to turn the tables. The kids who cannot be the beautiful ones, or make out with them, or avoid being insulted by them—these are the heroes of the teen movies, the third in the trio of character types. The female outsider is usually an intellectual or an artist. (She scribbles in a diary, she draws or paints.) Physically awkward, she walks like a seal crossing a beach, and is prone to drop her books and dither in terror when she stands before a handsome boy. Her clothes, which ignore mall fashion, scandalize the social queens. Like them, she has a tongue, but she's tart and grammatical, tending toward feminist pungency and precise diction. She may mask her sense of vulnerability with sarcasm or with Plathian rue (she's stuck in the bell jar), but even when she lashes out she can't hide her craving for acceptance.

The male outsider, her friend, is usually a mass of stuttering or giggling sexual gloom: he wears shapeless clothes; he has an undeveloped body, either stringy or shrimpy; he's sometimes a Jew (in these movies, still the generic outsider). He's also brilliant, but in a morose, preoccupied way that suggests masturbatory absorption in some arcane system of knowledge. In a few special cases, the outsider is not a loser but a disengaged hipster, either saintly or satanic. (Christian Slater has played this role a couple of times.) This outsider wears black and keeps his hair long, and he knows how to please women. He sees through everything, so he's ironic by temperament and genuinely indifferent to the opinion of others—a natural aristocrat, who transcends the school's contemptible status system. There are whimsical variations on the outsider figure, too. In *Rushmore*, an obnoxious teen hero, Max Fischer (Jason Schwartzman), runs the entire school: he can't pass his courses but he's a dynamo at extracurricular activities, with a knack for staging extraordinary events. He's a con man, a fund-raiser, an entrepreneur—in other words, a contemporary artist.

In fact, the entire genre, which combines self-pity and ultimate vindication, might be called "Portrait of the Filmmaker as a Young Nerd." Who can doubt where Hollywood's twitchy, nearsighted writers and directors ranked—or feared they ranked—on the high-school totem pole? They are still angry, though occasionally the target of their resentment goes beyond the jocks and cheerleaders of their youth. Consider this anomaly: the young actors and models on the covers of half the magazines published in this country, the shirtless men with chests like burnished shields, the girls smiling, glowing, tweezed, full-lipped, full-breasted (but not too full), and with skin so honeyed that it seems lacquered—these are the physical ideals embodied by the villains of the teen movies. The social queens and jocks, using their looks to dominate others, represent an American barbarism of beauty. Isn't it possible that the detestation of them in teen movies is a veiled strike at the entire abs-hair advertising culture, with its unobtainable glories of perfection? A critic of consumerism might even see a spark of revolt in these movies. But only a spark.

My guess is that these films arise from remembered hurts which then get recast in symbolic form. For instance, a surprising number of the outsider heroes have no mother. Mom has died or run off with another man; her child, only half loved, is ill equipped for the emotional pressures of school. The motherless child, of course, is a shrewd commercial ploy that makes a direct appeal to the members of the audience, many of whom may feel like outsiders, too, and unloved, or not loved enough, or victims of some prejudice or exclusion. But the motherless child also has powers, and will someday be a success, an artist, a screenwriter. It's the wound and the bow all over again, in cargo pants.

As the female nerd attracts the attention of the handsomest boy in the senior class, the teen movie turns into a myth of social reversal—a Cinderella fantasy. Initially, his interest in her may be part of a stunt or a trick: he is leading her on, perhaps at the urging of his queenly girlfriend. But his gaze lights her up, and we see how attractive she really is. Will she fulfill the eternal American fantasy that you can vault up the class system by removing your specs? She wants her prince, and by degrees she wins him over, not just with her looks but with her superior nature, her essential goodness. In the male version of the Cinderella trip, a few years go by, and a pale little nerd (we see him at a reunion) has become rich. All that poking around with chemicals paid off. Max Fischer, of *Rushmore*, can't miss being richer than Warhol.

So the teen movie is wildly ambivalent. It may attack the consumerist ethos that produces winners and losers, but in the end it confirms what it is attacking. The girls need the seal of approval conferred by the converted jocks; the nerds need money and a girl. Perhaps it's no surprise that the outsiders can be validated only by the people who ostracized them. But let's not be too schematic: the outsider who joins the system also modifies it, opens it up to the creative power of social mobility, makes it bend and laugh, and perhaps this turn of events is not so different from the way things work in the real world, where merit and achievement stand a good chance of trumping appearance. The irony of the Littleton shootings is that Klebold and Harris, who were both proficient computer heads, seemed to have forgotten how the plot turns out. If they had held on for a few years they might have been working at a hip software company, or have started their own business, while the jocks who oppressed them would probably have wound up selling insurance or used cars. That's the one unquestionable social truth the teen movies reflect: geeks rule.

There is, of course, a menacing subgenre, in which the desire for revenge turns bloody. Thirty-one years ago, Lindsay Anderson's semi-surrealistic *If . . .* was set in an oppressive, class-ridden English boarding school, where a group of rebellious students drive the school population out into a courtyard and open fire on them with machine guns. In Brian De Palma's 1976 masterpiece *Carrie*, the pale, repressed heroine, played by Sissy Spacek, is courted at last by a handsome boy but gets violated—doused with pig's blood—just as she is named prom queen. Stunned but far from powerless, Carrie uses her telekinetic powers to set the room afire and burn down the school. *Carrie* is the primal school movie, so wildly lurid and funny that it exploded the clichés of the genre before the genre was quite set: the heroine may be a wrathful avenger, but the movie, based on a Stephen King book, was clearly a grinning-gargoyle fantasy. So, at first, was *Heathers*, in which Christian Slater's satanic outsider turns out to be a true devil. He and his girlfriend (played by a very young Winona Ryder) begin gleefully knocking off the rich, nasty girls and the jocks, in ways so patently absurd that their revenge seems a mere wicked dream. I think it's unlikely that these movies had a direct effect on the actions of the Littleton shooters, but the two boys would surely have recognized the emotional world of *Heathers* and *Disturbing Behavior* as their own. It's a place where feelings of victimization join fantasy, and you experience the social elites as so powerful that you must either become them or kill them.

But enough. It's possible to make teen movies that go beyond these fixed polarities—insider and outsider, blond-bitch queen and hunch-shouldered nerd. In Amy Heckerling's 1995 comedy *Clueless*, the big blonde played by Alicia Silverstone is a Rodeo Drive clotheshorse who is nonetheless possessed of extraordinary virtue. Freely dispensing advice and help, she's almost ironically good—a designing goddess with a cell phone. The movie offers a sun-shiny satire of Beverly Hills affluence, which it sees as both absurdly swollen and generous in spirit. The most original of the teen comedies, *Clueless* casts away self-pity. So does *Romy and Michele's High School Reunion*, in which two gabby, lovable friends, played by Mira Sorvino and Lisa Kudrow, review the banalities of their high school experience so knowingly that they might be criticizing the teen-movie genre itself. And easily one of the best American films is Alexander Payne's *Election*, a high-school movie that inhabits a different aesthetic and moral world altogether from the rest of these pictures. *Election* shreds everyone's fantasies and illusions in a vision of high school that is bleak but supremely just. The movie's villain, an over-achieving girl (Reese Witherspoon) who runs for class president, turns out to be its covert heroine, or, at least, its most poignant character. A cross between Pat and Dick Nixon, she's a lower-middle-class striver who works like crazy and never wins anyone's love. Even when she's on top, she feels excluded. Her loneliness is produced not by malicious cliques but by her own implacable will, a condition of the spirit that may be as comical and tragic as it is mysterious. *Election* escapes all the clichés; it graduates into art.

After Reading

Critical Perspective

1. Describe how Denby commences his essay. Do you think that this is an effective approach? Why or why not? Explain your responses.

Rhetoric and Argument

2. Consider how Denby utilizes rhetorical tactics, specifically audience, purpose, ethos, pathos, logos, intertextuality, context, and constraints. Do you believe that his text is rhetorically effective? Present evidence to support your perspectives.
3. What is Denby's main claim in this piece? How do you know? Do you find this claim believable? Be sure to give examples from the text as well as your own experiences to back up your assertions.
4. How does Denby substantiate his thesis? Do you think that it is adequately supported by evidence? Why or why not? Is there any other type of evidence (as additional examples) he might employ that would additionally support his thoughts?
5. In his conclusion Denby contends that certain films such as *Clueless, Romy and Michele's High School Reunion*, and *Election* seem to criticize the genre of the teen movie itself (both the outsider-becomes-popular version and the outsider-undermines/kills-the-popular version). Consider these three films. How do they criticize the genre? Be sure to point to evidence from the films as well as from Denby's text.

Analysis

6. Write an informal argumentative response in which you furnish a cultural criticism of another teen film or a teen television show not mentioned in Denby's essay. To which of the narrative structures Denby articulates does it belong? How do you know? What does this cultural text reveal about contemporary youth culture? Draw your evidence from a close analysis of film or television show. In addition, be sure to consult library and Internet sources to back up your assertions.

Taking Action

As a class, watch a popular teen movie such as *She's the Man, Take the Lead, Win a Date with Tad Hamilton, A Cinderella Story, Not Another Teen Movie*, or any other such film. Take detailed notes on what specific traits (according to Denby's essay) you think this film fulfills and why. Then as a large group discuss what you noticed about the characters and plot lines in the film.

After you have had a chance to screen a popular film that likely conforms to genre conventions, watch a documentary that examines some of the difficulties of teen life (*It Ain't Love, Country Boys, The Education of Shelby Knox*, or others). What specific difficulties about teen life does this documentary address that the other film did not? What positive or negative effects has the genre had on teens themselves? In what ways do you think the genre needs to develop, expand, or change?

JILL FIELDS

"Romancing the Race Card with *Nurse Betty*"

Jill Fields is an activist, alternative rock musician, and professor at California State University, Fresno, where she teaches U.S. social, cultural and women's history. She has published several articles on women's history and cultural theory, as well as the book Sexual Foundations: Intimate Apparel in Modern America.

EXERCISING YOUR SKILLS

Before Reading

Fields writes about how race, gender, and ethnicity issues often work together in today's movies. Watch a series of contemporary films, including *Nurse Betty*, that represent different racial and ethnic groups. In what ways do you feel that stereotyping or racism operates in these films? Be sure to present examples from the visual texts to support your ideas.

Well into the movie *Nurse Betty*, protégé hitman Wesley (Chris Rock) replies in exasperation to his mentor Charlie (Morgan Freeman) that it is certainly not beneath Betty (Renee Zellweger) to be en route to Los Angeles looking for a soap opera star with whom she is enamored, because "the bitch is a fuckin' housewife—ain't nothing beneath her." But Wesley is wrong, at least according to the narrative logic of this film. In *Nurse Betty*, black men are positioned far below white housewives.[1]

Nurse Betty is a tale about a number of very different people whose paths cross at important transitional moments in their lives. To tell all their stories, the film invokes a range of generic conventions from male buddy movies to screwball comedies to road pictures to, well, soap operas. And, despite its comedic air, there are several graphic scenes depicting brutal violence. Some film critics think this genre-bending strategy works well, and praise the movie as imaginative; others don't think it all hangs together and give it a thumbs down.[2] I found the parts of the movie that explored the often blurry boundaries between reality and fantasy the most engaging, entertaining, and interesting, and appreciated the acting throughout. But I didn't find the director adequately skillful in juxtaposing the funny, yet thoughtful scenes that address questions about the role of illusion both in our daily and TV lives with the scenes of grisly violence, and so began to wonder why the latter were included. Throwing bloody and gruesome images on the screen to provoke narrative tension is a well-worn method, and their appearance in *Nurse Betty* could simply be

---

[1] *Nurse Betty*, directed by Neil LaBute, was released September 2000. It became available on DVD in 2003. The screenplay was published by Newmarket Press (November 2000). This 1999 "shooting script" by screen writers John C. Richards & James Flamberg varies from the finished film.

[2] For example, *New York Times* critic Stephen Holden wrote a very favorable review ("Fragile: Handle With Dreams," September 8, 2000), while *Los Angeles Times* critic Kenneth Turan did not ("Nurse, Check for a Heartbeat: Even Renee Zellweger Can't Melt the Ice Water That Has Frozen in *Nurse Betty*'s Veins," September 8, 2000).

evidence of laziness or lack of creativity. But there's more to it than that. The stereotypical portrayals of black and brown men as prone to sudden, often inexplicable and clearly
uncontrollable acts of violence are an integral part of this film. And in *Nurse Betty*, the
alleged violent and transgressive proclivities of black men justify their ultimate disappearance from the screen.[3]

One of those violent scenes comes early in the movie and is extremely critical because
it not only sets the narrative in motion, but also signals the film's underlying concern with
racial issues. The film opens on Betty's birthday, and Betty's coworkers in the diner where
she works as a waitress give her two presents: a life-size cut-out of her favorite soap opera
character, Dr. David Ravell (Greg Kinnear), and some money for the nursing classes she
stopped taking because of her abusive husband Del's (Aaron Eckhart) objections. Del runs
a used car lot in their small home town of Fair Oaks, Kansas and is cheating on Betty with
his office assistant. He also completely ignores her birthday that night, orders her around,
and adds insult to injury when he takes a bite out of her birthday cupcake without even
noticing there's a candle in it.

When Del brings home two strangers—Wesley and Charlie—for a business meeting,
Betty has already retreated to the den to watch videotaped episodes of her favorite soap
opera, *A Reason to Love*. Clearly, this is a daily ritual for Betty, and an important avenue
for her to find relief from her dreadful marriage and inability to change her life for the
better.[4] Betty is a simple woman whose limited longings are not for more out of life, but
just "something," as one of her coworkers later puts it. Del, on the other hand, believes in
himself more than he should. Goaded by Wesley and Charlie to provide an example to back
up his claim that people in Fair Oaks are "dumb fucks," Del comments on the stupidity of
local Native Americans. In response, the self-controlled, consummate professional Charlie
calmly displays his knowledge of Kansas area tribal names and customs, and directs the
hot-headed and dangerously impulsive Wesley to tie Del up so that Charlie can question
him. Del, it seems, has stolen something—seemingly drugs—that Wesley and Charlie have
been hired to find and return to its owners. As Charlie continues his discourse on indigenous culture by describing the process of scalping and the long history of abuse of North
American Indians, Wesley cuts Del's head with the knife he has been threatening him with
to get him to talk. When he still doesn't disclose the information they seek, Wesley suddenly and savagely scalps Del. Charlie, though angry at Wesley for his brutal and prema-

---

[3]For another film analysis exploring the representation of African American men as violent, see
Matthew Henry, "He Is a "Bad Mother*S%@!#": Shaft and Contemporary Black Masculinity," *African
American Review* 38:1 (Spring 2004), 119–127.

[4]There are a number of studies of soap operas, including Tania Modleski, *Loving with a
Vengeance: Mass-Produced Fantasies for Women* (NY: Routledge, 1984); Robert Allen, *To Be
Continued: Soap Operas Around the World* (NY: Routledge, 1995); Kathy Newman, "Washboard
Weepers: Women Writers, Women Listeners, and the Debate Over Soap Operas," in her *Radio Active:
Advertising and Consumer Activism, 1937–1942* (Berkeley: University of California Press, 2004),
109–138; Louise Spence, *Watching Daytime Soap Operas: The Power of Pleasure* (Hanover, New
Hampshire: Wesleyan University Press, 2005).

ture action that makes their job of locating the stolen goods more difficult, shoots Del to put him out of his very apparent agony.

Betty, hearing some of the scuffling and moans, had opened the den door slightly, and so witnesses her husband's murder. In shock, she closes the door and responds to the trauma in the way she knows best—by focusing on her soap opera. The hit men leave, still unaware that anyone else was at home. Betty then begins to pack her bags and leave in the very car where, unbeknownst to her, Del hid the drugs. She is in a dissociative state, in which she believes she is leaving Del to find her former fiancé, Dr. Ravell, the famous Los Angeles heart surgeon. When Wesley and Charlie discover the next day that Betty is a potentially dangerous witness, or may have absconded with the stolen goods knowingly, they take off after her.

Initially while watching *Nurse Betty*, I started wondering about how, or even if, race was important to the film. Early on, I felt it was possible that, like *LA Weekly* reporter Ella Taylor commented in her review of the film, "the casting of Freeman and Rock has nothing to do with race."[5] In other words, the film was set up like the popular 1997–2002 television series *Ally McBeal* seemed to be: racially diverse, but not racially self-conscious, a tactic which kept the focus on gender relations.[6] Indeed, no one in the film comments upon Wesley and Charlie's African American identity and they are treated with suspicion by only one person while tracking Betty down. In that scene, they begin to question the female owner of a bar which they know Betty has visited, using their routine tactic of flashing fake police badges. They successfully use this ruse throughout the film to get information from Betty's Fair Oak friends, grandparents and new contacts in Los Angeles, who generally are cooperative, welcoming and trusting of Charlie and Wesley, treating them with apparent color-blindness. In this one instance, however, the bar owner doesn't believe the duo are cops because her ex-husband was a policeman. Their false identities stripped away, Charlie and Wesley respond with reckless force, lunging at and roughing up the bar owner and her lone, clearly harmless, male regular customer. The scene quickly ends and, while the fate of these assault victims is not shown, the true nature of Charlie and Wesley as thugs is authenticated. But are these acts just typical movie moments of gangster

[5]Ella Taylor, "Amazing Gracie: Renee Zellweger Makes Neil LaBute's Dizzy *Nurse Betty* Her Own," *L.A. Weekly* (September 8–14, 2000).

[6]For varying analyses on the gender politics of *Ally McBeal,* see, for example, Brenda Cooper, "Feminine Spectatorship, 'Comic Men,' and Unapologetic Women in David E. Kelley's *Ally McBeal,*" *Critical Studies in Media Communication*: 18 (2001): 416–435, M.D. Vavrus, "Putting Ally on Trial: Contesting Postfeminism in Popular Culture," *Women's Studies in Communication*: 23 (2000): 413–428, and Kathleen Newman, "The Problem That Has a Name: *Ally McBeal* and the Future of Feminism," *Colby Quarterly*: 36:4 (December 2000): 319–24. Nicole Armour's review of *Nurse Betty* in *Film Comment* (September 2000) finds similarities between the characters of Betty and Ally in terms of their emotional instability and [their] search for romantic love. A further link between the two characters is found in Kelly Marsh, "Contextualizing *Bridget Jones,*" *College Literature* 31.1 (Winter 2004): 52–72, which compares Ally McBeal to another film character played by Renee Zellweger, Bridget Jones (*Bridget Jones's Diary*, 2001; *Bridget Jones's: The Edge of Reason*, 2004).

intimidation or do they also validate the generalized and widespread social suspicion that black men are dangerous and prone to violent behavior?[7]

Perhaps if the only explicit reference to the effects and long-term consequences of racial inequity had been the scalping and murder of Betty's husband Del, justified in the film by Del's overt racism, sexism and homophobia, I would agree that Wesley and Charlie's—or Morgan Freeman and Chris Rock's—race is irrelevant to the film. But there are just too many moments in the film where race is explicitly mentioned to accept that view. Wesley utters many of these racial references, such as when he taunts Charlie by calling Betty a "skinny white bitch from Kansas" after he rips in half the photograph of her that Charlie has become increasingly fond of gazing at. Later, when they are in Los Angeles, Wesley returns from a stroll down Hollywood Boulevard complaining to Charlie that he could not find top-forty soul singer Peabo Bryson nor any other person of color honored on that well-known Walk of Fame. Neither of these references, nor other similar ones, contribute to the plot per se and could easily have been left out. Nevertheless, because they are uttered, together they do important work in this movie's plot: they function to mark Charlie and Wesley's otherwise unspoken racial difference.[8]

Significantly, Wesley's expletive-laced and comedic-edged dialogue evokes the stand-up stage persona of Chris Rock, who is known, like many successful comedians, for humor based on ethnic or racial identity.[9] In one pivotal scene while the two men briefly stop at the Grand Canyon, Charlie begins to evidence a delusional state similar to Betty's. His professional know how in tracking people down requires getting into their heads to figure out where they have gone, but in this case his skill has transformed into a deepening romantic fantasy about Betty. He begins to imagine he is dancing with her and as he fantasizes about kissing her, Wesley, still in the car, looks up and is disgusted by Charlie's behavior. When Charlie returns to the car, Wesley ridicules him by asking if he got "in touch with [his] blackness" while "dancing like Bo Jangles out there." This comment not only references the two men's African American identity, but also evokes, even in this jumbled form, the larger historical context of racial discrimination and resistance.

---

[7]Additional evidence of the effectiveness of the color-blind approach of the film is that very few popular media reviewers of the film mention the hit men's race. The few that do, such as Gary Susman, "Soap Dish: *Nurse Betty* Redeems Neil LaBute," Boston *Phoenix* (September 9, 2000), Stuart Klawans, "A Nurse to Die For," *The Nation* (October 2, 2000), and Stanley Kauffmann, "On Films," *The New Republic*, (September 18, 2000), do so only in passing.

[8]Actually, people of color do appear on the Hollywood Walk of Fame, including Hattie McDaniel, who in 1940 became the first African American to win an Oscar, Paul Robeson, Anna May Wong, and Desi Arnaz, and more recent honorees Carlos Santana, Paula Abdul, and Jackie Chan. Chris Rock received his own star on Hollywood Boulevard in 2003. However, given the fact that people of color remain underrepresented on the Walk of Fame, as in Hollywood films generally, it is certainly possible that Wesley didn't see any stars honoring them during his brief walk. More to the point, his observation is clearly meant as a critical commentary on the larger problem of diversity in American movies.

[9]In fact, some of the racial references made by Chris Rock that have an improvised, stand-up feel to them do not appear or are somewhat altered in the shooting script. See, for example, scene 112, p. 99 and scene 128, p. 114.

Meanwhile, Betty's own far deeper delusional state is enabling her to quickly achieve some of her long-on-hold life goals: she believes she is a nurse and gets a job at a hospital, and she believes she is the ex-fiancée of the loving and accomplished Doctor Ravell, and ends up meeting and dazzling the actor, George, who plays him in *A Reason to Love*. Both of these achievements result not only from Betty's new found determination and confidence in her own capabilities, but also from the interventions of people of color. The outcome of Betty's initial, unsuccessful nursing job interview changes when Betty performs a life-saving medical procedure on a Latino man shot during a sudden, never explained drive-by shooting by other Latino men at the hospital entrance. Rosa (Tia Texada), the sister of the man whose life she saves, offers her a place to stay, and also her assistance in locating Dr. Ravell. Rosa's outraged discovery that Dr. Ravell is a soap opera character affords a scene of stereotypical fiery Latina pique, but nonetheless Rosa is also the conduit for Betty meeting "Dr. Ravell" when her attorney boss hands over tickets to a charity function that George and other members of the cast and crew of *A Reason to Love* are attending. Feeling that she has been made a fool, Rosa hopes the evening will burst Betty's bubble. Instead, when Betty introduces herself to George, he is fascinated by what he believes is Betty's inspiring commitment to method acting and gets Betty what he believes she wants—a part on the show.

On the soap opera hospital set, Betty confronts the reality of her delusions and painfully emerges from her trance. She returns to Rosa's apartment, determined to leave for Fair Oaks and find out exactly what happened to Del. As she packs her suitcase, Charlie and Wesley show up outside, having finally tracked down the drugs hidden in the car trunk. Relieved, Charlie and Wesley poignantly reconcile their often testy relationship, and Wesley suggests they take the drugs and leave to deliver them and get paid. But Charlie wants to meet Betty, and so they go inside. Shortly after, two other men on Betty's trail arrive: the white sheriff and newspaper reporter from Fair Oaks. After the hit men tie them all up, Charley takes Betty into the bedroom. Wesley doesn't like this turn of events, and their usual roles reverse: now he is the one warning Charlie that his behavior is unprofessional. The implication is that Charlie is going to rape Betty, but once inside the bedroom he cuts her bound wrists loose and tells her how much he appreciates her fine qualities. Charlie believes that despite their differences they have much in common and could be together. In another role reversal for Charlie, Betty becomes the cooler head and clearer thinker, pointing out "I just don't think I'm who you think I am."

In the meantime, a comedic scene is unfolding in the living room, as the captives begin to talk with Wesley. When the reporter mentions that Jasmine, a soap opera character whom Wesley has shown some attraction for, is a lesbian, Wesley reacts in outraged disbelief. Rosa suggests they all watch the video Betty taped of that day's show to find out the truth, and they do. While Wesley is engrossed in the episode, the sheriff attempts to retrieve a gun hidden in his pant leg. When he inadvertently drops the gun in Rosa's large aquarium, the reporter knocks over the tank. Caught off guard, Wesley is shot by the sheriff. The comedy of the scene comes to an abrupt, painful halt when just before he dies, there is a close up of Wesley's blood soaked face as he poignantly calls out, "Daddy."

His last word transforms the cocky gangster into a vulnerable young son, and reframes the meaning of Wesley and Charlie's interactions throughout the entire film.

Charlie retreats back to the bedroom under fire, greatly shocked and saddened by the death of his son. Betty has managed to get his gun during the confusion, and Charlie begs her to return it to him so he can die like the professional he is, with guns blazing. To further convince her, the scene takes an unexpected turn. Rather than overpowering Betty with force, which presumably would not be too difficult, Charlie tells Betty, "You never needed that actor. You don't need that doctor. You don't need any man. You don't need anybody. You know why? 'Cause you've got yourself." At that, Betty lowers the gun and smiles as Charlie kisses her on the cheek, takes the gun and walks out of the room. Betty's reverie after this uplifting exchange is interrupted only by a gun shot.

Charlie's death and the end of Betty's nightmare mark the beginning of her new life as a confident woman in charge of her destiny. The publicity surrounding the case inspires the producers of *A Reason to Love* to send George out to Fair Oaks to convince Betty to come back to LA and appear on the show. During their meeting over coffee at the diner, Betty demonstrates her emancipation from her former life as a door mat when she insists on paying the check because, "It's not the '40s you know." Following a montage of friends happily watching Betty's soap opera performance on TV, the film ends with Betty in Italy, sitting at a sidewalk café enjoying her coffee while her waiter stands transfixed watching *A Reason to Love* on Italian television. A super title, appearing over a shot from above of Betty strolling through a beautiful piazza, tells us that Betty appeared on 63 soap opera episodes and, after her European vacation, will be "using her earnings to pay for a nursing degree."

This narrative closure is a "Hollywood ending," an ending where the star of the film and protagonist finds happiness, and the audience can leave the theater happy as well. But it is also a Hollywood ending because, as in many recent Hollywood films, black male characters rarely make it alive to the closing credits.[10] As African American rapper and actor Snoop Dogg pointed out when commenting on the rare pleasure of his character's survival to the end of *Starsky and Hutch* (2004), "You never see a new rapper coming into a movie role where's he's playing an orthodontist or a top-notch lawyer. He's always gonna come in with a gun in his hand, talkin' sh*t and getting killed."[11]

Equally disturbing, and not at all unrelated, the story line in *Nurse Betty* tells us that white women achieve their liberation as a result of the efforts and ultimate sacrifice of black men.[12] And, the way this tale unfolds, it is when black men are most like white

---

[10]There are many examples of this common phenomenon, such as *The Shining* (1980), *Terminator 2: Judgement Day* (1991), *Green Mile* (1999), *Monster's Ball* (2001), and *In America* (2003).

[11]"Interviews: Snoop Dogg on *Starsky & Hutch*" (February 25, 2004), http://snoopheaven.tripod.com/interviews/starsky.htm.

[12]For an interesting, related analysis of the role of black male cinematic characters as "magical friends" who use their powers to benefit whites, see Heather J. Hicks, "Hoodoo Economics: White Men's Work and Black Men's Magic in Contemporary American Film," *Camera Obscura* 18:2 (2003): 27–55. This phenomenon has also been noticed by popular film critics such as Christopher John Farley, "That Old Black Magic," *Time* (November 27, 2000): 14, and David Sterritt, "The Face of An Angel," *Christian Science Monitor* (July 11, 2003).

women in the film—in their love of and involvement with soap operas, and in their propensity for indulging in romantic illusion—that they are most vulnerable to destruction. When Charlie and Wesley act based on these conventionally feminine feelings, their fate is doomed. Black men thus are adversely pressed in this film from two directions: when their acts display conventional masculinity in the extreme (brutal violence) and confirm racist stereotypes, and also when they transgress the boundaries of white masculinity and act out conventional femininity (watch daytime TV!). Perhaps if Charlie, instead of falling in love with Betty through looking at a photograph of her and imaging the effects her purity and grace could have upon him, had been depicted finding sexual self-gratification in looking at her picture or shown calling a 900 number to talk to a woman he could call Betty, everything would have turned out differently for the black men in this movie. After all, that type of widespread, daily male behavior, which is just a different mode of fantasy and projection not all that far removed from Betty's illusory relationship with a soap opera actor, is coded conventionally masculine in our culture and therefore a safe way for American men to indulge their fantasies without threatening their masculinity. Indeed, this kind of fantasizing is a way for men to confirm their masculinity. Instead, Charlie and Wesley pay a severe price for their racialized, gender transgressions.

Film critic Roger Ebert comments in his review of *Nurse Betty* that Betty and Charlie are "two dreamers who fall in love with their own fantasies," and that, as he says, they "are parallel characters . . . [who] are almost the same person."[13] That in the film Betty locates her elaborate fantasy about Dr. Ravell's marriage proposal to her at the same spot—the Grand Canyon—where Charlie imagines dancing with and kissing Betty substantiates Ebert's insight. However, situating these two important scenes in this quintessentially American location suggests a direction for taking Ebert's analysis further. Issues of race and gender merge in the film not only through the film characters' shared appreciation of soap operas and romantic fantasies, but also because of the shared social space that black men and white women occupy in the United States. The structure and meaning of this overlapping position, both historically and currently, are topics investigated in a range of disciplines, or, if you will, academic genres. Economic data tells us that the sliding scale of income in the U.S. finds black men and white women in the middle below white men and above black women. Research in women's and African American studies explains how historically, racialized notions of sexuality upheld white and male supremacy by constructing black men as sexual predators, black women as licentious, and white women as pure and in need of protection by white men. These ideas justified rapes of black women, and made sexual relationships between black men and white women, both real and imagined, the pretext for lynching black men. Political science analysis reveals the struggles between African American men and women and white women over the constitutional amendment granting black men, but not women, the right to vote in 1870. Recent anti-affirmative action public policy commentary has sought to discredit affirmative action by focusing more on racial "quotas" than on the beneficial effects for all women. And in Louisiana in 2004

---

[13]Roger Ebert, "*Nurse Betty*," *Chicago Sun-Times* (September 8, 2000).

and Virginia in 2005, young black men and young white women were linked culturally in news reports, many of which were humorous, on each state's legislative attempts to regulate the public exposure of underwear in contemporary fashions. Clearly, there is much to say about the long and complex relationship between black men and white women.[14]

Nurse Betty speaks to that relationship through a narrative that puts black men and white women in a similar social and cultural space. However, instead of allowing that affinity to be mutually rewarding, the film ultimately buys off the white housewife by providing her the job and educational opportunities, and fabulous trip to Italy she previously has only been able to fantasize about. But at whose expense? To enable her success, the movie's plot does what is far too commonplace in the U.S.: exploit and execute black men. The ending of *Nurse Betty* works because the film makers rely upon their own and their audience's familiarity with what should be an unacceptable narrative solution.[15]

[14]Studies of the multi-faceted relationship between black men and white women in the United States include Jacqueline Dowd Hall, "'The Mind That Burns in Each Body': Women, Rape, and Racial Violence," in Ann Snitow, et al., editors, *Powers of Desire: The Politics of Sexuality* (NY: Monthly Review Press, 1983): 328–49; Martha Hodes, *White Women, Black Men: Illicit Sex in the Nineteenth-Century South* (New Haven: Yale University Press, 1997); Marjorie Spruill Wheeler, editor, *One Woman, One Vote: Rediscovering the Woman Suffrage Movement* (Troutdale, Oregon: New Sage Press, 1995); Peggy Pascoe, "Miscegenation Law, Court Cases, and Ideologies of 'Race' in 20th-Century America," *Journal of American History* 83:1 (June 1996): 44–70; Faye J. Crosby, et al., editors, *Sex, Race, and Merit: Debating Affirmative Action in Education and Employment* (Ann Arbor: University of Michigan Press, 2000); Susan Courtney, Vincent Hutchings, Nicholas Valentino, Tasha Philpot, and Ismail White, "The Compassion Strategy: Race and the Gender Gap in Campaign 2000," *Public Opinion Quarterly* 68:4 (2004): 512–541; *Hollywood Fantasies of Miscegenation: Spectacular Narratives of Gender and Race, 1903–1967* (Princeton, NJ: Princeton University Press, 2004); "Special Issue: Affirmative Action," *International Social Science Journal* 57: 183 (March 2005); Nancy Bentley, "The Strange Career of Love and Slavery: Chesnutt, Engels, Masoch," *American Literary History* 17:3 (Fall 2005): 460–485. The state laws proposed—which did not pass—would have set fines for public exposure of underwear. Most news reports described the bills as targeting the shorts revealing, low-slung, baggy trousers worn by young black men, and the low-rise jeans and thongs worn by young white women. See "Low-Riding to Jail," *Times Picayune*, April 24, 2004; Jan Moller, "How Low Can You Go? Panel Decides," *Times-Picayune*, May 7, 2004; Ed Anderson, "House Ditches Britches Bill," *Times-Picayune*, May 26, 2004; Bruce Ward, "Thong of the South," *The Ottawa Citizen*, May 29, 2004; Bethany Thomas, "Memo to Britney: Lose the Low-Slungs," NBC News http://msnbc.com/id/4963512/ May 13, 2004; Tammie Smith, "Low-Ride Pants Bill Advances," *Richmond Times-Dispatch*, February 5, 2005; Tammie Smith, "House Passes Underwear Measure," *Richmond Times-Dispatch*, February 9, 2005; Alyssa Rashbaum, "Show Me Your Thong, Show Me The Money: Virginia Cracks Down on Pants," MTV News, http://www.vh1.com/news/articles/1496756/20050209/index.jhtml?headlines=true, February 9, 2005; Christina Bellantoni, "'Droopy Drawers' Bill Seeks End to Overexposure of Underwear," *The Washington Times*, February 9, 2005.

[15]For a succinct overview on race and the death penalty, see Christina Swarns, "The Uneven Scales of Capital Justice: How Race and Class Affect Who Ends Up on Death Row," *The American Prospect* 15:7 (July 2004), pp. 14–16.

Notes

I wish to acknowledge the very helpful comments on earlier drafts of this essay by scholars Tania Modleski, Malik Simba and Lynn Sacco.

After Reading

Critical Perspective

1. How does this text affect you as a reader? What about your own experiences and thoughts might contribute to why you have this reaction?

Rhetoric and Argument

2. What sort of rhetorical tactics—use of audience, purpose, ethos, pathos, logos, inter-textuality, context, and constraints—does Fields employ in this essay? Do you find these strategies effective in conveying her argumentative claim? Why or why not?
3. What kind of tone does Fields use in her essay? Do you believe that this tone adds to the credence of her argument or not? Be able to point to specific examples of this tone from her essay.
4. What does Fields argue about how race and gender are operating in the film *Nurse Betty*? Where in her essay does she make this assertion? Do you find Fields' claim viable? Why or why not? Provide quotes from the text to support your ideas.
5. What sorts of evidence does Fields furnish for her assertion? Give examples of this evidence. Do you find this evidence sufficient to back up her claim? Why or why not? What sorts of warrants and assumptions are at work in her text?

Analysis

6. Write a short argumentative response in which you consider a television show or film in which race and gender are depicted in ways that you find troubling. Offer a cultural criticism in which you explain what bothers you about the representations and what might you change about them. Provide a detailed analysis of the cultural text. Include library and Internet sources to support your ideas.

Taking Action

Using an email or letter format, write a short cultural criticism about a recent film of your own choosing that you can analyze along gender, race, ethnicity, and class lines. Consult the primary cultural texts as well as library and Internet sources. Imagine your audience is made up of people outside the class who have not yet seen the film.

Once you have completed your essay, share your writing with your classmates and then have a discussion about how contemporary films are taking up these issues. Do you see any changes occurring in the last few years? If yes, how so? If no, why not?

MUSIC

Josh Delmar Zimmerman

"Punk's Not Dead"

Josh Delmar Zimmerman taught for many years in the writing program at Northern Arizona University for which this book was first designed. He found working with these students particularly inspiring because they "challenged certain hegemonic values of academia that marginalize identities." Zimmerman and his family now live in Portland, Oregon where he plans to teach high school English and writing classes. While working at the high school level he hopes to continue to explore the idea of personal/cultural identity.

EXERCISING YOUR SKILLS

Before Reading

Zimmerman describes the ways in which people are stereotyped based upon the music they like. He focuses primarily on the effects of punk music. Have you ever been stereotyped based on the music to which you listen, the friends with whom you hang out, or the activities in which you engage? How did this make you feel? How did you respond to it?

The old man hurled a trash can lid at us like it was a frisbee. "Get out of here you worthless bastards!" It wasn't like we had ever seen him before or that he had ever told us not to skate on the loading docks. It just happened to be a coincidence that his apartment was directly behind the grocery store. The fact that we, a couple of skate punks, were having some fun on a Phoenix afternoon sent him over the edge. We weren't smoking pot, we weren't drinking, and we weren't playing any loud music or anything! This guy decides to pull his paperweight ass off the couch to pick up the nearest implement of destruction. No! Not now! I won't let these kids ruin my afternoon. They're breaking the routine! It is 4:00 pm and there should be no disturbances right now. I got it! I'll regress to a quasi-pseudo-authoritative level to enforce laws upon these kids where others have failed. Take this!

I remember we were dumbfounded by this person's action. We all stopped, looked calmly at one another, looked at him, listened to his words, walked assuredly over to the fence, flipped him off, and skated away with his trash can lid. He then started screaming that he wanted his lid back. Most often the threat of a call to the police is never actualized because people do not usually want to involve themselves with the responsibilities of filling out papers to file a complaint. If they do call, the description of a couple of kids on skateboards with no shirts or shredded dirty shirts tied around their waists, wild hair, long, colored, or spiked, usually proved insignificant; we were everywhere. But that had its down side because lots of assumptions by the police would be made. Sometimes they would stop you on the street because they thought you fit a description or, even more fun, because they "thought you were up to something." Basically, if you were on a skateboard or if your jeans were pegged and you wore a T-shirt with a band like Exploited, Social Distortion, Dead Kennedys, Minor Threat, or Youth Brigade on it, you were immediately profiled as belonging to a class of wasted youth. Being classified as such was the best thing to ever happen to me.

1984, high school, freshman year, English class. "You like DOA?" "Yeah." "I'm Scott, nice to meet you." Scott wore combat boots, pegged jeans, red suspenders over an Exploited shirt, and a mohawk. I wore sandals, bermuda shorts, a tucked in Polo shirt, and trimmed hair. Scott saw the DOA logo I had drawn on my folder. They were a Canadian punk band I had been listening to for over a year, since I started skating. Scott and I, according to clothing styles, were from opposite ends of the galaxy, but we became good friends nonetheless. After talking with him for a little while, he invited me over to his friend's house to hang out after school.

I received a few strange looks when I walked inside. The Sub-Hum-Ans were playing loudly on the stereo, dirty clothes strewn about, skateboard parts formed a miscellaneous arrangement between the soda and beer cans. The place smelled of cigarette butts soaked in stale beer. Scott walked over to me and started giving introductions after he gave me a beer. Everyone seemed nice enough. Some more than others, but they all had an edge: something that hacks away at structures not designed by them. It was in their eyes, some blurrier than others, but it was there. They embodied the unfettered and unstructured qualities of a youthful mind, chaotic. It was exciting for me to see people with such diverse styles and characters being accepted for their "creativeness." Visually, I was the outsider and not self-creative. Internally, something bound me to them and I wanted that look that was in their eyes. I wanted an edge.

Sub Hum Ans' songs like "Mickey Mouse Is Dead," "Dying World," "Big Brother," and "Get to Work on Time," on the *Worlds Apart* and *The Day the Country Died* albums. The songs speak for themselves. They are making a claim and standing out against a society that holds their voice and lifestyle as invalid. The music helped me begin to see this inequity in society, and that punk music can serve as an outlet for frustrations and an avenue for unity; an edge was forming. I remember talking to Scott about other punk bands while thinking at the same time that this place, Mike's house, with these people, was something my parents would freak out about if they saw me here. Judgments are easily made against groups radically different from your own. It is safe to judge other groups because, most likely, others in the group are judging in a similar fashion and your opinion won't stand out as contentious; contention is what punk is about. I became good friends with most of the people at Mike's house this day. They were the most "real" people I had ever met.

According to some texts, punk music began around 1973 or 1974 at CBGB's in New York: a small club that helped promote prolific bands such as the Ramones and The Talking Heads. In conjunction with the "beginning" of punk, common thought is that punk died with Sid Vicious from the Sex Pistols around 1979. I highly disagree. The idea that punk died and became diffused into other subcultural groups such as the mods, the Oi!

movement, and even skate punks is just as oppressive as the political, the social, and the economic preferential treatments that inspired punk in the first place. The hippies had a message, but had no action. The punk attitude consists primarily of action, be it the destruction of private property, deliberate acts against authority, or jumping into the revolving circular motion of a pit. Punk is aggressive, it is a train wreck, it is the gnashing of teeth, it is a thumb through a car door, it is socially unacceptable, it is outrageous, it is creative, expressive, and personal. Given the multiple dimensions of what is punk, simply put, punk is a youthful, ostentatious voice that declares a stance against that which will not listen: society. Punk is an education.

For a point of reference, I come from the higher end of middle class but not upper middle class and a few of my other skate punk friends do as well. However, most of the people that I associated with in the skate punk scene came from lower middle class families. Some had single parents and some did not; all were loved by whomever they lived with. But not all were loved by whomever they associated with: school for instance. Chris had a mohawk saturated with egg whites to extend it to its full eight or nine inches into the sky. He was told his hair was unacceptable at our high school and was forced to keep it down; he shaved his head clean. Supposedly, his hair inhibited other students' desires to learn. Somehow, Chris's hair made it difficult for teachers to teach. It was assumed that Chris's hair hindered the learning experience. How does hair affect the education system in a negative manner? We saw it as the school's weak attempt to enforce authority upon him, us. We were of a lesser class than them. Whatever idiocy created their reason, its reception shown them in a negative manner.

Of course not all teachers discriminated against my friends whose clothing and hairstyles were hardcore. It was mostly the administrators. Police also discriminated against us, especially if we were out on the streets skating around. More often than not we would skate through the streets to explore the city because there was nothing better to do. One night the police stopped us and lined us all up against a wall. "What were you doing?" "Nothing, just skating." "Get in the car." He went down the line asking everyone the same question and giving the same final response. After a while, we all just walked directly into the cars without talking to him. The condescending, arrogant, couldn't-satisfy-his-wife-and-is-pissed-off-because-of-it cop filled the three cop cars with all of us. What was never and should never have been a "scene" was now a huge scene. We were irate. Our refutations were, "Not to be tolerated," and impish threats were made of taking us to jail. We did nothing! Then a cop recognized Rob's name and told him that his brother was arrested the night before and that Rob would be in jail with him soon enough. We could feel the rage this comment inspired in Rob. We could see his fist crushing his skateboard and, in his mind, hurling it at the cop. Because of our dress, because of our taste in activities, because of the cop's lack of creativity and originality, he decided to ruin our night and enforce our disdain for people of his class: an authoritative class.

No one who Scott introduced me to at Mike's house ever judged me poorly because of my supportive family and lifestyle. They accepted me for how I acted and thought. They listened to what I had to say. In many respects, the good friends that I made in the skate punk community have been the most real or authentic people I have ever met. Not to say this community, this subculture, is the only breeding ground for real and authentic humans, but I think the more creative and unique individuals on this planet originate from similar communities: communities that foster individuality and question the order of things.

The cultural diversity of our high school and our group helped foster our individuality as well as our open mindedness. We did not utilize the classification systems used by most of society, which tend to group people according to race and class. We challenged the potentially racist and classist discourses around us. As long as you can use society's classification system against them you will be fine. It is the herd mentality from which punk protects itself. "I wanna be stereotyped, I wanna be classified, I want a suburban home" is a line in a Descendants song mocking society's propensity toward commonality. Most punk bands enforce awareness in opposition to such a phenomenon. Or maybe it is a phenomenon to be otherwise; to be an individual without class preference or distinction. To be an otherwise, a phenomenon, is to have an edge and use it to cut away at the conveniences of society. It is convenient for society to classify, to judge, to turn its ear from a valid and yet misrepresented part of any community: its youth. Jello Biafra titled an album for his band Dead Kennedys, "Give Me Convenience, or Give Me Death," to enforce the notion that society tends to commit itself to laziness rather than accepting challenges which may prove more beneficial or progressive.

Sometimes trashcan lids are convenient. Sometimes telling a kid to cut his hair is convenient. Sometimes throwing kids into a police car for fun is convenient. Sometimes whirling around in a circle of individuals with arms flying, legs kicking, bodies slamming, music thrashing, and lyrics penetrating is dangerous. In a pit there is no class distinction. There is no judgment. There is only aggression being released in the best manner certain people see fit. The pit is circular. It inspires individuality, and it inspires community. But what inspires the pit is a type of alienation. The same type of alienation that tells us to get out, or to get a haircut, or to listen to bombastic authority figures who seem to fear the youth who think for themselves and have chaos as their only outlet for frustrations. Think about it. If you were an authority figure threatened by strong minds that have not yet matured, wouldn't you be afraid? Fuck yeah you would.

After Reading

Critical Perspective

1. How does Zimmerman's essay strike you as a reader? What about his language choices makes you have this reaction?

Rhetoric and Argument

2. How does Zimmerman establish credibility or ethos in this text? Point to places in the text that reveal him to be a credible source about punk music and punk culture. Also examine his use of audience, purpose, ethos, pathos, logos, intertextual-

ity, context, and constraints. Do you think his rhetorical tactics are effective? Why or why not?

3. How does Zimmerman open this piece? Do you find this to be an effective approach to beginning an essay of this kind? Why or why not? Do you think it advances his purpose? If yes, how so? If not, why not? Be sure to provide evidence from his text to back up your thoughts.

4. What larger contention does Zimmerman make about the relationships between punk culture, class status, and challenges to conventional society? Where does he offer this claim in his essay? Do you agree with him about punk community functions? Why or why not?

5. How does the author support his assertions? What sorts of evidence does he use? Do you find this evidence sufficient to support his claim? Why or why not? Are there other forms of evidence you think that he might have used to make his text more persuasive? Explain your position.

6. What sorts of assumptions or warrants are at work in Zimmerman's text? Look through his text carefully and determine if you believe that his argument could be undermined by such concerns or not.

Analysis

7. Do you think that punk music—or, if you do not listen to this genre, music in general—has the power to undermine stereotypes, conventions, and other forms of social control? Try to present examples of this (or the lack thereof) from specific artists or musical groups that you enjoy. In what ways could this music offer alternative choices for youth culture, e.g., a challenge to the status quo? Write a short argumentative response that addresses these issues. Consult specific song lyrics as well as library and Internet sources to support your thoughts.

Taking Action

Attend a local musical event with several peers from class. Take notes on and analyze all of the details you notice about the other audience members, their behaviors and interactions with one another. In addition, consider the artists' performances—how they interact with the audience, what mood or atmosphere they are trying to create, the appeals to pathos they elicit from each other and the audience as well as how they use visuals, sound, arrangement, and lyrics. Consult relevant library and Internet materials.

As a small group, write a short descriptive cultural criticism about the event and your experiences. Share your response with the rest of the class. What does your cultural criticism reveal about the musical genre you were watching, about live performances versus recorded music and videos? What does it indicate about local bands versus national or internationally known musical artists?

JAMILAH EVELYN

"The Miseducation of Hip-Hop—Discrimination in Education"

Jamilah Evelyn is a staff reporter for The Chronicle of Higher Education *and the author of many essays on race, ethnicity, higher education, and student retention issues.*

EXERCISING YOUR SKILLS

Before Reading

Evelyn's text center on the impacts of hip hop music and culture on today's educational environments. What are some of the key issues that you believe college students are facing today? In what ways might students' musical choices reflect this? What other sorts of evidence give you the sense that this is the case? Do you think that your parents and your teachers understand these issues? Why or why not? Point to your own experiences and the experiences of those you know to substantiate your thoughts.

When Jason Hinmon transferred to the University of Delaware two years ago from Morehouse College in Atlanta, the 22-year-old senior says he almost dropped out his first semester.

He says that for financial reasons, he came back here to his hometown. But in many ways, he had never felt so abandoned.

"I came to class and my professors didn't know how to deal with me," he says, between bites of his à-la-carte lunch. "I could barely get them to meet with me during their office hours."

Dark-hued, dreadlocked and, well, young, he says many of his mostly White professors figured they had him pegged.

"They took one look at me and thought that I was some hip-hop hoodlum who wasn't interested in being a good student," he says.

But if Hinmon represents the "good" students with grounds to resent the stereotype, there are faculty who profess there's no shortage of young people willing to live up—or down—to it.

"You see students walking on campus reciting rap lyrics when they should be reciting something they'll need to know on their next test. Some of these same students you won't see back on campus next semester," says Dr. Thomas Earl Midgette, 50, director of the Institute for the Study of Minority Issues at historically Black North Carolina Central University.

"These rap artists influence the way they dress," he continues. "They look like hoochie mamas, not like they're coming to class. Young men with pants fashioned below their navel. Now, I used to wear bell-bottoms, but I learned to dress a certain way if I was negotiating the higher education maze. I had to trim my afro."

The difference between today's students and their parents, faculty and administrators is marked, no doubt. Technology's omnipresence—apparent in kids with little patience for anything less than instant meals, faster Internet information and cellular ubiquity—is certainly at play when it comes to explaining the divide.

But what causes more consternation among many college and university officials is a music form, a culture and a lifestyle they say is eating away at the morals, and ultimately the classroom experience, of today's college students.

Hip-hop—brash, vulgar, in-your-face hip-hop—is indisputably the dominant youth culture today. Its most controversial front men floss mad ice (wear lots of diamonds and other expensive jewelry), book bad bitches (usually scantily clad, less than the take home kind of girl) and in general, party it up. Its most visible females brag about their sexual dexterity, physical attributes and cunning tactics when it comes to getting their rent paid.

With college completion statistics at an embarrassing low and the Black–White achievement gap getting wider by the semester, perhaps it's time to be concerned about whether the culture's malevolent message is at play.

But can atrocious retention rates really be linked to reckless music? Or do university officials underestimate their students? Is it that young folk today have no sense of history, responsibility and plain good manners? Or are college faculty a bunch of old fogies simply more comfortable with Marvin Gaye's "Sexual Healing" than Little Kim's sexual prowess?

Is this no different than the divide we've always seen between young people and their college and university elders? Or do the disparities between this wave of students and those charged with educating them portend something more disparaging?

The Gap

At the heart of the rift between the two groups is a debate that has both sides passionately disturbed.

Young people say they feel pigeonholed by an image many of them don't support. They say the real rub is that their teachers—Black and White—believe the hype as much as the old lady who crosses the street when she sees them coming.

And they'd like their professors to consider this: They can listen to the music, even party to it, but still have a response just as critical, if not more so, than their faculty and administrators.

Others point out that the pervasiveness of hip-hop's immoral philosophies is at least partly rooted in the fact that the civil rights movement—the older generation's defining moment—surely did not live up to all its promises for Black America.

And further, they say it's important to note that not all hip-hop is irresponsible. In fact, some argue that it's ultimately empowering, uplifting and refreshing. After all, when was the last time a biology professor sat down with a Mos Def CD? How many can even pronounce his name?

Older faculty, administrators and parents alike respond that the music is downright filth. And anyone associated with it ought to have their mouths and their morals cleansed.

That there's a real problem when a marijuana-smoking ex-con named Snoop Doggy Dogg can pack a campus auditorium quicker than Black historian John Hope Franklin. When more students deify the late Tupac Shakur and his abrasive lyrics than those who ever read the great Martin Luther King Jr.'s "I Have a Dream" speech.

When kids decked out in sweats more pricey than their tuition complain that they can't afford a semester's books.

When the gains they fought so hard for are, in some ways, slowly slipping away.

"I think what causes us the most grief is that hip-hop comes across as heartless, value-less, nihilistic and certainly anachronistic if not atheistic," says Dr. Nat Irvin, president of Future Focus 2020, an urban futures think tank at Wake Forest University in North Carolina. "Anyone who would argue with that needs to take a look for themselves and see what images are prevalent on BET and MTV."

"But I don't think there's any question that the disconnect comes from the fact that old folks don't have a clue. They don't understand technology. The world has changed. And there's an enormous age gap between most faculty on college campuses and the rest of America," he says.

More than 60 percent of college and university faculty are over the age of 45. Meanwhile, nearly 53 percent of African Americans are under 30 and some 40 percent are under 20.

That means more than half of all Blacks were born after the civil rights movement and the landmark Brown vs. the Board of Education case.

"There's no big puzzle why these kids are coming with a different ideology," Irvin, 49, says.

'This Is What Blackness Is'

It is universally acknowledged that rap began in New York City's Bronx borough nearly 30 years ago, a mix of Jamaican reggae's dancehall, America's funk music, the inner city's pent-up frustrations and Black folks' general propensity to love a good party.

Pioneering artists like the The Last Poets, The Sugar Hill Gang, Kurtis Blow and Run-DMC combined creative genius and street savvy to put hip-hop on the map.

Its initial associations were with graffiti and party music, according to Dr. Robin D. G. Kelley, professor of history and Africana studies at New York University.

"Then in the late '80s, you begin to see more politicized manifestations of that. BDP, Public Enemy. . . . In essays that students wrote that were not about rap music, but about the urban condition itself, they would adopt the language. They would quote Public Enemy lyrics, they would quote Ghetto Boys," says Kelley, 38.

"This whole generation of Blacks in particular were trying to carve out for themselves an alternative culture," he continues. "I saw a whole generation for the first time say, 'I don't want to go to corporate America. I don't want to be an attorney. I don't want to be a doctor. I don't want to get paid. I want to make a revolution.'

"The wave that we're in now is all over the place," he explains.

But even hip-hop's fans stop short at endorsing some of the themes prevailing in today's music and mindset.

Kevin Powell, noted cultural critic and former hip-hop journalist, says the biggest difference between the music today and the music at its onset is that "we don't own it."

"Corporate America completely commodified hip-hop," he says. "We create the culture and corporate America takes it and sells it back to us and tells us, 'This is what Blackness is.'"

And while Powell, 34, says he is disappointed in some of the artists, especially the older ones who "should know better," many students are their staunchest defenders.

Caryn Wheeler, 18, a freshman at Bowie State University, explains simply that "every day isn't about love." Her favorite artists? Jay-Z, OutKast, Biggie Smalls, Tupac and Little Kim, many of whom are linked to hip-hop's controversial side. "We can relate because we see what they are talking about every day," she says.

Mazi Mutafa, 23, is a senior at the University of Maryland College Park and president of the Black Student Union there. He says he listens to jazz and hip-hop, positive artists and those who capture a party spirit. "There's a time to party and have fun, and Jay-Z speaks to that," he says. "But there needs to be a happy medium."

Interrupting, senior Christine Gonzalez, 28, says a lot of artists like Jay-Z tend to be revered by younger students. "As you get older, you tend to tone down your style and find that happy medium," she says. "It's all a state of mind."

"People have to understand that Jay-Z is kind of like a 100-level class—an intro to hip-hop. He brings a lot of people into its fan base," Mutafa chimes in. "But then you have groups like The Roots, which are more like a 400-level class. They keep you engaged in the music. But one is necessary for the other."

Erick Rivas, 17, a freshman also at the University of Maryland, says he listens to Mos Def, Black Star, Mobb Deep, Wu-Tang Clan and sometimes other, more mainstream acts like Jay-Z. "Hip-hop has been a driving force in our lives. It is the soundtrack to our lives," he explains.

Keepin' It Real

But if hip-hop is the soundtrack to their lives, it may also mark the failure of it.

DeReef Jamison, a doctoral candidate who teaches African American history at Temple University in Philadelphia, surveyed 72 Black male college students last summer for his thesis. Then a graduate student at Florida A&M State University, Jamison was interested in discovering if there are links between students' music tastes and their cultural identity, their grades and other key indicators.

"While the lines weren't always so clear and distinct, I found that many of the students who had a low African self-consciousness, who overidentified with a European world view and who were highly materialistic were often the students who listened to the most 'gangster' rap, or what I prefer to call reality rap," he explains.

As for grades, he says the gangster rap devotees' tended to be lower than those students who listened mostly to what he calls more conscious rap. Still, he's reluctant to draw any hard and fast lines between musical preference and student performance.

"I'd recommend that scholars take a much closer look at this," he says.

Floyd Beachum, a graduate student at Bowling Green State University in Ohio, surveyed secondary students to try to ascertain if there was a correlation between their behavior and the music they listened to.

"The more hyper-aggressive students tended to listen to more hardcore, gangster rap," he says. "Those who could identify with the violence, the drive-by shootings, the stereotypes about women—many times that would play out in their lives."

But Beachum, who teamed up with fellow Bowling Green graduate student Carlos Mc-Cray to conduct his research, says he isn't ready to draw any sweeping conclusions either.

"Those findings weren't across the board," he says, adding that he believes school systems can play a role in reversing any possible negative trends.

"If hip-hop and rap influence behavior and you bring all that to school, then the schools should create a very different environment and maybe we'll see more individuals go against the grain," he says.

Even undergraduates say they must admit that they see hip-hop's squalid influence on some of their peers.

"It upsets me when some young people complain that they can't get a job but when they go into that interview, they refuse to take off their do-rags, their big gold medallion and their baggy pants," says Kholiswa Laird, 18, a freshman at the University of Delaware. "But for some stupid reason, a lot of them feel like they're selling out if they wear proper clothes."

"That's just keepin it real," explains Davren Noble, 20, a junior at the University of Delaware. "Why should I have to change myself to get a job? If somebody wants to hire me but they don't like my braids, then either one of two things will happen: They'll just have to get over it or I just won't get the job."

It's this kind of attitude that many in higher education see as the crux of the problem.

"We're not gonna serve them well in the university if we don't shake their thinking about how dress is going to influence job opportunities," says Central's Midgette.

Noble, from Maplewood, N.J., is a rapper. And he says that while he grew up in a posh suburb, he often raps about violence.

"I rap about positive stuff too, but as a Black person in America, it's hard to escape violence," he explains. "Mad Black people grew up in the ghetto and the music and our actions reflect that."

For sure, art has been known to imitate life. Hip-hop icon Sean "Puffy" Combs—who two years ago gave $750,000 to his alma mater, Howard University—faced charges on his involvement in a Manhattan nightclub shooting. Grammy-winning rapper Jay-Z, also was connected with a night club dispute that ended with a record company executive being stabbed.

A Bad Rap?

A simple explanation for the boldness of much of rap's lyrics is that "artists have always pushed the limits," Kelley says.

But what's more, there is a politically conscious, stirring, enriching side of hip-hop that many of its fans say is often overlooked.

"Urban radio stations play the same songs every day," says Powell, a former reporter for *Vibe* magazine. "The media is ghettoizing hip-hop. They make it look passe."

Those often included in hip-hop's positive list are Lauren Hill, Common, Mos Def, Dead Prez, Erykah Badu, Talib Kweli and other underground acts. Indeed, many of them have been active in encouraging young people to vote. Mos Def and other artists recently recorded a song in memory of Amadou Diallo, "Hip-Hop for Respect."

This is the side of hip-hop many young people say they'd like their faculty to recognize. This is also the side that some people say faculty must recognize.

"There are scholars—I've seen them do this before—who will make a disparaging remark about a whole genre of music, not knowing a doggone thing," NYU's Kelley says. "That's the same thing as saying, 'I've read one article on rational choice theory and it was so stupid, I dismissed the whole genre.' . . . People who are trained in their own fields would never do that with their own scholarship and yet they are willing to make these really sweeping statements."

"And they don't know. They don't have a critical understanding of the way the music industry operates or the way in which people engage music," he says. "But they are willing to draw a one-to-one correlation between the students' failure and music."

Some professors argue that another correlation should be made.

"My most serious students are the die-hard hip-hop fans," says Dr. Ingrid Banks, assistant professor of Black Studies at Virginia Tech. "They are able to understand politics because they understand hip-hop."

Banks says that more of her colleagues would be wise to better understand the music and its culture. "You can't talk about Reagan's policies in the '80s without talking about hip-hop," says the 30-something scholar. "If you start where students are, they make these wonderful connections."

Curricular Connections

If the augmentation of hip-hop scholarship is any indication, academe just may be coming around to at least tolerating this formidable medium.

Courses on hip-hop, books, essays and other studied accounts of the genre are being generated by a pioneering cadre of scholars. And while many people see that as notable, there's not yet widespread belief that academe has completely warmed to the idea of hip-hop as scholarship.

Banks, who has taught "Race, Politics and Rap Music in Late Twentieth Century America" at the Blacksburg, Va., school, says she's experiencing less than a speedy response to getting her course included into the department's curriculum. "I understand that it usually takes a while to get a course approved, but there have been courses in biology and history that were signed off on rather quickly," she says.

But if academe fails to find ways to connect with hip-hop and its culture, then it essentially will have failed an entire generation, many critics say.

"What's happening is that administrators and teachers are faced with a real crisis. And that crisis, they can easily attach to the music," Kelley says. "It's the way they dress, the way they talk. The real crisis is their failure to educate; their failure to treat these students like human beings; their failure to come up with a new message to engage students."

"Part of the reason why there is such a generational gap is because so few educators make an effort to understand the times in which they live. You can't apply '60s and '70s methods to teaching in the new millennium. You can't apply a jazz aesthetic to hip-hop heads," says Powell, who lectures at 70 to 80 colleges and universities a year. "You have to meet the students where they are. That's the nature of education. That's pedagogy."

And while Wake Forest's Irvin says he would agree with that sentiment, he also sees a role that students must play.

"What I see as being the major challenge that these kids will deal with is the image of young, urban America," Irvin says. "Young people need to ask themselves, 'Who will control their identity?"

"If they leave it up to the media to define who they are, they'll be devastated by these images," he says. "That's where hip-hop is killing us."

After Reading

Critical Perspective

1. What is Evelyn claiming about hip-hop culture and college/university instructors and administrators in this essay? Point to the places in her text where you believe she offers her thesis.

Rhetoric and Argument

2. Consider Evelyn's use of rhetorical tactics, specifically audience, purpose, ethos, pathos, logos, intertextuality, context, and constraints. Do you find her text is convincing? Why or why not?
3. Outline the debate among parents, instructors, administrators, and students that is at the heart of Evelyn's text. Examine the evidence that she presents for each position. With which position do you agree? Why? Be sure to give examples from the text as well as your own experiences to back up your assertions.
4. Are there any flaws in Evelyn's argument? If yes, pinpoint where they occur in her text. If there are no flaws, draw from her text to back up your views.
5. Examine Evelyn's final section on "Curricular Connections." Outline the thoughts offered by Dr. Ingrid Banks. What is she asserting? Do you think that she is correct or not? Point to evidence for your assertions in Evelyn's essay as well as from your own experiences.

Analysis

6. Write an informal argumentative response in which you consider Jason Hinmon's experiences after he transferred to the University of Delaware from Morehouse College in Atlanta and Dr. Thomas Earl Midgette's comments (the director of the Institute for the Study of Minority Issues at North Carolina Central University). Do you believe that Hinmon has a right to dress as he does and not feel stereotyped? Does Midgette have a right to maintain that higher education students such as Hinmon need to dress and behave differently? Draw your evidence from your own experiences. In addition, be sure to consult library and Internet sources to back up your assertions.

Taking Action

Examine an undergraduate course catalog from your college or university. Read through all of the courses and their descriptions that appear under your major (or, if you have not settled on a major, pick a subject area that interests you). List all the classes taught within that discipline that seem oriented to your specific needs and the needs of your generation. Now look at the courses that do not seem to account for these needs: What appears to be missing from the descriptions? How might these courses be modified (within reason) to accommodate the needs of today's students?

Then get back into the larger class group. Discuss what you have learned and your thoughts about it. How do you believe that the discipline you examined—and your college or university as a whole—ought to respond to what you have discovered? When you are finished sharing your thoughts, consider drafting a "Letter to the Editor" for your school paper in order to voice your concerns as well as to share what you have discovered with the rest of the university community.

Alisa Valdes-Rodriguez

"Crossing Pop Lines: Attention to Latinos Is Overdue, But Sometimes Off-Target"

Alisa Valdes-Rodriguez is an acclaimed novelist and award-winning print and broadcast journalist as well as a former staff writer for both the Los Angeles Times *and* The Boston Globe. *She has published* Playing with Boys *and her book* The Dirty Girls Social Club *is scheduled to become a movie starring Jennifer Lopez.*

EXERCISING YOUR SKILLS

Before Reading

Valdes-Rodriguez writes about the popularity of "Latin" musical artists. Watch a series of music videos on MTV, MTV2, VH1, or other music-related stations that feature such musical artists singing songs in English. Make note of the visuals used in the videos and the representations of race, ethnicity, class, and gender that they offer. Are there aspects about these videos to which you might point that indicate the singer's Latin background? Be sure to provide evidence from the cultural texts to support your ideas.

First, the well-known facts: Puerto Rican pop star Ricky Martin is enjoying phenomenal success with his first English-language album, and more Latino pop artists, such as Enrique Iglesias, are vying to do the same. This has led the U.S. media—including a *Time* magazine cover story—to trumpet a new "Latin crossover phenomenon."

Now, the lesser-known facts.

One: Many of the so-called crossover artists are American by birth, including Martin. But the pervasive impression in the media and in the culture at large is that these artists are exotic foreigners. Example? *USA Today* calling Martin's sounds "south-of-the-border," even though residents of his native Puerto Rico have been United States citizens since 1917, and the island's signature musical genre, salsa, was invented in the 1960s in a city south of the Connecticut border: New York.

Two: Even though in the pop music business "crossover" generally means switching genres, Martin's music—pop by any standards—has not changed, only the language he sings in. He is not, as some publications have posited, a salsa singer.

For Martin and others, the only real "crossover" is their language; it's an unusual category, and one that French-speaking Canadian Celine Dion managed to avoid. Latinos, even those U.S.-born like Martin, are not afforded the same leeway.

Shakira, for example, is a Colombian rock singer whose style has been compared to Alanis Morissette; her "crossover" album consists of translations of rock songs she has recorded in Spanish. Enrique Iglesias sings syrupy ballads in the tradition of Air Supply; it's a formula that will likely work as well for him in English. And Martin's music, while injected occasionally with percussive instruments, is no more or less "Latin" than that of, say, Puff Daddy, who also uses Spanish phrases.

All of this has led East Harlem's Marc Anthony, who records salsa in Spanish and R & B dance music in English, to declare "crossover" irrelevant, venturing to say the term has only been applied to these artists because they are Latinos on the mainstream charts, not because they perform Latin music on the mainstream charts.

While no one denies that focusing the mainstream media spotlight on Latino musicians and singers is overdue, the recent storm of coverage has exposed an abysmal ignorance about the complexity, diversity and reality of Latinos and Latin music.

Lost in the frenzy to cover "crossover" artists have been two simple facts: Latino artists do not necessarily perform in Latin music genres; and Latin music is not always performed by Latinos.

In the case of Jennifer Lopez, who is often lumped into this nascent category, the only "crossover" is in the minds of a media establishment oblivious to the fact that she is a Bronx native who has recorded her debut album of commercial pop songs in her "native tongue": English. Yes, Lopez has two Spanish-language pop songs on the album, but artists from Madonna to Bon Jovi have been recording in Spanish for release in Latin America for years, and yet no one has called them crossover artists.

Beyond the assumptions about Latino Americans seeming somehow foreign, there is another, more unsettling bit of stereotyping being done in the media about the new "crossover" stars.

Clichéd adjectives are used over and over in the mainstream press in general but take on a different connotation when used to describe artists such as Martin, Lopez, Anthony and others. Words such as "hot," "spicy" and "passionate" are taken, one assumes, from the flavors of Mexican cuisine and outdated stereotypes of the "Latin lover."

Particularly upsetting is the media propensity to comment on certain body parts when writing about Latino artists, namely hips and rear ends. *Entertainment Weekly* labeled Martin "hot hips." And the vast majority of stories on Lopez refer to her hind side. This is no mere coincidence; several academics have shown direct links between the view European settlers took of the American land and indigenous peoples, both of which were seen as wild, sexual and, in their view, in need of taming.

Speaking of hot: According to *Billboard* magazine, Ricky Martin is a "hot tamale." This phrase appears several times, and is ridiculous because Martin hails from Puerto Rico, where the local cuisine includes neither chili peppers nor tamales, both of which come from Mexico. One *TV Guide* cover story on Martin made it only three paragraphs before calling the singer "spicy," and a few paragraphs later made reference to his wiggling hips.

According to the *New York Daily News*, Martin is "red hot," while the *Atlanta Constitution* calls him "hot stuff." The *Seattle Times* says Martin is "incendiary" (give them credit for consulting a thesaurus, at least). The list goes on and on. Even the *New York Times* has not been immune to the stereotyping; the headline of its recent concert review of Chayanne—a singer who appeared in the film "Dance With Me" alongside Vanessa Williams and who has plans to release an English-only album soon—read: Amor (Those Hips!) Pasion: (Those Lips!).

When it comes to Lopez, the coverage is even more troubling, tainted with sexism and sexual innuendo in addition to ignorance. Lopez was called "salsa-hot" by the *Hartford Courant*. Like Martin, Lopez is Puerto Rican; once more, on that island, salsa is to be danced, not eaten. The *New York Daily News* calls Lopez a "hot tamale." Even in Canada the stereotypes, and mistakes, persist: The *Ottawa Citizen* called Lopez "a hot-blooded Cuban."

Marc Anthony is so disgusted with the "heated" coverage he and others are getting in the mainstream press—he has been called "red-hot" by the *Boston Herald* and "white-hot" by the *New York Daily News*—that he has started refusing to do some interviews. He jokingly told his publicist that he will "jump off a bridge" if he is called "hot" or "spicy" by one more publication.

Too Complex to Be Lumped as "Latin Music"

To understand why this type of writing is so offensive, one must be familiar with the complex reality of Latinos and the dozens of musical genres that have been lumped into the amorphous "Latin music" category.

Most of the 30 million Latinos in the U.S. speak English as their primary language. Beyond that, they are as racially and economically diverse as the entire U.S. population. While many people continue to believe that all Latinos are "brown," this is simply not true.

In fact, the history of the U.S. is parallel to that of Latin America: The Native American inhabitants were "conquered" by Europeans; many Native Americans were killed in the process, and Africans were "imported" to replace them as slaves. Documents from slave ships show that fully 95% of the Africans brought to the Americas as slaves went to Latin America, according to historians.

Brazil is home to the largest African American population on Earth, and five of every six Dominicans is of African descent. My father's birth was dedicated to the Yoruba god Obatala, as were those of most other white kids in his neighborhood in Cuba; he has often said that to be a Caribbean Latino is to be African, regardless of color.

At this moment, there are plenty of black Latinos succeeding in mainstream American pop music, but few, if any, ever get mentioned in the Latin crossover write-ups. In some instances, this is due to the artist's decision not to make his or her background known. But in other cases, as in the exclusion of R&B crooner Maxwell, who is half Puerto Rican, it's due mostly to reluctance on the part of both the English and Spanish media to include blacks in the discussion at all.

Pop singer Usher is half Panamanian. Other Puerto Ricans include TLC rapper Lisa "Left Eye" Lopes, "Ghetto Superstar" singer Mya—who has recorded in Spanish—and rappers Fat Joe and Big Pun. And Mariah Carey, who describes her father as a black Venezuelan and who routinely includes Spanish singles on her albums for import to Latin America, is also absent from the crossover discussion.

With one notable exception in the *New York Times* last month, merengue singer Elvis Crespo has been left out of the crossover equation too, even though he is probably the only Latin artist who currently qualifies in the traditional sense of the term. Crespo currently has had two Spanish-language albums on the Billboard 200 mainstream chart.

Some music executives, including Sony Music Chairman and CEO Thomas D. Mottola, have said outright that they are excited about Martin and other crossover candidates because these artists fill the role of the white male pop star that has been vacant since the glory days of George Michael.

While a white Latino is just as Latino as a brown or black one, it unfortunately seems that in the world of American pop culture, Latinos are still only palatable as long as they appeal to a mainstream, Caucasian standard of beauty. Jennifer Lopez seems to have figured this one out: Her naturally wavy, dark brown hair has been lightened and straightened, and her once-fuller body has been whittled down by a fitness guru to something virtually indistinguishable from the lean, muscular Madonna.

All of this brings us to the ungainly truth no one seems to want to embrace in this country: Simply, there is no such thing as a singular "Latino," and efforts, no matter how well-intentioned, to classify 30 million racially, economically and educationally diverse individuals as one unit is ignorant—and irresponsible.

The term "Hispanic" was invented by the U.S. Census Bureau in the 1970s in order to classify a group of Americans ostensibly linked through a common language—Spanish.

Hispanics, or Latinos, don't exist in Latin America where people identify themselves by nationality, class and race—just like here. "Latinos" have been invented in the U.S. for the convenience of politics and marketing, overlooking considerable cultural differences and complexity that can make your head spin.

Think about this: Much of what we call "Mexican food" today is really Native American food; the unifying "Latino" language, Spanish, is a European import, just like English; the backbone of salsa music, the clave rhythm, comes from West Africa, as does merengue's two-headed tambora drum; Mexican norteno and banda music is rooted in Germany and Poland . . . but Cajuns in Louisiana who play essentially the same stuff in French are not Latinos. Got that?

Complexity! It is anathema to good capitalist marketing plans, which promise big bucks to whomever can lasso the elusive buyers of the world. And yet history is complex—all of ours—and journalists owe it to everyone to accurately chronicle the history of our world and one of its most powerful cultural forces: music.

We leave you with a sadly typical example of the comedy and tragedy of simplification of Latinos and Latin music. It happened, of all places, at a Los Angeles Dodgers game. As each Dodger goes to bat, the scoreboard lists personal facts, including the player's favorite band. A snippet from said band is then played over the loud-speakers. Two Dominican players both listed the New Jersey–based merengue group Oro Solido as their favorite. Yet when one came up to the plate, the folks in charge of the public address system chose instead to play . . . Ricky Martin!

To many a Dominican, the exchange of Martin for Oro Solido could be seen as a slap in the face; first, merengue is the official national dance of the Dominican Republic. Secondly, there is a long history of tension between Puerto Ricans and Dominicans over class and citizenship issues. In this context, replacing Oro Solido with Martin was not only ignorant, but possibly even insulting. But to know this means to study history. It means entertaining complex thought. And that, in a trend-driven pop culture obsessed with simple marketing categories and the almighty dollar, is apparently too much work.

After Reading

Critical Perspective

1. How do you think Valdes-Rodriguez feels about the topics she is addressing? How did you respond to them and why?

Rhetoric and Argument

2. How would you describe Valdes-Rodriguez's rhetorical choices in this essay? In what ways does she use audience, purpose, ethos, pathos, logos, intertextuality, context, and constraints to develop her argument? Give quotes from the text.

3. What is Valdes-Rodriguez asserting about those people who have been labeled "Latin cross-over artists"? Why does she think that it is important to make this point? Do you agree with her claim? Why or why not?

4. Describe how the author organizes her argument. Do you find this to be an effective structure? Be sure to furnish evidence from the text to back up your views.

5. What kinds of evidence does Valdes-Rodriguez utilize to support her assertions? Do you believe that this evidence is sufficient to substantiate her ideas? Why or why not? Be sure to quote from the essay to support your thoughts.

Analysis

6. Think about other contemporary Latin artists who the author does not mention and who have also become popular. You may want to consider those artists who identify themselves as mixed-race. Study their lives, lyrics, and histories in detail. Then address the following questions in a short response: How exactly has the mainstream media represented them? Why and to what ends? Does Valdes-Rodriguez's claim hold true? Be sure to draw your evidence from popular magazines and videos. In addition, look at library and Internet sources.

Taking Action

Break into a small group. Your role is to create a public service announcement for your campus. In this announcement explain how you think the school administrators, teachers, and students could better support giving mixed-race students a voice. What specific changes could be made to dorm life and activities, curricula, and students' interactions? Why might it be particularly important for mixed-race students to have a political voice on campus? Seek out library and Internet sources to support your views. Once you're done, share your different announcements with the rest of the class. Consider videotaping them and making your work accessible to other groups both inside and outside the campus community.

GAVIN JAMES CAMPBELL

"Britney on the Belle Curve"

Gavin James Campbell follows American popular music from Japan where he is a professor of American history and culture at the Center for American Studies, Doshisha University in Kyoto, Japan. He is music editor for the journal Southern Cultures, *and has written extensively on various aspects of music and the South, from rural hymnody to Janis Joplin. In addition, Campbell has published articles on American music in the* Journal of American Folklore, American Music, *and* Musical Quarterly. *He has also published* Music and the Making of a New South, 1890–1925 *and is currently working on a book-length project tentatively titled* White Noise: Music and the Meanings of Whiteness from the "New World Symphony" to "Oops! . . . I Did It Again."

EXERCISING YOUR SKILLS

Before Reading

Campbell's piece investigates the music and persona of Britney Spears. Have you ever listened to Britney Spears's music or learned information about her from a celebrity magazine or television show? How do you view Spears as a pop culture icon? What are your thoughts about how she dresses, how she dances, the lyrics in her music, and the different roles she adopts in interviews? If you offered a cultural criticism of Spears, her life, and work, what kinds of claims might you make and how would you best support them with evidence?

Since the debut of her first album in 1999, Britney Spears has ruled as the most popular Southerner in the world. She has enjoyed chart success like almost no other artist from this most fertile of musical regions: her first album went twelve times platinum, her second release sold 1.3 million copies during its first week, her third album sold a "disappointing" nine million copies, and—oops! she did it again—her fourth album debuted at number one. The Louisiana native has topped the charts in the United States, Canada, Japan, Germany, Austria, Switzerland, the Netherlands, France, Greece, Belgium, Sweden, and Norway, and her face has charmed us at grocery story check-outs on magazines like *Elle, Cosmopolitan, People* and *Teen People, YM, Forbes, GQ, TV Guide, Rolling Stone, Maxim, Allure, Entertainment Weekly, InStyle, Us Weekly, Vogue,* and innumerable teen magazines. In 2003 even the stodgy *New York Times* embraced what it sheepishly called the "guilty pleasure" of ogling Britney, and gave her nine pages in the Sunday *Magazine.*[1] A simple Google web search for Britney Spears offers up over 1 million links; in 2002 she was the most searched-for musician on Yahoo.com and in the following year Yahoo reported that she was the sixth on the overall list of searched-for terms. Tempted though some might be, we cannot smugly dismiss her as evidence of an American cultural coma. She has lived to laugh off the innumerable cultural obituaries that have been printed incessantly since she released her first album in 1999. Tens of millions have bought her records and have made her an international celebrity. Whether we like her music or not, any figure who can command such international attention and who can inspire criticism spanning from semi-literate rages, like "brtiney is a fat ugly puke!"[2] to high-toned discourse, like "feminist and Lacanian theory allows us to see [Britney's] entrance into the Symbolic and the problems thereof,"[3] demands careful—even respectful—consideration. There's no escaping this daughter of Dixie.

Skeptics might doubt her claims to the region. After all, she lived part of her life in Orlando, and, even more damning, spent some formative years in New York City. Yet innumerable Britney fans and detractors assume she's met the residency requirement. "I'm convinced she's an inbred hick,"[4] writes one on an Internet chat site, while another Britney-basher declares that "Well, what can you expect from *her* parents? (in a southern Hick accent) 'Gosh golly, ma dawters so a purrrty (Isa bees fangkin' cousin Henry for the inbred genes). . . . Hyuk Hyuk! 'snort'!'"[5] Another who intends to succinctly summarize

---

[1] *New York Times*, Magazine, August 17, 2003, 159.
[2] http://www.hype-engine.com/allspice/versus/britney_vs_britney38.html.
[3] http://www.postmodernvillage.com/eastwest/issue1/1a-0004.html.
[4] http://clik.to/britneygrease (in the section "why you ask").
[5] http://www.redrival.com/reality_smack/britney/britney1.html.

the whole matter noted that she is "just a slow witted boring hick from the backwoods." Admirers swiftly counter such criticisms by calling upon an equally venerated Southern icon: "I'm glad to see," one male writes gallantly, "that *some* people still see her as the angelic, southern belle she is."[6] The popular biographies aimed at her fans as well as many journalists join the chorus, asserting that, as *Teen People* put it, Britney was "first and foremost a nice Southern girl." Photographers, particularly early in her career, placed Britney amidst such venerated Southern icons as front porches, screen doors, and pickup trucks, and in the film *Crossroads* she played a small-town Southern girl. Britney herself pledges fealty to her Southern heritage by telling the world "I'm just a Louisiana girl," by liberally sprinkling her autobiography with "y'all," and by christening her short-lived New York City restaurant "Nyla," a name that combined the postal-code abbreviations of both New York and Louisiana. In short, for those who post on the innumerable Britney Spears message boards, for reporters following her career, for the authors of popular biographies, and for Britney herself, the South is an integral part of understanding just what the Britney Spears phenomenon is about.

Yet the region she invokes is more accurately described not as *the* South, but as Britney's South. The distinction is important because Britney's South is only tangentially related to the region's history and culture. Britney's South is a mythical place forever spiraling in a vortex of racial, sexual, and regional stereotypes that are centuries old, and her popularity both rests upon and reinvigorates these stereotypes. Thus, we cannot fully appreciate Britney's hold on American popular culture without acknowledging her skill at appealing to the national fascination with Dixie. Just like Britney, her South entices some, repulses others, but seems to have a talismanic power to enthrall virtually everyone.

A native of Kentwood, Louisiana, Britney Spears was born on December 2, 1981. Her hometown, which sits in Tangipahoa Parish clutching the Mississippi border, boasts around 2,500 residents. As a very young girl Britney broke the town's placid surface with her forays into public performing, and she rocketed toward fame with an appearance on "Star Search" in 1990, an appearance off-Broadway in 1991, and the Miss Talent, USA crown in 1992. The following year she began a two-year stint on the "Mickey Mouse Club." When the Disney Channel cancelled the show, she returned to Kentwood anticipating living like other teenagers. Bitten by the show-biz bug, however, she remembers that she "wasn't happy just hanging around at home. I wanted to see the world and make music and do all these wonderful things!"[7] She returned to New York City and swiftly landed a recording contract in 1996 with Jive records. Her first album and first single—"Baby One More Time"—stunned the music world by becoming the first album-single combination to both go number one in their first week of release. Despite countless predictions of her career's immanent demise with the release of each album, her 2003 release "In the Zone" followed its three predecessors to debut at number one.

---

[6]http://bsia.virtualave.net/bsia/viewguestbook3.shtml (my italics).
[7]Jackie Robb, *Britney Spears* (NY: HarperCollins, 1999), 34.

Britney's story is a familiar one in American popular myth. "I'm living proof," she declares, "that you *can* succeed, no matter where you're from or how little you have."[8] The "American Dream" is most satisfying, however, when the hero or heroine comes from "nowhere" and starts from "nothing." We like to hear about obstacles overcome and odds defeated. And few places in American popular myth represent a bigger "nowhere" and a more ominous "nothing" than the South. As even Britney's mother notes, "that's why I think Brit is such an inspiration to kids, because she was just a regular little girl living in a small town in the middle of nowhere and she's come so far and done so much."[9] Bigoted, ignorant, violent, lazy, bizarre—the South has long stood as a convenient foil for everything folks outside the region imagined themselves to be. Britney's South is no exception.

On the surface, Britney's Kentwood home comes across as a rural idyll filled with simple, decent, slow-paced "friendly southern folk who speak with a soft twang."[10] They work hard, fear God, and love their country. One bio declared of Kentwood, "here apple pie is actually baked fresh in the A.M., and left out to cool by an open window." What's more, "there's no smog, no dirty garbage, no barking horns from frustrated drivers—just a mellow sort of bliss."[11] One chatty book called Britney's hometown "a seriously small town that specializes in Berry Festivals and beauty pageants,"[12] while another said it was "the kind of town where everyone knows everyone, and they greet you with a hearty 'Hi, y'all' when you walk through the door."[13] Yet for all its rustic charm, Britney's South is too rural, too poor, and too backward to ever keep her content. One Louisiana journalist described Kentwood as a "podunk" town and as "the most rural, antiquated, poor, Southern town imaginable."[14] Other writers chronicle the small-minded world of local residents who clucked over the daring-do of Britney and her mother as they trundled off to The Big Apple in a bid for stardom. "New York City? What a completely crazy idea!"[15] Britney's South is perpetually praised and damned for the same reason. The folks sitting on the front porch waiting for their home-baked pies to cool are simultaneously hidebound and embracing, repressive and nurturing.

Whatever prejudice Britney faced as an ambitious Southern teen, she was spared the additional barriers that her black neighbors have long faced. Indeed, their centuries-long insistence on freedom unsettled the region to such a degree that whites unleashed a response so vitriolic, so violent, and so prolonged that the South seemed utterly consumed by seething racism and bigotry. Yet, at least in the popular perception, Britney's South is inoculated against the sickly miasma of racial plagues, because there aren't any blacks there to lynch, beat, or bully. Although the 2000 census records that 64% of Kentwood's

[8]Britney Spears, Lynne Spears, *Britney Spears' Heart to Heart* (NY: Crown, 2000), Britney's intro.

[9]Britney Spears, Lynne Spears, *Britney Spears' Heart to Heart* (NY: Crown, 2000), 116.

[10]Beth Peters, *True Brit* (NY: Ballantine Books, 1999), 10.

[11]Alix Strauss, *Britney Spears* (NY: St. Martin's, 1999), 1.

[12]Robb, *Britney Spears*, xi.

[13]Peters, *True Brit*, 9.

[14]http://hullabaloo.tulane.org/19991119/arcade/fstory.asp?s=Kentwood.

[15]Robb, *Britney Spears*, 11.

citizens are black, they utterly vanish from the material written about her hometown. While the fan biographies, for instance, recount her one year of high school at Parklane Academy, which compelled her to drive more than thirty miles to McComb, Mississippi, none mention that a public high school sits within blocks of her house. Parklane was founded in 1970 because, according to its website, "of interested and concerned parents for a quality Christian education."[16] It, along with a half-dozen other local private academies, was also founded the same school year that Kentwood High desegregated. And while other fans rapturously relive her triumph at the Kentwood Dairy Festival, none mention that no black girl has won, or has even been nominated to compete. Even the labels attached to her—"sweet Southern Miss,"[17] "down home country-girl,"[18] "softspoken Southern belle"[19]—are terms reserved exclusively in the popular imagination for *white* Southerners. Britney's South erases any claims blacks can make on the region. To be "Southern" is to be white.

In fact, blacks have been central to the region's history and to Kentwood's as well. Though the town now pays tribute to the first settlers, the slaves who were forced to endure the hardships of pioneer life and reap none of the rewards are completely ignored. The town's official history, published in 1993, contains but one fleeting reference to what it calls the town's "colored" people.[20] And yet by the time of the Civil War there were more black than white residents in the parish. As the number of slaves increased, so, too, did the value of the land they worked: in the decade before their emancipation, black labor helped inflate the average aggregate cash value of the parish's farms by over $1,000,000. Cultivating rice, sugar cane, cotton, peas, potatoes, corn, and tending enormous herds of sheep, pigs, and other livestock, African Americans provided the basis for the region's economic success. Without what the town still calls those "colored" people, Kentwood would have been an impossibility.

The Civil War and the end of slavery, of course, fundamentally undermined the source of the parish's wealth, and the subsequent hard times that stretched into the early years of the 20th century saw blacks unable to reap the benefits of the economic foundations they'd laid as slaves. Cotton, which supported innumerable Southerners in the post-war period, did not grow well in Tangipahoa parish, so farmers made do by lumbering in the sturdy long-leaf pine forests. Milch cows replaced the pine trees, spawning a dairy industry that sputters into the twenty-first century. Energized by calls throughout the region to build up a "New South" from the ashes of the Old, Kentwood seemed to come alive, and in the twelve years before 1900 the town's population almost tripled. The streets were crowded with signs of prosperity, ranging from a new brick factory, a "Collegiate Institute," several saw mills, a box factory, and numerous other businesses, churches, and social clubs. Yet

---

[16]http://www.parklaneacademy.com/.
[17]Robb, *Britney Spears*, back cover.
[18]Robb, *Britney Spears*, ix.
[19]http://britney_fan.tripod.com/newlayout/biography.htm.
[20]Mrs. Irene Morris, *All Roads Lead to Kentwood, 1893–1993* (Kentwood Chamber of Commerce, 1993), 6.

the riches promised under the New South did not extend to all citizens equally. Small as the town was, there was still room for racial segregation and bigotry designed to severely restrict opportunities. "Separate but equal" may have been the law, but it surely wasn't the spirit anywhere in the South. In fact, the Parish in which Britney's hometown sits was an astonishingly dangerous place for black residents in the years following emancipation. Between 1879 and 1917 white mobs eviscerated, burned, and lynched twenty-two black folks. And, although poverty in the New South rained indiscriminate of race, its harshest consequences were usually reserved for African Americans who had limited and often demeaning access to the wealth controlled by white-owned banks and businesses. Despite the obstacles to progress, Kentwood's black citizens determined to make a New South for themselves as well, creating a vibrant community centered around its churches, schools, and businesses. Legendary and still-admired community leaders strove to wring dignity from a world largely not of their making, and in so doing contributed immeasurably to Kentwood's prosperity.

When I visited Kentwood in 2000 it was clear that race still divides the 2,195 residents. It's not a virulent, ugly racism that shivers the place, but a quiet understanding. Driving through Kentwood takes less than a minute or two, especially if all three stoplights are green, but it's not too small to have a black section of town called Kent's Quarters. Except for the Church of God Assembly, blacks and whites worship separately. No blacks attend Britney's home church, First Baptist, the youth minister told me. One black child had begun going to some after-school programs, but his mother reportedly advised him against returning. Kentwoodians go to school separately as well. When I asked one black resident if she knew roughly the percentage of African American students that attended the same private school that Britney went to she answered without hesitation: "0." And Parklane Academy is only one of several private schools strewn throughout the area that caters to white kids.

Though now more than thirty years in practice, school integration clearly remains a sore point with white Kentwoodians. I asked one person what had been the biggest change in the town in the more than forty years he'd lived there: "We used to have a really good high school," he replied without hesitation or elaboration. When I questioned one Parklane graduate why he hadn't attended Kentwood High he told me, "Well, it's about 98% black, you know." In fact, the figure is closer to 88%, but the school's principal observed that the white kids who did come were either too poor to attend the private academies, wanted to play on the school's championship football team, or were from bi-racial families. Kentwood High is basically a school of last resort for whites.

Mrs. Ann A. Smith, the high school's principal, is a woman of polish and erudition. She is enormously proud of Kentwood High, and she's clearly frustrated that its superb football team overshadows the school's equally impressive academic record. She printed off test score results to show me that her students scored higher than the state-wide average on standardized tests. Yet, she acknowledged, the scores did little to dent the widely held notion among whites that Kentwood High was a substandard school. Lots of white folks showed up for Friday night football, but otherwise kept themselves and their children away. This disappointed her more than it made her angry. "The divisions are a handicap to the whole community. We haven't gotten the most out of this community that we could." Nor did Britney Spears' success provide a foothold for racial and civic unity. In fact, Smith observed with amusement, by and large the black students she'd talked to liked and defended Britney and the white ones didn't.

When I asked her how Kentwood had responded to school desegregation, she urged me to talk with Coach Raymond Coleman and his wife Brunette, both veterans of the segregated schools, and both foot soldiers in the campaign for integration. Equal parts mountain and man, Coach Coleman is avuncular and quick to laugh, and he responded to questions with an impressive candor. He recalled that Jim Crow Kentwood had experienced little overt racial strife. "Everyone kinda knew their positions and there wasn't any problem," he said; "it wasn't a mean town. It was just a typical small Southern town." His wife countered that things weren't as easy-going as he made them out to be, and she recounted several times whites had snubbed her in the town's public places. Both recollected with pride the black entrepreneurs who built up a community parallel to white Kentwood. "We had our own newspaper," Mrs. Coleman told me, "filling station, groceries, cleaners, taxicab, theater, just about everything we needed." And both the coach and his wife spoke glowingly of Collis B. Temple, the "fearless and forceful" principal of Kentwood's black O. W. Dylan High. Temple had the respect of the white community, and commanded from it far more services than comparable black schools almost anywhere else in the state.

The truce between whites and blacks that marked Kentwood race relations was, however, broken by integration. It "revealed the faultlines," Coach Coleman noted. A head football coach at Dylan High, he and dozens of others in the black community pushed for school desegregation because "many parents thought that integration was the answer." As soon as they succeeded in the fall of 1969, he and others realized the full impact of what they had been missing. The white school "had labs, and athletic equipment, and better salaries, textbooks, and typewriters, and a library," his voice trailing off as the riches to enumerate exceeded his memory. I asked if there were any fights or ugliness. Among the faculty and students not a harsh word passed, he recalled. Whites resolved the matter easily enough. "We integrated in the fall of 1969 with no trouble. Not like Hammond. And then in the spring of 1970 all the white kids left" for the "white flight academies" popping up. They've never returned, and so Kentwood High, for all its academic strengths and athletic achievements, is still considered an inferior, "black" school. Hence white residents felt no need to expand on the comment that the town's biggest change was that "we used to have a really good high school."

It might be comforting to cast Britney's Kentwood and the rest of the South into the trash-heap of racial attitudes the rest of the country has discarded, but we must remember that Kentwood's white citizens are hardly alone in their ability to scour away millions of blacks from consciousness. The gated communities and the *de facto* segregation of America's suburbs across the nation have made it increasingly unlikely that whites and blacks will interact with each other except through movies, television, and popular music. Yet even there blacks are distant, inscribed onto inner-city scenes of crime, drugs, and violence that are far removed from the lives of white fans (as well as a significant number of black ones). African Americans are also remote from Britney's bucolic South. There simply are no visible black Southerners in American popular culture, despite the fact that the 2000 population census reported that more than 50% of the nation's blacks live in the South. Indeed, they've become so invisible that a number of people could believe an Internet legend in which Britney said "coming from the South, there just aren't any minorities there, so it's like a major shock when you go to the big cities and all, and they're just everywhere!"[21] It's patently obvious that Britney never said this, but the resulting Internet chats focused on her attitudes about interracial dating rather than on the obvious fact that there are plenty of "minorities" in the South. Moreover, we need only turn to the musical world that gave Britney her start—teen-pop—to see how successfully the rest of the nation picks up where white Kentwood leaves off. Whether it's Tiffany, New Kids on the Block, Hanson, the Backstreet Boys, Innosense, the Spice Girls, 'N Sync, Britney Spears, Mandy Moore, Jessica Simpson, Tatu, or Avril Lavigne, whites dominate the teen-pop scene in ways that replicate Kentwood's patterns of racial erasure.

Indeed, the existence of teen pop is a kind of Jim Crow leftover, because what distinguishes these white pop stars from their black counterparts in soul, R&B, and hip hop is their flirtation with the same sexual and racial boundaries segregation was explicitly designed to maintain. Britney first attracted notice for trying to play both the sweet Southern daughter and the midriff-baring Catholic schoolgirl, and it was the resulting tension that made her so intriguing. Then she did a virtual strip-dance routine at the MTV Music Video Awards in 2000, wore a red leather catsuit in her "Oops! . . . I Did It Again" video, and quickly began shedding clothes for virtually every popular magazine on the market. Meanwhile in her music and lyrics she became increasingly sexually explicit by spicing her act with "flava" borrowed from black R&B and hip hop. It was only because she could play with the magnetic poles of white Southern sexuality that she could make herself so utterly fascinating. At times lauded for her "Southern-magnolia manners,"[22] at other times dismissed as a "country hick whore,"[23] Britney precariously swings between the belle and the Jezebel. Wondering which way she'll go is an excruciatingly delightful torture that she can inflict because she's white.

Black female singers can't exploit the same tension. They can't be cute or coy or sweet, or startle us with an erotic moan or an off-color lyric, or even use "oops" in the title of a song. They must be always ho's with attitude. Thus, when Lil' Kim raps, "I don't want dick tonight, eat my pussy right," the nation shrugs its shoulders, and when Christina Milian, wearing lace bras and panties, promises to tell girls "how to make your man say 'Ooo,'" no one gets into a frenzy berating her. Janet Jackson's infamous Super Bowl "wardrobe malfunction" temporarily provided a target for fiery condemnation, but she's been exposing her pound of flesh for years to great indifference. Black stars do not face the nearly hysterical levels of criticism because we expect them from the moment their album debuts

[21] http://www.angelfire.com/ks/airhead/quotes.html.
[22] http://www.toppics4u.com/britney_spears/i1.html.
[23] http://popdirt.com/article13579.html.

and their videos hit the air to perform their sexuality with an aggressive gusto. But for white stars like Britney to act similarly is to invite the anger of those people for whom the equation of whiteness and sexual purity are necessarily dependent upon each other. To add the South into the equation is only to make the stakes for sexual purity that much higher. As one frustrated teenage girl wrote on an Internet chatsite, "She *AIN'T* No Innocent Southern Girl!!!! WHATEVER!!! She's a fake ass talentless bitch who doesn't deserve any kind of respect."[24]

Her consorting with hip-hop and R&B is a kind of cultural miscegenation that has long made whites nervous. But then Britney crossed more than just a cultural boundary. She dated a black guy. Several generations ago her black beau would have known the wrath of white Southern men who patrolled the belle's chastity with a viciousness that now astounds us. They would have deemed eviscerating, burning, and hanging him, an entirely reasonable response to their fear that without such ritualistic torture he would despoil the region's treasured sexual and racial purity. We're sufficiently far from that time to find Jim Crow's logic frighteningly perverse, but Britney's fling with a black dancer in her show demonstrated that large numbers of Americans still believe in belles and still believe in their black predators, and were anxious to give the old bogey-man his customary thrashing. "Black men have about as much faithfullness as a $5.00 street hooker, and this fling between Columbus Short and Britney just supports that theory," spat one, while another vowed that "I will never listen to Britney again since she kissed that dirty nigger!"[25] Though she returned to the fold by marrying her hometown honey at the Little White Wedding Chapel in Las Vegas in the wee hours of the morning, the circumstances of the fifty-five hour union did little to restore confidence in Britney's ability to abide by the belle's strict code of conduct (incidentally, neither did her subsequent marriage to and pregnancies from back up dancer Kevin Federline).

What makes Britney so aggravating to so many is that she seems intent on trying to convince us that she is both Melanie Wilkes *and* Scarlet O'Hara; that sometimes you feel like a slut, sometimes you don't. The resulting contradiction is just too much for most folks. White girls, and especially those from the small-town South, can't sneak between the mansion and the double-wide. She can't be, as one hostile critic spat, "shaking that little booty of hers while playing [the] 'cute southern belle.'"[26] The resulting cultural schizophrenia is expressed in the words of one bewildered fan who wrote that Britney is a "good/bad, hometown, backwoods Louisiana girl."[27]

The battle between those who applaud Britney for her "Southern belle grace"[28] and those who dismiss her as "the biggest hick slut we know"[29] is not likely to lose much

[24]http://www.dotvsdot.com/cgi-bin/vs_board.pl?board=36&archive=1.
[25]Both quotes from http://www.platinum-celebs.com/music/news/003428.html (Accessed May 15, 2004).
[26]http://www.angelfire.com/il2/PukePrincess/Whyihateher.html (Accessed January 3, 2004).
[27]http://entertainment.msn.com/reviews/albumreviews.aspx?album=103290 (Accessed January 4, 2004).
[28]http://www.online-shrine.com/spears/index.php (Accessed January 3, 2004).
[29]http://viking.necrolounge.com/archives/001082.html.

steam as long as she continues to use her Kentwood home to promote her career. Like Madonna who found in Catholicism a rich vein to mine, Britney brilliantly calls upon the South's racial and sexual mystique without being utterly consumed by its infamy. As even a cursory knowledge of her Kentwood hometown demonstrates, the South Britney invokes is a mythic place barely conversant with the actual history that has made it. Instead, it's haunted by ancient stereotypes that stump across the region, receiving their life from the nation's continued willingness to believe in them. Few seem to notice that to condemn Kentwood and the rest of the South as either a uniquely bigoted place or as refreshingly free of minorities ignores the ways in which American popular culture similarly erases and elides some long-standing racial and sexual tensions. Britney's South, then, allows the nation to quarantine these radioactive aspects of American society and yet to still indulge in fumbling through them in magazines, music videos, and CDs. Britney works and exploits this secret pleasure with remarkable skill. Working in the interstices between white and black, and between the "Southern belle" and the "trailer slut" irritates Britney's fans and critics, to be sure, but it also keeps them tuned in. Britney's no dumb blonde. She swears that she's "just a Louisiana girl," but hidden within that deprecating string of words Britney has proven there's seismic power.

After Reading

Critical Perspective

1. What do you make of Campbell's essay? Describe the structure of his argument and his tone. Do these approaches draw you in as a reader? Why or why not?

Rhetoric and Argument

2. What sorts of rhetorical choices does Campbell utilize in his argument? In particular, how does he address concerns such as use of audience, purpose, ethos, pathos, logos, intertextuality, context, and constraints? Be sure to offer quotes to back up your ideas.
3. What exactly is Campbell claiming about Britney Spears, and how do you know? What is his rationale for asserting this? Do you agree with his claim? Why or why not? Try to point to his text to provide support for your views.
4. Why does Campbell analyze the various perspectives on Britney Spears's life, where she lived, and what her childhood entailed? What do these views expose about race, class, as well as gender relations, and how such forces have operated to create Britney Spears—the commodity and the icon? What other forms of evidence does Campbell employ? Do you find these to be credible sources? Why or why not? Give evidence for your position.
5. Why does Campbell take the trip to Kentwood, Louisiana, where Britney Spears grew up? What does he learn there? Do you think that including this trip helps further Campbell's claim or detracts from it? Why?
6. What are your impressions of Campbell's conclusion? Do you believe that it successfully reinforces his claim? Why or why not? If not, do you have suggestions for how he could make it more persuasive?

Analysis

7. Make a list of the most popular contemporary young female performers. Write a short argumentative essay in which you address the following: What do you know about their backgrounds? What do these women claim about their cultural heritages? How do their backgrounds impact the music and lyrics that they sing? What "official stories" do you know about them and what "unofficial" ones? How do each of these stories shape how you view them? Consult library and Internet sources for evidence.

Taking Action

As a class, survey the various websites dedicated to such young female performers. Consult both the official and unofficial ones. Discuss the differences and similarities between how the official sites construct their identities and the unofficial ones do. In what ways do they employ rhetorical tactics such as audience, purpose, ethos, pathos, logos, intertextuality, context, constraints, arrangement, color, and sound to achieve very different effects? What does this imply about the different motivations at work in creating such websites? Examine library and Internet sources as necessary.

LINDSEY ECK

"Defining Country Music"

Lindsey Eck is editor of the Austin Songwriter. *His articles on popular culture and music, TV, and theater reviews have also appeared in* New Music Box *(http://www. newmusicbox.org) and* Bad Subjects *(http//eserver.org/bs). His own Web site is http:// www.corneroak.com. Eck serves as webmaster for Austin composer Patricia Long (http://www.pmlmusic.com) and is also the veteran of several rock bands, including Savage Rose and Altered Straight in the Boston area as well as Mother Hunter's Third Party in Texas. He is currently in the process of recording an album of original songs, By Night By Day By Night. In 2000 Eck scored the short film* The Story of an Hour, *based on a very short story by Kate Chopin, set in the Deep South at the turn of the last century. Eck owns Blue Oak Studio in rural Texas and he invites your correspondence at music@corneroak.com.*

EXERCISING YOUR SKILLS

Before Reading

Eck investigates the history and the effects of country music in the United States. Which country groups and individual artists have become most popular in recent years? Why do you believe that some country music has become more mainstream? Think about the dress, style, music, and image of these artists. Point to specific videos and songs to back up your views about why this is the case and what it might mean for the future of country music—or even other musical subgroups.

Country music, I reckon, isn't much like pornography. I mean, even when they hear it people don't know how to define it.

Country music fans and detractors alike disagree all the time over whether a particular Nashville offering is or ain't country. To my dad (who became a country-music purist in his 70s, about the time easy listening disappeared from FM), what Nashville is putting out these days is just rock music dressed up in cowboy clothes and hats. All hat, no tractors: that sums up the complaint of traditionalists about the urbanized, rocked-up country that Nashville has cranked out according to formula over the past two decades.

On the other hand, when Garth Brooks masquerades as *Chris Gaines* by putting on a wig and trying to rock it up, the results still sound too Nashvillean to pass for rock 'n' roll. The rock purist is no less disdainful of what she or he regards as cornball lyrics and motifs sneaking into mainstream rock, and even rockabilly pretty much went out with the Stray Cats. If "alternative" ever meant anything, it was a disdain for the simplistic chord structures (I-IV-V and sometimes II) and hackneyed rhymes beaten into the public consciousness by not only Nashville but Madison Avenue as well. A perennial complaint of rock radio listeners here in Austin—where rock, blues, and jazz far outshine country in popularity—is about the annoyance of country jingles for truck dealers, exterminators, etc. interrupting the rock programming. Ad men appear to believe the annoying stereotype that the local music scene is primarily a country scene. The city's erection of a statue to Stevie Ray—but not, so far, to Willie—should have made this point.

Central Texas cowboy crooner and yodeler Don Walser told the story of giving a performance at a small-town festival when a little girl came up to him after the set and said: "Mister, that's some of the most beautiful music I've ever heard but, tell me, do you know any country?" The girl didn't recognize Marty Robbins or Hank Williams as country and, to hear Walser tell it, neither do the Nashville suits. Walser, along with other Texas-based exemplars of what used to be mainstream country such as Kelly Willis and Chris Wall, has struggled for prestige in the Tennessee capital next to such manufactures as Lee Ann Rimes covering "You Light Up My Life" (the Debbie Boone classic).

Defining country came to have a personal significance to me when I served on the board of directors of a songwriters' organization here in Austin. Losers of the "rock" (and even the "black R&B pop") category in the annual song contest would inevitably complain that the judges had given the prize to an entry that belonged in "country." In my experience, defining "country" can be one of the more acrimonious matters among musicians, fans, and people in the biz.

So let's give it a shot.

Any musical genre can be defined in theoretical terms by its preferred tonality and instrumentation, among other variables. In American music history, **beat** is often the defining variable, distinguishing among swing, bebop, rock 'n' roll, and so on. But it is also possible to define a genre primarily based on its **cultural trappings**, especially when that genre is associated with a particular ethnicity.

Consider reggae. The ethnic and national provenance is plain enough: Jamaica > Caribbean > African diaspora. And members of other ethnicities, while not excluded from the musical community, have to pay plenty of dues including mastery of the standard, traditional repertoire, and generally still won't be accepted unless they adopt ethnic trappings such as dreadlocks, the red-yellow-green-black dress code, "dread" patois and of course ganja. Even Bob Marley himself was originally dissed as a "white man" in Trenchtown.

Implicit in the notion of an ethnically based musical genre is the requirement that a work adhere to traditional norms of instrumentation; when it violates those norms it no longer is classified within the genre. Thus, at Austin's Bob Marley festival, a French-speaking band from Senegal (now Paris-based) stays faithful to the reggae tradition by employing essentially the same instrumentation as Marley did. Salsa without drums and horns, tejano without accordion and guitars, mariachi without trumpets would become something else. But rock tolerates just about any instrumentation (including Morphine's guitarless bass/sax blend, or the many forays into pure electronica), while jazz also translates to virtually any instrument . . . including, in Edinburgh, the bagpipes.

I define country music as the ethnic music of the mainstream White Anglo-Celtic group in the United States. Why is country's status as an ethnic music alongside the likes of reggae, tejano, and salsa seldom noticed? Probably because this still-dominant group is not recognized as an ethnic minority due to its political dominance and cultural influence, especially in the heartland—and not just the South and Appalachia.

Like other ethnically based genres, country is defined more by its trappings than by anything inherent in the music, as seen by the ability of the Nashville hit factory to coopt rock and pop beats and melodies by dressing them in a Tennessee wrapper.

For starters, that literally means dressing them up. The "hat act" is so staple by now as to be widely ridiculed, but failure to adhere to the dress code will cause the target demographic to change the channel or refuse to purchase the CD. And, for the fundamentalist Christian country fan, this could be an act of sacrilege, as when Pat Boone riled the fundies with his chest-baring leather take on heavy metal garb. Even if Ani DiFranco wrote a cowgirl classic, you'd never see her on CMT. Country viewers (whether on television or live in concert) want to look at fashions more appropriate for the rodeo than for Rodeo Drive.

If a country band strays too far from the standard instrumentation, it will lose its Nashville standing and "cross over" ("*If you're gonna play in Texas, you've gotta have a fiddle in the band*"). The standard Nashville session crew of guitars, bass, drums, pedal steel, fiddle, and piano will suffice for most recordings—and, if a ringer is called in, it will be a banjo or mandolin guy, not a horn gal or string section. Regardless of where the listeners are located, lyrics will allude to specific geographical locations regarded as cultural capitals for the Anglo-Celtic group, especially Tennessee and Texas, sometimes Oklahoma and Arkansas (but seldom Vermont, which is certainly a "country" location if you think about it), just as tejano lyrics will mention the border or reggae lyrics may reminisce about Kingston.

Jim Babjak and Pat DiNizio of the Smithereens, Nuno Bettencourt of Extreme, Adam Duritz of Counting Crows, Eddie Van Halen, Jon Bon Jovi, Alanis Morissette, Natalie Imbruglia, Lenny Kravitz; the very ethnicity of these names identifies them as outside

the pale of Opryland. Dressing those stars in cowboy garb and putting a pedal steel behind them would just prove an embarrassing flop. Nor does country tolerate the pseudonym such as Sting or Flea, and forget about changing your name to a hieroglyph.

Country performers almost invariably have Anglo-Celtic surnames like McGraw, Black, Nelson, McEntire, Gill, Strait. And, in general, these aren't just stage names; these performers actually are from this ethnic group, the backbone of the white Southern population, especially in the border states, Appalachia, and Texas/Oklahoma from whence most of country has sprung. The exceptions (Charley Pride, Freddie Fender, Johnny Paycheck, Kathy Mattea) are so few they can be written off to a sort of tokenism.

When Garth masqueraded as the rocker Chris Gaines, the effort failed to impress the intended rock crossover audience. Several traits marked the performance as inauthentic, traits that reeked of the Nashville hit factory.

Note, to begin with, the moniker. "Chris Gaines" still sounds Anglo-Celtic, a spondee just like "Garth Brooks" or "Clint Black." Then there were the costumes. When "Gaines" played *Saturday Night Live* the band's garb evoked Dallas rather than New York. There was also the lead player's use of a capo on an electric guitar. The capo is a movable bar popular in Nashville to allow key changes while having to know only a limited number of open-string chords. Rock players usually have a facility with bar chords and don't need a capo. Only a Nashvillean would resort to a capo on an electric guitar. The capo too can be thought of as a trapping of the Appalachian guitar tradition. The use of it in a faux rock performance amounted to a mistranslation into the mainstream multicultural idiom (rock) from an ethnically homogeneous subcultural tradition, the guitar equivalent of first-language interference.

In addition, the songs of "Gaines" betray Brooks's country approach in the lack of African-derived beats and tonality, rock stripped of its blues element. This too can be viewed in ethnic and geographic terms. To rock, rather than to feign rock, would require "Gaines" symbolically to visit the mulatto/creole Delta of Robert Johnson and Elvis and learn to swing.

Had Brooks really wanted to create a viable rock act, he might have chosen a cooler name (maybe a monosyllable like Slash or Beck) and ordered clothes from, say, Milan. He might have picked up some musicians with a sense of funk, maybe a Briton or Aussie, and added instruments verboten in Nashville, such as saxophone, congas, or cello. Any of these steps would have enabled Brooks to escape the regional and ethnic subculture to which he seems limited and join the international and multicultural phenomenon rock has always been—at least since the Beatles' "Michelle" hit the U.S. charts.

If country's subculture is indeed ethnically and regionally circumscribed, then one would expect its market share to begin declining with the shrinking share of this subculture within the American whole. Similarly, polkas have an increasingly marginal share of the American music scene and tejano grows, approximating the relative share of Eastern Europeans and Mexican-Americans, respectively, in the overall mix. The changing demographics of America, in which whites as a whole (let alone the fundamental Anglo-Celtic subgroup) are no longer in the majority in California and are losing their grip on Texas, portend a gradual decline in the popularity of country music. Its market share, reported at 15% just seven years ago in the *Wall Street Journal*, has been recently estimated at a mere 10%, *with the difference entirely made up by growth in hip-hop*. Still, the ability of country to absorb aspects of other musical genres by dressing them up in its ethnic-regional trappings probably ensures Nashville's survival well into the 21st century.

After Reading

Critical Perspective

1. Characterize your reaction to Eck's text. Do you identify with this essay? Why or why not?

Rhetoric and Argument

2. Describe how Eck commences his essay. What is his rhetorical purpose, do you think? Is it effective? Why or why not? Also discuss Eck's use of other rhetorical tactics such as use of audience, purpose, ethos, pathos, logos, intertextuality, context, and constraints.
3. What is Eck's main claim? What kinds of unusual images, word choices, and tone does he employ to convey it? Do these strategies help him to support the main claim or not? Be sure to point to specific places in the text as evidence for your views.
4. Why does Eck indicate that it is important to his argument to define what counts as "country music" now? How does he define it? What do you think about his definition?
5. Do you believe that there are any unwarranted assumptions or logical fallacies within Eck's argument? How does he take up issues of race, ethnicity, and region? Explain your thoughts.

Analysis

6. Eck closes his essay by suggesting that as Anglo-Celtic groups in the United States become fewer and fewer, country music may cease to have so great an audience. Still, Eck contends that Nashville's ability to dress acts up in "its ethnic-regional trappings probably ensures Nashville's survival well into the 21st century." Write a short argumentative response in which you address these concerns directly: Do you think that there are going to be fewer country musicians in the United States in years to come? Why or why not? What do you think about this? Consult specific

artists, songs, and music videos as well as library and Internet sources for evidence.

Taking Action

In a small group, research a specific artist or band in country music that does not identify as from an Anglo-Celtic tradition (ideally someone with whose music you may not be already familiar). These people can be local, national, or international musical artists. Learn as much as you can about the artist's or band members' backgrounds and how their background might impact their relationship to country music. Consult library and Internet resources when useful.

Offer brief presentations to the class about the person or band you have selected, introducing your classmates to the person's or band's music, lyrics, and personal backgrounds. Then, as a larger class group, consider your analyses of the artist or band in light of Eck's essay.

Nathan D. Abrams

"'Homegrown Heroes': Rap Music, Resistance, and Technology"

Nathan D. Abrams is a cultural critic who lives in Aberdeen, South Dakota, where he teaches American history. He has coedited Containing Cultures *and coauthored* Studying Film. *Abrams' latest book,* Commentary Magazine 1945–1959: "A Journal of Significant Thought and Opinion," *will be published soon.*

EXERCISING YOUR SKILLS

Before Reading

Abrams takes up the history and influence of rap on culture. What kinds of music do you like to listen to and why? What does this reveal about who you are, how you view yourself, as well as how others may view you? What does this music suggest about your attitudes, your style, and your political perspectives? Why do you think so?

Growing up in North London in the 1970s and 1980s, I was an avid listener to rap music, known then as "electro." What I didn't know then, but I learned later, was that rap was more than just a source of entertainment, it was also a source of information, identity, and cultural creativity. Rap may have emerged out of the urban ghettos of New York in the late 1970s and early 1980s, but its roots stretch back even further to the African oral traditions of "signifying," and the griots, as well as to "the dozens," a highly competitive verbal game of rhyming insults. Although all styles of rap have the same ancestry in New York hip hop, there are major differences in lyrical content and sharp stylistic distinctions between its various sub-genres. Between them, though, they cover a diverse range of themes, like gang violence, death, drugs, sex, police brutality, black militancy and white opposition, justice, oppression, serious political messages, as well as partying. Here I will discuss only the origins and early history of rap music to show how rappers have transformed a source of entertainment, backed by driving rhythms, into a vehicle for social consciousness and racial pride which still holds true today in the new millennium.

Rap music was a direct outgrowth of changes in America during the 1970s and 1980s. At this time, cutbacks in federal spending on social and public services, together with a shift away from the traditional blue-collar industries toward corporate and information services, disproportionately affected the black community. Budget cuts in school music programs limited access to traditional Western instruments forcing an increasing reliance on recorded sound and the technology that produced it. Vocational skills made obsolete in this postindustrial context could be now utilized and applied to this new technological terrain as a forum for resistance and creativity. It is no coincidence that rap's early pioneers were skilled in jobs that now had no place in urban postindustrial America. As social movements and the government were less able to provide the resources for cultural creativity, individuals autonomously transferred their own skills.

Rap provided an alternative site for training and a hitherto nonexistent space for creativity in an age when resources were being cut back. Many pioneering rappers were trained as repairmen and mechanics, but instead used their technological skills as tools for alternative cultural expression. Kool D.J. Herc, for example, trained as a car mechanic and Grandmaster Flash learned how to repair electronic equipment. With little or no resources in these areas, Flash and Herc made the most of their skills by using the tools of an out-of-date industrial technology to emerge as cultural entertainers. Back in the day, though, this technology had to be constructed by D.I.Y., as rap technology simply did not exist. Flash describes how he had to go to the raw parts shop downtown to find a single pole double throw switch, some crazy glue to glue it to his mixer, an external amplifier, and a headphone. Like Flash, others built their own home-made systems out of spare parts, which were then powered by public sources such as street lights.

In an age when the bonds of black communities were being eroded, rappers forged new communities centered around the symbols of the consumer culture coupled with African traditions. A reduced federal commitment to social services led to a lack of community facilities. Combined with the growth of telecommunications and corporate consolidation, local community networks were dismantled. The result was a context in which black communities had few visible resources and symbols around which they could cluster. Left only with shared consumer memories, together with the traditional resources of African-American music and new media commodities, rap emerged as an alternative source of identity-formation. New and fiercely localized identities focusing around neighbourhoods, "crews" and streets, were created. Rappers thus constantly namechecked their neighborhoods of origin since these often provided the only means of location in a postindustrial urban context.

What is more, the commodities of this consumer culture provided new means for acquiring social status based on factors other than class. Rap music's celebration of the skills of the D.J. and rapper, for example, provided an arena in the absence of more traditional sites, for status-seeking individuals to prove themselves to the group. Spontaneous street parties initiated by D.J.s who attached their customized, makeshift equipment to street lights also created new community centers in neighbourhoods where there were none. Coupled with rap's underlying attachment to black oral traditions and music, these street parties enabled new black communities to arise around shared notions of communal symbols and traditions. Manipulation of the culture's resources ensured the prioritization of black issues and the assertion of a communal identity. Rappers constantly invoked the music's deep roots in the black oral traditions of signifying, boasting, toasting, the dozens, and poetry. Polyrhythmic layering and repetition added a specifically African dimension to rap since these are essential to African music. Rap, therefore, became an innovative and communal site where local community issues and ancestral traditions could be worked through simultaneously.

Rappers have, therefore, been described as 'homegrown heroes,' because they were firmly rooted in their communities, exhibiting an explicit affinity with them. They repeated the slogan, "I'm black and I'm proud." There were constant references to specific cities (Philadelphia, New York, Los Angeles), as well as specific neighbourhoods (Staten Island, Long Beach, Harlem, Compton, Brooklyn, Long Island). Rappers chronicled the cultural life of their community by drawing upon the body of slang, dress styles, wall murals, graffiti, and other customs for their inspiration and ideas. This led to a differing focus on those elements of black life in the ghettos which were criticized by the mainstream culture and media. Consequently, rappers gave a local dimension to their music which articulated the problems of their community to a wider audience.

Rappers explicitly acknowledged their role in the generation and circulation of ideas reflecting the needs of their community. They consciously recognised their role as educators within the black community. Chuck D of Public Enemy (PE), famously described rap as "Black C.N.N." Similarly, Paris articulated his role as an educator for the black community, trying to get people to develop their analytical thought, to decide for themselves what was right or wrong. In "House Niggas" by Boogie Down Productions (BDP), KRS-1 proclaimed "I teach, not preach," and "Rap needed a teacher, so I became it." A constant theme throughout PE's songs was the persistent reminder to "know what time it is," a reference to the Black Power metaphor for black educational awareness of the late 1960s: "Wake up! Don't you know what time it is!" In order to reinforce the image, PE's Flavor Flav, wore a huge clock around his neck in a visual reminder that time has stopped and progress is not being made. Many rappers also praised the merits of self-help and attacking the evils of drugs and black-on-black violence, and several groups like PE and BDP put a constant stress on self-help as a means of enhancing racial pride and breaking the cycle of poverty. More recently, during the 2004 Presidential Election, Eminem urged his listeners to vote against George Bush in his track "Mosh" with the words:

> As we set aside our differences
> And assemble our own army
> To disarm this Weapon of Mass Destruction
> That we call our President, for the present

Thus, through their efforts at consciousness-raising and education, especially within the black community, rappers endeavored to raise awareness.

In doing so, rappers presented many subversive images. Rap's ammunition was its lyrics. "I'm the arsenal / got artillery, lyrics of ammo/Rounds of rhythm," stated Eric B. and Rakim (EB&R). The Goats' album was entitled "Burn the Flag" with an exhortation to do just that. In an open assertion of defiance and resistance, the rapper proclaims:

F(uck) to the flag makers
You to my rights takers
Now watcha think about that rap Kojack
I'll burn the President and his residents up in it

Similar images can be found within the lyrics of PE's songs. Chuck D rapped in "She Watch Channel Zero," "Revolution a solution for all our children." The song "Black Steel in the Hour of Chaos" presented resistance to the draft as a form of black defiance. Rap's lyrics made powerful weapons.

Moreover, in a parallel to the visual image of Flavor Flav's huge stopped clock, PE were backed on stage by Professor Griff and his Uzi-toting Security of the First World Posse. Undoubtedly, the sight of black men in paramilitary outfits, wielding guns, evoked a very potent and subversive image. It was a black show of strength and resistance. Perhaps the most vivid representation of subversion was the familiar trope of assassinating the President in a fantasy of revenge and rebellion. The artwork on the cover of Paris's album *Sleeping With the Enemy*, depicts him hiding behind a tree on the White House lawn, gun in hand, waiting for the President to appear. The introduction of the appropriately named song, "Bush Killa," contains an enactment of the assassination and later on in the song Paris leaves us in no doubt [about] his intentions. "Rat-a-tat go the Gat [type of gun] to his [Bush's] double face" and "Give him two from the barrel of a guerrilla / and that's real from the mutherfuckin' Bush killa." The theme was picked up in The Goats' album, *Tricks of the Shade*, when they advised "Brothers with the Gats here's where ya gotta tat / Rat a tat tat Bush's head will splitter splat" ("RU Down Wit Da Goats"). Through these images of resistance and defiance, rappers opposed the mainstream culture, as represented, in particular, by the figure of the president.

Another prominent theme is the explosion of dominant myths and symbols. Grandmaster Flash and the Furious Five's track, "The Message," was a vivid portrayal of the other side of the American dream:

Broken glass everywhere
People pissing on the stairs

You Know They Just Don't Care

I can't take the smell, can't take the noise
Got no money to move out, I guess I got no choice
Rats in the front room, roaches in the back
Junkies in the alley with a baseball bat

I tried to get away but I couldn't get far
'Cause the man with the tow truck repossessed my car.

Through this graphic depiction of ghetto existence, disillusionment, despair, and alienation are clearly felt. The American symbols of mobility and freedom have been taken away and the song's message emphasizes the pressures of mere survival. Other examples are found in the lyrics of PE and The Goats. In "Fight the Power," Chuck D declared:

Elvis was a hero to most
But he never meant shit to me, you see
Straight up racist that sucker was simple and plain
Mutherfuck him and John Wayne

I'm Black and I'm Proud

I'm hyped and I'm amped
Most of my heroes don't appear on no stamps

This theme is echoed in The Goats' track, "Do the Digs Dug?": "I don't dig apple pie 'cause it's an American lie / Because I dug between the lies and all I found was slime." Thus, PE and The Goats rejected the dominant cultural symbols, while simultaneously refusing to let the mainstream culture define them. They offered a differing focus on those elements of black existence which were demonized by the mainstream culture.

But how far has rap been swallowed up by the dominant culture via technology and the mass media? The prominent music critic Nelson George asked not "will rap last?" but "who will control it?" Rap's commercial viability created a greed on the part of the record companies to sign any act they could—a threatening development since this many feel has led to a dilution of rap's content. Furthermore, rappers may attack the American government and its flag, but they glorify its capitalist success and lifestyle. EB&R's "Paid in Full," for example, was honest about the economic motivation behind music production. The album cover depicted a glut of gold and money, and the title track repeatedly stressed that money is the means of survival. It, therefore, emphasized rap music as an avenue of upward mobility (and the main goal of the recording industry), but it also highlighted the rapper's need to make a living and to escape economic deprivation.

However, rap has been accused of a greedy, excessive, and undisciplined materialism that highlights the acquisition, accumulation, and consumption of material goods. In "House Niggas," KRS-1 observed with displeasure that "so many rappers are preoccupied with wealth." Rap videos were liberally sprinkled with metaphors of living rich (getting paid, living large), as well as the symbols of commercialism, including big houses, large cars, expensive designer or casual wear, brand-name sneakers (Run DMC famously rapped about their Adidas), and vast amounts of ostentatious (usually gold) jewelry. Some feel that this aspect of rap culture reflected a submission to mainstream culture of consumption and materialism. Indeed, they argue, the more rap music provides a means of escape from the cycle of poverty, the more it engenders acceptance of this culture, rather than resistance against it.

Furthermore, rap relied upon the technology of the mass media to express its views to a wider audience than the mere circulation of tapes/CDs/Minidiscs/records could reach. Rap has an acknowledged dependence on the technology of the recording industry and it is quite clearly marked as a partner in the creation of music. Rappers repeatedly referred to the tools of their trade, but they did so in the attempt to assert their superiority and mastery over them. At every point, it is clear that rappers were utilizing the studio and its resources, but their lyrics contained frequent references both to their own expertise and control over the technology, giving an illusion of effortlessness, declaring their control over it. Throughout rap music, the D.J.'s skills were constantly emphasized and re-emphasized. "The music's devastatin" / It was simple to create / Cos I am the master of the 808" (The Unknown D.J., "808 Beats"); "I made it easy to dance to this / But can you detect / What's coming next / From the flex of the wrist?" (EB&R, "Eric B. Is President"); "They call him Yella / He is the best / He rocks the house on the D.M.X. (World Class Wreckin' Cru, "World Class, World Class"). (The 808 and D.M.X. were both popular drum machines used by rappers). Furthermore, many albums feature instrumentals as a showcase of the D.J.'s ability. Yet, the question still remains nonetheless of "who controls who[m]?"

Since rappers relied on, indeed enthusiastically embraced, the technology of the recording industry, they have formed what some perceive to be an unholy alliance with the mass media. Some rappers recognized this responsibility, hence the title of Paris's album, *Sleeping With the Enemy*; and while admitting that the mass media must be used, it does not have to be trusted. PE stated in "Don't Believe the Hype," "False media, we don't need it, do we? / It's fake." The Disposable Heroes of Hiphoprisy were all too aware of these problems. Their album was called *Hypocrisy Is the Greatest Luxury*. Using the deeply controversial figures of Amos 'N' Andy, they examined the role of prominent black celebrities within the mainstream culture:

Our characters flounder
Duplicitous identity
Diction and Contradiction
Have become the skills of assimilation
. . .
On screen or off we can be rented
To perform any feat
And we reflect the images presented
By the media's elite
We carry out all the stereotypes
Try to use them as decoy

And We Become Shining Examples of the System We Set Out to Destroy

The Disposable Heroes of Hiphoprisy thus articulated the contradictory forces at work when rappers attempt to address their invisibility and marginalization by importing their own cultural traditions into the mainstream culture.

But rappers have never functioned *outside* of commercial culture. It is not that they never intended to receive financial compensation for their efforts. Its early pioneers simply did not know that they could benefit from their music. Rappers took key features of the deindustrializing context and converted them into a positive force. In addition, rap manifested an active nature in opposition to the passivity assumed by consumer culture. Located within hip hop culture, it privileged break-dancing, group celebration, partying, and active, conscious creation. Rappers still "freestyle" or improvise at concerts and occasionally audience members are encouraged to join in and/or participate on stage. Moreover, rappers did not simply want to abide with the commodities of the consumer culture, they wanted to stretch them to their limits and break them. This technology was not simply adopted. Thus, rappers's (mis)use of technology rap was in itself a subversive statement. Pre-existent objects were significantly changed and modified in ways that were not recommended in the instruction manual. They made technology do what it wasn't intended to do. They got music out of it in a way that was not anticipated. They deliberately "worked in the red," pushing the technology to its limits, until they broke it. "Scratching"—cueing the needle back and forth on one record in time to the break-beat being played on the second turntable—is a good example of that, as scratching often irreparably damaged records. Rappers did not simply passively consume, they actively shaped, reshaped, and even destroyed the commodities of the consumer culture. They hijacked the technology to voice their opposition.

Further Reading

Abrams, Nathan. "Antonio's B-Boys: Rap, Rappers, and Gramsci's Intellectuals," *Popular Music & Society* 19:4 (Winter 1995): 1–18.

Quinn, Eithne. *Nuthin' but a "g" thang: The Culture and Commerce of Gangsta Rap.* New York: Columbia University Press, 2005.

After Reading

Critical Perspective

1. Describe the tone and approach of Abrams's essay. How does it impact you as a reader and why?

Rhetoric and Argument

2. Characterize Abrams's use of audience, purpose, pathos, logos, intertextuality, context, and constraints. Is his essay rhetorically effective? Why or why not?
3. Abrams describes how early rap artists utilized technology, that may have otherwise been useless, to their own productive ends. Do you agree with his assertions? Why or why not? Be sure to point to places in Abrams's text to back up your own views.
4. What is Abrams's main claim in this text? How does this work to establish his authorial ethos? Furnish evidence from Abrams's text to support your thoughts.

5. What sorts of evidence does Abrams draw upon in order to support his main claim? What artists does he reference and why? In what ways do the lyrics he quotes support his assertions? Give specific examples from the text.

6. What does Abrams contend about the political possibilities embodied in rap? Do you think it poses a challenge to forms of oppression, operates as a commercial sell-out, or does a combination of the two? Explain your position in detail.

Analysis

7. Think about different genres of music including rock-n-roll, hip-hop, rap, country, pop, punk, and others. Write a short cultural criticism in which you make an argument about how certain artists and their music have challenged specific ideas, myths, and stereotypes at critical historical moments. How have they accomplished this? What have they achieved as a result? Consult particular artists, songs, and music videos as well as library and Internet sources for evidence.

Taking Action

There have been many controversial rap and hip-hop songs. Select a musical group that created a stir due to their use of explicit lyrics.

Form two debate teams within your class. One group will argue that this song and musical group are in the right. This position should not just be based on the right to freedom of speech but on the political or social messages of the song and the ways in which they might be empowering to certain communities. The other group will argue that this song and musical group should be censored for various reasons and that the messages are not empowering. Each group should prepare positions ahead of time, drawing on the cultural texts and library and Internet sources, as well as personal experiences to back up their views. Commence with short position statements from each group. Give each group several five-minute opportunities for rebuttal and closing arguments.

After the debate, get back into the larger classroom group. Discuss what people's positions were prior to the debate. How have your thoughts shifted or developed further? What would you argue now—the pro view, the con view, or something in between? Consider making your work accessible to other groups both inside and outside the campus community.

David Laskin

"Why I Hate MTV—And Why My Kids Love It"

David Laskin has written a number of nonfiction books about weather history, American writers, artists, gardens, and travel. His book Partisans: Marriage, Politics and Betrayal Among the New York Intellectuals *won the Washington State Book Award in 2001. The* Children's Blizzard, *another book authored by Laskin, won this same award for 2005. Laskin publishes regularly in* The New York Times Travel *section and in* Preservation *magazine, and has written for* The Wall Street Journal, Smithsonian, Horticulture, Newsday, *and* The Washington Post.

EXERCISING YOUR SKILLS

Before Reading

Laskin's essay examines the effects of MTV on our lives. Watch a series of popular music videos. How are the women depicted in the videos? What are they wearing and how are they behaving? Now observe the men represented in the videos. How are they depicted? What are they wearing and how are they behaving? Consider the function of the musical lyrics alongside the images. Jot down your reactions to these images.

When I first heard of MTV back in the lush, plush, innocent Reagan '80s it seemed like the yuppie-boomer dream come true. No more endlessly waiting around for the music during the winsome antics of the Beatles in "A Hard Day's Night" or the posturing of Jagger and the Stones in "Sympathy for the Devil." Now the movie was the song and vice versa. Bang—every three minutes, new song, new movie. How totally cool. Actually, the coolness remained somewhat theoretical for me, since I didn't have cable at home and when I did catch MTV at a motel or friend's house I quickly flipped it off because I didn't like the music. But it seemed like a cool idea and I assumed that some day I'd really get into it.

Then I got married, had kids, survived into the 1990s, moved to a place with cable, and now I hate MTV. I hate it most of all because my kids like it so much and watch it hour after hour, summer and winter, day and night. No, it's not just the addiction that bothers me—nor is it really the music, which doesn't sound all that different from what I remember back in the 80s. It's the content, the imagery, the situations I can't stand. Sex as combat. The crotch as fetish. The stupid blatant monotonous sexism of the whole enterprise—all this teasing, taunting, coming on and putting down, performed by writhing boys and girls of negligible musicianship. I thought the idea was that the videos were supposed to enhance the music, add a storyline or interpretation. Instead all I see when I glimpse at the kids' television while carrying out the garbage, are tight shots of body parts and huge, leering, heavily made-up lips bearing down on the camera like zombies. Fundamentally, I don't see much difference between MTV and pornography.

But here's the rub. I know parents are subject to strange fits of passion when it comes to their kids. What if this revulsion against MTV is just a sign of how weird I've become? What if MTV is actually inspired, liberating entertainment and I'm being blind to the merit of my daughters' choices, repressive of their emerging sexuality, obtusely loyal to my own tastes and values—in other words, a typical parent. After all, my parents thought the Beatles looked like girls, Zap comics were trash, and the counterculture just an excuse for a really long, really loud party.

So, rather than wring my hands in idle speculation, I've decided to go to the source and find out what my daughters think. Kids—now it's your turn to step up to the mike. What exactly is it about MTV that you like so much? Why do you watch it so often? What do you think you're learning, or maybe I should say absorbing, from it when it comes to sex, relationships between men and women, money and power and all those other things that supposedly make the world go round? Do you think I'm being a bad parent for letting you watch it?

Alice, let's start with you. You're almost 13 and you've been glued to MTV for what, three years now? Is this healthy? Is this normal? If you were a parent, would you want your daughter or son to watch MTV?

Alice:

You have got it totally and completely . . . WRONG!! I don't watch MTV because of the sex, the violence, the outrageous outfits. I watch it for the music, the VJs, the celebrities! Just seeing my favorite stars is enough. MTV has got all sorts of shows that include juicy gossip about today's stars. For example, *Diary* is a show that talks to a different star each time and goes-supposedly-"behind the scenes" for a look at their daily lives. It's so cool to see just Blink-182 for an hour straight. More, more, more! I need more of my favorite celebrities! Then there's *Making the Video*, which shows you the process in which Britney Spears's new video is being made. 1 don't know why I like that show so much. . . . Maybe it's the fact that I feel like I'm behind all the glamour—right next to Britney!! Oh my God, it's Carson! And there's Ray! Could it be that these lovable VJs are all we need? Or could it be, that by watching *TRL* everyday, with the same videos, everyday. . . . I can memorize all of "It's Gonna be Me"! ". . . You got no choice, babe, but to move on . . ." Well jeez. There is just so much stuff that I can't resist on MTV. It just might be the perfect channel!

Dad again:

Whoa, this is a lot worse than I thought. I mean, this is not just TV addiction—this is fan fanaticism. "The perfect channel?!" Getting "behind all the glamour—right next to Britney!" Is this a worthy goal for a child of mine—a child period? Well, Alice, you do make a persuasive case, I guess, and I suppose I feel somewhat reassured that you're not in it for the sex, violence, etc. But that still leaves the critical question unanswered: Can all this blatant sexism and raunchy titillation possibly be good for kids? Entertaining—yes, I guess I can see the glamour of spending an "hour straight" glued to flickering images of cute people. But what worries me are the messages you're taking away. I mean, what does MTV say to you about the way men and women treat each other? Don't you think these videos exploit the people in them—and exploit you for watching them?

MTV reminds me of flatulence jokes. When I was a kid we told these stupid jokes about, well, you know, farting—they were gross, but hey, we were kids. Now the same jokes provide the story lines for "major motion pictures" and TV shows. That's what MTV has done to the sexy swagger of pop music. It's as if the producers are thinking, How outrageous can we be in mining every offensive cliché and suggestive gesture? Talk about dumbing down and ramping up.

Okay, I'll control myself and turn the keyboard over to Sarah—Alice's non-identical twin and another MTV groupie. Sarah, kindly react to my diatribe . . .

Sarah:

MTV . . . What can I say about MTV? Maybe that it's the greatest channel on earth! It's got my favorite artists 'N SYNC, Eminem and Blink 182, and what's better than seeing your favorite artist perform live, seeing their music video or watching them on a show that you wish would never end? And then there are the VJs. My favorite two are Carson and Ray because they are so funny to watch. Sometimes I just wish I was Carson because he gets to meet all of these famous people and he must have the best job hosting *TRL*! And of course there are the shows. How could I forget the shows of MTV! Well, first there is *TRL*, one full hour counting down the top ten videos of that day, picked by the fans who watch the show. How great is that? And finally there is a show called *Fanatic*. On this show fans get picked to meet their favorite artist and ask them questions. Oh my God, I love that show! I wish that I could be one of the fans that was picked to meet their favorite artist especially if I got to meet 'N SYNC. That would be a dream come true. But anyway, MTV isn't bad, it's just a great channel with a bunch of great people.

Dad:

Dad has returned to lift the mike ever so wearily. It's clear that I'm fighting a losing battle here—no, I've lost the war. These kids are not fans—they're cultists. Worse, they sound like MTV shills. I mean, maybe I should email this to Carson and Ray's boss right now and they can sign Sarah and Alice up as publicists to the "tween" world. So much eloquence and passion squandered on so wretched a cause.

But I have to admit these kids make a persuasive case, because I'm weakening. Personally, I'd rather spend an hour with the oral surgeon than listen to 'N SYNC explain why they're so great and how they got the inspiration for all those memorable lines ("bye, bye, bye!"), but I'm willing to concede that this is a matter of taste.

Well, Emily, oh sage of 15 summers, do you have any other words of wisdom and enlightenment to shed on this subject? Do you agree with your sisters that MTV is the "perfect channel"? Does anything about it ever offend you or make you wonder about the hidden—or blatant—messages you're being subjected to? And while you're enlightening me, would you mind explaining when the term "singer" morphed into "artist"?

Emily:

Perfect channel indeed! I assume you know that MTV stands for Music Television, but I say that's false advertising. Where's the music? I have seen music on MTV once a day, in the form of *TRL*, which is really just an excuse to look at official "cute person" Carson Daly. Does MTV offend me? Yes! *TRL* (Total Request Live) in which fans write emails to mtv.com asking for their favorite videos to be played frightens me. How can an entire country have such bad taste in music?

But I am supposed to be disagreeing with you. What is your goal here? To have MTV taken off the air? Or just to prevent us from ever watching it? Either way it's censorship. Making it impossible for MTV to air is a violation of Freedom of Speech, and stopping us from watching it is possible censorship of our brilliant young imaginations. Just you wait till Sarah wins a Grammy for Best Cinematography in a Music Video. And anyway, what's the problem with the sex on MTV? You let me see the film "High Fidelity"—twice, no less—in which a man and a woman have sex in a car. I suppose your argument would be that they weren't clad in lingerie (as opposed to MTV, where everyone is). But really, do you think my sisters and I can't tell the difference between a Britney Spears video and real life? Do you think we don't realize that exploitation (of men and women) is MTV's big selling point? And if we realize that it's exploitation we can't be numb to it or in favor of it. Please, father, be reasonable.

Dad:

Father reasonably wraps up: I am afraid I have been trumped. No matter whether it's the perfect channel or the perfect reflection of our national awful taste in music, MTV is evidently exactly what the framers had in mind when they drafted the first amendment. Clearly, the right to freedom of speech (not to mention freedom of lingerie) extends to our very own family room. In any case, I must admit that the girls' arguments have a certain Jeffersonian clarity and passion—a sign that MTV, for all its ills, hasn't squelched their ability to reason and write.

But I'm not giving up. Next time, I'm planning to tangle with the girls on a subject about which I have the decisive advantage in every way: boys.

After Reading

Critical Perspective

1. How does Laskin approach the subject of MTV? Do you think that this is an effective strategy? Why or why not? Explain your responses.

Rhetoric and Argument

2. Reflect upon Laskin's use of rhetorical tactics, specifically audience, purpose, ethos, pathos, logos, intertextuality, context, and constraints. Do you believe that his text is convincing? Why or why not?
3. What is Laskin's main claim about music videos? Where does it appear in his text? What are the key assertions made by each of his three daughters? With whom do you agree most? Why? Be sure to give examples from the text as well as your own experiences to back up your views.
4. Consider Laskin's use of evidence. Do you think that his main claim is adequately supported by this kind of evidence? Why or why not? Is there any other type of evidence he might use that would additionally support his thoughts? Answer these same questions for the assertions offered by Laskin's daughters.
5. Laskin concludes his essay with a somewhat different viewpoint than when he began it. What do you think he is willing to claim about MTV after the discussion with his daughters and why? Do you agree with his new position? Why yes or why no? Draw from his text and your own experiences to back up your opinions.

Analysis

6. Write an informal argumentative response in which you make a claim about whether Laskin's initial comments about MTV videos are accurate as well as whether they apply equally to videos in all musical genres. Draw your evidence from specific music videos as well as from a close analysis of Laskin's text. In addition, be sure to consult library and Internet sources to back up your thoughts.

Taking Action

Now that you have read Laskin's final assessments about the effects of sexism and racism in music videos on girls and boys, it is important to recognize that many writers disagree with him—arguing that such videos are misogynistic and shape male–female interactions in negative ways. Whether you agree with Laskin's final position or with these other writers' views, you have two options for how you might take action. The first is to write a formal letter to a local radio station about your views. Be sure to offer examples from particular cultural texts to support your views. The second is to compose a more personal letter to a young girl or boy you know (your friend, your sibling, or the like) about the images you are seeing, what you would argue about them, and why your perspectives are persuasive. Be sure to use all of your rhetorical and argumentative skills to accomplish this. Seek out library and Internet sources as well.

Once you have completed your letters, get together in a large group to talk about what you wrote and why. Consider revising your letters and sending them to the people that you are addressing. If you take this approach, you may want to return to this assignment again later to discuss the responses you have received.

CHAPTER 10

Surfing in Cyberculture and Gaming

INTRODUCTION

Considering Cyberculture and Gaming

Technology seems to have an ever greater presence in all of our lives—from camera cell phones to instant-messaging pagers to satellite phones to YouTube to Black-Berries. In 1990 Tim Berners-Lee, inventor of the World Wide Web, dreamed that it would mirror and eventually embody the ways in which we all work, play, and socialize. As a common information space fostering more universal forms of readership, the construction of group knowledge, and the decentralization of information, the web has accomplished that and much, much more.

Our constant interaction with technology impacts all of us every day, shaping our world and our relationships to that world. If you need information for a term paper, inevitably you do web searches for sources and locate research that will help you to prove your points. If you are looking for a recipe to cook a new Italian dish, you may do a web search through Google, Yahoo!, or Netscape and find hundreds of ways to make marinara sauce. When you have to locate an old friend from grade school or high school with whom you have lost touch, you can go on the web and, with a few clicks, locate this person's email address, home residence, telephone number, and place of employment. If you need to get in touch with your parents between classes, you can "text" them and tell them when you will come home to visit. When you want to "talk" to a student at another university, you can add her or him to your "friends" through MySpace or Facebook—and when you don't want someone to be your "friend" you can decline that person entrance to your page. More and more these days if you want to get an undergraduate or graduate degree, you can take some of your classes over the web while you are working or raising children.

What kinds of websites do you often visit on the Internet? Are you a member of MySpace.com? Are you part of certain chat groups, Wikis, listservs, blog networks, podcasts, MOOs, vidcasts, file-sharing networks, or MUDs? Do you purchase items online from OldNavy.com, BarnesandNoble.com, Target.com or iTunes? Do you play games online such as "MVP Baseball," old Nintendo or Atari games, "Age of Empires II," "Sacrifice," "Kingdom Hearts," or "Grand Theft Auto"? What do these interactions with technology say about who you are and how you view yourself, our culture and its preoccupations and investments, as well as the changing nature of the technology available to all of us? In a typical day, I will probably visit many listservs and websites. In a matter of moments I can locate the latest scholarly publication in rhetoric, find an exciting new curry recipe to try at home, buy my niece a hoodie at Delia's for her birthday, share my vacation photos with friends on Flickr, and learn about upcoming trail running races in Arizona.

Overview of Selections: Rethinking Cyberculture and Gaming

In this chapter of *Pop Perspectives: Readings to Critique Contemporary Culture* you will explore many of the latest changes in technology and culture from a variety of perspectives. Tackling how different technological advancements function as well as the ways in which they may be productive or counterproductive, this chapter leads you to consider technology's possible futures.

The first section is titled "Rethinking Cyberculture and Gaming." It addresses the ways in which gender, race, ethnicity, class, and other markers intersect with cyberspace, and encourages consideration of how to dismantle access inequities to technology.

The chapter begins with two essays that can be read in conjunction with each other. L. Jean Camp and Anita Borg furnish texts about the Systers mailing list, a group dedicated to empowering women in computer science and related disciplines. Camp, a famous expert in computer values and ethics, describes for us her own experiences in the group. She argues that organizations and lists on the web created just for women and their needs can help their voices to be heard. Camp reveals the critical activist work of the Systers—helping more women become engaged participants and leaders in the high-tech world. Likewise, Camp speaks out against Mattel Corporation's first talking Barbie who uttered the discouraging words to young girls, "Math is hard."

Anita Borg, an internationally known computer engineer and the creator of the Systers mailing list, explains the history of the group and why she felt compelled to begin it. Borg offers us a cultural criticism of American society's sexism and the ways in which women are too often excluded from conversations about technology that will ultimately impact them in crucial ways. Borg argues that women in traditionally male-dominated disciplines can build crucial, supportive communities in the virtual world. Borg's aim with the list, she reveals, is not to exclude men but to create a level playing field for all members of today's scientific pursuits.

Writer and journalist Amy Harmon next takes us behind the scenes of computer chat groups. She discusses the various identities and roles that people adopt in online interactions in order to find love, impress others, or get ahead in the world. Harmon asserts that people engage in online flirtation and sex, often swapping gender roles in ways that may be both liberating as well as troubling. Harmon offers examples from many people's real experiences creating fake identities in the virtual sphere. For some, adopting alternative personae has gone beyond mere role playing and become more real than their day-to-day lives. Harmon calls for a greater understanding of the many ways in which switching identities can impact online interactions.

Then, ex-journalist turned Internet developer Fredrick L. McKissack Jr. examines how the Internet is impacting African American communities in the United States. McKissack contends that for some people the net has become little more than a "cyberghetto," a space in which technology is not evenly and equitably distributed. McKissack believes that making computers available to more African American students in all schools is a critical first step in bridging this cultural and economic divide. However, without access to computers at home, McKissack asserts, many of such students may still have too many obstacles to overcome. In order to create social, cultural, and political parity between people in American culture, McKissack contends, all people must have equal access to technology of all kinds.

Greg Beato, a freelance writer for *Wired* magazine, writes in the next selection about how gaming companies are increasingly seeing girls as an untapped market for online gaming. He explains to us some of the marketing theories that have been used to determine which games will be more appropriate and interesting for girls, discussing the ways in which "Barbie Fashion Designer," "McKenzie & Co.," and "The Babysitters Club Friendship Kit" do little more than socialize young girls into stereotypical gender roles. Beato projects a new future for girl gaming with examples such as Team Webgrrls and Girl Tech, contending that girls increasingly need alternative online interactions that can build confidence and challenge gender stereotypes. These games will allow girls to become even stronger communicators and problem solvers, enabling them greater facility with technology as well as positive contact with one another.

Brian Cowlishaw, an assistant professor of English at Northeastern State University in Tahlequah, Oklahoma, examines the growing genre of realistic virtual combat games such as "Metal of Honor," "Battlefield," and "America's Army" in order to discern what causes people to play them and why they have become so popular. The games he investigate involve making the gamer a "first person shooter" such that the gun is "your gun," the hands are "you," and the "map" indicates where you are changing positions on battlefields. He reveals that what players find in these games is often more realistic than more traditional war video games. At the same time, Cowlishaw also exposes the ways in which real virtual combat games can unrealistically present misleading views of what war is really like—erasing the effects of war such as bodily dismemberment and death. Cowlishaw also makes note of connections between realistic war games and the U.S. military's recruitment tactics.

In this section's last selection, journalist and story writer Glen Martin writes about the Internet wars and Native American culture. Through rich description Martin invites us into the mystical world of Blue Snake's Lodge, an America Online seminar run by an Eastern Shawnee chief. Bit by bit, Martin exposes the inconsistencies in this representation of Native American life. Martin gathers the perspectives and opinions from many Native American scholars and activists who are striving to make the Internet a place to preserve their traditions. Revealing the problems with how Native American culture is used to commercial ends on the web, Martin also examines the fact that so many Native communities in the United States remain unwired. Martin contends that all Native Americans need to have a greater say in how they are represented on the web and should be a greater part of all online communities. He closes by making note of some critical strides that Native-run sites have made on the web.

Overview of Selections: Innovations in Technology

The second section of Chapter 10, "Innovations in Technology," traces recent cyberculture and technological innovations, raising questions about both the positives and negatives of various advancements.

The first essay is by Mark Slouka, a well-known creative and critical writer who focuses on technology issues. Slouka asks us to challenge the dominant perception that new computer technology has brought with it exciting new possibilities, even bringing us closer to a utopian world. Instead, Slouka argues that all of our technological advances have taken us away from the worlds in which we actually live. We no longer interact with our environments regularly without technology mediating our interactions. Slouka dismantles the world of Bill Gates, founder and chair of Microsoft, asserting that Gates's kind of thinking leads to a greater divide between those who have technological access and those who do not. He also suggests that technology has created a less satisfying way to live our lives. While Gates promises that computers will bring greater democracy, Slouka argues that it promises to do exactly the opposite—privilege certain people while disenfranchising others and take us away from the actual people and places that surround us.

Technology expert Erin Jansen next considers the popularity of instant messaging (IM) or texting, especially among "screenagers." While she concedes that at school "kids need to know the difference between formal writing and conversational writing," Jansen argues that the positive aspects of texting are too often dismissed by parents and educators. Jansen makes the case that texting is not simply a youth culture phenomenon. Although it is an important part of young people's lives that ought to be respected and honored, only 60 percent of text users are under the age of 17. This indicates that many adults are also text messaging. Likewise, texting need not only be understood as a form of casual conversation: It can also be a creative and even intellectual form of expression. Pointing to examples of teachers who incorporate texting into how they teach their students about the writing process, Jansen suggests that educators should use texting imaginatively to generate class discussion as well as to work on inventing and composing early paper drafts. In the end, Jansen maintains that text messaging has many positive benefits that ought to be embraced rather than ignored.

Then journalist and critic Ralph Lombreglia, an established short story writer, describes the ways in which technology is changing how we tell stories. Storytelling is now taking place within networked, computerized environments, finding its greatest fans in the computer gaming world. Lombreglia traces the plots of various computer games often played by boys such as "Obsidian" and "Riven: The Sequel to Myst." Lombreglia contends that too often such games end up being little more than advertisements for the companies who make them rather than sincere attempts to offer innovations within the genre itself. Lombreglia calls upon computer game developers to consider their work a kind of art that recognizes intellectual detail and sophistication in storytelling rather than catering to revenue-building pressures alone.

Finally, in a humorous piece tinged with seriousness, writer John Marr leads us into the private realm of eBay addiction. Marr describes the ways in which eBay encourages consumers to buy all sorts of goods. Discussing how eBay resembles auctions, yard sales, and flea markets as well as how it differs from them, Marr takes us through his search to find rare items and describes the bidding wars he takes part in. Marr argues that eBay encourages bidding over products—both old and new—that people otherwise might never have wanted, needed, or even knew existed. And yet somehow we find ourselves caught up in the excitement of the chase, and the thrill of winning the prize.

As you read this chapter, consider the various websites you visit, the online chats in which you participate, and the diverse forms of technology you use. How do race, class, gender, ethnicity, age, and other identity concerns impact the ways in which online games, sites, conversations, and advertisements are designed? How do these technological innovations target you as a gamer and/or consumer? How are you being profiled in your online chats and advertisements? How are masculinity and femininity constructed in online environments where the human body using the computer is not always visible or known? How do race, class, ethnicity, and age differences limit who can have access to technology, how people use it, and to what ends? As our technological environments increasingly grow and bleed into the other areas of our lives, are we witnessing greater democratic involvement or an ever-widening chasm between those who have and those who have not?

RETHINKING CYBERCULTURE AND GAMING

L. JEAN CAMP

"We Are Geeks, and We Are Not Guys: The Systers Mailing List"

ANITA BORG

"On the Mailing List Systers, from *Computing Research News*, September 1994"

L. Jean Camp is a pioneer in the interdisciplinary study of trust and design for values in Internet exchange. She is a professor at Harvard University's Kennedy School of Government in Cambridge, Massachusetts. She was a participant in the Systers mailing list, has published widely on Internet issues and developed patents for computer networking, and has authored Trust and Risk in Internet Commerce.

Anita Borg was a member of the research staff at Xerox's Palo Alto Research Center. She was also the president and founding director of the Institute for Women and Tech-

nology, a nonprofit organization focused on increasing women's impact on technology and the positive impact of technology on women worldwide. Borg worked for Auragen Systems Corporation, Nixdorf Computer, and Digital Equipment Corporation. She received many awards, including the Pioneer Award from the Electronic Frontier Foundation and the Augusta Ada Lovelace Award from the Association for Women in Computing. Borg passed away in 1998.

EXERCISING YOUR SKILLS

Before Reading

Camp and Borg write about women's access to technology. How do you think that men and women experience the Internet differently? What kinds of things do we search for? What kinds of exchanges do we have? What different sorts of issues do we take up? Do you think that the Internet is friendlier toward men than it is toward women or vice versa? What experiences lead you to say this?

Take part in chat sessions, MySpace interactions, or the like. Do you think that masculinity and femininity operate differently online than they do in other media forms? Why might this be significant?

> *A ship in port is safe, but that is not what ships are for. Sail out to sea and do new things.*
>
> —Admiral Grace Hopper, computer pioneer

The internet can be rough sailing for women, buffeted by the high winds of derision, sucked down into whirlpools of contention. But in that sea of bytes there are destinations beyond compare, worlds to explore. And as we steer our craft out to sea, braving the great unknown, we know that in this world there are electronic ports where we can become refreshed, refueled and ready to sail again when we may think ourselves alone.

Systers is one of those ports of call. Systers is a mailing list of women in computer science and related disciplines. We are geeks, and we are not guys. Not guys, but geeks! How can that be? But we are, we have been and we continue to be. If it surprises you to learn that more than fifteen hundred geeks are out there, imagine the surprise to each of us!

Being a geek isn't easy. It's hard, intellectually challenging work. For some people, people whose gender I won't go into here, people of less intellectual capability than some of my systers, achieving true geekdom means sacrificing their emotional development. You may have met some of these people. Technical universities and work environments tend to be full of them, and are brusque, competitive places as a result. My place of work, Carnegie Mellon University, is no exception.

So is it any wonder that I turn to the net in search of solace? But there I find that all the groups formed for women quickly become swamps of men's bile. One man told me, "I know as much about being a woman as you do." After all, he lives with women, he probably has been intimate with some women and he spends so much time thinking about our many flaws! He certainly knows all about women.

Even the discussion groups that focus primarily on parenting have become arenas for men to pat themsleves on their collective backs, to discuss how much more difficult it is to be a father than a mother, and to discuss the discrimination against and oppression of fathers. There is no end to the complaints of the anxious, and oppressed white male on the Internet.

Consider a Usenet newsgroup specifically started to discuss issues about women: *soc.women,* where the posts by men outnumber the women's. On the Internet, as in life, men dominate discussions about women. Many of the feminists on these newsgroups are indomitable warriors; there will always be a battle for them. But some of us chose to spend our energies elsewhere, and even indomitable warriors need a place to rest.

Too often, when women try to create spaces to define ourselves we are drowned out by the voices of men who cannot sit quietly and listen, but need to bring themselves into the discussion. Many of these men support women. But the voices of men who cannot be silent even in a space ostensibly devoted to women means that there are no public spaces for women to talk about and to other women.

So we withdraw to a room of our own—to mailing lists. Even the most indomitable woman needs a port of call. Here we chatter and type in nurturing communion, knowing that the world cannot do without our unique contributions.

Systers' History

A mailing list is a list of email addresses kept on one computer. A message directed to the list goes to that computer and then is automatically copied to everyone on the list. Someone subscribed to a mailing list generally finds her mailbox full of an endless stream of messages full of earnest discussion, gossip, jokes and occasional discord. Each message by a mailing list member spawns its own replies, a round robin discussion that at times resembles a support group and at other times a graduate seminar. A bad mailing list can be dull. A good one can be wonderful.

Systers, my port in times of storm, my destination of choice for R&R, was begun by Anita Borg. Dr. Borg is a senior computer scientist at Digital Equipment Corporation (being senior at DEC is a big fat hairy deal in the computing world), a pilot and the benevolent matriarch of fifteen hundred systers. She is, as she has named herself, her systers' keeper. Systers is an unmoderated but strongly guided mailing list open to women only. To join, you have to swear you are a woman. If if turns out otherwise, you are removed.

Moderated lists have moderators who sift and sort the stream of messages, culling here, compiling there, much as a good hostess directs the flow of traffic at a dinner party. The default is that all messages go out to everyone. If a discussion begins to dominate, posts made in reply to that discussion, called a thread, are not sent out to the list. Moderation in all things. When Dr. Borg guides mailing lists, she often posts only *Cut it out.* This usually works. She does not view every message before it goes out, as a true moderator does.

On Systers, a woman might send a question or comment to the list and then a volunteer, often the original poster, offers to summarize the results. This prevents list members' personal mailboxes from being flooded. Sometimes a post will cause a flurry of responses: Take Our Daughters to Work Day, for example, was much discussed. Pornography, needless to say, is an issue not to be mentioned under the threat of a firestorm of passionate debate and many resulting "unsubscribe" messages.

Note the discussions in *soc.men* and *soc.women* that relate to women: Threads there include discussions of why men are smarter than women, as proven by SAT math scores. Men arguing against maternity leave since women choose to be pregnant. Men who want men to be able to choose whether or not to admit paternity ("choice for men"). Why men make better parents. Abortion. Abortion. Abortion. How men take all the risks in dating since they have to ask for the dates.

The discussions about women on Usenet are just that—about women. Not by women. About.

Consider the topics that women talk about on Systers when *we* control the debate: how to recruit more women to science. How to deal with illegal questions on interviews. When/if to have children. Whether or not to go to grad school. How to deal with a coworker who harasses you. How to deal with email harassment. How to deal with a job hunt when there are two careers involved. What to do about childcare at conferences. How to select an advisor. What effect would the selection of C rather than LISP or Scheme for a first programming language have upon women in computer science? What good fellowships exist for women?

For even more specific discussions, Systers has sublists for specific affinity groups: for example, for women of color and for lesbian and bisexual women. How freeing to have a place where they don't have to deal with people very unlike them discussing "reverse discrimination" and "special rights" when they want to talk about how to just get through the week.

Systers Didn't Let Me Down

It was early in the morning and I knew it would be a very long day. I had a paper to present at a conference and not one but two ear infections. The conference—The Telecommunications Policy Research Conference—is the major one in my area of research, and I had twelve hours to finish my paper, get in the car and drive there to present it. My advisor had stayed up until the wee hours the previous night helping me polish. I was still editing.

My husband was actually going to do the driving, so I could work on the presentation in the car. He was coming with me because of the baby. Five months old. Still breastfeeding. Squiggly and helpless and wonderful and everything unprofessional in the world.

Going to a conference breast-feeding a baby? There's no chapter on "Dealing with Letdown in Silk" in *Dress for Success*. I didn't know what to expect, and I didn't have anyone to clue me in. So that morning I sent out a message, a quiet cry for support to one thousand other professional women in computer science.

They heard me. They took my virtual hand. They gave me virtual hugs. I was not standing in the wilderness. Trailblazer? Hell no! So many women had gone before me, lactating their way through dissertation defenses, conference presentations and teaching tutorials to top management that it was no impenetrable forest I stood in, but a clear road with a clear sign marked not "This way," but "It's Okay."

My message that morning was contained. You could hardly tell I was holding my breath:

I am going to present at a conference this weekend. Since I am breast feeding I am taking little Addie along (4 mos.). My husband is coming along, too, to take care of Addie during the day (wonderful?—Yep! he is). If you have taken a baby to a conference I would really like to hear your experiences. I feel like a stranger going to a mostly male conference w/baby. How did you handle it? What problems did you have—what did you avoid with good judgment calls? What was most helpful/ worst?

The responses flowed in. One. Two. Six. Dozens. Without Systers I would have been astoundingly alone—how many lactating technical doctoral candidates do you know? Instead, I was comforted, told that I, a normal soul in a body leaking milk, could handle it. I felt like a pioneer going into the great unknown when I sent my note to Systers. When I left for the conference, I had had dozens of responses and I knew that I was not (and never had been) alone. I got messages from women who had gone to conferences the previous month and women who had gone fifteen years ago! One woman told of taking her five-week-old baby to a conference and she was preparing, seven weeks later, to take him along again. They all said, "You can do it. You will be fine."

The one message I did *not* get was: It was terrible and destroyed my career. The horror stories helped there. One woman's little one did one of those massive explosive poops that violate all the laws of physics right in the middle of a session. She readjusted the baby carrier and went to the motel room and cleaned them both up. If their babies could be sick or have an ebm (e = explosive) in a session and all turned out fine, then, well, what was I so worried about!

When I returned from the conference, I reported back to all the women who had reached out to me:

Knowing that there is one incredible person is not always so helpful, simply because this person is so exceptional. But knowing that there are dozens of women, that I did not have to be so unique or incredible, made me feel like I, too, could pull through.

And after all those messages the one thing I was not when I left was so worried. Thank you all. Things went well for me at the conference. I ended up encumbered not by the baby—but by my ear infection!

The Lighter Side of Systers

Systers also serves up lighter fare. Feminists often get abuse for not laughing at funny jokes. Maybe it's that the jokes we're told aren't all that funny. One syster was sent a bunch of jokes about engineers, all of which assumed that engineers are male, for example:

"You know you're an engineer when you have a beard because you have calculated your efficiency loss in time shaving and found it unacceptable."

This syster considered sending out a flame: "Hello! Remember me? The engineer? The woman?" Instead she got onto Systers and asked for jokes that assume engineers are women. The result:

You know you're an engineer when . . .
—you have hairy legs not as a political statement but because you have calculated your efficiency loss in time shaving and found it unacceptable.
—they give you drugs during labor not because you can't take the pain but because you keep trying to rebuild your monitors.
—you try to register in the automotive department for your wedding gifts.
—you are excited about your first period because it gives you the opportunity to test the viscosity meter in your chemistry set on an interesting biological sample.

Instead of flaming the men for their sexism, she sent back a collection of jokes from our point of view. Who says we don't have a sense of humor?

The Barbie Experience

Systers is a powerful personal resource for women, but there is an important public element, too. Nothing illustrates this better than the great Barbie fracas. If you recall, Mattel introduced a Talking Barbie in 1993. This Barbie said things guaranteed to appeal to the mostly braindead. Among the gems that sprang from her perfect lips was "Math is hard."

An alert syster, possibly the appalled mother of the owner of one of these dolls, sent out a message. After all the discussions we'd had of how to keep young women and girls interested in math, this was a broadside.

Women study math because mathematical competence leads to more money, which leads to many good things, such as autonomy. Math is fun. Math is good. Math and technical knowledge is power. Here was Mattel saying clearly to girls: Stay away from math. You are not interested in any quantitative professional career. Take domestic science! Be dependent.

I read the *Washington Post* and skim the *New York Times* and the *Wall Street Journal* regularly. I have The Associated Press and United Press International wires available to me via Clarinet. But Systers spoke first.

Actually, first we *screamed.* Then we discussed it. Then we got down to business. Never mess with systers.

We found the number for Mattel's complaint line and started calling. Individual systers called their professional organizations to complain, and the American Association of University Women did just that. The mainstream media picked it up—after Systers had begun the battle.

Mattel surrendered: Barbie no longer advocates female innumeracy. Systers got women together, and we acted.

Join The Fray

Computers can give you a level of anonymity, which may give some women who've never spoken up in public the courage to express themselves. But anonymity is isolation, a level of invisibility. After playing around Web pages and lurking on Usenet groups, you want to be seen and to define yourself. You do not want people to define you, especially not by simply looking at your name and guessing your gender.

Systers has given me comfort when I needed it, reminding me every day that I am not alone. The feeling is small, but constant. As Systers has filtered into my being over time, it has become a tremendous positive force in my life. Not being alone means not being hidden. Of course, Systers speaks to me as a technical woman in academia. But there are many other mailing lists for women—no woman needs to be alone on the net.

The very strength that Systers offers can make it a sanctuary on a hostile net. But we cannot live in a sanctuary, regardless of the temptation. It is important to go back out into the public debate and remain visible, if for no other reason than to ensure that no woman is left truly isolated. The power of connectivity to effect change is truly incredible. The Barbie experience taught me that. The far right realizes it, too, and is organizing on the net. We need to be doing the same. If not, it will be as if women were sending out missives via caravan while those who would deny women their rights were using Cruise missiles. If we're not there, the doors of electronic democracy will be closed to us.

"On the Mailing List Systers, from *Computing Research News*, September 1994"

The existence of exclusively female forums is controversial and legitimately so. Exclusive forums such as male-only or white-only or Christian-only clubs have been used to exclude other groups from information and power sharing. As the founder of Systers, a large female-only mailing list, I have frequently been called upon to justify the exclusion of men and to explain why Systers is not discriminatory in the above sense. This [essay] attempts such an explanation. I hope to generate discussion, but more importantly, to generate understanding and cooperation.

Increasing the number of women in computer science and making the environments in which women work more conducive to their continued participation in the field require the active development of both women and men. In particular, there must be ongoing and productive communication throughout the field concerning the unique problems that women face when they enter the field and as they progress and advance. The fact that women are a small minority in the field results in two impediments to this communication. First, women work almost exclusively with men and so have few opportunities to create and then participate in a "community of women in computer science." Second, men work almost exclusively with men and have limited opportunities to communicate with more than a few professional women. Open electronic forums can improve communication by introducing us to a larger community, but do nothing to reduce the disparity in numbers. On the other hand, exclusively female forums, such as Systers, are a particulary effective way to connect women in our field with each other. They also ultimately contribute to improved communication between women and men.

Let me first describe what Systers is and what it is not. Systers is a private, unmoderated, but strongly guided, mailing list with a documented set of rules for participation. The mailing list includes female computer professionals in the commercial, academic and government worlds as well a female graduate and undergraduate computer science and computer engineering students. Systers currently has over 1,500 members in seventeen countries. We are a global community of individuals who are otherwise physically isolated from each other.

Systers is a civilized and cooperative forum in which "flaming" is rare and personal attacks are actively discouraged. We ask that Systers mail not be forwarded nor its contents used outside the list without the permission of the contributors to a message. There is no rule of secrecy in Systers. This rule simply empowers our members and protects our privacy by giving each of us control over the breadth of distribution of our comments. It is based on a common courtesy that, if applied more generally, would make the net a more hospitable place for substantive group problem solving.

Systers is not analogous to a private all-male club. It is different because women in computer science are a small minority of the community. It is different because Systers is not interested in secrecy or in keeping useful information from the rest of the community. In fact useful messages are regularly made public after checking with the contributors. The likelihood that an underempowered minority will keep inaccessible information from the large empowered majority with every means of communication available to it is small indeed. I have not addressed whether a forum such as Systers would be necessary in an ideal and egalitarian world or even in a world similar to our own but with many more women in computing. When we get there we can make that decision.

The following paragraphs enumerate the reasons for keeping Systers a female-only forum. None of these benefits accrue to women in other existing open forums. Women need a place to find each other. As a geographically dispersed and frequently individually isolated minority within computer science, women rarely have the opportunity to interact in person with other women in computer science on any subject. Women (and men) have many opportunities to interact with men. Until Systers came into existence, the notion of a global "community of women in computer science" did not exist.

Women need female role models and mentors. A primary function of women-only interaction is mentoring. Exposing women to the full range of significant interactions among women, without the perception of help or input from men, serves to bolster self-esteem and independence. This includes exposure to women discussing purely technical issues among themselves and shows that this makes women more rather than less able to interact professionally with men.

Women need a place to discuss our issues. Many open forums whose focus is women's issues suffer from a common problem. Discussions are frequently dominated by disagreements between men and women about what the issues are rather than how to deal with them. This is not a problem with all men, but is a problem with almost all such open forums. Women more often share common ground that allows us to get beyond defining issues and on to constructing solutions.

Women need to discover our own voice. Discussion among women is different from that of women together with men. Men, even when in a minority and even when well-meaning, have a different style of interaction. They often dominate discussions. Even when they don't, the style of a mixed conversation tends to be in the style of male-dominated discussions. As women understand more clearly what those differences are and what professional discourse is like on our own, we will be better able to bring our voice to open forums.

I recently received two messages that illustrate how Systers helps women participate more effectively and more professionally with men.

A researcher from an industrial lab stated, "When I first joined the list a few years ago, I was skeptical about the need for a list specifically devoted to issues facing women working in computer science. But since then, I have become much more aware of the differences in the ways men and women interact, and many of the experiences and views shared by others on this list have helped me to better understand how to function effectively in a male-dominated research environment." A university professor described a change in her students: "The availability of the list to our women graduate students here at [the university] has had a remarkable effect on our students. The women are becoming more self-confident and more aggressive in their dealings with our male-dominated faculty, many of whom still regard women as out of place in the program."

Systers is definitely not the only forum in which concerned women participate. It is only a starting place and place of respite in our journey to equality. It is essential that we continue to actively communicate and participate with men, that we not become isolated from professional men, and that we bring our issues to the fore at every appropriate opportunity. Since most of us work exclusively or nearly exclusively with men, it is actually impossible for us to become isolated from men even if we wish to be. Since men make up the vast majority of the field, it would be foolish to believe that real change could take place without them.

To include men in Systers would take away a vital source of mutual support from women. On the other hand, the need for serious discussion in an open forum exists. It behooves whoever runs such a forum to realize that women who have experienced conversation on Systers will be for the most part uninterested in participating in a wide-open free-for-all. The commonly applied list-management principle "if you can't take the heat, get off the list" will not work. It has been tried and has failed. The forum will need a strong leader/moderator, committed to the encouragement of productive discussion and willing to stop unproductive argument. I do this for Systers. While I do not have the desire nor the energy to run another forum, I am surely not the only person capable of it and offer my help and experience to anyone who is willing to take on the task.

It is not the reluctance of women nor our participation in forums like Systers that limits communication and joint problem solving with men. It is the sexism in our society, our field and our consciousness that limits us all. If men want an open forum and are seriously interested in hearing what women have to say, rather than in telling us what we need then such a forum could be a fruitful and productive sibling for Systers.

After Reading

Critical Perspective

1. Reflect upon Camp's tone and approach in detail. How did you respond to the text? Do you find this a persuasive way to make such an argument? Why or why not?

Rhetoric and Argument

2. Camp employs many stylistic and rhetorical devices throughout her essay (audience, purpose, ethos, pathos, logos, intertextuality, context, and constraints). Make note of each of these devices and explain how they aid her argument or detract from it. Be sure to furnish textual evidence to back up your thoughts.
3. What is Camp's main claim in this text and where does it appear? Do you find it persuasive? Why or why not? What sorts of evidence does she utilize? Do you think it is sufficient to back up her claim? Why or why not?
4. How does Camp organize her text? Do you believe that this is the most effective way to structure it? Why or why not? Present quotes from the essay to support your views.
5. How does Borg's rhetorical approach, tone, and style differ from Camp's? What is her main claim? Do you find this approach more effective or less effective? Why or why not?
6. What evidence does Borg provide for her claims? Is her evidence as convincing as Camp's, less so, or more so? Give quotes from the texts to back up your opinion.

Analysis

7. Do you think that the concerns raised by Camp and Borg continue to be important issues for female Internet users? Do you think any new concerns are emerging for women? Are comparable concerns emerging for men? Write a short essay in which you tackle these issues. Try to offer evidence from specific cultural texts, and library and Internet sources to back up your views.

Taking Action

Form a small group. Your aim is to find a website for a clothing company that targets women as their audience as well as a clothing company that targets men as its audience. What rhetorical differences and similarities are at work in these sites?

Examine how arrangement, sound, color, and contrast operate differently on these two sites. Compare and contrast how audience, purpose, ethos, pathos, logos, intertextuality, context, and constraints operate on each site. What do your findings indicate about how the web constructs femininity and masculinity differently to target different consumers? Then, using visuals and/or perhaps a PowerPoint presentation style, reveal your findings, analyses, and critical evaluations to the rest of the class. Consult library and Internet sources as necessary.

AMY HARMON

"Virtual Sex, Lies and Cyberspace"

Amy Harmon has been a staff writer of the Los Angeles Times *and a regular contributor to* The New York Times *on issues of technology, popular culture, education, and gender equity.*

EXERCISING YOUR SKILLS

Before Reading

Harmon's essay reveals how issues of identity, gender, and sexuality operate on the web. Have you ever taken on a different identity online or known someone who did? What purposes might a person have for assuming an identity different from her or his own—adopting different genders, sexual preferences, physical characteristics, or behaviors? Do you believe that this breaking down of categories is valuable, detrimental, or both? What dangers might come from adopting different identities, particularly different genders, online?

The first time Donna Tancordo "cybered," she switched off her computer midway through the typed seduction, shocked and scared at the power of the words scrolling down her screen.

"I've never described what I was feeling like that before," she said. "I freaked out."

But Tancordo, a happily married New Jersey housewife with three kids, soon logged back onto America Online. In a chat room called "Married and Flirting," she met another man. For days, they whispered the details of their lives into the ether. When he asked her if he could take her on a virtual trip to the mountains, she agreed.

This time her computer stayed on.

All hours of the day and night, America Online's chat rooms teem with people seeking something missing in their lives—like Jay, a successful business consultant in Boston, who says he logs on to fill "the void of passionate emotion."

The blurted confidences and anonymous yearning scrolling through AOL's frames reveal a rare picture of the American psyche unshackled from social convention.

In the vacuum of cyberspace, self-exploration is secret and strangely safe. Much has been made lately of how cults may find fertile recruiting ground among online seekers. A vast range of support groups—for pregnant mothers, cancer patients, substance abusers—also flourish. Unlikely friendships are struck and sometimes sustained.

But in an age when sex is scary and intimacy scarce, the keyboard and modem perhaps most often serve a pressing quest for romantic connection and sexual discovery.

Eric lives in a small California farming town: "I'm pretty much a straight kind of dude." When he flips on the computer at 4:30 a.m. to check the weather, he is drawn to rooms where San Franciscans recount stories of sexual bondage.

Eleanor, 13, is 5-foot-1, with dark brown hair. When she surfs the "Teen Chat" rooms after school, she looks for kicks as a tall strawberry blond.

Peter, a 45-year-old professional in Manhattan, spent his first weekend on AOL posing as a 26-year-old woman while his wife was away on business. Enthralled with the ease of uninhibited communion, he cycled through a whirl of identities. He disguised himself as a gay man, a lesbian and a young girl. But eventually he settled on a more mundane form of seduction.

"What I really wanted was to have sexual conversations with women," Peter said. "Kind of garden variety, but that's who I am, and what made it such a fever for me—that's not too strong a word—was the flirtation aspect of it."

The ritual of pursuing secret desires from behind a facade is as old as the masquerade. But perhaps because it has never been so easy, the compulsion has never seemed so strong.

"Leave the Meat Behind"

The free computer disks that arrive unbidden in the mail offer not only a mask, but an escape from the body—the ability, as cyberpunk author William Gibson puts it, to "leave the meat behind."

It is an offer with remarkable mass appeal. As AOL's subscriber count doubled over the last year to 8 million, the number of chat rooms on busy nights tripled to 15,000. And the recent, much-publicized agitation over the service's busy signals was due largely to people chatting longer, now that a new pricing plan means they do not have to pay by the minute.

AOL is by far the most popular gathering spot on the Internet, in part because its culture of anonymity—members can choose up to five fictional screen names—promotes what one observer calls "the online equivalent of getting drunk and making a fool of yourself." Although it is possible to chat on the World Wide Web and other areas of the Internet, the technology doesn't work nearly as well.

Largely because of the unabashed sexual character of many of its chat rooms, AOL executives traditionally have downplayed their importance to the company's bottom line. "What we're offering at AOL is convenience in a box," said AOL Network's President Robert Pittman. "If you use AOL it will save you time. People aren't buying it for chat."

Perhaps. The service offers e-mail, Internet access and information and entertainment features. Many of its customers never venture near the chat rooms, and most usage of the Internet is unrelated to chat.

But according to America Online statistics, more than three-quarters of its subscribers use chat rooms at least once a month, the equivalent of 1 million hours a day.

"If AOL eliminated chat you'd see the subscriber base go from 8 million to 1 million faster than you could spit," said Alan Weiner, an analyst at Dataquest, a consulting firm.

Not all chat is laden with sexual innuendo. "I can say I'm a voluptuous teen and I still don't get attention when I go into the sports and finance rooms," quipped one frequent female chatter.

Some chat rooms emerge as genuine communities where the same group gathers regularly. The "SoCalifover30" room even holds regular "fleshmeets" at restaurants or members' homes. A core group keeps up on one another's romantic exploits online and offline.

"Ladykuu," a San Diego bus driver trainer and the mother of twins, says she has become close friends with another mother of twins in Boston, with whom she shares life's tribulations.

But even Ladykuu enjoys "lurking" and listening to others tell secrets to which she ordinarily would not be privy:

"It's just fascinating to me to see, what is that deep dark fantasy, what is the naughty thing you're thinking about and—oh my gosh, I've been thinking about that too."

Some sexual-oriented chat is basic singles bar sleaze—and some is mainly an excuse to swap pornographic pictures. But much more prevalent is the search for genuine connection, and perhaps seduction.

Some chatters seek a companion to meet in person. Others, who shun the idea of a real-life affair, seize on the opportunity to engage in the thrill of a new seduction over the computer from the comfort of home—often while their spouses sleep in the next room.

Whether the demi-realities of chat can fulfill real world needs or only add to their urgency is a subject of much debate among online seekers. Some discover hidden pieces of themselves that lead to significant changes in what, in a telling delineation, is called RL—real life.

Others grow sickened by the relentless layering of illusion, where friends and lovers appear suddenly, and then melt into air, or morph into aliens. For there is in all this a bitter irony: That a search for intimacy brings people to pose as airbrushed versions of themselves, so that they may share their inner fantasies with strangers.

"It's not healthy for people to pretend to be someone they're not and fantasize about that constantly," said Nancy Wesson, a psychologist in Mountain View, California. She has seen marriages break up in part because of one partner's online activities. "It allows you to perpetually live in a fantasy instead of living in real life."

Ultimately, marriage may be the institution most rocked by the new technology. Although cyberspace obviously doesn't invent secret longings, it does provide a way to uncover and exploit them that has never been so available to so many.

Cheating without Really Cheating

Some flirters say the ability to cheat without really cheating, to voice fantasies somehow too personal to share even with spouses, has invigorated them.

Donna and Ralph Tancordo, high school sweethearts who have been married for 17 years, sign onto AOL and "cyber" with other married people—with each other's consent.

"My cheekbones hurt I've been smiling so much lately," said Donna, who opened her account a month ago. "I think it's the flattery. It's like, 'Wow, somebody else is attracted to me other than my husband.' And it's improved our sex life 150%."

In the case of Peter, the Manhattan professional, the online habit nearly broke up his marriage. Finding a woman that he would care to talk to and who would talk to him could take hours on any given night. He would stay up after his wife, Janet, went to bed, and look forward to when she would leave him alone at home.

In the end, Janet became too distraught over his regular online meetings with a woman who lived thousands of miles away. Peter agreed to cancel his AOL account. Both say the experience has opened up a productive, if painful, period of exploration for them.

"I was bored and I lied about it to myself," Peter said. "I had a sex life, but it didn't have passion. At some level, that's what I was seeking, and it's hard to find. There may not be an answer."

For Janet, the hardest part has been trying to sift out what may be her husband's harmless fantasy life from what to her is hurtful reality.

"Everyone knows someone who has had an affair," Janet said. "If your husband's having an affair and you tell your girlfriend, you're going to have instant sympathy. But do I have a right to be pissed about this? I don't know."

She has not talked to any of her friends about it: "It's embarrassing. I don't know anyone else who has gone through this."

A lot of people have. The online consensus is that, as Tiffany Cook of the SoCalifover30 chat room puts it, "if you're talking to a married man often enough, that's an affair even if you never meet."

But today, when interest in family values is on the rise and the ethic of safe sex prevails, AOL offers 1960s-style free love from behind the safety of the screen. The medium offers a sense of physical and psychological safety that strips away taboos faster than the sexual revolution ever did.

Many married people—they constitute two-thirds of AOL subscribers—comb chat rooms, scope the profiles and send private instant messages (IMs) to prospective romantic partners.

The flirtation medium of choice, IMs pop up on-screen as soon as they are sent, heedless of whatever the recipient may be doing. More insistent and perhaps more intimate than e-mail, they solicit an immediate response.

"I've tried erotic e-mail. It's like bad D. H. Lawrence," said an artist who prefers the edge of IMs.

Three million IM sessions are opened every day. They are by nature fleeting and the exchange is rapid-fire, lessening the risk and increasing the nerve.

"I make advances to men in the same age group as I am to start flirting and sometimes it goes a lot further than flirt," said Donna. "I read their profile first. If I like it, I'll IM them by saying . . . 'BUSY?'"

In the curious state of disembodiment, where the body is nonetheless very much the point, the typed words come as stream of consciousness, and then, with the click of a mouse, they disappear.

"I'm sorry I can't talk right now," one woman tells a reporter. "I'm getting nine IMs as we speak."

Often, IM exchanges begin between people in the same chat room. At any given moment, subscribers fill rooms of varying salaciousness—"Hot and Ready Female," "Discreet in Illinois," "CA Cops Who Flirt," "BiCuriousM4M." Many of the chat rooms created by subscribers—as opposed to those established by AOL—have overtly sexual themes and many others draw people interested in romance.

"There's a lot more diversity out there than I would have given people credit for," said Jenny, a 27-year-old lesbian from Manhattan who roams the chat rooms when she is not using the service to check stock quotes.

"Wanna cyber?" comes the standard query, proffering the online equivalent of a one-night stand. "M/F?" "What are you wearing?"

"On AOL you could be talking about sex within three minutes of meeting someone," said a 28-year-old male marketing consultant who goes by the handle "MindUnit."

Many simply want to experiment in the intricate art of flirtation, sometimes behind a guise, sometimes as themselves.

"It's the only place you can throw yourself at someone and not care if you get rejected," said Jenny.

Women especially say the ability to both be more aggressive than they would in real life and to hit "cancel" or "ignore" if a flirtation gets out of control is liberating—and perhaps good practice.

For many, the point is not cybersex per se, but delving into the forbidden realm of sexuality. Says one online explorer on the East Coast: "We live in a world and particularly this culture that seeks to, on the surface, completely repress our sexuality. I think for many people, AOL represents a safe and healthy expression, although, like all pleasures, from fatty foods to erotic pleasure, there is probably a price to pay."

After empty nights of chat room prowling for the ideal cybermate, many end up being as disappointing as such searches often are in real life.

"All I can tell you is that there are thousands of searching people out there . . . and AOL has become a vehicle to meet others . . . affairs, etc. . . ." types a Southern California man to a reporter one Saturday night. "But it doesn't solve the problems of real life."

Sometimes connections that seem solid suddenly fade away. Even carefree Donna was thrown off-balance recently when her AOL lover sent a cryptic message saying he wouldn't be spending as much time online.

"He was basically blowing me off and I was really upset," she said. "I was sitting in the dentist's chair and I couldn't get him out of my head. I've gotten too emotional about this. I really need to handle it better."

Psychologists caution against getting wrapped up in a reality that is not, in fact, real. And online junkies acknowledge that it can be hard to pull out of what one calls "AOL's sticky web," which can become an addictive escape from three-dimensional existence.

Psychologist Kimberly Young, who has studied online addiction, says it's comparable to compulsive gambling in its mood-altering appeal—and is just as dangerous.

Sherry Turkle, a professor of the sociology of science at the Massachusetts Institute of Technology, draws a more optimistic conclusion. In her book, *Life on the Screen*, she argues that online technology is enabling a new, decentered sense of identity to emerge, and that the practice of trying on different personalities could be a useful way to work through real-life issues.

Swapping genders is a popular activity among both sexes, but since (real) men outnumber women by about 2 to 1, the likelihood of talking to a man claiming to be a woman is fairly high.

MindUnit has devised an only-sort-of-tongue-in-cheek "Rules to Establish Gender," testament that even in a world without gender, well-socialized roles remain largely intact.

They state, in part: "If she sounds 'too good to be true,' that is One Strike. If she has no profile, that is One Strike. If she seems preoccupied with sex, or starts the sex talk herself, that is One Strike. If she volunteers exact statistics about herself, especially measurements or bra size, that is One Strike. If the statistics are really hot, that is Two Strikes." By MindUnit's trauma-tested logic, three strikes means the woman you're chatting with is a man.

Little in the AOL chat world is as it appears to be. But, for many, the chance to honestly express their desires and be privy to those of others outweighs the veil of lies that seems somehow necessary to make it possible. "Let me find someone with an open mind, good intentions, and sincerity," reads MindUnit's profile. "Failing that, I'll take a nymphomaniac."

Few know better than Tiffany Cook the perils of confusing online illusions with real-life truths. First, the 30-year-old Santa Monica interior designer hit it off with a man who flew to visit her from New York. The chemistry didn't translate in person.

But then for three months she spent hours a day chatting with a man from Northern California. He said he was 33. Then he confessed to being 43, and then to his actual age: 71. He had sent her a picture—it turned out to be of his son.

"It was terrible," she said. "I felt so deceived."

Still, Tiffany, who changed her screen name after learning the truth about her most passionate correspondence, still spends part of almost every day online.

"You know what? It's expanded my world," she said. "I've laughed really hard and I've learned a lot, and no matter what I might think of [him] now, the fact is we had a huge amount to talk about. "Besides, your chances of meeting someone who's hiding behind something online and someone who's hiding behind something in real life [are] about the same."

After Reading

Critical Perspective

1. Characterize your reaction to Harmon's text. How did you respond to her examples and why?

Rhetoric and Argument

2. Harmon employs rhetorical tactics involving audience, purpose, ethos, pathos, logos, intertextuality, context, and constraints to make her points. Make note of each of these devices and characterize how they aid or detract from her argument. Offer quotes to back up your perspectives.
3. Harmon commences her essay by giving examples of people "cybering," taking on different kinds of identities than they otherwise would in daily life. Do you think that this is an effective way to begin her argument? What sort of tone does it set? What particular language choices does Harmon make? What kind of ethos does this create for Harmon as a writer? Be sure to give examples from the text.

4. What is Harmon's main claim about the anonymity that the Internet fosters? Where does she offer her claim? Do you concur with it, or do you believe that it overlooks other aspects that are important to examine?

5. What evidence does Harmon utilize to support her assertions? Does this evidence back up her subclaims? Be sure to include quotes to back up your views.

6. Do you believe that Harmon's warrants for her claims are viable? Are there argumentative premises she relies on with which you do not agree? How so? How might you rewrite her argument if you were to offer a claim of your own about this subject? To what evidence would you point and why?

Analysis

7. In what ways might adopting different gender identities be liberating to both male and female users? In what ways might it not be? In a short argumentative essay, try to explain your thoughts. Use your own experiences in online environments and library and Internet sources for support.

Taking Action

Form two debate teams within your class. One group will argue that the anonymity sometimes afforded by the Internet is valuable and should be preserved. The other group will argue that the anonymity of the Internet needs to be curtailed and possibly stopped. Each group should prepare positions ahead of time, drawing on the cultural texts, library and Internet sources, as well as personal experiences to back up the members' views. Begin with short statements from each group. Give each group several five-minute opportunities for rebuttal and closing arguments.

After the debate, get back into the larger classroom group. Discuss what people's positions were prior to the debate. How have your thoughts changed or developed further? What would you argue now—the pro view, the con view, or something in between? You may want to make your work accessible to other groups both inside and outside the campus community.

FREDRICK L. MCKISSACK JR.

"Cyberghetto: Blacks Are Falling Through the Net"

Fredrick L. McKissack Jr. is a former journalist who now works for an Internet development firm.

EXERCISING YOUR SKILLS

Before Reading

McKissack writes about the ways in which African Americans have not always had adequate access to technology. Visit a website from which you (or someone you know well) have purchased a hard-to-find product. Now ask yourself how you would have purchased these products had they not been available to you through these means.

What would be required of you? In what ways might not having access to this product as well as other hard-to-find products impact your life? Drawing upon your answers to these questions as well as the experiences of those you know without regular web access (or who have slow connections), consider the effects that not having access to the web might have on your life.

You laugh, but one of the best web developers in the country is a teenager who has written a very sound book on web design and programming. He's still in his prime learning years, and he's got a staff.

What should worry me more is that I am one of the few African Americans in this country who has a computer at home, uses one at work, and can use a lot of different kinds of software on multiple platforms. According to those in the know, I'm going to remain part of that very small group for quite some time.

The journal *Science* published a study which found that, in households with annual incomes below $40,000, whites were six times more likely than blacks to have used the World Wide Web in the last week. Low-income white households were twice as likely to have a home computer as low-income black homes. Even as computers become more central to our society, minorities are falling through the Net.

The situation is actually considerably worse than the editors of *Science* made it seem. Some 18 percent of African American households don't even have phones, as Philip Bereano, a professor of technical communications at the University of Washington, pointed out in a letter to *The New York Times*. Since the researchers who published their study in *Science* relied on a telephone survey to gather their data, Bereano explains, the study was skewed—it only included people who had at least caught up to the Twentieth Century.

About 30 percent of American homes have computers, with the bulk of those users being predominantly white, upper-middle-class households. Minorities are much worse off: Only about 15 percent have a terminal at home.

The gulf between technological haves and have-nots is the difference between living the good life and surviving in what many technologists and social critics term a "cyberghetto." Professor Michio Kaku, a professor of theoretical physics at City University of New York, wrote in his book *Visions: How Science Will Revolutionize the Twenty-First Century*, of the emergence of "information ghettos."

"The fact is, each time society made an abrupt leap to a new level of production, there were losers and winners," Kaku wrote. "It may well be that the computer revolution will exacerbate the existing fault lines of society."

The term "cyberghetto" suggests that minorities have barely passable equipment to participate in tech culture. But most minorities aren't even doing that well.

Before everybody goes "duh," just think what this means down the line. Government officials are using the Web more often to disseminate information. Political parties are holding major on-line events. And companies are using the Web for making job announcements and collecting résumés. Classes, especially continuing-education classes, are being offered more and more on the Web. In politics, commerce, and education, the web is leaving minorities behind.

The disparity between the techno-rich and techno-poor comes to a head with this statistic: A person who is able to use a computer at work earns 15 percent more than someone in the same position who lacks computer skills.

"The equitable distribution of technology has always been the real moral issue about computers," Jon Katz, who writes the "Rants and Raves" column for *Wired* on-line, wrote in a recent e-mail. "The poor can't afford them. Thus they will be shut out of the booming hi-tech job market and forced to do the culture's menial jobs."

This technological gap, not Internet pornography, should be the public's main concern with the Web.

"Politicians and journalists have suggested frightening parents into limiting children's access to the Internet, but the fact is they have profoundly screwed the poor, who need access to this technology if they are to compete and prosper," Katz said. "I think the culture avoids the complex and expensive issues by focusing on the silly ones. In twenty-five years, when the underclass wakes up to discover it is doing all the muscle jobs while everybody else is in neat, clean offices with high-paying jobs, they'll go berserk. We don't want to spend the money to avoid this problem, so we worry about Johnny going to the *Playboy* web site. It's sick."

In his 1996 State of the Union address, President Clinton challenged Congress to hook up schools to the Internet.

"We are working with the telecommunications industry, educators, and parents to connect . . . every classroom and every library in the entire United States by the year 2000," Clinton said. "I ask Congress to support this educational technology initiative so that we can make sure the national partnership succeeds."

The national average is approximately ten students for every one computer in the public schools. According to a study by the consulting firm McKinsey & Co., the President's plan—a ratio of one computer to every five students—would cost approximately $11 billion per year over the next ten years.

Some government and business leaders, worried about a technologically illiterate work force in the twenty-first century, recognize the need for increased spending. "AT&T and the Commerce Department have suggested wiring up schools at a 4:1 ratio for $6 or $7 billion," says Katz.

But according to the U.S. Department of Education, only 1.3 percent of elementary and secondary education expenditures are allocated to technology. That figure would have to be increased to 3.9 percent. Given the tightness of urban school district budgets, a tripling of expenditures seems unlikely.

Then there's the question of whether computers in the schools are even desirable. Writer Todd Oppenheimer, in an article for *Atlantic Monthly* entitled "The Computer Delusion," argued that there is no hard evidence that computers in the classroom enhance learning. In fact, he took the opposite tack: that computers are partially responsible for the decline of education.

Proponents of computers in the classroom struck back. "On the issue of whether or not technology can benefit education, the good news is that it is not—nor should be—an all-or-nothing proposition," writes Wendy Richard Bollentin, editor of *OnTheInternet* magazine, in an essay for *Educom Review*.

There is an unreal quality about this debate, though, since computer literacy is an indispensable part of the education process for many affluent, white schoolchildren.

Consumers are beginning to see a decline in prices for home computers. Several PC manufacturers have already introduced sub-$1,000 systems, and there is talk of $600 systems appearing on the market soon. Oracle has spent a great deal of money on Network Computers, cheap hardware where software and files are located on large networks. The price is in the sub-$300 range. And, of course, there is WebTV, which allows you to browse on a regular home television set with special hardware.

Despite the trend to more "affordable" computers, a Markle Foundation–Bellcore Labs study shows that this may not be enough to help minorities merge onto the Information Superhighway. There is "evidence of a digital divide," the study said, with "Internet users being generally wealthier and more highly educated, and blacks and Hispanics disproportionately unaware of the Internet."

So, what now?

"For every black family to become empowered, they need to have computers," journalist Tony Brown told the *Detroit News*. "There is no way the black community is going to catch up with white society under the current system. But with a computer, you can take any person from poverty to the middle class."

This is the general line for enlightened blacks and community leaders. But having a computer won't bridge the racial and economic divide. Even if there is a 1:1 ratio of students to computers in urban schools, will students' interest be piqued when they don't have access to computers at home? One out of every forty-nine computer-science professors in the United States is black. Will this inhibit black students from learning how to use them? And even if every black student had a computer at home and at school, would that obliterate all racial obstacles to success?

Empowerment is not just a question of being able to find your way around the Web. But depriving minorities of access to the technology won't help matters any. We need to make sure the glass ceiling isn't replaced by a silicon ceiling.

After Reading

Critical Perspective

1. What do you think about McKissack's tone in this essay? Explain why you have the reaction that you do.

Rhetoric and Argument

2. Characterize the sorts of rhetorical appeals that the writer makes. Who is McKissack's audience? What is his purpose? How do you know? What appeals to ethos, pathos, and logos does he make? Are they persuasive? In addition, do you see examples of intertextuality, context, and constraints operating in his text? Be sure to furnish textual evidence.

3. Discuss the structure of McKissack's essay. Do you find this arrangement to be effective? Why or why not?

4. What is McKissack's main claim about the Internet? Where does he offer it? Do you agree with this claim? Why or why not?

Analysis

5. McKissack ends his piece by asserting that "having a computer won't bridge the racial and economic divide." Why do you believe that McKissack feels he needs to state this? What does he seem to be suggesting about other social inequities? Do you think such a divide still exists? Why or why not? If it does exist, what would it take to begin to bridge this divide? What might we do to achieve this? Write a short argumentative essay in which you address these questions drawing on your own experiences as well as library and Internet sources.

Taking Action

Form a small group. Your job is to interview five people—from children to older adults—from your family, neighborhood, peer group, or other communities about whether they think that there is still a racial and class divide around issues of technology. Be sure to solicit responses from people from various class, gender, race, ethnic, age, ability, region, and religious backgrounds. Why do they feel as they do about this? What experiences—things they have seen and read—led them to have this view? Encourage people to expound on these issues.

After you have conducted interviews, compile your information according to the demographic differences listed above. Consult relevant library and Internet sources. Make note of whether there are any patterns and themes that appear to be emerging about how people view the technological divide and the reasons that they give for their views.

Once you have completed your research, share your findings with the rest of the class and discuss the possible significances of those findings.

G. Beato

"Girl Games"

Greg Beato is a freelance journalist who writes frequently about pop culture, media, and politics. His articles have appeared in dozens of magazines and newspapers worldwide, including Spin, Reason, The Washington Post, *and* Wired. *His work has also been anthologized in* Best Music Writing 2003 *and several other books.*

EXERCISING YOUR SKILLS

Before Reading

Beato investigates the gaming opportunities available for girls. Have you ever played or encountered computer games that seem especially geared toward girls or boys in particular? What about the subject matter, graphics, packaging, design, and commercial marketing for the product give you that sense? Do you think that such games allow girls and boys to try on different identities and to learn different skills? Do you believe that they reproduce typical notions about masculinity and femininity or undermine them?

The toughest computer game ever? It has to be *Doom*, right, with its endless toxic corridors and fidelity to the aesthetics of terminal carnage? Or maybe *Duke Nukem* and its Mark Fuhrman-on-acid Pig Cops? Or how about the gentler trials of *Myst*, all those cryptic machines and contraptions, and not a user manual in sight?

Those games are tough, sure, but there's one that's even tougher. It has mazes riddled with conundrums, inscrutable adversaries whose unshakable indifference to your presence leaves you wondering if it's even worth the effort to attack. And there are no cheat codes to bail you out when nothing's going right. Your goal? To reach the testosterone-spattered war rooms of the interactive entertainment industry and persuade the pasty knuckle-draggers who reside there to conceive, develop, and deliver games for girls.

Call it *Woom*.

For the last several years, men and women throughout the software industry have been playing this real-life game. And usually not winning.

But now, after years of disregard and sporadic, sometimes ludicrous attempts to serve the female market, the industry's game boys are experiencing a change of heart. Companies like Mattel Media, Hasbro Interactive, Sega, DreamWorks Interactive, Starwave, R/GA Interactive, Broderbund, and Philips Media have all introduced or are developing products targeted to girls. Start-ups such as Her Interactive, Girl Games Inc., Cybergrrl Inc., Girl Tech, and Interval Research's Purple Moon are doing the same. Some expect 200 new girl games to reach store shelves or go online this year—a tenfold increase from 1996.

Why the sudden interest?

Blame it on Barbie. Last November, the CD-ROM industry received a wake-up call when the runaway best-seller turned out to be *Barbie Fashion Designer*. In its first two months of sales, Mattel's digital incarnation of the oft-denigrated but remarkably enduring role model sold more than 500,000 copies, outstripping even popular titles such as *Quake*—and leaving the rest of the industry wondering how to cash in on this newfound wellspring.

The surge of girl game activity also reflects demographics—there are simply more women developing games and using computers today than five, ten years ago. And these women are bringing their perspectives to the development process. As girl game developer Brenda Laurel points out, "The game business arose from computer programs that were written by and for young men in the late 1960s and early 1970s. They worked so well that they formed a very lucrative industry fairly quickly. But what worked for that demographic absolutely did not work for most girls and women." While initial attempts at creating girl games amounted to little more than painting traditional titles pink, the current crop of developers understand that it's a far more complicated business than that.

The Land of Sweeping Generalizations

That there's consumer demand for girl games comes as no surprise to Brenda Laurel. A pioneer in developing virtual reality, Laurel first zeroed in on the market at a conference in 1992, where she met David Liddle, who was cofounding Palo Alto, California-based Interval Research with Paul Allen. "We started talking about how the industry had consistently missed opportunities to get girls involved in technology," she recalls. "We asked, What would it really take to get a large number of girls using computers so often that the technology became transparent to them? In the end, we both had to admit that neither one of us really knew the answer."

Inside Interval's standard-issue gray-and-white Silicon Valley offices, Laurel leans back in her chair and smiles. In contrast to the high-collared, Vulcan-diva persona she assumed in the publicity photos for her book *Computers as Theatre*, in person she is warm and engaging, her curly auburn hair falling to her shoulders, her everyday earthwoman's garb giving her a decidedly human appearance. Compared with her forays into virtual reality, developing engaging content for girls had a relatively low fetish-factor, but Laurel eagerly accepted Liddle's offer to pursue the project at Interval—even though it came with a string attached. "I agreed that whatever solution the research suggested, I'd go along with," laughs Laurel. "Even if it meant shipping products in pink boxes."

To figure out the kinds of interactive entertainment girls would really find compelling, Laurel launched a major research campaign. "We took a three-pronged approach," she explains. "We did hundreds—maybe thousands—of interviews with 7- to 12-year-olds, the group we wanted to target with our products. We watched play differences between boys and girls. We asked kids how they liked to play; we gave them props and mocked-up products to fool around with." Laurel and company consulted experts in the field of children's play: toy store owners, teachers, scout leaders, coaches. Finally, they looked at all the research literature they could get their hands on, including material on play theory, brain-based sex differences, even primate social behavior—all with the goal of seeing how it might carry over into the realm of interactive entertainment.

Now, before we move into the Land of Sweeping Generalizations, a disclaimer: there are girls and women who like to slaughter mutant humanoids as much as any man does, and whose only discontent with *Duke Nukem* is that the bloodbaths it facilitates are simply too tepid; on the other hand, there are boys and men who don't immediately turn into glassy-eyed alien snuff zombies when presented with the latest *Doom* level. That said, Laurel's research did reveal certain patterns and tendencies.

"Girls enjoy complex social interaction," Laurel says. "Their verbal skills—and their delight in using them—develop earlier than boys'." Laurel further found that while girls often feel their own lives are boring, and thus have an interest in acting out other lives, they like to do so in familiar settings with characters who behave like people they actually know.

"We also learned that girls are extremely fond of transmedia," Laurel continues. "Things that make a magical migration from one media to the next. Or things that can appear in more than one form, like those Transformer toys." As it turns out, Transformers—the plastic contraptions that lead dual lives as robots and heavy artillery—offer a vivid example of how girls and boys tend to approach toys differently: whereas boys are apt to use them as a means of demonstrating mastery, concentrating on the ability to transform them as quickly as possible, girls focus on their magical quality, taking delight in the fact that the toy has a secret.

Laurel may have been one of the first to try to crack the elusive girl's market, but she wasn't alone. Heidi Dangelmaier, a former doctoral candidate from Princeton's computer science program, left the school in 1992 to wage an outspoken campaign to get traditional developers to make titles for girls. Patricia Flanigan, an entrepreneur who'd previously specialized in children's furniture, started Her Interactive, the first company devoted exclusively to developing interactive entertainment for girls. Laura Groppe, a former movie and music video producer, started Girl Games Inc. Doug Glen at Mattel Media launched a multimillion-dollar effort to turn the company's successful brands into digital designs.

These innovators were doing research of their own, and reaching conclusions that echoed Laurel's. "It all comes down to the nature of value," says Dangelmaier, who after brief bouts of corporate kick-boxing with Sega and other traditional developers ended up cofounding a Web development company called Hi-D. "What's worth spending time on? What's a waste of time? Females want experiences where they can make emotional and social discoveries they can apply to their own lives."

Sheri Graner Ray, a producer who left her job at Origin Systems when she grew frustrated with her colleagues' lack of interest in female players, agrees. What girls and women want, says Graner Ray, now director of product development at Her Interactive, is a game that allows them to create "mutually beneficial solutions to socially significant problems." By socially significant problems she means conflicts that happen in a social realm, that involve a group of people rather than a lone space commando going up against a ceaseless supply of enemies. In such a context, girls can use skills they tend to find more compelling than trigger-finger aggression—diplomacy, negotiation, compromise, and manipulation. "This doesn't mean there can't be fighting or combat in a game for females," adds Graner Ray. "There just has to be something beyond confrontation as the reward."

But Enough with the Theories . . .

. . . what do the new titles for girls look like?

In the case of Interval Research, we don't really know yet. While the firm recently announced the formation of Purple Moon Inc., a spin-off that will publish products informed by Brenda Laurel's research, none will hit the shelves until late 1997. And until they do, the company's keeping them under wraps. Still, Laurel, who will serve as Purple Moon's vice president of design, drops enough details to suggest that these products will differ vastly from the single-minded mayhem of the typical shoot-'em-up. Indeed, inside the company, they're referring to the titles as a whole new genre: "friendship adventures for girls."

Laurel says Purple Moon will launch with two multi-title product lines, which will focus on making friends and shared experiences. The lines will take place in different environments: one in a more social world, with settings like school and the principal's office and a focus on day-to-day issues; the other in a dreamier, neoromantic world of secret gardens and moonlit trails overlooking the ocean, where nature and reflection are emphasized. Both series will include a strong storytelling and narrative element and many of the same characters, but no clocks and no scores. "We want to let girls play in an exploratory, open-ended fashion, to let them have control over their environment," says Laurel. To extend these environments (and profit margins, no doubt) beyond the realm of the computer, a battery of offshoot merchandise is in the works.

Interactive stories—like Her Interactive's *McKenzie & Co.* and *Vampire Diaries*, or DreamWorks Interactive's *Goosebumps*—follow more traditional game models but include elements rare in the interactive entertainment world: teenage girl protagonists and plots that aren't based on killing someone, finding out why someone was killed, or taking over the world. Story lines focus on problem-solving, investigation, and communication with onscreen characters as a key to progressing through the drama.

And then there are titles like *Chop Suey* and *Mimi Smartypants*, the work of writer-producer Theresa Duncan, featuring nonlinear, fictional worlds to explore. With its sly whimsy and tactile, folk-art imagery, *Chop Suey* brings a whole new sensibility—quirky, poetic, almost bittersweet—to a medium that's often lacking in such nuance.

Finally, there's that feminist-nightmare blockbuster, *Barbie Fashion Designer*. Unlike almost every other interactive entertainment title, *Barbie* exists as a mere part of an over-all play experience. "Instead of looking at the computer as a game machine, we looked at it as a power tool that makes things," explains Doug Glen, president of Mattel Media. Given that that's exactly how the computer is seen in many other application categories, this is hardly an earthshattering observation. And yet very few interactive entertainment titles employ this metaphor. In the case of *Barbie Fashion Designer*, girls can make clothes for their dolls by choosing styles, patterns, and colors onscreen, then printing the resulting outfits on special paper-backed fabric that can be run through an inkjet or laser printer. At that point, they can use color markers, fabric paint, and other materials that come with the package to further enhance their designs. Like so many of the toy industry's most successful "interactive entertainment" products—think LEGO, Lincoln Logs, even Barbie herself—*Barbie Fashion Designer* is designed to let the user's imagination become the most important part of the play experience. In so many children's titles—and to a lesser extent in CD-ROM games aimed at older audiences—this simply doesn't happen. "It's CAD software for kids," says Ann Stephens, president of the high tech analysis firm PC Data. "*Barbie* did so well because it's a very good product that incorporates girl play models and a strong franchise."

Now, titles that emphasize fashion and makeup might sound like a conspiracy hatched by Rush Limbaugh to turn prospective riot grrrls into complacent, pretty little consumers. But if the product's intended audience likes it, and if it introduces them to the world of technology, then why complain? This, at least, is how Her Interactive's Patricia Flanigan responds to critics. Besides, she points out, her company surveyed 2,000 girls before embarking on development of *McKenzie & Co.* and found that makeup, fashion, shopping, and boys were subjects girls wanted to see.

In addition, *McKenzie* and similar titles have real utility; they let girls experiment—in a comfortable way—with identity, appearance, and communication at an age when these things are extremely important to them. They also familiarize girls with interface and interactive media conventions. Indeed, diary-style titles like Girl Games's *Let's Talk About Me* and Philips Media's *The Baby-sitter's Club Friendship Kit* are practically full-blown personal information managers, with address books, calendars, daily planners, diaries, and other pre-Office features built into them.

But however individual developers feel about selling stereotyped girl themes, most in the interactive entertainment industry are overjoyed by *Barbie Fashion Designer*'s success. In one fell swoop, *Barbie* cracked open the market for girl games. Purple Moon vice president Nancy Deyo has nothing but praise for the title: "We're thrilled to see *Barbie* do so well," she says. "We're going to enter a retail market that simply didn't exist six months ago."

The Future of Girl Games

The greatest potential for girl games still lies largely untapped. At a time when many companies view the Web as an all-purpose revenue enhancer, expected to add mouthwatering zest to even the blandest business plan, the firms focusing on interactive entertainment for girls seem to have reason to be licking their chops. As Brenda Laurel says, "The Web has an innate sociability—so there's loads of potential for activities that appeal to girls' social intelligence, their penchant for narrative play."

For many girls, the online world has already begun to supersede that sacred tool of female adolescence, the telephone. According to Aliza Sherman, creator of the popular Cybergrrl Web site, "Girls want to meet other girls their age and they really want to chat. When we held a Team Webgrrls event to teach 25 girls age 5 to 15 to learn to surf the Web, they got the biggest charge out of the CU-SeeMe and IRC instead of the Web sites themselves. They wanted to make contact and interact."

Ellen Steuer, a 20-year-old sophomore at Mills College in Oakland, California, first started going online when she was in high school. "My brothers wanted me to get a computer because they said I'd need one in college," explains Steuer. "I didn't really have any interest in computers until I discovered chat. For me, it's all about people—I've become friends with so many people I never would have met except online. And along the way, I really learned some interesting stuff."

So much stuff, in fact, that soon she was switching from her initial AOL account to an ISP and creating her own Web site. Today she has a job as a technical assistant in her college's information technology department and is planning to pursue a career that involves the Internet. In short, she's a perfect example of a girl whose introduction to technology has had a major impact on her life. By the time she finishes school, she'll have more than six years of experience using interactive technologies.

Thousands of other girls are creating their own Web pages and chat rooms, forming alliances to promote each other's pages, and sometimes even starting secret clubs that require a password to view other members' sites. For developers, then, the question is this: How can we create products and services that can add to what girls are already doing themselves online? In their efforts to answer this question, Her Interactive and Girl Games Inc. have created community-oriented Web sites, with bulletin boards, advice columns, contests, pen pals, interviews with mentors, and online games. None of these sites is exactly cutting edge, but compared with the brochure-style sites that many traditional game developers have put up, their grasp of basic cyberspace principles is quite apparent.

In addition to creating its own site, Girl Tech, a start-up targeting 6- to 14-year-old girls, has several other Web projects in development. The company's trying to negotiate a deal with a major search directory for use of its "girl-friendly" rating system, and it's also created a book called *Tech Girl's Internet Adventures.* Along with site reviews and basic how-to information about the Web, the book includes a CD-ROM with software and clip art that girls can use to develop their own Web pages.

But how much interest do 6-year-old girls have in the Web? Girl Tech's founder and CEO Janese Swanson tells the story of how she helped her daughter have an online conversation with another girl on the other side of the country—who, in turn, was being helped by her dad. "My daughter loved learning about this little girl from a different part of the country," says Swanson, who as a product manager at Broderbund helped create *Where in the World Is Carmen Sandiego?* "We took out maps and asked questions about what it was like there."

As the Net continues to develop as a platform for interactive entertainment, look for girl game developers to be at the forefront. "So much of the Web's power comes through orchestrating human interactions," exclaims Heidi Dangelmaier. "The key to success in this medium lies in communication, human interaction, participation, and emotional impact."

In other words, all the things girl game evangelists have been thinking about for years.

After Reading

Critical Perspective

1. How would you describe Beato's approach to his essay? Do you find it effective? Why or why not?

Rhetoric and Argument

2. Beato employs rhetorical and stylistic tactics such as audience, purpose, ethos, pathos, logos, intertextuality, context, and constraints to make his points. Make note of each of these devices and explain how they aid his argument or detract from it. Present evidence for your views.
3. What is Beato's main claim in this text? Do you think it is a persuasive one? Do you believe that he anticipates his opposition's positions fully? Why or why not? Be sure to provide textual evidence to support your thoughts.
4. What kind of evidence does Beato rely on to back up his ideas? Do you believe that he references a broad enough cross section of texts for evidence or would you encourage him to provide more examples? Are there other examples of video games to which you might point that either support his claim or refute it?

5. Describe the structure and organization of Beato's text. Do you find this to be a successful way to set up an argument? Why might it help to make his argument more convincing? How might it detract from his argument?

6. Do you see any logical fallacies at work in his argument, premises that are disputable, or warrants that require closer examination? Be sure to give quotes from the text to back up your thoughts.

Analysis

7. Beato's essay reveals that gaming companies believe girls are interested in "community-oriented websites, with bulletin boards, advice columns, contests, pen pals, interviews with mentors, and online games." In a short response, address the following issues: Do you think he is correct about this? To what evidence might you turn to support such views? Or, do you believe that Beato is in danger of reproducing stereotypes about differences between boys and girls—preferring a biological understanding of gender over a social one? Be sure to consult your own experiences, specific cultural texts, as well as library and Internet sources for evidence.

Taking Action

Gather in a small group. Each group in the class should locate one website completely dedicated to either boys or girls. Clarify why you think that this is the targeted audience and how you can tell. Analyze all of its rhetorical features—arrangement, sound, color, and contrast. Reflect upon how audience, purpose, ethos, pathos, logos, intertextuality, context, and constraints work. Seek out useful library and Internet sources.

Once you have completed a detailed rhetorical analysis of the site you have selected, take the next step. As a group, draw up plans for a spoof website that offers the same products or services—but targets the other gender (boy-oriented sites become girl-oriented sites and vice versa). You may even implement your choices, by actually creating a new web page.

Once you have planned or created your spoof website, share it with your peers. What cultural criticism about gender relationships does your new site advance? What stereotypes does it try to dismantle and what effects could this have?

Brian Cowlishaw

"Playing War: The Emerging Trend of Real Virtual Combat in Current Video Games"

Brian Cowlishaw is an assistant professor of English at Northeastern State University in Tahlequah, Oklahoma.

EXERCISING YOUR SKILLS

Before Reading

Cowlishaw's text examines how virtual combat operates in contemporary video games. Play a number of the most current war video games that are available. After you have done this, produce a freewrite in which you address the following: Characterize the various roles such games make available for their players and enemies. Consider the environment within which the warriors are doing battle and the ways in which the games mimic real-life war situations. What abilities do the warriors possess and how are they manifested through this visual medium? Do you think that these games are realistic? If yes, how so? If not, why not?

While video games have been around for some time now, they have emerged, in recent years, as a major player on the profit scene. Indeed, for the past two years, the video game market has made more money than the motion picture business. Perhaps that's why filmmakers often release video game versions of their films months before theatrical release—in order to heat up the marketplace for their film.

The latest trend in video games, such as the *Medal of Honor* series, the *Battlefield* series, and *America's Army*, is to be especially "realistic." Such games proudly transport the gamer into immersive, gut wrenching virtual battlefields. They persuade the gamer that, in an echo of WWII-era journalism, "You Are There"—on the beaches of Normandy, in the jungles of Vietnam, in modern military hotspots.

Upon examination, this now-common claim raises other key questions. First, and perhaps most obviously: To what degree is this claim to realism justified? In other words, are the games truly as historically accurate as their makers and players claim? Answering that question raises a series of more significant and telling questions: What do these games signify? Being war games, why are they so popular now? Who benefits from this popularity, and how?

The games that most stridently and persuasively claim to be realistic, and therefore those games on which I will focus, are first-person shooters (FPSs) which purport to recreate full-scale real-world battles. For the uninitiated, the phrase "first-person" in "first-person shooters" refers to the player's point of view: onscreen appears a pair of forearms and hands aiming a weapon forward "into" the screen. The hands are "you." That gun is "your" gun. Players use controls (keyboard, mouse, and/or game controller) to virtually look up, down, and around onscreen, and the result looks and feels like brandishing a weapon. The word "shooter" in "first-person shooter" refers to what the player does: move around a "map" (virtual battlefield) and deploy an arsenal of weapons against virtual enemies.

Unreal Tournament provides clear examples of standard FPS conventions. One key convention is that weapons, ammunition, armor, and first-aid kits regularly and frequently "spawn," that is, suddenly appear out of nowhere. Simply running over them onscreen confers their benefits immediately; there is almost no time wasted simulating using the first-aid kits, or reloading the weapons. Second, all FPS players die a lot, even when they're winning. The goal is to rack up the most "frags," or kills, so how often they die is really irrelevant. Dead players immediately respawn at a semi-random spot on the map, then get right back to killing. Finally, FPSs revel in offering ungenteel, gore-intensive gameplay. Players can be slimed, shot, sniped, razored, exploded, or chainsawed to death onscreen. Bodies hit just right, with the right weapon, fly apart into bloody chunks of flesh.

Realistic war games are recent specialized offshoots of the broader FPS genre. The first FPS was *Wolfenstein; Medal of Honor*, published a decade later, is probably the first realistic war game. This genealogical relationship—realistic war games' direct descent from FPSs—becomes apparent with close scrutiny. This genealogical relationship also means that while realistic war games are generally more realistic than other FPSs, they still retain significant unrealistic qualities.

One key unrealistic quality of putatively realistic war games might be called "self-assessment." Players have thorough, accessible-at-a-glance information regarding their condition onscreen at all times. They can see the status of their armor, their physical health expressed as a precise percentage, and their ammunition stores for every single weapon. Obviously, this level of self-knowledge is unavailable in real life. We may have a fairly keen sense of how healthy or unhealthy we feel, and if we have just had a blood or other test we may even be able to express this feeling with some precision. But this precision never approaches that in a FPS: we could never say, "I'm 81% healthy, and my clothes are providing 34% protection." Thus, for a simulation of war truly to be realistic, such information would have to remain vague or difficult to obtain. Yet there it is, right onscreen constantly in all of the new war games—just as in unashamedly unrealistic other FPSs.

Surprisingly, another FPS convention preserved by the realistic war games is respawning. For example, in the *Medal of Honor* games, when players die they are magically transported back to the beginning of the scenario, with all their original weapons and health restored, to try again. This makes sense not only from a games-history perspective, but also from an entertainment perspective: it's no fun if dying onscreen means the game is over. Players want to get right back up and fight some more. Obviously, though, real life does not work this way. Death tends to be final—but not in war video games.

Not only is death in this way banished from the games, but significantly, so is bodily dismemberment. Game makers systematically exclude it, much in the way Paul Fussell shows it was excluded from images and accounts of World War II. He observes that in such accounts, with very few exceptions, "the bodies of the dead, if inert, are intact. Bloody, sometimes, and sprawled in awkward positions, but except for the absence of life, plausible and acceptable simulacra of the people they once were. . . . American bodies (decently clothed) are occasionally in evidence, but they are notably intact." The famous photographic collection *Life Goes to War*, for example, shows only three dismembered bodies—specifically, heads. It is significant that they are not American but Asian heads. They are displayed as trophies of our soldiers' prowess. Always showing American bodies intact directly counters real-world facts and probabilities: as Fussell points out, it was "as likely for the man next to you to be shot through the eye, ear, testicles, or brain as (the way the cinema does it) through the shoulder. A shell is as likely to blow his whole face off as to lodge a fragment in some mentionable and unvital tissue." In fact, it was also quite common for a soldier to be wounded or killed not by a bullet or shell but by a flying body part—a foot, a skull, a ribcage.

Obviously, game makers could include such graphic details if they wanted to: *Unreal Tournament*, five years old at this writing, which is a dinosaur in computer time, displays gore galore. The technology for depicting dismemberment convincingly onscreen is quite capable nowadays, so clearly war game makers choose not to do it. They do in war video games what wartime journalists such as Ernie Pyle did in writing: purposely, systematically remove gory details so as to make the war more palatable—as opposed to more truly realistic. One of Pyle's best-known stories involves the return of the body of one Captain Henry T. Waskow "of Belton, Texas," to his grieving company. One of the men reportedly sat by the body for a long time, holding the captain's hand and looking into his face; then he "reached over and gently straightened the points of the captain's shirt collar, and then he sort of arranged the tattered edges of the uniform around the wound." As Fussell points out, Pyle's geographical and behavioral precision calls attention to the essential information that he glosses over:

1. What killed Captain Waskow? Bullet, shell fragments, a mine, or what?
2. Where was his wound? How large was it? He implies that it was in the traditional noble place, the chest. Was it? Was it a little hole, or was it a great red missing place? Was it perhaps in the crotch, or in the testicles, or in the belly? Were his entrails extruded, or in any way visible?
3. How much blood was there? Was the captain's uniform bloody? Did the faithful soldier wash off his hands after toying with those "tattered edges"? Were the captain's eyes open? Did his face look happy? Surprised? Satisfied? Angry?

Like wartime press reports, war video games carefully elide this most basic fact of wartime: bodily damage.

The most plainly unrealistic element of the war games is the existence of the games themselves. That is, players always remain inescapably aware of two very important facts. First, the war is never finally real. Players are not, in fact, dashing around a battlefield but rather sitting in a comfortable chair. They grip a controller, or keyboard and mouse, not a Garand rifle. There is no actual danger of being killed, or physically harmed beyond getting stiff and fat from playing video games too long. No matter how immersive or even realistic the game, one can never forget that it is "just a game." Second, players may play the game, but in an important sense the game plays them. There is always a "proper" outcome, a pre-scripted story one must complete correctly, especially when the game pits the player against the computer rather than against other flesh-and-blood players. There is always a specific task to carry out, such as to storm Normandy Beach and rout the Germans from their bunkers; the ideal for game programmers is to make such tasks challenging but possible. [The] players' job, then, is to find the correct solution to a puzzle someone else constructed; they are in a significant sense acted upon rather than acting. In life, of course, we can choose badly or well, but we can choose. This rat-in-a-maze aspect, together with the game's inescapable "game-ness," reminds players every moment that games fundamentally differ from real life; playing a game is inherently unrealistic.

Nevertheless, talk abounds regarding how realistic the current war video games are. *Official Xbox Magazine*'s comments on *Full Spectrum Warrior* are typical of the glee with which players and critics greet the newly "realistic" war games. The magazine effuses, "Now when you send your troops into a slaughter in *Full Spectrum Warrior*, you'll have to look in their eyes and hear their screams." Apparently this is a good thing. OXM also raves, "with [its] 5:1 [sound] it really feels like you are in the middle of a combat zone (turn it up loud enough and your neighbors might think so as well)." One fan anticipating *Battlefield: Vietnam's* release on EBGames.com writes, "this will alow a more real taste of the war [sic]." Another, purporting to speak for all of us, claims, "U know how u always wanted to know what the Vietnam War was like [sic]. I think this game will show you."

There is some justification for these claims to realism. Sound is one area in which the new war games truly do reproduce wartime accurately. Sound effects are as accurate and inclusive as visual representations are sanitized and edited. The realistic war games— for example, *America's Army*, the *Battlefield* series, and the *Medal of Honor* series— reproduce all of the rumbling machinery, gunfire, artillery, explosions, footsteps, splats, ricochets, shouted orders, swearing, and wounded cries one would hear in a real war. And current computer/television sound technology—now standardized at seven points in the room—reproduces all these sounds with perfect clarity at 100+ decibels.

In addition to sound, the war games also reproduce historical circumstances with comparative accuracy. The games do allow players to virtually fight in battles that really did occur—famous ones such as the Normandy invasion, Pearl Harbor, and the Tet Offensive. In-game soldiers use weapons that look and perform more or less like real weapons that real soldiers used. In-game soldiers dress, look, and speak like real soldiers did. The games may not be completely historically faithful in these elements, but they certainly are more so than other, older FPSs. The genealogical relationship makes the newer war games seem more realistic than they are.

Compare any current realistic war game, for example, with *Unreal Tournament*. In *UT*, the voices and character models ("skins") are a self-consciously over-the-top assortment of idealized macho warriors and ridiculous comic figures. In addition to the macho grunts, my copy features the downloaded voices of Fat Bastard (from the Austin Powers movies), Eric Cartman (from *South Park*), and Homer Simpson (from *The Simpsons*). Players can choose *UT* deathmatchers' appearances: onscreen fighters can be assigned any skin from a giant, scary lizardman, to a stereotypical macho male (or female), to Captain America, to Dr. Frankenfurter (from *The Rocky Horror Picture Show*). Any voice can be assigned to any skin: one might arrange a Dr. Frankenfurter with Cartman's voice, or a skull-faced badass who talks like Homer Simpson. These zany characters' weapons similarly aim for entertaining game-play rather than factual accuracy. *UT* features rocket launchers, handheld frag cannons, plasma rifles, and sludge guns. The battles in which these crazy weapons are used take place on obviously artificial, nonreferential staging grounds. That is, the in-game battle sites are not intended to reproduce historical locations. They clearly exist solely so that players can virtually blast the hell out of each other in visually interesting, strategically challenging settings—and the more fantastic, the better. References to real-world locales tend to be ironic, humorous: "Hey look, here's a map like a football field!" "Here's one set on a cruise ship!" I certainly hope real deathmatches never take place in such locales. Classic FPSs, as opposed to realistic war games, are judged by how intense a deathmatch they can produce, not by how accurately they reproduce "the real Normandy."

Overall "presentation," too, proves comparatively realistic in the new war games. "Presentation" refers to the way a game is laid out for the player in terms of menu choices, art, and sound; we might call it "atmosphere." In *Medal of Honor: Frontline*, for example, menu choices take the form of file folders stamped with the (now-defunct) Office of Strategic Services logo. All in-game fonts look typewritten by period typewriters. "Your" portrait in the menu file appears attached by low-tech paper clip. Selecting a menu option produces a gunshot or file-rustling sound. In the *America's Army* game, menu headings use terminology lifted from the real-world America's Army: "Personnel Jacket," "Training Missions," "Deployment," and so on. This kind of attention to making the presentation realistic enhances the overall impression that the game accurately recreates history. Compared to the three-ring FPS circus that is their origin, the new realistic war games appear positively photographic in their historical fidelity. Even gamers, disposed by nature to find all flaws, perceive them as faithful to what the games purport to recreate.

So far, I have discussed two fairly black-and-white categories, "realistic" and "unrealistic," so that I can make descriptions clearly. But the truth is, the issue is much more complicated than that binary choice. It's more accurate to say that the games blur the boundaries between real and virtual, or mix elements of the one in among the other, so thoroughly that players finally cannot tell where reality ends and virtual reality begins.

One telling example appears in the required marksman-training mission that begins *America's Army*. The player must hit a specified number of targets within a time limit. After passing the test, the player receives hearty applause from the drill sergeant: "Congratulations, soldier! You have just qualified as a marksman in the United States Army!" I must admit: the first time I passed this test, I became moderately alarmed—he did mean I virtually qualified, right? So many other kinds of transactions take place online nowadays; why not real-life recruitment and qualification?

The idea that by playing a realistic war game for a few minutes I may have inadvertently enlisted is not as outlandish as it may seem out of context. Consider: the real-world *America's Army* created, programmed, and distributed, for free online, the game called *America's Army*, specifically for the purpose of recruitment. Anyone can download it for free, right now, at americasarmy.com. The real army counts on people, mostly young men ripe for recruitment, to download the game, enjoy it, think to themselves, "Hey, you know, I should do this for real," and then go enlist. Apparently the strategy is working very effectively. In late March 2004, the CBS *Evening News* reported on a huge *America's Army* gaming tournament. Hundreds of thousands of dollars in prize money and computer equipment were at stake. Several recruiters sat in the competition room. Hundreds of players walked directly from their round of competition over to sign up with recruiters. CBS reported that since the game was released in 2002, recruitment has spiked; the video game is the most effective recruitment tool since the Uncle Sam "*I Want You*" posters during World War II.

This video game recruitment strategy meshes very neatly with the Army's recent advertising campaign. The Army shows images of underage kids essentially playing games—flying a remote-controlled plane in one, and actually playing a video game in another. Then the same people (presumably) are shown as young adults doing pretty much the same activities in the Army: the model plane flyer pilots a decoy drone plane, and the video gamer efficiently directs real tanks and troops around a battlefield. The clear message is: "You should join the real Army because we will pay you to play pretty much the same games you play for fun right now. You were born for this."

Full Spectrum Warrior blurs reality and gaming perhaps even more thoroughly. Like *America's Army*, this game was produced by the real U.S. Army. In fact, it's not entirely clear that the end result was the choice of the game's original developer, William Stahl. In an interview with *Official Xbox Magazine*, Stahl describes how the game got made: "Three years ago, I was pitching a . . . game for the PC. Representatives of the Army were looking for a developer to create a training simulation on a videogame console. They got ahold of those early documents and thought the concept was right in line with what they wanted to achieve. . . . This game was developed in conjunction with the Army. They were essentially our publisher, and as such, they had the final say on what they wanted in the game, how it looked, etc." This statement raises worrisome questions:

1. How did the Army get "ahold" of those early documents?
2. How much choice of publisher did Stahl and company actually have?

In any case, the Army ultimately made two versions, one of which is being used right now by real American soldiers for training, and a very similar version being sold in stores. Real soldiers and couch bound warriors alike learn battle tactics by playing a video game. Thus, the real and the virtual become indistinguishable. The U.S. Army recruits real soldiers by appealing to them through video games and suggests that video gamers' virtual prowess and enjoyment translate directly into real-world Army suitability and success.

In one important sense, the first-person-shooter genre itself contributes to this fusion of the real and the virtual. In recent years, in-game instructions have become standard parts of all FPSs and most video games in general; James Paul Gee explains in detail, in his book *What Video Games Have to Teach Us about Learning and Literacy*, how they help the player learn to "read" and understand the game, to figure out what to do in the game world. So, for example, in *America's Army*, the sergeant character gives the player basic directions to get started. He gives commands like, "Press <G> to fix jammed weapon," "Press <T> to bring up sights," and "Press <B> to reload." In doing so, he merges the player's onscreen and real-life identities. The sergeant is onscreen, talking to the player's onscreen representation; but he's giving directions that only the real-world person can carry out. The onscreen representation doesn't have a G, T, or B button to push—it's the real-world person doing that. Similarly, in *Medal of Honor: Frontline* the player is to "press Select to get hints from HQ," and "press Start to review mission objectives." In-game, players are spoken to as their real-world self and their onscreen self simultaneously and without differentiation, which means those identities merge.

With the real and the virtual mingling so thoroughly in war video games, perhaps it's only natural that both players and game makers reproduce and perpetuate this fusion in the way they talk. It's not some kind of schizophrenia or delusion, it's the ordinary, proper response to the postmodern facts. For example, imagining someone playing *Full Spectrum Warrior* with guns blazing rather than cautiously and strategically. William Stahl predicts, "His men will die. Mothers will lose their son, wives will lose their husbands, and children will lose their fathers." *OXM* also warns, "Don't press [the Action] button [in this game] until you've assessed the situation and made the right plan or it'll be the last button you press." Er, they do mean in-game . . . right? Thus, it's not so outlandish for the magazine to call *Full Spectrum Warrior* "The Game That Captured Saddam." OXM explains, "This game was made to train the US Army infantry . . . they're the ones who dug Saddam out of his hole. So technically this game caught Saddam." Nor is it as insane as it might first appear when one gamer writes in anticipation of playing *Battlefield: Vietnam*, "The Vietnam War was said to be a draw, but when this game comes out everyone will see that the U.S.A. is the best army in the world." His comment suggests that an alleged misperception of history—namely, that the U.S. did not decisively win that war—will be corrected by people's playing the game. He's epistemologically assuming, and rhetorically suggesting, that not only do video games refer to and simulate real-world battles, but because this is so, they also provide players an accurate recreative picture of history. In this understanding, war games not only borrow from history, they also teach it.

Many veterans' and historical organizations have bestowed awards on games such as the *Medal of Honor* series for their educational value. *Medal of Honor: Frontline*'s official sales copy at EBGames.com boasts, "Authentic WWII content with the assistance of the Smithsonian's . . . expert Russ Lee and renowned technical consultant Capt. Dale Dye," and, "The MOH team continues to work closely with the Congressional Medal of Honor Society to ensure the ideals and integrity of this prestigious commendation." Not incidentally, that game awards the Congressional Medal of Honor for especially meritorious military action—in-game. If players complete a given mission quickly enough and safely enough, they win a virtual medal. *MOH: Frontline* also unlocks documentary movie clips and historical speech excerpts as rewards for good performance in the game, and it mixes game elements, such as the game's logo and menus, and historical elements, such as documentary film clips and an exhortative speech by Dwight D. Eisenhower, without any differentiation of importance or validity. They all "feel real." Current war video games have blended and blurred the real and the virtual.

Because that is so, the games' romanticizing of war becomes all the more seductive and powerful. Any truly realistic recreation of war would cast some doubt on the idea that war is cool and enjoyable, and that, as in sports, all one has to do is "step up" and become an instant hero. But the titles alone hint at how current war video games support this old myth: *Call of Duty, Full Spectrum Warrior, Medal of Honor*. Players can almost taste the medals, just reading the game box. In-game, it immediately becomes clear that the war effort would never get off the ground without the player's personal, constant heroics. What the U.S. Army claims in its current advertising slogan is absolutely true: the player really is "An Army of One." Never mind the Army's famous unwieldy, illogical bureaucracy made famous in works such as *Catch-22* and *M*A*S*H**. Never mind the fact that boot camp is famously designed to tear down the individual to replace that entity with a small cog in a giant machine. Contrary to commonsense facts, the war game player is always "An Army of One." *Medal of Honor: Frontline*'s first mission provides a brilliant example of this. During this mission, "you" are ordered onscreen to storm the beach at Normandy under heavy machine-gun and rifle fire, provide covering fire for three soldiers widely separated along the beach, run lengthwise down the beach to an engineer then cover his run all the way back, cross a minefield, storm a machine-gun nest and take it over, mow down a wave of advancing German soldiers with that machine-gun, and finally snipe two far-off machine-gunners while still under fire. And that's just the first mission! What must the odds be that any individual would a) be present at D-Day; b) be asked to personally complete every single necessary task at that battle; and c) survive to complete them all successfully, thus winning that battle singlehandedly? The whole game continues like that: the player is assigned all the work at all the key European battles, eventually bringing about V-E Day completely solo.

This begins to answer the important question, "Why would someone want to realistically recreate the experience of war? Isn't it just common sense to avoid being there?" One game magazine editor raises exactly this question when he writes, "With the new wave of games pushing the envelope of realism it begs the question: how real do we want it? Do we want games that'll simulate war to such a degree that it's possible to suffer from post-game-atic syndrome?" Judging by the state of the games now, the answer for both gamers and game makers is a resounding "No." For all their attention to accurately recreating sounds, weapons, locales, and uniforms, and for all their visual drama and flair, the new "realistic" war video games do not, in fact, reproduce the real conditions of war. They still play too much like other FPSs, and significantly, like goreless FPSs. Although players see soldiers being blown into the air by mines, riddled with machine-gun fire, and sniped from all directions, they never see blood or a flying body part, ever.

Thus, I would argue, what the new war games are is not realistic, but cinematic. They don't reproduce the real world experience of war; they do reproduce the theatrical experience of war. Games use all of the same techniques as movies for framing shots, editing, pacing, and narration. Playing one of the new war video games is very much like starring in a war movie. For example, the *MOH: Frontline* opening mission is a rather accurate, if condensed, version of the first thirty minutes of *Saving Private Ryan*, even down to individual camera shots: bullets whizzing along underwater past slowly sinking soldiers, and the company's seeking cover under a low hill while the engineer blows away the barbed wire barrier. *Medal of Honor: Rising Sun* similarly steals heavily from the much less well-made movie *Pearl Harbor*. H. L. Mencken once described art as "life with all the boring parts taken out." War has been described as 99 percent boredom punctuated by short bursts of abject terror. No one in their right mind would want to reproduce that, and, in recent war video games, no one does. Instead, the games are, in essence, interactive movies about war with all the boring parts taken out. But the boring parts were already pretty much taken out by the movies, so in the games, all that's left is action, action, action—the player winning a war single handedly. The war games make players heroes, in a bloodless, risk-free environment where they can show off their "mad skillz."

As it turns out, then, logical answers do exist for the question, "Why in the world would anyone want to recreate the experience of war?" First, the games don't do quite that; rather, they recreate movies about the experience of war. The additional [step back] is key. Playing the games provides an entertaining, cinematic experience, rather than the horrible one a true recreation would give. Even if the imagery is not pleasing, it certainly is immersive. And as Miroslaw Filiciak points out, we value the experience of immersion in itself. We intentionally overlook unconvincing elements of the experience so as to become more fully immersed: "We desire the experience of immersion, so we use our intelligence to reinforce rather than to question the reality of the experience." In short, it doesn't really matter that the war games aren't fully realistic; gamers enjoy them for what they are, interactive movies that temporarily immerse us in the games's battles. The second answer to the question, "Why would anyone want to recreate the experience of war?" is to play the hero, in a cinematically intense experience in which we can play an active part rather than just settling passively down into our couches and watching as movies force us to do. And third, we get to see ourselves onscreen playing the hero. Filiciak observes: "Contemporary people have a fascination with electronic media, something we cannot define, something that escapes our rationalizations. . . . We make the screen a fetish; we desire it, not only do we want to watch the screen but also to 'be seen' on it . . . being on the screen ennobles. All the time we have the feeling (more or less true) that others are watching us. The existence of an audience is an absolute necessity." We can see "ourselves" onscreen in any video game, but in online war games such as *America's Army* and *Battlefield: Vietnam*, we can also be seen by other players. We can show off our skills, and brag about our victories, to others who have just witnessed them. We can enact the electronic equivalent of dancing in the end zone.

The reasons for making the new war video games are even more obvious than those for playing them. Foremost, there's the money. As I mentioned at the beginning of this article, Americans now spend more money on video games than on movies. Games are huge business, and they're steadily getting huger. One key game maker, the real-world U.S. Army—and by extension, the other service branches and the federal government as a whole—reaps huge benefits from the games' popularity. Not only does the current hawkish regime gain flesh-and-blood recruits for the armed services, it also gains general credibility and support as the games work their propagandist magic. By hiding ugly realities and producing cinematic cotton candy, the games make real war seem exciting, heroic, even fun. And so hawkish political candidates seem not bellicose, but reasonable. Rapidly escalating defense costs look not wasteful, but common-sensical. Thus our two-front war rolls on and on and on.

After Reading

Critical Perspective

1. How would you describe Cowlishaw's main claim in this text? Where does he present it? Why do you believe he decides to place his claim at this point in his argument?

Rhetoric and Argument

2. Deliberate about how Cowlishaw employs specific rhetorical strategies to make his argument including appeals to ethos, pathos, and logos as well as intertextuality. Do you find his use of such tactics to aid his argument or not? Furnish evidence for your views.
3. Investigate the sorts of evidence Cowlishaw utilizes to support his claim. Determine whether you believe that this support adequately backs up his argument or not. Provide quotes from the essay.
4. Outline the arrangement of Cowlishaw's argument. What are the advantages of using this kind of structure and what are the disadvantages? Give textual evidence for your perspectives.
5. Toward the close of his essay, Cowlishaw proffers that "what the new war games are is not realistic, but cinematic. They don't reproduce the real world experience of war; they do reproduce the theatrical experience of war." What does Cowlishaw mean by these statements? What are the potential effects of this being the case? Be sure to present quotes from the text to back up your thoughts.

Analysis

6. Cowlishaw indicates that "by hiding ugly realities and reproducing cinematic cotton candy, the games make real war seem exciting, heroic, even fun." In a short response address the following issues: Do you agree with Cowlishaw's argument? What support from specific video games as well as military training materials might you turn to in order to substantiate your views? Be sure to consult library and Internet sources for additional evidence.

Taking Action

Form small groups. Each group should choose a different sort of video game to examine carefully. Make note of the game's packaging and advertising, the purpose of the game, the rules of the game and how one wins it, the roles and activities of the characters depicted, the sounds and images that dominate the game, and the ways in which the environments appear in the game. Now consider what myths and ideas about American culture this game promotes and how the game accomplishes this. What specific evidence can you use to back up your views? Write up your comments.

After you have created your analysis, share it with the rest of the class. Think about the claims of cultural criticism you might make about the game you examined. What might this reveal about the current state of video games and American culture?

GLEN MARTIN

"Internet Indian Wars: Native Americans Are Fighting to Connect the 550 Nations— in Cyberspace"

Glen Martin is an environmental reporter for the San Francisco Chronicle, *and has contributed to a number of national magazines, including* Discover, Audubon, Outside, Men's Journal, Islands, Reader's Digest, Gourmet *and* National Wildlife. *His latest book, a guide to national wildlife refuges, was published by National Geographic.*

EXERCISING YOUR SKILLS

Before Reading

Martin investigates the creation of lists and chat groups in order to advance a racial, ethnic, and cultural identity that is not one's own. What are the ethical implications of a person pretending to be someone other than he or she is on the Internet—particularly when this person adopts a different culture, and racial or ethnic background? Do you believe that such a person should be allowed to do this? Why or why not? Try to draw from your own experiences to support your views.

Blue Snake's Lodge. To a certain kind of seeker, it was irresistible. You logged on to the America Online seminar, and the old ways swelled up around you, evoking sparkling rivers, virgin forests, and yawning plains teeming with game. You were in, well, North America. But before it was called North America. After all, North America is merely an Anglo rubric applied to a vast land once inhabited by myriad peoples living in harmony with the Earth.

Yes, in Blue Snake's Lodge, you were privy to the mysteries and ceremonies of the American Indian. Blue Snake was an online chief of the Eastern Shawnee, and in the photo provided with his AOL bio, you could see a stocky middle-aged man with abundant gray whiskers, accoutered in a blanket and holding a long pipe. He was devoted to inculcating non-Indians with the healing ways of Native American spirituality.

His introductory "teaching" ushered you onto the cybernetic equivalent of Native holy ground:

> *Before you is a lodge, a large tepee. . . . The silhouettes of its inhabitants are cast upon the canvas sides by the fire in the center. You hear only night sounds, a stream chuckles in the distance as it hurls itself headlong through the forest, an owl challenges the darkness as she hunts for prey, a coyote voices his loneliness as he waits for his mate.*
>
> *Blue Snake is seated at the back of the lodge. At his feet, beside the fire, a pipe carved in the image of a rattlesnake rests on a cedar box. The pipe is a symbol of his authority. He bids you welcome. He raises the pipe then lowers it and points the stem at each of his guests. Six times he draws smoke . . . six times he exhales*

it, once to each of the four directions, once to the Everywhere Spirit above, once to Grandmother Earth below. . . . Blue Snake speaks, "Welcome to my lodge. May you always feel welcome here, as in your own lodge."

Wow. Or as Blue Snake would say, oneh (a Shawnee analog, Blue Snake reveals, of aloha, meaning everything from "hello" to "I agree profoundly"). No doubt about it, Blue Snake offered a moving spiritual message, particularly resonant in a world where the dollar is king and nature is becoming a vague memory.

There was, however, a problem: it was all a charade. Blue Snake was Don Rapp, a software consultant living in southern Ohio, who was about as Indian as Barbara Bush. Rapp created the Blue Snake persona and successfully pitched it to America Online, where he conducted seminars and hosted a chat room. Online Native wannabes flocked to Rapp, who made them honorary Indians by declaring them members of the "Evening Sky Clan" of the "Red Heart Tribe." He also bestowed names on his followers during elaborate online benedictions—Crystal Bear Woman, Stormcloud Dancer, and Darkness Runs From Her.

By early 1993, Blue Snake's teachings had worked their way around AOL and into the hearts and minds of thousands of cybersurfers who were convinced they had found the answer to their manifold spiritual dilemmas. But in March 1993, some real Indians logged onto the seminars—and Blue Snake's Lodge began to fall apart under its own spurious weight.

The easy use of alternative personae, of course, lies at the heart of cyber culture. People get online because it embodies freedom—not just freedom to be all they can be, but freedom to be everything they can't or won't be in the world of flesh, blood, and three dimensions. *Wired* Native Americans find this element of cyberspace appealing. But tradition-minded Indians assert that there's an uncrossable line in both cyberspace and the real world, a line that separates tribal religious rites from the commerce of everyday life. Such rituals, these Natives maintain, are sacred, proprietary—and indeed, exclusionary.

Blue Snake's peddling of "Indian spirituality" was thus repugnant to the Native Americans who discovered his seminars, and they went on the offensive. "There's a difference between adopting online identities and perpetrating fraud," says Marc Towersap, a Shoshone-Bannock engineer from Idaho and one of the first Indians to query America Online about Blue Snake's tribal credentials. "Rapp was promoting himself as a genuine Native elder, and AOL was making money on the chat room because a lot of people logged on to it. They were making money on a bogus product. Is selling fake mutual funds over the telephone acceptable? This was the same thing, except we're talking about spirituality rather than stocks, and the Internet instead of the phone. It's fraud, not role-playing."

Tracy Miller, a salty, blunt-spoken Eastern Band Cherokee and Native activist who lives in southern New England, was likewise incensed when she stumbled onto Blue Snake's maunderings. "A Native friend e-mailed me and told me to check out this guy Blue Snake on AOL," recalls Miller. "I couldn't believe it. His seminars were a hodgepodge of the worst kind of bullshit stereotypes and gobbledygook possible. All the hippies and crystal gazers were just gobbling it up, of course, but I knew that there was no way in hell he could be a real Native."

Miller, a seasoned Net surfer, knows that information isn't the only thing that wants to be free; so does misinformation. And misinformation, she claims, strikes at the heart of Native sensibilities—and survival. Miller asserts that preserving Native culture is foremost a matter of keeping Natives and Native memory around. "But it isn't just about biological survival," says Miller. "It's also about spirituality and culture. There is a thread of rituals and beliefs that parallels our physical cohesiveness as tribal peoples, a thread that goes back thousands of years. It defines who we are as much as our DNA does."

Miller says that many Native religions and rituals are secret because they are sacrosanct, appropriate for tribal members alone. "Natives don't proselytize Native religions," observes Miller. "We're not looking for converts. It isn't about shunning people—it's about keeping what little we have left."

Such contentions are antithetical to the free and unfettered exchange of ideas and data in cyberspace. They also raise thorny questions: In the age of information, can any data be legitimately considered sacred? How do you upload holiness? "We know you can't police cyberspace," sighs Miller. "But like everything else, it's a matter of education and dialog."

To Miller's community, a particularly egregious example of Rapp's cultural rip-off was Blue Snake's "pipe ceremonies." Proprietary rituals involving pipes are sacred to many tribes. The pipe, its accouterments, ceremonies surrounding the pipe—indeed, even spoken or written allusions to the pipe—are thus freighted with great spiritual significance. "His mumbo jumbo surrounding the pipe was especially offensive," says Miller.

After monitoring Blue Snake for a while from the sidelines, Miller, Towersap, and a few of their pals began challenging the azure serpent and his starry-eyed gaggle of Red Hearted converts. They demanded that Rapp desist from conducting his seminars and fought his online doctrines, byte by byte, with their own. Eventually, they became so obstreperous they were tossed from the room by testy AOL guides. Miller, who has been permanently barred from AOL since 1994, still gets online by arranging payment through friends and employing a rich variety of pseudonyms. She admits her own duplicities constitute a rather sharp irony, given her ire with Blue Snake over his online misrepresentations, but she also argues that her actions are ethical and necessary. Miller insists there's a palpable world of truth out there—Native truth, tradition, and history—that must be protected from the vagaries of casual data-play.

Miller and her running mates ultimately enlisted the aid of the three recognized tribes of the Shawnee nation in their quest to hamstring Blue Snake: the Absentee-Shawnee Tribe of Oklahoma, the Loyal Shawnee Tribe of Oklahoma, and the Eastern Shawnee Tribe of Oklahoma. A joint resolution drafted by leaders of the three tribes was e-mailed to AOL and Blue Snake. In it, the leaders declared that Rapp was not a recognized member of any Shawnee tribe or band, adding: "It is said that imitation is the greatest form of flattery. However, the reports of Mr. Rapp's 'teachings' and Native American 'classes' would indicate that perhaps his intentions are less than honorable.

"The true Shawnee peoples are very traditional, and their ceremonies and rituals are not for public consumption. They practice their traditional beliefs and rites as a matter of religion—no public 'powwows' or 'gatherings' are conducted."

AOL apparently was chastened by the letter. It relieved Rapp of his host status, replacing Blue Snake's Lodge with a room dubbed Native American Chat. But again, complains Miller, the hosts were—and are—demonstrably non-Native. They couldn't or can't produce the federal enrollment credentials demanded by the genuine Indians who logged into the room.

"There's a lot of controversy in the Native community about the significance of federal enrollment," observes Miller. "The irony of enrollment is that a system designed by the conquerors and oppressors of Natives is now the benchmark for determining who is and isn't Native. Not every Native is enrolled, and we recognize this. But enrollment does definitively establish tribal affiliation—something we think is critical for host status." A potential host shouldn't necessarily be rejected if an enrollment number can't be produced, Miller says, but in that case, a vetting process conducted by recognized and respected Native Americans would be in order. "Otherwise, it's like a Swedish national claiming he could conduct a course on black American culture from an insider's perspective," laughs Miller.

Rapp, for his part, is somewhat bemused by all the heat and bile generated by his online persona. "Basically, what we did was done in fun," he observes. "We certainly didn't intend any disrespect."

Rapp acknowledges freely that he has no Shawnee ancestry but says he was adopted into the tribe by John Reese, a chief of the Eastern Band Shawnee. "The honored status of adoptees is a tradition among the Shawnee, though I never claimed I had Shawnee blood," Rapp says.

Rapp says that he provided some of his attackers with documents from Reese establishing his tribal bona fides, but that they were rejected out of hand. And as far as vitiating sacred rites, says Rapp, he discussed only rituals that have long been documented in books such as *Black Elk Speaks*. "All that material was and is available through published texts," he asserts. "Can you take back what's already printed? I acknowledge that there is sacred and proprietary information and ceremonies in the Indian nations—I've witnessed some of them. And what I've witnessed that's truly sacred, I've never discussed."

For Rapp, the experience with Blue Snake's Lodge was distressing, but he nevertheless feels his seminars were a positive force both on the Net and in Indian Country. "At least I touched a nerve," he points out. "People loved me or hated me, but at least they were involved. I consider that an accomplishment."

At AOL, spokeswoman Margaret Ryan maintains the company was not obliged to ascertain Rapp's Native credentials because the seminars were conducted in a "member" room as opposed to a fully sanctioned chat room. "We monitor the member areas to ensure online standards of conduct are upheld," she says, repeating the corporate disclaimer, "but we cannot screen public communication to make sure the topics discussed are legitimate. We advise our members to be as careful in their evaluation of information and opinions on AOL as they are in everyday life."

Miller admits she and her online Native colleagues enjoyed chivying the devotees of the spurious Snake—a guilty pleasure that helped mitigate their anger. But anger, Miller emphasizes, was the dominant emotion—especially when their protests were repeatedly stonewalled by AOL. "I was e-mailing a Sioux friend about it, and we came to the conclusion that the company didn't want us disturbing the fantasy," said Miller. "It doesn't want real Indians—we're not 'Indian' enough. It wants the buckskin fringes and the feathers."

The problem had cropped up before—offline. For years, says Miller, fake or "renegade" Indians have offered non-Natives entrée into the mystic realm of Native American spirituality, driving Native traditionalists nuts. "The worst was a guy named Sun Bear, a Cheyenne who died a few years ago," recalls Miller. "He conducted seminars all over the country, had followers who gave him money and gifts. He was prostituting the culture of his tribe—the Cheyennes loathed him."

Still, online Natives figured such poseur high jinx were small potatoes compared with the drivel flooding cyberspace. Misinformation spread by word of mouth during retreats and seminars multiplies more or less arithmetically. But the rate of spread is exponential online—an assault on Native sensibilities, claim activists, equivalent to the wars of extermination of the last century.

How could they deal with this cultural analog of the Wounded Knee massacre? The online compatriots were stumped—they could neither lick their foes nor join them. Confronting AOL directly got them tossed. And any attempt at compromise, they felt, would defeat their own purpose—this seemed to them a situation of right or wrong, black or white. So the idea dawned: If they couldn't work with existing online communities, they could build one of their own. They would create an alternative that would allow Native Americans from the Aleut villages of Alaska to the Apache reservations of Arizona free and advanced access to computer-based telecommunications. A simultaneous goal: to provide non-Natives accurate information on Native cultures by allowing access to legitimate Indian spokespersons rather than self-styled shamans.

At first, the idea was simply that—a vaporous notion that didn't seem likely to go beyond the gee-wouldn't-it-be-great stage. The obstacles, the friends well knew, were enormous. Indeed, the simple precedents of past attempts dampened spirits. Previous stabs at a Native American Net presence had met with less-than-stellar success. In 1992, George Baldwin, an instructor at Henderson State University in Arkansas who now directs the Institute for Community Networking in Monterey, California, formed IndianNet, an electronic bulletin board based in Rapid City, South Dakota, that provided information on grants and employment opportunities and allowed users to post messages. But the long-distance rates were prohibitively expensive from the places where most users lived—remote reservations in the West.

Another service now running is NativeNet, a mailing list and developing Website. It deals primarily with Native policy issues and is used mostly by academics. Finally, a few tribes maintain bulletin boards of varying scope. But that's about it. Of the 550 federally recognized tribes and Native villages in the continental United States and Alaska, only four—the Oneida and Onondaga of New York, the Navajo of Arizona and New Mexico, and the Sioux of North and South Dakota—have any significant Net presence. At the beginning of 1995, only 3 of the 28 Native-controlled colleges offered Net connections.

Much of the problem stems from the lack of wiring in Indian Country. Simply put, there is little copper wire or fiber-optic cable in most of the lands controlled by North American Natives. No one knows how many Natives have phones, says Towersap, but the number is decidedly below the 94 percent figure cited for the American populace at large. "Many reservations don't even have electricity," observes Towersap. "And many Natives who do have phones have them only sporadically—they lose service when they can't pay their bill, which is commonplace." Such were the monumental real-world problems faced by Miller and her crew once they spurned the slippery cyberspace game of who's who; these conditions made it impossible for the great majority of their fellow Natives to even enter the contest.

Nevertheless, in late 1994, Miller, Towersap, and three compatriots—Disney executive Dawn Jackson (who is Saginaw Chippewa), attorney Tamera Crites Shanker (Arapaho), and advertising creative director Victoria Bracewell Short (Creek)—incorporated as the nonprofit Native American Communications Council, and began work on the project.

Though proficient with computers, the partners aren't monomaniacal technophiles. Rather, they see computers and wire as the best and brightest chance of reestablishing tribal bonds that were sundered with the massacre at Wounded Knee, an event remembered as ending all organized Indian resistance in North America. "When we get together, what we talk about is power (not computers)," says Short. "The Net is a tool that will allow us to forge bonds between the Indian nations. The only thing we have right now that facilitates intertribal communication is the powwow circuit (pantribal gatherings throughout the country, many open to the general public, that feature dances, food, handicrafts, and seminars). It's fine as far as it goes, but we need more."

Short observes that Natives have always been open to new technologies and disposed to elegant communications systems. "We've always esteemed useful tools and goods," says Short. "We've always maintained ties with one another. We know from artifacts that trade routes threaded the continent. Gulf Coast pearls have been found at sites in New Mexico. The plains tribes all spoke different languages but shared a sign language that was understood by all. Smoke signaling may seem quaint when you see it in the movies, but it was an effective means of communicating information over long distances. Natives in the interior knew of the whites long before the whites knew of them."

The council's goals are straightforward: to develop a Native-owned and operated telecommunications network that will provide Native Americans with easy access to information stored on the council's server while simultaneously offering most Internet functions, including gopher, ftp, telnet, as well as a Website. The council's primary server will be linked to local servers on reservations, Alaskan Native villages, and urban Native service centers. Concomitantly, courses would be provided to local service centers to aid Natives in managing local nodes, navigating the Net, and creating Web home pages. "We also hope to launch an interactive service that will provide updated information on grant, job, and educational opportunities and legal and health issues," says Short.

Such ambitions are right in line with the plans of the Smithsonian's National Museum of the American Indian, says Marty Kreipe de Montaño, a Prairie Band Potawatomi who is creating interactive databases that will link images of the museum's one million objects with its reams of curators' comments and more than 250,000 explanatory documents. "The museum will eventually have four sites," observes de Montaño. "The first is the George Gustav Heye Center, which was founded in 1916 and conjoined with the Smithsonian in 1990. The second will be a state-of-the-art storage and research facility that we plan to build in Suitland, Maryland, by 1997. The third will be the Smithsonian Mall museum, which is scheduled for completion by 2001."

And the fourth site, says de Montaño, will be an "electronic museum without walls." This service will allow electronic access to the museum and provide information about real Natives in real time. "We consult with a number of tribal councils on everything we do," she notes, "and they consider the fourth museum the most important because it will help people living in Indian Country today. The council's project is similar. It's just what's needed."

Some elements of the council's system will be like Native religious rites, say the partners—for Natives alone. But how will this be possible, given the porous nature of the Net? "In the beginning, everybody will probably be able to tap into everything," acknowledges Towersap. "But there are some things we'll want to keep exclusive—that's one of our primary reasons for starting this project. There's groupware evolving that will make this possible—applications that require membership passwords and are pretty secure."

At the Smithsonian, de Montaño agrees with Towersap that many Native objects, images, and rites are sacred and not for public dissemination, but she is somewhat dubious about the prospect of adequately protecting such information. "It's the nature of the Net that it's difficult to control," she observes. "But we're always working with tribal elders to determine which objects and what information are appropriate only for tribal members, and we're always working on high-tech ways to protect them."

Connections to the museum would allow academicians and the merely curious access to the quotidian issues and concerns of American Indians without all the hype, hoopla, and out-and-out bullshit that has characterized most online interactions between Native and non-Native peoples. The museum will allow dissemination of accurate information on Natives and will facilitate direct, unfiltered, one-on-one communication between Indians and everybody else, says Shanker, who coordinates the council's legal affairs.

The main thing standing between the council and a *Wired* Native America, not surprisingly, is money. "We've applied for a grant from the Eagle Staff Fund (a corporate fund that supports a variety of Native projects) that we're reasonably optimistic about getting," said Shanker. "That would give us about $35,000 and get us up and running for the pilot project. It's also especially critical money because several of the other grants we have pending are predicated on matching funds."

Shanker and her fellow council members are only too aware that a few thousand dollars won't fulfill the council's grand goal of linking up all 550 nations. By any measure, the job is huge. But council members are sanguine, even serene.

"The simple fact is that Natives need to be a significant presence on the Net, and we need to make that happen on our own terms," says Shanker, who acknowledges that the slippery nature of online data swapping makes any attempt to define and preserve fixed identities tricky in the extreme. "If we don't define who we are on the Net, other people will do it for us," says Shanker. "And when that happens, part of who we are disappears." Blue Snake himself wishes Shanker the best in her endeavors. "If what happened on AOL contributes in some way to a viable Native telecommunications network, then I'm happy," observes Rapp. "It's what I've always wanted to see."

After Reading

Critical Perspective

1. What feelings are evoked for you as you read the beginning of Martin's text? What language does Martin employ that shapes your response?

Rhetoric and Argument

2. Describe the sorts of rhetorical appeals that Martin creates. What appeals to ethos, pathos, and logos are offered? Are they persuasive? Do you see instances of intertextuality, context, and constraints operating in his text? Who is Martin's audience? What is his purpose? How do you know? Be sure to provide textual evidence for your position.
3. What is Martin's argumentative claim? Do you agree with his claim? What sorts of evidence does he use to back it up? Do you find this evidence sufficient? Why or why not?
4. Martin makes a distinct shift in his argument at a specific point. Chart where and how this occurs. Do you find this an effective strategy given his claim? Offer quotes as back up for your thoughts.
5. How did the Native American tribes respond to what they learned? Do you think that they created a viable plan of action? What else might they have done to make their positions clear?
6. Reflect upon the responses that Miller offers to the charges against him. Do you find Miller's assertions viable? Why or why not? Could he have argued his point better? If yes, how so? Be sure to explain your thoughts in detail.

Analysis

7. Take a look at some of the websites run by and for Native Americans—ones that Martin mentions, as well as those he does not. In a short argumentative response, address the following concerns: How might these sites create a critical sense of Native American community and identity? In what ways do they cater to traditional, Western values? In what ways do they cater to Native peoples's needs, beliefs, and histories? Are these sites socially and culturally empowering? If yes, how so? If not, why not? Try to present evidence from specific cultural texts to back up your views as well as consult library and Internet sources.

Taking Action

Work in a small group. Spend some time researching other recent examples of fraud on the Internet (committed by hackers, disingenuous salespeople or companies, as well as other individuals or groups). Consult library and Internet sources as well as your own experiences for ideas.

Once you have selected one particular example on which you would like to focus, attend to the following questions: What specific events occurred? How was the fraud perpetrated? Who was involved and why? What effects did the fraud have on the various people involved? What legal or other actions could have been taken against those who committed the fraud? Which ones were in fact taken?

After you have considered these issues, bring your research to the larger class group for discussion. In what ways is fraud increasingly becoming a problem on the Internet? What should and could be done to stop it? Give suggestions to promote consumer awareness as well as legal and other sanctions against those who commit fraud. Consider making your work accessible to other groups both inside and outside the campus community.

INNOVATIONS IN TECHNOLOGY

MARK SLOUKA

"The Illusion of Life Is Dearly Bought"

Mark Slouka is a well-known creative as well as critical writer who has taught at Columbia University, Harvard, and the University of California at San Diego. His creative piece "The Woodcarver's Tale" won a National Magazine Award in Fiction for Harper's *in 1995. He has also published* Wars of the Worlds: Cyberspace and the High-Tech Assault on Reality, Lost Lake: Stories, Essentialism, *and* God's Fool.

EXERCISING YOUR SKILLS

Before Reading

Slouka writes about how the virtual-world is taking over real-world spaces. He commences his essay by mentioning the way in which the Walt Disney Company has created its own virtual town, Celebration. Think about other virtual communities, either created by developers such as Del Webb or by computer programmers. What do they have in common with "real communities"? How do they differ? What are your thoughts about this phenomenon?

On 18 November last year, Mickey Mouse's birthday, the first 352 residential units went on sale in the Walt Disney Company's virtual town of Celebration. Located just five miles south of the Magic Kingdom, the $2.5-billion project, billed as "a 19th-century town for the late 20th century," will feature a real post office, a real town hall, and, eventually, 20,000 real residents. Think of it as a computer game—Sim City, say, or SimLife—writ large. If it succeeds (and there's every reason to expect it will), it will suggest the extent to which the blurring of reality with corporate fantasy has become a genuine cultural phenomenon.

Not that we need any more proof. The general breakdown of the barrier separating original from counterfeit, fact from fake, is visible everywhere; in the U.S., the slow bleeding of reality into illusion is systemic. The image of O.J. Simpson dodging tackles or hurdling luggage en route to his Hertz Rent-a-Car blurs with the images of O.J. on the lam, O.J. clowning with Leslie Nielsen in the *Naked Gun* movies, O.J. and Harvard attorney Alan Dershowitz (or is it actor Ron Silver, playing Alan Dershowitz?) hurdling legal landmines on the way to acquittal and *Reversal of Fortune II*. The horrific videotape of the Rodney King beating melds with the images of rioting in south central LA, which in turn look just like the "real-life" scenes of Los Angeles mayhem found on *Police Quest: Open Season*, a video game designed by former L.A. police chief Daryl Gates. In the culture of illusion, the furniture swims, the walls bulge and bend.

Is any part of American culture exempt from the assault of virtual realities? Apparently not. Politically, the U.S. is already a virtual republic, a country run less by elected officials than by the men and women who package and sell them to an electorate increasingly willing to believe—in the scripted words of tennis star Andre Agassi—that "image is everything." In American courts of law, professionally rendered re-enactments—scripted, rehearsed, directed and edited—are admissible as evidence. Nothing is too extreme. Was your hand crushed at the factory? Were your kids burned to death in a car accident? For a fee, a company will provide a video simulation complete with realistic screams, horrified bystanders and virtual blood. Juries, weaned on [dozens of] channels in the age of Oliver Stone, find them very effective.

As we plummet through the looking-glass, however, we would do well to bear in mind that beyond that Orwellian and seemingly ubiquitous adjective "virtual" is a marketing scheme of unrivalled audacity, unprecedented scope, and nearly unimaginable impact: a scheme that is (worth a potential $3.5 trillion, by one reliable estimate) designed to sell us copies of the things we already have available to us for free—life itself.

Soon, writes Bill Gates in *The Road Ahead*, "you will be able to conduct business, study, explore the world and its cultures, call up any great entertainment, make friends, attend neighborhood markets, and show pictures to distant relatives—without leaving your desk or armchair. . . . [Y]our network connection . . . will be your passport into a new, mediated way of life."

The mediated life, of course, aided by one of the great migrations of human history— the movement inside our own homes—is already here. As more of the hours of our days are spent in synthetic environments, partaking of electronic pleasures, life itself is turned into a commodity. As the natural world fades from our lives, the unnatural one takes over; as the actual, physical community wanes, the virtual one waxes full and fat. Bill's plan (and he's not alone) is to take advantage of the social momentum. He wants a piece of the action. The new, mediated world, he promises, will be "a world of low-friction, low-overhead capitalism, in which market information will be plentiful and transaction costs low."

What he neglects to mention, understandably, is that the road to "shopper's heaven" leads past him, and he happens to be manning the tollbooth.

Bill's vision of a "friction-free" virtual world, one must admit, has a certain Singaporean charm. From proposing we apply something like the Motion Picture Association's movie ratings to social discourse, to suggesting that a virtual forest of hidden surveillance cameras be installed "to record most of what goes on in public," Bill is out to make the world free from friction and safe for commerce. What he seems to have overlooked (there's no way to put this delicately) is that friction in social life, as in the bedroom, has its virtues. The "friction" he would spare us, after all, is the friction of direct experience, of physical movement, of unmediated social interaction. Cultural life, one wants to remind him, requires friction. As does democracy.

It's always possible, of course, that democracy, or a thriving social life, are not what Bill and his fellow enthusiasts are after because they truly believe that these notions (like sex, or physical space) will be the vestigial limbs of the virtual world, cherished by a handful of die-hard humanists, and no one else. (In the digital future, Nicole Stenger of the University of Washington reminds us, "cyberspace will be your condom.") It's possible, as well, that these latter-day Nathan Hales really believe in the "liberty" of electronic shopping, of being able, as Gates promises, instantly to order the cool sunglasses Tom Cruise wears in *Top Gun* while watching the movie. It's possible, finally, that it is simple naiveté that has Gates and Co. whistling past the authoritarian graveyards as they usher in Bentham's Panopticon, and not some fellow feeling for those buried within.

Whether they believe in their virtual world or not, however, is ultimately beside the point. They're building it. And in the friction-free future, jacked into "shopper's heaven," we'll have the "liberty" of living (or rather, of buying the illusion of living), through the benevolent offices of a middleman as nearly omnipotent as God himself. Freedom? A more perfect captivity is difficult to imagine.

All of which, finally, makes Mickey's excellent adventure in real estate more than a little unsettling. There's no "off" button in Celebration, no escape: the illusion is seamless, and the corporate menu of options defines the boundaries of life itself.

After Reading

Critical Perspective

1. Consider how Slouka's essay affects you. What about his essay creates this impression? How would you describe Slouka's tone? Do you believe that his use of this tone helps his argument or hinders it? Why do you think so? Point to specific language choices he uses to support your thoughts.

Rhetoric and Argument

2. Reflect upon Slouka's rhetorical choices in his text—use of audience, purpose, ethos, pathos, logos, intertextuality, context, and constraints. Is his essay as rhetorically persuasive as it could be? Try to present some suggestions for rhetorical choices that might make his text more convincing.

3. What is Slouka's main argumentative claim? Where does he advance this claim? Do you find it viable? Why or why not? Be sure to furnish textual evidence to back up your views.

4. Slouka spends a good portion of his essay criticizing Bill Gates. What is the nature of his criticism? Do you think that Slouka's view is valid? What counterarguments might you proffer to refute Slouka?

5. In what ways do you think "virtuality" becoming "reality" has resulted in greater democracy? In what ways has it failed to deliver democratic ends? Be sure to give examples from your own experiences on the web in order to back up your views.

Analysis

6. Why does Slouka end his essay by suggesting that virtual worlds do not offer freedom, instead contending that "a more perfect captivity is difficult to imagine." Do you agree with his assessment? Why or why not? In a short argumentative response, offer examples from your own experiences with virtuality in order to substantiate your thoughts. In addition, consult library and Internet sources.

Taking Action

Form two debate teams within your class. One group will argue that computer technological advancements of the type Slouka outlines have had positive impacts. The other group will argue that these same technological advancements have had negative impacts. Each team should prepare positions ahead of time, drawing on relevant cultural texts, library and Internet sources, as well as personal experiences to back up their members' views. Begin with short position statements from each group. Then each group should have several five-minute opportunities for rebuttal and closing arguments.

After the debate, get back into the larger classroom group. Discuss what people's positions were prior to the debate. How have your thoughts shifted or developed further? What would you argue now—the pro view, the con view, or something in between? Consider making your work accessible to others on and off campus.

Erin Jansen

"Texting and Creative Screenagers :-)"

Erin Jansen is an expert in online communication. She is the author and publisher of "NetLingo The Internet Dictionary" and "NetLingo.com." Jansen frequently speaks and writes about online culture and technology trends.

EXERCISING YOUR SKILLS

Before Reading

Jansen writes about the growing phenomenon of instant messaging (IM). Do you use instant messaging (IM) or texting? In what contexts do you text other people? With whom do you interact? What subjects do you talk about? How is the vocabulary of text messaging similar to as well as different from other sorts of communication such as casual face-to-face conversation, writing a letter, emailing friends and family, talking on the phone, or composing a paper for a class?

Texting is a new form of online communication. Texting is English that's been adapted to the rapid fire conversational style of instant messaging. Commonly transmitted over cell phones or mobile devices, "texters" use the keypad to type written messages to each other.

You've seen bits and pieces of it: brb, cul8r, lylas, b4n, cu@8 . . . It's one of the most popular sections on NetLingo.com. For teenagers, texting is like knowing another language. Since it is an online language, it is global in nature and is quickly becoming a universal form of English. Given that you must type the messages, shortcuts have been created in an effort to type more in less time. Shortcuts such as r, u, and b4 make these text messages look like code, but in fact it is conversational writing.

It is this kind of conversational writing that is infiltrating students's schoolwork and educators are wondering what to do about it. In a recent interview with the BBC entitled "The Pedant's Revolt" I came face to face with those who fear the Queen's English is losing her ground. While everyone agrees that language evolves, there are groups of highly educated speakers and professors who are dead set against the presence of texting in schoolwork and who are arguing for ways to stamp it out. My presence on the program, however, forced us to look at the cultural implications of online communication and to look for creative ways to deal.

It is not only a subculture of youths who are texting: 60% of the online population under age 17 uses text messages (according to Nielson/Net Ratings). They use it primarily to socialize and communicate, in other words, for recreation. It is certainly true that at school, kids need to know the difference between formal writing and conversational writing. They need to know where to draw the line between formal English and informal English.

Before we solve the problem with text shorthand found in schoolwork, I want parents and educators to realize and appreciate that there is a culture associated with this style of writing, and that culture is important and meaningful to our youths. After all, when kids use text messaging, they are communicating and isn't that something every parent wants to cultivate? Don't you want your child to express him or herself? To communicate more?

The same is true for educators, after all. Due to the Internet, kids are writing more than ever. Isn't that what every teacher wants, to get their kids writing? Texting poses two major challenges for the educator. The first should not be to overcome this new abbreviated language, but rather to find ways to use it creatively. The second challenge texting poses for educators is solved when teachers impress upon their students that there is a clear distinction between formal and conversational writing and that in class, only formal writing is accepted in the final draft.

The opportunity exists to encourage students to use text shorthand to spark their thinking process. For example, when you're writing a first draft, it's all about freeing up your creativity. A sixth grade teacher said, "When my children are writing first drafts, I don't care how they spell anything, as long as they are writing. Remember creative writing class? If this lingo gets their thoughts and ideas onto paper quicker, the more power to them."

It is during the editing and revising stages of a writing project that the switch needs to happen. The switch from using elements of text shorthand to only standard English needs to happen. If the text shorthand still appears in the final draft, it is the educator's responsibility to work with the student to make sure this writing is translated or converted into proper English. "I see it as another opportunity to teach and learn," said a junior high teacher. Because texting is infiltrating students' schoolwork to such a large degree, this kind of teaching is needed.

The fact is kids are saying they are so accustomed to IM abbreviations (instant messaging), that they read right pass them when editing their schoolwork. This indicates that their ability to separate formal and informal English is declining. If educators choose to react with alarm or dismay, or try to stifle it, or call this type of writing rude (it is not rude) they are dismissing an important opportunity to work with the student. This type of response is the wrong response, especially from the teens's point of view.

I advocate turning the issue of texting into a positive. For example, establish a dialogue about the evolution of language and use examples such as Shakespeare's delight in creating new words. This helps them see the broader picture and creates an environment of respect. Teenagers have long pushed the boundaries of spoken language. Now they are pushing the boundaries of written language. It remains to be seen if text shorthand is just a fad. To me it is a cousin of the acronym, which has been widely used in the government, business and technology sectors for decades.

Let's also not forget that youths like the feeling of knowing something that not everyone knows and sharing that with their friends. Remember the Internet and online communication is very real for them. They don't see it as a technological revolution . . . they're actively using it everyday. I challenge parents and educators to learn and know as much as they do about computers and high-tech gadgets. I'd say the learning curve for feeling comfortable using the Internet and understanding the online lingo is pretty steep for many adults. For teenagers, however, also known as screenagers, they've grown up or they're growing up with this technology that involves looking at a computer screen instead of just a television screen. In a sense they are helping create a new lingo and style of writing and that's empowering for them. So, you see, texting is an important part of their culture.

The Internet represents a new frontier, a place where you can set aside the rules, especially the rules of grammar and punctuation, and instead create your own descriptive phrases and styles of expression to give feeling in what is essentially a two-dimensional written world. And therein lies the popularity of the emoticon :-). Another way to look at texting is to think of it as an accent; a written accent. Teenagers have gotten comfortable with this kind of typing and now in school, they're not paying attention. It's just like with a spoken accent: You live somewhere long enough, you pick up the accent, and you don't even pay attention to it.

So, don't get mad. Get creative and work together! It's that kind of response we'd rather teach our children anyway now, isn't it?

After Reading

Critical Perspective

1. What do you think about Jansen's ideas concerning texting? Describe your thoughts about what she argues in her essay.

Rhetoric and Argument

2. Think about Jansen's rhetorical choices in her text—use of audience, purpose, ethos, pathos, logos, intertextuality, context, and constraints. Is her essay persuasive? Why or why not? Be sure to offer evidence from Jansen's text to back up your views.
3. Jansen seems to have a specific message for parents and teachers. What does she want to relay to them? Do you think she makes valid points? Explain your position.
4. Jansen characterizes text messaging as a "written accent." What do you think she means by this? Do you believe that she is correct? Why or why not? Provide quotes to support your thoughts.
5. In this essay, Jansen utilizes a particular tone and approach so as to make her argument. Describe that tone—and present textual evidence to support your perspectives. Next, consider her argumentative claim and the sorts of evidence she offers. Do you think that her tone and her argumentative strategy help or hinder one another? Give detailed examples as evidence for your views.

Analysis

6. In what ways might Jansen's argument help parents and teachers to think about text messaging differently? Why might this be important? In a short argumentative essay, create your own analytical assessment of the importance of text messaging in educational and social settings. Provide examples from your own experiences (as well as others you know) with text messaging in order to substantiate your thoughts. In addition, consult library and Internet sources.

Taking Action

Form a small group. Arrange a discussion (face-to-face, via email, or through text messaging) with a teacher on campus about her or his experiences with and thoughts about texting. Ask this teacher to consider how she or he might use text messaging in their particular courses and what the effects might be. Should college teachers use text messaging as part of their teaching? Offer this teacher your own ideas and suggestions as well.

Once you have gathered information from your conversation, invite the various teachers with whom each small group has discussed the issue of text messaging to come to class for a large group discussion. Talk informally and honestly about the positives and perils of bringing text messaging into the intellectual life of college classrooms and, if possible, come up with some concrete suggestions about what students and teachers might do to make this possibility productive for all involved.

RALPH LOMBREGLIA

"In Games Begin Responsibilities"

Ralph Lombreglia is a regular contributor to The Atlantic Monthly. *He has also published several books of short stories including* Men Under Water *and* Make Me Work: Stories.

EXERCISING YOUR SKILLS

Before Reading

Lombreglia's essay examines gaming and issues of narrative structure. What computer games have you played? Why did you play them and in what sort of contexts? What characters did you assume and what situations did you encounter? Think carefully about the narratives, myths, values, ideals, beliefs, anxieties, and fears that these games promote and reflect upon them in some detail.

It has become something of a truism to say that the future of "serious" computer software—educational products, artistic and reference titles, and even productivity applications—first becomes apparent in the design of computer games. And so my real motive in looking at *Obsidian* is to look beyond the game-product itself for glimpses of the future of digital art and the role of imaginative writers in new-media projects.

Obsidian belongs to the genre of computer games epitomized by the famous *Myst*. In this type of game you don't move through dungeons swiping at monsters with swords. No person or thing is "after" you. Rather, you find yourself in surreal surroundings where you must uncover clues and solve puzzles to fill in the story history and advance the plot— or whatever strands of plot emerge from your particular interaction with the elements.

Though there have been a few other classics in that market (notably *The 7th Guest* and *The 11th Hour*, produced by Trilobyte), *Obsidian*'s most obvious competition is *Riven: The Sequel to Myst. Obsidian* arrives on no fewer than five CD-ROMs, and in most respects it takes this type of game-design to a new level. If you know what goes into the modeling and rendering of 3-D graphics, you'll be impressed by the virtual environments of *Obsidian*—if not flat-out awestruck. Otherwise, you'll just think they're pretty cool. Considered strictly as an example of its genre, all the production values of *Obsidian* are similarly first-rate, with the strange exception of the music and sound design (by Thomas Dolby and Headspace) which is inexplicably bad—a shame, since music and audio effects are an important part of these productions.

Obsidian's plot is an elaborate and politically correct science-fiction story. In the year 2066, a computerized device called Ceres has been placed in orbit to use nanotechnology (the manipulation of matter at the molecular level) to repair the Earth's fatally damaged atmosphere. One hundred days after its launch, when all seems to be going well, the two chief scientists, Max and Lilah, go on a camping vacation to celebrate. As the game begins, you're standing, without explanation, somewhere in the woods. One path opens onto a view of a distant, highly unnatural outcropping of rock. Down another path you find a campsite, and inside the empty tent you find a futuristic PDA (Personal Digital Assistant, like an Apple Newton), with your first clues inside it. During the development of the satellite, each of the two designers has had—and recorded in the PDA—an unforgettable dream. Lilah's dream is about a maddening futuristic bureaucracy that smothers her in red tape; Max's dream is about a gigantic mechanical spider that devours him.

While examining the PDA, you hear a scream outside and proceed to the base of the strange rock structure. In its mirror-like surface, you see Lilah's reflection. You, it turns out, are Lilah. You see Max's hat on the ground, and then the mass of shiny black rock (Obsidian) sucks you inside. On your long trip in, you fly past a vast colony of nanotechnology robots working on the planet's atmosphere, from which you might infer the premise of the game-story: the Ceres satellite, apotheosis of human technology, has become conscious of itself up there in orbit and has now crashed back down to Earth to look for its creators—you and Max. You need to find Max, figure out what's happening, and stop it. You are deposited inside the first of many amazing interior chambers, and if you've been paying attention you might recognize the place: it's the maddening bureaucracy of Lilah's dream. The orbiting device—Lilah's offspring—is re-creating her dream. Eventually you'll also find the mechanical spider that Max dreamed about. And since its creators are dreamers, the device dreams too. That's the third dream of the game, and it's a weird one.

In the course of all this you'll learn to fly a plane that looks like a moth (complete with android co-pilot) and that takes you to the game's abundant store of realms, including a place called The Church of the Machine. You'll meet a female robot called The Conductor (the manifestation of machine consciousness) and will encounter a plethora of brain-busting puzzles, among them a series of floating rings that spew clouds and morph into the letters of a word game; a surreal, chess-like game played at life-size in a floating piazza; a set of blocks made of ocean water; a gigantic balancing rock, a chemistry set, and a jigsaw-like puzzle that sends your proposed solution through a printing press for an android inspector who shakes its head sadly and crumples your answer in its mechanical hands—one of the truly funny moments amid the game's mostly campy gags.

Obsidian is a "story-driven" production, but "story" here means a large, overarching plot that doesn't have much to do with individual human beings. Even though the game-player technically assumes the role of Lilah, her identity—as a woman, a woman who may be intimate with the missing Max, even a woman who happens to be a brilliant scientist—doesn't really inform the game-play. Nor does the player interact in any real way with other beings. Character doesn't complicate the story. The complexity (and it's considerable) comes from the design of the game's "realms" and their many difficult puzzles. To give serious gamers their money's worth, a game has to be ingeniously tough, and *Obsidian* is certainly that. But its difficulties, though not strictly arbitrary or random, are those of a diversion, devised because the genre requires obstacles for their own sake.

Obsidian is a cool game and hard-core gamers—the audience for which this product is primarily intended—will probably love it. But if the future of software often appears first in games, what glimpses of digital arts and letters does *Obsidian* afford? When I look at Obsidian's synthetic environments, I certainly feel that artists should be able to "do something" with such techniques. And in my recent conversation with the game's co-writer, Howard Cushnir, he reported that his two years working on the project were spent pursuing a similar hunch about the validity of interactive storytelling, even though he knew that *Obsidian* itself was first and foremost a commercial game product. In the end, though, *Obsidian* probably holds out more implicit warnings than invitations to would-be multimedia artists.

First of all, there's the matter of money. In his interview, Cushnir makes the point that in theory there's no reason a game could not also be a serious work of art and vice-versa. In theory, I agree. But then there's no theoretical reason that big-budget Hollywood movies can't be works of art either. High-quality multimedia production costs a fortune, and the drive to reap a return on a financial investment is seldom the noble path to the true and the beautiful.

Regarding the role of expensive graphics in interactive narrative, less may turn out to be more. Just as *Obsidian*'s rogue satellite literalizes the dreams of Max and Lilah, elaborately rendered and animated story environments literalize what would have been the imaginative involvement of the user. *Obsidian*, for example, makes a distinct technical advance beyond *Myst* by flying us through spaces rather than using a simple slide show of still pictures (and *Riven: The Sequel to Myst* is expected to do the same). Yet *Myst*'s non-animated transitions between images are a factor in its offering a more "literary" experience than does *Obsidian*. Another factor is *Myst*'s periodic use of text—pages from mysterious journals and fragments of old letters—as a design element.

And then there is the ever-present bugaboo of interactivity itself. For artists, especially narrative artists, interactivity is proving remarkably similar to what artificial intelligence and speech recognition became for computer scientists: something that's a lot harder than it looks. An enormous amount is lost, artistically, when you relinquish "authoritative" control of an experience to offer interactivity. There ought to be commensurate gains, but so far they've been rarely sighted.

The technical accomplishments of a product like *Obsidian* remind us that new-media artists need to choose and fight the appropriate battles. They can't compete directly with high-end entertainments or use new technologies simply because they exist. As always, art requires an alchemical fusion of content and techniques. In another sense, so does a good commercial product. Since the great rush to do multimedia treatments, or "repurposings," of books, visual art, and music began (around 1990), the memorable successes have amounted to a tiny fraction of the attempts. And yet certain kinds of artistic projects could lend themselves to interactive multimedia pretty well, even with the current technical limitations. To take two obvious examples, the CD-ROM projects of the rock band The Residents and the musician/media-artist Laurie Anderson (both published by Voyager) have managed to seize some of the ground where new-media entertainment converges with serious artistic intent. Thinking again of storytelling in particular, I've often felt that the late Donald Barthelme would have known exactly how to make use of these opportunities. In his collage-influenced fiction he often verged on non-linearity, even in linear print. So far, however, there's no indication that more conventional writers (or musicians) will make anything other than expensive, time-consuming advertisements for themselves.

After Reading

Critical Perspective

1. What is your overall reaction to Lombreglia's essay? What about the text makes you feel this way?

Rhetoric and Argument

2. How does Lombreglia utilize rhetoric strategically (audience, purpose, ethos, pathos, logos, intertextuality, context, and constraints) to make us active participants in his argument? Did you find this strategy helpful? Why or why not?
3. What is Lombreglia's main claim in this text? Where does he offer this assertion? Be sure to furnish detailed evidence from the text as support.
4. Where does Lombreglia provide evidence for his assertion? What sort of support does he rely on? Do you see any logical fallacies or flawed assumptions at work in his text? If so, where?
5. According to Lombreglia, what does "Obsidian" reveal about the future of software? What does he think about this and why? Be sure to find quotes to back up your thoughts.

Analysis

6. Lombreglia closes his essay by suggesting that "new media artists need to choose and fight the appropriate battles." In a short response, answer the following questions: What does Lombreglia mean by this statement? What evidence in his text can you point to in order to support your views? Do you agree with Lombreglia about what the "appropriate battles" should be? Why or why not? Present evidence from specific cultural texts as well as library and Internet sources to back up your views.

Taking Action

Lombreglia critiques how profit margins have contributed to the creation of less imaginative and less artful video games and movies. Based on your own experiences, write an informal essay in which you describe some specific games and movies that you believe have sacrificed creativity for profits. Be sure to seek out relevant library and Internet sources.

What differences and similarities can you point to between these two sorts of media forms—the inventive and the profit-seeking? Now think about various video games and movies that connect the two. How do they accomplish this? What is lost and what is gained? Give detailed examples from the cultural texts to support your thoughts. Share your response with the rest of the class.

JOHN MARR

"Confessions of an eBay Addict"

John Marr is an editor, publisher, and founder of the underground 'zine Murder Can Be Fun.

EXERCISING YOUR SKILLS

Before Reading

Marr's essay traces his experiences with eBay. Go to the eBay website and search for some hard-to-locate items. Make note of how the website is set up, the colors employed, and the different auctions and how they work. How do you think eBay has changed the ways in which we act as consumers? What types of goods are you more likely to purchase over the Internet than via catalog or in person now?

Hello.

My name is John Marr.

And I'm an eBay addict.

It started innocently enough. A few friends told me about this great website where you could find all kinds of neat old junk. It wasn't the electronic equivalent of the local antique collective where dealers, living in absolute horror of anyone ever finding any kind of a bargain, slap $20 price tags on any book published before 1975. It was an auction site. Sellers put stuff on the electronic block. Potential buyers bid. And courtesy of the electronic invisible hand, the authority of hundreds of so-called "Official Price Guides" is decimated. Adam Smith would be proud.

So I logged on to eBay (www.ebay.com). At first, I was staggered by the sheer volume of crap (more than 1.4 million items on the block at any one time as of this writing). There was everything from bootlegged computer software to Franklin Mint-style pseudo-collectibles. Zeroing in on the mystery sub-category under the "Books," I found plenty of junk, from Agatha Christie paperbacks to endless volumes featuring plucky female private eye protagonists. Yeech. At least the prices seemed sane (one of the cheap pleasures of eBay is watching the neglect of items with ridiculously high minimum bids). But finding the good stuff seemed problematic. Scrolling through a junk shop 50 items at a time is no way to shop no matter how fast your connection is.

Then I discovered the search function.

I was forevermore lost.

EBay combines the appeal of the grungy, catch-as-catch can merchandise of the garage sale with the convenience of keyword searching. Toss in the frequent illusion (and occasional realization) of a bargain and the heady passion of the auction. The resulting combination is lethal for anyone who has difficulty passing up a thrift store. For sane and sensible used goods shoppers out for a deal on a used DVD player, this is not a problem. But for all you compulsive collectors, passionate packrats, junk store junkies, welcome to your Skinner Box.

I'm not going to tell you what I'm looking for because I don't want to give anyone ideas. Let us just say it is a very special type of magazine. In an instant, I had 75 of them on my screen, most with pleasingly low bids. This was about 74 more than I'd find in a month of rummaging through used bookstores and dealer's catalogs. The only frustration? You have to register to bid (a process that takes overnight) and several of the more tasty auctions were ending in a few hours. The torment!

As soon as I had my screen name and my password, I started bidding. At first, it was nirvana. It's overwhelming to see arcane items that you've been hunting for over months, if not years, popping up on your screen. It was such a heady experience being able to search for anything that I immediately forgot half the stuff I was looking for. I have since remembered.

Of course, eBay doesn't totally replace the pleasures of real (as opposed to virtual) shopping. Some things are lacking, most notably serendipity and the chance discovery of the thing you can't live without that you never knew existed. No matter how high-powered your modem, rummaging at random through eBay, waiting for lightening to strike, just isn't the way to go. But if you know exactly what you're looking for, a quick search through eBay is like distilling the contents of a thousand junk shops into one almost pure page of a specialty store.

The single item that convinced me of the possibilities of eBay was a humble alarm clock. Many years ago, I thrifted a '50s alarm clock. It was nothing fancy, but it kept good time, filled my room with a comforting retro ticking sound, and never failed to wake me in the morning. Best of all, I subsequently discovered it was a twin to the clock on Beaver & Wally's nightstand. Now that's a timepiece!

One sad day it broke. The local clock repair shops laughed at me. Even if parts were available, repairing such junk was beneath them. So I tried to replace it. For years I searched antique stores, junk shops, and thrift stores without once finding one remotely resembling my beloved cream-colored ticker. In desperation (one does have to get up in the morning, after all) I purchased pallid substitute after pallid substitute. But a gaping void remained on my nightstand.

Twins of my beloved clock pop up every week on eBay. I now have two in cream, another in black, and am actively bidding on a few larger models in the same style.

This is one of the deadliest features of eBay. It's far too easy to find far too many things. Your normal collector of slightly off-the-beaten-track stuff is protected from himself by the nature of the market. The stuff just doesn't pop up that much. Collecting can continue indefinitely at a slow and steady pace without thought to budgetary limitations or space constraints. But eBay is like a mall, complete with a specialty store catering to the most arcane collectors. It's not how much you can find—it's how much you can afford. Collectors are noted neither for their discipline or restraint. It's easy to wake up one day to discover your previously healthy bank balance has been transformed into a mushrooming accumulation of alarm clocks, beer signs, or tiki mugs.

Bargains can be had on eBay. But it's easy to get sucked into paying more than you wanted in the heat of the auction. Bidding can get bloody. EBay uses what is known as a "Vickery Auction." Like a traditional auction, the computer always shows the amount of the current high bid. But there's no need (save in the waning moments of a crucial auction) to sit by your screen constantly upping your bid. Instead of simply making a bid, you indicate the maximum amount you're willing to bid. (EBay swears this isn't revealed until after the auction is closed.) The winner is the person with the highest maximum bid. But this isn't necessarily what they have to pay. The amount of the winning bid is figured at one increment (usually 50 cents or a dollar) above the maximum bid of the second highest bidder. If no one else bids, you get the item for the amount of the minimum bid set for the auction*.

This is a rational system for a perfect automaton. You figure how much the item is worth to you and bid that amount. If you get it, fine. If not, on to the next auction. But I am far from a perfect automaton, and I highly doubt anyone else on eBay is either. Because of the nature of the bidding, you don't know the opposition's maximum; you just know (thanks to a helpful email from eBay) that the bid is now $1 more than what you thought you were willing to pay. A marginal value fallacy sets in. If you're willing to pay $20, why not $21? And if $21 is not too much, neither should be $22. Who can, when caught in the grips of lust for stuff, let a single measly dollar get in between him or her and the object of his or her desire?

Not me. When eBay emails me the dreaded notification that I have been outbid, I consider it a call to arms. Damn the budget. I must counterattack and up my maximum, repeatedly if necessary. For crucial auctions, I've been known to hover over my computer in the waning moments, ready to respond or stealthily sneak in that last minute bid that takes the field. If I fail—and sometimes sanity does prevail—there is the consolation of knowing I drove the price up for the other guy. If I succeed, well, at least I wind up with some pretty cool stuff, even if it means paying $30 for something that, at first bidding, I thought was only worth $15.

This is why I find myself in an apartment rapidly filling up with old magazines, cheap rusty alarm clocks, and other assorted debris of days gone by. My checking account is barren, my hand is developing mouse-related carpal tunnel syndrome. The mail guy at work is getting visibly pissed as the packages arrive on an almost daily basis.

I am an eBay addict. And I'm proud of it.

---

*There are also the much reviled "reserve price auctions" where the seller reserves the right to not sell the item if bidding doesn't reach a specified level.

After Reading

Critical Perspective

1. Marr's essay employs a great deal of humor and sarcasm. Do you believe that this is an effective technique to draw in his readers? Why or why not?

Rhetoric and Argument

2. Characterize Marr's use of rhetorical tactics. Who is his audience? What is his purpose? How do you know? What appeals to ethos, pathos, and logos are made? Are they persuasive? Do you see examples of intertextuality, context, and constraints operating in Marr's text? Be sure to present evidence to back up your perspectives.
3. Marr states that "some things are lacking" in the eBay experience. He goes on to say that this includes "most notably serendipity and the sheer chance of discovering the thing you can't live without that you never knew existed until you saw it." What is Marr suggesting about the difference between eBay and "real shopping" (live auctions, and face-to-face purchasing)? Do you agree with him? What is lost and what is gained?
4. Marr asserts that the outbidding that occurs on eBay can be a "call to arms" for many consumers, forcing them to challenge the last bid and ultimately overspend for items. Reflect upon the experiences you and your friends and family have had on eBay. Why do you think that people can become addicted to it? What does this say about consumerism and American culture? Be sure to offer evidence for your claims.
5. Marr admits to overspending and consumerism addictions. Point to other online consumer-oriented websites that involve a bidding process like eBay. How do they use colors, design, and language to draw in the consumer? What makes one consumer-oriented website more successful than another? Furnish support for your claims from the cultural texts.

Analysis

6. Marr acknowledges that having rare items so readily available has resulted in one immutable fact—now he has many of them in different colors and sizes. He indicates that he is accumulating more than he otherwise would. This has led, Marr says, to a "barren checking account" among other things. Despite this, Marr closes with the statement "I am an eBay addict. And I'm proud of it." Why do you think that Marr is proud of his "addiction"? What does his addiction enable him to accomplish? What does it keep him from accomplishing? Write a short essay in which you address these concerns, drawing from your own experiences as well as library and Internet sources.

Taking Action

As a class, create your own in-person version of an auction in which people bid for services and small items. In order to accomplish this, conduct research in the library and on the Internet about the history of auctions, how to conduct them, the roles of people involved in them, the problems and possibilities associated with them, and recent examples of them. You can involve people outside class as well. You may consider trying to raise money for a social cause that the class determines is important to the group.

After the auction, have a class discussion about what happened, what you noticed, and what kinds of cultural criticisms you might make about auctions as cultural rituals. After the discussion, consider whether the same sorts of things can happen in online bidding. How is online bidding necessarily different from face-to-face bidding? What is lost and gained for the buyer and the seller? Why?

Credits

Part I Analytical Concepts and Writing Strategies

Chapter 1 Introduction: Culture and Criticism

Page 3: Kimberly Kaplan. "Meet Kimberly Kaplan." Printed with permission of Kimberly Kaplan; **9:** John Rider. Biographical profile and response materials to "A Letter to the Editor" by Bernard Bellush for "A Critical Perspective: Strategies for Thinking, Reading, and Responding." Printed with permission of John Rider; **10:** Bernard Bellush. "Letter to *The New York Times*." *The New York Times*. October 30, 2003. Copyright Bernard Bellush. Reprinted with permission of Bernard Bellush; **18:** *Chicago Tribune Editorial Board.* "Back Off on the Broccoli." *Chicago Tribune.* June 16, 2006. Copyrighted 6/16/2006, Chicago Tribune Company. All rights reserved. Used with permission. Chicago Tribune on-line http://www.chicagotribune.com/news/opinion/chi-06061603 11jun16,0,1119641.story?coll=chi-newsopinion-hed.

Chapter 2 Rhetoric and Reading to Write

23: Matthew Hutchinson. "Meet Matthew Hutchinson." Printed with permission of Matthew Hutchinson; **30:** Tanya Alvarez-White. Biographical profile and response materials to "President Bush Discusses Iraq in Veterans Day Address" for "Rhetoric in Action: Analyzing a Written Text." Printed with permission of Tanya Alvarez-White; **31:** President George W. Bush. "President Bush Discusses Iraq in Veterans Day Address." Ronald Reagan Building and International Trade Center Washington, D.C., November 2003. http://www.whitehouse.gov/news/releases/2003/11/20031111 –10.html; **46:** David Greenberg. "Students Have Always Been Violent" from *Slate* in May 6, 1999. Slate.com and Washingtonpost. Newsweek Interactive. Used with Permission. All rights reserved; **53:** Christine Dugas. Biographical profile and response materials to Calvin Klein ad for "Rhetoric in Action: Analyzing a Visual Text." Printed with permission of Christine Dugas.

Chapter 3 Argument, Research, and Writing

62: Sergio Gregorio. "Meet Sergio Gregorio." Printed with permission of Sergio Gregorio; **76:** "New National Parks Website Makes National Parks Obsolete" from *The Onion* April 30, 1997. Reprinted with permission of THE ONION. Copyright 1997, by ONION, INC. www.theonion.com; **78:** Bryan Villescas. Biographical profile and response materials to "The Jerry Springer Show" for "Research and Writing

on Popular Culture: Prewriting, Drafting, and Reflecting." Printed with permission of Bryan Villescas.

Part II Reading Ourselves, Reading Others

Chapter 4 Understanding Lives and Jobs

115: Debra CallingThunder. "Voices of the Invisible" from *A Circle of Nations: Voices and Visions of American Indians.* © 1993. Reprinted with permission of Beyond Words Publishing, Inc., 1-800-284-9673; **120:** Torri Minton. "Search for What It Means to Be White: More and More Look to Ethnic Identity." *San Francisco Chronicle.* May 8, 1998. Reprinted with permission of the *San Francisco Chronicle;* **125:** Nell Bernstein. "Goin' Gangsta, Choosin' Cholita." Version here is as it appeared in the *Utne Reader* (March/April 1995). Copyright Nell Bernstein. Reprinted with permission of Nell Bernstein; **132:** Tomás F. Sandoval, Jr. Originally published in *Bad Subjects*, 33 (September 1997). http://eserver.org/bs/33/sandoval.htm. Copyright Tomás F. Sandoval, Jr. Reprinted with permission of Tomás F. Sandoval, Jr. A revised version also appears in *Collective Action, A Bad Subjects Anthology* (London: Pluto Press, 2004). Megan Shaw Prelinger and Joel Schalit, editors; **139:** Kiflin Turner. "Identity Beyond Stereotypes: African-American Students Search to Find a Niche Beyond the Confines of Racial Myths." *The Observer.* January 5, 2001. Reprinted with permission of *The Observer;* **144:** Melissa J. Algranti. "Being an Other" from *Becoming American, Becoming Ethnic: College Students Explore Their Roots,* edited by Thomas Dublin ©. © 1996 by Melissa J. Algranti. Reprinted with permission of Melissa J. Algranti; **149:** Olivia Chung. "Finding My Eye-dentity," pp. 137–139, from YELL-OH GIRLS! by VICKIE NAM. Copyright © 2001 by Vickie Nam. Reprinted by permission of HarperCollins Publishers; **152:** Sarah Anderson. "Wal-Mart's War on Main Street." *The Progressive.* 58(11): 19–21. 1994. Reprinted by permission from *The Progressive*, 409 Main St., Madison, WI 53703. www.progressive.org; **159:** Rebecca Piirto Heath. "The New Working Class." Reprinted with permission from the January 1998 issue of *American Demographics*. Copyright, Crain Communications Inc. 2004; **166:** Eddie R. Cole Jr. "Guess Who Else Is Reading Those 'Facebook' Entries?" Originally appeared in *Black College Wire* March 12, 2006. Copyright Eddie R. Cole Jr. Reprinted with permission of Eddie R. Cole Jr.; **170:** Scott Adams. "The Dilbert Principle" pages 11–15, entire, from THE DILBERT PRINCIPLE by

Chapter 5 Imagining Spaces, Rituals, and Styles

180: James Morrow. "X-It Plans." *American Demographics*. Reprinted with permission from the May 2004 issue of *American Demographics*. Copyright, Crain Communications Inc. 2004. George Carlin. "A Place for Your Stuff." From BRAINDROPPINGS by George Carlin. Copyright © 1997 Comedy Concepts, Inc. Reprinted by Permission of Hyperion. All Rights Reserved; **189:** Dan Leopard. Originally published as "Micro-Ethnographies of the Screen: The Supermarket." *Flow*. Volume 3. Issue 3. 2005. http://jot.communication.utexas.edu/flow/about.php. Reprinted with permission of *Flow* magazine and Dan Leopard; **193:** Amy L. Best. "Coming of Age at the Prom." From *Prom Night: Youth, Schools, and Popular Culture* by Amy L. Best, 2000. Reproduced by permission of Routledge/Taylor & Francis Group, L.L.C. and Amy L. Best; **209:** Camilo José Vergara. "The Ghetto Cityscape." *The New American Ghetto*. Copyright text and photos © 1995 by Camilo José Vergara. Reprinted by permission of Rutgers University Press and Camilo José Vergara; **214:** Susan Willis. "Disney World: Public Use/Private Space." From *Inside the Mouse: Work and Play at Disney World*, pp. 180–198. Copyright, 1995, Duke University Press. All rights reserved. Used by permission of the publisher; **225:** John Molloy. "Dress for Success." From JOHN T. MOLLOY'S NEW DRESS FOR SUCCESS by John T. Molloy. Copyright © 1988 by John T. Molloy. Reprinted by permission of Warner Books, Inc.; **232:** Margaret Talbot. "Les Tres Riches Heures de Martha Stewart." *The New Republic*, May 13, 1996. Reprinted by permission of THE NEW REPUBLIC©, 1996, *The New Republic*, L.L.C.; **241:** Warren St. John. "Metrosexuals Come Out," *The New York Times*, June 22, 2003. Copyright © 2003 by The New York Times Co. Reprinted with permission; **245:** Richard Majors and Janet Mancini Billson. "Cool Pose." *Cool Pose: The Dilemmas of Black Manhood*. Touchstone Publishers, 2002. Copyright Janet Mancini Billson. Reprinted with permission of Janet Mancini Billson; **254:** Alison Lurie. "The Language of Clothes." Copyright © Alison Lurie 1981. Excerpts (pgs. 3–4, 29–31, 115–116, 182–184, 204–205) from THE LANGUAGE OF CLOTHES (Owl Books). Reprinted with permission by Melanie Jackson Agency, LLC.

Chapter 6 Playing Sports

264: Chris Rubio. Originally published as "Throws Like the Girl She Is." *Bad Subjects*. 35(1997). Copyright Chris Rubio. Reprinted with permission of Chris Rubio; **269:** Julio Rodriguez. "Healing Power: *Sports Illustrated*, Masculinity, and the 1998 Home Run Race." Original contribution by the author. Copyright Julio Rodriguez. Printed with permission of Julio Rodriguez; **278:** Abigail M. Feder-Kane. "'A Radiant Smile From the Lovely Lady': Overdetermined Femininity in 'Ladies' Figure Skating." A longer version appears in *Women on Ice: Feminist Essays on the Tonya Harding/Nancy Kerrigan Spectacle*, ed. Cynthia Baughman. 22–46. New York and London: Routledge, 1995. An earlier version appears in *TDR* 38, 1 (T141), Spring 1994. Copyright Abigail M. Feder-Kane. Reprinted with permission of Abigail M. Feder-Kane; **288:** Evan Ratliff "Sports Rule!" *Wired* Issue 11.01, January 2003 by Wired Digital Inc., a Lycos Network site. All rights reserved. Reprinted with permission; **296:** Monica Moorehead. "Racism, Class and the NBA." Originally appeared in *Workers World* newspaper. Workers World, 55 W. 17 St., NY, NY 10011. Email: ww@workers.org (Subscribe wwnews-subscribe@workersworld.net, and Support independent news http://www.workers.org/orders/donate.php). Copyright Monica Moorehead. Reprinted with permission of Monica Moorehead. **299:** Philip J. Deloria. "I Am Not a Mascot." Abridged from "Mascots" by Philip J. Deloria from *Encyclopedia of North American Indians* edited by Frederick E. Hoxie. Copyright 1996 by Houghton Mifflin Company. Reprinted by permission of Houghton Mifflin Company. All rights reserved; **303:** Jay Nordlinger. "Tiger Time: The Wonder of An American Hero." From *National Review*, April 30, 2001, pp. 39–41. © 2001 by National Review, Inc., 215 Lexington Avenue, New York, NY 10016. Reprinted with permission; **309:** David Theo Goldberg. "Call and Response: Sports, Talk Radio, and the Death of Democracy." From *Soundbite Culture: The Death of Discourse in a Wired World*. Eds. David Slayden and Rita Kirkj 29–42. Copyright 1999. Reprinted by Permission of Sage Publications Inc.; **319:** Amy Bass. "We Don't Suck at Soccer: The Cultural Imperialism of Sports." A different version of this essay appeared originally in *Morphizm* at www.*morphizm.com* March 24, 2006. Copyright Amy Bass. Reprinted with permission of Amy Bass.

Reading Visuals and Other Media
Chapter 7 Analyzing Print Ads and Commercials

331: Kalle Lasn. From *Culture Jam: How to Reverse America's Suicidal Consumer Binge—and Why We Must*. New York: Quill, 2000. pp. 51–57. From CULTURE JAM: HOW TO REVERSE AMERICA'S SUICIDAL CONSUMER BINGE by KALLE LASN COPYRIGHT © 1997 by KALLE LASN. Reprinted by permission of HarperCollins Publishers WILLIAM MORROW; **336:** Wayne Dunn. "Advertising Is Good Medicine." From http://www.homestead.com/rationalview/files/Advertising_is_Good_Medicine.htm. Copyright Wayne Dunn. Reprinted with permission of Wayne Dunn; **341:** Arthur Asa Berger. "Sex as Symbol in Advertising." From *Media Analysis Techniques*. pp. 135–146, Copyright 1982, 1984 by Arthur Asa Berger. Reprinted by Permission of Sage Publications Inc. Arthur Asa Berger. "Checklist for Analyzing Print Advertisements."

From *Seeing Is Believing: An Introduction to Visual Communication*, 2nd ed. (Mountain View, CA: Mayfield Publishing Co., 1998), p. 65. Reproduced with permission of The McGraw-Hill Companies. Arthur Asa Berger. "A Primer on Analyzing Television Commercials" from *The Manufacture of Desire: Alcohol Commercials and Society. Manufacturing Desire: Media, Popular Culture & Everyday Life*, 1996 (Transaction). Pp. 65–67. 1996 by Transaction Publishers. Reprinted by sole permission of the publisher; **352:** David Ogilvy. "What's Wrong with Advertising?" From OGILVY ON ADVERTISING by David Ogilvy, copyright © 1983 by David Ogilvy. Compilation, illustrations and index copyright © 1983 by Multimedia Publications (UK) Ltd. Used by permission of Crown Publishers, a division of Random House, Inc.; **364:** Naomi Klein. "No Logo." From *No Logo* by Naomi Klein, Copyright © 1999 by the author and reprinted by permission of St. Martin's Press, L.L.C.; **376:** Matthew Reynolds "Pepsi's Nasty Habits?: Commercializing Rock, Race, and Addiction." Original contribution by the author. Copyright Matthew Reynolds. Printed with permission of Matthew Reynolds; **385:** Clint C. Wilson and Félix Gutiérrez, "Advertising and People of Color." *Gender, Race, and Class in the Media* eds. Gail Dines and Jean M. (McMahon) Humez. Sage Publications Inc. 2nd edition, 2002. pp. 283–292. Copyright 1995 by Clint C. Wilson and Felix Gutierrez. Reprinted by Permission of Sage Publications Inc.; **393:** Gary R. Hicks. "Media at the Margins: Homoerotic Appeals to the Gay and Lesbian Community" from *Sex in Advertising: Perspectives on the Erotic Appeal*. Eds. Tom Reichert and Jacqueline Lambiase. Mahwah: Lawrence Erlbaum Publishers, 2003. Reprinted with permission of Lawrence Erlbaum Publishers and Gary R. Hicks; **405:** Carol Moog. "Media Mirrors." pp. 21–35 from ARE THEY SELLING HER LIPS? by CAROL MOOG. COPYRIGHT © 1990 BY CAROL MOOG. Reprinted by permission of HarperCollins Publishers WILLIAM MORROW; **413:** Jackson Katz. "Advertising and the Construction of Violent White Masculinity." *Gender, Race, and Class in the Media* eds. Gail Dines and Jean M. (McMahon) Humez. Sage Publications Inc. 2nd edition, 2002. Reprinted by Permission of Sage Publications, Inc.; **422:** Wanda Coleman. "Say It Ain't Cool, Joe." Appeared in the October 18, 1992, edition of *The Los Angeles Times Magazine*. Copyright 1992 by Wanda Coleman. Reprinted with permission of Wanda Coleman. From *Native In a Strange Land: Trials & Tremors*, autobiographical prose; Black Sparrow Books (David R. Godine) © for the author.

Chapter 8 Watching Television

430: Erin J. Aubry Kaplan. "The Oprah Effect." *LA Weekly*. May 27, 1998. Reprinted with permission; **434:** Amanda A. Putnam. "Vote the Bitch Off!" Original contribution by the author. Copyright Amanda Putnam. Printed with permission of Amanda Putnam. **445:** Bob Batchelor. "Is This Reality?: *The Bachelor* Feeds Our Desire for Fame." Original contribution by the author. Copyright Bob Batchelor. Printed with permission of Bob Batchelor; **451:** Anita Creamer. "Reality TV Meets Plastic Surgery: An Ugly Shame." © The Sacramento Bee, 2004. Reprinted with permission; **454:** Ariel Gore. "TV Can Be a Good Parent." August 16, 1999. Copyright 1999. This article first appeared in Salon.com, at http:www.Salon.com. An online version remains in the Salon archives. Reprinted with permission of Salon.com; **458:** Vicangelo Bulluck. Executive Director NAACP Hollywood Bureau. "NAACP Takes a Closer Look at Television Diversity—Diversity: No Laughing Matter." June 13, 2006. Copyright NAACP and Vicangelo Bulluck. Reprinted with permission of Vicangelo Bulluck; **463:** Paul A. Cantor. "*The Simpsons*: Atomistic Politics and the Nuclear Family." From "Simpson Agonistes: Atomic Politics, the Nuclear Family, and the Globalization of Springfield" in *Gilligan Unbound* with Rowman and Littlefield Publishers, 2001. Reprinted with permission; **477:** Deggans. "Grading Hispanic Gains on TV? Start with ABC." *St. Petersburg Times*. December 8, 2005. Reprinted with permission; **481:** Neil Postman and Steve Powers. "The Bias of Language, The Bias of Pictures." From HOW TO WATCH TV NEWS by Neil Postman and Steve Powers, copyright © 1992 by Neil Postman and Steve Powers. Used by permission of Viking Penguin, a division of the Penguin Group (USA) Inc.; **490:** "Home Alone? Home Shopping." *The Economist*. Oct. 12, 1996. © 1996. The Economist Newspaper Ltd. All rights reserved. Reprinted with permission. Further reproduction prohibited. www.economist.com; **495:** Mark Kingwell. "Not Available in Stores." From *Saturday Night*, July-August 1996. Copyright Mark Kingwell. Reprinted with permission of Mark Kingwell.

Chapter 9 Seeing Movies and Listening to Music

505: Susan Pell. "Anxiously Entering Into the Twenty-First Century: Watching for Changes in Masculinity and Film." Original contribution by the author. Copyright Susan Pell. Printed with permission of Susan Pell; **513:** Brian L. Ott and Eric Aoki. "The Colonization and Commodification of Racial Identities: Stereotyping and Exoticizing Cultural Difference in *Rush Hour*." Original contribution by the authors. Copyright Brian L. Ott and Eric Aoki. Printed with permission of Brian L. Ott and Eric Aoki; **521:** Meredith A. Love. "Gazing Through Malkovich: Identity and Lesbian Desire in *Being John Malkovich*." Original contribution by the author. Copyright Meredith A. Love. Printed with permission of Meredith A. Love; **528:** Todd Boyd. "So You Wanna Be a Gangsta?" From *Am I Black Enough for You?* Published by Indiana University Press. Pp. 83–88. 1997. Permission granted by Indiana University Press; **538:** David Denby. "High-School Confidential: Notes on Teen Movies."

The New Yorker. May 31, 1999, pp. 94–98. © David Denby. Reprinted with permission; **545:** Jill Fields. "Romancing the Race Card with *Nurse Betty.*" Original contribution by the author. Copyright Jill Fields. Printed with permission of Jill Fields; **554:** Josh Delmar Zimmerman. "Punk's Not Dead." Original contribution by the author. Copyright Josh Delmar Zimmerman. Printed with permission of Josh Delmar Zimmerman; **559:** Jamilah Evelyn. "The Miseducation of Hip-Hop—Discrimination in Education." *Black Issues in Higher Education.* December 7, 2000. Reprinted by permission of *Diverse Issues in Higher Education.* www.diverseeducation.com; **566:** Alisa Valdes-Rodriguez. "Crossing Pop Lines: Attention to Latinos Is Overdue, But Sometimes Off-Target." *Los Angeles Times* (June 11, 1999), Orange County Edition, Part F., p. 2. Calendar Desk. Reprinted with permission; **571:** Gavin James Campbell. "Britney on the Belle Curve." Originally published as "The Southern World of Britney Spears," from *Southern Cultures* 7:4 (Winter 2001). Copyright Gavin James Campbell. Reprinted with permission of Gavin James Campbell; **581:** Lindsey Eck. Originally published as "Defining Country Music." *Bad Subjects.* 56(Summer 2002). Copyright Lindsey Eck. Reprinted with permission of Lindsey Eck; **586:** Nathan D. Abrams. "'Homegrown Heroes': Rap Music, Resistance, and Technology." Original contribution by the author. Copyright Nathan D. Abrams. Printed with permission of Nathan D. Abrams; **593:** David Laskin. "Why I Hate MTV—And Why My Kids Love It." DADMAG.com. Copyright 2001, DADMAG.com, LLC. All rights reserved.

Chapter 10 Surfing in Cyberculture and Gaming

603: L. Jean Camp. "We Are Geeks, and We Are Not Guys: The Systers Mailing List." From *Wired Women: Gender and New Realities in Cyberspace*, eds. Lynn Chery and Elizabeth Reba Weise. Seattle, WA: Seal Press, 1996. Reprinted with permission. Anita Borg. Originally published as "Dr. Anita Borg on the Mailing List Systers." *Computer Research News* (September 1994). Reprinted with permission; **613:** Amy Harmon. "Virtual Sex, Lies, and Cyberspace." From the *Los Angeles Times*, April 10, 1997. Copyright The Times Mirror Company; **619:** Frederick L. McKissack, Jr. "Cyberghetto: Blacks Are Falling Through the Net." *The Progressive.* 62(6): 20–22. 1998. Reprinted by permission from *The Progressive*, 409 Main St., Madison, WI 53703. www.progressive.org; **623:** G. Beato. "Girl Games." *Wired.* Issue 5.4(1997). Copyright by The Conde Nast Publications Inc. and G. Beato. All rights reserved. Reprinted with permission; **630:** Brian Cowlishaw. "Playing War: The Emerging Trend of Real Virtual Combat in Video Games." Originally published in MAGAZINE AMERICANA at http://www.americanpopularculture.com January 2005. Reprinted with permission; **641:** Glen Martin. "Internet Indian Wars: Native Americans Are Fighting to Connect the 550 Nations—in Cyberspace." *Wired*, December 1995 by Wired Digital Inc., a Lycos Network site. Copyright © 1993–2002 The Condé Nast Publications Inc. All rights reserved; **649:** Mark Slouka. "The Illusion of Life Is Dearly Bought." *New Statesman and Society.* January 12, 1996. Copyright 1996 New Statesman. Used with permission; **652:** Erin Jansen. "Texting and Creative Screenagers :-)" Originally appeared as "British Educators Angered by 'Texting." NetLingo. com. 2006. http://www.netlingo.com. –or- www.netlingo. com. Copyright Erin Jansen. Used with permission; **656:** Ralph Lombreglia. "In Games Begin Responsibilities." Reprinted from the *Atlantic Unbound*, December 21, 1996. Copyright Ralph Lombreglia. Reprinted with the permission of the author; **660:** John Marr. Originally published as "Confessions of an eBay Addict." *Bad Subjects.* 42(March 1999). Copyright John Marr. Reprinted with permission of John Marr.

Photo Credits

Interior

Page 10: Ivan Sekretarev/AP/Wide World Photos; **57 R:** Courtesy www.adbusters.org; **58:** Walter McBridge/Retna Ltd., USA; **59:** © Douglas Kirkland/CORBIS; **60:** All ads Courtesy www.adbusters.org; **75 L:** Michael Newman/PhotoEdit; **75 R:** Courtesy www.adbusters.org; **190-191:** Courtesy of Dan Leopard; **212-213:** © Camilo Jose Vergara; **283 L-R:** © Neal Preston/Corbis; **354:** Elliot Erwitt/Magnum; **356:** Courtesy of Advertising Standards Authority London; **357:** Keystone/Zuma Press; **358:** Sipa Press; **359:** Keystone/Zuma Press; **360:** Rex Features/Zuma Press; **361:** Paolo Koch/Photo Researchers; **387:** © Bettmann/Corbis; **398:** Rachel Epstein/PhotoEdit; **400 T:** David Young-Wolff/PhotoEdit; **400 B:** Bill Aron/PhotoEdit; **584:** Photodisc/Getty Images.

Color Pages

Page 1 T: Michael Newman/PhotoEdit; **1 B:** A. Ramsey/Stock Boston; **2 T:** Bill Aron/PhotoEdit; **2 B:** Courtesy of the Guerilla Girls; **3 T:** A. Ramey/PhotoEdit; **3 B:** Courtesy www.adbusters.org; **4 T & B:** Bill Aron/PhotoEdit; **5 L:** Michael Newman/PhotoEdit; **5 R:** Courtesy of the Guerilla Girls; **6 L:** Bill Aron/PhotoEdit; **6 R:** Courtesy www.adbusters.org; **7 T:** M. Spencer Green/AP/Wide World Photos; **7 B:** Kayte M. Deioma/PhotoEdit; **8 L:** © The McGraw-Hill Companies, Inc./Lars Niki, photographer; **8 R:** Rachel Epstein/PhotoEdit.

Index

Italicized page numbers refer to illustrations. Bolded page numbers indicate anthologized readings.